Society Today and Tomorrow

THE MACMILLAN COMPANY
NEW YORK · CHICAGO
DALLAS · ATLANTA · SAN FRANCISCO
LONDON · MANILA
IN CANADA
BRETT-MACMILLAN LTD.
GALT, ONTARIO

Society Today and Tomorrow

READINGS IN SOCIAL SCIENCE

EDITED BY

ELGIN F. HUNT, *Lecturer in Economics, Northwestern University*

AND

JULES KARLIN, *Chairman of the Social Science Department, Wilson Junior College*

THE MACMILLAN COMPANY   NEW YORK

First Printing

Library of Congress catalog card number: 61–6684

*The Macmillan Company, New York
Brett-Macmillan Ltd., Galt, Ontario*

Printed in the United States of America

To Agnete and Dorothy

To Agnes and Dorothy

Preface

SOCIETY TODAY AND TOMORROW was prepared primarily as a book of readings for the introductory college course in social science, but its wide variety of selections will, it is hoped, also interest the adult layman and students of the various disciplines within the social sciences. Some of the selections are short, some are rather long; some expound more fully than the average textbook certain important concepts; some present unusual or controversial points of view; and some are written with a light touch and leavened by a sense of humor. Always in choosing readings the editors have tried to keep in mind not only their readability, relevance, clarity, and interest, but also the quality of the insights which they provide into the nature of society and its problems.

Social science is a relatively new approach to the understanding of man and society, one which involves learning to think in terms of relationships, and in terms of process and change. As the social scientist sees it, human life itself is made up of countless active relationships of individuals to other people and to things, and the notion of the single, wholly self-contained individual, a prisoner within himself, is a myth. Furthermore, the social scientist views the human personality as a plastic, changing entity, which emerges gradually from a complex network of relationships, the most important of which are those with other people.

The ancient Greek maxim "know thyself," which formerly meant probing inward introspectively to "our very depths," has been reinterpreted by the social scientist to mean a search into the motives, the values, the ideas, the institutions, and the general social forces which have become a part of the individual person. Hence when he looks for the source of our major troubles, the social scientist seeks it in some weakness, disturbance, or distortion of our human relations.

Through complex historical processes, the social system has become subject to increasingly rapid change. We have witnessed unprecedented advances in science and technology and we have seen the United States transformed from a rural society to a predominantly urban mass society. But our failure to grasp cause and effect relationships and to foresee social trends has left us largely unprepared for such disastrous events of the twentieth century as two world wars, a major depression, numerous revolutions, and the protracted period of world tension which we call "the cold war." These immense developments demand reorganization of our lives, but we are not at all sure of the direction in which we should move. Today we are genuinely troubled about the uncertainties of the future.

If we could see the future more clearly, in a broad social and historical context, some of our doubts and fears might be allayed. In the present volume we draw on the work of outstanding social scientists for the purpose of developing greater social understanding and a more adequate image of our changing society. We emphasize social change, and we believe that the material of this book, as we have organized it, will enable and encourage the reader to perceive order and form in the drift of events. The title of our volume is intended to suggest continuity among past, present, and future; we have therefore attempted, in various parts of the book, to include selections which indicate what lies ahead.

While we have covered the main areas of social life, we have tried at the same time to produce a work which is compact and manageable. Further, it has been our aim to offer a reasonably integrated body of facts and ideas without glossing over conflicting opinions or overextending favored ideas. Though man's social life is a unity, it is a very complex unity, and we do not believe that anything is gained by attempting to disregard or to "scramble" such traditional social science disciplines as history, sociology, economics, and political science. Each has a contribution to make to the understanding of human society. We do believe, however, that their interrelations should be emphasized, and we have drawn upon all of them for integrating concepts.

In its organization this book is divided into an introduction and six major parts. The first part offers up-to-date analyses of such basic concepts as man and animal, community and society, class and caste, status and role, and culture and cultural relativity. The second part continues with discussions of some of the important problems of personal and social adjustment. The problems of family living, juvenile delinquency and crime, racial prejudice, and mental illness are dealt with in terms of difficulties in interpersonal relations. It is shown that serious problems arise when these relations become either too limited and harsh, or are distorted by dread, hate, and intolerance. Later parts of the book deal with the economy, government, and the quest for peace within the sphere of international relations. The major problems within the areas of our economic and political life, and our international relations, are linked to rapid social change in an industrial society. The sixth and final part of the book is devoted to readings which consider vitally significant social trends, and which attempt to glimpse and to prophesy the emerging shape of the future.

The editors wish to express their appreciation to all who have helped make this book possible. Recognition is given in footnotes to the authors and publishers of individual selections. Members of the Wilson Junior College social science faculty who aided the editors in finding suitable readings include Leon Novar, Andrew Korim, and Rudolph Haerle. Special thanks are owed to the staff of the Chicago Teachers College and Wilson Junior College Library, and to Mrs. Harry L. Foster of the University of Chicago Libraries. Finally, invaluable secretarial assistance was given by Mrs. Elgin F. Hunt, who handled the great volume of necessary correspondence and the many other details connected with preparing the manuscript for the publisher.

Elgin F. Hunt
Jules Karlin

Chicago, Illinois

Contents

INTRODUCTION

1. The Twentieth Century: Dawn or Twilight?   3
   Joseph Wood Krutch

Part One: Basic Factors in Social Life

1. MAN AND SOCIETY   15

2. Man adn Animal: The City and the Hive   17
   Suzanne K. Langer

3. Society: Primary Concepts   24
   Robert M. MacIver and Charles H. Page

4. The Dangers of Nonconformism   32
   Morris Freedman

2. SOCIAL SCIENCE AND ITS METHODS   35

5. The Sociological Imagination: The Promise   36
   C. Wright Mills

3. THE ROLE OF CULTURE   46

6. Cultural Relativism and Social Values   47
   Robert Redfield

7. Universals of Culture   55
   George P. Murdock

8. An Indian's Solioquy   56
   Burt W. Aginsky

4. CULTURE AND THE NATURAL ENVIRONMENT   59

    9. Environmental Limitation on the Development of Culture   60
       Betty J. Meggers

5. PRIMITIVE AND MODERN SOCIETIES   67

   10. How Human Society Operates   68
       Robert Redfield

6. SOCIAL CHANGE AND SOCIAL PROBLEMS   79

   11. The Meaning of Social Change   80
       Kingsley Davis

   12. The Hypothesis of Cultural Lag   88
       William F. Ogburn

7. TECHNOLOGY AND SOCIAL CHANGE   93

   13. Technology and Social Change   94
       Robert M. MacIver and Charles H. Page

   14. Automation's Brave, New World   99
       Bernard Karsh

8. POPULATION   105

   15. World Population   106
       Julian Huxley

   16. How We Stack Up in the World—"Small Town" Tells the
       Story   *Jack Mabley*   111

Part Two
Social Adjustment and Social Problems

9. PERSONAL ADJUSTMENT   115

   17. Centrality of the Problem of Anxiety in Our Day   116
       Rollo May

   18. The Air-Conditioned Conscience   124
       Frederic Wertham

10. THE FAMILY   129

   19. The Family: Genus Americanum   130
       Ruth Benedict

   20. Thoughts on the Future of the Family   136
       Barrington Moore, Jr.

11. RURAL AND URBAN COMMUNITIES   148

21. On the Impact of Urbanism on Society   149
    Philip M. Hauser

22. Suburbia: Dream or Nightmare?   157
    Maurice R. Stein

23. Problems of Metropolitan Areas   168
    Luther Gulick

12. SOCIAL STRATIFICATION   174

24. The New Social Stratification   175
    Robert M. MacIver

25. The Myth of the Happy Worker   184
    Harvey Swados

13. RACIAL AND CULTURAL GROUPS   192

26. The Slow, Painful Death of the Race Myth   193
    Arnold M. Rose

27. Tre Authoritarian Personality   200
    Samuel H. Flowerman

14. CRIME AND DELINQUENCY   206

28. Causes and Cure of Crime and Juvenile Delinquency   207
    Statement by Committee on Human Rights and Welfare
    of the American Humanist Association

29. Juvenile Delinquents: The Latter-Day Knights   211
    Joseph Margolis

15. EDUCATION   218

30. How Education Changes Society   219
    Robert J. Havighurst

31. The Change in Soviet Schooling   226
    Ernest J. Simmons

Part Three
Economic Organization and Social Problems

16. ECONOMIC BEHAVIOR AND ITS ORGANIZATION   235

32. Economics and Economic Wants   236
    E. T. Weiler and W. H. Martin

33. Economic Planning   240
    J. A. Nordin and Virgil Salera

34. "Take-Off" into Economic Growth   245
    Interview with W. W. Rostow

17. THE AMERICAN ECONOMY   252

35. The Growth of Competition   253
    Sumner H. Slichter

36. Strengthening Free Institutions in the United States   257
    John Jewkes

37. The State and the Economic System   262
    Hans Morgenthau

18. ECONOMIC STABILITY AND FULL EMPLOYMENT   267

38. The Passing of Keynesian Economics   268
    Sumner H. Slichter

39. Can We Cure Depressions?   273
    Debate between Abba P. Lerner and Harry Braverman

19. ECONOMIC INEQUALITY AND SOCIAL SECURITY   280

40. Fringes Are Not Frills   281
    Benson Soffer

41. The Canadian Plan for Hospital Care   285
    U.S. News and World Report

20. LABOR RELATIONS AND THE PUBLIC WELFARE   288

42. The Capitalism of the Proletariat: A Theory of American
    Trade-Unionism   *Daniel Bell*   289

43. Wage Induced Inflation   302
    George Terborgh

21. AGRICULTURE AND THE PUBLIC WELFARE   307

44. Farm Policy: The Problem and the Choices   308
    John Kenneth Galbraith

45. Let's Set the Farmer Free   315
    Earl M. Hughes

22. THE CONSUMER   321

46. Advertising on Trial   322
    Victor R. Fuchs

47. A Sad Heart at the Supermarket 326
Randall Jarrell

48. The Use of Income Resulting from Economic Growth 332
John Kenneth Galbraith

Part Four
Political Organization and Social Problems

23. **THE ROLE GOVERNMENT** 339
49. Man and Government 340
Robert M. MacIver

24. **DEMOCRACIES AND DICTATORSHIPS** 357
50. From Individualism to Mass Democracy 358
Edward Hallett Carr

51. Totalitarian Theory of the State 371
R. Wallace Brewster

25. **DEMOCRATIC GOVERNMENT IN AMERICA** 374
52. Excerpts from The Federalist 375
James Madison

53. America's Big Tug-of-War 380
Sidney Hyman

26. **POLITICAL PARTIES AND ELECTIONS** 386
54. Government by Concurrent Majority 387
John Fischer

27. **GOVERNMENT FINANCE AND THE SOCIAL WELFARE** 398
55. The Gap Between Social Needs and Public Expenditures 399
Barbara Ward

56. Truth vs. Myths 403
William Henry Chamberlain

57. Parkinson's Second Law 404
C. Northcote Parkinson

Part Five: International Relations

28. **THE WORLD COMMUNITY OF NATION-STATES** 413
58. The Making of Nations 414
Frederick L. Schuman

59. The Changing Character of the United Nations   420
    Sydney Bailey

29. INTERNATIONAL ECONOMIC RELATIONS   427

60. Trade Not Aid   428
    Myron H. Umbreit, Elgin F. Hunt, and Charles V. Kinter

61. U.S. Response to Soviet Growth   431
    Jean Monnet

**30. NATIONALISM, IMPERIALISM, AND COMMUNIST EX-
PANSION**   437

62. A New Look at Nationalism   438
    Hans Kohn

63. Some Reflections on Colonialism   443
    Hans Kohn

31. THE SEARCH FOR PEACE   447

64. The Probability of War in Our Time   448
    Gerhart Niemeyer

65. War or Peace: What Are the Chances?   457
    Drew Middleton

Part Six: The Shape of the Future

66. The Human Condition: Prologue   465
    Hannah Arendt

67. Planning for the Year 2000   470
    J. Bronowski

68. The Economic Revolution   475
    Barbara Ward

69. The Future as History   487
    Robert L. Heilbroner

Society Today and Tomorrow

Introduction

[1] The Twentieth Century: Dawn or Twilight?*

by JOSEPH WOOD KRUTCH

In many measurable respects ours is the most successful civilization
that ever existed. The average life span was never so long and what we
have learned to call "the standard of living" was never so high nor enjoyed by so large a proportion of the population. By comparison with any
other race that ever lived we are amazingly well fed, well clothed, and
well housed. We suffer less physical pain, we enjoy more conveniences,
and we know more about the laws of the physical universe in which
we live. These are the things we have striven for and these are the
things we have won. They may be more precarious than we like to admit,
but we possess them. We are, or at least we seem to be, singularly blessed.

No previous civilization has ever before achieved so successfully its
immediate aims because no other ever answered so successfully the questions it thought most important to ask or solved so triumphantly the problems it thought most important to solve. To the achievement of the tangible goods we enjoy we have devoted almost the whole of our intelligence and our energy, and because the questions answered and the
problems solved have centered around the achievement of power or the
creation of wealth, man is now a creature more powerful and more
wealthy than ever before. If a dissatisfied minority has persisted in expressing its dissatisfaction by calling us "materialists" we have usually
replied, not so much by defending materialism as such, as in terms of a

faith which is the very essence of modernity: namely, the assumption that material welfare is the *sine qua non* of every other kind and that every other kind may be expected to increase as the material does.

Old-fashioned philosophers often urged men to be wise, or virtuous or spiritual, first and either to despise material goods or to trust that they are to be won through wisdom and virtue; rather than, as we insist, the other way around. Man, we reply, may not live by bread alone but he certainly cannot live without it, and beyond that admission we hesitate to go—partly no doubt because we have reason in experience to fear that those who stress less tangible items in his diet are often preparing to deny him his bread.

Those who are disapprovingly aware that all this constitutes a novel emphasis sometimes call it "Americanism," though both as a theory and as a method it goes back to the seventeenth century, when "control of nature" was first proposed as the most important and most rewarding enterprise upon which the human race could embark. It is "American" only to the extent that here in the United States the method has been most successfully applied to even the smallest details of everyday life and most consistently put into the service of democratic and egalitarian ideals.

Ours is not only a powerful, a wealthy and a materialistic civilization, but also, within the limits imposed by its philosophy, an astonishingly kindly and generous one. This is an aspect of it which the conventional European critic is likely to leave out of account and, in all sincerity, fail to understand. Our "materialism" is a complicated and novel phenomenon the like of which he has never met before because, though his own civilization has been moving more slowly in the same direction, its philosophy has been less successfully implemented and its attitudes less tempered by kindliness or generosity. When such a critic says that we do not care about anything except money he is both right and wrong.

More than a century ago, De Tocqueville noted with amazement how American private citizens had a habit of spontaneously getting together to right some wrong or to relieve some need. He thought the phenomenon unique and he was probably right. Yet it has not only persisted but entered upon a new international phase. We are almost as distressed by suffering and want in distant places as we are by distress and want at home. And we are almost as determined to do something about it. No other nation in all history ever before gave away so much in money or goods. We seem determined to "do good" all over the globe.

Faced with these facts, the European critic shrugs. He hints that we have low, ulterior motives. Materialists, he thinks, would not be so generous. And since we are, by premise, materialists there must be a catch somewhere in all this generosity. Yet he often seems more puzzled than convinced by his own argument. Both European virtues and European vices are traditionally different from ours and he can't make us out.

What really troubles him (and might well trouble us) is something which he is not able to put into words and which the American has never felt any need to analyze because it is not, in his own experience, a paradox. That something is simply this: Materialism and stinginess, thinks the European, inevitably go together—and in his experience they usually have. But generosity and materialism are not at all incompatible—as the whole panorama of the American temperament abundantly demonstrates. We are not materialists in the sense that we love money for its own sake. We are not misers. We are spendthrifts who lavish wealth on ourselves, on our families, on our fellow citizens, and nowadays on the inhabitants of the four quarters of the globe. But we are materialists—generous materialists—in the very simple sense that we believe everything worth having can be had if we are willing to spend enough money to get it.

Nearly everything which makes American life both richer and poorer, both better and worse, than life in any other civilized community ever has been before goes back to the virtues and limitations of this generous materialism. We believe, for example, in education—more passionately and more uncritically than any nation ever believed in it before. We believe in it so thoroughly that we are willing to spend prodigious amounts of public funds. In nearly every American community, citizens vote to tax themselves at higher and higher rates to pay for the education of other people's children. But there are few to whom it ever occurs that putting more money into schools is not a sure way of getting more education, or that any deficiencies which happen to become manifest will not be remedied by putting more into school buildings. Being convinced that you cannot have what you refuse to pay for makes us generous; believing that you will get what you pay for, or at least that if you don't there is no other way of getting it, constitutes materialism.

Your true American never misses an opportunity to make money. He assumes that no one else does either. Perhaps, therefore, we actually are more devoted to the pursuit of the dollar than most other nations are to their pounds, francs, or marks. But we are not particularly anxious to hold on to it when we catch it. Acquisitiveness, not miserliness, is our vice. We are very ready to forgive a man for doing whatever is necessary to make a profit. We are quite resigned, to take small examples, to having the symphony concert interrupted by a commercial or the highway disfigured by billboards. We do not expect anyone to forgo a profit even if making it annoys everybody else. But we expect the profiteer to give generously to charity and to vote for public improvements which will cost him much more than he personally will ever get out of them.

The American is not being hypocritical when he tells you that he is frantically making money because he wants his children to "have all the advantages." He does. And he will spend freely the money he has made to buy these advantages; even, not seldom, to buy some of them for other people's children as well. He is not a materialist in the sense of being one who believes that education, travel, fun, even "culture" are foolish frills. But he is a materialist in the sense that he is quite sure no child can have "advantages" without having money to pay for them, and almost as sure that if he does have money to pay he will get the "advantages." Thoreau thought money not required to buy one necessary of the soul. The typical American believes that no necessary of the soul is free, and that there are few, if any, which cannot be bought.

None of this is consciously cynical. If it were, our civilization would not be the world's wonder that it is: materially richer than any that ever existed before and providing a larger proportion of the population with a considerable share of that material richness than any other rich civilization ever did. In fact, our attitude is so far from being consciously cynical that not one American in ten can be made to recognize any inadequacy in "generous materialism" as a philosophy, a religion, or a way of life. He will call it merely "realistic" and "practical"; nothing more or less than "benevolence without humbug." He will sincerely suspect that anyone who so much as hints at a qualification is seeking an excuse for denying the common people their proper share of material things.

Only during the past hundred years have moral and social philosophers squarely faced the fact that it is easier—at least—to be law-abiding, well educated, and responsive to "the finer things of life" if you are not hungry and cold. Material welfare, they have decided, is a *sine qua non* for welfare of any other kind. But most Americans have taken a further step which does not logically follow, and despite the fact that Europeans still blame us, they and the rest of the world are following us as well as they can. We have forgotten that a *sine qua non* is not always the "one thing necessary" as well.

If the assumption has been turning out to be not so obviously true as was expected, not many will yet acknowledge the fact. Yet the vast majority of our well-fed, well-housed, and well-clothed population has not turned toward intellectual or artistic pursuits, but has simply taken a greater and greater interest in even more food, even better houses, and even more expensive clothes. The more abundant its material riches have become the more thoroughly it has tended to believe that only material riches count. To those who have already a chicken in the pot and a car in the garage the next desirable thing to be acquired is less likely to be, say, a book than a television set and another car.

What philosophers used to call "the good life" is difficult to define and impossible to measure. In the United States today—increasingly also in all "progressive" countries—we substitute for it "the standard of living," which is easy to measure if defined only in terms of wealth, health, comfort, and convenience. But the standard of living does not truly represent the goodness of a life unless you assume that no other goods are real or at least that the less tangible and less measurable bear a direct functional relation to the tangible.

Even when measuring the standard as such we put greater and greater stress upon its most trivial and, indeed, most dubious aspects. A recent magazine article about Russia by one of the most widely read commentators on the world situation includes these remarkable sentences: "[In Moscow] the day-to-day routine of most citizens is inexpressibly dreary. No local citizen has ever read a gossip column or played canasta. No one has ever seen a supermarket, a drive-in movie, a motel or a golf course. Nobody has ever shopped by mail or paid a bill by check. No one has ever seen an electric toaster, a sidewalk café, a shoeshine parlor or a funeral home. I never saw a girl with dark glasses or encountered a Russian with a cigarette lighter."

Is life necessarily "inexpressibly dreary" without these things? Is our ability to supply them the best proof of the superiority of our civilization to that of Russia? If the answer to both the questions is "no," if these are not major, indispensable items in the good life, then it is obvious that either this writer (who has repeatedly demonstrated his ability to be understood and accepted by a large section of the more serious-minded public) has a wrong notion of what constitutes a high standard of living or the relation between such a high standard and the good life is by no means an identity.

Unless one is prepared to accept as inevitable such confusions as his, or to regard them as a small privilege to pay for prosperity and the other blessings of modern society, then it must appear that not even kindliness and generosity are sufficient to make the good life an inevitable consequence of wealth and power.

Wealth can come to be loved for itself alone, but also and more insidiously for the trivialities and vulgarities it enables one to obtain. Power can be used to oppress and abuse, but it can also become insidiously a threat to those who wield it and the occasion, as in the modern world it is, not of confidence but of an insecurity more acute than any powerful nation ever suffered from before.

Even those who recognize these paradoxes and are troubled by them are reluctant to consider the possibility that they suggest a revision of the fundamental premises which have made our civilization what it is. They may be both offended by the vulgarities of an almost too prosperous economy and frightened by threats which exist only because man has achieved so successfully the power he has for two centuries been seeking. They may even share Albert Einstein's doubt that the modern American is any happier than was the Indian whose continent he took. But they still take it for granted that if there is any right road it is the one we have been following.

If we are no happier than the Indians, that may be because some perversity in the human animal makes more than a certain degree of happiness impossible to him. If that is not the case, and if superabundant bread has so far created a society which only gossip columns and drive-in movies redeem from utter dreariness, then perhaps, so most people seem to believe, this is only because we need still more wealth still more equitably distributed. If power has not brought security, if indeed the most astonishing of new acquisitions has enormously increased the sense of insecurity, then perhaps what we need to know is how to "control nature" even more successfully. At least if none of these perhapses is true then few seem able to imagine any other which could be. Certainly few are prepared to abandon faith in wealth and power as such or able to imagine what else might reasonably be pursued instead.

Ours is not only the richest and most powerful civilization that ever existed, but also one of the most uneasy both without and within—within, perhaps because we feel some undefined lack in wealth and power; without, for a plain and simple reason.

Side by side with the optimism which success in achieving our immediate aims has seemed to justify, there has grown among intellectuals what some see as a perverse cult of despair and a readiness to accept as inevitable "the decline of the West." And though the average man certainly does not share this pessimism, he is likely to have heard enough about it and about the grounds upon which it is based to be puzzled by certain ambiguities.

On the one hand technology and that ability to "control nature" in which he so profoundly believes is so far from being in a state of decline that it still follows a sharply ascending curve. There are new worlds to conquer and space travel will begin tomorrow. Yet he cannot, on the other hand, fail to be aware that intercontinental missiles are already here and that our enemies may quite possibly have better ones than we have. Do these recent developments mark a new stage in man's triumphant conquest of nature or the beginning of the catastrophe with which a decline will end?

Progress is strangely mixed up with threats, and the release of atomic energy is, among many "firsts," the first technological triumph widely regarded as possibly, all things considered, a misfortune. To be sure, old fogies have always viewed with alarm. They thought twenty-five miles an hour in an automobile too fast; they shook their heads over the airplane; and it is possible that some conservatives among cave men were sure that no good would come of the wheel. But doubts about the atom are not confined to old fogies. They are shared by some of the very men who tinkered with it so successfully. The suspicion that man may at last have become too smart for his own good is nervously entertained in some very respectable quarters. Observing one of those bright new exploding stars called nova in the night sky, a famous American astronomer is said to have remarked with resignation, "Well, there goes another place where they found out how to do it."

The most prevalent opinion among our so confused contemporaries seems to be that tomorrow will be wonderful—that is, unless it is indescribably terrible, or unless indeed there just isn't any. *If* we are wise enough and lucky enough to escape all the various catastrophes which threaten, then there is no limit to the power and the glory ahead, no limit to the wealth, comfort, and convenience either. But the nagging "if" remains. Have we caught a Tartar or has the Tartar caught us? "He who rides a tiger does not dare to dismount."

There have been ages of hope and ages of despair before now. Historians of ideas inform us that for a thousand years nobody believed in Progress. They inform us also that the general opinion shortly before the year one thousand was that the world was about to end, although, five hundred years later, the notion that the possibilities open to man were limitless was already beginning to be widely assumed. But were the two opinions ever before held simultaneously and progress itself regarded as the possible cause of impending catastrophe?

A recent public relations advertisement by North American Aviation reads: "Supersonic supremacy is the absolute condition of America's future security. It is a day-to-day thing. It must grow with major advances." What we are being told—truthfully enough, it seems—is that we must run as fast as we possibly can if we are to remain where we are. The reward of heroic effort will not be some boon we never enjoyed before, and it will not be the conquest and enrichment which the proponents of military might used to promise. It will be merely the possibility of staying alive. This seems a rather insecure sort of security, though "security" is what it is here called.

If we turn to those of our contemporaries who are professionally occupied, not with the atom, but with the life of our fellow human beings, there is no escaping the fact that man as he appears in the most esteemed contemporary literature, American or European, is an unattractive creature and his life a distressing thing. Our novelists and poets may be wrong. Probably they do exaggerate somewhat and the majority of even their readers does not believe that either man or human existence is quite so unrelievedly dismal as they are made out. But at least this is what the most eloquent and respected among the writers do make out modern man and modern life to be.

It is true that the literary man as spokesman and prophet does not stand very high today even among the more educated classes. Any contemporary *Heroes and Hero Worship* would have to put the Hero as Man of Letters low in the hierarchy and the Hero as Man of Science at the top. But suppose we turn to these modern heroes. From some of the best of them you will get cold comfort. Here, for instance, is J. Robert Oppenheimer:

"Nuclear weapons and all the machinery of war surrounding us now haunt our imaginations with an apocalyptic vision that could well become a terrible reality: the disappearance of man as a species from the surface of the earth. It is quite possible. But what is more probable, more immediate and in my opinion equally terrifying is the prospect that man will survive while losing his precious heritage, his civilization and his very humanity."

Perhaps the physicists do have the best brains now functioning and it is something to have them used, as here they are, to think about man as well as about the things man makes.

Mr. Oppenheimer has reason to know that doing so has its dangers, and the eight leading scientists (including two Nobel Prize men) who consented some time ago to celebrate the centenary of Seagram's whiskey on TV by taking part in a symposium discussing the prospects for man a hundred years hence, were perhaps only playing safe when they confined themselves largely to predicting such blessings as delicious vegetable steaks, mail delivery from earth satellites, recreational resorts on space platforms, and machines which had abolished all physical labor. Thus they put themselves in the same class as those who write articles for the "service magazines" inviting us to drool over a future full of electronic cookers, family helicopters (at least two in every garage) and two-way household television-telephones *in color.* The most appropriate comment seems to have been that in the New York *Nation:* "The future of the human race resides in its humanity, not in its ability to construct honeymoon hotels on Venus."

But what is this "humanity" which the *Nation* is interested in and Oppenheimer fears we may lose? It is easier to say what it isn't or to define it negatively. It is that part of man's consciousness, intellect, and emotion which is neither exclusively interested in nor completely satisfied by either mere animal survival on the one hand, or wealth, power, and speed alone. It is that part of him which is least like a machine and therefore least satisfied by machines. It is the part that would like to know itself and that cherishes values to which nothing in the inanimate world seems to correspond and which the nonhuman world of living things only dubiously (though none the less comfortingly) seems to encourage.

Perhaps we are being a bit provincial to call this "humanness." Man existed for many millennia without, so we guess, exhibiting much of it. Perhaps Mr. Oppenheimer is right in supposing that he might endure indefinitely after he had lost it. Many contemporary men—and especially many contemporary youths—to whom only automobiles, airplanes, and television sets seem interesting, have already lost most of it. Perhaps it is primarily a phenomenon of recent man and, in the form we best understand, of Western man. Perhaps what some of us tend to call "the human being" first came into easily recognizable existence about the year 475 B.C. and began to disappear about seventy-five years ago. But though the world may soon belong to other creatures, there are some of us who cannot say simply, "Cultures come and go," without a regret for the passing of what seems to our possibly prejudiced minds more worthy of admiration than anything which ever existed before.

We need not, as some do, insist that the decision whether or not humanness in this limited sense will endure is wholly outside our power to influence. But there can be little doubt that the weight, the pressure, and the demands of the machine we have created make the preservation of "human" life more difficult than ever before—at least since the time when man ceased to be wholly at the mercy of the natural forces he has now mastered almost too well. If we should devote more of our time, energy, and brain power to the cultivation of "the humanities" in the broad sense that our definition of "humanness" implies, then we would have to face the fact now so insistently urged upon us that "we need more scientists for survival," and that therefore much more rather than any less of the available brain power must be devoted to the machine and its management, to public education more and more exclusively devoted to "turning out the scientists necessary to our survival." . . . .

We cannot now "control the machine" because we are hypnotized by it; because we do not really want to control it. And we do not want to control it because in our hearts we believe it more interesting, more wonderful, more admirable, and more rich in potentialities than we ourselves are. We cannot break the hypnosis, cannot wake from our submissive dream, without retracing one by one the steps which brought us more and more completely under its spell.

Those steps were not taken yesterday and they cannot be retraced unless we are both willing and able to reassess the values which the hypnosis has imposed upon us. That would involve a willingness to ask how many of the "advantages" which power has conferred upon us really are advantageous. It would mean also getting rid of all our love of the machine for its own sake, of our delight in the small gadget as well as in the great. But if we did do all that these things imply, then we might begin to recover from our hypnosis.

If there are any signs of such an awakening they are faint and dubious. The main current tends to run in the long-familiar direction. To the average citizen knowledge means science, science means technology, and (a last debasement) the meaning of technology is reduced to "know-how." It took a Russian satellite in the sky to shake our complacency and it was shaken only because it suggested that the Russians had more "know-how" than we. And the lesson most commonly drawn has been that education should put even greater stress upon the development of such know-how, leaving even less time for "fundamental thinking."

Someday we may again discover that "the humanities" are something more than ornaments and graces. Sociology and psychology may again find man's consciousness more interesting than the mechanically determined aspects of his behavior and we may again be more concerned with what man *is* than with *what he has* and *what he can do*. We might again take more pride in his intellect than in his tools; might again think of him as pre-eminently *Homo sapiens* rather than *Homo faber*—man the thinker rather than man the maker. We might—at some distant day—come to realize again that the proper study of mankind is man.

But that time is certainly not yet. We have forgotten that know-how is a dubious endowment unless it is accompanied by other "knows"—by "know what," "know why," and—most important of all at the present moment—"know whether." Quite blandly and as a matter of course we still ask what are the needs of industry, not what are the needs of man. . . .

PART ONE

Basic Factors
in Social Life

CHAPTER ONE

Man and Society

*W*HAT *distinguishes man from animal? While accepting the theory of evolution, Susanne Langer finds a deep gulf between the two forms of life. An entirely new process in the human brain has made possible the use of symbols, especially words, for things and ideas. Man is defined as a symbol-making and symbol-using animal. Entering into communication with each other through words, human beings have created their own peculiar environment consisting of symbols, tools, rules, patterns of life and thought. While remaining a creature of biological needs, man is not strictly confined to the narrow limits of animal existence. Through the social world he has created, man can strive for self-realization and individuation: "We are not the Masses [of the beehive]: we are the Public."*

What then is the relationship between man and society? In their treatment of the primary concepts in terms of which society can be understood, MacIver and Page make a number of distinctions between society as a web of relationships, community as the matrix or ground of social life, and associations as specific organizations which grow within the matrix. They emphasize the essential harmony between society and man, believing, along with Langer, that the social world is so organized as to afford individuals the conditions under which they can develop individuality and freedom.

In every society there must be basic agreement on the norms of social behavior and on essential social values. Only a limited amount of deviation can be permitted. But modern industrial societies are complex, and within them are a variety of groups whose cultural patterns differ some-

*what from one another. In the fourth selection Freedman suggests that the
"nonconformist" in our society is usually conforming, often rather slav-
ishly, to the attitudes of a minority group with which he chooses to
identify himself.*

[2] Man and Animal: The City and the Hive*

by SUSANNE K. LANGER

Within the past five or six decades, the human scene has probably changed more radically than ever before in history. The outward changes in our setting are already an old story: the disappearance of horse-drawn vehicles, riders, children walking to school, and the advent of the long, low, powerful Thing in their stead; the transformation of the mile-wide farm into a tic-tac-toe of lots, each sprouting a split-level dream home. These are the obvious changes, more apparent in the country than in the city. The great cities have grown greater, brighter, more mechanized, but their basic patterns seem less shaken by the new power and speed in which the long industrial revolution culminates.

The deepest change, however, is really a change in our picture of mankind; and that is most spectacular where mankind is teeming and concentrated—in the city. Our old picture of human life was a picture of local groups, each speaking its mother-tongue, observing some established religion, following its own customs. It might be a civilized community or a savage tribe, but it had its distinct traditions. And in it were subdivisions, usually families, with their more special local ties and human relations.

Today, natural tribes and isolated communities have all but disappeared. The ease and speed of travel, the swift economic changes that send people in search of new kinds of work, the two wars that swept over all boundaries, have wiped out most of our traditions. The old family structure is tottering. Society tends to break up into new and smaller units —in fact, into its ultimate units, the human individuals that compose it.

This atomization of society is most obvious in a great cosmopolitan city. The city seems to be composed of millions of unrelated individuals, each scrambling for himself, yet each caught in the stream of all the others. Ever since this shakeup in society began, a new picture of society has been in the making—the picture of *human masses,* brought together by some outside force, some imposed function, into a super-personal unit; masses of people, each representing an atom of "manpower" in a new sort of organism, the industrial State.

* Reprinted from *The Antioch Review,* Fall, 1958 (Vol. 18, No. 3). Antioch Press, Yellow Springs, Ohio. By permission of the publishers and the author.

The idea of the State as a higher organism—the State as a super-individual—is old. But the old picture was not one of the masses driven by some imposed economic power, or any other outside power. The super-individual was a rational being, directed by a mind within it. The guardians of the State, the rulers, were its mind. Plato described the State as "the man writ large." Hobbes, two thousand years later, called it "Leviathan," the great Creature. A city-state like ancient Athens or Sparta might be "a man writ large," but England was too big for that. It was the big fish in the pond. The mind of Hobbes's fish was perhaps subhuman, but it was still single and sovereign in the organism.

Another couple of centuries later, Rudyard Kipling, faced with a democratic, industrialized civilization, called his allegory of England "The Mother Hive." Here, a common will, dictated by complicated instincts, replaced even Leviathan's mind; each individual was kept in line by the blind forces of the collective life.

The image of the hive has had a great success as an ideal of collaborative social action. Every modern Utopia (except the completely wishful Shangri-La) reflects the beehive ideal. Even a statesman of highest caliber, Jan Smuts, has praised it as a pattern for industrial society. Plato's personified State and Hobbes's sea monster impress us as fantasies, but the hive looks like more than a poetic figure; it seems really to buzz around us.

I think the concept of the State as a collective organism, composed of multitudes of little workers, guided by social forces that none of the little workers can fathom, and accomplishing some greater destiny, is supported by another factor than our mechanized industry; that other factor is a momentous event in our intellectual history: the spread of the theory of evolution.

First biologists, then psychologists, and finally sociologists and moralists have become newly aware that man belongs to the animal kingdom. The impact of the concept of evolution on scientific discovery has been immense. Gradually the notion of the human animal became common currency, questioned only by some religious minds. This in turn has made it natural for social theorists with scientific leanings to model their concepts of human society on animal societies, the ant hill and the beehive. . . .

Despite Man's zoölogical status, which I wholeheartedly accept, there is a deep gulf between the highest animal and the most primitive normal human being: a difference in mentality that is fundamental. It stems from the development of one new process in the human brain—a process that seems to be entirely peculiar to that brain: the use of *symbols for ideas*. By "symbols" I mean all kinds of signs that can be used and understood whether the things they refer to are there or not. The word "symbol" has, unfortunately, many different meanings for different people. Some people reserve it for mystic signs, like Rosicrucian symbols; some mean by it *significant images,* such as Keats' "Huge cloudy symbols of a high romance"; some use it quite the opposite way and speak of "mere symbols," meaning empty gestures, signs that have lost their meanings; and some, notably logicians, use the term for mathematical signs, marks that constitute a code, a brief, concise language. In their sense, ordinary words are symbols, too. Ordinary language is a symbolism.

When I say that the distinctive function of the human brain is the use of symbols, I mean any and all of these kinds. They are all different from signs that animals use. Animals interpret signs, too, but only as pointers to actual things and events: cues to action or expectation, threats and promises, landmarks and earmarks in the world. Human beings use such signs, too; but above all they use symbols—especially words—to think and talk about things that are neither present nor expected. The words convey *ideas,* that may or may not have counterparts in actuality. This power of thinking *about* things expresses itself in language, imagination, and speculation—the chief products of human mentality that animals do not share.

Language, the most versatile and indispensable of all symbolisms, has put its stamp on all our mental functions, so that I think they always differ from even their closest analogues in animal life. Language has invaded our feeling and dreaming and action, as well as our reasoning, which is really a product of it. The greatest change wrought by language is the increased scope of awareness in speech-gifted beings. An animal's awareness is always of things in its own place and life. In human awareness, the present, actual situation is often the least part. We have not only memories and expectations; we have a *past* in which we locate our memories, and a *future* that vastly over-reaches our own anticipations. Our past is a story, our future a piece of imagination. Likewise our ambient is a place in a wider, symbolically conceived place, the universe. We live in *a world.*

This difference of mentality between man and animal seems to me to make a cleft between them almost as great as the division between animals and plants. There is continuity between the orders, but the division is real nevertheless. Human life differs radically from animal life. By virtue of our incomparably wider awareness, our power of envisagement of things and events beyond any actual perception, we have acquired needs and aims that animals do not have; and even the most savage human society, having to meet those needs and implement those aims, is not really comparable to any animal society. The two may have some analogous functions, but the essential structure must be different, because man and beast live differently in every way.

Probably the profoundest difference between human and animal needs is made by one piece of human awareness, one fact that is not present to animals, because it is never learned in any direct experience: that is our foreknowledge of Death. The fact that we ourselves must die is not a simple and isolated fact. It is built on a wide survey of facts, that discloses the structure of history as a succession of overlapping brief lives, the patterns of youth and age, growth and decline; and above all that, it is built on the logical insight that *one's own life is a case in point.* Only a creature that can think symbolically *about* life can conceive of its own death. Our knowledge of death is part of our knowledge of life.

What, then, do we—all of us—know about life?

Every life that we know is generated from other life. Each living thing springs from some other living thing or things. Its birth is a process of new individuation, in a life-stream whose beginning we do not know.

Individuation is a word we do not often meet. We hear about individuality, sometimes spoken in praise, sometimes as an excuse for being slightly crazy. We hear and read about "the Individual," a being that is forever adjusting, like a problem child, to something called "Society." But how does individuality arise? What makes an individual? A fundamental, biological process of *individuation,* that marks the life of every stock, plant or animal. Life is a series of individuations, and these can be of various sorts, and reach various degrees. . . .

Our power of symbolic conception has given us each a glimpse of himself as one final individuation from the great human stock. We do not know when or what the end will be, but we know that there will be one. We also envisage a past and future, a stretch of time so vastly longer than any creature's memory, and a world so much richer than any world of sense, that it makes our time in that world seem infinitesimal. This is the price of the great gift of symbolism.

In the face of such uncomfortable prospects (probably conceived long before the dawn of any religious ideas), human beings have evolved aims different from any other creatures. Since we cannot have our fill of existence by going on and on, we want to have *as much life as possible* in our short span. If our individuation must be brief, we want to make it complete; so we are inspired to think, act, dream our desires, create things, express our ideas, and in all sorts of ways make up by concentration what we cannot have by length of days. We seek the greatest possible individuation, or development of personality. In doing this, we have set up a new demand, not for mere continuity of existence, but for *self-realization*. That is a uniquely human aim. . . .

The greatest possible individuation is usually taken to mean, "as much as is possible without curtailing the rights of others." But that is not the real measure of how much is possible. The measure is provided in the individual himself, and is as fundamental as his knowledge of death. It is the other part of his insight into nature—his knowledge of life, of the great unbroken stream, the life of the stock from which his individuation stems.

One individual life, however rich, still looks infinitesimal: no matter how much self-realization is concentrated in it, it is a tiny atom—and we don't like to be tiny atoms, not even hydrogen atoms. We need more than fullness of personal life to counter our terrible knowledge of all it implies. And we have more; we have our history, our commitments made for us before we were born, our relatedness to the rest of mankind. The counterpart of individuation from the great life of the stock is our rootedness in that life, our involvement with the whole human race, past and present.

Each person is not only a free, single end, like the green palm leaf that unfolds, grows in a curve of beauty, and dies in its season; he is like the whole palm leaf, the part inside the trunk, too. He is the culmination of his entire ancestry, and *represents* that whole human past. In his brief individuation he is an *expression* of all humanity. That is what makes each person's life sacred and all-important. A single ruined life is the bankruptcy of a long line. This is what I mean by the individual's involvement with all mankind.

All animals are unconsciously involved with their kind. Heredity governs not only their growth, color and form, but their actions, too. They carry their past about with them in everything they do. But they do not know it. They don't need to, because they never could lose it. Their involvement with the greater life of the race is implicit in their limited selfhood.

Our knowledge that life is finite and, in fact, precarious and brief, drives us on to greater individuation than animals attain. Our mental talents have largely freed us from that built-in behavior called instinct. The scope of our imagination gives each of us a separate world, and a separate consciousness, and threatens to break the instinctual ties of brotherhood that make all the herrings swim into one net, and all the geese turn their heads at the same moment. Yet we cannot afford to lose the feeling of involvement with our kind; for if we do, personal life shrinks up to nothingness.

The sense of involvement is our social sense. We have it by nature, originally just as animals do, and just as unconsciously. It is the direct feeling of needing our own kind, caring what happens. Social sense is an instinctive sense of being somehow one with all other people—a feeling that reflects the rootedness of our existence in a human past. Human society rests on this feeling. It is often said to rest on the need of collaboration, or on domination of the weak by the strong, or some other circumstance, but I think such theories deal with its modes, and ignore its deeper structure; at the bottom of it is the feeling of involvement, or social sense. If we lose that, no coercion will hold us to our duties, because they do not feel like commitments; and no achievements will matter, because they are doomed to be snuffed out with the individual, without being laid to account in the continuity of life.

Great individual development, such as human beings are driven by their intellectual insights to seek, does of course always threaten to break the bonds of direct social involvement, that give animal life its happy unconscious continuity. When the strain gets hard, we have social turmoil, anarchy, irresponsibility, and in private lives the sense of loneliness and infinite smallness that lands some people in nihilism and cynicism, and leads others to existentialism or less intellectual cults.

It is then that social philosophers look upon animal societies as models for human society. There is no revolt, no strike, no competition, no anti-anything party, in a beehive. As Kipling, fifty years or more ago, represented his British Utopia that he called the Mother Hive, that ideal State had a completely cooperative economy, an army that went into action without a murmur, each man with the same impulse, the moment an enemy threatened to intrude, and a populace of such tribal solidarity that it would promptly run out any stranger that tried to become established in the State and disrupt its traditions. Any native individual that could not fit into the whole had to be liquidated; the loss was regrettable, but couldn't be helped, and would be made up.

Yet the beehive really has no possible bearing on human affairs; for it owes its harmonious existence to the fact that its members are *incompletely individuated*, even as animals go. None of them perform all of a creature's essential functions: feeding, food-getting, nest-building, mating, and procreating. . . . So there is not only division of labor, but division of organs, functional and physical incompleteness. This direct involvement of each bee with the whole lets the hive function with an organic rhythm that makes its members appear wonderfully socialized. But they are really not socialized at all, any more than the cells in our tissues are socialized; they are associated, by being un-individuated.

That is as far away from a human ideal as one can get. We need, above all, a world in which we can realize our capacities, develop and act as personalities. That means giving up our instinctive patterns of habit and prejudice, our herd-instincts. Yet we need the emotional security of the greater, continuous life—the awareness of our involvement with all mankind. How can we eat that cake, and have it, too?

The same mental talent that makes us need so much individuation, comes to the rescue of our social involvement: I mean the peculiarly human talent of holding ideas in the mind by means of symbols. Human life, even in the simplest forms we know, is shot through and through with *social symbols*. . . .

Most people have some religious ritual that supports their knowledge of a greater life; but even in purely secular affairs we constantly express our faith in the continuity of human existence. Animals provide lairs or nests for their immediate offspring. Man builds for the future—often for nothing else; his earliest great buildings were not mansions, but monuments. And not only physical edifices, but above all laws and institutions are intended for the future, and often justified by showing that they have a precedent, or are in accord with the past. They are conveniences of their day, but symbols of more than their day. They are symbols of Society, and of each individual's inalienable membership in Society.

What, then, is the measure of our possible individuation, without loss of social sense? It is the power of social symbolism. We can give up our actual, instinctual involvements with our kind just to the extent that we can replace them by symbolic ones. This is the prime function of social symbols, from a handshake, to the assembly of robed judges in a Supreme Court. In protocol and ritual, in the investment of authority, in sanctions and honors, lies our security against loss of involvement with mankind; in such bonds lies our freedom to be individuals.

It has been said that an animal society, like a beehive, is really an organism, and the separate bees its organic parts. I think this statement requires many reservations, but it contains some truth. The hive is an organic structure, a super-individual, something like an organism. A human city, however, is an *organization*. It is above all a symbolic structure, a mental reality. Its citizens are the whole and only individuals. They are not a "living mass," like a swarm of semi-individuated bees. The model of the hive has brought with it the concept of human masses, to be cared for in times of peace, deployed in times of war, educated for use or sacrificed for the higher good of their state. In the specious analogy of animal and human society, the hive and the city, lies, I think, the basic philosophical fallacy of all totalitarian theory, even the most sincere and idealistic—even the thoroughly noble political thought of Plato.

We are like leaves of the palm tree, each deeply embedded in the tree, a part of the trunk, each opening to the light in a final, separate life. Our world is a human world, organized to implement our highest individuation. There may be ten thousand of us working in one factory. There are several millions of us living in a city like New York. But we are not the Masses: we are the Public.

[3]   Society: Primary Concepts*

by ROBERT M. MacIVER and CHARLES H. PAGE

SOCIETY

What We Mean by Society.   Our first, the most general of our terms, is *society* itself. Social beings, men, express their nature by creating and re-creating an organization which guides and controls their behavior in myriad ways. This organization, society, liberates and limits the activities of men, sets up standards for them to follow and maintain: whatever the imperfections and tyrannies it has exhibited in human history, it is a necessary condition of every fulfillment of life. Society is a system of usages and procedures, of authority and mutual aid, of many groupings and divisions, of controls of human behavior and of liberties. This ever-changing, complex system we call society. It is the web of social relationships. And it is always changing.

The Psychical Condition of Social Relationships.   Society, we have said, is the changing pattern of social relationships. What do we mean by social relationship? We may approach the answer by contrasting the social with the physical. There is a relationship between a typewriter and a desk, between the earth and the sun, between fire and smoke, between two chemical constituents. Each of these is affected by the existence of the other, but the relationship is not a social one. The psychical condi-

* From *Society: An Introductory Analysis* by Robert M. MacIver and Charles H. Page. Reprinted by permission of Holt, Rinehart and Winston, Inc. Copyright, 1949.

tion is lacking. The typewriter and the desk are in no intelligible sense *aware* of the presence of one another. Their relationship is not in any way determined by mutual awareness. Without this recognition there is no social relationship, no society. Society exists only where social beings "behave" toward one another in ways determined by their recognition of one another. Any relations so determined we may broadly name "social."

The Range of Social Relationships. Social relationships are as varied as society is complex. The relations of voter to candidate, mother to child, employee to employer, friend to friend, are but a few of the varying types. The generality of the concept of "social" is borne out when we note the almost countless terms our language employs to name the many kinds of social relationships between men. Some of them we label "economic," some "political," some "personal," some "impersonal," some "friendly," some "antagonistic," and so on. But they are all *social* relationships when they are grounded in mutual recognition.

Among such relationships there are some which express mere conflict or unmitigated hostility, such as those between two armies in time of war. Armies in the field are certainly aware of nothing so much, and their activities are animated by nothing so much, as the presence of one another. Such relationships are "social." However, the great majority of social relationships involve a principle which the example of the armies expressly denies. This is the sense of community or belonging together. As sociologists, we study both the conditions that unite and those that separate human beings. But if there were no sense of community, if there were no co-operative undertakings by man, there would be no social systems, no society or societies—there would be practically nothing for sociologists to study. Hence the relationships which are central to sociology are those which involve both mutual recognition and the sense of something held or shared in common.

Society Not Confined to Man. From our definition it should be clear that society is not limited to human beings. There are animal societies of many degrees. The remarkable social organizations of the insects, such as the ant, the bee, the hornet, are known to most school children. It has been contended that wherever there is life there is society, because life means heredity and, so far as we know, can arise only out of and in the presence of other life. But in the lowest stages of life, social awareness, if it exists, is extremely dim and the social contact often extremely fleeting. Among all higher animals at least there is a very definite society, arising out of the requirements of their nature and the conditions involved in the perpetuation of their species.

As above defined, there may be society also between animals of differ-ent species, as between a man and a horse or dog or, say, between sheep and their shepherd dog. Our concern is with society among the human species.

Society Involves Both Likeness and Difference. It is often said that the family, in some form, was the first society. It is certainly true that the sex relationship is a primary and essential type of social relationship. It is clear that this relationship involves *both* likeness and difference in the beings whom it relates. So with society in its various manifestations. . . .

Without likeness and the sense of likeness there could be no mutual recognition of "belonging together" and therefore no society. Society exists among those who resemble one another in some degree, in body and in mind, and who are near enough or intelligent enough to appreciate the fact. Society, as F. H. Giddings expressed it, rests on "consciousness of kind." In early society and among some of our "primitive contemporaries," the sense of likeness is focused on kin-membership, that is, real or sup-posed blood relationships. The conditions of social likeness have broad-ened out in modern societies. But the basic conception of likeness that primitive man identified with the kin remains in even so extensive a prin-ciple of union as nationality. And if the struggling principle of "one world" is to win out it must necessarily rest upon the recognition of the funda-mental *likeness* of the entire human race.

Society, however, depends on difference as well as on likeness. If people were all exactly alike, merely alike, their social relationships would be as limited, perhaps, as those of the ant or bee. There would be little give-and-take, little reciprocity. They would contribute very little to one an-other. What we have noted above to be true of the sex relationship is present, in various forms, in all social systems. For they all involve rela-tionships in which differences complement one another, in which exchange takes place. In society each member seeks something and gives some-thing. . . .

Man as a Social Animal. We have still to mention the fundamental attribute, fundamental beyond even the sense of likeness, on which society depends. It was expressed by Aristotle when he said that man was a social animal.[1] It is evidenced in man's reflection on society ever since the be-ginnings of recorded thought, the reflection that it was not good for man to be alone. Man is dependent on society for protection, comfort, nurture, education, equipment, opportunity, and the multitude of definite services which society provides. He is dependent on society for the content of his thoughts, his dreams, his aspirations, even many of his maladies of mind

[1] Aristotle significantly adds that the person who is incapable of sharing a common life is either below or above humanity, "either a beast or a god."

and body. His birth in society brings with it the absolute need of society itself.

No wonder, then, that solitary confinement is one of the most fearful of all punishments, for it prevents the satisfaction of this fundamental need. Whatever the claims of "independence" we may hear from some persons, no man is free of the need of society. When the hermit leaves the society of men he imagines he can find another society in communion with God or with "Nature," or he is driven by some obsession to a kind of self-punishment. If he is not mad at the outset he becomes so in the end. For normal humanity must have social relationships to make life livable.

COMMUNITY

Definition of Community. The second of our primary concepts is that of *community*. Let us begin with examples. It is the term we apply to a pioneer settlement, a village, a city, a tribe, or a nation. Wherever the members of any group, small or large, live together in such a way that they share, not this or that particular interest, but the basic conditions of a common life, we call that group a community. The mark of a community is that one's life *may* be lived wholly within it. One cannot live wholly within a business organization or a church; one can live wholly within a tribe or a city. The basic criterion of community, then, is that all of one's social relationships may be found within it.

Communities Need Not Be Self-sufficient. Some communities are all-inclusive and independent of others. Among primitive peoples we sometimes find communities of no more than a hundred persons, as, for example, among the Yurok tribes of California, which are almost or altogether isolated. But modern communities, even very large ones, are much less self-contained. Economic and, increasingly so, political interdependence is a major characteristic of our great modern communities.

We may live in a metropolis and yet be members of a very small community because our interests are circumscribed within a narrow area. Or we may live in a village and yet belong to a community as wide as the whole area of our civilization or even wider. No civilized community has walls around it to cut it completely off from a larger one, whatever "iron curtains" may be drawn by the rulers of this nation or that. Communities exist within greater communities: the town within a region, the region within a nation, and the nation within the world community which, perhaps, is in the process of development.

The Bases of Community. A community then is an area of social living marked by some degree of *social coherence*. The bases of community are *locality* and *community sentiment*.

[1] *Locality:* A community always occupies a territorial area. Even a nomad community, a band of gypsies, for example, has a local, though changing, habitation. At every moment its members occupy together a definite place on the earth's surface. Most communities are settled and derive from the conditions of their locality a strong bond of solidarity. To some extent this local bond has been weakened in the modern world by the extending facilities of communication; this is especially apparent in the penetration into rural areas of dominant urban patterns. But the extension of communication is itself the condition of a larger but still territorial community.

The importance of the conception of community is in large measure that it underscores the relation between social coherence and the geographical area. This relation is easily revealed in such examples as an Eskimo village or a frontier town or the semi-isolated communities of French Quebec. Whatever modifications in the relation of social bonds and territorial abode have been introduced by civilization, yet the basic character of locality as a social classifier has never been transcended.

[2] *Community sentiment.* Today we find, what never existed in primitive societies, people occupying specific local areas which lack the social coherence necessary to give them a community character. For example, the residents of a ward or district of a large city may lack sufficient contacts or common interests to instill conscious identification with the area. Such a "neighborhood" is not a community because it does not possess a feeling of belonging together—it lacks community sentiment. Later we shall analyze the various elements of community sentiment. Here it is sufficient to stress that locality, though a necessary condition, is not enough to create a community. A community, to repeat, is an area of common living. There must be the common living with its *awareness* of sharing a way of life as well as the common earth. . . .

The Spread of Civilization and the World Community. The wholly self-contained community belongs to the primitive world. In the modern world the nearest approach to it is found in the huge nation-community included within the frontiers of a single state. This has been especially the case when the state has sought to "co-ordinate" the whole national life as did National Socialist Germany, or when, as in Soviet Russia, it establishes a form of economy very different from that of most other nations. But Nazi Germany was never self-sufficient, nor is the U.S.S.R., as American exporters of heavy machinery will testify. Modern civilization, we know, unleashes forces which break down the self-containedness of communities great or small.

These forces are partly *technological,* such as the improvement of the means of communication and transportation; partly *economic,* such as the demand for markets and for wider areas of economic exchange necessitated by the newer processes of industrial production; and partly *cultural,* since the thought and art and science of one country are, whatever the temporary barriers of "ideological" and political construction, inevitably carried on the wings of civilization to others. In the face of these forces, there are no national "secrets," atomic or otherwise, of permanent duration.

Certainly Wendell Willkie's *One World* has been in the making for centuries. We have been approaching a stage where no completely self-contained community can be found on any scale unless we extend the limits of community to include the whole earth. Men's current efforts to develop political agencies of world scope are consistent with the trend of the spread of civilization. In our view, the counterefforts of some men ignore the realities of expanding community itself.

The Great and Small Communities. We have noted the historical expansion of community to the dimensions of the nation and, perhaps, the world. The smaller communities, however, still remain, though only in degree. The nation or the world-state does not eliminate the village or neighborhood, though they may be changed in character. As civilized beings, we need the smaller as well as the larger circles of community. The great community brings us opportunity, stability, economy, the constant stimulus of a richer, more varied culture. But living in the smaller community we find the nearer, more intimate satisfactions. The larger community provides peace and protection, patriotism and sometimes war, automobiles and the radio. The smaller provides friends and friendship, gossip and face-to-face rivalry, local pride and abode. Both are essential to the full life process. . . . The significance of the term "community" is more clearly brought out when we contrast it with our next major concept, association.

ASSOCIATIONS

Associations as Means of Pursuing Ends. There are three ways in which men seek the fulfillment of their ends. First, they may act independently, each following his own way without thought of his fellows or their actions. However seemingly desirable, this unsocial way has narrow limitations wherever men live together. Second, they may seek them through conflict with one another, each striving to wrest from the others the objects that he prizes. But this method, if not channeled strictly by regulation, is precarious and wasteful and is opposed to the very existence of society. True, as we shall see later, conflict is an ever-present part of social life, but for the most part it is, like economic competition, socially limited and regulated. Finally, men may pursue their ends in company, on some co-operative basis, so that each is in some degree and manner contributing to the ends of his fellows.

This last method, co-operative pursuit, may be spontaneous, such as the offering of a helping hand to a stranger. It may be casual. It may be determined by the customs of a community, as in the case of farmers assisting their neighbors at harvest time. On the other hand, a group may organize itself expressly for the purpose of pursuing certain of its interests together. When this happens, an *association* is born.

We define an association, then, as a group organized for the pursuit of an *interest or group of interests* in common.

Association and Community. It follows from our definition that an association is not a community, but an organization within a community. A community is more than any specific organizations that rise within it. Contrast, for example, the business or the church or the club with the village or city or nation. With respect to the business or church or club, we can ask such questions as why they exist and what they stand for. And we can answer in terms of the particular *interests* around which they are organized. But if we ask *why* communities exist, we can expect no such definite answer. (We can ask why a community, say a city, exists *where it is situated*, but this is a different question.)

Another contrast between the community and the association is revealed by considering the interest aspect of associations. Because the association is organized for particular purposes, for the pursuit of specific interests, we belong to it only by virtue of these interests. We belong to an athletic club for purposes of physical recreation or sport, to a business for livelihood or profits, to a social club for fellowship. Membership in an association has a limited significance. It is true that an association may engage our whole devotion. Or the interests of an association may be wider than or different from those officially professed. But we belong to associations only by virtue of some *specific* interests that we possess. Consequently, there can be a multitude of associations within the same community. And the individual, of course, may belong to many. The late President Butler of Columbia University reported membership in twenty clubs in addition to dozens of other associations.[2]

Associations may become communities, at least temporarily. There are the examples of seventeenth-century trading company outposts which became communities in every respect, or of military units compelled to

[2] W. F. Ogburn and M. F. Nimkoff, *Sociology* (Boston, 1940), pp. 258-260.

create their own communities when isolated for a period of time. And there are borderline cases between community and association, such as the monasteries, convents, and prisons discussed in the previous section. The two major social organizations which may seem to lie on the borderline between associations and communities are the family and the state. We shall consider these two at length later, but each demands brief comment in this introductory treatment of primary concepts.

The Family as an Association. In some of its forms, especially in some primitive and extremely rural societies, the family has many of the attributes of a community. In these cases, people toil, play, and even worship almost wholly within the orbit of the family. It circumscribes largely or even wholly the lives of its members.

However, in modern society, as in all complex civilizations, the family becomes definitely an association, so far as its adult members are concerned. For the original contracting parties it is an association specifically established with certain ends in view. These interests are vastly important but nevertheless limited. The functions of the family are more and more limited and defined as the social division of labor increases.

But even in the most complex society, the family, for the new lives that arise within it, is more than an association. To the child the family is a preliminary community which prepares him for the greater community. By imperceptible degrees it is transformed for him also, as he grows up, into an association of, often intense, but *limited* interest. Eventually he will normally leave it to establish a new family.

The State as an Association. The state is frequently confused with the community. In reality the state is *one* form of social organization, not the whole community in all its aspects. We distinguish, for example, the state from the church, the political from the religious organization. The confusion of community and state is increased by the usage of the same term to indicate either. Thus "United States" refers either to our national state association with its governmental apparatus or to the national community which it governs.

It is highly important, for the understanding of social structure and particularly of the evolution of that structure, that we should realize the associational character of the state. The state is an agency of peculiarly wide range, but nevertheless an agency. The state may assume at times absolutist or "totalitarian" form, claiming to control every aspect of human life. Even if this claim were *fully* realized—which never could be the case—the state would not become the community, but an association controlling the community.

Human beings are, without choice to be sure, citizens or subjects of the state. But they are also members of families and churches and clubs, they are friends or lovers, scientists or laborers or artists associating with their kind. However significant the citizen role may be, it is only *one* of many roles that each man exercises as a social being.

The state, we must recognize, is different in important respects from all other associations . . . [but] the state as a form of social organization is, like the church or business or club, an association.

[4]   *The Dangers of Nonconformism**

by MORRIS FREEDMAN

Not long ago I heard one of this country's professional intellectuals— a former university president, a present foundation president—address a university gathering of several hundred persons. The gentlemen attacked the blight of conformism in the United States; he deplored the fact that men in gray flannel suits had become "interchangeable"; he lamented the loss of true individualism. What struck me while listening to his urbane talk was his own "interchangeable" appearance: neat, three-button blue suit, plain tie, precisely coiffured graying hair, erect carriage: the very model of a model executive, not only interchangeable with dozens of men in similar positions and in "gentlemen of distinction" ads, but ready to be played in the movies by a dozen or so actors—Walter Pidgeon, Cary Grant, Gregory Peck, Ray Milland. It struck me as somewhat odd, too, that several hundred persons should applaud in unison a speech urging nonconformity, and that during the question period one of the questions that did not "conform" with the speaker's views should be greeted with derision.

Of course one man's conformism may be another man's heresy. But what seems to have taken place in American intellectual life in recent

* From *The American Scholar*, Winter 1958-1959 (Vol. 28, No. 1), pp. 25-32, *passim*. Reprinted by permission of the author.

years is the rising of just about any nonconformity to the status of respectable orthodoxy. . . .

It has been well-established that nonconformists, instead of responding to the values of tabloid newspaper, subway car, or television advertisements, respond to a no less specific and no less rigid set, particularly those in the advertisements of *The New York Times, The New Yorker*, the *Saturday Review* and the like, or of the commercials of FM stations that broadcast classical music all day. Although the nonconformist may refuse with a shudder to engage in the barbaric practice of drinking instant coffee, he will no less eagerly sip *espresso*. If you can construct a stereotype of the man in the street, you can build an equally plausible one of the man out of the street. . . .

It was not so long ago that a position taken by a Luce publication would have been instinctively opposed by large numbers of nonconformists; but *Life* in recent years has so well caught the importance of being fashionably nonconformist that it is now a leader in establishing accepted nonconformist thought, which, of course, some while ago spilled over from the highbrow crest onto the extensive middle-brow plateaus. On the matter of education, for example, *Life* and other media shaping mass nonconformist ideology have now laid down the party line, making it intellectually suicidal to suggest that possibly the educators have their own peculiar problems to solve before they can reshape their curricula to respond to the present pressures. On most campuses, I venture, a professor in liberal arts would be read out of the ranks if he said a good word about colleges of education, let alone about educational television, which combines two bogeys. . . .

Let me catalogue from my own recent experience a number of other positions, attitudes, and habits of behavior and thought no nonconformist in good standing can hold these days. These are, of course, subject to rapid change, like fashions in ladies' dress. Also, I should say, it is not essential to reject *all* to remain a respectable nonconformist—only most of them.

It is impossible, then, for the nonconformist to say a good word about Dulles, Nixon, Lyndon Johnson, or (since Dwight MacDonald's critique in *Commentary*) James Gould Cozzens, or a bad one about Henry James, Adlai Stevenson, Lionel Trilling, or Freud; to express approval of any television show (except *Omnibus*, Ed Murrow, or Sid Caesar), or of any American movie (except the inexpensive and badly lighted ones, or the solemn westerns, like *High Noon*); to dislike any foreign films (except those imitating American ones); to believe that you can buy ready-made a good hi-fi set; to wear a non-Ivy-league suit or long hair if a man, or to wear or not wear a sack dress if a woman (I am not sure what feminine nonconformism calls for at the moment); to prefer American cars to European; to believe that there may be any justice in the official position on Oppenheimer; to defend Western diplomacy on any basis; to invite company to dinner without candles on the table and chamber music in the background; to criticize Arthur Miller or Tennessee Williams as play-wrights or otherwise; to like Tchaikovsky or Irving Berlin, or to dislike Leonard Bernstein or Mozart; to express admiration for Marilyn Monroe or any other American movie star; to disparage Alec Guinness; and so on. . . .

There is no more self-righteously, high-mindedly closed a mind than that of a nonconformist. He will begin every conversation with some such gambit as "I know this isn't a popular position, but. . . ." He will insist that no one since Galileo or Joan of Arc has had as much courage as he. Challenge him, and he will dismiss you as a peasant not worth his atten-tion. "If you don't know what's wrong with American culture," I heard one champion nonconformist say down his nose to someone who mildly demurred on the subject, "then there's no point even talking with you."

CHAPTER TWO

Social Science and Its Methods

*W*HAT *ought social scientists to do, and what is their function in society? C. Wright Mills expresses strong dissatisfaction with what most present-day social scientists are doing. He accuses them of being preoccupied with trivial factual studies in the form of "abstract empiricism" or with vague generalities in the form of "grand theory." There is too great a concern with method, in the narrow sense, and too little concern with making man aware of mankind through cultivation of the sociological imagination. To Mills this means the ability to relate parts to wholes, to see individual lives and problems in terms of history and institutional changes—it means viewing the "present as history." The sociological imagination can be applied to help men understand themselves by uncovering the links between their individual experiences and historical processes. Social science was born out of the belief that man as a rational animal should be free to manage his affairs. Knowledge of the sort provided by the use of the sociological imagination promises to make it possible for people to guide their social destinies.*

[5] The Sociological Imagination: The Promise*

by C. WRIGHT MILLS

Nowadays men often feel that their private lives are a series of traps. They sense that within their everyday worlds, they cannot overcome their troubles, and in this feeling, they are often quite correct: What ordinary men are directly aware of and what they try to do are bounded by the private orbits in which they live; their visions and their powers are limited to the close-up scenes of job, family, neighborhood; in other milieux, they move vicariously and remain spectators. And the more aware they become, however vaguely, of ambitions and of threats which transcend their immediate locales, the more trapped they seem to feel.

Underlying this sense of being trapped are seemingly impersonal changes in the very structure of continent-wide societies. The facts of contemporary history are also facts about the success and the failure of individual men and women. When a society is industrialized, a peasant becomes a worker; a feudal lord is liquidated or becomes a businessman. When classes rise or fall, a man is employed or unemployed; when the rate of investment goes up or down, a man takes new heart or goes broke. When wars happen, an insurance salesman becomes a rocket launcher, a store clerk, a radar man; a wife lives alone; a child grows up without a father. Neither the life of an individual nor the history of a society can be understood without understanding both.

Yet men do not usually define the troubles they endure in terms of historical change and institutional contradiction. The well-being they enjoy, they do not usually impute to the big ups and downs of the societies in which they live. Seldom aware of the intricate connection between the patterns of their own lives and the course of world history, ordinary men do not usually know what this connection means for the kinds of men they are becoming and for the kinds of history-making in which they might take part. They do not possess the quality of mind essential to grasp the interplay of man and society, of biography and history, of self and world. They cannot cope with their personal troubles in such ways as to control the structural transformations that usually lie behind them. . . .

The very shaping of history now outpaces the ability of men to orient

---

* From *The Sociological Imagination*, by C. Wright Mills, pp. 3-24, 132-134 *passim.* © 1959 by Oxford University Press, Inc. Reprinted by permission.

36

themselves in accordance with cherished values. And which values? Even when they do not panic, men often sense that older ways of feeling and thinking have collapsed and that newer beginnings are ambiguous to the point of moral stasis. Is it any wonder that ordinary men feel they cannot cope with the larger worlds with which they are so suddenly confronted? That they cannot understand the meaning of their epoch for their own lives? That—in defense of selfhood—they become morally insensible, trying to remain altogether private men? Is it any wonder that they come to be possessed by a sense of the trap?

It is not only information that they need—in this Age of Fact, information often dominates their attention and overwhelms their capacities to assimilate it. It is not only the skills of reason that they need—although their struggles to acquire these often exhaust their limited moral energy.

What they need, and what they feel they need, is a quality of mind that will help them to use information and to develop reason in order to achieve lucid summations of what is going on in the world and of what may be happening within themselves. It is this quality, I am going to contend, that journalists and scholars, artists and publics, scientists and editors are coming to expect of what may be called the sociological imagination.

The sociological imagination enables its possessor to understand the larger historical scene in terms of its meaning for the inner life and the external career of a variety of individuals. It enables him to take into account how individuals, in the welter of their daily experience, often become falsely conscious of their social positions. Within that welter, the framework of modern society is sought, and within that framework the psychologies of a variety of men and women are formulated. By such means, the personal uneasiness of individuals is focused upon explicit troubles and the indifference of publics is transformed into involvement with public issues.

The first fruit of this imagination—and the first lesson of the social science that embodies it—is the idea that the individual can understand his own experience and gauge his own fate only by locating himself within his period; that he can know his own chances in life only by becoming aware of those of all individuals in his circumstances. In many ways it is a terrible lesson; in many ways, a magnificent one. We do not know the limits of man's capacities for supreme effort or willing degradation, for agony or glee, for pleasurable brutality or the sweetness of reason. But in our time we have come to know that the limits of "human nature" are frighteningly broad. We have come to know that every individual lives, from one generation to the next, in some society; that he

lives out a biography, and that he lives it out within some historical sequence. By the fact of his living, he contributes, however minutely, to
the shaping of this society and to the course of its history, even as he is
made by society and by its historical push and shove.

The sociological imagination enables us to grasp history and biography
and the relations between the two within society. That is its task and its
promise. . . . No social study that does not come back to the problems
of biography, of history and of their intersections within a society has
completed its intellectual journey. . . .

That, in brief, is why it is by means of the sociological imagination that
men now hope to grasp what is going on in the world, and to understand
what is happening in themselves as minute points of the intersections of
biography and history within society. In large part, contemporary man's
self-conscious view of himself as at least an outsider, if not a permanent
stranger, rests upon an absorbed realization of social relativity and of
the transformative power of history. The sociological imagination is the
most fruitful form of this self-consciousness. By its use men whose men-
talities have swept only a series of limited orbits often come to feel as if
suddenly awakened in a house with which they had only supposed themselves to be familiar. Correctly or incorrectly, they often come to feel that
they can now provide themselves with adequate summations, cohesive
assessments, comprehensive orientations. Older decisions that once appeared sound now seem to them products of a mind unaccountably dense.
Their capacity for astonishment is made lively again. They acquire a new
way of thinking, they experience a transvaluation of values; in a word, by
their reflection and by their sensibility, they realize the cultural meaning
of the social sciences.

Perhaps the most fruitful distinction with which the sociological imagination works is between "the personal troubles of milieu" and "the public issues of social structure." This distinction is an essential tool of the
sociological imagination and a feature of all classic work in social science.

Troubles occur within the character of the individual and within the
range of his immediate relations with others; they have to do with his
self and with those limited areas of social life of which he is directly and
personally aware. Accordingly, the statement and the resolution of troubles properly lie within the individual as a biographical entity and within
the scope of his immediate milieu—the social setting that is directly open
to his personal experience and to some extent his willful activity. A trouble is a private matter: values cherished by an individual are felt by him
to be threatened.

Issues have to do with matters that transcend these local environments of the individual and the range of his inner life. They have to do with the organization of many such milieux into the institutions of an historical society as a whole, with the ways in which various milieux overlap and interpenetrate to form the larger structure of social and historical life. An issue is a public matter: some value cherished by publics is felt to be threatened. Often there is a debate about what that value really is and about what it is that really threatens it. This debate is often without focus if only because it is the very nature of an issue, unlike even widespread trouble, that it cannot very well be defined in terms of the immediate and everyday environments of ordinary men. An issue, in fact, often involves a crisis in institutional arrangements, and often too it involves what Marxists call "contradictions" or "antagonisms."

In these terms, consider unemployment. When, in a city of 100,000, only one man is unemployed, that is his personal trouble, and for its relief we properly look to the character of the man, his skills, and his immediate opportunities. But when in a nation of 50 million employees, 15 million men are unemployed, that is an issue and we may not hope to find its solution within the range of opportunities open to any one individual. The very structure of opportunities has collapsed. Both the correct statement of the problem and range of possible solutions require us to consider the economic and political institutions of the society, and not merely the personal situation and character of a scatter of individuals.

Consider war. The personal problem of war, when it occurs, may be how to survive it or how to die in it with honor; how to make money out of it; how to climb into the higher safety of the military apparatus; or how to contribute to the war's termination. In short, according to one's values, to find a set of milieux and within it to survive the war or make one's death in it meaningful. But the structural issues of war have to do with its causes; with what types of men it throws up into command; with its effects upon economic and political, family and religious institutions, with the unorganized irresponsibility of a world of nation-states. . . .

In so far as an economy is so arranged that slumps occur, the problem of unemployment becomes incapable of personal solution. In so far as war is inherent in the nation-state system and in the uneven industrialization of the world, the ordinary individual in his restricted milieu will be powerless—with or without psychiatric aid—to solve the troubles this system or lack of system imposes upon him. In so far as the family as an institution turns women into darling little slaves and men into their chief providers and unweaned dependents, the problem of a satisfactory marriage remains incapable of purely private solution. In so far as the overdeveloped megalopolis and the overdeveloped automobile are built-in features of the overdeveloped society, the issues of urban living will not be solved by personal ingenuity and private wealth.

What we experience in various and specific milieux, I have noted, is often caused by structural changes. Accordingly, to understand the changes of many personal milieux we are required to look beyond them. And the number and variety of such structural changes increase as the institutions within which we live become more embracing and more intricately connected with one another. To be aware of the idea of social structure and to use it with sensibility is to be capable of tracing such linkages among a great variety of milieux. To be able to do that is to possess the sociological imagination. . . .

In every intellectual age some one style of reflection tends to become a common denominator of cultural life. Nowadays, it is true, many intellectual fads are widely taken up before they are dropped for new ones in the course of a year or two. Such enthusiasms may add spice to cultural play, but leave little or no intellectual trace. That is not true of such ways of thinking as "Newtonian physics" or "Darwinian biology." Each of these intellectual universes became an influence that reached far beyond any special sphere of idea and imagery. In terms of them, or in terms derived from them, unknown scholars as well as fashionable commentators came to re-focus their observations and re-formulate their concerns.

During the modern era, physical and biological science has been the major common denominator of serious reflection and popular metaphysics in Western societies. "The technique of the laboratory" has been the accepted mode of procedure and the source of intellectual security. That is one meaning of the idea of an intellectual common denominator: men can state their strongest convictions in its terms; other terms and other styles of reflection seem mere vehicles of escape and obscurity.

That a common denominator prevails does not of course mean that no other styles of thought or modes of sensibility exist. But it does mean that more general intellectual interests tend to slide into this area, to be formulated there most sharply, and when so formulated, to be thought somehow to have reached, if not a solution, at least a profitable way of being carried along.

The sociological imagination is becoming, I believe, the major common denominator of our cultural life and its signal feature. . . . By means of it, orientation to the present as history is sought. As images of "human nature" become more problematic, an increasing need is felt to pay closer yet more imaginative attention to the social routines and catastrophes which reveal (and which shape) man's nature in this time of civil unrest and ideological conflict. Although fashion is often revealed by attempts to use it, the sociological imagination is not merely a fashion. It is a quality of mind that seems most dramatically to promise an understanding of the intimate realities of ourselves in connection with larger social realities. It is not merely one quality of mind among the contemporary range of cultural sensibilities—it is *the* quality whose wider and more adroit use offers the promise that all such sensibilities—and in fact, human reason itself—will come to play a greater role in human affairs. . . .

In the absence of an adequate social science, critics and novelists, dramatists and poets have been the major, and often the only, formulators of private troubles and even of public issues. Art does express such feelings and often focuses them—at its best with dramatic sharpness—but still not with the intellectual clarity required for their understanding or relief today. Art does not and cannot formulate these feelings as problems containing the troubles and issues men must now confront if they are to overcome their uneasiness and indifference and the intractable miseries to which these lead. The artist, indeed, does not often try to do this. Moreover, the serious artist is himself in much trouble, and could well do with some intellectual and cultural aid from a social science made sprightly by the sociological imagination. . . .

Of late the conception of social science I hold has not been ascendant. My conception stands opposed to social science as a set of bureaucratic techniques which inhibit social inquiry by "methodological" pretensions, which congest such work by obscurantist conceptions, or which trivialize it by concern with minor problems unconnected with publicly relevant issues. These inhibitions, obscurities, and trivialities have created a crisis in the social studies today without suggesting, in the least, a way out of that crisis.

Some social scientists stress the need for "research teams of technicians," others for the primacy of the individual scholar. Some expend great energy upon refinements of methods and techniques of investigation; others think the scholarly ways of the intellectual craftsmen are being abandoned and ought now to be rehabilitated. Some go about their work in accordance with a rigid set of mechanical procedures; others seek to develop, to invite, and to use the sociological imagination. Some —being addicts of the high formalism of "theory"—associate and disassociate concepts in what seems to others a curious manner; these others urge the elaboration of terms only when it is clear that it enlarges the scope of sensibility and furthers the reach of reasoning. Some narrowly study only small-scale milieux, in the hope of "building up" to conceptions of larger structures; others examine social structures in which they try "to locate" many smaller milieux. Some, neglecting comparative studies

altogether, study one small community in one society at a time; others
in a fully comparative way work directly on the national social structures
of the world. Some confine their exact research to very short-run sequences
of human affairs; others are concerned with issues which are only apparent in long historical perspective. Some specialize their work according
to academic departments; others, drawing upon all departments, specialize according to topic or problem, regardless of where these lie academ-
ically. Some confront the variety of history, biography, society; others do
not. . . .

I believe that what may be called classic social analysis is a definable and usable set of traditions; that its essential feature is the concern with historical social structures; and that its problems are of direct
relevance to urgent public issues and insistent human troubles. I also
believe that there are now great obstacles in the way of this tradition's
continuing—both within the social sciences and in their academic and
political settings—but that nevertheless the qualities of mind that constitute it are becoming a common denominator of our general cultural
life and that, however vaguely and in however a confusing variety of
disguises, they are coming to be felt as a need.

Many practitioners of social science, especially in America, seem to me
curiously reluctant to take up the challenge that now confronts them.
Many in fact abdicate the intellectual and the political tasks of social
analysis; others no doubt are simply not up to the role for which they are
nevertheless being cast. At times they seem almost deliberately to have
brought forth old ruses and developed new timidities. Yet despite this
reluctance, intellectual as well as public attention is now so obviously
upon the social worlds which they presumably study that it must be
agreed that they are uniquely confronted with an opportunity. In this
opportunity there is revealed the intellectual promise of the social
sciences, the cultural uses of the sociological imagination, and the political
meaning of studies of man and society. . . . A truly remarkable variety
of intellectual work has entered into the development of the sociological
tradition. To interpret this variety as A Tradition is in itself audacious.
Yet perhaps it will be generally agreed that what is now recognized as
sociological work has tended to move in one or more of three general
directions, each of which is subject to distortion, to being run into the
ground.

Tendency I.   Toward a theory of history. For example, in the hands of
Comte, as in those of Marx, Spencer, and Weber, sociology is an encyclo-
pedic endeavor, concerned with the whole of man's social life. It is at
once historical and systematic-historical, because it deals with and uses

the materials of the past; systematic, because it does so in order to discern "the stages" of the course of history and the regularities of social life.

The theory of man's history can all too readily become distorted into a trans-historical strait-jacket into which the materials of human history are forced and out of which issue prophetic views (usually gloomy ones) of the future. The works of Arnold Toynbee and of Oswald Spengler are well-known examples.

Tendency II. Toward a systematic theory of "the nature of man and society." For example, in the works of the formalists, notably Simmel and Von Weise, sociology comes to deal in conceptions intended to be of use in classifying all social relations and providing insight into their supposedly invariant features. It is, in short, concerned with a rather static and abstract view of the components of social structure on a quite high level of generality.

Perhaps in reaction to the distortion of Tendency I, history can be altogether abandoned: the systematic theory of the nature of man and of society all too readily becomes an elaborate and arid formalism in which the splitting of Concepts and their endless rearrangement becomes the central endeavor. Among what I shall call Grand Theorists, conceptions have indeed become Concepts. The work of Talcott Parsons is the leading contemporary example in American sociology.

Tendency III. Toward empirical studies of contemporary social facts and problems. Although Comte and Spencer were mainstays of American social science until 1914 or thereabout, and German theoretical influence was heavy, the empirical survey became central in the United States at an early time. In part this resulted from the prior academic establishment of economics and political science. Given this, in so far as sociology is defined as a study of some special area of society, it readily becomes a sort of odd job man among the social sciences, consisting of miscellaneous studies of academic leftovers. There are studies of cities and families, racial and ethnic relations, and of course "small groups." As we shall see, the resulting miscellany was transformed into a style of thought, which I shall examine under the term "liberal practicality."

Studies of contemporary fact can easily become a series of rather unrelated and often insignificant facts of milieu. Many course offerings in American sociology illustrate this; perhaps textbooks in the field of social disorganization reveal it best. On the other hand, sociologists have tended to become specialists in the technique of research into almost anything; among them methods have become Methodology. Much of the work—and more of the ethos—of George Lundberg, Samuel Stouffer, Stuart Dodd, Paul F. Lazarsfeld are present-day examples. These tendencies—

to scatter one's attention and to cultivate method for its own sake—are fit companions, although they do not necessarily occur together.

The peculiarities of sociology may be understood as distortions of one or more of its traditional tendencies. But its promises may also be understood in terms of these tendencies. . . .

What social science is properly about is the human variety, which consists of all the social worlds in which men have lived, are living, and might live. These worlds contain primitive communities that, so far as we know, have changed little in a thousand years; but also great power states that have, as it were, come suddenly into violent being. Byzantine and Europe, classical China and ancient Rome, the city of Los Angeles and the empire of ancient Peru—all the worlds men have known now lie before us, open to our scrutiny.

Within these worlds there are open-country settlements and pressure groups and boys' gangs and Navajo oil men; air forces pointed to demolish metropolitan areas a hundred miles wide; policemen on a corner; intimate circles and publics seated in a room; criminal syndicates; masses thronged one night at the crossroads and squares of the cities of the world; Hopi children and slave dealers in Arabia and German parties and Polish classes and Mennonite schools and the mentally deranged in Tibet and radio networks reaching around the world. Racial stocks and ethnic groups are jumbled up in movie houses and also segregated; married happily and also hating systematically; a thousand detailed occupations are seated in businesses and industries, in governments and localities, in near-continent-wide nations. A million little bargains are transacted every day, and everywhere there are more "small groups" than anyone could ever count.

The human variety also includes the variety of individual human beings; these too the sociological imagination must grasp and understand. In this imagination an Indian Brahmin of 1850 stands alongside a pioneer farmer of Illinois; an eighteenth-century English gentleman alongside an Australian aboriginal, together with a Chinese peasant of one hundred years ago, a politician in Bolivia today, a feudal knight of France, an English suffragette on hunger strike in 1914, a Hollywood starlet, a Roman patrician. To write of "man" is to write of all these men and women—also of Goethe, and of the girl next door.

The social scientist seeks to understand the human variety in an orderly way, but considering the range and depth of this variety, he might well be asked: Is this really possible? Is not the confusion of the social sciences an inevitable reflection of what their practitioners are trying to study? My answer is that perhaps the variety is not as "disorderly" as the mere listing of a small part of it makes it seem; perhaps not even as disorderly as it is often made to seem by the courses of study offered in colleges and universities. Order as well as disorder is relative to viewpoint: to come to an orderly understanding of men and societies requires a set of viewpoints that are simple enough to make understanding possible, yet comprehensive enough to permit us to include in our views the range and depth of the human variety. The struggle for such viewpoints is the first and continuing struggle of social science.

Any viewpoint, of course, rests upon a set of questions, and the overall questions of the social sciences come readily to the mind that has firm hold of the orienting conception of social science as the study of biography, of history, and of the problems of their intersection within social structure. To study these problems, to realize the human variety, requires that our work be continuously and closely related to the level of historical reality—and to the meanings of this reality for individual men and women. Our aim is to define this reality and to discern these meanings; it is in terms of them that the problems of classic social science are formulated, and thus the issues and troubles these problems incorporate are confronted. It requires that we seek a fully comparative understanding of the social structures that have appeared and do now exist in world history. It requires that smaller-scale milieux be selected and studied in terms of larger-scale historical structures. It requires that we avoid the arbitrary specialization of academic departments, that we specialize our work variously according to topic and above all according to problem, and that in doing so we draw upon the perspectives and ideas, the materials and the methods, of any and all suitable studies of man as an historical actor. . . .

CHAPTER THREE

The Role of Culture

*T*HE concept of culture is a key concept of social science. Culture was first defined as that complex whole which includes knowledge, belief, art, morals, law, custom, and any other capabilities and habits acquired by man as a member of society. Today culture is defined more briefly as a way of life of a people, a legacy of tradition handed down from generation to generation—it is that part of the environment created by man. Because of the accumulation of tradition, even the simple things that people as animals want are expressed in cultural patterns—an animal eats when it is hungry, a human being waits for lunch. In the selections which follow Robert Redfield criticizes the doctrine of "cultural relativity." If everything is right in terms of its own logic, then nothing including tyranny can be condemned. Murdock finds broad similarities as well as diversities in culture. He describes those aspects of culture found wherever men are found. The third selection offers an American Indian's judgments on our way of life.

[6]   Cultural Relativism and Social Values*

by ROBERT REDFIELD

In this . . . chapter I will consider some of the questions that arise when we look at all the primitive or the precivilized cultures with a view to the goodness or the badness of them. My own behavior, as an anthropologist, is relevant to the subject now to be discussed, for I am interested here in the way anthropologists do or do not place values on the things they see in prehistoric or in contemporary nonliterate or illiterate societies, and what comes of it if they do. I shall venture to anthropologize the anthropologists, and shall not leave myself out of their number.

. . . Writing of Petalesharoo, the Pawnee Indian who in the face of the customs of his tribe rescued a woman prisoner about to be put to death ceremonially and strove to end human sacrifice among his people, I called him "a hint of human goodness." Plainly I placed a value on his conduct. Looking back twenty-five years, I recall when as a student I first heard the story of Petalesharoo from Professor Fay-Cooper Cole, anthropologist. He told the story with great human warmth, and I know that then I responded sympathetically. Now I begin to wonder if he or I *could* tell the tale barely, neutrally, without implying admiration of the deed.

In the course of these pages, I have not infrequently indicated my admiration for some act, my approval of some turn in human events. The long story of human affairs which I have been sketchily recounting is a story in which I have not pretended to be disinterested. It is the human biography; it is your story and mine; how can we help but care? I have not tried to conceal a certain sense of satisfaction that in the childhood of our race, before there were cities, precivilized men, like the preliterates of today, recognized moral obligations, even if the moral rules were not my rules. I think this better than the unrestrained selfishness which Hobbes imagined wrongly to characterize the behavior of men before political society developed. So when in the course of these discussions I have encountered in some uncivilized society a custom which I liked or disliked, I think I have in many cases shown how I felt about it. I re-

* From *The Primitive World and Its Transformations* by Robert Redfield, pp. 139-165, *passim*. Ithaca, N.Y., Cornell University Press. © 1953 by Cornell University. Reprinted by permission.

gret that the Siriono in the Bolivian forest abandon their dying kinsmen without a word, while I come to understand the rigors of their life that make such conduct excusable. I am pleased that the Yagua in their big communal houses respect even a child's desire to be alone, and refrain from speaking to him when he turns his face to the wall. . . .

This is, perhaps, a shocking admission. What right have I, who admit to caring about the human career, to speak as an anthropologist? For are not anthropologists enjoined to adopt in their work a rigid objectivity? Professor Kroeber has written that "there is no room in anthropology for a shred of ethnocentricity, of homino-centricity." My ethnocentricity appears in the positive valuations I have placed on the increase and widening of humane standards, for are not such standards a special pride of Euro-American civilization? And my homini-centricity is patent: I have placed myself squarely on the side of mankind, and have not shamed to wish mankind well.

My predicament stimulates an examination of some of the problems of objectivity and value judgment that arise in anthropology. There are a good many of these problems, and I shall try to sort them out and to reach at least the first points of understanding as to what is involved in some of them. . . .

Since Westermarck wrote two books to show that it is not possible to establish one way of thought or action as better than another, if not before that time, anthropologists have taken this position. It has come to have a name: cultural relativism. Most anthropologists would, I think, accept the term as naming their position, or would take the position without perhaps accepting the name. Cultural relativism means that the values expressed in any culture are to be both understood and themselves valued only according to the way people who carry that culture see things. In looking at a polygamous society and a monogamous society, we have no valid way to assert that one is better than the other. Both systems provide for human needs; each has values discoverable only when we look at marriage from the point of view of the man who lives under the one system or the other. This is, necessarily then, also to be said in comparing cultures which practice torture, infanticide, in-group sorcery, and homosexuality with those that do not. The gist of cultural relativism as stated by Professor Herskovits, who has discussed the concept at length, is that "judgments are based on experience, and experience is interpreted by each individual in terms of his own enculturation."

With this proposition I do not disagree. I fail to see that having accepted it one finds it necessary to accept everything else that Professor Herskovits says about cultural relativism. It is possible, I think, to agree that everybody passes judgments as guided by the experience he was brought up to have and recognize, and yet to assert some reasonable basis for preferring one thought or action to another. . . .

However this may be, I am persuaded that cultural relativism is in for some difficult times. Anthropologists are likely to find the doctrine a hard one to maintain. The criticisms of philosophers will be directed more sharply against it. Moreover, the experiences of anthropologists are changing, and these changed experiences will work changes in their judgments as to the relativity of values. (It occurs to me that this proposition is itself an application of the principle!) It was easy to look with equal benevolence upon all sorts of value systems as long as the values were those of unimportant little people remote from our own concerns. But the equal benevolence is harder to maintain when one is asked to anthropologize the Nazis, or to help a Point Four administrator decide what to do for those people he is committed to help. The Point Four man is committed to do something to change that people, for he cannot help them without changing them, and what is the anthropologist to say when the Point Four man asks him just what he ought to do? Perhaps the anthropologist can keep on saying: "Do A, and X will result, but Y will result from doing B—*you* choose which to do." But I doubt that if the anthropologist says only this, he and the administrator will get on very well together. And perhaps the anthropologist, if he continues this neutrality, and yet sees a smash coming, will be just a little restless at night.

At any rate, I should like to point out that the doctrine of cultural relativism does enjoin the benevolence. It is a doctrine of ethical neutralism, but it is not a doctrine of ethical indifference. Ruth Benedict's *Patterns of Culture* is an exemplification of cultural relativism. She wrote in large part to tell us that all cultures are "equally valid." But this meant, for her, not that we are to value none of them, but that we are to value all of them. The book is a call to positive sympathetic valuation of other ways of life than our own. Malinowski has gone so far as to write of "the respect due even to savages." And Herskovits states the positive element in the doctrine very clearly. He is not confused into supposing that cultural relativism is a mere scientific method, a procedure instrumental in reaching statements as to fact. No, he says, "cultural relativism is a *philosophy* which, in recognizing the values set up by every society to guide its own life, lays stress on the dignity inherent in every body of custom, and on the need for tolerance of conventions though they may differ from one's own." And again: "Emphasis on the worth of many ways of life, not one, is an affirmation of the values of each culture."

However, the two parts of this doctrine are not logically or necessarily interdependent. The first part says that people are brought up to see the value in things that their local experience has suggested. The second part says that we should respect all cultures. But there is no true "therefore" between these two parts. It cannot be proved, from the proposition that values are relative, that we ought to respect all systems of values. We might just as well hate them all. It is Professor Herskovits who has intruded upon the objectivity of science a moral judgment, which I personally admire, but for which he can show no demonstration of proof.

The anthropologist is, then, ethically neutral, but unlike him of whom the partisan demanded, "Just who are you neutral *for?*", the anthropologist is neutral for everybody. This, at least, is the way anthropologists represent their position. It seems to me that their success in living up to their doctrine may be questioned.

The difficulties of doing so were remarked by not a few of the anthropologists themselves when in 1947 the Executive Board of their American professional association submitted a statement to the Commission on Human Rights of the United Nations. The statement urged the Commission to recognize that, not only should the personality of the individual be accorded respect, but that "respect for the cultures of differing human groups is equally important." It declared the principle of cultural relativity and told the UN Commission that therefore any attempt it might make to write something about human rights ("formulate postulates") "that grow out of the beliefs or moral codes of one culture must to that extent detract from the applicability of any declaration of Human Rights to mankind as a whole." So the Commission was advised to incorporate in the Declaration of Human Rights a statement of the right of men to live in terms of their own traditions.

I understand that the UN Commission did not follow this advice. I imagine that some anthropologists are rather relieved that they did not. Such a declaration might seem to authorize the head-hunting peoples to continue head hunting, for would they not, by continuing head hunting, be living in terms of their own traditions? Of course the anthropologists who drafted this statement were not thinking of the head hunters. They knew, as well as you or I, that the head hunters and the cannibals will not be permitted to live in terms of these particular traditions if it is our heads and bodies they go for. They were thinking of the great and influential world civilizations—Indonesian, Indian, Chinese, African, Euro-American. But even here it is not clear just what the writers of the declaration expected to guarantee to these traditional ways of life—the right of a Mississippi human group to maintain its traditional white supremacy, of Russia to maintain a dehumanizing, fear-ridden way of life? At the time the anthropologists wrote their statement it was perhaps nazism that presented to their minds most plainly the difficulties with their statement, for they wrote the following sentence: "Even where political systems exist that deny citizens the right of participation in their government, or seek to conquer weaker peoples, underlying cultural values may be called on to bring the people of such states to a realization of the consequences of the acts of their governments." If we call upon underlying values to save us, it is we, on the outside of the culture, who are making them effective. And what if the underlying approved values are not there? The sentence is, to put it bluntly, a weasel; by including it, the declaration was made self-contradictory. You either respect all values or you do not. If the Nazis had come to have values approving the subjugation of everybody else, we, or the United Nations, would have either to respect this traditional way of life or not respect it. . . .

As soon as the anthropologist puts his attention on the particular human individuals in a primitive society, it becomes difficult to avoid the suggestion if not the fact that he is valuing one culture, or cultural situation, as better than another. It is not uncommon for an anthropologist, now studying a primitive culture disorganized by its contact with civilization, to see that the people he is studying are less comfortable than they were. Some of them, indeed, as those Oceanic natives whom Rivers described, appear now on their way to extinction just because they do not find life worth living any more. The anthropologist can hardly convince us—or himself—that so far as he is concerned a disorganized culture that fails to provide a desire to live is as valid as any other. Equal validity can be safely attributed only to cultures that arrange it so people do what they want to do and are convinced that it is the right thing to do.

But even among such cultures, the well-integrated and the motive-providing, it is not always possible for the anthropologist to avoid at least the suggestion that he is preferring one of them to another. Ruth Benedict was a cultural relativist who told us that cultures are equally valid. Nevertheless, in reading some of her pages, one doubts that she found them equally good. In the seventh chapter of *Patterns of Culture* she introduces the concept of "social waste." Here she leads the reader to see a resemblance between the values of Kwakiutl society and those of his own (Middletown); both emphasize rivalry. But rivalry, wrote Benedict, is "notoriously wasteful. It ranks low in the scale of human values." One asks, Whose scale? Is there a universal scale of values which ranks rivalry low? She goes on to point out not only that "Kwakiutl rivalry produces a waste of material goods," but also that "the social waste is obvious."

In Middletown, also, rivalry is "obsessive." Thus she is led to the conclusion that "it is possible to scrutinize different institutions and cast up their cost in terms of social capital, in terms of the less desirable behavior traits they stimulate, and in terms of human suffering and frustration." Apparently "social waste" includes a poor choice of desired behavior traits, human suffering, and frustration. In this passage Benedict is saying how, within one society (that of Middletown) one might make an evaluation, a sort of scoring, of the social waste that follows from one set of institutions rather than another. . . .

It is that disturbing fellow, the living human individual, who makes trouble for the scientist's stern principle of perfect objectivity. Whenever the anthropologist looks at him, something human inside the anthropologist stirs and responds. It is easy enough to be objective toward objects; but the human individual refuses to be only an object. When he is there before you, he insists on being judged as human beings are judged in life, if not in science. While the anthropologist is looking at the bones of the dead, at flint implements, or at institutions formally conceived and named—the Omaha kinship system or the tribal ideology—he is not much distracted by these claims upon his own human nature. But when the anthropologist meets and talks with some particular Indian or Oceanic islander, then he is apt to feel for that native while he is trying to describe him objectively. If the society is one that is running along the traditional ways of life, the field ethnologist is apt to respond with sympathy and indeed with favor toward the culture that keeps men's lives going in directions that they find good. If the ethnologist is himself gifted in communicating the human warmth of an exotic scene, as was Malinowski, an account results which communicates not only the humanity of the life described, but something of the enjoyment and satisfactions which the ethnologist himself experienced in coming to know that life. If the culture is one which puts the people who live by it into constant and fearful anxieties, the anthropologist is apt to show the disfavor he feels toward such a life. Reo Fortune's Dobuans are familiar; so I mention here instead the Tzeltal Indians of Chiapas, where Alfonso Villa Rojas found a people often sick, always believing that each sickness was the result of some moral transgression committed by the sufferer or, more terribly, by some one of his near kinsmen, and who are continually ridden by anxiety and compulsions to confess sins. Villa has described this people objectively, in the sense that his report is well documented and obviously trustworthy. But it would be untrue to assert that he has not shown, strongly in conversation and of course much more reservedly in his written description, his own unfavorable view of such a life. Furthermore, if one reads such an account of a people whose traditional ways of life have been disrupted, as, for example, McGregor's account of a reservation community of Sioux Indians, one finds oneself making value judgments that seem to reflect those of the writer, as to the somewhat unhappy predicament in which these people find themselves.

I think that the objectivity claimed by the anthropologist must admit of difficulties and qualifications. Professor Herskovits declares that "a basic necessity of ethnographic research . . . calls for a rigid exclusion of value judgments." This seems a little too strongly put. Rather, I should say, ethnographic research calls for as much objectivity as can be combined with the necessity to come to know the values of the people one is studying. The exception to allow the ethnographer to respect—i.e., value positively—all cultures, has already been noted. Professor R. H. Tawney is then expressing an opinion with which we may suppose that Professor Herskovits would agree when he writes that the student of a society must bring to his study "respect and affection." The necessity to understand the values of the people one is studying requires, I should say, the projection into unfamiliar words and action of human qualities—sympathy, pride, wish to be appreciated, and so on. Otherwise the ethnologist will not find out what the people he is studying are proud about or what, for them, deserves appreciation. My own opinion is that it is not possible to make use of these human qualities in field work, as I think one must, without also valuing what one sees. In the very necessity to describe the native, one must feel for him—or perhaps against him. The feelings are mixed with valuations. In Indian communities in which I have worked, I have found myself constantly liking and disliking some people as compared with others, some customs as compared with others, and some aspects of the total culture as compared with others. I remember, after having spent a good deal of time in Chan Kom, Yucatan, how I had come to admire a certain quality of decency and dignity about the people, and how bored I had become with their—to me—overemphasis on the prudent and the practical. If they would only once admire a sunset or report a mystic experience, I used to hear myself thinking. I would not know how to find out about a culture without this sort of valuing. Objectivity requires that I hold in suspense each formulation I make about the native life. It requires me to become aware of the values I have that may lead me in one direction rather than another. It demands that I subject my descriptions to the tests of documentation, internal consistency, and if possible the evidence and judgments of other observers. But I do not think that it asks of me that I divest myself of the human qualities, including valuing. I could not do my work without them. . . .

Perhaps we should ask of the field ethnologist, not that he divest himself of values, for that is impossible, nor that he emphasize in every case values predominating in his own times with regard to applied science, increased production, and adjusted personalities, but that he make plain what he does find that is good or bad about the people he reports. And then, also, perhaps he can help to bring it about that he is followed in the same community to be studied by an ethnologist with a contrasting value emphasis! It was *The New Yorker* that suggested that we do not want balanced textbooks; we want balanced libraries. We do not want ethnologists so balanced that they have no humanity. We want a balanced profession, a varied lot of anthropologists. . . .

My praise of Petalesharoo here receives explanation, if not justification. Petalesharoo acted against the customary practice of his people. It is a little easier to do that after civilization than before; in precivilized societies it was harder. So Petalesharoo gets my praise on that count. And when he acted, he acted in conformity with the trend of the human career of which he was ignorant, but which I know about, being some thousands of years older in civilization than was he. So it is not remarkable that I praise him. Perhaps also you, my reader, do too.

If you do, and you are not an anthropologist, no one will scold. But I am an anthropologist, and have taken the oath of objectivity. Somehow the broken pledge—if it is broken—sits lightly on my conscience. In me, man and anthropologist do not separate themselves sharply. I used to think I could bring about that separation in scientific work about humanity. Now I have come to confess that I have not effected it, and indeed to think that it is not possible to do so. All the rules of objectivity I should maintain: the marshaling of evidence that may be confirmed by others, the persistent doubting and testing of all important descriptive formulations that I make, the humility before the facts, and the willingness to confess oneself wrong and begin over. I hope I may always strive to obey these rules. But I think now that what I see men do, and understand as something that human beings do, is seen often with a valuing of it. I like or dislike as I go. This is how I reach understanding of it. The double standard of ethical judgment toward primitive peoples is a part of my version of cultural relativity. It is because I am a product of civilization that I value as I do. It is because I am a product of civilization that I have both a range of experience within which to do my understanding-valuing and the scientific disciplines that help me to describe what I value so that others will accept it, or, recognizing it as not near enough the truth, to correct it. And if, in this too I am wrong, those others will correct me here also.

[7]   *Universals of Culture**

by GEORGE P. MURDOCK

Early reports of peoples lacking language or fire, morals or religion, marriage or government, have been proved erroneous in every instance. Nevertheless, even today it is not generally recognized how numerous and diverse are the elements common to all known cultures. The following is a partial list of items, arranged in alphabetical order to emphasize their variety, which occur, so far as the author's knowledge goes, in every culture known to history or ethnography: age-grading, athletic sports, bodily adornment, calendar, cleanliness training, community organization, cooking, cooperative labor, cosmology, courtship, dancing, decorative art, divination, division of labor, dream interpretation, education, eschatology, ethics, ethnobotany, etiquette, faith healing, family, feasting, fire making, folklore, food taboos, funeral rites, games, gestures, gift giving, government, greetings, hair styles, hospitality, housing, hygiene, incest taboos, inheritance rules, joking, kin-groups, kinship nomenclature, language, law, luck superstitions, magic, marriage, mealtimes, medicine, modesty concerning natural functions, mourning, music, mythology, numerals, obstetrics, penal sanctions, personal names, population policy, postnatal care, pregnancy usages, property rights, propitiation of supernatural beings, puberty customs, religious ritual, residence rules, sexual restrictions, soul concepts, status differentiation, surgery, tool making, trade, visiting, weaning, and weather control.

Cross-cultural similarities appear even more far-reaching when individual items in such a list are subjected to further analysis. For example, not only does every culture have a language, but all languages are resolvable into identical kinds of components, such as phonemes or conventional sound units, words or meaningful combinations of phonemes, grammar or standard rules for combining words into sentences. Similarly funeral rites always include expressions of grief, a means of disposing of the corpse, rituals designed to protect the participants from supernatural harm, and the like. When thus analyzed in detail, the resemblances between all cultures are found to be exceedingly numerous. . . .

The true universals of culture, then, are not identities in habit, in defin-

* From *The Science of Man in the World Crisis,* edited by Ralph Linton, pp. 123-125 *passim.* New York, Columbia University Press, copyright 1945. Reprinted by permission.

able behavior. They are similarities in classification, not in content. They represent categories of historically and behaviorally diverse elements which nevertheless have so much in common that competent observers feel compelled to classify them together. There can be no question, for example, that the actual behavior exhibited in acquiring a spouse, teaching a child, or treating a sick person differs enormously from society to society. Few would hesitate, however, to group such divergent acts under the unifying categories of marriage, education, and medicine. All of the genuinely widespread or universal resemblances between cultures resolve themselves upon analysis into a series of such generally recognized categories. What cultures are found to have in common is a uniform system of classification, not a fund of identical elements. Despite immense diversity in behavioristic detail, all cultures are constructed according to a single fundamental plan—the "universal culture pattern" as Wissler has so aptly termed it.

The essential unanimity with which the universal culture pattern is accepted by competent authorities, irrespective of theoretical divergences on other issues, suggests that it is not a mere artifact of classificatory ingenuity but rests upon some substantial foundation. This basis cannot be sought in history, or geography, or race, or any other factor limited in time or space, since the universal pattern links all known cultures, simple and complex, ancient and modern. It can only be sought, therefore, in the fundamental biological and psychological nature of man and in the universal conditions of human existence. . . .

[8]   *An Indian's Soliloquy**

by BURT W. AGINSKY

While doing field research in northern California with an Indian group which had suffered a great deal under the disruptive influences of Spanish and Americans, I became familiar with an old Indian man well over one hundred years of age. He had lived through a period which encom-

* From *The American Journal of Sociology*, Vol. XLVI, pp. 43-44, published by The University of Chicago Press. Reprinted by permission.

passed the days before any whites had come into his territory, the Spanish raids, the white massacres, the herding of his people upon reservations, and the variegated civilized tortures accompanying these deprivations. One day after a long period of discussion concerning the changing family situation he talked eloquently for a period of about two hours. As soon as it was possible I returned to my headquarters and recorded what he had said in as close an approximation as I could.

An old Pomo Indian once said to me: "What is a man? A man is nothing. Without his family he is of less importance than that bug crossing the trail, of less importance than the sputum or exuviae. At least they can be used to help poison a man. A man must be with his family to amount to anything with us. If he had nobody else to help him, the first trouble he got into he would be killed by his enemies because there would be no relatives to help him fight the poison of the other group. No woman would marry him because her family would not let her marry a man with no family. He would be poorer than a newborn child; he would be poorer than a worm, and the family would not consider him worth anything. He would not bring renown or glory with him. He would not bring support or other relatives either. The family is important. If a man has a large family and a profession and upbringing by a family that is known to produce good children, then he is somebody and every family is willing to have him marry a woman of their group. It is the family that is important. In the white ways of doing things the family is not so important. The police and soldiers take care of protecting you, the courts give you justice, the post office carries messages for you, the school teaches you. Everything is taken care of, even your children, if you die; but with us the family must do all of that.

"Without the family we are nothing, and in the old days before the white people came the family was given the first consideration by anyone who was about to do anything at all. That is why we got along. We had no courts, judges, schools, and the other things you have, but we got along better than you. We had poison, but if we minded our own business and restrained ourselves we lived well. We were taught to leave people alone. We were taught to consider that other people had to live. We were taught that we would suffer from the devil, spirits, ghosts, or other people if we did not support one another. The family was everything, and no man ever forgot that. Each person was nothing, but as a group joined by blood the individual knew that he would get the support of all his relatives if anything happened. He also knew that if he was a bad person the head man of his family would pay another tribe to kill him so that there would be no trouble afterward and so that he would not get the family into trouble all of the time.

"That is why we were good people and why we were friends with the white people when they came. But the white people were different from us. They wanted to take the world for themselves. My grandfather told me that the white people were homeless and had no families. They came by themselves and settled on our property. They had no manners. They did not know how to get along with other people. They were strangers who were rough and common and did not know how to behave. But I have seen these people of yours are even worse. They have taken everything away from the Indians, and they take everything away from one another. They do not help one another when they are in trouble, and they do not care what happens to other people. We were not like that. We would not let a person die of starvation when we had plenty of food. We would not bury our dead with no show. We would kill another person by poisoning him if he was an enemy, but we would not treat a stranger the way they treat their own brothers and sisters. Your people are hard to understand. My brother lived with your people for twenty years, and he said that he was used to you; but he cannot understand yet why you people act as you do. You are all the same in one way. We are all the same in another. What is wrong with you? The white people have the land. They own the courts, they own everything, but they will not give the Indians enough money to live on. It is hard to understand.

"With us the family was everything. Now it is nothing. We are getting like the white people, and it is bad for the old people. We had no old peoples' homes like you. The old people were important. They were wise. Your old people must be fools."

CHAPTER FOUR

Culture and the
Natural Environment

*B*ETTY J. *Meggers considers the relations of environment to culture. The evidence she examines suggests that the environment exerts a limiting effect on the cultures it supports. This limiting effect is insurmountable in relation to hunting and subsistence food-gathering patterns of life. In the case of agricultural economies, a breakthrough is achieved and culture becomes progressive; the level to which a culture can develop is dependent upon the agricultural potentialities of the environment it occupies. As these potentialities improve, culture will advance. The concept of differential potential is offered as an explanation of both the regional distribution of cultures and the lack of stability of certain culture areas through time.*

[9]   Environmental Limitation on the Development of Culture*

by BETTY J. MEGGERS

The relationship of culture to environment is one of the oldest problems in the science of anthropology and has provided a leading source of controversy. Early students, impressed with the ways in which cultures were adjusted to unique features of their local environments, developed the concept of environmental determinism. As more field work was done by trained observers, the variability in culture patterns became more evident and the idea of determinism was rejected. Then, as individual cultures were grouped into culture areas and recognized as specific manifestations of a general pattern, the role of environment once again compelled attention. . . .

There are few anthropologists today who would disagree with the general statement that environment is an important conditioner of culture. However, efforts to establish the relationship more specifically seem to give negative results. The potentialities of a particular habitat can be seen reflected in the subsistence pattern, the material culture, and by extension, in the social and religious aspects of the culture that is exploiting it, but when cultures of similar subsistence patterns or general features are compared they are not found to occupy similar environments. Hunting tribes, for example, may live in semi-deserts, swamps, forests, grasslands, or mountains, and in the arctic, the tropics or the temperate zone. Conversely, areas that seem similar geographically may differ greatly culturally. This has led to the conclusion expressed by Forde:[1]

> Physical conditions enter intimately into every cultural development and pattern, not excluding the most abstract and non-material; they enter not as determinants, however, but as one category of the raw material of cultural elaboration. The study of the relations between cultural patterns and physical conditions is of the greatest importance for an understanding of human society, but it cannot be undertaken in terms of simple geographical controls alleged to be identifiable on sight. It must proceed inductively from the minute analysis of each actual society.

Given the traditional conceptions of environment, no other conclusion is possible. However, in view of the very definite evidence that cultures have

---

* From "Environmental Limitation on the Development of Culture," by Betty J. Meggers. *American Anthropologist*, LVI (1954), pp. 801-824, *passim*. Reprinted by permission of the author and publisher.
[1] Daryll Forde, *Habitat, Economy and Society* (London, 1934), p. 464.

an ecological aspect, which can be shown to have a determinative character particularly on the lower levels, it does not seem likely that no more general relationship exists. It is more probable that, in attempting to discover it, we have not been distinguishing the fundamental factors involved. All the efforts to correlate culture with environment have utilized the landscape classifications set up by geographers. James, for example, has summarized world environments under eight principal types: dry lands or deserts, tropical forests, Mediterranean scrub forests, mid-latitude mixed forests, grasslands, boreal forests, polar lands and mountain lands. It has frequently been noted that these categories do not represent cultural uniformities or even similarities. Desert cultures range from food gatherers to high civilizations; both polar lands and boreal forests, on the other hand, are exploited by food gatherers. Since environment does have an important effect on culture, and since the usual geographical classifications fail to discriminate culturally significant units, it is logical to search for some other basis for distinction.

DEFINITION OF ENVIRONMENT

The primary point of interaction between a culture and its environment is in terms of subsistence, and the most vital aspect of environment from the point of view of culture is its suitability for food production. Until the discovery of agriculture, this was relatively equal over the major portion of the earth's surface. In some areas game, wild plants or fish were more abundant than in others, but the range of variation was slight in comparison with what it became following the adoption of agriculture. The cultivation of cereals was designated by Tylor as "the great moving power of civilization," and the cultural revolution that followed in its wake has since been commented upon frequently. Most anthropologists, however, do not carry the analysis beyond the effect that agriculture has had on culture, to the effect that environment has on the productivity of agriculture. Differences in soil fertility, climate and other elements determine the productivity of agriculture, which, in turn, regulates population size and concentration and through this influences the sociopolitical and even the technological development of the culture. Once this point is raised, it is evident that differential suitability of the environment for agricultural exploitation provides a potential explanation for differences in cultural development attained around the world.

To be culturally significant, a classification of environment must recognize differences in agricultural potential. Areas that permit only limited, shifting cultivation because of the poverty of the soil must be distinguished from those of enduring fertility where intensive agriculture can be practised over long periods of time. An examination of the methods of food production suggests that four types of environment can be recognized, each with a distinct agricultural and cultural implication:

Type 1.—Areas of No Agricultural Potential.   This includes the greatest variety of natural landscapes because only one of the many components necessary for agriculture need be absent for the area to be unsuitable. The defective element may be soil composition, temperature, rainfall, short growing season, elevation, terrain, etc. Type 1 regions include tundra, some deserts, tropical savannas, swamps, some mountain ranges, and similarly uncultivable types of land.

A few areas with no agricultural potential are suitable for a pastoral economy. These constitute a special category of Type 1 because food gathering is replaced by food production and a higher level of cultural development can be attained than is typical of Type 1 areas. Some Type 3 areas have also supported pastoral cultures on the aboriginal level. However, since pastoralism is a minor source of food production compared to agriculture among the cultures of the world, and lacks both the environmental adaptability and the variety of potentiality for cultural development characteristic of agriculture, it will receive only brief mention in this discussion.

Type 2.—Areas of Limited Agricultural Potential.   Here agriculture can be undertaken, but its productivity is minimized by limited soil fertility, which cannot economically be improved or conserved. When the natural vegetation cycle is broken by clearing, planting and harvesting, the delicate balance between what is taken from and what is returned to the soil is upset. The soil is poor to begin with, and exposed fully to the detrimental effects of the climate, it is quickly exhausted of plant nutrients. The addition of fertilizer is not feasible on a primitive level or economically practical on a modern one. Since the major cause of this condition is abundant rainfall and high humidity, Type 2 environments may be restricted to the tropics, and a good example is the South American tropical forest and selva. This does not mean, however, that all tropical environments are necessarily Type 2.

Up to the present time, no method of maintaining such areas in continuously profitable, intensive food production has been found, in spite of our extensive knowledge of plants and soils. Permanent and intensive production has been achieved in some places by the introduction of tree crops (cacao, coffee, bananas, citrus, etc.) and jute, but with the possible exception of the banana, none of these could provide an adequate subsistence base. Should a solution appear in the future, the "limited" designation for

Type 2 might have to be modified, but since the obstacles to the increased productivity of food crops are infinitely greater than in Type 3, a distinction between the two should still be made.

Type 3.—Areas of Increasable (Improvable) Agricultural Potential. Areas of this type contain all the essentials for agricultural production that exist in Type 2. However, being in more temperate climates where rainfall and humidity are less detrimental, soil exhaustion is caused mainly by the raising of food crops. Under a slash-and-burn type of utilization, the productivity of the land is not much greater than that of Type 2 areas. However, crop returns can be appreciably increased by techniques such as rotation, fallow and fertilization, and the same fields can be kept in almost constant production over long periods of time if not permanently. Temperate forest zones like Europe and the eastern United States belong in this category.

Other Type 3 environments are less readily improved because the deficient element is not soil fertility, but water. The Imperial Valley of California is such a case, where agriculture is made possible by water brought long distances over mountains.

Further methods of increasing agricultural potential are by the introduction of more suitable plants, such as the replacement of dry rice by wet rice in Madagascar, and the introduction of new or improved tools like the animal-drawn plow in the North American plains.

Type 4.—Areas of Unlimited Agricultural Potential. Here the natural environment approximates as closely as possible the ideal conditions for agriculture. Climate, water and terrain are suitable and soil fertility is for the purposes of this discussion inexhaustible, so that the land can support intensive food production indefinitely. The "cradles of civilization" all belong to Type 4.

The classification of an area into one of these types is theoretically independent of the time factor. Since the introduction of agriculture in most of the world, there has been little alteration in climate or topography that has affected the agricultural potentiality of the environment. Where changes have occurred because of climatic shifts, such as the gradual northward extension of the limit of agriculture in North America, the area can be reclassified in accord with its new potential.

For purposes of practical ease in identifying an area as to type, the year 1950 can be taken as a base line. If an area is improvable by modern agricultural techniques, it is Type 3, regardless of what might have been its primitive or aboriginal usage. If it cannot be shown to have been so improved, or to be comparable to some area where similar natural deficiencies in agricultural potential have been compensated for with modern knowledge and techniques, then it is Type 2 or Type 1, depending on whether agriculture is feasible or impossible. Type 3 areas, as will be seen, are most dependent on such technical advances to develop their potential. Type 4 areas are highly productive even with relatively primitive means of exploitation. . . .

If we accept as a working hypothesis the existence of a definite cause and effect relationship between these four kinds of environment and the maximum cultural development they can continuously support, the next step is to examine from this point of view some of the evidence that has been assembled about cultures. Since limitations of space do not permit coverage of the world, the greatest temporal, spatial and cultural variety may be included by using South America as a test area. . . .

CULTURE AND ENVIRONMENT IN SOUTH AMERICA

. . . The evidence suggests that the environment exerts an insurmountable limiting effect on the cultures it supports as long as it permits only a hunting and gathering subsistence pattern, and that this limitation extends to all areas of the culture, even those that seem remotely or not at all related to the subsistence requirements. No amount of inventive genius or receptivity to borrowing that might be theoretically attributable to the people psychologically is sufficient to overcome this barrier. . . .

In the Andean culture area with a Type 3 and Type 4 environment, the highest cultural development in South America was achieved. The Peruvian coastal valleys furnish the longest uninterrupted prehistoric sequence, partly because favorable conditions for preservation accompany favorable conditions for human occupancy. Art and crafts, social organization, and religion were elaborated to an extent that rivaled what had been achieved in Europe in the same centuries. Cotton and woolen textiles were produced by a variety of techniques, some so complex that they cannot be duplicated on modern machine looms, and often ornamented with elaborate designs. Pottery was mass-produced and of high quality. Metallurgy included casting, alloying, plating of gold, silver and copper. Massive fortifications, agricultural terraces, palaces, temples and lesser buildings were constructed of carefully fitted stone masonry or adobe. Minor arts and crafts existed in profusion. Settlements ranged from small villages to cities, some of which were administrative centers attaining an estimated population of 100,000. A network of roads facilitated communication and transportation of goods between towns.

The functions of government were handled by a hierarchy of officials of increasing rank and responsibility, culminating in the divine and absolute monarch. Class distinctions were clearly defined and hereditary, with distinctive garments, insignia and other privileges for individuals of the upper class. Governmental supervision touched all aspects of life; the duties and obligations of each individual were fixed, all activities were regulated. It is almost superfluous to add that occupational division of labor was advanced to modern proportions. The religious organization paralleled the governmental one, with a hierarchy of priests headed by a close relative of the ruler. These presided over temples dedicated to gods of varying importance and housing images and ceremonial paraphernalia. The gods were approached with blood sacrifice, fasting, prayer and offerings, and ceremonies were held in accord with the ritual calendar.

The existence of so elaborate a civilization depends upon the intensive production of food and its effective distribution. Large irrigation works increased cultivatable land in the valleys on the coast, and terracing with fertilization was employed in the highlands. Specialization in crops permitted each region to grow what was best suited to its climate, altitude and soil. The surpluses of one year or area were stored for distribution in time of need. These methods were so productive that many thousands of commoners could be levied for military service, labor on public works or similar specialized tasks that contributed nothing to the basic subsistence. The closeness of the correlation between these advanced technological and sociological features and the highly productive subsistence base is demonstrated by the failure of the Inca Empire to extend its boundaries into regions with lesser agricultural potential. The failure to expand farther north or south might be laid to the slow communication and consequent difficulties in maintaining control, which were compounded as distance from the center increased. This could not excuse lack of expansion to the east, however, nor would it have prevented the diffusion of advanced pottery and weaving techniques, which were not adopted to any extent by neighboring tribes.

The evidence summarized above leads to the following conclusion: In determining the degree of evolution that a culture or culture area can attain, geographical location (in terms of proximity to centers of diffusion), intelligence (or genius) and psychological receptivity to new ideas are not as important as environment as it is reflected in the subsistence resources. If the temperature, soil, altitude, rainfall, growing season, terrain or some other factor will not permit agricultural production, then only unusual circumstances in the form of a bountiful and permanent supply of wild food (as on the Northwest Coast), or the adoption of a pastoral food production (as in parts of Asia) will permit the cultural adaptation to go beyond nomadic family bands with a minimum of material equipment and social organization. Where other factors are favorable, but the soils are of limited natural fertility that cannot be artificially increased, agriculture can be carried on although it requires constant clearing of new fields to be maintained. Even with such limitations, the effect on culture is remarkable, bringing a radically altered settlement pattern and an increase in the inventory of material traits. However, unless a method of continuing fields under permanent production is found, the culture can never proceed beyond a simple level. Where soils are of increasable or unlimited fertility and capable of permanent productivity, cultural evolution has no environmental limitation.

CHAPTER FIVE

Primitive and Modern Societies

IN the selection that follows Redfield outlines the way in which all human societies, primitive and modern, operate; indicating the functions they perform as well as their essential characteristics. A society is people who share a common way of life, a culture, and feel themselves in some important way to be a unit. The simplest answer Redfield offers to the question, How does a whole society operate? is that it operates because, on the whole, people do what is expected of them. Modern societies differ from the simplest societies in their dependence upon political institutions to keep the behavior of people more or less within the rules, in line with prevailing expectations.

67

[10]   How Human Society Operates*

by ROBERT REDFIELD

What Is a Society?   A society is people with common ends getting along with one another. A brawl in a barroom is not a society, nor is there yet a society when ten exhausted shipwrecked sailors clamber up on a lonely beach—at least there is none until they begin to work out their common problems of getting a living and of living together. A society has, then, organization. It is people doing things with and to and for each other to the interests of each and all in ways that those people have come to accept.

In this sense a group of boys organized to play baseball or to exchange postage stamps is a society, but here we have in mind those societies in which people are organized not for some special purpose or interest, but for all the business and pleasure of living. The societies that are the subject of this chapter are composed of men and women and children living together, generation after generation, according to traditional ways of life. Such societies are whole societies, in that they exist for all human needs and interests. They are enduring societies in that children are born and raised to become adults with ways of life much like those of their parents and grandparents. A nation is such a society, and so is an Indian tribe. So, too, is a town or village, and even a single family in so far as its members have traditions that are transmitted to each succeeding generation and make that family, through time, distinguishable from other families. On the other hand groups of nations taken together are great societies; one speaks of Western society in contrast to Oriental society. In some sense all the people of the world taken together constitute a single society. But it is of the separate tribes and nations that we are chiefly thinking here. Because there have been and still are so many and so various primitive societies, one learns a good deal about society in general by referring, as will be done in this chapter, to one or another of these simple societies.

A society is easily seen as people doing work. It has other aspects, too. A society is also people sharing common convictions as to the good life. This is to say that it is not merely a system of production and of services —an anthill is that—but that a human society exists in the fact that its members feel that certain conduct is right and other conduct wrong, and act more or less accordingly. And a third aspect of human society is to be

* From *Man, Culture, and Society,* edited by Harry L. Shapiro, pp. 345-368, *passim.*

recognized in the sentiment its members have of belonging together as against other people who do not belong. A society is people feeling solidarity with one another.

A Society as People Doing Work.   In every society the work is divided. Everyone takes advantage from work done by others of a kind which he does not do and in exchange serves those others by doing useful things that are not done by them. The division of labor between men and women is universal, in that everywhere what women do is on the whole different from what men do; on the other hand what each sex does varies with the society: in Polynesia the men did the cooking; among the Hidatsa Indians the women did the farming. Equally obvious is the division of labor that goes with differences in age. Beyond these bases for the organization of work, there are those which depend on differences in temperament, or on training, or on the accidents of opportunity, or on the variations in demand.

In some small, isolated, primitive societies there is almost no division of labor except between the sexes and the age-groups, and except some individuals who act as magicians or as leaders of ceremonies. Every adult man does about what every other does, and so it is with women. With the development of tools and techniques, with increase in population, and with the advancement of communication and transportation, the division of labor has become far more complete and complex. In the Guatemalan village of San Pedro de la Laguna, fifty-nine different kinds of specialists are to be recognized in a population of less than two thousand. A classified telephone directory suggests but by no means completely lists the thousands and thousands of kinds of specialists that make up a modern city.

An obvious result of this increasing division of labor is the increasing ease in the number and kinds of commodities and services which people can enjoy. But another effect is to limit the view which any one individual has of the operations and goals of his society to a very small segment of the whole, with corresponding difficulties for industrial management, for democratic government, and for personal happiness. Another result is greatly to extend the number and distribution of people who divide labor with one another. Millions of people, from China to the Congo to Akron, come to depend upon one another for services and products exchanged, and yet these people have no common purposes and understandings; they hardly know that one another exist. The organization of work tends to become worldwide while national and other local groups distrust, dislike, or fear one another. So men come to depend upon one another while yet without common sentiments and values.

A Society as People Sharing Convictions about the Good Life.   The organization of work takes place in ways other than the mere division of labor. Slavery is a way of organizing work. The market, to be discussed below, is another way. And a third, perhaps the basic form of the organization of work, arises from the fact that in a society people share common sentiments and beliefs as to what it is good to do. People work, not only because in most cases they are uncomfortable or even starve if they do not, but because work is a part of the meaning of life. To the primitive agricultural Indian, farming is a necessary part of decent and appropriate human existence, an essential way of maintaining relationship with the supernaturals, a test and duty of honorable manhood. In such a society one prays as one works, and work is, in part, religion. In aristocratic societies of recent times on the other hand, work was appropriate only to the underprivileged masses; while in modern Western society work is again a general positive value, and men work for wealth and power and to excel their neighbors. . . .

A Society as People Feeling Solidarity with One Another.   A society also operates by virtue of the confidence its members feel in one another and of the loyalty they have to their own group. It is said that the dangers of a great war between the present great powers of this earth would be quickly averted if Mars would attack this planet. Perhaps it would be sufficient for us earth-dwellers merely to know that there were Martians. We would feel a new sense of solidarity for all fellow earth-beings as contrasted with those inferior or iniquitous Martians. At any rate it appears that the members of every society, small or great, think very well of themselves as contrasted with the members of comparable societies. What is seen on a small scale in gangs, appears again in nations. Every tribe and nationality, in some parts of the world every valley or cluster of hamlets, refers to itself in favorable terms and to others unfavorably. Many primitive tribes reserve the term for "people" or "human beings" to themselves alone, while everywhere the terms used to refer to neighboring peoples are contemptuous, derogatory. It would seem, indeed, that the resentment and scorn shown toward other peoples are strongest with regard to neighboring people, as though, as Sigmund Freud remarked, one could least well bear to see what is so much like oneself and yet so different.

In cases where one society is divided into subgroups, each with its own loyalty, but yet a loyalty subordinated to that of the entire tribe or nation, this fact of appreciation of the lesser in-group and depreciation of the out-group contributes to the effective operation of the society. There is a special kind of strength in a tribe divided into clans, for each clan is a warm and supporting intimate group for every individual within it; its limited solidarity is intensified by the contrast and competition with other clans. A similar effect is brought about by the grouping of colleges within a university, and perhaps was realized among the nations of Europe in the nineteenth century, when all the nations were held together by a degree of common tradition and by common commercial and banking interests, so that national pride flourished while wars were limited to moderate destructiveness. . . .

Warfare. Of many forms of organized violence, warfare is that one which has political consequences. The rivalry between closely related groups that is an aspect of the in-group sentiments just referred to, often leads, obviously enough, to organized violence. The brawls between gangs of boys in the city characteristically are regulated by custom and form; and this formal aspect of violence between closely related groups is marked in the primitive societies. Usually such violence, which is not war, follows upon the commission by some individual of an act which in a modern society would be called a crime. Among Australian aborigines the offender is required to stand and receive spears thrown at him. Among the Eskimo the quarrelers publicly sing insulting songs at one another. All these cases of limited and regulated fighting are ways to adjust differences between constituent groups of a larger unit; they are more closely related to law than to war. Distinguished also are the very common instances, in primitive society, of armed raids upon unfriendly groups to take heads, scalps, or other trophies, or to bring back human sacrifices. This resembles war, in that the groups engaged are persistingly hostile, and the military enterprises are organized and lethal. Yet in many of these cases there is a strong element of sport: such organized conflict is a dangerous game, in which glory may be won and lives lost. This element persisted in the warfare of western societies until very recently. Other cases of this general group involve a religious motive: the head or the scalp is taken to bring supernatural power to the taker's group, or the captive is brought home as an offering to the deities.

In none of these cases is warfare an instrument of tribal or national policy. True warfare is probably to be recognized in those military activities in which political power is extended to include culturally related peoples, and in those in which the rivalries of two culturally different groups are put to the test of armed conflict. In the operation of societies such warfare plays a double role. It both destroys and constructs societies. In ancient Mexico the Aztecs entered upon warfare with neighboring peoples; the object was in large part the obtaining of captives for sacrifice, but a result was the subordination of many neighboring peoples of similar culture to the Aztec military power. In ancient Peru warfare led to a much stronger political and administrative organization: a state over a thousand miles in extent was the result. Similar political consequences followed from warfare among the Maori of New Zealand and among several African tribes. With this political motive an economic motive enters in, not among the most primitive people, but where there is enough property and wealth to attract the military marauder. And mixed also, as causes, are the personal ambitions of military leaders. . . .

Property. Among the common understandings which constitute the ultimate basis of society are those which attach to things that may be used, enjoyed, or disposed of. Where the understandings limit or otherwise define such rights and obligations of one individual or one group as to others, we speak of "property." Property operates to keep use and enjoyment and disposal in expected channels; it contributes to the working of society in wide and far-reaching ways: to confer and to limit power and the basis for getting more power; to serve as a criterion for status; to provide motives for effort. Wanting to own things, men may work, steal, or go to war. Owning things, men may enter social groups otherwise barred to them, exercise influence over political decisions, or assume correspondingly great responsibility for serving the common good.

Property is thought of most immediately in connection with such tangible goods as tools, automobiles, houses, and land. It exists also, with respect to such intangibles as magical spells, power-inducing songs addressed to supernaturals, hunting and fishing rights, patents and copyrights. In some societies personal names are owned in that they may be disposed of by sale or gift; in our society, a trade name may be registered and so owned. On the whole, the conceptions of ownership have become more complex with the developing complexity of society. Land, in particular, has become subject to private and exclusive ownership, with rights of sale and disposition by will; in most primitive societies such precise and exclusive rights to land are not recognized; nevertheless, individual or familial rights over hunting and fishing territories may be sanctioned in custom in some very simple societies. . . .

Status, Prestige, and Rank. Society operates through the division of labor and the social organization of production and consumption. Society operates through understandings as to proper conduct which have become traditional. Society operates through the guidance provided by conventional rights and obligations connected with the individuals and the groups making up the society. These, as already indicated, constitute the "status" of the individual or the group. What is expected of any particular person, or group of them, or of the occupier of any particular role or office, is known in advance, and this foreknowledge enables the people of the society to do what is expected and what is consistent, more or less, with the ideals that the people have in common. In this way, too, society operates.

Society may thus be seen as a system of status relationships. Many of these take the form of relationships of kinship. . . . Also mentioned already is the status of the members of the in-group as contrasted with that of the out-group. And easily added are the differences in status of a man as contrasted with a woman, or a priest, policeman, or potentate as contrasted with a man who is none of these things. Conduct is expected of the one, and is due to him, different from that expected of or due to the other. In every society there are status-groups connected with differences in age. Any school reveals them, where they are connected with the grades through which the child passes. In many primitive societies this sort of classification in terms of status is made without schools; boys and men pass through a series of ranked groups, each perhaps with its name, its rights and duties, its growing prestige. In many cases certain of these age-groups enjoy a special clubhouse, or have special secrets or ceremonies. Such a ladder of attainment defines what is expected of everyone according to successive categories, from birth to death. . . .

Custom and Law. The simplest answer that can be made to the question, how does society operate, is that it operates because on the whole people do what is expected of them. But why do people do what is expected of them? To this question there are many true answers. It is easier to do what one has done before than to do something else; a habit that everyone in a society has we call a custom. Further, the things that one has done, and that one's father's father has done, as well as some things that have been thought over and struggled for, have come to be so rooted in sentiments and in explanations and justifications that they have the force of what we speak of as conscience: they are felt to be right, ultimately and necessarily right. And still further, one does what is expected of one because it is often extremely inconvenient, even dangerous, if one does not. That is why I do not start out tomorrow to drive on the left-hand side of an American road. There is an efficiency, an ease, about doing what is expected of one. In a more special form, the expediency of doing what other people expect appears in the exchanges of services and benefits which help us all to get along. I do a thing helpful to another knowing that he is then more apt to do something helpful to me. If I pay my bills, lend my lawnmower, keep out of those of my neighbor's affairs which correspond to those of mine that I want him to keep out of, and yet listen to enough of his troubles so that I may tell him mine, we all get along pretty well. It is, however, to be emphasized that it is the nature of human society to regard these considerations of expediency, important as they are, as less worthy than those which are rooted in conscience and the sense of duty. Society is not, basically, so much a body of traffic rules and favors exchanged as it is a system of moral conviction.

At a more obvious level society operates because conduct is sanctioned. A sanction is a consequence, pleasant or unpleasant, that follows the doing of something and is known to follow it. Some such consequences are internal—the pangs of conscience—but others fall upon the transgressor from without. Of those that so fall, many are imposed by almost anybody in a diffuse and generalized way, as is illustrated by the looks I receive from the people who know me if I do something of which they disapprove. Perhaps what I do is not otherwise punishable. If a specific consequence follows through the exercise of some centralized authority, we begin to think of the transgression and its consequence as an affair of the law. Legal sanctions have a quality of preciseness about them: the misconduct is defined in advance in clear terms, and the consequence is also precisely known. Commonly the procedure for matching the transgression to its appropriate consequence—complaint or arrest, charge, hearing, trial, judgment—is specific and formal. Also, for the matter to be one of law and not just custom, the consequence that is the sanction is carried out not entirely if at all by the particular person that suffered from the transgression, but by someone or some body that stands for the society as a whole and acts for it. Law is the whole society settling a local dispute or punishing or redressing a wrong in the interests of the whole society and according to its common conscience. . . .

Political Institutions.   In the simplest societies there is nothing that is "political" if we use that word for institutions to express or enforce the common will or the ruler's will formally and publicly. In the Andaman Islands the natives lived in small bands without chief, council, law, or administrative regulation. If a man lost his temper and smashed things, the rest of the people just let him alone till he got over it. No one exercised any general authority to rule or to decide or to negotiate on behalf of the community. In such a society there is no state, no political government. Political institutions do clearly appear, however, in many tribal societies; there is a chief who has power to decide issues or to lead in the making of decisions; there may be a council; there may be groups to police the people.

The dependence of modern complex societies upon political institutions for their operation is obvious. The making, enforcing, and interpreting of law is the manifold business of thousands of individuals and hundreds of bodies: from legislatures, courts, and executives to the citizens who vote or obey orders, bring law suits or defend them, pay taxes, and discuss public issues with their neighbors or write a letter to some newspaper. These political institutions keep people's behavior more or less within the rules. They also are a means to the reconsideration of the rules and for the changing of the rules. They operate in that frontier of rule-making and rule-observing where conflicts occur, or at least differences of opinion, and the enforcement and interpretation of the rules helps to keep at least some of the people conscious of them, and so pushing to change them. Formal political institutions not only keep societies going in the good old ways; they also provoke a challenge of those ways. . . .

Religion. Some of the sanctions that keep men doing what is expected of them are neither the exterior sanctions of the law or of public opinion, nor the wholly interior sanctions of conscience. The sentiments that arise within a man that prevent him from doing that of which he would be ashamed, or that condemn him for doing it, in certain situations seem to come from outside him, yet not to come from this earthly world. Then it is a religious sanction that affects him. The convictions about the good are associated with unseen powers; these powers *are* the good, or represent it. A man's relationships to them have a unique quality; they are supremely critical for his ultimate welfare; and before the powers or their symbols he feels awe. The consequence of his action that is the sanction in this case may be a punishment, a suffering here on earth or a suffering in some other life. It may be a hand withered, or a soul damned. The suffering—or the reward, should his conduct be right, not wrong— may be simply the sense that the unseen powers are satisfied or dissatisfied, the feeling that one is or is not in harmony with ultimate goodness, final and unearthly authority.

Religion has been briefly defined as the adoration of goodness. It is goodness that is its essence; religion is not concerned with the trivial, nor with the morally neutral. It is about what most matters. But though an aspect of the moral life, it is not the same as morals. There are peoples— and many of these are primitive, uncivilized—whose religions are the worship of propitiation of supernatural beings who do not enforce the rules of good conduct among men. In such religions it is the worship and the propitiation, the ritual and the relationship between man and god, that matter; earthly morality is supported by conscience and the interplay of reciprocal obligations among people. In other religions, of which Christianity, Islam, and some primitive ones are examples, what a man should do to or for another *is* a matter of divine concern. On the whole, the ethical aspects of religion have grown stronger in the course of human history.

Religion is, moreover, activity; it is something going on in mind and in overt act; it is belief and rite. The power that is beyond men and that holds the welfare of men, mundane and spiritual, is thought about, conceived in certain forms and powers, and approached in prayer and offering and sacrifice. Commonly the power is conceived with qualities that are personal; the god may be angered, appeased, gratified. But in some religions, as in forms of Buddhism, the rites and beliefs have to do with conduct and with spiritual qualities. A religion is yet a religion even though it does not center about a god or gods.

Religion thus contributes to the operation of society through the power and authority and sacred meaning which it provides to the support of man's conduct and to his understanding of his place in the universe. . . .

The Expressive Life. In many of the preceding pages of this chapter the operation of society has been described as a matter of work and discipline. It has been suggested how people become and continue as a society by virtue of the fact that they labor together for common ends, and how they are kept at it by the convenience of co-operation and by the rewards and penalties which are provided by law, the general opinion, or the conscience of the individual. In this account the sober, the practical, and the constraining have perhaps been too strongly emphasized. Perhaps the impression has been given that society gets along wholly or chiefly because people do what they are compelled to do, or that work is the sole or the basic form of activity.

As a matter of fact, a very great part of human social behavior is quite the opposite of work. In work one does what a particular end demands in just the way it demands it and when the end requires it. To hoe corn effectively is usually work because one must move the hoe just so, one must do the hoeing just when the weather and the weeds make it necessary, and one may not stop when one would care to. But a very great deal of human activity is simply expressive. It is activity which responds to the impulse of the individual to be active; it is activity which takes a form that shows what the individual is thinking and feeling; it is a fruit of the human impulse to create. Some expressive activity takes place when it occurs to the individual to express himself; much takes place at times fixed by the expectations and rhythms of society, but even then without having to meet the demands of practically useful effort.

Laughing, joking, improvising with language, storytelling, praying, arranging flowers, painting pictures, enjoying or playing a ball game or Beethoven, and dancing are all forms of expressive activity. The expressive forms of behavior in large part give each society its own special character as they give special flavor to each personality. Different societies may have the same tools and the same work habits, but if their art and storytelling are different, the societies are then different. "What do you dance?" is the first enquiry a man of a certain Bantu tribe puts to a stranger. What a man dances in that part of Africa is the key to a man's whole life, the way to ask about a foreign society. . . .

All these forms of expressive action help in the operation of society by providing opportunities for carrying out the expectations which are the basis of society and by depicting to its members the related conceptions and ideals. Games involve the ideas and ideals as to sportsmanship which the society entertains; playing them disciplines player and audience toward these ideals and tests each player by them. In many primitive societies some games are representations of religious ideas. A game played by the ancient Maya represented the movement of the divine sun through the heavens; yet the game was sport too. "Pure art" is a relatively new and unusual conception; in most times and places art is or has been a form for the expression of the religious conceptions, or for the earthly ideas and ideals. The totem poles carved by Indians of the Northwest Coast proclaimed the social position and divine connections of the family connected with the pole. . . .

This chapter suggests some of the answers to the question expressed in its title: How does a human society operate? In its first pages the answer given was that a society is kept in operation by arrangements whereby a number of people can do the work that needs to be done to keep them going and whereby they can feel that they belong together and share a kind of life which they believe to be good. There is a world of necessity into which people are born; to survive they must live together; to live together they must have tacit agreements as to who does what, and is what. They must, in short, regulate their common life. The regulation is a matter of conventional understandings partly as to what each one should do, and partly as to what is, generally and for everybody, the good life. The plan of the good life finds expression, it was then added, in religion, myth, and art. We can think of the operation of society as machinery for social control and also as a sort of charter or drama of a scheme of all things.

But there is another way to think of the operation of society that is, probably, implicit in what has been written here. We may also think of society as operating so as to realize impulses and meet needs of human beings. Instead of asking, as we have, What operations keep this society going? we can ask, What is there about society that keeps human beings going? Any human being must have protection and food, and we can see society as providing for these necessities. Human beings have also sexual demands or needs, and every society provides some arrangement for meeting these. Moreover, beyond this, human beings have characteristics that are not shared with the animals but are peculiarly human. While it is perhaps not possible very definitely to describe the human impulses and needs beyond those that are shared with animals, it is hardly possible to deny that there are some; and society may thus be seen as a way of providing for the development and expression in everyone of human nature. In this sense, society operates by doing for us what our natures, given society, demand.

CHAPTER SIX

Social Change and Social Problems

SOCIETIES, like all other phenomena of nature, are in incessant change. What is the direction of social change? Are we moving toward some desired goal, or toward catastrophe? Does social change possess form and regularity, depending upon certain laws of change? Can the causes and sources of social change be discerned and, perhaps, be controlled for the great benefit of mankind? These are questions Kingsley Davis considers. They are most important questions. Since men are social creatures, social change means change in people—to change society is to change man.

The rapidity of social change in modern times raises the important problem of social adjustment. This is the issue which concerns Ogburn. His thesis is that the various parts of modern culture are not changing at the same rate, some are changing rapidly, some more slowly. Since the various parts of culture are interdependent, the result is often seen in dislocation, maladjustment of parts, and social problems. Material conditions and material culture change most rapidly, while the non-material, the adaptive part of culture often changes slowly—thus a lag develops which may last for years.

[11] *The Meaning of Social Change**

by KINGSLEY DAVIS

To see a picture of the strange clothes that were worn only yesterday, to read the history of the queer customs and ideas that once were current, to hear predictions of the marvels that are destined for tomorrow—to do these things is to realize the incessant changeability of human society. Individuals may strive for stability and security; societies may foster the illusion of permanence; the quest for certainty may continue unabated and the belief in eternity persist unshaken, yet the fact remains that societies, like all other phenomena, unremittingly and inevitably change.

This fact of change has long fascinated the keenest minds and still poses some of the great unsolved problems in social science. What, for instance, is the *direction* of social change? Is it toward some goal, toward some catastrophe, or toward mere extinction? . . . What is the *form* of social change? Is it more rapid now than in the past, and will it be more rapid in the future? . . . What is the *source* of social change? Is it a matter of borrowing or a matter of independent invention? . . . What is the *cause* of social change? Is it some key factor that explains all change, a prime mover that sets everything else in motion, or is it many different factors operating together? . . . And finally, what is necessary for the *control* of social change? Can we regulate and guide it in the direction of our heart's desire? . . . These are the tantalizing questions—tantalizing not only because of their difficulty but because of their human significance. Since men are social creatures, social change means human change. To change society is to change man.

For obvious reasons social change has been a perennial happy hunting ground for spurious theories and illogical beliefs. It has been approached too often with the reformer's zeal and with a philosophical or religious question uppermost. The strictly scientific literature on it is scant indeed, and none too good. If the following discussion can clarify some of the issues and suggest a few truths, it will have achieved its purpose. Necessarily social change has been discussed in various connections in early parts of the book. The present chapter aims merely to state the problem and define the major theoretical issues.

Social versus Cultural Change. By "social change" is meant only such alterations as occur in social organization—that is, the structure and func-

---

* From Kingsley Davis, *Human Society*, pp. 621-631. Copyright 1948 and 1949 by The Macmillan Company, and used with their permission.

tions of society. Social change thus forms only a part of what is essentially a broader category called "cultural change." The latter embraces all changes occurring in any branch of culture, including art, science, technology, philosophy, etc. as well as changes in the forms and rules of social organization.

To illustrate, let us cite on the one hand the rise of organized labor in capitalistic society and, on the other, the occurrence of systematic sound shifts in the Indo-European languages. The first represents a basic alteration in the relation of employer and employee, and has had repercussions throughout the economic and political organization of modern civilization. The second is just as definitely a change. The sound shifts in the various languages after separation from the original and long extinct Aryan mother-tongue were strikingly regular and parallel, so that the philologists could reduce them to a few basic principles such as Grimm's Law. But this phonetic change neither arose from nor affected the social organization of the peoples who spoke the Indo-European languages. It was purely a linguistic phenomenon, a cultural rather than a social change.

Cultural change is thus much broader than social change. Since our interest is focused on the narrowed topic we shall not become involved in such matters as the evolution of phonetic sounds, the history of art forms, the transition of musical styles, or the development of mathematical theory. Of course, no part of culture is totally unrelated to the social order, but it remains true that changes may occur in these branches without noticeably affecting the social system. Sociologically, therefore, we are interested in cultural change only to the extent that it arises from or has an effect on social organization. We are not interested in it for itself apart from social change.

Change versus Interaction. From the standpoint of atomic physics an iron bar is not quiescent. Instead its protons and electrons are constantly active. Yet the shape of the bar remains relatively fixed, altering only when it is smelted, bent, rusted, broken, welded, etc. Similarly the individuals in a society are constantly interacting, yet the structure governing such activity—the forms and rules of interaction—may remain relatively stable for long periods of time. The activity itself should not be confused with changes in the structure, which alone comprise social change.

For example, the principle of monogamous wedlock has remained fixed in American law from the beginning. Marriage has changed in many ways but not in this one particular. Yet many millions of Americans have entered wedlock under this principle and have left it through death or divorce. Each such step has meant an important change to them as individuals but not a change in the social order. Just as linguistic change does not refer to the activity of speaking but rather to the forms of speech, so social change does not refer to social interaction but rather to the normative conditions of interaction.

Certainly there is a close connection between social interaction and social change, for it is mainly through interaction that change comes about. The development of organized labor occurred, in part at least, because of strains in the interaction of employer and employees under the old system. In other words interaction is possible because there is a structure, and change is possible because there is interaction.

The distinction between interaction and change may seem elementary, but in practice it is not always clear. For instance, where does the phenomenon called "the circulation of the elite" belong? Pareto, who has discussed this phenomenon at great length, seems to believe he is discussing social change. Yet if the conditions by which the elite are recruited remain the same, there is no social change but merely social circulation or "metabolism." If, on the other hand, as Pareto seems to intimate, the displacement of one elite by another alters the social structure, it is social change—even though it may occur in cycles.

Short- versus Long-Run Changes. It seems wise to emphasize fairly long periods—generations or centuries at least— in first approaching the topic of social change. This helps to eliminate the confusion between interaction and change, and saves us from too great a preoccupation with the ephemeral present. What seems important today, what seems a vital change, may be nothing more than a temporary oscillation having nothing to do with essential trends. This is what historians mean when they say that time alone can place the events of the day in their true perspective. In any case, in discussing social change, one should specify the length of time one has in mind.

Whole Societies versus Parts. Any social system differs in different epochs. Some of its parts may remain virtually stable but as a whole it changes. This fact has led many authors to try to delineate types of societies and to interpret social change as the successive shifting from one type to another. The task has proved extremely difficult, because societies differ in such myriad ways that any typology seems rough and vague. Scholars have been forced to talk about the "spirit," the general "ethos," or the "essence" of one society as against another. The very names they have given the alleged types disclose the nebulous and sometimes metaphorical character of their speculations. For instance Spengler distinguishes "Faustian," "Apollonian," and "Magian" cultures; Sorokin, "Ideational," "Sensate," and "Idealistic"; and Ruth Benedict, "Apollonian" and

"Dionysian." MacIver points out that these terms are so indefinite that the same ones are applied to the most advanced societies (e.g. by Spengler) and to the most primitive ones (e.g. by Ruth Benedict). In addition different scholars looking at the same society are apt to characterize it differently, according to which particular traits they emphasize.

Perhaps the analysis of change in the parts of society may throw light on changes in the whole. As we shall see later, the way the different parts of society figure in the process of change is by no means clear, however.

Description versus Analysis. The poorest way to understand social change is simply to recapitulate all past changes. Twenty tomes would not suffice for such recapitulation, nor would any amount of repetition give it relevance.

Information, no matter how reliable or extensive, which consists of a set of isolated propositions is not science. A telephone book, a dictionary, a cookbook, or a well-ordered catalogue of goods sold in a general store may contain accurate knowledge, organized in some convenient order, but we do not regard these as works of science. Science requires that our propositions form a logical *system*, that is, that they stand to each other in some one or other of the relations of equivalence and opposition already discussed.[1]

If a mere narrative were adequate for an understanding of social change the best means would be a moving picture of everything that happens. This film could then be run off whenever the subject of social change arose. The only trouble would be that showing the picture would take as long as it took the events to happen in the first place. We would have to repeat life in order to understand life.

The study of social change has often tended in the direction of sheer history, with no real light on causation; or, discouraged by the avalanche of facts, it has tended in the direction of sheer generalization, with mere citation of examples instead of systematic proof or disproof. To strike a golden mean requires that the facts be marshalled, organized, and dealt with in terms of theoretical propositions susceptible of verification. Only in this way, by a *method* of analysis, can this kaleidoscopic phenomena of history be reduced to scientific order.

The Rate of Change. One must conceive of a balance of opposed forces, some favoring change, others opposing it. To the extent that they cancel each other, stability reigns. To the extent that forces favoring change prevail, a rate of change results.

But the "rate of change" has two different applications according to whether one thinks of whole societies or of parts. In the first application

[1] Morris R. Cohen and Ernest Nagel, *An Introduction to Logic and Scientific Method* (New York: Harcourt, Brace, 1934), p. 128.

the rate refers to the rapidity of change in different societies or in the same society at different times. Thus modern Europe is commonly believed to have changed more rapidly than Medieval Europe and, in the nineteenth century, the United States more rapidly than Latin America. In the second application the rate refers to the rapidity of change in various parts of the same society, usually in the same period. Thus it is a disputed question as to whether in Western civilization during the last three centuries, economic and political institutions have changed more rapidly than familial and religious institutions.

No matter in which context, the comparison of rates of change is exceedingly difficult. To begin with, there are few ways of measuring change in an entire society. By what procedure, for example, can one prove statistically that the Roman society of the first century A.D. was changing more or less rapidly than the Greek society of the fifth century B.C.? It seems best to break the problem down into component parts. One may compare the changes in religion in the two places at the specified times, and also the changes in government, kinship, business, and what not. This has the advantage that in each case things of the same order are being compared—government with government, business with business, etc. In the end one may arrive at a tentative summation of the relative rates of change in the two societies during the two periods, although the techniques of measurement in the various fields would be hard to contrive.

When a comparison is made between different parts of society, an important basis of comparability is lost. How can it be proved, for instance, that the replacement of private by public ownership of railroads is a greater or lesser change than the passage of a prohibition amendment, or that the development of air transportation is a greater or lesser change than the spread of college education? It may seem absurd to speak of relative rates of change in such noncomparable matters—like asking if a giraffe moves faster than a cell divides—but it is sometimes done.

It is extremely difficult if not impossible to prove that in fact the rate of change in a particular part of culture is faster than the rate in other parts. On logical grounds we suspect that any such diversity of rate, if it occurs at all, occurs for a very limited time. The notion of "lag" implies that in order to have an "adjusted society" all parts of culture must eventually "catch up" with the most rapidly changing parts; and since a society must be fairly well "adjusted" in order to keep going, the size of the lag cannot grow continually larger. If there were a permanent difference in the rate of change, no matter how small, it would eventually produce a gap that would be intolerably wide. This reasoning suggests that over a long period the rate of change in two different parts of culture cannot be very different. We must conclude, therefore, that comparisons of rates of change between different parts of social organization have at best a dubious validity, and that comparisons between different whole societies, though difficult, may have a better claim to validity.

The Direction of Change. Though it appears difficult to say that within a given period a change from believing in three gods to believing in one is faster or slower than a change from horse-drawn to motor-drawn vehicles, one possible way of making the two comparable is to take into account the direction of change. If the ultimate result is going to be a belief in six gods, a change from a belief in three to a belief in one is not speed at all but retrogression. If in the same society the ultimate vehicle is to be a sun-driven motorcar, a change from horse-powered to gasoline-powered vehicles may be a step toward that result and therefore "faster" than the other change. Thus changes in different parts of culture could be compared with respect to the rapidity with which they approach the eventual result.

In most discussions of social change some direction is assumed. Often, however, this assumption is not inherent in the facts but is contributed by the wishes of the observer. The direction is interpreted as tending towards some goal that the individual would like to see reached, and it is against this goal (not the actual end-result) that "speed" or "slowness" is measured. Frequently it *is* possible to discern a consistent trend in changes that have taken place in the past—for example, the trend of modern technology toward greater productivity. But such a trend may not continue forever. It may reverse itself, in which case there would still be change but in the opposite direction. Again, the length of time under discussion must be kept in mind.

Attempting to take account of the direction of change is necessary procedure both in organizing the facts and in arriving at causal principles. But a trend cannot be extrapolated unless there are logical and empirical grounds lying outside the given phenomenon for expecting a continuation of the trend. For instance, the fact that a given population has been growing rapidly does not mean that it will continue to grow at the same rate. An analysis of the various demographic and social factors affecting population growth may indicate that it will grow even more rapidly or considerably less so. When "factors" are mentioned we are obviously in the realm of causal analysis, which is fundamental both for a consideration of rates and for a consideration of direction.

The Forms of Social Change. Closely linked with the question of direction is the problem of the *form* of social change. This seemingly boils down to a single issue—namely, whether change is cyclical or linear. An extreme statement of the cyclical hypothesis would be that social phenomena of whatever sort (whether specific traits or whole civilizations) recur again and again, exactly as they were before. An equally extreme statement of the linear hypothesis would be that all aspects of society change continually in a certain direction, never faltering, never repeating themselves. Put so baldly, neither of these statements would prove acceptable to most people. Yet what sort of an answer can be given? Is there any sort of compromise? Yes, if we confine ourselves to what is known rather than to the eternal, there is a possible compromise.

It is quite obvious that any trend will show minor fluctuations, for nothing changes at identically the same rate from one year to the next; and it is equally obvious that recurrences will not be absolutely perfect, for nothing returns to exactly its original state. Proponents of the linear or the cyclical view really take refuge in the unknown. They argue that although fluctuations and trends are both observable, social change is "ultimately" one or the other. Their opinions thus become philosophical dogmas rather than scientific hypotheses.

We cannot know anything about *all* of social change. We can know only about the social change that is observable. At best we have reasonably full data concerning a few thousand years of human history, out of millions of past years and no telling how many future ones. Any claim that a mode of change has always persisted and always will persist clearly goes beyond empirical knowledge. The question of what is the ultimate nature of social change is therefore simply a philosophical puzzle that has no place in social science. When we confine ourselves to what is knowable, we find both trends and fluctuations. Indeed, whether a given change is cyclical or linear depends largely on the span of time under consideration. A decline in business appears as a trend if only a few years are taken, whereas in a larger time context it appears as merely one phase of the business cycle.

The Source of Social Change.   For a long time a controversy raged in cultural anthropology as to which is the more important, invention or diffusion. Though not quite dead, it is a dying controversy—not because one side is winning but because the question is proving pointless.

The emphasis on diffusion was in the main a protest against the evolutionary point of view, which had implied that culture develops through a series of self-generating stages. The diffusionists pointed out that independent invention occurs with extreme rarity. The fact that a particular society has a given cultural trait is not usually due to its having evolved to that stage, but to the fact that it borrowed the trait from another society. Indeed, by the simple process of borrowing, a primitive society may become civilized within a century or so (as the Maori are doing today in New Zealand) and thus jump across a cultural chasm that took thousands of years to bridge by independent invention.

The diffusionists were correct in their criticism of the extreme evolutionary point of view. Yet they too overstated their case. Some of them went so far as to claim that two similar traits in two different societies could not possibly be due to invention in both places. The civilizations of South and Central America, for example, could not have arisen by themselves, but must have obtained their civilized traits from Egypt by way of India, Java, and Polynesia.

Obviously, the opposition between these two points of view is much like that between environmentalists and hereditarians, or linear and cyclical theorists.[2]

As usually happens in the perpetration of scientific fallacies, the error has been introduced into the framing of the question. Hence we are tempted at first sight to jump to the erroneous answer. The correct reply to the . . . question, however, must insist that the very opposition, sharp and precise though it appears, between diffusion and invention, is really misleading.

Let us inquire, then, what precisely an "invention" is. In the case of every modern invention, we know that it is invariably made and re-made time after time in different places, by different men along slightly different roads, independently of one another. It is enough to mention the famous disputes about the discovery of the infinitesimal calculus, the steam engine, the telephone, the turbine, the wireless; the endless priority wrangles in science; the difficulties of establishing rights to a patent; and so on. The fact is that each invention is arrived at piece-meal, by infinitely many, infinitely small steps, a process in which it is impossible to assign a precise share to any one worker or still less to connect a definite object and a definite idea with a single contribution. In the wireless, for instance, the man to whom the invention is popularly ascribed has little more than commercialized the already existing practical appliances. The real work can be traced back through Righi, Braun, Hertz, Clerk-Maxwell, Faraday, Ampere, and so on back to Galvani and Galileo. But these are only the summits—illuminated by the flash-light of sensational coincidence and the limelight of success as well as by the elevation of their genius. The real pathway of ideas and achievements goes through hundreds and thousands of humbler workers and laboratory mechanics, and mathematicians and engineers who jointly make the final success possible. Thus the invention of the wireless can be treated as a single event and ascribed to one man or another only after its nature has been completely misconceived.

In the same way "diffusion" turns out to be a complex abstraction, not a separate entity. No idea, no practice, no technique ever passed from

[2] Reprinted from *Culture: The Diffusion Controversy* by G. Elliott Smith *et al.*, by permission of W. W. Norton & Company, Inc. Copyright 1927, 1955, by W. W. Norton & Company, Inc.

one society to another without some modification being added to it. The borrowed culture trait must be somehow modified and adapted so as to fit into the existing cultural context. It follows that diffusion and invention are always inseparably mixed. To oppose them as if they were mutually exclusive is to raise a false issue.

[12]   *The Hypothesis of Cultural Lag**

by WILLIAM F. OGBURN

This rapidity of change in modern times raises the very important question of social adjustment. Problems of social adjustment are of two sorts. One concerns the adaptation of man to culture or perhaps preferably the adapting of culture to man. The other problem is the question of adjustments, occasioned as a result of these rapid social changes, between the different parts of culture, which no doubt means ultimately the adaptation of culture to man. This second problem of adjustment between the different parts of culture is the immediate subject of our inquiry.

The thesis is that the various parts of modern culture are not changing at the same rate, some parts are changing much more rapidly than others; and since there is a correlation and interdependence of parts, a rapid change in one part of our culture requires readjustments through other changes in the various correlated parts of culture. For instance, industry and education are correlated, hence a change in industry makes adjustments necessary through changes in the educational system. Industry and education are two variables, and if the change in industry occurs first and the adjustment through education follows, industry may be referred to as the independent variable and education as the dependent variable. Where one part of culture changes first, through some discovery or invention, and occasions changes in some part of culture dependent upon it, there frequently is a delay in the changes occasioned in the dependent part of culture. The extent of this lag will vary according to the nature of the cultural material, but may exist for a considerable number of years, during which time there may be said to be a maladjustment. It is desirable to reduce the period of maladjustment, to make the cultural adjustments as quickly as possible.

The foregoing account sets forth a problem that occurs when there is a rapid change in a culture of interdependent parts and when the rates of change in the parts are unequal. The discussion will be presented according to the following outlines. First the hypothesis will be presented, then examined and tested by a rather full consideration of the facts of a single instance, to be followed by several illustrations. Next the nature and cause of the phenomenon of cultural maladjustment in general will be analyzed. The extent of such cultural lags will be estimated, and finally the significance for society will be set forth.

A first simple statement of the hypothesis we wish to investigate now follows. A large part of our environment consists of the material conditions of life and a large part of our social heritage is our material culture. These material things consist of houses, factories, machines, raw materials, manufactured products, foodstuffs and other material objects. In using these material things we employ certain methods. Some of these methods are as simple as the technique of handling a tool. But a good many of the ways of using material objects of culture involve rather larger usages and adjustments, such as customs, beliefs, philosophies, laws, governments. One important function of government, for instance, is the adjustment of the population to the material conditions of life, although there are other governmental functions. Sumner has called many of these processes of adjustment, mores. The cultural adjustments to material conditions, however, include a larger body of processes than the mores; certainly they include the folkways and social institutions. These ways of adjustment may be called, for purposes of this particular analysis, the adaptive culture. The adaptive culture is therefore that portion of the nonmaterial culture which is adjusted or adapted to the material conditions. Some parts of the nonmaterial culture are thoroughly adaptive culture such as certain rules involved in handling technical appliances, and some parts are only indirectly or partially so, as for instance, religion. The family makes some adjustments to fit changed material conditions, while some of its functions remain constant. The family, therefore, under the terminology used here is a part of the nonmaterial culture that is only partly adaptive. When the material conditions change, changes are occasioned in the adaptive culture. But these changes in the adaptive culture do not synchronize exactly with the change in the material culture. There is a lag which may last for varying lengths of time, sometimes indeed, for many years.

An illustration will serve to make the hypothesis more clearly understood. One class of material objects to which we adjust ourselves is the forests. The material conditions of forestry have changed a good deal in the United States during the past century. At one time the forests were quite plentiful for the needs of the small population. There was plenty of wood easily accessible for fuel, building and manufacture. The forests were sufficiently extensive to prevent in many large areas the washing of the soil, and the streams were clear. In fact, at one time, the forests seemed to be too plentiful, from the point of view of the needs of the people. Food and agricultural products were at one time the first need of the people and the clearing of land of trees and stumps was a common undertaking of the community in the days of the early settlers. In some places, the quickest procedure was to kill and burn the trees and plant between the stumps. When the material conditions were like these, the method of adjustment to the forests was characterized by a policy which has been called exploitation. Exploitation in regard to the forests was indeed a part of the mores of the time, and describes a part of the adaptive culture in relation to forests.

As time went on, however, the population grew, manufacturing became highly developed, and the need for forests increased. But the forests were being destroyed. This was particularly true in the Appalachian, Great Lakes and Gulf regions. The policy of exploitation continued. Then rather suddenly it began to be realized in certain centers of thought that if the policy of cutting timber continued at the same rate and in the same manner the forests would in a short time be gone and very soon indeed they would be inadequate to supply the needs of the population. It was realized that the custom in regard to using the forests must be changed and a policy of conservation was advocated. The new policy of conservation means not only a restriction in the amount of cutting down of trees, but it means a more scientific method of cutting, and also reforestation. Forests may be cut in such a way, by selecting trees according to their size, age and location, as to yield a large quantity of timber and yet not diminish the forest area. Also by the proper distribution of cutting plots in a particular area, the cutting can be so timed that by the time the last plot is cut the young trees on the plot first cut will be grown. Some areas when cut leave a land which is well adapted to farming, whereas such sections as mountainous regions when denuded of forests are poorly suited to agriculture. There of course are many other methods of conservation of forests. The science of forestry is, indeed, fairly highly developed in principle, though not in practice in the United States. A new adaptive culture, one of conservation, is therefore suited to the changed material conditions.

That the conservation of forests in the United States should have been earlier is quite generally admitted. We may say, therefore, that the old policy of exploitation has hung over longer than it should before the institution of the new policy. In other words, the material conditions in regard to our forests have changed but the old customs of the use of forests which once fitted the material conditions very well have hung over into a period of changed conditions. These old customs are not only not satisfactorily adapted, but are really socially harmful. These customs of course have a utility, since they meet certain human needs; but methods of greater utility are needed. There seems to be a lag in the mores in regard to forestry after the material conditions have changed.

The foregoing discussion of forestry illustrates the hypothesis which it is proposed to discuss. It is desirable to state more clearly and fully the points involved in the analysis. The first point concerns the degree of adjustment or correlation between the material conditions and the adaptive nonmaterial culture. The degree of this adjustment may be only more or less perfect or satisfactory; but we do adjust ourselves to the material conditions through some form of culture; that is, we live, we get along, through this adjustment. The particular culture which is adjusted to the material conditions may be very complex, and, indeed, quite a number of widely different parts of culture may be adjusted to a fairly homogeneous material condition. Of a particular cultural form, such as the family or government, relationship to a particular material culture is only one of its purposes or functions. Not all functions of family organization, as, for instance, the affectional function, are primarily adaptive to material conditions.

Another point to observe is that the changes in the material culture precede changes in the adaptive culture. This statement is not in the form of a universal dictum. Conceivably, forms of adaptation might be worked out prior to a change in the material situation and the adaptation might be applied practically at the same time as the change in the material conditions. But such a situation presumes a very high degree of planning, prediction and control. The collection of data, it is thought, will show that at the present time there are a very large number of cases where the material conditions change and the changes in the adaptive culture follow later. There are certain general theoretical reasons why this is so; but it is not desirable to discuss these until later. For the present, the analysis will only concern those cases where changes in the adaptive culture do not precede changes in the material culture. Furthermore, it is not implied that changes may not occur in nonmaterial culture while the material culture remains the same. Art or education, for instance, may undergo many changes with a constant material culture. Still another point in the analysis is that the old, unchanged, adaptive culture is not adjusted to the new, changed, material conditions. It may be true that the old adaptive culture is never wholly unadjusted to the new conditions. There may be some degree of adjustment. But the thesis is that the unchanged adaptive culture was more harmoniously related to the old than to the new material conditions and that a new adaptive culture will be better suited to the new material conditions than was the old adaptive culture. Adjustment is therefore a relative term, and perhaps only in a few cases would there be a situation which might be called perfect adjustment or perfect lack of adjustment.

It is desirable, however, not to make the analysis too general until there has been a more careful consideration of particular instances. We now propose, therefore, to test the hypothesis by the facts in a definite case of social change. In attempting to verify the hypothesis in a particular case by measurement, the following series of steps will be followed. The old material conditions will be described, that part of the adaptive culture under consideration will be described, and the degree of adjustment between these two parts of culture shown. Then the changed material conditions and the changed adaptive culture will be defined and the degree of adaptation shown. It is necessary also to show that the unchanged adaptive culture is not as harmoniously adjusted to the new conditions as to the old and not as harmoniously adjusted to the new conditions as is a changed adaptive culture.

CHAPTER SEVEN

Technology and Social Change

*T*ECHNOLOGICAL *change and mechanization are the most novel and pervasive aspects of our civilization. Every major problem that confronts man today either has its origin in or is strongly affected by technological change. Modern capitalism, as important as it is in its effects on social life, may be a mere by-product of the growth of technology. The selection from MacIver and Page well illustrates how profoundly mechanization has altered our mode of life and our habits of thought. Karsh explores some of the great effects that automation—the new industrial revolution —is likely to have on the life of our times. Automation is defined as the accomplishment of a work task by a power-driven mechanism entirely without the direct use of human energy or skill. This revolution in production is bound to affect society in many ways—"The rhythms of automation will give a new character to leisure, to work and to living." Karsh offers an overview of an emerging new life for man.*

[13] Technology and Social Change*

by ROBERT M. MacIVER and CHARLES H. PAGE

Modern Society and the Machine Age. The approach to social change through technology has . . . a particular appeal and significance for our own age. The rapid changes of our society are obviously related to and somehow dependent upon the development of new techniques, new inventions, new modes of production, new standards of living. We live more and more in cities, and "in the city—and particularly in great cities —the external conditions of life are so evidently contrived to meet man's clearly organized needs that the least intellectual . . . are led to think in deterministic and mechanistic terms."[1] *The most novel and pervasive phenomenon of our age is not capitalism but mechanization,* of which modern capitalism may be merely a by-product. We realize now that this mechanization has profoundly altered our modes of life and also of thought.

[1] *Mechanization and social changes.* Attitudes, beliefs, traditions, which once were thought to be the very expression of essential human nature, have crumbled before its advance. Monarchy, the divine ordering of social classes, the prestige of birth, the spirit of craftsmanship, the insulation of the neighborhood, traditions regarding the spheres of the sexes, regarding religion, regarding politics and war, have felt the shock. The process, beginning with the external change and ending with the social response, is easy to follow and to understand. Take, for example, the profound changes which have occurred in the social life and status of women in the industrial age. Industrialism destroyed the domestic system of production, brought women from the home to the factory and the office, differentiated their tasks and distinguished their earnings. Here is the new environment, and the new social life of women is the response. The rapid transitions of modern civilization offer a myriad of other illustrations.

The swift transitions of our industrial mechanized civilization have not only been followed by far-reaching social changes, but very many of these changes are such as appear either necessary accommodations or congenial responses to the world of the machine. In the former category

---

* From *Society: An Introductory Analysis* by Robert M. MacIver and Charles H. Page, pp. 553-557. Reprinted by permission of Holt, Rinehart and Winston Inc. Copyright 1949 by Robert M. MacIver and Charles H. Page.

[1] R. E. Park, chapter on "Magic, Mentality, and City Life," in Park and E. W. Burgess, *The City* (Chicago, 1925).

come the higher specialization of all tasks, the exact time-prescribed routine of work, the acceleration of the general tempo of living, the intensification of competition, the obsolescence of the older craftsmanship, the development, on the one hand, of the technician and, on the other, of the machine operative, the expansion of economic frontiers, and the complicated, extending network of political controls. In the latter may be included the various accompaniments of a higher standard of living, the transformation of class structures and of class standards, the undermining of local folkways and the disintegration of the neighborhood, the breaking up of the old family system, the building of vast changeful associations in the pursuit of new wealth or power, the increasing dominance of urban ways over those of the country, the spread of fashion, the growth of democracy and of plutocracy, the challenge of industrial organized groups, particularly the organizations of labor, to the older forms of authority.

[2] *Mechanization and changes in values.* With these conditions are bred corresponding attitudes, beliefs, philosophies. A great mass of contemporary social criticism seeks to depict and often to arraign the cultural concomitants of the machine age. Its tenor is generally as follows: Different qualities are now esteemed because the qualities which make for success, for wealth, and for power are different. Success is measured more in pecuniary terms, as possession is more detachable from social and cultural status. A form of democratization has developed which measures everything by units or by quantities and admits no differences in personal values save as they are attached to external goods or are the means of their acquisition. Men grow more devoted to quantity than to quality, to measurement than to appreciation. The desire for speed dominates, for immediate results, for quick speculative advantages, for superficial excitations. The life of reflection, the slow ripening of qualitative judgments, is at a discount. Hence novelty is sought everywhere, and transient interests give a corresponding character to social relationships. The changing interests of civilization absorb men to the relative exclusion of the more permanent interests of culture. Men grow pragmatic in their philosophies. "Things are in the saddle and ride mankind." The mechanistic outlook explains life itself in behavioristic terms, as a series of predetermined responses to successive stimuli. The unity of life is dissipated, since from the mechanistic point of view all things are means to means and to no final ends, functions of functions and of no values beyond.

[3] *Direct and indirect effects of technological change.* That the tendencies thus described are at least accentuated by the mechanization both

of work and of the means and conditions of recreation is clearly established by a great mass of evidence. It can scarcely be a mere coincidence
that in the periods and in the countries of rapid technological advance
there should have developed corresponding or congenial ways of thinking and of living. Nevertheless we should be wary of concluding too
hastily that social relations are in all important respects predominantly
determined by technological changes. This conclusion would hold only
if culture also, the values men set before them as ends for which to live,
were essentially the product of technology. But culture in turn seeks to
direct technology to its own ends. Man may be the master as well as
the slave of the machine. He has already rejected many of the conditions
that accompanied and seemed to be imposed by the earlier technology of
the industrial revolution. He has taken some steps in all civilized countries to place a variety of controls on factory toil, on the squalor of factory towns, on the shoddiness and ugliness of many factory-made goods,
on the risks and fatigues of many factory operations. Man is a critic
as well as a creature of circumstance.

Therefore we should distinguish between the more direct and less
direct social consequences of mechanization or other technological process. Certain social consequences are the inevitable results of technological
change, such as a new organization of labor, the expansion of the range
of social contacts, the specialization of function, and the encroachment
of urban influences on rural life. Other concomitants, not being inevitable
conditions of the operation of the new techniques, are more provisional or
more precarious, such as the increase of unemployment, the intensified
distinction between an employing and a wage-earning class, the heighten-
ing of competition, and the prevalence of mechanistic creeds. In the remaining sections of this chapter we shall endeavor to show that the deterministic theories which make technological change the dominant or
overruling cause of social change are one-sided or misleading. But first
it is well to insist on the positive aspect, and show by citing some recent
developments how real and how important an agency of social change
is the quest of modern man to discover and to utilize new techniques,
new and more efficient methods of accomplishing his ends.

How Technological Advance Initiates Social Change.   Every technological advance, by making it possible for men to achieve certain results
with less effort or at less cost, at the same time provides new opportunities and establishes new conditions of life. The opportunities, or some of
them, are frequently anticipated in the development or exploitation of
the new devices; the new conditions of life are in large measure the neces-

sary and unanticipated adjustments to the new opportunities. A few illustrations will bring out the distinction.

[1] *New agricultural techniques and social change:*   Take, for example, the advance of agricultural technology. The improvements in the breeds of cattle, in the use of fertilizers, in the varieties of seed, in mechanical laborsaving devices, and so forth, have had as their direct objective the increase in the quantity and quality of agricultural production. But as concomitants of the attainment of this objective there have gone changes in farm economy and in the manner of life of the farming household. And beyond these again there have gone changes in the relation of agriculture to industry, migrations from the farm to the city because of the lessened numbers required to supply the agricultural needs of the whole community, the decay or abandonment of marginal farm lands, tendencies to agricultural depression, new struggles for foreign markets and new tariff barriers. And these changes in turn have stimulated new and difficult economic problems. Thus the achievement of the immediate objective of agricultural technology has led by an inevitable nexus to changes of an entirely different order.

[2] *Advances in communication and social change:*   Even more far reaching and complex are the social changes that spring from the development of the techniques of communication. For communication is at once a primary condition of social relations and a basis of nearly all other forms of technological advance. The course of civilization has been marked by a constant development of the means of communication, but never so rapidly as in our own days, when electricity is not only being adopted as motive power in place of steam, not only is a factor in the improvement of automobile and airplane, not only makes the motion picture a vast commercial enterprise and television a promising adventure, but also, resuming its distance-annihilating range, becomes in the radio a voice that is heard simultaneously by millions over the face of the earth. The impact of these changes on society is too enormous and too multifarious to be dealt with here except by way of incidental illustration. Every step of technological advance inaugurates a series of changes that interact with others emanating from the whole technological system. The radio, for example, affects a family situation already greatly influenced by modern technology, so that its impetus toward the restoration of leisure enjoyment within the home is in part counteracted or limited by opposing tendencies. Again, the radio combines with other technological changes to reduce the cultural differentiation of social classes and of urban and rural communities. On the other hand, by enabling an individ-

ual speaker to address great multitudes, it makes possible the rapid rise of new parties or social movements, provided the broadcasting system is not itself politically controlled. In the latter event it tends to produce the opposite result, becoming a most powerful agency of propaganda monopolized by the ruling power. This last illustration should serve to show that what we call the "effects" of invention are in large measure dependent variables of the social situation into which they are introduced.

[3] *The control of atomic energy and social change:* The most spectacular illustration, however, is that afforded by the epoch-making discovery of a way to make atomic energy serviceable to human objectives. Like so many other discoveries of modern science, this new agency is available equally for destructive or for constructive purposes. As an agent of war it forebodes the most appalling annihilation of all the works of man. As an agent of peace it may ultimately bring an unprecedented era of plenty.

The General Direction of Social Change with Advancing Technology. Bearing in mind the caution contained in the last paragraphs we may still ask whether there is any major direction in which society moves under the continual impact of technological change.

[1] *Specialization:* We have seen that technology itself tends always in the same direction, attaining ever greater efficiency in the performance of *each* of the various functions to which its devices are applied. In doing so it specializes functions more and more, and thus tends to create an ever-increasing division of labor, with whatever social consequences depend thereon. The social significance of this growing division of labor has been given classic treatment by Durkheim, though some of his conclusions, such as that greater liberty and a diminution of class differences are concomitants of specialization, are stated in too sweeping and universal a form. More certain is the correlation between technological advance and a more elaborate social organization with higher interdependence between its parts, greater mobility of the members with respect to location and to occupation, more elaborate systems of laws and of governmental controls, new concentrations both of economic and of political power, greater instability of the institutional order, greater leisure and generally higher standards of living for large numbers. These conditions seem to be directly bound up with growing technological efficiency, and they in turn have further repercussions on every aspect of social life. They also create some extremely important social problems, one being the unbalance of the economic system that accompanies the accelerated processes of technological change. But within our limits we can do no

more than suggest some of the immediate social concomitants of technological advance.

[2] *The modern significance of the technological factor:* It is scarcely too much to say that every major problem of modern society is either initiated by or at least strongly affected by technological change. Conflicts between states, as they strive for dominance, for security, or for prosperity, are in no small measure concerned with competing ambitions to secure or control areas rich in oil, coal, or other resources of crucial importance to modern industry. Again, the specialization of functions in a modern economy gives rise to a multitude of organized groups, each of which seeks its own economic advantage and each of which has the power of withholding a service that modern interdependence renders indispensable. On the other hand, these groups are affiliated with or incorporated into massive federations or combinations. These in turn exercise a correspondingly greater power, so that the disputes arising out of their clashing interests sometimes threaten to disrupt the whole social order.

[14] *Automation's Brave, New World**

by BERNARD KARSH

It seems clear that automation, aside from its economic implications, will have profound social effects. Just as the industrial revolution—the rise of the factory—impressed its rhythms on society, so the rhythms of automation will give a new character to leisure, to work and to living. Affected will be not only the relation of the worker to his work, but his relations with other workers and with his employers; and, beyond this, significant changes in working hours and a redistribution of factories, in a geographic sense, could set up additional profound pressures on the present patterns of our society.

* Reprinted from *The Nation*, October 5, 1957, pp. 208-210, published by Nation Associates, Inc. By permission.

Automation is defined in various ways, but it may be summarily defined as the accomplishment of a work task by an integrated power-driven mechanism entirely without the direct application of human energy, skill, intelligence or control. Automation is more than simple mechanization, and it is advancing on at least two levels of technology. One level is the so-called continuous-flow automation which is typified by machines that replace men's muscles, eliminate physical effort and substitute electricity for manpower, and which are coupled to devices eliminating human judgment in the administration or direction of the control of the machine. This has sometimes been called machines to run machines. The automatic mechanism watches what the machine is doing, makes sure it follows the instructions, and automatically corrects mistakes.

Another phase of automation is sometimes called business automation. This is the use of computing and decision-making machines, so-called "electronic brains," which hand out administrative, statistical and clerical policies. Conceivably, an entire plant can be operated under the administration of these types of machines. Doing so would involve analyzing sales reports, ordering and checking the flow of materials, scheduling and controlling the operations, making out invoices, recording payments, and so on—all by machine.

Experiments are now going forward at an increasing rate to combine these two phases into a single computer-run system. Whether this technology is old or new is not relevant for our purpose here. Its most important consequences will be felt and are now being felt as a result of the tremendous pace with which it is being developed and put to use.

First, automation may change the basic composition of the labor force, creating what Daniel Bell calls a new "salariat" instead of a "proletariat," as automated processes reduce the number of industrial workers required in factory production. In the automobile industry, for example, the number of production workers declined by 3.5 per cent from 1947 to 1956, while the number of workers engaged in the processing of information increased 24.3 per cent (*Business Week*, April 20, 1957).

Changes of similar magnitude have occurred in the aircraft and farm-equipment manufacturing industries. And changes of even greater magnitude have occurred in the same period in the chemical and oil-refining industries. These industries are among the leaders in the adoption of automated equipment. A few specific examples of the impact of automation on production manpower requirements may suffice to give some indication of the direction in which manufacturing industry is headed.

Fourteen glass-blowing machines, each operated by one worker, now produce 90 per cent of the glass light bulbs used in the United States and all the glass tubes (except picture tubes) used in radio and television sets. In the radio and television industry, new machines etch or stencil on a board what were formerly hand-wired circuits; once the components are fed into the machines, complete radio sets can be produced. On one radio-assembly line, turning out 1,000 radios a day, two workers now produce more than 200 workers did with the old methods. . . .

These technical changes may have several effects. With automated processes doing the work of large numbers of human workers, management may no longer have to worry about a large labor force. This means that new plants can be located away from major cities and closer to markets or sources of raw materials and fuels. It is often cheaper to build a completely automated factory from the ground up than to automate piecemeal an existing factory. Thus, there is an impetus toward constructing new plant facilities either on the peripheries of large cities or away from them altogether. This, in time, may leave the giant, sprawling, industrial metropolis as a dwelling place for human beings instead of a location for unsightly factories. The radio-manufacturing, chemical and automobile industries are already developing along these lines. And since automation involves the continuous flow of materials and information in a highly integrated and coordinated fashion, it can be more efficiently applied in single-story factories which have been specifically built for the purpose. Thus, space allocation tends to be more efficient and factories of smaller size.

When the myriad of special-purpose production machines, each tended by a single worker, is replaced by a single, huge, multi-purpose, punch-card or tape-controlled machine, communication among workers, as well as the formation of work groups, becomes more difficult. At least one British union, for example, has already asked for "lonesome pay" for workers overseeing automated processes. Trade-union solidarity is fostered, at least in part, by the intimate relationship between workers thrown closely together in the work-place and by the development among them of common perceptions of their divorcement from management. With fewer workers in a given plant, and with these workers spatially isolated from each other, the corporation can exercise far greater social control over its workers. The works manager, presumably, can know all the men personally, and the spatial and social integration of workers in a non-automated factory may be replaced by a spatial and social integration of workers with supervisors. Under these conditions, a new kind of trade union identification may occur and a new kind of company town may be in the making.

The decentralization of industry may equally revolutionize the social topography of the country as a whole. As new plants are built on the outskirts of towns and as workers come to live along the fringes of the spreading city, the distinction between urban and suburban becomes increasingly obliterated.

But more than topographical changes are involved. Bell suggests that under automation, depreciation becomes the major cost. Labor is cheap in relation to the tremendous cost of an automated machine. Workers can be laid off when they become unproductive, but it is enormously expensive to permit a machine to be idle. To write off the big capital investment, more and more of the automated plants may expand shift operations in order to keep the plant running twenty-four hours a day. And so more and more workers may find themselves working odd hours. When this occurs, the cycles of sleeping, eating, working and social life become distorted. Thus friendship patterns change sharply; moreover, when the wife and children follow a "normal" routine while the man sleeps through the day, home life becomes disjointed.

It is often said that the era of automation represents a "second industrial revolution" in the sense that a computer or a feedback-controlled transfer machine takes from man the necessity that he use his brain, or a good part of it, in his work, just as the first industrial revolution, ushered in by the power-driven machine, represented an extension of man's muscle power. But whatever the degrading effects, workers who use power-driven tools do use them, in a sense, as an extension of their own bodies. The machine responds to the worker's commands and adds new dexterity and power to his muscle skills. But as a button-pusher on an automated machine, a man now stands outside his work and whatever control existed is finally shattered. Restricting output, for example, becomes a very difficult, if not impossible, thing to do. An oil-worker simply cannot slow down a cracking tower in order to get some satisfaction from the "boss." There is very little, if anything, the man who tends the huge broach in the Cleveland engine plant of Ford can do to affect the operation of that machine. A modern continuous tin mill operates almost wholly independently of the worker who watches lights, dials, gauges, perhaps a television picture tube or a spectroscope. In operations of this kind, muscular fatigue is replaced by mental tension.

A single instance may give some clue to this problem. *The New York Post* reported the experiences of a Ford worker as told to a Senate subcommittee:

Then there are workers who can't keep up with automation. Such as Stanley Tylack. Tylack, sixty-one and for twenty-seven years a job setter at Ford, was shifted from the River Rouge Foundry machine shop to the new automated engine plant. He was given a chance to work at a big new automatic machine. Simply, straightforwardly, he told his story. "The machine had about 80 drills and 22 blocks going through. You had to watch all the time. Every few minutes you had to watch to see everything was all right. And the machines had so many lights and switches—about 90 lights. It sure is hard on your mind. If there's one break in the machine the whole line breaks down. But sometimes you make a little mistake, and it's no good for you, no good for the foreman, no good for the company, no good for the union." And so Stanley Tylack, baffled by the machine he couldn't keep up with, had to take another job—at lower pay.

Mr. Tylack's experience suggests, of course, that the tedium of routine tasks may be preferred by some workers. It also suggests that we may not yet know what kind of skills, experience, personality and similar attributes are required to operate the new machines. It seems clear that a skilled tool and die maker who, by virtue of his high skills and seniority, is entitled to take a dial-watcher's job, may not possess the psychological requirements of that job at all. But this need not be a problem in an age of automation, since the machine-tender and dial- and light-watcher can be replaced by other machines, and this is happening very quickly.

Here is where there may be a real social gain for these new processes. Diebold and Drucker have pointed out that automation requires workers who can think of the plant as a whole. The locus of attention is shifted from the machine to the whole plant and the individual "cut-and-fit" method of production gives way to a continuous-flow process which eliminates the contribution of the machine-tender or batch-mixer. There is left, on the one hand, the unskilled worker, the broom pusher, whose job may be too menial to automate and, on the other, the highly skilled worker who designs, constructs, repairs, and programs the machine. There is less trivialization, less minute specialization of function, and a need to know more about more than one job. There is a need for highly-trained technical personnel who are able to see the process as a whole and who can conceive of the factory—not the machine or the individual worker—as the unit of production. Workers who can link the programmer with the lathe, the computer with the consumer, the sand pile with the casting, and the pipeline with the gasoline storage tank become the foremost need. It becomes necessary to know the drill and the finish grinder and to relate their jobs to each other.

The skills required in this new setting are altogether of a different order than before. The increased professionalization required by automation suggests that some of the loss of status attending earlier technological changes may be regained. Thus, there may be in the making a reversal of the historic trend toward ever greater specialization of function with its trivialization of work, and the reintegration of labor may begin to emerge.

Also very important may be the elimination of systems of work measurement in manufacturing and data processing. Modern industry, says Bell, began not with the factory but with the measurement of work. But under automation, with continuous flow, a worker's worth can no longer be evaluated in production units. Wage-incentive plans are based on the premise that human worth at the workplace can and should be measured by the number of units produced. It is reasoned that under the unit-worth concept, workers would produce more units for more money and there would be no limit to production if pay were made proportional to output. But with automation the human worker will be concerned with nonsystematic work activity and will stand outside direct production activity. Highly skilled workers will be more concerned with adapting the production system to special situations, and this is an activity whose value can be measured neither by production units nor by the time units, as Adam Abruzzi points out in *Work, Workers, and Work Measurement*. Hence, incentive plans, with their involved techniques, may vanish.

Abruzzi suggests that a new work morality may arise in place of a morality based on a unit-worth concept. The "one best way" definition of worker worth will give way, the stop watch and the slide rule will disappear as instruments for the measurement of worth, and fractionalized time or production units will no longer be useful measures. Worth will be judged on the basis of organization and planning and the continuously smooth functioning of the operation.

The individual worker loses his importance and is replaced by the team, and greater value is placed on the operating unit as a whole. Whyte's *The Organization Man* may indeed replace the traditional individualism which has characterized American society for so long.

CHAPTER EIGHT

Population

MORE than fifty million newly-born babies will be brought into the world this year. Every year the rate of growth in world population increases. Can modern production and technology keep pace with what has been called the "population explosion"? Julian Huxley deals with the race between the increase in the number of people and the rise of food production. The challenge of population growth differs for different parts of the world. There were fifteen million births in China, six million in India, and more than three and one-half million in Russia in the year 1958. In considering the truly staggering rate of population growth in relation to changing birth and death rates, Huxley suggests possible changes in population policy as a remedy. Mabley presents a graphic picture of how peoples of the world differ from one another—and especially from Americans—in ways that can create tension and conflict.

[15]   *World Population**

The problem of population is the problem of our age. In the middle of the 20th century anyone who travels around the world, as I have recently done, cannot fail to be struck by the signs of growing pressure of population upon the resources of our planet. The traveler is impressed by the sheer numbers of people, as in China; by the crowding of the land, as in Java; by the desperate attempts to control population increase, as in Japan and India; and at the same time by the erosion, deforestation and destruction of wildlife almost everywhere. The experiences of travel merely highlight and illustrate a fact which for some time has been obtruding itself on the world's consciousness: that the increase of human numbers has initiated a new and critical phase in the history of our species.

This crisis was recognized by the holding of a Conference on World Population in Rome in 1954. Held under the aegis of the United Nations, the Conference was a milestone in history, for it was the first official international survey of the subject of human population as a whole. In 1949 the UN had convened a scientific conference on world resources at Lake Success. As Director General of UNESCO, invited to collaborate in this project, I had suggested that a survey of resources should be accompanied by a similar survey of the population which consumed the resources. I was told that there were technical, political and religious difficulties. Eventually these difficulties were smoothed over; censuses were taken; and a conference on population was duly held in 1954. During the five years it took to arrange for a look at the problem the world population had increased by more than 130 million.

Let me begin by setting forth some of the facts—often surprising and sometimes alarming—which justify our calling the present a new and decisive phase in the history of mankind. The first fact is that the total world population has been increasing relentlessly, with only occasional minor setbacks, since before the dawn of history. The second fact is the enormous present size of the population—more than 2.5 billion. The third is the great annual increase: some 34 million people per year, nearly 4,000 per hour, more than one every second. The human race is adding to its numbers the equivalent of a good-sized town, more than

* From article, "World Population," in *Scientific American*, March, 1956, vol. 194, no. 3, pp. 64-67. Reprinted by permission of author and journal.

90,000 people, every day of the year. The fourth and most formidable fact is that the rate of increase itself is increasing. Population, as Thomas Malthus pointed out in 1798, tends to grow not arithmetically but geometrically—it increases by compound interest. Until well into the present century the compound rate of interest remained below 1 per cent per annum, but it has now reached 1⅓ per cent per annum. What is more, this acceleration of increase shows no sign of slowing up, and it is safe to prophesy that it will continue to go up for at least several decades.

In short, the growth of human population on our planet has accelerated from a very slow beginning until it has now become an explosive process. Before the discovery of agriculture, about 6,000 B.C., the total world population was probably less than 20 million. It did not pass the 100 million mark until after the time of the Old Kingdom of Egypt, and did not reach 500 million until the latter part of the 17th century. By the mid-18th century it passed the billion mark, and in the 1920's it rose above two billion. That is to say, it doubled itself twice over in the period between 1650 and 1920. The first doubling took nearly two centuries, the second considerably less than one century. Now, at the present rate of acceleration, the population will have doubled itself again (from the 1920 figure) by the early 1980's—*i.e.*, in the amazingly short space of 60 years.

Each major upward step in numbers followed some major discovery or invention—agriculture, the initiation of urban life and trade, the harnessing of non-human power, the technological revolution. During the present century the most decisive factor in increasing population has been of a different sort—the application of scientific medicine, or what we may call death control. In advanced countries death rates have been reduced from the traditional 35 or 40 per thousand to less than 10 per thousand. The average life span (life expectancy at birth) has been more than doubled in the Western world since the mid-19th century. It now stands at about 70 years in Europe and North America, and the process of lengthening life has begun to get under way in Asian countries: in India, for example, the life expectancy at birth has risen within three decades from 20 to 32 years.

BIRTH RATES V. DEATH RATES

Population growth appears to pass through a series of stages. In the first stage both the birth rate and the death rate are high, and the population increases only slowly. In the second stage the death rate falls sharply but the birth rate stays high; the population therefore expands more or less explosively. In the third, the birth rate also falls sharply, so that the increase of population is slowed. Finally both the birth and the death rates stabilize at a low figure; thereafter the population will grow only slowly unless it is spurred by some new development, such as access to new food sources or a change in ideas and values.

In the Western world the reduction of the death rate came gradually, and its effect on population growth was buffered by factors which tended at the same time to reduce the birth rate—namely, a rising standard of living and industrialization, which made children no longer an economic asset.

Matters have been very different in the still underdeveloped countries of Asia. There death control has been introduced with startling speed. Ancient diseases have been brought under control or totally abolished in the space of a few decades or even a few years. Let me give one example. In England malaria took three centuries to disappear; in Ceylon it was virtually wiped out in less than half a decade, thanks to DDT and a well-organized campaign. As a result of this and other health measures, the death rate in Ceylon was reduced from 22 to 12 per thousand in seven years—a fall which took exactly 10 times as long in England. But the Ceylon birth rate has not even begun to drop, and so the population is growing at the rate of 2.7 per cent per annum—about twice the highest rate ever experienced in Britain. If this rate of growth continues, the population of Ceylon will be doubled in 30 years.

Almost all the underdeveloped countries are now in this stage of explosive expansion. When we recall that rates of expansion of this order (2 to 3 per cent) are at work among more than half of the world's 2.5 billion inhabitants, we cannot but feel alarmed. If nothing is done to control this increase, mankind will drown in its own flood, or, if you prefer a different metaphor, man will turn into the cancer of the planet.

Malthus, a century and a half ago, alarmed the world by pointing out that population increase was pressing more and more insistently on food supply, and if unchecked would result in widespread misery and even starvation. In recent times, even as late as the 1930's, it had become customary to pooh-pooh Malthusian fears. The opening up of new land, coupled with the introduction of better agricultural methods, had allowed food production to keep up with population increase and in some areas even to outdistance it. During the 19th century and the early part of the 20th food production increased in more than arithmetical progression, contrary to the Malthusian formula. We now realize, however, that this spurt in food production cannot be expected to continue indefinitely: there is an inevitable limit to the rate at which it can be increased. Although Malthus' particular formulation was incorrect, it remains true that there is a fundamental difference between the increase of population, which is based on a geometrical or compound-interest growth mechanism, and the increase of food production, which is not.

There are still some optimists who proclaim that the situation will take care of itself, through industrialization and through the opening of new lands to cultivation, or that science will find a way out by improving food-production techniques, tapping the food resources of the oceans, and so on. These arguments seem plausible until we begin to look at matters quantitatively. To accelerate food production so that it can keep pace with human reproduction will take skill, great amounts of capital and, above all, time—time to clear tropical forests, construct huge dams and irrigation projects, drain swamps, start large-scale industrialization, give training in scientific methods, modernize systems of land tenure and, most difficult of all, change traditional habits and attitudes among the bulk of the people. And quite simply there is not enough skill or capital or time available. Population is always catching up with and outstripping increases in production. The fact is that an annual increase of 34 million mouths to be fed needs more food than can possibly go on being added to production year after year. The growth of population has reached such dimensions and speed that it cannot help winning in a straight race against production. The position is made worse by the fact that the race isn't a straight one. Production starts far behind scratch: according to the latest estimates of the World Health Organization, at least two thirds of the world's people are undernourished. Production has to make good this huge deficiency as well as overtake the increase in human numbers.

A POPULATION POLICY

Is there then no remedy? Of course there is. The remedy is to stop thinking in terms of a race between population and food production and to begin thinking in terms of a balance. We need a population policy.

The most dangerous period lies in the next 30 or 40 years. If nothing is done to bring down the rate of human increase during that time, mankind will find itself living in a world exposed to disastrous miseries and charged with frustrations more explosive than any we can now envision.

Even primitive societies practice some form of population control—by infanticide or abortion or sexual abstinence or crude contraceptives. Since the invention of effective birth control methods in the 19th century, they have been very generally practiced in all Western countries. Their spread to other cultures has been retarded by various inhibitions—religious, ideological, economic, political. It is worth noting that one retarding factor in the past has been the reluctance of colonial powers to encourage birth control in their colonies, often out of fear that they might be considered to be seeking to use population control as a weapon against an "inferior" race.

Today the underdeveloped countries are making their own decisions; what is needed is a new and more rational view of the population problem everywhere. We must give up the false belief that mere increase in the number of human beings is necessarily desirable, and the despairing conclusion that rapid increase and its evils are inevitable. We must reject the idea that the quantity of human beings is of value apart from the quality of their lives.

Overpopulation—or, if you prefer, high population density—affects a great many other needs of mankind besides bread. Beyond his material requirements, man needs space and beauty, recreation and enjoyment. Excessive population can erode all these things. The rapid population increase has already created cities so big that they are beginning to defeat their own ends, producing discomfort and nervous strain and cutting off millions of people from any real contact or sense of unity with nature. Even in the less densely inhabited regions of the world open spaces are shrinking and the despoiling of nature is going on at an appalling rate. Wildlife is being exterminated; forests are being cut down, mountains gashed by hydroelectric projects, wildernesses plastered with mine shafts and tourist camps, fields and meadows stripped away for roads and aerodromes. The pressure of population is also being translated into a flood of mass-produced goods which is washing over every corner of the globe, sapping native cultures and destroying traditional art and craftsmanship.

The space and the resources of our planet are limited. We must set aside some for our material needs and some for more ultimate satisfactions—the enjoyment of unspoiled nature and fine scenery, satisfying recreation, travel and the preservation of varieties of human culture and of monuments of past achievement and ancient grandeur. And in order to arrive at a wise and purposeful allocation of our living space we must have a population policy which will permit the greatest human fulfillment.

If science can be applied to increase the rate of food production and to satisfy our other needs, it can and should also be applied to reduce the rate of people production. And for that, as for all scientific advance, we need both basic research and practical application. Basic research is needed not only on methods of birth control but also on attitudes toward family limitation and on population trends in different sections of the world. Once we have agreed on the need for a scientific population policy, the necessary studies and measures to be applied will surely follow.

This does not mean that we should envisage a definite optimum population size for a given country or for the world as a whole. Indeed, to fix such a figure is probably impossible, and to use it as a definite target is certainly impracticable. For the time being our aim should be confined to reducing the over-rapid population growth which threatens to outstrip food supply. If we can do this, our descendants will be able to begin thinking of establishing a more or less stable level of population.

[16]   How We Stack Up in World—"Small Town" Tells the Story*

by JACK MABLEY

Suppose that in our imagination we could compress the total population of the world, more than 2½ billion people, into one town of 1,000 people.

Dr. Henry Smith Leiper, a leader in Congregational Christian churches and in the American Bible Society, has done just that. This image of the world is graphic.

In this imaginary town—the world reduced in exact proportion to a community of 1,000—there would be 60 Americans. The remainder of the world would be represented by 940 persons.

The 60 Americans would receive more than 35% of the income of the entire town, with the other 940 dividing the rest.

About 330 in the town would be classified as Christians, and 670 would not be so classified.

Fewer than 100 would be Protestant Christians, and some 230 would be Roman Catholics.

At least 80 townspeople would be practicing Communists, and 370 others would be under Communist domination.

White people would total 303, with 697 nonwhite.

* From *The Chicago Daily News*, May 16, 1960, p. 3. Reprinted by permission of the author.

The 60 Americans would have an average life expectancy of 70 years; the other 940 less than 40 years average.

The 60 Americans would have 15 times as many possessions per person as all the rest of the people.

The Americans would produce 16 per cent of the town's total food supply. Although they eat 72 per cent above the maximum food requirements, they would either eat most of what they grew, or store it for their own future use, at enormous cost.

Inasmuch as most of the 940 non-Americans in the town would be hungry, and have little prospect of ever having enough food, the disparity in the food supply might understandably lead to some ill feeling among the townspeople.

The Americans also would enjoy a disproportionate share of electric power, coal, fuel, steel, and general equipment.

The lowest income group among the 60 Americans would be much better off than the average of the rest of the town.

Half of the 1,000 people would never have heard of Jesus Christ, or what he taught. On the other hand, more than half would be hearing about Karl Marx, Lenin, Stalin and Khrushchev.

The 60 Americans and about 200 others representing Western Europe and a few favored classes in other areas in South America, South Africa, Australia, and a few wealthy Japanese, would be relatively well off.

But the majority of the 1,000 people would be ignorant, poor, hungry, and sick.

The American families would be spending at least $850 a year for military defense. . . .

Dr. Leiper didn't mention this, but a good many of the townspeople living in different blocks would be building guns—for self defense, naturally—with which they could, if necessary, wipe out the whole American settlement.

It is, in fact, a very nervous community. But most of the 60 Americans would be too interested in eating and increasing their holdings to take much notice.

PART TWO

Social Adjustment and Social Problems

CHAPTER NINE

Personal Adjustment

OUR age has been called the "Age of Anxiety." Rollo May accepts this characterization, but adds that anxiety has now become overt. During the past two decades it has emerged as a most pervasive and explicit social problem. This is partly evidenced in the large number of emotional disturbances and behavioral disorders which afflict our people. May explores the fields of literature, philosophy, religion, psychology, sociology, and economic and political thought for authentic insights as to how anxiety has come to be regarded as the "nodal" or central problem of our times.

Wertham discusses the "peace-of-mind" books which people buy in great numbers to relieve their anxieties and cure all their emotional problems. He finds that these books are superficial and do not teach people to face life as it is; but they may help them to escape from social responsibilities by developing in them an "air-conditioned" conscience.

[17]   Centrality of the Problem of Anxiety in Our Day*

by ROLLO MAY

NOW *there are times when a whole generation is caught . . . between two ages, two modes of life, with the consequence that it loses all power to understand itself and has no standards, no security, no simple acquiescence.*
—Herman Hesse, *Steppenwolf.*

Every alert citizen of our society realizes, on the basis of his own experience as well as his observation of his fellow-men, that anxiety is a pervasive and profound phenomenon in the middle of the twentieth century. The alert citizen, we may assume, would be aware not only of the more obvious anxiety-creating situations in our day, such as the threats of war, of the uncontrolled atom bomb, and of radical political and economic upheaval; but also of the less obvious, deeper, and more personal sources of anxiety in himself as well as in his fellow-men—namely, the inner confusion, psychological disorientation, and uncertainty with respect to values and acceptable standards of conduct. Hence to endeavor to "prove" the pervasiveness of anxiety in our day is as unnecessary as the proverbial carrying of coals to Newcastle.

Since the implicit sources of anxiety in our society are generally recognized, our task in this introductory chapter is somewhat more specific. We shall point out how anxiety has emerged, and has to some slight extent been defined, as an *explicit* problem in many different areas in our culture. It is as though in the present decade the explorations and investigations in such diverse fields as poetry and science, or religion and politics, were converging on this central problem, anxiety. Whereas the period of two decades ago might have been termed the "age of covert anxiety"—as we hope to demonstrate later in this chapter—the present phase of our century may well be called, as Auden and Camus call it, the "age of overt anxiety." This emergence of anxiety from an implicit to an explicit problem in our society, this change from anxiety as a matter of "mood" to a recognition that it is an urgent issue which we must at all costs try to define and clarify, are, in the judgment of the present writer, the significant phenomena at the moment. Not only in the understanding and treatment of emotional disturbances and behavioral disorders has anxiety become rec-

* From *The Meaning of Anxiety* by Rollo May, pp. 3-15 *passim.* Copyright 1950 The Ronald Press Company. Reprinted by permission.

116

ognized as the "nodal problem," in Freud's words; but it is now seen like-wise to be nodal in such different areas as literature, sociology, political and economic thought, education, religion, and philosophy. We shall cite examples of testimony from these fields, beginning with the more general and proceeding to the more specific concern with anxiety as a scientific problem.

In Literature. If one were to inquire into anxiety as exhibited in the American literature, say, of 1920 or 1930, one would be forced in all prob-ability to occupy oneself with symptoms of anxiety rather than overt anxiety itself. But though signs of open, manifest anxiety were not plenti-ful in that period, certainly the student could find plenty of symptomatic indications of underlying anxiety. *Vide*, for example, the pronounced sense of loneliness, the quality of persistent searching—frantically and com-pulsively pursued but always frustrated—in the writings of a novelist like Thomas Wolfe.

In 1950, however, our inquiry is simpler because anxiety has now emerged into overt statement in contemporaneous literature. W. H. Auden has entitled his latest poem with the phrase which he believes most ac-curately characterizes our period, namely, *The Age of Anxiety*. Though Auden's profound interpretation of the inner experience of the four per-sons in this poem is set in the time of war—when "necessity is associated with horror and freedom with boredom"—he makes it very clear that the underlying causes of the anxiety of his characters, as well as of others of this age, must be sought on deeper levels than merely the occasion of war. The four characters in the poem, though different in temperament and in background, have in common certain characteristics of our times: lone-liness, the feeling of not being of value as persons, and the experience of not being able to love and be loved, despite the common need, the com-mon effort, and the common but temporary respite provided by alcohol. The sources of the anxiety are to be found in certain basic trends in our culture, one of which, for Auden, is the pressure toward conformity which occurs in a world where commercial and mechanical values are apotheo-sized. . . . *What has been lost is the capacity to experience and have faith in one's self as a worthy and unique being, and at the same time the capacity for faith in, and meaningful communication with, other selves, namely one's fellow-men.*

The French author, Albert Camus, . . . designates this age as "the century of fear," in comparison with the seventeenth century as the age of mathematics, the eighteenth as the age of the physical sciences, and the nineteenth as that of biology. Camus realizes that these characterizations are not logically parallel, that fear is not a science, but "science must be somewhat involved, since its latest theoretical advances have brought it to the point of negating itself while its perfected technology threatens the globe itself with destruction. Moreover, although fear itself cannot be considered a science, it is certainly a technique."

Another writer who graphically expresses the anxiety and anxiety-like states of people in our period is Franz Kafka. The remarkable surge of interest in the 1940's in the writings of Kafka is important for our purposes here because of what it shows in the changing temper of our time; the fact that increasing numbers of people are finding that Kafka speaks significantly to them must indicate that he is expressing some profound aspects of the prevailing experience of many members of our society. In Kafka's novel *The Castle,* the chief character devotes his life to a frantic and desperate endeavor to communicate with the authorities in the castle who control all aspects of the life in the village, and who have the power to tell him his *vocation* and give some meaning to his life. *Kafka's hero is driven "by a need for the most primitive requisites of life, the need to be rooted in a home and a calling, and to become a member of a community."* But the authorities in the castle remain inscrutable and inaccessible, and Kafka's character is as a result without direction and unity in his own life and remains isolated from his fellows. What the castle specifically symbolizes could be debated at length, but since the authorities in the castle are represented as the epitome of a bureaucratic efficiency which exercises such power that it quenches both individual autonomy and meaningful interpersonal relations, it may confidently be assumed that Kafka is in general writing of those aspects of his bourgeois culture of the late nineteenth and early twentieth centuries which so elevated technical efficiency that personal values were largely destroyed.

Herman Hesse, writing less in literary symbols than Kafka, is more explicit about the sources of modern man's anxiety. He presents the story of Haller, his chief character in the novel *Steppenwolf,* as a parable of our period. Hesse holds that Haller's—and his contemporaries'—isolation and anxiety arise from the fact that the bourgeois culture in the late nineteenth and early twentieth centuries emphasized mechanical, rationalistic "balance" at the price of the suppression of the dynamic, irrational elements in experience. Haller tries to overcome his isolation and loneliness by giving free rein to his previously suppressed sensuous and irrational urges (the "wolf"), but this reactive method yields only a temporary relief. Indeed, Hesse presents no thoroughgoing solution to the problem of the anxiety of contemporaneous Western man, for he believes the present period to be one of those "times when a whole generation is caught . . . between two ages." That is to say, bourgeois standards and controls have been broken down, but there are as yet no social standards to take their place. Hesse sees Haller's record "as a document of the times, for Haller's sickness of the soul, as I now know, is not the eccentricity of a single individual, but the sickness of the times themselves, the neurosis of that generation to which Haller belongs . . . a sickness which attacks . . . precisely those who are strongest in spirit and richest in gifts."

In Sociological Studies. The emergence of awareness of anxiety as an overt sociological problem in an American community during the third and fourth decades of our century is seen when we compare the Lynds' two studies of Middletown. In the first study, made in the 1920's, anxiety is not an overt problem to the people of Middletown, and the topic does not appear in the Lynds' volume in any of its explicit forms. But anyone reading this study from a psychological viewpoint would suspect that much of the behavior of the citizens of Middletown was symptomatic of *covert anxiety*—for example, the compulsive work ("businessmen and workingmen seem to be running for dear life" in the endeavor to make money), the pervasive struggle to conform, the compulsive gregariousness (*vide* the great emphasis on "joining" clubs), and the frantic endeavors of the people in the community to keep their leisure time crammed with activity (such as "motoring"), however purposeless this activity might be in itself. But only one citizen—whom the Lynds describe as a "perspicacious" observer—looked below these symptoms and sensed the presence of covert apprehension: of his fellow townsmen he observed, "These people are all afraid of something; what is it?"

But the later study of the same community made in the 1930's presents a very different picture: *overt anxiety is now present.* "One thing everybody in Middletown has in common," the Lynds observe, "is insecurity in the face of a complicated world." To be sure, the immediate, outward occasion of anxiety was the economic depression; but it would be an error to conclude that the inclusive *cause* of the emerging anxiety was economic insecurity. The Lynds accurately relate this insecurity in Middletown to the *confusion of role* which the individual was then experiencing; the citizen of Middletown, they write, "is caught in a chaos of conflicting patterns, none of them wholly condemned, but no one of them clearly approved and free from confusion; or, where the group sanctions are clear in demanding a certain role of a man or woman, the individual encounters cultural requirements with no immediate means of meeting them." This "chaos of conflicting patterns" in Middletown is one expression of the pervasive social changes occurring in our culture, which are intimately connected with the widespread anxiety of our times. The Lynds observe that, since "most people are incapable of tolerating change and uncertainty in all sectors of life at once," the tendency in Middletown was toward a retrenchment into more rigid and conservative economic and social ideologies. This ominous development as a symptom of, and defense against, anxiety points toward the discussion of the relation between anxiety and political authoritarianism in the next section.

In the Political Scene.   Turning to the political scene, we again find pronounced anxiety evidenced both in symptomatic and in overt forms. Without going into the complex determinants of fascism, we wish to note that it is born and gains its power in periods of widespread anxiety. Tillich describes the situation in Europe in the 1930's out of which German fascism developed:

> First of all a feeling of *fear* or, more exactly, of indefinite anxiety was prevailing. Not only the economic and political, but also the cultural and religious, security seemed to be lost. There was nothing on which one could build; everything was without foundation. A catastrophic breakdown was expected every moment. Consequently, a longing for security was growing in everybody. A freedom that leads to fear and anxiety has lost its value; better authority with security than freedom with fear!

In such periods, people grasp at political authoritarianism in the desperate need to be relieved of anxiety. *Totalitarianism in this sense may be viewed as serving a purpose on a cultural scale parallel to that in which a neurotic symptom protects an individual from a situation of unbearable anxiety.* With some very significant differences, communistic totalitarianism fulfills a similar function. As we shall endeavor to indicate later in this study, fascism and communism are not only economic phenomena, but are also the product of the spiritual, ethical, and psychological vacuum which characterized the breakdown of the bourgeois tradition in Western Europe. As Martin Ebon phrases it, communism is a product of "the desperate wish to find a purpose in what seems confusion and emptiness." In this confusion and emptiness one thing did exist, namely anxiety; and we are submitting that totalitarianism gains its foothold to a considerable extent because, like a symptom, it "binds" and provides some relief from the anxiety.

In addition to anxiety in the above symptomatic forms, *unsystematized* anxiety has been increasingly evident in the sociopolitical scene in the past decade. The frequent references to Roosevelt's sentence in his first inaugural, "The only thing we have to fear is fear itself," testify to the fact that large numbers of people have become increasingly aware of "fear of fear," or more accurately, anxiety, in the face of the radical sociopolitical changes in our day. The emergence of the atom bomb brought the previously inchoate and "free-floating" anxiety of many people into sharp focus. The stark possibilities of modern man's situation are stated in an impassioned expression of the crystallization of anxiety at that moment by Norman Cousins:

The beginning of the Atomic Age has brought less hope than fear. It is a primitive fear, the fear of the unknown, the fear of forces man can neither channel nor comprehend. This fear is not new; in its classical form it is the fear of irrational death. But overnight it has become intensified, magnified. It has burst out of the subconscious into the conscious, filling the mind with primordial apprehensions. . . . Where man can find no answer, he will find fear.

Even if we should escape being confronted with actual death in a shooting and atomic war, the anxiety inhering in our portentous world situation would still be with us. The historian Arnold Toynbee has stated his belief that overt warfare on a world scale is not probable in our lifetime, but that we shall remain in a "cold" war for a generation, which will mean a perpetual condition of tension and worry. To live in a state of anxiety for a generation is, indeed, a horrendous prospect! But the picture is not inevitably black: Toynbee holds that the tension in the persistent cold war can be used constructively as our motivation for bettering our own socioeconomic standards in the West. The present writer agrees with Toynbee that our political and social survival depends both on our capacity for tolerating the anxiety inherent in the threatening world situation (and thus not irrationally precipitating war as a way out of the painful uncertainty) and also on our capacity for turning this anxiety to constructive uses.

In Philosophy and Religion. The fact that anxiety has emerged as a central problem in contemporaneous philosophy and religion is not only a general, but also a specific indication of the prevalence of anxiety in our culture. It is a specific indication in the respect that anxiety has become most prominent in the thought of those theologians, like R. Niebuhr, who are most intimately concerned with the economic and political issues of our day; and in those philosophers, like Tillich and M. Heidegger, who have experienced in their own lives the cultural crises and upheavals of Western society in the past three decades.

Tillich describes anxiety as man's reaction to the threat of *nonbeing*. Man is the creature who has self-conscious awareness of his being, but he is also aware that at any moment he might cease to exist. Thus in philosophical terms anxiety arises as the individual is aware of being as over against the ever present possibility of nonbeing. "Nonbeing" does not mean simply the threat of physical death—though probably death is the most common form and symbol of this anxiety. The threat of nonbeing lies in the psychological and spiritual realms as well, namely the threat of *meaninglessness* in one's existence. Generally the threat of meaningless-ness is experienced negatively as a threat to the existence of the self (the experience of the "dissolution of the self" in Goldstein's term). But when this form of anxiety is confronted affirmatively—when the individual both realizes the threat of meaninglessness and takes a stand against the threat —the result is a strengthening of the individual's feeling of being a self, a strengthening of his perception of himself as distinct from the world of nonbeing, of objects.

Niebuhr makes anxiety the central concept of his theological doctrine of man. To Niebuhr every act of man, creative or destructive, involves some element of anxiety. Anxiety has its source in the fact that man is on one hand finite, involved like the animals in the contingencies and necessi-ties of nature; but on the other hand has freedom. Unlike "the animals he sees this situation [of contingency] and anticipates its perils," and to this extent man transcends his finiteness. "In short, man, being both bound and free, both limited and limitless, is anxious. Anxiety is the inevitable con-comitant of the paradox of freedom and finiteness in which man is in-volved." Much will be said later in the present study about anxiety as the precondition of neurosis; it is significant that Niebuhr, in parallel theological terms, makes anxiety "the internal precondition of sin. . . . Anxiety is the internal description of the state of temptation."

In Psychology. "Anxiety is the most prominent mental characteristic of Occidental civilization," R. R. Willoughby asserts. He then presents statistical evidence for this assertion in the form of the rising incidences in three fields of social pathology which he believes may reasonably be understood as reactions to anxiety, namely *suicide,* the *functional forms of mental disorder,* and *divorce.* Suicide rates for the last 75 to 100 years show a steady increase in the majority of the countries of continental Europe. With regard to the functional forms of mental illness, Willoughby holds, "it seems probable . . . that there is a real rise in incidence of men-tal disease even when the greatest reasonable allowance is made for in-creasing facilities for hospitalization and insight in diagnosis." The di-vorce rates for every country except Japan have shown a steady upward trend in the twentieth century. Willoughby believes the incidence of di-vorce is a measure of the inability of the members of the culture to toler-ate the additional stress of the critical marital adjustment, and the higher incidence must presuppose a considerable load of anxiety in the culture.

We would not question Willoughby's purpose in introducing these statistics, namely, to substantiate the "commonsense proposition that there is in our civilization a large and increasing incidence of anxiety." But there might rightly be considerable question as to whether the relation between these statistical evidences and anxiety is as direct as he holds. Suicide can be due to other motivations than anxiety—revenge is one example. And the rising incidence of divorce would seem to be due to changing social attitudes toward divorce as well as to the prevalence of anxiety. But certainly the three groups of statistics Willoughby presents indicate radical social upheavals in our society which involve psychological and emotional trauma. To the present writer it seems more logical to regard rising divorce, suicide, and mental disease rates as symptoms and products of the traumatically changing state of our culture, and to regard anxiety also as a symptom and product of that cultural state. And certainly a culture described by these statistics would be a culture which generates much anxiety.

Anxiety has gradually come to be seen as a central problem in learning theory, in dynamic psychology, and specifically in psychoanalysis and other forms of psychotherapy. While it long has been recognized that apprehensions and fears, particularly those related to approval or punishment from parents and teachers, exerted much power over the child in school, not until recently have there been scientific recognitions of the innumerable subtle expressions and influences of anxiety permeating the child's educational and classroom experience. For this appreciation of anxiety as a focal problem in learning theory, and the scientific formulation thereof, we are indebted to such learning psychologists as Mowrer, Miller, and Dollard.

More than three decades ago, Freud singled out anxiety as the crucial problem of emotional and behavioral disorders. Further development of psychoanalysis has only substantiated his proposition, until it is now recognized on all sides that anxiety is the "fundamental phenomenon of neurosis," or in Horney's term, the "dynamic center of neuroses." But not only in psychopathology; in the actions of "normal" people as well as "abnormal," it is now recognized that anxiety is much more prevalent than was suspected several decades ago. From the viewpoint of dynamic psychology, Symonds accurately notes that "it would surprise most persons to realize how much of their behavior is motivated by a desire to escape anxiety by either reducing it or disguising it in one way or another." Whether we are concerned with "normal" or pathological behavior, Freud was correct in saying that the solution to the "riddle" of anxiety "must cast a flood of light upon our whole mental life."

[18]   *The Air-Conditioned Conscience**

by FREDERIC WERTHAM

There exists right now a flourishing literature which for brevity and
from its star example may be called peace-of-mind literature. These peace-
of-mind books have not been studied as a group before. To lump them
all together may be unfair to some individual book, and may not be quite
scientific. But although there are no sharp boundaries, it is a group
readily identified and with many common features. They are all "How
To" books: How to Use Psychiatric Principles to Become a "Cock-Eyed
Optimist."

Nothing will give you more quickly a picture of this whole literature
than a look at some of the titles: "Let's Explore Your Mind," "Emotional
Security," "Chart for Happiness," "The Complete Life," "Managing Your
Mind," "Emotional Hygiene," "The Comforts of Unreason," "Making Our
Minds Behave," "How to Psychoanalyze Yourself," "Personal Mental Hy-
giene," "Peace of Mind," "Peace of Soul," "Emotional Maturity," "On Be-
ing a Real Person," "How Sane Are You?" "How to Think Straight," "How
Never to Be Tired," "How to Remember," "Mastering Your Nerves," "How
to Stop Worrying and Start Living," "Life Is for Living," "Self-Analysis,"
"A Guide to Confident Living," "The Mature Mind," "Living Wisely and
Well," "Psychiatry for Everyman," "Psychiatry for You," "And We Are
Whole Again," "What Your Dreams Mean," "How to Think About Our-
selves," "Understandable Psychiatry," "The Mind in Action," "Be Glad
You're Neurotic," "Emotional Problems of Living," "Release from Nerv-
ous Tension," "How to Conquer Your Handicaps," "Make Up Your
Mind," "Don't Be Afraid," "How to Get Rid of Fear and Fatigue," etc.

Roughly, these books can be divided into three categories. The first
are the how-to-do-anything books or how-to-be-happy books based primarily on faith in oneself. They imply that anyone can do anything or be
anyone. They seem to say that you can be transformed into a Tarzan or
an Einstein if only you go about it in the right way and are persistent
enough. In the second group are those offering similar help on the basis
of faith in psychiatry. And in the third group the emphasis is on faith

* Reprinted from *Saturday Review of Literature*, Oct. 1, 1949, pp. 6-8, 26-27. Copyright 1949 by The Saturday Review, Inc. Reprinted by permission of Harold Matson
Company.

in religion—made more intriguing by psychoanalytic overtones, either consonant or dissonant.

The existence and wide popularity of these books raises a number of problems. There can be little doubt that the vogue of such self-improvement books indicates that there are lots of troubled people who need what these books promise—or think they need it. Since psychotherapy is restricted mostly to the well-to-do, the upper classes, and those who need it least, many people evidently seek from books what they cannot get otherwise. What is the significance of this sort of book in terms of general mental health? And what do they mean in terms of the society that breeds and reads them?

I have asked many people which of these books they have read and what they got out of them. In many instances I have tried to evaluate their effect objectively. There is no doubt that quite a number of these books contain grains of common sense and sensible statements of psychiatric observations which may sometimes be of some help, or at least give the illusion of helping. They have influence because they seem to be disinterested and objective, and because they carry the authority of the printed word plus the authority of the scientific foundations they claim to have.

One of the most typical replies I received was this: "I liked especially the case histories. A man got helped and I said to myself, why can't I help myself. It made me feel better to read that people can come out of all their troubles." That is, of course, a good attitude for people to take. The only question is, as Napoleon said, what did you do the next day? As another man told me, "I felt better after reading that book. But the next time it just didn't ring the bell."

A very decent and most harassed young woman told me: "I like these books. They foster understanding for self-discipline for two people to live together, let alone all society. They show that the same mechanism operates in religion and in psychiatry—both in the spiritual realm beyond material reward. They make you self-sufficient and give you inner peace. They give you the reasonable satisfaction which one needs to have if one wants to remain sane."

This answer illustrates the sweeping solace these books give on a theoretical plane, which is really a plane of unreality. For they are addressed to anyone or everyone and take no cognizance of individual differences. The readers are people who consciously or unconsciously reach out for guidance, help, and strength. They think they are getting individual understanding when what they really receive is generalized consolation. They don't like the rules by which their ordinary life must be lived, so they enjoy reading about rules which they would like to live by but don't have to. Whatever their own problem, they read avidly in these books that other people have the same problem. Not having the discipline of scientific clinical observation, they see themselves in any case history or any generalization. They find their fears about the present, and the future particularly, relieved, for as one man told me, "There was something in your childhood that causes all that, and that is the only thing that is wrong—and after I had read that I had peace of mind for twenty-four hours."

There, of course, is the rub. For many of these readers will fall victim of the implied threat that—as in the comic-book story of Dr. Sigmund Adler—they are "too far gone" and had better hurry to the nearest psychoanalyst. If advertising ever existed, this literature is it. As if in this day and age, when mental-hygiene clinics have waiting lists filled up for a year in advance, people still need to be "enlightened" in this respect! The trouble is that while the reader has the illusion that he is being directly and personally talked to he may be given all kinds of misinformation as if it were proven fact. In one of the recent articles which are miniatures of this kind of literature the writer (who is identified as the wife of an "eminent psychoanalyst") gives the shocking misinformation that electric-shock therapy is a good test to determine whether you are mentally disturbed or not! A similar article contains this misinformation: "The patient must spend an hour a day with the doctor for a period of perhaps one to five years, and the cost may range from $1,000 to $25,000. Anyone offering a much quicker or cheaper psychoanalysis, except as charity, may safely be labeled a quack."

Where these books deal with sex they commendably alleviate fears about perversions—while at the same time, however, describing them just in case you should not know them yet.

There is no doubt that many people have enlarged their vocabulary through this sort of reading. They have gained a surface understanding of deep psychology and learned a lot of new glib words, which are especially useful in social conversation if the other person doesn't know them yet. The difficulty is that a whole barbaric vocabulary has crept not only into conversation but also into literary writing: "ego strength," "return to the womb," and many other such expressions. When recently a pocket edition of "Manhattan Transfer" was published some people took it for granted that it was a book about psychoanalysis in New York. Psychoanalysis has reached into the psychotheological books, too. And you can find in them such strained expressions as "souls stretched out on psychoanalytic couches."

But this is not just a question of words. More and more people are using psychoanalytic terminology not as a tool but as a substitute for thinking. Recently a judge sentenced an eighteen-year-old youth to death, disregarding the jury's recommendation of clemency. He stated that he based himself on the probation report which said of the defendant: "His personality is permeated with psychosexual habits of thought and conduct." What would the judge think if he learned that he also (and all other human beings) is "permeated with psychosexual" thoughts?

One attraction of these books is that they give simple, pat answers. Linking science, common sense, and spirituality, many of them do not leave out the material side of things. They talk about security, especially emotional security; but financial securities hover in the background. They seem to imply that the end justifies the means—if you have the means. And since they have to be best sellers a good title for some of them would be "The Bacon and I."

As for teaching how to get on with other people, they preach a kind of Machiavellianism not for princes but for the little man. Somehow these books convey the idea that you can be selfish with justification as long as you make yourself feel that you are unselfish; that you can enrich yourself at the expense of others as long as you persuade yourself that you only give "service" to them. In your personal relations you are taught to be cunning and diplomatic—all, of course, on the basis of psychology. And since you should not feel guilty, you certainly are not supposed to feel guilty about the insincerity entailed in all this. Recently I examined a man who seemed to me to have mastered the art of "using psychology" as taught in this literature to perfection. He won the confidence of many lonely women and certainly influenced them. (The complication was that he took their money and, when the "psychology" didn't work any more, killed a few of them.)

All these books breathe an atmosphere of optimism. Everybody can be happy or should be happy and if he *isn't* happy he should be happy that he isn't happy. This attitude seems to have spread even to one of our biggest universities, which recently announced a "Project Concerned with the Cheerful Aspects of Human Behavior. The subjects will not be the mentally distressed, but the strikingly happy and successful persons. Through detailed and intensive study of these individuals it is hoped that light will be thrown on the factors essential to effective and happy living." (Cost: $54,000.)

This optimism is different from the simple kind found in the old new-thought and uplift literature. It exists against a background of anxiety and evoked hypochondriasis. As a matter of fact, the negative emotional reactions aroused by this literature consist in a new kind of mental hypochondriasis which is a mixture between the cure and the disease. People have commented that in "Death of a Salesman" we never learn what Willy Loman is selling. But it is easy to guess what kind of books he reads—the peace-of-mind literature with the optimism of which life catches up in the end. What these books do *not* teach is to face life as it is. They are like tax guides which teach us not how to pay but how to evade taxes.

Books like "Peace of Mind," which seek most thoroughly to blend psychoanalysis and religion, work in the suggestive twilight of abnormal psychology and supernatural revelation. It is not quite clear whether they smuggle psychoanalysis into religion or religion into psychoanalysis. The parallel between psychoanalysis and religion is, as Freud pointed out, a false one. The road to Damascus is not the road to Vienna. Even the road to Bollingen is a thing for itself.

The outstanding feature common to these books is that they seem to be addressed to individuals who live mostly in a social vacuum. The influence of the environment in producing worry, tension, or anxiety is either completely disregarded or accepted as inevitable. There are no social forces, no social history, no social interaction, no social responsibility. In one of the most successful recent books an untrue statement about Negroes is repeated as if it were scientific fact: They don't "have the kind of heart disease brought on by worry because they take things calmly." Social evils are rationalized and therefore justified as the result of individual faults amenable to self-improvement or psychoanalytic or psychotheological influence. The lesson is, clearly, that it is not the social scene but its isolated inhabitant that needs to be analyzed. Repressive measures of governments do not exist; there are only repressing mechanisms in the mind of the individual. If you can't help yourself the remedy you seek must be individual, not social. Instead of fighting against such attacks on civil liberties as "guilt by association," you should lie on psychoanalytic couches and ruminate about guilt by free association. Among all the case histories in this literature, there is no suggestion that there are maladies which as Dostoievsky said "arise from the abnormal conditions of society." There is almost no awareness of society's responsibility toward old, infirm, sick, and handicapped people—not to mention the normal ones.

Is there anything new in this literature? I think there is. It is, of course, a type of escape literature. It will not help you in the long run to an escape from anxiety, from suffering, or from doubts. But it does go a long way to help you to an escape from social responsibility. One can extract from these books a new concept, never before so fully elaborated—the concept of an air-conditioned conscience.

CHAPTER TEN

The Family

HOWEVER *widely it may differ in form, it is generally agreed that the family as an institution for regulating sexual relations and rearing children is found in all human societies. In modern societies the patriarchal family of the past has given way before the swift onrush of economic and social change. Technological advance has reduced the economic functions of the family, while the state has taken over in part certain other functions, including education. Thus the family has come gradually to play a less dominant role in the life of individuals. This process has gone farthest in urban areas.*

In this chapter Benedict deals with hazards confronting the American family, but she is optimistic about its ability to meet them. Moore, on the other hand, raises certain questions which have a bearing on the very survival of the family. The major theme of sociologists has been that the family is making up for the lost or weakened functions by strengthening certain other functions such as companionship and the fulfilling of emotional needs. To Moore this seems little more than a middle-class hope. The crucial question is, To what extent does the modern family perform the essential function of developing in children healthy personalities?

[19]   The Family: Genus Americanum*

by RUTH BENEDICT

A great many people today speak as if the family were in some special sort of danger in our times. We hear a great deal about "saving the family" and about "preserving the home." Authors and lecturers describe how the family is threatened by divorce, or by mothers who work outside of the home, or by unemployment, or by lack of religious training of children. Each of them, depending on his experience in his own home and on his observations in the families he knows, selects something which he thinks should be changed—or should be preserved—and says that, if this or that were done, the family would be "saved."

To an anthropologist such phrasings are dangerously misleading. He has studied the family among naked savages and in contemporary civilizations and he knows that it has survived in all human societies known in the record of mankind. Just as surely he knows that the family takes all kinds of different forms. It is not merely that unlettered primitive nomads have family arrangements different from Western industrial nations; even in Western nations around the Atlantic shores the family differs profoundly. The ethics of marriage, the specific close emotional ties which the family fosters, the disciplines and freedoms for the child, the nature of the dependency of the children upon the parents, even the personnel which makes up the family—all these differ in Western civilized nations. The anthropologist knows that the changes taking place in the home in any decade in any country do not mean that the family is now about to disintegrate under our eyes unless we do something about it. The problem as he states it is quite different: how do legal and customary arrangements in the family tally with the arrangements and premises of the whole way of life which is valued in any tribe or nation? If, for instance, the father has a heavy, authoritarian hand upon his children, the anthropologist asks: Is this in keeping with authoritarianism in the state and in industry? Or is it at odds with a society which values non-authoritarianism and the pursuit of happiness? He asks the same kind of question about a nation's laws of inheritance from father to son, about the divorce laws, about the architectural layout of the house, about the reasons that are given to children when they are told to be good.

Customs enshrined in the family in any tribe or nation are likely to be sensitively adjusted to the values and customs of each particular people.

* From *The Family: Its Function and Destiny*, edited by Ruth Nanda Anshen, pp. 159-166. Copyright 1949 by Harper & Brothers, New York. Reprinted by permission.

This is no mystic correspondence; the persons who make up the family are the same people who are the citizens of that nation—the business men, the farmers, the churchgoers or non-churchgoers, the readers of newspapers, and the listeners to the radio. In all their roles they are molded more or less surely into a people with certain habits, certain hopes, and a certain *esprit de corps*. Americans come to share certain slogans, behavior, and judgments which differ from those of Frenchmen or Czechs. This is inevitable. And in the process the role of the family also becomes different. By the same token, just as economic and political changes occur over a period of time in the United States or in France or in Czechoslovakia, the family also changes.

An anthropologist, therefore, when he reads about the failure of the family, finds in such criticism a somewhat special meaning. He remembers how often the family is made a convenient whipping boy among many peoples who disapprove of the way their world is going. He has seen it in Amazon jungles and on the islands of the Pacific. The author remembers an American Indian tribe which used to talk about the family in a most uncomplimentary fashion. They were a people who, not long before, had roamed over the great plains hunting buffalo and proving their courage by war exploits. Now they lived on a reservation, and tending crops was no adequate substitute for their old way of life. Their old economic arrangements of boastful gift giving, their political life, and their religious practices had either been destroyed by circumstances or had lost their meaningfulness. Life had become pointless to them. These men talked with gusto about the failure of the family. They said that in the family the children no longer learned manners, or religion, or generosity, or whatever it was the individual Indian favored as a cure-all. The family, too, weighed a man down, they said; it was a burden to him.

To the anthropologist studying this tribe, however, the family was precisely the best arranged, most trustworthy institution in their whole culture. It was hard beset and it had not escaped the tragic effects of the general disintegration of tribal life, but it was what provided the warm, human ties and the dependable security which were left in that Indian tribe. The children were loved and cared for, the husbands and wives often had comfortable relations with each other, and the family hospitality had a graciousness that was absent in more public life. At birth and marriage and death the family still functioned as an effective institution. And there seemed to be no man or woman of childbearing age who was not married or would not have preferred to be.

The writer thinks of this Indian tribe when she hears Americans talk about the decay of the family. Instead of viewing the family with such alarm, suppose we look at it as it exists in this decade in this country and see how it is arranged to fulfill its functions in American schemes of life. Let us leave aside for the moment the questions of whether conditions are provided that would keep it from preventable overstrain and of whether as human beings we are able to get all the satisfaction we might out of this institution; let us consider only the arrangements of the family as we know it and how these fit in with our values and with the way we should like to plan our lives.

Suppose we take marriage first. Marriage sets up the new family, and it seems to make a great deal of difference whether a society dictates that the new home shall be begun in tears and heartache or with rejoicing. Many human societies would not recognize a marriage without a wailing bride and a sullen groom. Often the bride has to be surrounded by her mourning women, who lament her coming lifelong separation from her parents and her brothers and sisters, as well as her future misery as she goes to work for her mother-in-law. Often they cut her long hair and remove her jewelry as a sign that she is now a worker and no longer alluring. The groom's role, too, may be that of an unwilling victim. Often marriages are arranged by the parents without giving the two young people any chance to know each other.

All these circumstances are absent in marriage in the United States. The young people are hardly hampered in their choice of a mate; if occasionally parents deplore their choice, public opinion allows the young couple to outface them and expects the parents to accept the inevitable with as much decency as they can muster. We expect that the bride and groom will be in love or will have chosen each other for reasons known to themselves. Whether they marry for love or for money or to show they can win a sought-after mate from a rival, in any case they are making a personal choice and are not acting on command. Because in every field of life American culture puts such a high value on this kind of freedom and so bitterly resents its curtailment in peace time, the fact that the young people do make their own choice of a mate is an important and auspicious arrangement. The arranged marriage which is traditional in France or the careful class restrictions which have been observed in Holland would be difficult to manage in the United States. The wide range of choice of a mate and the fact that the young people make their own selection are conditions which could hardly be made more satisfactory for Americans with their particular habits and demands.

After marriage, too, the new family has a wide range of choices about where to live, how the wife shall occupy herself, when to start a family, and a host of other important matters. Such freedom is extremely unusual in the world. Sometimes the couple must live with the husband's family, sometimes with the wife's. Often in other countries, until one or two children are born, the young man continues to work for his father and has no say about the farm or the flock and no money which he can control. But in the United States a young couple plans the family budget before the wedding and what they earn is theirs to spend.

The way the new family in this country sets up its own separate home makes possible a rare and delightful circumstance: the two of them can have an incomparable privacy. No matter how hard it has been to arrange for privacy before marriage, as soon as the wedding is over everybody expects them to have their own latch key and their own possessions around them. If they cannot manage this, they feel cheated and other people think something is wrong. It is the same if they have to give a home to a parent. In most civilized countries this is a duty to which as a good son and good daughter they are bound, but if it is necessary in the United States their friends and neighbors will regard them as exceptionally burdened. Even the scarcity and high wages of domestic servants give the young family a greater privacy. Considering that they have chosen each other to their own liking, this privacy in the home is made in order to gratify them; the only problem is whether they can use it to their own happiness.

When they cannot, and when they find that their choice of a mate was not fool-proof just because they made it on their own, there is in the United States great freedom to get a divorce. Our growing divorce rate is the subject of much viewing-with-alarm; yet in a culture built as ours is on ever expanding personal choice, an important goal of which is the pursuit of happiness, the right to terminate an unhappy marriage is the other side of the coin of which the fair side is the right to choose one's spouse. Weak and stunted individuals will of course abuse both privileges, yet it is difficult to see how divorce could consistently be denied in a culture like ours. Certainly if we accepted it more honestly as a necessary phase of our way of life, however sorrowful, and put honest effort and sympathy into not penalizing the divorced, we should be acting more appropriately and in our best interests. At any rate, the high divorce rate in the United States is no attack on marriage, for it is precisely the divorced—those who have failed in one or two attempts—who have the highest rate of marriage. Between the ages of twenty-five and thirty-five not even the unmarried or the widowed marry at so great a rate as the divorced.

Besides free choice and privacy, the American family has unusual potential leisure because of the labor-saving devices, prepared foods, and
ready-made clothes available under modern conditions. The basic labor-
saver is running water in the sink, and Americans have little idea how
many millions of homes in civilized countries do not have it. Thus we
are saved an endless round of drudgery that ties down women—and men
also—in countries where homes have no running water, no gas and
electricity, no farm tools but those which are driven into the earth by
human hands or are swung in human arms, and no use of ready-made
soaps and foods and clothes. Americans put high value on lessened
drudgery, but they deprecate having free spaces of truly leisure time; the
more time they save the more they fill up their days and nights with a
round of engagements and complications. They are unwilling to admit
that they have leisure, but the schedules of their lives prove clearly how
much they have.

Universal schooling in the United States also frees the family of many
duties when children have come. It is hard for Americans to imagine
the difference which regular school hours makes in a mother's role. For
a great part of the working day, American children are the responsibility of the teacher and not the mother. As nursery schools spread
over the country, younger and younger children get trained care outside
the home and the mother's labors are correspondingly relieved. As the
children grow older the mother's leisure increases, until finally she
reaches that middle age with its round of card parties and clubs and
window shopping and movies which engross and waste the energy of so
many millions of American women. Her husband is earning more
money now than when he was younger, and her children have flown;
she has a plethora of privileges and freedom and leisure. In one sense she
has everything.

It is obviously unfair to talk about the incomparable freedom from
drudgery which the American home offers without emphasizing that
interval of a few years when there is no leisure for the mother in the
home—the years when the babies are little. In our great cities where each
family is strange to all the others, a mother is likely to have to be a baby
tender every hour of the day, with no one to relieve her. Along with
these duties she must do all her cooking and washing and cleaning. And,
as all our magazines and women's pages reiterate, she must make efforts
to keep her husband. She must keep herself looking attractive, must keep
up social contacts, and be a companion to him. To European wives this
program looks formidable. "I was always told that American women
were so free," a Polish woman said to me, "but when I came here and

saw how they had to manage with the babies and the house without any older women of the family to help, and then how they had to play around with their husbands in the evening to keep them happy, I decided I wouldn't change places with them for anything. In Poland a woman doesn't have to 'keep' her husband; it's all settled when they're married."

The striking fact about the nursery years in the United States is that in comparison with those in other countries they are so short and that nevertheless we do not really treat them as an interim. Mothers who are going through this period give remarkably little thought to the leisure that will come soon. They are often vocal enough about the turmoil of their present lives, and sometimes bitter, but the fact that the nursery years last so short a time in the United States and could be treated as an interim—like a professor's going into the government during war time —is all too seldom part of their thinking. No doubt this is due in part to a lag in our culture, since even with our grandparents conditions were different; but in part it is a result of the sentiment which selects this period, no matter how short, as the fulfillment of a woman's chief duty in life. A social engineer looking at the family, however, would certainly put his major effort into better arrangements for the overburdened mother during these years and into thinking about effecting some transition from this period into that next one during which, in the United States, millions of women become idle parasites upon society—and dull and unhappy into the bargain.

Another notable feature of the American family is its peculiarly non-authoritarian character. The old rules that a child should be seen and not heard and the adage, "Spare the rod and spoil the child," are anachronistic in the United States; they are dispensed with even in immigrant groups which honored them in their native country. The rule of the father over the family is still a reality in some European nations, but in the United States the mother is the chief responsible agent in bringing up her children; here the father's opinions are something the children are more likely to play off against the mother's, to their own advantage, rather than a court of last authority from which there is no appeal. Children take the noisy center of the stage at the breakfast table and in the living room in a way that is quite impossible in European countries. The fact that they are expected to know right from wrong in their tenderest years and to act upon it on their own is often commented on by European mothers who have lived here. A Dutch mother once spoke to the author about how hard we are on our children because we expect this of them; she said, "I don't expect it of my children before they are seven; until then, I am there to see that they act correctly." But an American mother expects a child of three or four to be a responsible moral agent, and she gives him great latitude in which to prove that he can manage his little affairs by himself.

All this lack of strong authoritarianism in American families accords well with the values that are chiefly sought after in this country. No strong father image is compatible with our politics or our economics. We seek the opportunity to prove that we are as good as the next person, and we do not find comfort in following an authoritarian voice—in the state or in the home, from landowner or the priest—which will issue a command from on high. We learn as children to measure ourselves against Johnny next door, or against Mildred whose mother our mother knows in church, and this prepares us for living in a society with strongly egalitarian ideals. We do not learn the necessity of submitting to unquestioned commands as the children of many countries do. The family in the United States has become democratic.

These free-choice and non-authoritarian aspects of the family, along with its privacy and potential leisure, evidence only a few of the many ways in which it has become consistent with major emphases in our national life. They seem, when one compares them with arrangements in other civilized nations, to be quite well fitted to the role the family must play in a culture like the United States. . . .

[20] *Thoughts on the Future of the Family**

by BARRINGTON MOORE, JR.

Among social scientists it is almost axiomatic that the family is a universally necessary social institution and will remain such through any foreseeable future. Changes in its structure, to be sure, receive wide recognition. The major theme, however, in the appraisal American sociolo-

* Reprinted by permission of the publishers from Barrington Moore, Jr., *Political Power and Social Theory*, Cambridge, Mass.: Harvard University Press, Ch. V, pp. 160-178. © Copyright 1958, by The President and Fellows of Harvard College.

gists present is that the family is making up for lost economic functions by providing better emotional service. One work announces as its central thesis that "the family in historical times has been, and at present is, in transition from an institution to a companionship." In the past, the authors explain, the forces holding the family together were external, formal, and authoritarian, such as law, public opinion, and the authority of the father. Now, it is claimed, unity inheres in the mutual affection and comradeship of its members. Another recent work by a leading American sociologist makes a similar point. The trend under industrialism, we are told, does not constitute a decline of the family as such, but mainly a decline of its importance in the performance of economic functions. Meanwhile, the author tells us, the family has become a more specialized agency for the performance of other functions, namely, the socialization of children and the stabilization of adult personalities. For this reason, the author continues, social arrangements corresponding rather closely to the modern family may be expected to remain with us indefinitely.

In reading these and similar statements by American sociologists about other aspects of American society, I have the uncomfortable feeling that the authors, despite all their elaborate theories and technical research devices, are doing little more than projecting certain middle-class hopes and ideals onto a refractory reality. If they just looked a little more carefully at what was going on around them, I think they might come to different conclusions. This is, of course, a very difficult point to prove, though C. Wright Mills, in a brilliant essay, has shown how one area of American sociology, the study of crime, is suffused with such preconceptions. While personal observations have some value, one can always argue that a single observer is biased. Here all I propose to do, therefore, is to raise certain questions about the current sociological assessment of the family on the basis of such evidence as has come my way rather casually. In addition, I should like to set this evidence in the framework of an intellectual tradition, represented, so far as the family is concerned, by Bertrand Russell's *Marriage and Morals,* that sees the family in an evolutionary perspective, and raises the possibility that it may be an obsolete institution or become one before long. I would suggest then that conditions have arisen which, in many cases, prevent the family from performing the social and psychological functions ascribed to it by modern sociologists. The same conditions may also make it possible for the advanced industrial societies of the world to do away with the family and substitute other social arrangements that impose fewer unnecessary and painful restrictions on humanity. Whether or not society actually would take advantage of such an opportunity is, of course, another question.

It may be best to begin with one observation that is not in itself conclusive but at least opens the door to considering these possibilities. In discussions of the family, one frequently encounters the argument that Soviet experience demonstrates the necessity of this institution in modern society. The Soviets, so the argument runs, were compelled to adopt the family as a device to carry part of the burden of making Soviet citizens, especially after they perceived the undesirable consequences of savage homeless children, largely the outcome of the Civil War. This explanation is probably an accurate one as far as it goes. But it needs to be filled out by at least two further considerations that greatly reduce its force as a general argument. In the first place, the Soviets, I think, adopted their conservative policy toward the family *faute de mieux*. That is to say, with their very limited resources, and with other more pressing objectives, they had no genuine alternatives. Steel mills had to be built before crèches, or at least before crèches on a large enough scale to make any real difference in regard to child care. In the meantime the services of the family, and especially of grandma (*babushka*), had to be called upon. In the second place, with the consolidation of the regime in the middle thirties, Soviet totalitarianism may have succeeded in capturing the family and subverting this institution to its own uses. At any rate the confidence and vigor with which the regime supported this institution from the early thirties onward suggests such an explanation. Thus the Soviet experience does not constitute by itself very strong evidence in favor of the "functional necessity" of the family.

If the Soviet case does not dispose of the possibility that the family may be obsolete, we may examine other considerations with greater confidence, and begin by widening our historical perspective. By now it is a familiar observation that the stricter Puritan ethics of productive work and productive sex have accomplished their historical purposes in the more advanced sections of the Western world. These developments have rendered other earlier elements of Western culture and society, such as slavery, quite obsolete, and constitute at least prima facie evidence for a similar argument concerning the family. Let us ask then to what extent may we regard the family as a repressive survival under the conditions of an advanced technology? And to what extent does the modern family perform the function of making human beings out of babies and small children either badly or not at all?

One of the most obviously obsolete features of the family is the obligation to give affection as a duty to a particular set of persons on account of the accident of birth. This is a true relic of barbarism. It is a survival from human prehistory, when kinship was the basic form of social organization. In early times it was expedient to organize the division of labor and affection in human society through real or imagined kinship bonds. As civilization became technically more advanced, there has been less and less of a tendency to allocate both labor and affection according to slots in a kinship system, and an increasing tendency to award them on the basis of the actual qualities and capacities that the individual possesses.

Popular consciousness is at least dimly aware of the barbaric nature of the duty of family affection and the pain it produces, as shown by the familiar remark, "You can choose your friends, but you can't choose your relatives." Even if partly concealed by ethical imperatives with the weight of age-old traditions, the strain is nevertheless real and visible. Children are often a burden to their parents. One absolutely un-Bohemian couple I know agreed in the privacy of their own home that if people ever talked to each other openly about the sufferings brought on by raising a family today, the birth rate would drop to zero. It is, of course, legitimate to wonder how widespread such sentiments are. But this couple is in no sense "abnormal." Furthermore, a revealing remark like this made to a friend is worth more as evidence than reams of scientific questionnaires subjected to elaborate statistical analyses. Again, how many young couples, harassed by the problems of getting started in life, have not wished that their parents could be quietly and cheaply taken care of in some institution for the aged? Such facts are readily accessible to anyone who listens to the conversations in his own home or among the neighbors.

The exploitation of socially sanctioned demands for gratitude, when the existing social situation no longer generates any genuine feeling of warmth, is a subtle and heavily tabooed result of this barbaric heritage. It is also one of the most painful. Perhaps no feeling is more excruciating than the feeling that we ought to love a person whom we actually detest. The Greek tragedians knew about the problem, but veiled it under religion and mythology, perhaps because the men and women of that time felt there was no escape. In the nineteenth century the theme again became a dominant one in European literature, but with the clear implication that the situation was unnecessary. Even these authors, Tolstoi, Samuel Butler, Strindberg, and Ibsen, in exposing the horrors and hypocrisies of family life, wove most of their stories around the marital relationship, where there is an element of free choice in the partner selected. Kafka's little gem, *Das Urteil*, is a significant exception. With magnificent insight into the tragedy on both sides, it treats the frustrations of a grown-up son forced to cherish a helpless but domineering father. Henry James' short story, *Europe*, is an effective treatment of the same relationship between a mother and her daughters. Despite some blind spots and limitations, the artists, it appears, have seen vital aspects of the family that have largely escaped the sociologists.

In addition to these obsolete and barbaric features one can point to certain trends in modern society that have sharply reduced rather than increased the effectiveness of the home as an agency for bringing up children. In former times the family was a visibly coherent economic unit, as well as the group that served to produce and raise legitimate children. The father had definite and visible economic tasks, before the household became separated from the place of work. When the children could see what he did, the father had a role to be copied and envied. The source and justification of his authority was clear. Internal conflicts had to be resolved. This is much less the case now.

It is reasonably plain that today's children are much less willing than those of pre-industrial society to take their parents as models for conduct. Today they take them from the mass media and from gangs. Radio and television heroes, with their copies among neighborhood gangs, now play a vital part in the socialization process. Parents have an uphill and none too successful struggle against these sources. Like adult mobs, children's groups readily adopt the sensational, the cruel, and the most easily understood for their models and standards. These influences then corrupt and lower adult standards, as parents become increasingly afraid to assert their own authority for fear of turning out "maladjusted" children.[1]

The mass media have largely succeeded in battering down the walls of the social cell the family once constituted in the larger structure of society. Privacy has greatly diminished. Newspapers, radios, and television have very largely destroyed the flow of private communications within the family that were once the basis of socialization. Even meals are now much less of a family affair. Small children are frequently plumped down in front of the television set with their supper on a tray before them to keep them quiet. Since the family does less as a unit, genuine emotional ties among its members do not spring up so readily. The advertising campaign for "togetherness" provides rather concrete evidence that family members would rather not be together.

The mother, at least in American society, is generally supposed to be the homemaker and the center of the family. Has she been able to take up the slack produced by the change in the father's role? Is she, perhaps,

[1] It is sometimes claimed that the modern family still represents a bulwark against mass and totalitarian pressures. No doubt this is true in the best cases, those few where parents are still able to combine authority and affection. These are, however, mainly a relic of Victorian times. By and large it seems more likely that the family constitutes the "transmission belt" through which totalitarian pressures toward conformity are transmitted to the parents through the influence of the children.

the happy person whose face smiles at us from every advertisement and whose arts justify the sociologists' case? A more accurate assessment may be that the wife suffers most in the modern middle-class family, because the demands our culture puts upon her are impossible to meet. As indicated by advertisements, fiction, and even the theories of sociologists, the wife is expected to be companion, confidante, and ever youthful mistress of her husband.

If the demands could be met, many wives might feel very happy in this fulfillment of their personality. The actual situation is very different. The father is out of the house all day and therefore can be neither overlord nor companion. With the father absent, radio and television provide the mother with a watery substitute for adult companionship. A young colleague told me recently that his wife leaves the radio on all day merely to hear the sound of a grown-up voice. The continual chatter of little children can be profoundly irritating, even to a naturally affectionate person. The absence of servants from nearly all American middle-class households brings the wife face to face with the brutalizing features of motherhood and housework. If she had the mentality of a peasant, she might be able to cope with them more easily. Then, however, she could not fulfill the decorative functions her husband expects. As it is now, diapers, dishes, and the state of the baby's bowels absorb the day's quota of energy. There is scarcely any strength left for sharing emotions and experiences with the husband, for which there is often no opportunity until the late hours of the evening. It is hardly a wonder that the psychiatrists' anterooms are crowded, or that both husband and wife seek escapes from psychological and sexual boredom, the cabin fever of the modern family. For the wife, either a job or an affair may serve equally well as a release from domesticity.

A further sign of the modern family's inadequacy in stabilizing the human personality may be seen in the troubled times of adolescence. This stage of growing up has been interpreted as a rejection of adult standards of responsibility and work by youngsters who are about to enter adult life. It seems to me that this period is more significantly one of pseudo-rebellion, when the youngsters copy what they see to be the real values of adult life instead of the professed ones. Even in the more extreme forms of youthful rebellion, relatively rare among respectable middle-class children, such as roaring around in noisy cars to drinking and seduction parties, the adolescents are aping actual adult behavior. Adolescents then do things they know many grown-ups do when the latter think they are escaping the observant eyes of the young. A "hot-rod" is, after all, nothing but an immature Cadillac. Where the Cadillac is the symbol of success, what else could be expected? Adult standards too are made tolerable through commercialized eroticism that lures us on to greater efforts and greater consumption from every billboard and magazine cover. Thus the whole miasma of sexual and psychological boredom in the older generation, pseudo-rebellion and brutality in the younger one, is covered over by a sentimental and suggestive genre art based on commercial sentiment.

No doubt many will think that these lines paint too black a picture. Statistics could perhaps be accumulated to show that families such as the type sketched here are far from a representative cross-section of American middle-class life. Such facts, however, would not be relevant to the argument. As pointed out elsewhere in these essays, the representative character of certain types of social behavior is not necessarily relevant to estimates of current and future trends. This kind of statistical defense of the status quo represents that of a certain maiden's virtue by the claim, "After all, she is only a little bit pregnant."

To refute the appraisal offered in these pages it would be necessary to demonstrate that they misrepresent basic structural trends in the family in advanced industrial countries. The most important argument of this type that I have encountered asserts that the proportion of married people in the population has steadily risen while the proportion of single individuals has steadily dropped. Therefore, people obviously prefer famliy life to bachelorhood, and the gloomy picture sketched above must be nothing more than vaporings of sour-bellied intellectuals thrown on the dumpheap by the advance of American society.

Before discussing the question further, let us look at some of the relevant facts. The table below shows changes in the proportions of single, married, and divorced persons in the United States from the age of fourteen onward. The source, an authoritative and very recent statistical survey of the American family, has standardized the proportions for age, using the 1940 age distribution as a standard, in order to eliminate changes due merely to shifts in the age composition of our population, which would merely confuse the issue.

Percentage Distribution of Persons 14 Years and Over by Marital Status and Sex in the Civilian Population 1890–1954

| | MALE | | | FEMALE | | |
Year	Single	Married	Divorced	Single	Married	Divorced
1954	28.4	66.7	1.8	22	65.8	2.2
1950	29.4	65.5	1.5	22.5	64.8	2.1
1940	34.8	59.7	1.2	27.6	59.5	1.6
1930	34.7	59.1	1.1	26.9	59.7	1.3
1890	36.7	57.9	0.2	27.8	57.7	0.4

The figures do show a rise in the proportion of married persons and a decline in the proportion of single ones. They also show that the proportion of married persons is overwhelmingly larger than the number of divorced ones. But the biggest change has been in the proportion of divorced people. For men it has risen ninefold since 1890 and for women more than fivefold. A bigger proportion of people are married now than in 1890, but a *much* bigger proportion have abandoned the marital state. In the long run, the latter change might turn out to be the more important one.

Even the statistical evidence, in other words, does not uphold in a completely unambiguous manner the sociologists' argument for the family. Sometimes an attempt to save the case is made by interpreting the rise in divorce as something that allows greater freedom for the individual to choose marital partners on the basis of congeniality. Thereby divorce allegedly strengthens the family's function as a source of emotional support. By talking about greater freedom for the individual in this fashion one has already taken a long step toward the opponents' view that marriage as such may be superfluous.

The point cannot be considered merely in the light of the facts as they exist now or have existed in the past. To do this in social questions is basically unscientific. Those who dismiss negative appraisals of the family with the crude observation that they reflect personal bias or mere "European decadence" deserve an equally crude reply: "So what if Americans prefer to get married! That simply shows how stupid they are."

Acrimony here unfortunately conceals a genuine issue. It is perfectly possible that conditions exist, perhaps even now, that permit better institutional arrangements than most people would be willing to accept. The word better, of course, implies a definite standard of judgment. One can debate such standards endlessly, and perhaps cannot reach agreement without at some point making arbitrary assumptions. I shall not enter this debate here except to say that any social institution is a bad one that imposes more suffering on people than is necessary when they have sufficient material resources and scientific knowledge to do away with this suffering. This standard, anthropologists tell us, is that not only of Western culture, but of all culture.

What then, are the prospects for the future? We need not take a completely determinist view. Indeed, the perceptions that both plain people and opinion makers have about the present enter in as a significant component among the forces shaping the future and thereby provide an entering wedge for rational adaptation.

Among those who accept a substantial part of the preceding image of the family as basically correct, one frequently hears the prescription that what American culture really needs is a higher evaluation of the social role of the housewife and of motherhood. The trouble with this prescription, I would suggest, is that it merely increases the element of self-deception already so prevalent in our culture. Under present conditions motherhood *is* frequently a degrading experience. There is nothing to be gained by concealing the facts in the manner of an advertising campaign designed to raise the prestige of a particular occupation. We would not think of trying to eliminate the hazards of coal mining in this way. Why should we try to do it with motherhood? If it is true that under present circumstances the experience of motherhood narrows and cramps the personality rather than promotes the development of its capacities, some other way will have to be found if it is to be a real solution.

The trend towards a continually more efficient technology and greater specialization, which dominates the rest of our culture, may conceivably provide an answer. In regard to the division of labor it is important to recall one widely known but neglected fact. In the past, whenever human beings have acquired sufficient resources and power, as among aristocracies, they have put the burden of childrearing on other shoulders. Twenty years ago Ralph Linton pointed out that "aristocrats the world over . . . are reluctant to take care of their own children. Anyone who has had to take care of two or three infants simultaneously will understand why. This arduous business is turned over to slaves or servants. . . ."

Since the decline of slavery, a basic trend in European society has been to transfer to machines more and more tasks formerly carried out by slaves. By and large, this change has been accompanied by the growth of large organizations to perform tasks formerly scattered among many small groups. This trend may well affect the family. Specialized human agencies, developing from such contemporary forms as the crèche, play school, and boarding school, might assume a much larger share of the burden of child rearing, a task that could in any case be greatly lightened by machinery for feeding and the removal of waste products. Can one sensibly argue that the technical ingenuity and resources required to solve this problem are greater than those necessary for nuclear warfare? Are we to regard as permanent and "natural" a civilization that develops its most advanced technology for killing people and leaves their replacement to the methods of the Stone Age?

Against this viewpoint it is usually argued that human infants require some minimum of human affection, even fondling, if they are to survive, and that therefore some form of the family is bound to remain. The premises may be correct, but the conclusion does not follow. A nurse can perform these tasks of giving affection and early socialization just as well as the parents, often better. The argument does not prove anything therefore about the inevitable necessity of the family.

At the same time this point of view does call attention to certain important problems. Industrial society is not likely to produce household nurses, or any form of "servant class" in abundance. On the other hand, as everyone knows who has been in a hospital, nurses in a bureaucratic setting have a strong tendency to treat persons under their care "by the book," without much regard for their individual tasks and requirements. This is a well-known trait of bureaucracy, which tends to treat people and situations alike in order to achieve precision and efficiency. Infants and small children on the contrary require individual attention. For some years they may need to feel that they are the center of the universe. How then can the characteristics of bureaucracy be brought in line with those of maternal affection?

Though this may be the most difficult problem facing any qualitative transformation of the family, it is not necessarily insoluble. In the first place, as Bertrand Russell points out, a good institutional environment may be better for the development of the human personality than a bad family one. In the second place, an increase in the resources allocated to a bureaucratic organization can greatly increase its flexibility and capacity to satisfy variations in individual temperament. Any first-class hotel knows how to cope with this problem. In a few of the best ones in Europe the guest can have privacy and the illusion of being the center of the universe. Finally, one might legitimately expect that the persons who are drawn to serve in any such child-rearing institutions of the future would have more than the average amount of fondness for children, as well as general human warmth and kindliness. Under proper circumstances and management such institutions could give full scope to these benevolent sentiments.

Certain other considerations suggest an alternative that has at least the merit of being much more palatable to the vast majority of people today, since it is more in line with our deep-rooted cultural traditions. These considerations are essentially two. One is the possibility of some innate biological trait roughly resembling the "maternal instinct." The other lies in technological developments that might allow for wider dissemination of machinery to lighten household tasks and to take over the more routine aspects of child rearing. The dish-washing machine, laundromat, and, as a much more extreme device, the "Skinner box" represent prototypes of this technological development that could strengthen decentralized arrangements for rearing children.

I do not know what students of human physiology now believe about the maternal instinct. Common observation is enough to show that it cannot be an instinct like sex or hunger. There are many women who never become fond of children, or who soon cease to be fond of them. For them the institutional outlet just sketched would be the most satisfactory way of providing for their offspring. But for others, possibly the majority, the gestation period with its trials and burdens may be enough to create in the mother a desire to retain the infant under her care, after which she could become reluctant to give it up. If machinery were available to lighten child-rearing and household tasks on a far wider scale than is now the case, mothers might be able to satisfy the more positive desires of motherhood. One that seems to be quite important in the middle class is the desire to mold the child according to some ideal image, though it is now contradicted by fears of damaging the child that derive from superficial popularizations of Freud.

For the home to become again the place where human beings take the first important steps toward realizing their creative potentialities, parents would have to become willing once more to assert their authority. In turn this authority would have to acquire a rational and objective basis, freed of current attempts to revive religious taboos. Thus there would have to be a philosophical as well as a social revolution whose implications we cannot here pursue. One aspect, nevertheless, deserves to be stressed. Rational arguments can be given only to persons competent to understand them. For obvious reasons children are not able to absorb all rational arguments at once, though the present system of education undoubtedly postpones the development of this faculty where it does not destroy it altogether. Therefore parents will have to learn not to be afraid of saying to a child, "You are not old enough yet to understand why you have to do this. But you must do it anyway." The "progressive" family, where every decision turns into an incoherent and rancorous debate, actually contributes to reactionary tendencies in society by failing to equip the next generation with adequate standards of judgment.

There are, however, some grounds for doubting that this conservative solution will eventually prevail as the dominant one. The disappearance of the wider economic functions of the family would make it very difficult, and probably impossible, to restore the emotional atmosphere of a cooperative group in which the father has a respected authority. Furthermore, the bureaucratic division of labor has proved the most effective way of solving recurring and routine problems in other areas of life. Though a considerable part of the task of raising children is not routine, a very great portion is repetitive. For these reasons one may expect that semibureaucratic arrangements will continue to encroach on the traditional structure of the family. No doubt many individual variations, combinations, and compromises will remain for some time to come. Yet one fine day human society may realize that the part-time family, already a prominent part of our social landscape, has undergone a qualitative transformation into a system of mechanized and bureaucratized child rearing, cleansed of the standardized overtones these words now imply. As already pointed out, an institutional environment can be warm and supporting, often warmer than a family torn by obligations its members resent.

Such a state of affairs, if it comes at all, is well over the visible horizon now. Quite possibly it may never come at all. If it does come, there is not the slightest guarantee that it will solve all personal problems and land us in a state of airconditioned euphoria. Values that many people hold high today may go by the board, such as the affection older couples show for one another who have shared the same pains in life until they have grown but a single scar. It is also possible that a world of reduced family burdens might be one of shallow and fleeting erotic intrigues, based really on commercial interests. Hollywood could conceivably be the ugly prototype of such a future world, especially in its earlier transitional phases. The most that might be claimed by any future apologist for such institutions, if they ever come to pass, is that they gave greater scope to the development of the creative aspects of the human personality than did the family, which had begun to damage rather than develop this personality under advancing industrialism. And the most that can be claimed for the arguments supporting this possibility is that they correspond to some important trends visible in the family itself as well as in the rest of society. Nevertheless, it would appear that the burden of proof falls on those who maintain that the family is a social institution whose fate will differ in its essentials from that which has befallen all the others.

[CHAPTER ELEVEN]

Rural and Urban Communities

*T*HE term city has a variety of meanings: statistical, political, economic, and sociological, and hence it can be regarded from a number of perspectives and levels of understanding. Statistically, the city is an aggregation of people living within a comparatively small area, merely a matter of numbers. Politically, it is a unit of government recognized by some state. Sociologically, the city is a mode of life created by man: the product, Hauser suggests, of the cumulative effects of various revolutions ranging from the neolithic to the industrial. Urban areas today face further revolution. Hauser surveys the possible impact of the changes in our cities upon human nature and society. Stein is concerned with the effects of the widespread flight from urban chaos into the "dream" of suburbia, while Gulick deals with the problem of organizing suburbs and central cities into more effective metropolitan units.

[21] On the Impact of Urbanism on Society*

by PHILIP M. HAUSER

Man as the only culture-building animal on the globe not only adapts to environment but creates environment to which to adapt. The urban or metropolitan area is one of man's more complex cultural constructs which, on the one hand, is an impressive symbol of achievement and, on the other, the matrix of serious and pressing problems. Product of the cumulative effects of the various "revolutions," ranging from the "neolithic" to the "industrial," the urban area today faces the prospect of adjustment to still further revolutions. These revolutions are being generated by electronic and atomic technology, which together with developing rocketry may produce new and as yet unvisualized dimensions of change, or even result in the annihilation of the metropolis altogether.

It is generally believed that the neolithic revolution with its invention of domesticated plants produced the first relatively widespread and fixed human settlements. The emergence of an agricultural economy and increasing dependence on its products led gradually to the abandonment of the nomadic existence. Neolithic settlements were relatively small population groupings, villages rather than towns, whose size was limited by technological, economic, social and political factors. The appearance of larger population aggregations, the town and the city, depended on developments which did not appear until the metal ages. The emergence of a metropolitan area of a million or more is probably a modern phenomenon dependent on the technology and the economic, social and political organization identified with the industrial revolution.

Since the first city of one million or more inhabitants was probably nineteenth century London, it may be said, in broad perspective, that it took man, or closely related ancestors, some one hundred thousand to one million years to produce the modern metropolis. But the metropolis not only is the consequent of such developments; it is also a determinant of further development. Urbanism has profoundly affected the social order; it has modified the nature of human nature and has produced vast changes in the political order.

It is to the consideration of aspects of these changes, or aspects of "urbanism as a way of life," that this essay is addressed.

* From *Confluence: An International Forum*, Spring 1958, Vol. 7, No. 1, pp. 57-69, *passim*. Reprinted by permission.

The fact that living in the city makes a difference in the way of life has been noted by the writers of antiquity, as well as by more recent observers. . . . Increased size and density of population produce the equivalent of a mutation in social structure and organization. Great variations in physical spacing and accessibility of people to one another lead to quite different social orders. In the most abstract documentation of this observation, it may be indicated that in a density situation of 35 persons per square mile (common in non-urban areas) the individual can, within a 3 mile radius, reach fewer than 1,000 persons. If the population density is 10,000 persons per square mile (a common figure in cities) the person has access within a 3 mile radius to over 280,000 people. . . .

The urban social order is the opposite of the folk society which Redfield described as small, isolated, homogeneous, with simple technology, with simple division of labor, largely independent economically, characterized by strong organization of conventional understanding with no systematic knowledge in books and with no "market" complex. Wirth, in describing the "urban mode of life," emphasized the way in which the physical mechanism of the city, including the pattern of land use, land values, transport and communication facilities, influenced urban living. He emphasized the dominance of the city over its hinterland. He pointed to the way in which the essential abstract characteristics of the city—"size," "density" and "heterogeneity" resulted in "the substitution of secondary for primary contacts, the weakening in the bonds of kinship and the declining social significance of the family, the disappearance of the neighborhood, and the undermining of the traditional bases of social solidarity."

In connection with the general impact of urbansm on the social order as described above, it must be noted that in the United States "heterogeneity" played a peculiarly important role because this nation has been largely peopled by diverse ethnic groups from Europe and by the Negro from Africa. Our cities during the nineteenth and early part of the twentieth century were made up predominantly of the foreign born and their immediate descendants. During the last four or five decades, and especially since the onset of World War II, our cities have been subject to relatively large streams of Negro migrants, shifting from the South to the North and to the West. Thus the emergence of the urban mode of life in the United States has, in comparison with most other Western nations, been more vitally affected by the admixture of diverse ethnic and racial groups. This process is by no means complete. In Chicago, in 1950, for example—and this is not an atypical situation—the "foreign white stock" as defined by the United States Census (that is, the foreign born plus native of foreign or mixed parentage) made up about 45% of the population; and the non-white made up an additional 15%. Thus the third generation or [more] white population of Chicago, and of many of our large metropolitan areas, constitute a minority.

The changes described are of course reflected in changes in social institutions. Because the family has in our society traditionally been recognized as the primary social unit, it is a convenient unit through which to trace many of the influences of urbanism on social institutions. The colonial family in early American history was the keystone of social organization. For example, it was a basic and largely self-sufficient economic unit; it provided for the security and protection of its members; and it was the center for their affectional and recreational life.

Even this most solidly rooted of our social institutions, however, has not been able to withstand the impact of urbanization. Compared with the colonial family, the modern urban family is smaller; it is more often childless and has fewer children, if fertile. The urban family collectively and individually is much more mobile; it possesses comparatively little economic or social unity; is much more frequently broken by separation or divorce; and, as my colleague William F. Ogburn demonstrated some time ago, has long since lost many of its various historic functions, or shared them with new, specialized, urban institutions. The relationship of husband and wife, parents to children, children to each other and of the "small" to the "large" family have been redefined in the urban setting. The relations of family members to one another compete in depth, range, influence and satisfaction with extra-family relationships.

As old institutions, including the family, were modified, new institutions emerged in response to new needs. These have given rise to specialized types of agencies such as the police department, public health services, insurance, workmen's compensation laws, unemployment compensation, labor unions and civilian defense organizations. In brief, the urban environment has forced modification of our inherited institutions and has precipitated the need for the formation and development of new institutions.

One of the most important differences between the urban and "folk" environment as it affects the conduct of the person is to be found in the extent to which he is faced with the necessity of exercising choice, of substituting rational for traditional ways of doing things. In the "folk" setting there is generally a prescribed way of dealing with most situations, certainly with the most important recurrent situations in life. In the city there are almost always alternatives—and the person is forced to make a choice.

These basic changes in the nature of human nature in the urban setting are expressed, of course, in changes in modes of thought and action and in personality types. . . .

Enforced rationalism and urban living, together with rapid social change, provide the matrix for social and personal disorganization, blatant manifestations of the frictions of urbanism as a way of life. . . .

The juvenile delinquent and the criminal are manifestations of the breakdown of inherited social controls. They are symptoms of the deteriorating influence in the urban environment of such social institutions as the family and the church, of the waning grip of our mores, of the inadequacy, as yet, of the emergent new controls represented by such substitute institutions as the school, the court, the prison and the reformatory. The pauper, early industrial sweated labor, the radical and revolutionist, the unemployed, the aged dependent and the striker are some of the by-products of rapid change and its attendant frictions in our economic organization and in its impact on other aspects of total social organization. The corrupt political boss, the "big fix," the grafter, the "short pencil" operator and the unscrupulous lobbyist mirror the disorganization of political institutions caught in the vortex of rapid social change. Modern war, as a symptom of social disorganization, can be described largely as an outgrowth of the new forms of international contact and international economic, social and political interdependence which precipitate new frictions and problems for the peaceful resolution of which an adequate international social heritage—adequate international institutions, processes and patterns of conduct and thought—have not yet emerged.

Urban existence in breaking down the inherited vestiges of a "folk" order is producing many forms of disorganization. But it has also opened up new vistas for self-expression and new opportunities for shaping both man's environment and his destiny. For the same processes of social change that produce social and personal disorganization free man's mind from the constraints of the past and promote the exercise of ingenuity and creativity. It is not merely a coincidence that the great centers of learning, invention, innovation, art and culture have historically been located in urban areas.

In the new urban matrix of social interaction, a new human nature has been bred which is still in process of social evolution. The "city mentality," characterized by its sophistication, objectivity, utilitarianism and rationalism, is on the one hand a product of the urban environment, and on the other a major force producing and influencing changes in our social heritage, in our economic, social and political institutions and in the urban environment itself.

III

Many of our pressing contemporary problems in government and in politics are symptoms of the strains arising from the anachronism represented by our twentieth century industrial, urban, economic and social order and eighteenth and nineteenth century forms of government and political structure.

The city as the symbol of the twentieth century order is the nub of the many sore political problems of the day. The great metropolitan areas of the country have long since outgrown their inherited governmental structures. Arising as geographic, economic, demographic and social entities, they are nevertheless subjected to layer upon layer of local governmental structure. The 168 Standard Metropolitan Areas delineated by the Federal government in 1950 contained over 16,000 governmental units (including school districts) with powers to tax and to spend. They thus averaged some 100 governmental units per Standard Metropolitan Area; and the larger SMA's had about a thousand governmental units.

The city in the United States is usually the corporate creature of a state, with boundaries rigidly defined by a state charter. In contrast, the economic, population and social phenomena which it symbolizes, but of which the metropolitan area rather than the city is the expression, are not so rigidly defined.

As a result chaos is evident in many of our metropolitan areas in respect to problems with which prevalent forms of governmental structure are ill-equipped to deal. These include such area-wide problems as traffic control, highways, public transport, water and air ports, water supply, sanitation, housing, crime, recreation, health and welfare and the like. The pressures created by the area-wide problems may be expected to mount. It may be anticipated in the coming decades that new governmental mechanisms will emerge to complement or to supplant present forms of local government.

An acute aspect of problems of local government is evident in the conflict of interests between central cities and the metropolitan rings or suburbs. Mayor Zeidler of Milwaukee in a recent paper has predicted increasing political cleavage between central cities and their suburban areas, and has suggested that suburban areas may unite with downstate areas in coalition against central cities.

Certainly there is a basis for drawing such a generalization in recent voting behavior. But such projections overlook at least several factors which may conceivably produce a quite different situation, perhaps even within the next two decades.

For one thing, by 1975, of a total possible population of 228 million in the United States, about two-thirds—or about 150 million persons—are likely to be resident in Standard Metropolitan Areas, with only a third of the population in the remaining areas of the country. Of the population within the Standard Metropolitan Areas, only half will be resident in central cities and the remainder will live in suburban areas. Certainly it will be true that suburban area populations together with non-standard metropolitan area populations will greatly surpass central city populations, in fact surpass them by a ratio of two to one. But the community of interest between metropolitan suburban populations and non-metropolitan area populations is easily exaggerated. The following are among the considerations that indicate that community of interest between suburban and central city populations will grow closer rather than further apart, and tend to preclude suburban-non-metropolitan area coalition.

Standard Metropolitan Areas are at present absorbing 97 per cent of the total population increase of the nation, with disproportionate increases in outlying suburban areas which, between 1950 and 1955, grew 7 times as rapidly as central cities (28 per cent as compared with 4 per cent). The rapidity of metropolitan area growth, especially suburban growth, together with the fact that a relatively large proportion of suburban growth is derived from the central cities through migration, is likely to mean that suburban areas will more closely resemble central cities in the next two decades than they have in the past decade. That is, the continued process of metropolitan area growth is extending so far beyond central city boundaries that large parts of suburban areas will contain working-class and lower-middle-class populations of the type which was previously located in inner zones of central cities when metropolitan areas as a whole were smaller. Many political analysts tend to assume that migrants from central cities to suburbs become conservative and Republican when they come in association with the higher social-economic strata previously associated with suburban living. But these political analysts fail to recognize that by the time the suburbs contain 50 to 56 per cent of the population in Standard Metropolitan Areas, which may be the case by 1975, they will no longer be made up entirely of upper- and upper-middle-class groups.

Another acute aspect of contemporary problems in local government and politics is evident in the widespread concern about the growing Negro population in central cities. Some political analysts assume that the Negro migrant to the central cities will retain his low social-economic characteristics and previous political behavior; and visualize that "a kind of economic caste system will develop." They believe that lower-class Negroes will remain in central cities with the suburbs containing the white upper-income groups.

This assumption completely ignores the past history of migration to cities and the processes by which migrants have been absorbed into "urbanism as a way of life." The Negro migrant to the central city will, without question, follow the same patterns of social mobility blazed by the successive waves of immigrants who settled in our central cities. Just as the immigrant underwent a process of "Americanization," the in-migrant Negro is undergoing a process of "urbanization." The Negro is already rising and will continue to rise on the social-economic scale as measured by education, occupation, income and the amenities of urban existence. Furthermore, the Negro, in time, will diffuse through the metropolitan area and occupy outlying suburban as well as central city areas.

These observations should not be construed to deny the possibility, in the short run, of central cities becoming vast non-white areas of lower economic status than the suburbs. The forces described above, however, are likely, in the longer run, to produce an admixture of low and high economic status and white and non-white populations both in the central cities and in the suburbs. . . .

Quite apart from the problems of governmental structure and levels of government, urbanism has greatly affected the role of government itself, the character of public administration, the nature of representative government, the political party system and the substance of political issues.

There is no doubt that the complex of technological, economic and social changes which constitute "urbanism" is the major factor in the rapidity with which governmental functions have proliferated, often despite the express intent of administrations. The urban way of life, the increasing interdependence of the elements of the social order and the increasing inability of traditional and inherited social institutions to cope with the new problems of urban living have led inexorably to the multiplication of government functions, powers and personnel; and the process is still under way.

The complex and often technical character of the urban problems has changed the requirements of "governing." In the urban setting, public administration requires many technical and professional skills. The "expert" has emerged as a new and powerful element in government, and bureaucracy has become an indispensable tool in the functioning of society.

Urbanization has also brought great changes in the nature of representative government. Representative government as provided for in the United States was an adaptation of the "democracy" of the Greek city state. It is one thing, however, for a representative to speak for a small,

homogeneous, rural, agricultural constituency; and quite another thing to
"represent" a heterogeneous population of one-quarter to one-half million
persons with diverse and sometimes conflicting interests. The emergence
of the public opinion poll may be regarded as an invention in the urban
scene for the measurement of the "will" of the urban population. It may
play an increasingly important role in representative government in the
years to come.

Urbanism is also increasing the strains to which our two party system is
being subjected. The historic differences which led to the formation of our
political parties are more and more obscured by the problems of our complex urban order. As a result there is a wider range of interests, political
philosophies and policies within each of our great political parties than
between them. The increased choice forced upon the urbanite, discussed
above, extends also to the choice of political parties. The urban voter is
more apt to choose than to inherit his political preferences; therefore the
increasing importance of the "independent" vote. In the state of transition
in which we still find ourselves, the citizen, in voting, often has little notion of just what men, principles and policies he is supporting; and the
elected official often operates with no better awareness of the policy preferences of the electorate. . . .

IV

The problems of urbanization—social, personal and political—are but
symptoms of the frictions produced by the differential rates of change in
our social heritage. But reorganization can never be achieved without a
certain amount of disorganization. We can be comforted by the many
obvious advantages and advances which the industrial revolution and the
city have brought with them, including an ever-rising standard of living
and an unprecedented opportunity for personal expression and creativity.

The adjustments necessary to achieve an integrated and consistent social heritage can conceivably be attained in time through "natural" processes—through the forces which produce the "strain toward consistency"
in our culture. This process of social evolution perhaps parallels the biological "struggle for existence" and the "survival of the fittest," but in the
area of culture traits and culture complexes.

Unlike the rest of the animal kingdom, however, man has it within his
power to speed up the social evolutionary process—to accelerate the adjustment of social and political institutions and ideologies to the new requirements forced by technological and structural change. Indeed, one of
the most important influences of urbanization lies in the emancipation of
the person from the rigidities and restraints imposed upon him by tradi-

tion, in the new opportunity—in large measure forced upon him by the nature of urban existence—to be a rational animal and to intervene in the processes of social change so as to exert some control over its tempo and its direction.

[22]   *Suburbia: Dream or Nightmare?**

by MAURICE R. STEIN

Students of the American community in the fifties have had their attention drawn to the suburbs much as the attention of their counterparts in the twenties was drawn to the slums. On the face of it, the reasons would appear to be quite different: the slum is the center of urban disorganization while the suburb would appear to be that of urban aspiration. Closer attention to the details of suburban life suggests, however, that it is actually the setting for the dominant "disorders" of our time.

THE EXURBANITES

A popular and perhaps impressionistic study like Spectorsky's *The Exurbanites* starts with exactly this premise and provides a good deal of valuable information about the latest and most extreme form of suburbia. . . .

The Exurbanites deals with a special category of suburbanites: the men who work in the communications industries in New York City. These men, in an effort to establish refuges for themselves from the urban "rat races" at which they are regularly employed, have infiltrated and finally taken over sections of several outlying counties including Westchester, Fairfield, Bucks and Rockland Counties. As luck (or perhaps their social situation) would have it, these people moved out to the "exurbs" in groups. Each exurban area tended to attract slightly different elements from the vast com-

* From Maurice R. Stein, *The Eclipse of Community: An Interpretation of American Studies*, pp. 199-226, *passim*. Copyright © 1960 by Princeton University Press, Princeton, N.J. Reprinted by permission.

munications industry and Spectorsky has a very interesting comparative analysis of the Bucks, Fairfield, and Rockland settlements. His major analytic strategy is to link the social patterns of the sub-community to the particular occupational status and problems of its residents. . . .

Spectorsky pursues this theme from its initial definition wherein exurbanites are shown to be motivated by a reaction against their daily labors involving symbol creation and manipulation, through the effects of that peculiar social institution, the commuters' train, to their final entanglement with budgets that remain constantly beyond their incomes. Homes in the exurbs are designed to provide rustic comforts so that the "lucky" residents can balance their symbol-dominated work-days by thing-dominated leisure activities based on intimate contact with nature. At the same time, this contact with the wide-open spaces includes a sophisticated circle of neighbors and friends whose business and home lives are in the same state of precarious equilibrium.

Spectorsky describes the institutional system arising in each of the New York City exurbs in telling detail. Jobs in the communications industry are highly competitive, and apparently the criteria for judgment leave much to be desired as regards objectivity. The individual employee is therefore always subject to important uncertainties as to how his superiors view him. Since keeping his place in the exurban social system entails living well beyond his income at any given time and moving still further beyond it with each increase of income, he is always subject to terrible anxieties with no conceivable relaxation in sight. For that matter, as Spectorsky depicts the situation, the higher one gets, the more pressure one is subject to.

The job is not, however, the only source of pressure. In his chapter on women and children, the author points toward a number of family dilemmas arising from the isolation of the women in their rural strongholds. With all the expensive modern appliances that money can buy, life for these latter-day frontierswomen remains tied to schedules that are tremendously demanding. Their time is portioned out in taking care of their rambling houses, transporting their husbands to the trains and their children to school as well as to their play areas, and finally preparing themselves to greet their travel-and-work-tense husbands at the end of each busy day. Coming from careers and colleges themselves, these wives cannot help envying the professional and social outlets available to their husbands in the city. Boredom and impatience are the female's lot. She can focus on her children as an escape, perhaps experiment extra-maritally, or even take to drinking. Whichever way she turns, further frustration seems to lie in wait.

Perhaps the most painful chapter in the book is the one reporting on the leisure of the exurbanites. Liquor plays a pervasive role. Cliques abound, with the unfortunate result that the sociable account executive trying to escape from office problems finds himself thrown together with other account executives in the same situation so that the temptation to lapse back into office conversation and moods is inescapable. And since social life is coordinated with career goals, an unsuccessful party or excessive unpopularity can react back on job chances. Most exurban relaxation takes place at full speed: Sunday finds everyone tired from Saturday's round of vigorous family activities and evening partying. By this time the novelty of the children has worn off for father. Mother, trying to avoid spending this day as she does weekdays, arranges informal evening "dropping around." Spectorsky describes some of the party games that are occasionally played on these occasions. Their main purpose seems to be eliciting embarrassing expressions from the unwary while everyone else tries to release their hostilities without exposing themselves. The ingenious cruelty shown in this enterprise is amazing.

To interpret the strange suburban worlds described in *The Exurbanites*, the sociologist can begin by placing them in the context of a theory of community development. In part, these sub-communities are successors to Greenwich Village. Here the Pseudo-Bohemians who spent their early years in the Village while working their way up the hierarchies of the communications industry now try to recapture some of the values of their youth without sacrificing the comforts that accompany commercial success. This accounts for the heavy emphasis on "self-expression" in the exurbs. While most of them have given up anything more than a lingering dream of artistic success, they still seek to "express" themselves in their homes and life styles. Heavy emphasis is placed on original but good taste judged according to the most advanced ideas of the better fashion magazines.

By the time they have made the exurban grade, they are already too enmeshed in an over-extended budget to consider seriously returning to genuinely artistic employments with the consequent economic sacrifice that this usually requires. Yet Spectorsky notes in his last chapter the persistence of such fantasies, with the would-be "creative artists" cherishing the illusion that they will eventually write a great novel while their businessmen counterparts dream of going into business for themselves. As their obligations increase, the futility of these secret dreams becomes increasingly apparent. At the same time, they are confronted with the dilemmas of their more limited dream: escaping from the "rat race" to their exurban manorial life. Soon these expensive exurban homes, with the up-

keep, improvement, and commuting problems they entail, begin to appear like a trap at least as crushing as the "rat races" for which they were
supposed to compensate. Even the limited dream of exurban bliss is dissipated, while the secret dream of eventual creative accomplishment is
even more traumatically shattered. Growing awareness of self-betrayal
can be avoided by manic hyperactivity, by cynicism, or, for the introspectively inclined, by extended psychotherapy.

This condensed summary, harsh though it may sound, does not capture
more than a bit of the detailed excoriation of the exurban plight which
Spectorsky presents. The wish to escape from the harsher human consequences of bureaucratic role-playing has led a group of talented and economically privileged people to pattern a way of life that intensifies instead
of alleviates the anxieties inherent in their occupational roles. Doctors in
the community report an abundance of psychosomatic ills, including some
like sexual impotence and frigidity which further disrupt already disturbed family lives. Perhaps because of the author's involvement and his
hostility, the book fails to capture any sense of stable satisfactions that
this round of life could convey. Some of the uncertainties and anxieties derive from the special early creative aspirations of communications workers; others seem to stem from the exceptionally competitive character of
the industry itself. Both are reinforced by the fact that the skills sold are
exactly those earlier intended as vehicles of creative expression. This is the
modern version of the cycle described by Lynd, wherein desire for consumers' goods motivates people to play otherwise unrewarding production
roles; the circumstances are a bit more complicated here, but the principle
is the same. Middletown is not as far from Bucks County either in problems or social structure as the residents of both might assume.

THE TRANSIENTS

A different kind of suburb, bearing only slight physical resemblance to
exurbia, is the housing "development" or "project" which is making its
appearance at the outer edges of most American cities. These new suburbs, most of them erected during and since the war, have standard ranch-
type houses or, in lower-income brackets, standard box-type dwellings.
Sometimes they are all built by the same firm, as in Levittown or Park
Forest, the community studied by William H. Whyte. His analysis of this
community appears as Part vii of his book *The Organization Man.* Since
residence in these suburbs is usually only a temporary affair, Whyte has
aptly called his study "The Transients." These are the stopover communities in which upwardly mobile junior executives house themselves while

serving their apprenticeship. In Park Forest, about 35 per cent of the population turned over annually.

Whyte's study provides a penetrating glimpse into the patterns of social life arising among these transient neighbors. Park Forest is a planned community built in an outlying part of Chicago by a single entrepreneur. The houses are similar though not identical, since provision for standardized variation has been built into the plan. Since most of the residents are rather low in the occupational hierarchies, incomes are comparatively small and excessive expenditure frowned upon. The goal is to hit just that dead level of spending which will demonstrate good taste without a hint of extravagance.

Park Forest differs from exurbia in that its residents are not employed by a single industry. They are distributed among the lower executive ranks of many corporate enterprises, including even the army. But this fact of diversity in kinds of enterprises does not mean that their work situations or problems are different in any important social respects. All must focus their attention on gaining approval from their superiors and all accomplish this by demonstrating their "flexibility and capacity to adjust." They are Organization Men and must display virtues of their tribe. Thus, the whole social life of the community becomes a training ground in "adjustment."

All of the institutions of the community arrange themselves around the needs of the corporation. Since business has learned the lesson that an efficient executive needs a happy home, family life becomes most important. The families of Park Forest learn how to look happy. Since the houses are close together and privacy all but impossible, this is not a part-time task but one that usurps most of the wife's energies and a good deal of the husband's when he is around the house. During the day the women have interminable "kaffee-klatches." Everyone is forced to participate, even the more retiring, and the groups themselves develop techniques for "reeducating" would-be laggards. This neighborliness, forced in part by propinquity, is encouraged by the feeling that the wish to be alone is somehow neurotic or childish. Fulfillment comes from group participation.

This slogan is imbibed by the children at their mother's kaffee-klatch and reinforced by their early training in the play group, nursery school, and finally grammar school. Getting along with others is the prime virtue and popularity its symbol. Much of the curriculum of the Park Forest school is devoted to "life adjustment" courses having this as their theme. Their high school exemplifies this best: over half of its seventy formal course offerings fall into this category. Parents support this trend, maintaining that the high school is primarily responsible for teaching their children to be good citizens and to get along with people.

Religion in Park Forest is also caught up in "togetherness." The Protestant denominations consolidated in a United Protestant Church and employ a minister who has learned to deemphasize religious doctrine so as to avoid offending anyone, while at the same time providing plentiful opportunities for social activities which his transient parishioners need to give them a sense of stability. Administering the invariably extensive affairs and finances of this church provides these young executives with an opportunity to see the over-all operations of a large-scale organization and thereby does its part in training them for the responsibilities they will someday carry.

The social life of these Park Foresters embodies the same principle. Their parties must be modest but show some signs of originality in the kind of food served and entertainment provided. There are periodic waves of food fashions so that the housewife is never completely at loss for acceptable new dishes. Riesman's concept of "marginal differentiation" expresses well the kind of "individuality" that Park Forest encourages. Wandering too far from the margin brings penalties, as the housewife who was discovered reading Plato and listening to The Magic Flute learned. In this community, even the ways of "being different" are standardized.

With all of this "togetherness," the junior executive and his family must still look forward to the day when his promotion will both permit and require a rapid departure from Park Forest. Friendships cannot become so deep as to interfere with this shift upward nor can they become so deep that a friend's failure to move upward can disturb one's own upward rise. The "inconspicuous consumption" defined by Riesman is a form of "antagonistic cooperation" and this, after all, is the main operating mode of the upwardly mobile in large corporations. It is important to be "friends" with one's colleagues, superiors, and subordinates though the exact etiquette for expressing friendship with each differs considerably. Equally important, however, is the requirement that one not become so friendly with anyone that this interferes with effective competition. Friendliness is always subordinate to the goal of successful mobility. . . .

CRESTWOOD HEIGHTS

Crestwood Heights, a study of a Canadian upper-middle-class suburb by John Seeley, R. Alexander Sim, and Elizabeth Loosley, reports on the social life of the destination suburbs to which the more successful transients migrate. This is the first full-scale sociological study of a suburb. Brilliantly executed, it is a fit successor to the classic community studies. . . .

Crestwood Heights is a well-to-do suburb [of Toronto]. Many of the residents are independent business and professional men, while the "employees" are usually senior executives at or close to policy levels. Houses are expensive and living even more so. One point of interest is the fact that this suburb is in transition from a predominantly or exclusively Gentile to a predominantly Jewish neighborhood. The processes of invasion and succession involved in this transition are never brought into focus, though they crop up at several points. Though this failure to deal with the community in terms of a process model is unfortunate, the inattention to Jewish-Gentile differences has an interesting rationale. The authors found that outside of church and a few ritual occasions, these differences were negligible with regard to social behavior. There is obviously some segregation within the sub-community. Jews and Gentiles both associate with members of their own faiths more than with each other and intermarriage, though it does occur, evokes considerable censure. The two religious groups may attend church on different days, worship a different god, and observe different rituals but the capacity of any of this to alter the deeper meanings of their lives is slight. Above all else, they are successful businessmen (or female appendages of successful businessmen) and their Judaism or Christianity remains conveniently in the background except on religious holidays or when intermarriage threatens. Characteristically, the main area in which concern over religion is expressed occurs in the high school, where fraternity or sorority "discrimination" does become an object of some controversy. . . .

One suspects that much of the depth of the book derives from the authors' interest in mental health and their utilization of this interest as a lever for entry to the community. They worked out of the mental health agency in the school and in so doing were forced up against members of the community whose disturbed conditions had led them to consult the clinic. For the most part, these were families with "problem children" though adults in difficulty also must have come within their purview if only because disturbed children invariably have in the background disturbed parents. The parent-child relationship proved to be an important lead to the problems of this sub-community, one that naturally grew out of concern with mental health. And in this suburb it could hardly have been avoided.

The social structure of child-rearing deserves close scrutiny, since it is in itself one of the most problematic aspects of Crestwood Heights life.

After a long description of the "confusions" that exist the authors summarize: "The whole area of child care and control is at present in a state of considerable flux in Crestwood Heights. Fathers may differ from mothers at almost every point in the complex socialization process. Families are divided between permissive and authoritarian ways of handling children, and so are individuals at different times or—worse—the same time." [1] At the same time, there is a tremendous desire that the child be "normal" for his age so that signs of difference send the family off to the experts. Even the normal socialization routines have been turned over by confused parents to nursery schools and other secondary agencies. The child is expected to learn independence at an increasingly early age:

". . . The busy mother, who must run the house without the aid of a maid, entertain for husbands and friends, attend meetings, and have 'outside interests,' is literally compelled to ration strictly her physical contacts with her child. Thus in early infancy preparation continues for achievement-in-isolation, for the individual pursuit of materialistic goals in which human relationships must often be subordinated. . . ."

Beneath all Crestwood social patterns we find the same harnessing of life to occupational success explicitly adopted in Park Forest. Male careers do not involve quite the desperate struggle that Exurbia requires, but they do remain the anchoring point for the family's activities as well as the single factor on which continued residence in this privileged suburb depends. So the career of the male is focal, with female careers being subordinated to motherhood. This is usually painful for the serious woman, leaving her with even more ambivalence toward the already fragmented maternal role. Male career cycles have a terrible inevitability with performance peaks usually being reached in the late thirties only to taper off in the fifties and with virtual obsolescence arriving at an ever-earlier age. In addition, the limitations of the "peak" have to be absorbed, since no ceiling on ambition is ever quite acceptable in this sub-culture. Children seeing the career struggles of their parents soon become concerned with their own futures, yet parents cannot always arrange to pass on the fruits of their economic success to their children. All too often these fruits are consumed so that the child who has led a sheltered existence with all of his material wants satisfied must still carve out his own competitive career when he leaves home.

In a brilliant chapter the authors analyze the suburban home to show how it functions as property, as a stage, as a focus for family living, and as a nursery. It is a tremendously expensive and lavish enterprise. The Crestwood child soon learns that the display functions take precedence

---

[1] Seeley, John R., Sim, R. Alexander, and Loosley, Elizabeth W., *Crestwood Heights,* Basic Books, Inc., New York, 1956, p. 203.

over his impulses whenever the two conflict. The goal is "artless" staging of whatever setting the woman of the house has decided upon as a basis for justifying her claim to having "good taste." She makes her choice with the help of fashion magazines and interior decorators. Like child-rearing patterns, styles in home furnishing change periodically, giving the housewife another fashion to keep abreast of if she wishes to hold on to her position in the community. . . .

One of the lessons soon learned by the child is the appreciation of properly displayed property. He begins to feel this as a source of ego-enhancement so that new items are always preferred to old. As the child accumulates property for his own room, the advertising theorem that happiness comes from acquisition is painlessly inculcated. He watches his mother light up when she gets a shiny new kitchen appliance, so that cooking for her, as the advertisers would have it, does take on new meaning. But as the appliance ages and loses its capacity to bring appreciative responses from the neighbors it has to be quickly replaced by another. . . .

Life in the home is chopped up into time intervals all carefully scheduled to regulate the diverse affairs of the busy family. Very often the schedules of individual members are such that the whole family almost never spends time together during the week. Compensatory efforts are made at cramming intense "family life" into the equally busy week-end leisure schedules. The rhythm of the office has penetrated the home so that even television programming has to be taken into account: ". . . the resultant schedules are so demanding that the parents feel themselves constantly impelled to inculcate the virtues of punctuality and regularity in themselves and the child, at meal hour, departures for picnics, and such occasions. Being on time for school becomes more important than eating breakfast. The intimacy of primary relations can be punctured easily: the flow of after-dinner conversations will often be broken clearly and sharply at nine by a vigilant host who has scheduled a television viewing as part of the hospitality of the evening; . . . if a television program for children changes its schedule without warning, the family meal hour may have to be changed, unless the adult members are prepared to accept enforced silence and semi-darkness." In school, students learn to parcel out their time in the same fashion as their fathers and mothers. There is little room for spontaneous association or activity in this "time conscious" community.

Viewed more comprehensively, life time is transformed into a disposable commodity . . . and the emphasis on youth . . . seems to have become more pervasive . . . Evidence of this condition follows:

"Mrs. A has taken her four-year-old daughter to the hairdresser for a permanent . . .

". . . The Nursery School is taking two-year-olds now . . .

". . . Ten-year-old children in our school have dates, go to movies in twosomes, and have evening dresses.

". . . Our twelve-year-old boy wants to buy a tuxedo. He says everyone else in his class is buying or renting one for the Prom."

All of this and more constitute the pattern of "rushing at experience." The result is a mockery of adult patterns of independence, competition, and sex because they are adopted long before any of them can possibly be integrated into the growing personality: "This rushing at experience has consequences for the child as he gradually forms a conception of himself as an 'aging individual.' The boy who rides a horse, wears long pants, and has a girl friend before puberty, has lost some of the means of validating his biological manhood at the moment in his physical and social maturation when such signs are most needed. The boy's changing voice and the girl's first menstrual period are not accorded the public attention that one might expect from a culture where sexual matters are so often exposed to discussion. In contrast, there is, of course, no lack of ceremony in the areas where individual achievement and competition within the group are encouraged. These activities, which are often of a vigorous nature, and the rewards which attend them, together with opportunities for controlled eroticism (such as dances and mass behavior at football games), help to prolong adolescence and make it not simply tolerable, but 'exciting.' "

Little can be added to this fine interpretation except to underscore the fact that the high estimation of youthfulness is accompanied by a tendency to transform it into a replica of adulthood. A more complex conception of the relation between adulthood and childhood which recognizes distinctive differences as well as continuities has given way to a confusion between the two. This confusion ramifies through the life cycle so that every age level is forced to feel ambivalent about the stage it is passing through. . . .

It is important to notice what is happening here. The human life cycle has been leveled by a cultural system which ignores the values that can be found in various ages. By refusing to recognize the major life transitions in such a fashion as to render both prior and later stages meaningful and worthwhile, Crestwood Heights condemns its children and its adults to permanent anxiety in regard to their present identities as well as those of the future. And even if this anxiety can be channeled into competitive achievement, the price would seem to be permanent emotional immaturity. . . .

Schools are the main institutional mechanism in Crestwood Heights for coping with socialization. The child is handed over at an increasingly early age. Directives from school-affiliated experts exert their influence even earlier. The centrality of the schools in Crestwood Heights is exemplified by their size and spatial prominence. The authors contend that the community actually grew up around the school and suggest that its status can be compared with that of the church in less secular societies. . . .

Crestwood schools are administered and staffed by a crew of college-trained educators and "human relations" specialists whose influence grew as family confusion mounted. Life in a complex scientifically inclined suburb like this one required the services of a great many experts on all kinds of matters: ". . . The once relatively simple matter of feeding the family requires the services of domestic science specialists; consumers' guides; hygienists and health teachers in general; pediatricians; specialists who can advise on the meaning of food and food preparation in the maintenance of happy married relationships; and communications experts, journalistic and novelistic, who will give clues as to what 'the best people' are *really* eating, regardless of all the foregoing considerations . . ." Much of this desperately sought expertise requires some training in the social sciences. We observe efforts at applying social science knowledge that is only loosely confirmed in response to urgent demands arising from the confusions of suburban life. Some institutional mechanism had to emerge to meet this need. Applied social science then has become a vital part of suburban functioning since it is the branch of science which claims to have knowledge about the vital life problems at the "collective, social or interpersonal" levels, on the one hand, and on the more intimate "intrapersonal or individual" level, on the other. Marriage counselors, psychotherapists, aptitude testers, child guidance experts, public relations men, and other related occupations are familiar fixtures in the suburban milieu.

Crestwood Heights presents a brilliant picture of the social system in which these experts and their clients are enmeshed. Starting from anxieties deeply rooted in the socio-cultural situations of their clients, social science "experts" are called upon to give assistance with symptomatic problems while leaving untouched the larger community context in which these problems arise. Sometimes the "expert" has access to a highly systematized body of techniques for providing help, as does the well-trained psychotherapist; all too often, however, he has to cope with problems going far beyond the limited practical or even theoretical development of his discipline.

The important influence that the "human relations" experts exert on this sub-community derives from their ability to shape the beliefs of the women. The men pay less attention even though there are signs that they too are beginning to listen—e.g., the utilization of "human relations" theories in both production and marketing phases of many businesses. . . .

Exurbia, Park Forest, and Crestwood Heights are only three versions of a sub-community species which clearly contains other variants. They share the dedication to status and status-fronts along standardized "individual" lines; although the exurbanites would underscore "individual," while Park Forest emphasizes "standard" criteria more heavily. . . .

In all of these suburbs, children are at the focus of attention. Neither the exurbanites nor the Park Foresters seem to confront as many difficulties in deciding how to rear their offspring as do the Crestwood families, but all three share a willingness to abdicate in favor of the schools. Religion seems trivial in all three, turning into one more status symbol counting well below most others in the all-important secular realm. The growing influence of psychoanalytic doctrines and experts characterizes all three, although the exurbanites undoubtedly form the vanguard in this respect. . . .

[23]   *Problems of Metropolitan Areas**

by LUTHER GULICK

In the twelve years since the end of World War II, the United States has experienced one of the most spectacular periods of economic development in its history. Industrial production has reached heights far beyond the most optimistic predictions of the pre-war years. Living standards, particularly in the lower income groups, have advanced to a point where the elimination of poverty has become a practicable goal. The American economy has played a vigorous role in restoring the war-shattered economies of Europe and Asia.

Yet at the moment of our greatest prosperity we find ourselves confronted with an evil that threatens to throttle a large part of our business activity and to rob us of the fruits of our ever-advancing technology. That

* Reprinted from *Problems of United States Economic Development*, Vol. I, January 1958, published by Committee for Economic Development, 711 Fifth Ave., New York 22, N.Y.

is the stagnation and dry-rot which has attacked our great metropolitan centers.

Just what is this "metropolitan problem?" It is the discontent of millions of human beings. It is a vast and growing dissatisfaction with life in and around the great cities. People are not satisfied with their homes and housing, with their trip to and from work, and with the aggravations, costs and delays of traffic and parking. They are distraught by the lack of schools and recreational facilities for their children and themselves, and they are concerned by social pressures, neighborhood conditions, youthful delinquency and crime. People find shopping difficult and more regimented, and the ever more needed services hard to get and expensive. They struggle with water shortages, with bad drainage and sewer conditions, with dirt and noise which they don't like. They find the city centers "old style," inconvenient, dismal and repulsive, and the old busses, streetcars, trains and other methods of mass movement uncomfortable and slow, even though they are cheap in comparison with rising wages. And when people move to the suburbs and take work in a new suburban factory, store or other enterprise, they find that many of the evils they sought to escape move in right after them, with mounting taxes to plague them there too. It all adds up to the greatest American domestic problem, the "problem of the metropolitan region."

It is significant that nobody has risen up to say to the metropolitan regions, "Let the cities strangle themselves. In 50 or 75 years, with conditions getting worse and worse, the old cities will die of congestion anyway. Why waste effort and money? Cities have died before. Let them die again. People and industry and business will move to better suited locations, nice new cities will arise; in the old cities population will thin out, values will come down; then will be the time to do extensive rebuilding, if more cities are needed, following the lines of discoveries and inventions in the new towns."

Why is it nobody has come forward with this line of argument?

Is it because there is a partial recognition even in the mind of the greatest laissez faire conservative that a great city, a metropolis, is a social and economic structure, a living complex, which is far more than the brick, mortar, rails, streets, electric wires, water and sewers, and other facilities on which it rests, and is worth saving? Is the death of such a city through uncontrolled obsolescence a disaster out of all proportion to the capital value of the buildings, streets, and material investments which house it? Is it because the human suffering which would be involved in urban liquidation is a force which no democratic political system could endure?

Or is it because in every great city there is a whole host of direct economic interests most of which will be liquidated inexorably and individually if the city of which they are a part dies? This is certainly true of the central real estate interests, the business center, most financial institutions, the merchants, the newspapers, the hotels, the amusements, those who manufacture or distribute to local consumers, those who are engaged in transportation and trucking, in fact most labor, especially organized labor. Education and cultural institutions have a stake in the existing community, as do the local social and political organizations. Even the professional and service groups are now aware that their future is linked with the growth, not the decadence of the city where they are.

With all these vitally affected economic interests, why don't these vigorous representatives of individual initiative rise up and "solve the metropolitan problems" themselves by private initiative?

The reason is they cannot. And they cannot because a city knits us all up in its social and economic network in such a fashion that our life—economic, social and cultural—is all tied together. And we can only do together the things that now need doing.

Perhaps this will be understood if we examine the cause of the breakdown. It is not from size. The state is bigger. The nation is bigger. Size is not a handicap but an advantage in both cases. It is the little nations and little states that are in trouble, not the big ones. But when it comes to cities, to urban concentrations, it is the big ones that are tumbling all over themselves.

Nor does the breakdown come from lack of management knowledge and ability to deal with big enterprises and big government. Advances in management theory and practice in the past generation, both in business and government, now put within our reach most of the ideas and tools that are needed to manage any enterprise of any size with a high degree of efficiency.

Certainly it is not due to lack of money. Where is the wealth and the economic power in America? It is right in the cities. And the richer the city in its basic economy, the bigger are its current problems of unsolved urban congestion and growth!

The breakdown of local government in the metropolitan area comes straight out of bad political engineering and nothing else.

That which has happened is perfectly clear. There has been a sudden change in the governmental needs and the effective demands of human beings living in the new-patterned metropolitan complexes. The structure of government, political and administrative, was never designed or evolved to meet these new needs. For many of the new requirements there is no machinery at all; for others there was a system, but that system is now sadly inadequate and obsolete, and the effort of inadequate jurisdictions to deal with the problems which have grown beyond them, results in awkward arrangements, makeshifts, frustration and generally partial or complete failure.

The reason for the breakdown of local government in the metropolitan regions is found in four facts:

1. *A governmental vacuum*—many of the things that now need doing for the people who live in the metropolitan area have never been assigned to or undertaken as a task by any government, Federal, state or local.

2. *Fractionalization of assigned duties*—many problems of local services and controls have coalesced while the governmental jurisdictions have remained as they were. Thus each has but a fraction of a now unified problem to handle.

3. *Political imbalance*—produced by population and economic movements with respect to inflexible boundaries which leave many a governmental unit with an unbalanced population and a truncated economy, neither of which is equal to the governmental activities now required.

4. *The lack of clear-headed and courageous political leadership and a recognition that we face a metropolitan problem*—due in large measure to ignorance, jurisdictional fractionalization and political imbalance.

Transportation is probably the most important and the most neglected single problem. In no metropolitan region is there any official agency which has the duty or the power to know, think, plan or act concerning the entire transportation question. Nowhere has anybody been given the job of looking at the total geographic region of any metropolitan complex and the total transportation system to decide what can and should be done. Here and there a part of the job has been assigned to one governmental unit or to another, to one "authority" or another, or to some temporary commission. In most areas now, the through highway aspect is being considered by the state highway department and the U.S. Bureau of Public Roads. But the urban renewal aspect is in the hands of another series of local and Federal agencies, and the rapid transit operation is divided between local operators which cover only the central city and the private rail and bus lines which operate inside and outside and are subject to control by state and Federal rate-making and franchise-granting agencies. And there is a complete divorcement of consideration relating to rubber, and to rail, and to air-borne transport.

Thus no governmental body has been given the broad job of seeing to it that the metropolitan region as a whole is given a decent, effective and economical total system of transportation. We live and snarl in a governmental vacuum.

The second reason for the breakdown of government in the metropolitan regions is that the few functions and responsibilities for action which have been assigned, are now all split up into undoable pieces. This is what we call "fractionalization."

Wherever the success of an administrative operation requires close day to day timing or co-operation in relation to some other activity, there are great disadvantages and increased chances of failure if the two activities are assigned to separate and independent jurisdictions. Among the illustrations may be noted:

Street paving and sewer installations
Traffic controls and street sweeping
Exterior repairs and interior redecoration of a building
Water conservation and street flushing
Parking facilities and traffic regulation
License issuance and control of standards
Mosquito and pest controls of neighboring regions
Pollution controls in adjacent communities

The third major reason for the breakdown of government in metropolitan regions is political imbalance. The structure, the responsibilities, the election system and the powers, fiscal and other, of an American city have been designed for a "normal" balanced social and economic community. When the population changes greatly, especially when the upper and midde income groups depart, and the city comes to be dominated by the less educated, less assimilated, less politically experienced and less economically self-supporting individuals, it can hardly be said that the community is appropriately structured politically to carry on its normal assignments.

This becomes especially important when the economic base of the community is also sharply modified in the process. Democracy needs balanced constituencies, balanced leadership groups, balanced economic interests, balanced taxable resources, and powers of government which are balanced and appropriate to these other elements.

Government is now falling down on its part of the job. It is falling down because the major tasks are not now assigned to any level of government, and those tasks which are partly assigned are split up into undoable fractions among jurisdictions which are politically and economically incapable of functioning as to these problems. Set up as we now are, we cannot even develop the political responsibility or leadership called for.

The place to start in designing the required lines of action is to name the things that need to be done and then work out the machinery for doing them.

One thing at least has been achieved in recent years. We now have the universal recognition that there is a metropolitan problem, that the problem is serious and growing, and that something effective must be done about it and fast.

CHAPTER TWELVE

Social Stratification

THERE are two major concepts of the term "class." In one of its meanings a class is an economic group, set off from other groups or classes in the community through its relations to economic production. This is the Marxian emphasis. More recently social scientists have stressed the kind of class system or social stratification reflected by social attitudes. Here the emphasis lies with class consciousness and status. So, for example, when the "middle class" is referred to, the reference is to the millions of Americans who share, in general, common values, attitudes, and aspirations. MacIver is convinced that Marx erred in thinking that economic disparity was the sole condition of social class. Social stratification is a result of social differentiation—whatever distinguishes man from man carries with it the implication of class. The dream of mankind of a classless society is, therefore, bound to end in disappointment. Swados is concerned, not with the myth of the classless society, but with the myth of the "happy worker" which he subjects to severe criticism.

[24] *The New Social Stratification**

by ROBERT M. MacIVER

In two lands the dream of a classless society has been dynamic. In both of them it has been expressive of social change in the present and of tendencies toward changes to come. But in neither has the dream been fulfilled in the goal of classlessness. Where the dream has been cherished social stratification has been transformed but not abolished, for, as we shall see, social stratification, though forever changing, is in some sense as inherent in society as society is inherent in man.

North America, or rather an important section of it, has cherished that dream. It was the dream of the pioneer West and it gradually took form in the processes of nineteenth century expansion. It was the dream to which Walt Whitman gave literary expression. In it there was something more than the older claim that men were born free and equal, for this was a social dream whereas that was only a political one. . . .

The other land where the dream of classlessness has been cherished is Soviet Russia. This was a very different dream. It was more dramatic, more revolutionary, more positive. It did not emerge from a social situation already congenial to it, but as a revulsion from a social situation that was rapidly dissolving. Hence it came as a revelation, as a grand new dogmatic faith. It did not merely ignore or deny social stratification. It conceived instead the sweeping abolition of class differences between human beings everywhere. It saw in the stupendous revolution that it worked the first and greatest stage toward total classlessness. Here the classless society was not construed as simply a matter of men's attitudes toward their fellows. Of course they were all equally "comrades," but they were "comrades" not because they thought of themselves as such but because they had abolished the foundations of distinction. They had abolished capitalism. By ending the private ownership of the means of wealth they thought they had destroyed forever the foundations of class. This dream also came short of fulfillment. . . .

In spite of their ardent dreams neither North America nor Soviet Russia attained the classless society. The reason why in both cases the dream was unfulfilled is a simple and ineluctable one. Social stratification is a function of social differentiation. Whatever distinguishes man from man, or rather group from group, carries with it the implication of class.

* From *Our Emergent Civilization,* edited by Ruth Nanda Anshen, pp. 103-122 *passim.* Copyright 1947 by Harper & Brothers. Reprinted by permission.

Marx erred if he thought that one particular economic disparity was the sole condition of social class. This economic factor was indeed an important determinant of the particular type of class structure that existed throughout the Western world. But it was not the *sine qua non* of class. Some of the most powerful class systems in the world, such as the caste system of India, did not depend upon it. Even where this factor was powerful it was far from being all-powerful. The magic of birth and of inherited status also played a part. The economic factor was important because wealth was also power. But there are other sources of power independent of the possession of wealth. Moreover, if wealth is a source of power, power is also a source of wealth. Wealth in the last resort does not consist in the possession of specific titles to material things but in the ability to control, to exploit or to dispose of these things. He who commands men commands also wealth. He has service where other men serve. He rides where other men walk.

In North America the dream of a classless society weakened the older bonds of class. It was a liberating dream. It was also a trusting dream, for it believed that progress was inevitable. Because it believed too easily it suffered disillusionment. In Soviet Russia also the dream was one of liberation. But here it was a swift and universal liberation to be achieved not through the quiet processes of providentially directed change but through an infallible system of action clearly expounded from the first. This dream was charged with the highest dynamism. It brought one form of liberation in a manner beyond the dreams of any previous age. But it brought also a new form of servitude. Revolution does not abolish social stratification; it only changes it, for better or for worse. What is new in a changing society is primarily the character of the social stratification. What is also new is the changing basis of power. . . .

Since social differentiation is highly variant, the class system is different everywhere, not only as between countries but also as between different areas of the same country. It has a different pattern in a North Dakota village from that exhibited in a Midwestern town. It is quite different in a Vermont community from that characteristic in a community of like size in Virginia. Sometimes, particularly in the smaller towns, the main stratification is a simple dichotomy, often signalized by residence, as between those who live on the opposite sides of the tracks or between those who live on the hill and those who inhabit the valley. Sometimes the main stratification divides the community into three groups, as in a New England small town I have in mind, where there is an élite of the old residents and the upper professional class, a middle group of small traders and craftsmen, and a lower social level of millworkers and so forth.

Not infrequently in such towns each class has a particular church associated with it. There are also other organizations that have a class significance. There are clubs exclusive to the élite and there are usually particular organizations representative of the middle groups. It is such facts as these that justify us in applying the term "social stratification." Although there may be a general air of pervading fellowship to the outside view, the more intimate relationships are roughly within the boundaries of each group. Within these boundaries the men plan together and play together and the women pay calls on one another. Within these boundaries, for the most part, they marry and give in marriage.

Over these local differences there is superimposed the broader pattern of national differences. We miss any appreciation of the character of social classes unless we recognize that it is both an intricate and an extremely variable phenomenon. Each country has its own distinctive type. It is idle dogmatism to conceive social stratification as the simple corollary of economic power or economic exploitation, to imagine that it arose solely out of a particular economic relationship, or that it exists only so long as that relationship endures. Within the great range of what is called capitalistic society there are many marked differences in the character of social classes. It is very different in the United States or in Canada from what it is in England. The English class configuration is very different from the French one. The French is very different from the German. We cannot know the pattern of any one country by studying that of another. Each has its distinctive system. If sometimes they approach fairly closely, often they show most significant divergences.

Beyond these differences, again, there spreads a still broader and perhaps somewhat more elusive pattern. Every civilization, every age, tends to create an appropriate over-all scheme of social stratification. The great secular trends of every age influence the modes of relationship between men and groups. With these trends go changes in the underlying schemes of valuation. As these changes are taken up into the living culture of the people they have their impact on class forms and class relationships. We shall now turn briefly to consider some of these broader changes in the scheme of values and in the conditions of social valuation and shall then proceed to consider how they have been and are at work to create a new social stratification.

If there is a new form of social stratification characteristic of the age in which we live or taking shape within it for the time ahead, it is because our age is itself subjected to social forces and cultural influences that differentiate it from the past. Thus our social valuations have undergone and are undergoing change. The direction of some of the major trends of our society is already clearly indicated, particularly in the economic and technological areas. Others are more obscure and more ambivalent. Some of these processes have already been operative over several generations; others are only slowly unfolding themselves.

Most manifest are certain economic and technological trends. These have a specific impact not only on the nature of wealth, on its organization and distribution, but also on the nature and the distribution of power. It is becoming difficult for us to realize that only a few generations separate us from the time when land was still the most prized and overwhelmingly dominant form of possession. With the growing competition of other forms of wealth went the decay of feudalism. Thus began the dissolution of class rigidities, a process greatly advanced by the later developments of capitalism. When land was the main form of wealth— land, that is, regarded simply as the storehouse of products, matured by nature and merely gathered or harvested by man—the essential division of mankind was that of the landed proprietor and the landless worker. This relationship was a relatively fixed one. Land in a feudal sense was the static, the one permanent good. It was not produced by the will of man. It could not be multiplied. It was inherited as a right or won as the prize of power. Authority went with it, authority as undisputed and as absolute as the right of possession. The landless man could rarely pass the barrier between him and the landowner. The lines of social demarcation were hard and fast.

Against this system the growth of industrial capital—as distinct from mere financial capital—began to assert its power. The new wealth, which unlike the old had the secret of reproduction, came into being through the enterprise and under the control of the middle classes, not of the landed classes; hence it had no relation to prior status. It was not associated with authority. Being itself a fluctuating and unstable, though mightily extensible thing, it was not inherently such as to command the reverence that went with a title to land. He who owned land owned what God had given. He owned part of the indestructible firmament of things. He had the authority that belongs to the eternal. But though industrial wealth carried no intrinsic authority, though the mode of acquisition was despised by the landowner, it was indubitable wealth and it could buy the landed poor and in the end the landed rich. Thus its status increased and it began to shake the seats of ancient power.

The new industrial wealth did much more than merely compete with and in the end dominate the old wealth in land. There were inherent in the economics and technology of industry forces which in various other ways brought profound changes in the relationships of men. For our purpose here we shall single out one of these. From the beginning of the industrial revolution *function,* in the first instance economic function, began to gain social significance. The function of landowning, being in itself static, was relatively passive, receptive and differentiated. The main office associated with it, that of social and political control, was derivative, not inherent. By contrast the function of industrial production was directly and continuously active. It was forever disposing, changing and establishing the relationships of men and groups. It operated through a network of interdependence. From any one focus it ramified to all the earth. It was not, like the function of the landowner, walled within the bounds of a self-sufficient estate. It created a whole series of contingent and intermediate functions. It made a society vastly more diversified than it was before. Gradually it brought a distinction between the owners of the new apparatus of wealth and those who organized or controlled it. Just as function became more complex, so did power. . . .

The middle classes were the bearers of the new order, and they carried through, first in England and then in other lands, an assault on the old establishment of power and therewith on the ancient entrenchments of caste. The nobility ceased to be set off as a race apart from the commoners. The men of means entered the portals once so jealously guarded. The nobleman found it expedient, and profitable, to join hands with the industrialist, and often to marry his daughter. Social mobility was everywhere on the increase. It penetrated line after line. The middle classes in turn found that the forces of which they were the beneficiaries were far from being exhausted at that stage. The hitherto powerless also learned to organize. Labor unions discovered the secret of modern power, the secret of function.

In our space we can give only a synoptic and simplified picture of the great transformation, so as to dwell rather more upon its effects on the system of class.

It is necessary, however, to stress the cultural concomitance of the new economic order. In the first place, the cultural gulf that had previously existed between social strata was gradually narrowed until the line of demarcation became blurred or wholly obliterated. Under the older oligarchical regime the culture of the gentry and the culture of the folk were far apart, save for such indoctrination of the latter as was congenial to the former. The different classes thought different thoughts and practiced different mores. Each had its own manner of speech just as each had its own garb. Since their life chances were totally different, there was a total difference in their outlook on life. The ruling classes had their own system of education; the lowborn acquired, apart from the localized traditions and customs of the folk, only the relatively unspecialized arts of earning a living. The vast mass of men were illiterate, as hopelessly cut off from knowledge as from power. In the industrialized countries of the world all that has been changed. The greater realm of human culture has been opened to the rank and file. The printing press and universal schooling and a thousand agencies of communication have broken down the barriers. Except where extreme poverty still prohibits it, the acquisition of culture has become selective, open to high and to low alike according to their fitness to receive it.

Under these conditions a sentiment alien to the class spirit and therefore scarcely known to the older world, that of nationality, has grown powerful. Nationality equalizes man. All alike, rich and poor, high and low, possess it in equal measure. It cannot be possessed in degree. Class, on the other hand, is based on inequality and on a sense of superiority which demands a corresponding inferiority on the other side. Class is exclusive, essentially hierarchical. So long as class was dominant nationality could not prevail. As the pretensions of class were challenged, the sentiment of nationality came in to assert the greater solidarity. It was not until the end of the eighteenth century that this new sentiment found its opportunity.

All other social values were at the same time in process of transformation, and not least among them the values of religion. In the old order religion was the strong buttress of authority, except in those instances where authority itself dared to challenge religion. Otherwise religion tended to give to mundane authority a supermundane sanction of the most impressive kind. It conferred on authority the aegis of eternity. The foundations of social order were divinely ordained. The religious hierarchy was prone to look on social change as dangerous. Those who rebelled against the social order were presumptuously resisting the dictates of an all-wise providence. On the whole, dogmatic religion tended to freeze the *status quo*. As it was expressed in one of the hymns sung in Anglican churches:

> The rich man in his castle,
> The poor man at the gate,
> God made them, high and lowly,
> And ordered their estate.

Even in our world today it is notable that systems of authoritarianism seek to confer a kind of religious sanction on their doctrines, seek to establish the sacrosanctness of their absolute power, although these modern equivalents are not nearly so enduring as the ancient faiths. In broad terms this kind of religion has lost its hold on modern peoples. The character of religion itself has been undergoing a subtle and complex change. What has been most obviously challenged is the projection by the old faiths of a tradition of authority over the secular destinies of men. It may be that religion as a principle claiming ethical authority, as a guide of personal behavior, has not undergone much obvious change. It is hard in any event to trace, sometimes even to see, the influence of religion on the everyday behavior of men. But certainly the hierarchical principle of religion, as it bears on the stratification of men in society, has suffered eclipse.

Bereft of these cultural supports, the authority of man over man has lost its ancient anchorage. Authority is no longer viewed as predetermined, as given in the eternal order of things. Authority of some kind there must always be, but the new authority must find some other refuge than the ancient sanctity. There were now only two grounds on one or the other of which authority could sustain itself. The alternatives were either to find a new sanctity, no longer transcendental but immanent, in the social objectives proclaimed by government or else to make authority something that does not depend on the ruler at all but only on his relation to the ruled. . . .

Modern civilization involves a vast network of strategic controls over a highly complicated mechanism of interdependent functions. In some societies these strategic controls are unicentered. In other words, they are politically manipulated. The most complete embodiment of the unicentered principle is exhibited in Soviet Russia, where the political omnicompetence has wholly absorbed the economic function. There are also various approximations to this order in fascist types of states where the economic controls have been largely subordinated to politically conceived ends. In a much simpler fashion another approximation is found in such a country as Mexico, where since the antifeudal revolution the politicos somewhat freely manipulate the economic processes of the country. In these very diverse instances the division of classes becomes wholly or in large measure the simple one between the ruling class, with its inner clique and its outer cohorts, and the class of the ruled. The traditional social classes, relying on tradition, inheritance, birth, sanctity or other magical properties, have in these countries fought generally a losing battle against the new political hierarchy. They tend to disappear as coherent classes. They are either liquidated or else they somehow merge into the new order of things. It is noteworthy that the new political hierarchy in these countries is not determined by prior status. The Georgian peasant or the Austrian semiskilled worker or the Italian journalist or the Latin-American adventurer, may become the apex of the new pyramid.

A quite different picture is presented by those areas which maintain some kind of socio-capitalist system, including a considerable majority of the greater industrialized countries. Here the restratification of society is much more complex. Here there is some kind of moving adjustment between the still-expanding domain of government and the increasingly centralized systems of corporate enterprise, financial and industrial. Here too the function of control has in great measure severed itself from traditional limitations, from the older determinants of status. The divorce is by no means complete, since a minor type of traditionalism develops within the new order. Wealth to no inconsiderable extent tends to confer higher function, particularly with respect to the economic controls. The executive is increasingly likely to be the son of an executive. But since there are practical tests that must be met to hold the more exacting jobs, there are important limitations to this tendency. As for the political bureaucracy, a different test must here sooner or later be met: the capacity of its heads to make the effective kind of competitive public appeal. Hence the new stratification remains mobile. It cannot harden to anything like the rigidity of the older stratification.

In a broad sense we may perhaps think of this transformation as the "managerial revolution." But we must then include in the category of managers the upper political leaders, the party manipulators, and various other kinds of "social engineers." We must include, for example, the heads of the great labor organizations. The relative domain of one type of leadership or another, or of one group or another, fluctuates. The socio-capitalist order, unlike the socialist or the fascist order, is multicentered. There is much stress and strain between rival controls. The spheres of control are differentiated but by no means separated. While the political control always claims over-all authority, that is only the formal aspect. What the voice of that authority proclaims depends on the changing relations of various economic and politico-economic forces. Moreover, the source of power is often disguised. The great cartel runs a secret imperium of its own. The consortium of finance pursues its particular ends through devices the outsider cannot fathom. The organizations of industry on every level muster power against power, control against competing or opposing control. The bureaucracy of government is subject to the coalitions and the conflicts of these various interests, while at the same time it struggles to maintain its hold on office against ever-renewed insurgent political movements. Everywhere, however, it is the control function, the larger organizing function, that according to its scale holds or seeks the primacy in modern society, creates the relations of subordination and superordination, and thus presides over the stratification of the modern world.

This statement may somewhat oversimplify the complex and ever-changing fact. There are other determinants, but they are subsidiary. The ancient magic of class is not wholly dissipated. There are foci of reaction or resistance. There are also forces inherent in the creative culture which exercise great influence on social standards and convey status on their exponents or interpreters. It is indeed conceivable that with the permeation and diversification of new cultural movements, within a society that produces a sufficiency for the material needs of all and that is moving at the same time toward the abolition of abject poverty and economic insecurity and toward the conferment of new leisure on all the people, there will come a time when the increased ranks of the groups that minister to cultural needs will possess a much higher role than now exists within the social order. Here one important difference between the wholly socialized system and the socio-capitalist system is apparent. In the latter the creative culture is not subject to the direct control of the political function. It can follow its own spontaneity, subject no doubt to various economic pulls but nevertheless inherently free. Since in the last resort the stratification of society expresses the prevailing social valuations, this kind of system is much less restrained from following new paths and seeking new goals.

Before we conclude this brief survey we should point out the main factors that in the socio-capitalist order resist the processes of restratification we have sought to indicate. It may well be that the fate of this order itself, over against the new authoritarian order, will depend on the success with which it is able to overcome these resistances. For the factors to which we refer are not merely unreconciled with the spirit of the new order, the emergent civilization. They generate types of hostility within it which if unchecked may well cause its overthrow.

We place first the struggle for dominance between nonfunctional groupings, in particular between the various ethnic groups that compose many of the larger societies. The extreme type is the dominance of group over group in the name of racial superiority. This type of dominance constitutes the most formidable obstacle to the trends of modern civilization. Not only does it assert the primacy of class distinctions that have no intrinsic relation to function but it turns the classes thus distinguished into castes, the ultimate form of dissociation between members of the same community. This, for example, is the bitterly inflexible class structure that comprises the white and the colored groups of the United States. Another form of the assertion of racial supremacy, that which distinguished the Nazi regime, identifies race with nation and in a different way resists the whole trend of modern civilization. In this form it devotes itself to military conquest and to that end superimposes another stratification altogether. The myth of race and that of ethnic superiority combine to create one of the last strongholds of traditionalism, one of the last defenses of the ancient magic.

A further limiting factor on the processes of restrafication is the existence of great military establishments. Not only do they also claim a functional superiority that is utterly irrelevant to all the functions characteristic of modern civilization but also, because they divert the energies of peoples toward the preparation for war, they blunt the efficacy of all other social tendencies. In the older times the ruling class was also a warrior class and the fusion confirmed the social distance between this class and the rest of the people. When modern civilization has not been threatened by war it has worked toward the reduction of the status of the military class, since the function of that class is alien to the whole functional scheme of things. Thus the decline of the influence of a warrior class on government has been an important development of modern society. . . .

[25] *The Myth of the Happy Worker**

by HARVEY SWADOS

"FROM where we sit in the company," says one of the best personnel men in the country, "we have to look at only the aspects of work that cut across all sorts of jobs—administration and human relations. Now these are aspects of work, abstractions, but it's easy for personnel people to get so hipped on their importance that they look on the specific tasks of making things and selling them as secondary. . . ."

—The Organization Man,
by William H. Whyte, Jr.

The personnel man who made this remark to Mr. Whyte differed from his brothers only in that he had a moment of insight. Actually, "the specific tasks of making things" are now not only regarded by his white-collar fellows as "secondary," but as irrelevant to the vaguer but more "chal-

* Reprinted from the *Nation*, CLXXXV, No. 4 (1957), 65-68, by permission. (Copyright 1957, by Harvey Swados.)

lenging" tasks of the man at the desk. This is true not just of the personnel man, who places workers, replaces them, displaces them—in brief, manipulates them. The union leader also, who represents workers and sometimes manipulates them, seems increasingly to regard what his workers do as merely subsidiary to the job he himself is doing in the larger community. This job may be building the Red Cross or the Community Chest, or it may sometimes be—as the Senate hearings suggest—participating in such communal endeavors as gambling, prostitution, and improving the breed. In any case, the impression is left that the problems of the workers in the background (or underground) have been stabilized, if not permanently solved.

With the personnel man and the union leader, both of whom presumably see the worker from day to day, growing so far away from him, it is hardly to be wondered at that the middle class in general, and articulate middle-class intellectuals in particular, see the worker vaguely, as through a cloud. One gets the impression that when they do consider him, they operate from one of two unspoken assumptions: (1) the worker has died out like the passenger pigeon, or is dying out, or becoming accultured, like the Navajo; (2) if he *is* still around, he is just like the rest of us—fat, satisfied, smug, a little restless, but hardly distinguishable from his fellow TV-viewers of the middle class.

Lest it be thought that (1) is somewhat exaggerated, I hasten to quote from a recently published article apparently dedicated to the laudable task of urging slothful middle-class intellectuals to wake up and live: "The old-style sweatshop crippled mainly the working people. Now there are no workers left in America; we are almost all middle class as to income and expectations." I do not believe the writer meant to state—although he comes perilously close to it—that nobody works any more. If I understand him correctly, he is referring to the fact that the worker's rise in real income over the last decade, plus the diffusion of middle-class tastes and values throughout a large part of the underlying population, have made it increasingly difficult to tell blue-collar from white-collar worker without a program. In short, if the worker earns like the middle class, votes like the middle class, dresses like the middle class, dreams like the middle class, then he ceases to exist as a worker.

But there is one thing that the worker doesn't do like the middle class: he works like a worker. The steel-mill puddler does not yet sort memos, the coal miner does not yet sit in conferences, the cotton millhand does not yet sip martinis from his lunchbox. The worker's attitude toward his work is generally compounded of hatred, shame, and resignation.

Before I spell out what I think this means, I should like first to examine some of the implications of the widely held belief that "we are almost all middle-class as to income and expectations." I am neither economist, sociologist, nor politician, and I hold in my hand no doctored statistics to be haggled over. I am by profession a writer who has had occasion to work in factories at various times during the thirties, forties, and fifties. The following observations are simply impressions based on my last period of factory servitude, in 1956.

The average automobile worker gets a little better than two dollars an hour. As such he is one of the best-paid factory workers in the country. After twenty years of militant struggle led by the union that I believe to be still the finest and most democratic labor organization in the United States, he is earning less than the starting salaries offered to inexperienced and often semi-literate college graduates without dependents. After compulsory deductions for taxes, social security, old-age insurance, and union dues, and optional deductions for hospitalization and assorted charities, his pay check for forty hours of work is going to be closer to seventy than to eighty dollars a week. Does this make him middle class as to income? Does it rate with the weekly take of a dentist, an accountant, a salesman, a draftsman, a journalist? Surely it would be more to the point to ask how a family man can get by in the fifties on that kind of income. I know how he does it, and I should think the answers would be a little disconcerting to those who wax glib on the satisfactory status of the "formerly" underprivileged.

For one thing, he works a lot longer than forty hours a week—when he can. Since no automobile company is as yet in a position to guarantee its workers anything like fifty weeks of steady forty-hour paychecks, the auto worker knows he has to make it while he can. During peak production periods he therefore puts in nine, ten, eleven, and often twelve hours a day on the assembly line for weeks on end. And that's not all. If he has dependents, as like as not he also holds down a "spare-time" job. I have worked on the line with men who doubled as mechanics, repairmen, salesmen, contractors, builders, farmers, cab-drivers, lumberyard workers, countermen. I would guess that there are many more of these than show up in the official statistics: often a man will work for less if he can be paid under the counter with tax-free dollars.

Nor is that all. The factory worker with dependents cannot carry the debt load he now shoulders—the middle-class debt load, if you like, of nagging payments on car, washer, dryer, TV, clothing, house itself— without family help. Even if he puts in fifty, sixty, or seventy hours a week at one or two jobs, he has to count on his wife's paycheck, or his son's, his daughter's, his brother-in-law's; or on his mother's social security, or his father's veteran's pension. The working-class family today is not typically held together by the male wage earner, but by multiple wage earners often of several generations who club together to get the things they want and need—or are pressured into believing they must have. It is at best a precarious arrangement; as for its toll on the physical organism and the psyche, that is a question perhaps worthy of further investigation by those who currently pronounce themselves bored with Utopia Unlimited in the Fat Fifties.

But what of the worker's middle-class expectations? I had been under the impression that this was the rock on which Socialist agitation had foundered for generations: it proved useless to tell the proletarian that he had a world to win when he was reasonably certain that with a few breaks he could have his own gas station. If these expectations have changed at all in recent years, they would seem to have narrowed rather than expanded, leaving a psychological increment of resignation rather than of unbounded optimism (except among the very young—and even among them the optimism focuses more often on better-paying opportunities elsewhere in the labor market than on illusory hopes of swift status advancement). The worker's expectations are for better pay, more humane working conditions, more job security. As long as he feels that he is going to achieve them through an extension of existing conditions, for that long he is going to continue to be a middle-class conservative in temper. But only for that long.

I suspect that what middle-class writers mean by the worker's middle-class expectations are his cravings for commodities—his determination to have not only fin-tailed cars and single-unit washer-dryers, but butterfly chairs in the rumpus room, African masks on the wall, and power boats in the garage. Before the middle-class intellectuals condemn these expectations too harshly, let them consider, first, who has been utilizing every known technique of suasion and propaganda to convert luxuries into necessities, and second, at what cost these new necessities are acquired by the American working-class family.

Now I should like to return to the second image of the American worker: satisfied, doped by TV, essentially middle class in outlook. This is an image bred not of communication with workers (except as mediated by hired interviewers sent "into the field" like anthropologists or entomologists), but of contempt for people, based perhaps on self-contempt and on a feeling among intellectuals that the worker has let them down. In order to see this clearly, we have to place it against the intellectual's changing attitudes toward the worker since the thirties.

At the time of the organization of the C.I.O., the middle-class intel-

lectual saw the proletarian as society's figure of virtue—heroic, magnani-
mous, bearing in his loins the seeds of a better future; he would have
found ludicrous the suggestion that a sit-down striker might harbor anti-
Semitic feelings. After Pearl Harbor, the glamorization of the worker was
taken over as a function of government. Then, however, he was no longer
the builder of the future good society; instead he was second only to the
fighting man as the vital winner of the war. Many intellectuals, as government employees, found themselves helping to create this new portrait of
the worker as patriot.

But in the decade following the war, intellectuals have discovered that
workers are no longer either building socialism or forging the tools of
victory. All they are doing is making the things that other people buy.
That, and participating in the great commodity scramble. The disillusionment, it would seem, is almost too terrible to bear. Word has gotten
around among the highbrows that the worker is not heroic or idealistic;
public-opinion polls prove that he wants barbecue pits more than foreign
aid and air-conditioning more than desegregation, that he doesn't particularly want to go on strike, that he is reluctant to form a Labor Party,
that he votes for Stevenson and often even for Eisenhower and Nixon—
that he is, in short, animated by the same aspirations as drive the middle
class onward and upward in suburbia.

There is of course a certain admixture of self-delusion in the middle-
class attitude that workers are now the same as everybody else. For me
it was expressed most precisely last year in the dismay and sympathy with
which middle-class friends greeted the news that I had gone back to work
in a factory. If workers are now full-fledged members of the middle class,
why the dismay? What difference whether one sits in an office or stands
in a shop? The answer is so obvious that one feels shame at laboring the
point. But I have news for my friends among the intellectuals. The answer
is obvious to workers, too.

They know that there is a difference between working with your back
and working with your behind. (I do not make the distinction between
hand-work and brain-work, since we are all learning that white-collar
work is becoming less and less brain-work.) They know that they work
harder than the middle class for less money. Nor is it simply a question of
status, that magic word so dear to the hearts of the sociologues, the new
anatomizers of the American corpus. It is not simply status-hunger that
makes a man hate work which pays *less* than other work he knows about,
if *more* than any other work he has been trained for (the only reason my
fellow-workers stayed on the assembly line, they told me again and
again). It is not simply status-hunger that makes a man hate work that is

mindless, endless, stupefying, sweaty, filthy, noisy, exhausting, insecure in its prospects, and practically without hope of advancement.

The plain truth is that factory work is degrading. It is degrading to any man who ever dreams of doing something worthwhile with his life; and it is about time we faced the fact. The more a man is exposed to middle-class values, the more sophisticated he becomes and the more production-line work is degrading to him. The immigrant who slaved in the poorly lighted, foul, vermin-ridden sweatshop found his work less degrading than the native-born high school graduate who reads "Judge Parker," "Rex Morgan, M.D.," and "Judd Saxon, Business Executive," in the funnies, and works in a fluorescent factory with ticker-tape production-control machines. For the immigrant laborer, even the one who did not dream of socialism, his long hours were going to buy him freedom. For the factory worker of the fifties, his long hours are going to buy him commodities . . . and maybe reduce a few of his debts.

Almost without exception, the men with whom I worked on the assembly line last year felt like trapped animals. Depending on their age and personal circumstances, they were either resigned to their fate, furiously angry at *themselves* for what they were doing, or desperately hunting other work that would pay as well and in addition offer some variety, some prospect of change and betterment. They were sick of being pushed around by harried foremen (themselves more pitied than hated), sick of working like blinkered donkeys, sick of being dependent for their livelihood on a maniacal production-merchandising setup, sick of working in a place where there was no spot to relax during the twelve-minute rest period. (Some day—let us hope—we will marvel that production was still so worshiped in the fifties that new factories could be built with every splendid facility for the storage and movement of essential parts, but with no place for a resting worker to sit down for a moment but on a fire plug, the edge of a packing case, or the sputum- and oil-stained stairway of a toilet.)

The older men stay put and wait for their vacations. But since the assembly line demands young blood (you will have a hard time getting hired if you are over thirty-five), the factory in which I worked was aswarm with new faces every day; labor turnover was so fantastic and absenteeism so rampant, with the young men knocking off a day or two every week to hunt up other jobs, that the company was forced to over-hire in order to have sufficient workers on hand at the starting siren.

To those who will object—fortified by their readings in C. Wright Mills and A. C. Spectorsky—that the white-collar commuter, too, dislikes his work, accepts it only because it buys his family commodities, and is constantly on the prowl for other work, I can only reply that for me at any rate this is proof not of the disappearance of the working-class but of the proletarianization of the middle class. Perhaps it is not taking place quite in the way that Marx envisaged it, but the alienation of the white-collar man (like that of the laborer) from both his tools and whatever he produces, the slavery that chains the exurbanite to the commuting timetable (as the worker is still chained to the time-clock), the anxiety that sends the white-collar man home with his briefcase for an evening's work (as it degrades the workingman into pleading for long hours of over-time), the displacement of the white-collar slum from the wrong side of the tracks to the suburbs (just as the working-class slum is moved from old-law tenements to skyscraper barracks)—all these mean to me that the white-collar man is entering (though his arms may be loaded with commodities) the grey world of the working man.

Three quotations from men with whom I worked may help to bring my view into focus:

Before starting work: "Come on, suckers, they say the Foundation wants to give away *more* than half a billion this year. Let's do and die for the old Foundation."

During rest period: "Ever stop to think how we crawl here bumper to bumper, and crawl home bumper to bumper, and we've got to turn out more every minute to keep our jobs, when there isn't even any room for them on the highways?"

At quitting time (this from older foremen, whose job is not only to keep things moving, but by extension to serve as company spokesmen): "You're smart to get out of here. . . . I curse the day I ever started, now I'm stuck: any man with brains that stays here ought to have his head examined. This is no place for an intelligent human being."

Such is the attitude towards the work. And towards the product? On the one hand it is admired and desired as a symbol of freedom, almost a substitute for freedom, not because the worker participated in making it, but because our whole culture is dedicated to the proposition that the automobile is both necessary and beautiful. On the other hand it is hated and despised—so much that if your new car smells bad it may be due to a banana peel crammed down its gullet and sealed up thereafter, so much so that if your dealer can't locate the rattle in your new car you might ask him to open the welds on one of those tail fins and vacuum out the nuts and bolts thrown in by workers sabotaging their own product.

Sooner or later, if we want a decent society—by which I do not mean a society glutted with commodities or one maintained in precarious equilib-rium by over-buying and forced premature obsolescence—we are going to have to come face to face with the problem of work. Apparently the Russians have committed themselves to the replenishment of their labor force through automatic recruitment of those intellectually incapable of keeping up with severe scholastic requirements in the public educational system. Apparently we, too, are heading in the same direction: although our economy is not directed, and although college education is as yet far from free, we seem to be operating in this capitalist economy on the totalitarian assumption that we can funnel the underprivileged, under-educated, or just plain underequipped, into the factory, where we can proceed to forget about them once we have posted the minimum fair labor standards on the factory wall.

If this is what we want, let's be honest enough to say so. If we conclude that there is nothing noble about repetitive work, but that it is neverthe-less good enough for the lower orders, let's say that, too, so we will at least know where we stand. But if we cling to the belief that other men are our brothers, not just Egyptians, or Israelis, or Hungarians, but *all* men, including millions of Americans who grind their lives away on an insane treadmill, then we will have to start thinking about how their work and their lives can be made meaningful. That is what I assume the Hungarians, both workers and intellectuals, have been thinking about. Since no one has been ordering us what to think, since no one has been forbidding our intellectuals to fraternize with our workers, shouldn't it be a little easier for us to admit, first, that our problems exist, then to state them, and then to see if we can resolve them?

[CHAPTER THIRTEEN]

[CHAPTER THIRTEEN]

Racial and Cultural Groups

*M*OST *social scientists would agree that the available evidence provides no basis for believing that groups of mankind differ in their innate capacity for intellectual, emotional, and cultural development. The concept of race is regarded as a scientific device for the classification of the various groups possessing physical differences from other human groups. There is, however, a prevailing myth of the biological inferiority of some racial groups. It is indeed difficult to destroy this myth because it is supported by deep prejudice and vested interest. In this chapter Rose considers this myth, and some of the wider implications of strained racial relations.*

Flowerman describes the authoritarian personality. He finds that "authoritarians see the world and its people as menacing and unfriendly." They tend to be extreme conformists, undemocratic, and to have strong prejudices against "outgroups" such as Mexicans and Negroes.

[26]   The Slow, Painful Death
of the Race Myth*

by ARNOLD M. ROSE

The history of American race relations provides an almost perfect example of the process by which popular myths are created to permit the simultaneous existence of two apparently incompatible elements of a social complex; one of these elements is usually an aspect of the social structure and the other an aspect of ideology.

Since changes are now occurring in both elements of the race relations complex—in social structure, for example, toward industrialization and away from agriculture in the South, and in ideology toward, among other things, a belief that America's position in world affairs requires the enforcing of democratic principles at home—the older myths are no longer "socially necessary." They are therefore being peeled away—first by historians, then by schoolteachers and public leaders—thereby exposing facts of American history that have been hidden from the mass of the American people.

Slavery was discovered to be economically profitable in America, notably in the Southern states and especially after the invention of the cotton gin, which, with the improvement of transportation, made it possible to change Europe's clothing from wool to cotton. Slave-produced cotton and sugar (and slave-breeding in Virginia) not only created a number of great fortunes, but also gave their owners political power and social status in the rapidly growing nation.

This situation, of course, was in direct contradiction to the American ideological commitment to liberty and equality. The means of reconciling, and hence of retaining, the two incompatible forces was to create several myths. One of these was the belief (based on such legends as that God had ordained that the sons of Ham should forever be servants to the other offspring of Noah) that the Bible sanctioned slavery. This belief can still be found today in the more backward areas of the South, but there have been enough enlightened clergymen to prevent its general acceptance.

Another early religious justification of slavery was the notion that it

* Reprinted from "History with a Present Meaning," *Commentary*, 24 (December 1957), pp. 542-546. Copyright American Jewish Committee. By permission of the publisher and author.

served as a means of converting heathens into Christians, but this provided a sanction only for the slave trade and not for the continued retention of Negroes as slaves.

A more potent myth, and one accepted by the richer and better-educated groups in the South during the period 1800-1860, was based on certain ideas concerning the nature of "true democracy." Democratic political activity and the cultivation of the arts and sciences were said to be full-time activities. As in ancient Athens and republican Rome, manual labor in the South was to be performed by slaves, who would be well treated but necessarily excluded from politics and "culture."

This idea had great influence on the philosophy, politics, manners, architecture, and literature of the ante-bellum South, but it was weakened by the South's failure to produce a great artistic and scientific culture. For all practical purposes it died when the Civil War destroyed even the appearance of artistic achievement and forced the South to compete with the "cruder" North on the latter's terms.

But the most powerful myth of all—which swept the North as well as the South, which grew rather than declined after the Civil War, and which has begun to weaken only in recent years—is that of racism.

Racism, of course, had its origin in European thought—in the writing of Linnaeus, Buffon, and others—and has played an important role elsewhere in the West. In its American form it implied the following beliefs: (1) The races are biologically unequal, with Negroes being much lower on the evolutionary scale than whites; (2) a high level of civilization is the product and the expression of the biological character of a superior race, and Negroes are therefore inherently incapable of producing a high civilization of their own, or of maintaining the one developed by the whites of the Western world. Negroes, then, are fitted only to be servants or laborers in America; (3) it follows that any biological amalgamation of the races would lead to a decline of Western civilization and the ultimate destruction of its institutions (including Christianity, the monogamous family, the modern state, and large-scale economic enterprise); (4) to maintain racial purity, the possibility of sexual intercourse between members of the two races must be guarded against by social segregation.

Some of the most important aspects of American social life and history have been distorted to conform to the racist mythology, but the facts are gradually coming to be known more widely. Many of the "new" findings have now been conveniently brought together in John Hope Franklin's *From Slavery to Freedom* and Rayford W. Logan's *The Negro in the United States.* What are the findings?

Most startling, perhaps, is the discovery that there has been a significant admixture of Negro blood in the white American population, especially in the South. The process began in Colonial times, when there was fairly free inter-marriage of Negroes with lower-class whites. Even when legal and social barriers were erected against intermarriage, their purpose was to avoid interference with slavery, not to prevent biological amalgamation, and free Negroes continued to be assimilated into the larger white population.

It was not until racism developed at the end of the 18th century that the barrier against intermarriage became rigorous. But even after the rise of racism, sex relations between white men and Negro women continued to be frequent; the only effect of racism was to insure that the offspring would be allocated to the Negro race—at any rate, in those cases where the offspring were definitely known to have Negro mothers.

For coincident with the birth of racism was the inauguration of a practice it theoretically prohibited—the "passing" of persons socially defined as Negroes, but whose physical appearance and ancestry were predominantly white, from the Negro population into the white world. This practice was of course attended with extreme secrecy, and it is impossible to get exact statistical information, but estimates made for the period around 1900 indicate that several tens of thousands of persons with Negro ancestry were "passing" into the white population every year. The racist myth prevented open recognition of this fact, but Southern whites occasionally acknowledge it in private conversations. No "harm" resulted either to the population or to the culture, although some consistent racist might attribute Southern backwardness to this "mongrelization" of the whites.

Another element of the racist mythology was that Negroes were happy in their subordinated role, first under slavery and then under the elaborate system of segregation and discrimination that developed after the Civil War. The large number of suicides, revolts, and escapes under slavery, now reported by the historians, and the frequent organization of protest moves since the end of slavery, give the lie to this belief. A whole series of psychological and sociological studies have demonstrated that the effect of segregation on Negroes has been a sense of frustration, inferiority, and inadequacy.

Some years ago, the psychiatrists Abram Kardiner and Lionel Ovesey, in *The Mark of Oppression,* showed how discrimination and specific incidents of prejudice left deep wounds on the personalities of some Negroes. More recently, the sociologist E. Franklin Frazier (himself a Negro) has exposed the delusions of the Negro upper and middle classes in his *Black Bourgeoisie,* a book that disturbs many Negroes, just as the others mentioned here have disturbed many whites.

Frazier says bluntly—and documents his statements—that Negro business has largely been a failure; that "influential Negroes" have never really had much influence; that whites have never accorded much respect to the "respectable" Negroes, whether that respectability was based on the older morals and manners or on the more modern display of wealth through conspicuous consumption; that Negro politicians have served white interests or their own personal interests, but seldom the Negro cause; that the Negro middle class is rootless because it has broken with both the older genteel tradition and the folk tradition of the lower classes; that most Negro "achievements" played up in the Negro press are not really so important and in any case are ignored by the whites; that Negro "society" is a farcical imitation of white "society."

Frazier holds that the Negro middle and upper classes are characterized by a sense of inferiority, a fear of competition with whites, anxiety about loss of status, intellectual suffering, various escapist activities, self-hatred, antagonism toward other minorities (especially Jews), and the use of material possessions and of children as compensations (which Frazier labels "fetishes"). He also believes that the respectable Negro male exploits "charm and personality" to impress others, instead of adopting the "masculine role" called for by American culture. He accuses the "black bourgeoisie" of finding rationalizations for discrimination instead of marshaling an attack upon it. Frazier will only succeed in getting upper and middle class Negroes to accept these assaults on their myths if Negroes have in fact already achieved greater psychological security in the United States than they ever enjoyed before.

Supreme Court decisions involving Negro rights were, with some exceptions, an official source of myth-making until as late as 1944. Indeed the Court's decisions since 1944 demonstrate how fantastic some of the old decisions were. For example, the 1944 majority opinion in *Smith v. Allwright* simply held that, since the Fifteenth Amendment prohibited restriction of the franchise without due process of law, and since a primary was an election, it was illegal to prevent Negroes from voting in a primary. Previously the Court had repeatedly avoided a clear-cut statement as to whether a primary was actually an election, in spite of the fact that in the one-party South the general election almost always merely confirmed the results of the Democratic primary.

The epoch-making 1954 Supreme Court decision in *Brown v. Board of Education* invoked the well-known fact that segregation in the public schools had detrimental psychological effects on Negroes, and hence was illegal under the Fourteenth Amendment, which holds that "no state shall make or enforce any law which shall abridge the privileges or immunities of any citizen of the United States."

The 1954 decision was a direct reversal of the majority opinion in *Plessy v. Ferguson* (1896) which was based on the following idea: "Laws permitting, and even requiring, their separation in places where they are liable to be brought into contact do not necessarily imply the inferiority of either race to the other. . . . We consider the underlying fallacy of the plaintiff's argument to consist in the assumption that the enforced separation of the two races stamps the colored race with a badge of inferiority. If this be so, it is not by reason of anything found in the act, but solely because the colored race chooses to put that construction upon it."

This was simply a followup to the mythological reasoning in the Slaughterhouse Cases (1873). Here the Court made an undefined distinction between "citizens of the United States" and "citizens of the State," attributed the disputed right to the latter, excused itself from specifying any rights belonging to the former, declared that state governments could make any law abridging the privileges or immunities of "citizens of the State," and hence nullified the major clause of the Fourteenth Amendment.

Another notable decision in the same myth-making vein was in the Civil Rights case (1883) in which the Court declared unconstitutional the Civil Rights Act of 1875, to insure the constitutionality of which the Fourteenth Amendment had been specifically passed and ratified.

The myth-making character of the Court's decisions did not go unnoted in their time. Justice John Marshall Harlan, a Kentucky Unionist, wrote a vigorous dissenting opinion in the Civil Rights case which began with this statement: "The opinion in these cases proceeds, it seems to me, upon grounds entirely too narrow and artificial. I cannot resist the conclusion that the substance and spirit of the recent amendments of the Constitution have been sacrificed by a subtle and ingenious verbal criticism." Yet the majority decision in the Civil Rights case still stands today as the law of the United States. Harlan's dissenting opinion in *Plessy v. Ferguson*, however, has been vindicated by the Court's unanimous 1954 ruling. In that dissent Harlan wrote, "Our Constitution is color-blind, and neither knows nor tolerates classes among citizens. In respect of civil rights, all citizens are equal before the law."

The Reconstruction period, 1867-1875, is another area in which myth drove out history. According to the popular mythological view, Negroes and carpetbaggers then dominated the Southern state governments, which were cesspools of corruption, and did nothing to protect white womanhood from rape by savage Negroes. The actual facts are that only one Southern legislature (and that one for only two years) had a majority of Negroes; as it happens a majority of that particular state's population (as of several other states) was Negro. There were no Negro governors, and the twenty-two Negroes who served in Congress (1869-1901) were on as high an educational level as their white colleagues.

There was never a great number of "carpetbaggers"—most of the Northerners who moved South during the Reconstruction period were Federal officials who came to administer the programs that Congress had enacted, or schoolteachers (mainly New England spinsters) who came to start the South's first public school program (for whites as well as Negroes). As for the "Scalawags"—native Southerners, mostly of the poorer classes, who cooperated with Federal Reconstruction—they assumed a temporary prominence which they lost after 1875, when they joined the former Confederate leaders in subordinating the Negro. Nor were the Southern state governments any more corrupt than the Northern and Federal governments of the same period. The golden cuspidors in the halls of Southern legislatures that even so distinguished a historian as Allen Nevins gave credence to (a mistake he later apologized for) are legendary.

There is no evidence of a Reconstruction crime wave, and while rapes did occur they were not nearly so frequent as lynchings, which the mythology interpreted as the Southern white community's reaction to rape. When statistics were collected after the 1890's, it was discovered that only a fourth of the lynch victims were even accused of rape, and since there was usually no preceding trial, it is impossible to tell how many of the accusations were just.

The Reconstruction, as its name implies, was actually a period in which the Federal government tried to re-establish a modicum of social welfare and order in a disorganized and wartorn South. Contrary to the belief of the myth-makers that it was a time of unmitigated turmoil and terror, Reconstruction's real failure was that it did not go far enough. The Negroes were not provided with a basis for economic independence, and this situation—as Franklin points out—made it easier for upper-class Southerners to restore a system of white supremacy.

The post-Reconstruction period also has its myth—that the restored power of the former slave-owners in state government brought order, peace, and gradual progress to the South. The facts are that violence and illegal activity were institutionalized and absorbed into the law-enforcement agencies themselves, so that Southerners—both white and Negro—

have never known the security of life, limb, or property taken for granted in the North.

Moreover, the South made no economic progress until it began to adopt Northern patterns of industrialization and mechanization, starting in the 1920's. Meantime, around 1900, the Negro was pushed down to an economic and social level such as he had not experienced even during the days of slavery. The mythology has it that segregation was a traditional Southern institution; actually most practices of segregation were created by state law during the 1890's and received their basic legal sanction in *Plessy v. Ferguson*.

The Negroes of the United States have been a subjugated people, and their behavior and living standards show the marks of oppression. It is impossible to tell precisely what they would accomplish if they had the same opportunities and liberties that other Americans have. Significant progress toward equality only began after 1942, and already there is a marked improvement in living standards and behavior patterns among a considerable number of Negroes.

It still remains true that Negroes are conscious of themselves first as Negroes and then as Americans: as Franklin puts it, the main question for Negroes today is not whether the world will be destroyed by the atomic bomb, but whether their homes will be destroyed by a bomb thrown by their white neighbors. Nevertheless Negroes are Americans—indeed they are ultra-American, as Frazier somewhat disgustedly points out, in considering some of the foibles of American culture—and they ask nothing more nor less than equal treatment and acceptance as Americans.

The economic, political, and legal changes since 1942 are rapidly insuring equal treatment. But full acceptance awaits the clearing away of the rubble of mythology. Books like those of Franklin, Logan, and Frazier are among the first efforts in this direction, although they suffer from their lack of contact with other work that has been done in the field, and from the general absence of detailed technical studies of relevant historical demography, constitutional law, popular symbolism, etc., etc.

Some of the detailed studies now being made, like Dudley and Beverly Duncan's *The Negro Population in Chicago*, while competent, do not meet the need. The Duncans fail to place Chicago's changes in the context of larger American changes, and their conclusions are dated, since they rely entirely on the last published census and ignore subsequent important trends. But the quality of monographic researches on the Negro is improving rapidly, and the gaps in scholarship will clearly be bridged soon. This research, to be significant, will require the combined efforts of historians and sociologists, who at the moment are unfortunately working in isolation.

[27]   *The Authoritarian Personality**

by SAMUEL H. FLOWERMAN

Findings of recent scientific investigations reveal that the real menace to democracy is not the brutal dictator but the anonymous man-in-the-crowd on whose support the dictator depends for power. Social scientists have found that this nameless individual is not a creation of the dictator but a ready-made "authoritarian personality"—a person whose family background and social environment have made him perculiarly attuned to antidemocratic beliefs. It requires authoritarian personalities to take hold of authoritarian ideas; it takes authoritarian personalities—thousands and even millions of them—to build an authoritarian state.

Concern about authority and the relationship between the ruler and the ruled is not new. It runs through the fabric of recorded history of civilization. Philosophers and poets—from at least as far back as ancient Egypt and Greece to present-day Existentialists—have wrestled with the dilemma of how to attain the highest level of development of the individual within some system of order governing man's relation to man. In the United States a spate of studies about various aspects of personality development has been going forward for several decades. And research workers, most of them trained here, have been conducting studies in post-war Germany in an effort to understand why a people will produce, nurture and follow a dictator. The bulk of these inquiries tend to yield somewhat consistent results: there is something special, something different about the "authoritarian man."

Perhaps the most detailed study of all time in this field was made by a team of social psychologists in California, working for almost five years. They recently completed an investigation of the democratic and antidemocratic ideas and attitudes of the American man-in-the-crowd, seeking keys to their origin. Teams from other parts of the country have added to their findings. The California group—T. W. Adorno, Else Frenkel-Brunswik, Max Horkheimer, Daniel Levinson and R. Nevitt Sanford—interviewed and tested more than two thousand persons in the San Francisco Bay area, Los Angeles, Portland, Ore., and Washington, D.C.

Among the groups tested were factory workers, officer candidates in a maritime training school, veterans, members of service clubs (Rotarians

* From "Portrait of the Authoritarian Man," by Samuel H. Flowerman, *The New York Times Magazine,* April 23, 1950, pp. 9, 28-31. Reprinted by permission.

and Kiwanis), office workers, male inmates of a prison, members of parent-teacher associations, out-patients in a psychiatric clinic, church groups, and college students.

While the California study is not a statistical study but rather examines various groups psychologically, it was found that authoritarian men did exist in many groups and in many places. Based on the California study and other readings and observations over a number of years, social scientists feel that it can be said that about 10 percent of the population of the United States probably consists of "authoritarian men and women" while as many as another 20 percent have within them the seeds that grow into authoritarianism.

Lest the conclusion be drawn that there are only two kinds of people, authoritarians and anti-authoritarians, it should be said that the social scientists' findings rate persons on a scale from very low to very high, as regards their authoritarian tendencies, with perhaps the bulk of the population clustered around the middle.

From the findings of the California study has emerged this composite psychological portrait of the Authoritarian Man:

He Is a Supreme Conformist. The Authoritarian Man conforms to the nth degree to middle-class ideas and ideals and to authority. But conforming is no voluntary act for him; it is compulsive and irrational. It is an attempt to find security by merging with the herd, by submitting to some higher power or authority. Not only does he feel compelled to submit; he wants others to submit, too. He cannot run the risk of being different and cannot tolerate difference in anyone else.

In a mild form, such compulsive submission to authority may find a Casper Milquetoast chewing each mouthful of food thirty times because some bogus health expert has said he should. In its extreme form it finds people reduced to sheep, herded into marking "yes" on ballots that do not have "no," bleating "Heil!" to the commands of a Hitler, and doing his bidding even when it means oppressing, even killing, other people.

Authoritarians see the world and its inhabitants as menacing and unfriendly. Being so threatened, so anxiety ridden, they must seek security somehow, somewhere. The best security for the authoritarian is to surrender to a powerful authority. He agrees, for example, that "What the world needs is a strong leader"; and "There are two kinds of people, the weak and the strong."

To him, life is a power system into which he must fit. He doesn't have to wield the power himself so long as he can be near power, sharing it vicariously. It is this latter tendency which makes the authoritarian such a good camp-follower.

But the authoritarian is a loyal camp-follower only so long as the leader remains strong. Let the leader falter, let him be defeated; then, "Down with the old, up with the new."

So today in Germany many people agree that Hitler was bad, but only because he was unsuccessful in the long run; their basic way of life is still authoritarian—they simply await a new, stronger, more powerful leader.

He Is Rigid and Shows Limited Imagination.   He is a mechanical man, a kind of robot who reacts to only a limited number of ideas and can't be budged out of the channels in which he has been conditioned to operate. This doesn't mean that the Authoritarian Man is a person of low intelligence; but it does mean that his personality restricts his intelligence and imagination. He is generally incapable of figuring out alternate solutions to problems.

The extent to which this rigidity operates was demonstrated by Dr. Milton Rokeach, a junior member of the California team and now at Michigan State College. Dr. Rokeach worked out a series of simple problems in arithmetic and map reading. He presented these problems to groups of adults and children, whose authoritarianism had already been determined. All the people in the experiment were taught to solve the problems by using a complicated method, but nothing was said about other, easier, solutions; they were simply instructed to get the right answers. As Dr. Rokeach's guinea pigs continued to work down the list of problems they soon reached a series of examples that could be solved either the hard way or very simply. Authoritarians continued to solve the problems the hard way. The non-authoritarians shifted readily to the easy solutions—they were able to use more channels.

He Is Herd-minded.   And to be herd-minded—"ethnocentric" is the scientists' term—implies being prejudiced. To the authoritarian, people who are—or seem to be—different are strange, uncanny and threatening, although they may be few in number and unimportant in influence. He tends to exalt his own group and reject members of other groups. (To be sure, there are some exceptions to this praise of one's own group. Sometimes members of minority groups take over the prejudices of the majority groups and engage in what psychologists call "self-hate.")

The person who dislikes one "out-group" generally dislikes many other "out-groups." In this respect he is like the hay-fever victim, who is usually allergic to more than one kind of pollen.

The authoritarian puts neat—and often false—labels on people. In his group he may see individuals; outside his own group he sees only masses or types. So he will frequently say of members of "minority" groups that

"that kind" is "lazy," "sex-crazy," "dishonest in business," "money-mad," "smelly," and so on. What is more, he tends to see "them" everywhere.

He Is a Phony Conservative. He waves the flag, he sounds like a patriot, but at heart hates the very traditions and institutions he professes to love. In his most rabid form the phony conservative is the anti-democratic agitator who is more destructively radical than the radicals he claims he is attacking.

The California team distinguishes between the true conservative and the phony conservative. The true conservative may be patriotic, believe in American traditions and institutions, and support their continued existence; he may also believe in a laissez-faire economy. But he is also for giving every individual an equal "break" regardless of his group membership. And it is in regard to this last point that the true conservative can be distinguished from the counterfeit flag-waver.

He Is a Moral Purist. The authoritarian frowns on sensuality, a trait he is ready to find in members of other groups. He regards his own group as morally pure. Authoritarian men—and women—tend to agree, for example, that no "decent man" would marry an unchaste woman. Even male prisoners jailed for sex crimes support statements condemning sex crimes; and they are also more conforming, more anti-Semitic, more anti-Negro, and more pseudo-conservative than their fellow-prisoners.

It would be a grave mistake to regard the authoritarian as a lunatic or freak, although doubtless there are such extreme cases. If anything, the democratic person may appear outwardly to be less well-adjusted because he "internalizes" his problems to a greater degree and blames himself for many of his difficulties. The authoritarian "externalizes" his problems and blames other people and other forces. On the surface, the authoritarian may seem to be less troubled, but this is often because he has buried his smoldering resentment and hostility within himself.

By contrast with his opposite the extremely democratic personality is a man with a mind of his own; he is a flexible individual, adjusting readily to new situations. He is sensitive to the part he plays in conflicting situations and he is ready to take responsibility for his own behavior.

The model anti-authoritarian tends to like all sorts of people regardless of whether they are members of his group. He is without prejudice against religious or racial minorities. He regards persons as individuals, not types. Nor is he inclined to judge the moral standards of others. It is easy for him to see some good in the world and some hope for its future. Most important, he refuses to surrender his individuality to a "big shot," although he may submit to rational authority by choice when he believes

that such authority is based upon equality, superior ability, and co-operation, and that it is subject to dismissal for a job badly done.

The findings of these studies suggest that people are not deliberately
and systematically taught the ABC's of authoritarianism. Authoritarianism
is a term which describes personality; and personality is developed in the
crucible of inter-personal relationships, the most important of which is
the relationship between parent and child.

As a child the typical authoritarian was usually subjected to harsh discipline and was given little affection in a home in which the father was a
tough boss. In such a home children must "knuckle under" and submit.
There is little opportunity to act as an individual. Fear rules, and parents
and other figures of authority are regarded as menacing, punitive and
overpowering. This fear, based on the inability to disagree, is carried over
into adult life; when the opportunity to assert one's self occurs, it is seized
by way of compensation. The slave of one generation becomes the domineering master of the next generation.

On the other hand, as a child the democratic individual most often
grew up in a home where the mother had much to say. Children in these
families knew affection and had a feeling that they counted as individuals.
They exercised the right to disagree, although often not without conflict
and guilt. As adults they regard their parents as flesh-and-blood characters
with the traits of real people. In childhood, the democratic person was
able to choose equality and independence instead of blind, passive submission. As an adult, the democratic person is not so easily pushed around
because he has no compulsive need, based on fear, to submit to the authority of the "big shot."

To be sure, there are reasons for the development of authoritarian personalities which are not to be found in the home. There are the major environmental upheavals—depressions and unemployment, inflations, wars,
earthquakes, revolutions, floods—which alter ways of living and believing. There are also the chance experiences which an individual encounters
in a lifetime. Sometimes the harshness of a child's home may be offset by
kindly teachers, decent playmates, and other significant figures who treat
the child affectionately as an individual. Sometimes a child grows up in
such a way as to be able to throw off the effects of his slavery.

But these rebels are perhaps the exception, whereas the slave personality occurs more often when childhood has been spent in an authoritarian
house. Certainly research findings indicate that so far the key to the difference between the authoritarian and democratic personalities lies in the
relationship between parents and children. Learning to disagree with
one's parents may be the capstone of a democratic personality.

How great is the threat of authoritarian development in this country? There are several deeply ingrained trends in American culture which probably offset to a considerable degree the spread of authoritarianism.

Americans traditionally scoff at authority. An American President reads a State of the Union message before Congress and is heckled, only to answer right back. Prize-fight referees are booed when they award unfair decisions against Negro boxers in favor of white boxers. Players and spectators "razz" baseball umpires. Radio programs and movies make fun of cops, school teachers, and principals, and especially fathers.

American homes are mother-oriented—and if anything—child-dominated. Women control the family purse strings of America, handle immediate problems of discipline, and are favored by over-sentimentality in a Victorian sense.

We have an American creed of fair play, of equality, and of upward mobility among social and economic classes. We are an individualistic, freedom-loving, rational, practical people. Americans are suspicious of flag-waving and of military authority.

Yet there are those who note that our American creed is "honored more in the breach than in the observance." Wide gaps separate what we claim to believe and what we feel and do. Like any national group, we are susceptible to anti-democratic ideologies; we have authoritarian personalities among us.

[CHAPTER FOURTEEN]

Crime and Delinquency

*T*HE statement on the causes of crime and delinquency was prepared by a committee of the American Humanist Association and is of general interest. While identifying many specific causes of crime, the committee places greatest emphasis on the tragic weakening of the ethical influence of the family and other face-to-face groups in the present mass organization of an industrial society. All else, they assert, fades in significance for the understanding and prevention of crime.

Margolis attaches similar importance to the larger social aspects of combatting delinquency and crime. The problem, as he sees it, is one of maintaining the allegiance of the juvenile to the values of adult society. From this point of view punishment is a force often misapplied, since it aims at restraining the juvenile and not at recovering his allegiance; but it is precisely this allegiance that the adult world must win back.

[28]   Causes and Cure of Crime and Juvenile Delinquency*

a statement by the
COMMITTEE ON HUMAN RIGHTS AND WELFARE
of the AMERICAN HUMANIST ASSOCIATION

The alarming increase in crime in this country, particularly in the amount and violence of juvenile delinquency and teen-age gang warfare, is now a major problem. Its menace is the greater because it reflects serious deficiencies in the whole fabric of society, rather than merely the defects of the individuals immediately involved. The problem is exceedingly complex and will be solved only by solving national economic, social and cultural problems. It involves all major social relations and should be approached in its total ramifications.

It is essential that every group that is concerned with the ethical foundations of the society in which it occurs, and is concerned with the opportunity of citizens to live safe and satisfying lives, make every effort to recognize and act on the following:

1. First, to change public opinion from an archaic, punitive, self-exculpating attitude to one in which the chief effort is to discover causal factors; second, to set in motion the broad, social mechanisms which, when combined, will cure the society of its evils. It is essential that the public realize that only through therapy and reeducation can delinquents and criminals be brought into wholesome social relations and thus individual rehabilitation accomplished. It is essential that the public understands that prevention of delinquency depends on wholesome, character-productive environments for growing children.

Crash programs of public and private agencies merely add temporarily to the sense of personal security of the non-delinquent, magnify the punitive and retaliatory measures taken against the victims of circumstances, and invariably place the blame on home, school or some other institution. They must be abandoned in favor of sensible, well thought-out efforts to get at causes and to develop remedies.

2. Fundamentally the trouble lies in large part in the level to which ethical standards have sunk. Society does not sufficiently abhor wrong-do-

* From *The Humanist*, No. 6, 1959, pp. 360-363. Published by The American Humanist Association, Yellow Springs, Ohio. Reprinted by permission.

ing to give young and old the moral integrity to resist egoistically centered amoral or socially antagonistic impulses. All classes of society are here at fault. A competitive, acquisitive society is interlaced with non-moral ideals. Youngsters cannot be expected to cherish impractical ideals when they see success and status accorded to the wealthy and powerful, many of whom have prospered by methods inconsistent with the highest ideal-ism. Home, school, church and recreational agencies must be stimulated to advocate and exemplify ethical standards on a realistic basis even when those standards conflict with contemporary mores.

3. A basic obstacle to adequate treatment of the delinquent and the criminal lies in the failure to provide money for the purpose. There is sufficient knowledge of what to do but funds to accomplish it are woe-fully insufficient. Citizens, public officials and taxpayers need a deeper sense of the broad social significance of the problem. Sights must be raised materially in order that there be a possibility of meeting the issue. Among the specific measures that constitute a minimal program of treatment are:

a) Early detection of pre-delinquents in the elementary grades, possi-bly with the use of the test worked out by Sheldon and Eleanor Glueck (see reference at end of this statement).

b) Attitudes of public and private officials are of primary importance in the treatment of the delinquent, and specifically in the treatment of the pre-delinquent, and of the youngster who is experiencing his earliest con-tacts with enforcement agencies. The spirit of "treat 'em rough" creates far more anti-social feelings and delinquent behavior than it cures. Too often resistance on the part of youth to authorities or social workers is traceable to this cause. In a large number of cases delinquents have had a history of socially offensive behavior known to parents, teachers and rec-reation workers over a considerable period. During that time sympathetic cooperation between officials and private agency workers with parents could set in motion activities and changes in relationships that make later apprehension by the police unnecessary. The same attitude in the relation of parole officers to the offender who has been released would assure re-habilitation more often and more satisfactorily. The officers should have case loads that allow time to be sympathetic and in addition should be given every encouragement for efforts to understand and help.

c) A third item in a minimal program of treatment is the establish-ment of adequate detention homes run by trained personnel, in which the new offender is separated from the hardened cases.

d) A fourth item is the use of reception and classification centers for assignment of offenders to suitable institutions.

e) A fifth item consists of adequate institutions to house the youth and adults in quarters and under the care of personnel trained to direct the re-education of various types of offenders.

f) Of special interest and promise is the question of revival in principle of the Civilian Conservation Camps in a strictly educational, and not in a military frame of reference. Work, study, recreation should constitute the three-fold slogan in their inception, direction, equipment and design, with the purpose of developing the sense of belonging to a community. The primary responsibility for instituting such camps rests on the national government, but there is need for close collaboration by the separate states. While pre-delinquents and the youngsters of the less troublesome categories might be served, the camps should not be regarded as "re-habilitative" or punitive in nature. They should be open to high-school graduates or to youths seeking productive summer experiences. The work involved should be of a kind and importance to stimulate a sense of social pride in young adults. Opportunities exist for much needed work projects that are not profitable for private enterprise, such as conservation tasks or the opening up of waste lands to beneficial uses.

g) Too much stress can not be placed on the constant need to empha-size the ultimate goal of all treatment, namely, restoration of the individual to the community as a responsible, self-directing, socially-interacting person. Therapeutic treatment and practical experience in a cooperative environment are the principal elements in the process.

4. The great consideration is prevention. A heavy responsibility rests on the community to see that crime and delinquency are eliminated or re-duced to an absolute minimum through measures to provide the sort of developmental influences that result in a reliable citizenry. A few meas-ures stand out as the critical points in a program of prevention:

a) The first to be mentioned, although priority is impossible to allocate, is adequate school facilities and teaching force, with classes of moderate size and a curriculum adapted to the needs and capacities of pupils with divergent needs. (1) A foremost aim of schooling should always be the development of a sense of responsibility in the student. To that end care-ful attention needs to be given in each school system to the determination of the age at which children are allowed to leave school and the years during which less than full-time schooling is permitted. Particularly and most importantly, work-study programs need to be adopted more widely, and broadened in systems in which they already play a part. Both man-agement and labor should be intimately involved in the planning and ad-ministration of such programs. (2) Counselling of a professional kind for students on every academic level is a must. In tension-filled neighbor-hoods counselling service needs to be extended far beyond the usual pro-

vision. (3) With the change in the home brought about by invention of
modern home-aids, and with the changing role of parents in the lives of
their children, goes the inevitable need of parent education and guidance.
It is of paramount importance in the reduction of juvenile delinquency.
PTAs should be strengthened both by public and private effort until all
parents are reached with sympathetic professional service. Education of
children in a modern age is woefully incomplete without parallel education of fathers and mothers, an education closely related to the work of
the teachers in the various grades. (4) Since one of the strongest incentives to delinquent behavior comes about through failure of the student to
achieve in school, and since that failure is due in a large percentage of
cases to inadequate reading ability, it is incumbent on each community to
provide adequate facilities for remedial reading instruction. (5) In areas
into which newcomers of a culture other than the prevalent one are
drawn, special facilities must be created, particularly in the schools, to aid
in every possible way the understanding and use by the newcomers of our
language and of our customs.

b) Youth has a right to constructive participation in the economic
structure of the community. The responsibility therefore devolves upon
the community to see that vocational training is available for all youth,
and that they have jobs to do regardless of the restrictions of the market.

c) Decent housing and neighborhood planning to allow for wholesome
family life constitute a preventive factor of more than obvious significance. Not all youngsters living in slum conditions become delinquent;
not even a major portion of them do. And yet, without question, bad housing and slovenly neighborhoods do add their weight in the total burden
that swamps many a boy and girl.

d) All that has been said above, important as it is, fades in significance
for the prevention of crime and delinquency and the building of a wholesome society, before one fundamental, basic factor. It is the tragic weakening of the influence of the face-to-face groups in the present mass organization of an industrialized society. The home has far less influence on
the child than it once had, less than it is supposed to have by the advocates of fines for the parents of delinquents, less than it should have to
create strong and active ethical concepts and habits for the child's self-
direction. The play group, which in time supercedes the parent for the
place of strongest sway over the child, becomes a force for antisocial
ideals and activities in a neighborhood deprived of decent housing, play
space and equipment, and intelligent, experienced adult oversight. The
grade groups in many schools, located in pauperized tension areas, have
lost the developmental power necessary to help correct the lack of whole-

some daily activities and influences that are characteristic of a growing number of neighborhoods in urban (and also in some rural) areas.

Of first priority then, both in its moral demand on civic planning and organization and in its demand on national, state and municipal public and private funds, stands the need for more, infinitely more numerous settlements, recreation centers, group work agencies, area coordinators in the public school systems, neighborhood civic agencies, community organizations and all other nonsectarian, nonpolitical, noncommercial local enterprises. Only out of the provision for participation by children in unbiased, friendly, cooperative activities can children learn the fundamental concepts of the good life, and parents find their modern role in the development of wholesome future citizens.

[29]   *Juvenile Delinquents:*
*The Latter-Day Knights**

by JOSEPH MARGOLIS

No one can hope to discover the cause of juvenile delinquency, just as no one can hope to discover the cause of crime. These are labels applied to large clusters of acts that may have in common nothing more than the breaching of the law by minors or merely the breaching of the law. If we fasten on such fractional uniformities, we are inevitably led to expect simple and adequate causal correlations. We speak, accurately enough, of an upsurge in juvenile delinquency, which, because it is an isolable trend, we expect to be assigned an equally isolable source. But if we asked instead for the cause of crime, we should at once realize that "crime" is an umbrella term held over the heads of some extraordinarily different kinds of things. And even if we invented a term to cover criminal activity committed between the ages of thirty and thirty-nine (say, "trigintennial criminality"), we would still find it odd to inquire into its causes.

* From *The American Scholar*, Vol. 29, No. 2, Spring 1960. © copyright 1960 by the United Chapters of Phi Beta Kappa. Reprinted by permission of the publisher.

This does not mean that it is pointless to search out as many correlations as the traffic will bear between juvenile delinquency and the kinds of lives delinquents actually lead. The trends are clear enough and ugly, and they excite our honest hopes for corrective action. Nothing is lost, for instance, in noticing that delinquency is very highly correlated with the various patterns of the "broken home." But one senses that delinquency is too amorphous a phenomenon to respond to the specific of patching homes. And the causally relevant sequences may even come to minimize the juvenile condition of the delinquents and the delinquent condition of the juveniles. Our concern is, properly, with the fact that it is juveniles, in mounting numbers, who are responsible for our crime records. But this, after all, is an outcome completely detached from any insight into the kinds of careers offending juveniles have come to prefer.

I think we are nowadays shocked by delinquency. We are startled and horrified by certain of the most dramatic aspects of much juvenile delinquency. But, above all, we are puzzled by it, failing to find its core of sense and purpose. We notice apparently unmotivated crimes, attacks on total strangers, inordinate punishment for seemingly trivial and imagined slights, bloodthirstiness and excessive violence, the exhilarated state of delinquents during their exploits, their disdain of, and relative independence from, the legal and ethical codes of society. Much of the special bravado that we associate with this kind of delinquency, I admit, collapses when the law uses its teeth; but this is not significant, since the delinquent simply behaves as a hostile captive isolated from the little world in which he finds his former conduct appropriate.

I shall not attempt to isolate the causes of juvenile delinquency. I wish only to make the well-known facts about a certain kind of delinquency fall into place in a coherent pattern whose causal analysis would prove more fruitful than the steady, piecemeal accumulation of statistical data. What we require at the present time is a promising model for interpreting the various patterns of delinquent behavior. Perhaps the model I propose is inadequate; it is, however, at least an attempt at correcting our conception of what the delinquents in question think they are doing in carrying on the way they do. Apparently, we don't understand them, for it is perfectly clear that we regard their behavior as senseless, pointless, unprovoked, inexplicable. But we must be mistaken, from their point of view, since there is among them as much seriousness, devotion to imagined duties, sense of honor and trust and co-operation (however perverse), even heroism and self-sacrifice, industry, incentive and reward, foresight and planning as can be found in any legitimate group endeavor. There is among them, moreover, an impressive enthusiasm, *esprit,* solidarity and even pride that would be genuinely hard to duplicate.

Let me exaggerate somewhat the description of two important features that regularly appear in these delinquency patterns. The first is that "there is a war on." The second is that "there must be witnesses." Although I say these are exaggerations, they would not be unlikely first impressions. The sense of a war stems partly from the quite regular skirmishes ("rumbles") between highly organized, usually well-armed, and even territorially distinct rival gangs. It stems also from the understandable hatred (however unpardonable) of this juvenile underworld toward law-enforcement agencies, a hatred that spills over not infrequently into overt hostilities. And it stems finally from the cruel and usually senseless victimization of random members of the law-abiding community.

But in fact there is no war, there are only patterns that strongly resemble warfare. Even the skirmishes between rival gangs are initiated largely by invitation (although it may not be possible to refuse it): "Do you want a rumble?" is, apparently, a common announcement that sufficient reason has been found for a skirmish to be staged. Nevertheless, there seems to be an understanding between warring companies that a return engagement is always to be expected and that no surrender or compensation could establish peace; moreover, each group seems primarily occupied with the way its own champions conduct themselves. The police are simply a perpetual threat, for the activities of these gangs happen typically to be criminal. That is, I do not believe these delinquents wish merely to be law-breakers; they are fully prepared to break the law and, hence, permanently alienate the police. And again, the victims meaninglessly selected from the law-abiding community are merely victims, the unfortunate innocent bystanders of a gang code that affects them in an altogether contingent way. The code imposes obligations on the membership; compliance leads inevitably to the violence we know so well. But the important matter is compliance and not the breach of law. We, within our adult, law-abiding world, are struck by the frequent horror of these acts; whereas the juveniles themselves have hardly considered the victim's personal plight or the anguish of society at large. They are genuinely thoughtless in this respect, so engrossed are they (apart from their immaturity) in leading lives dictated by their own intimate society and in assessing, by their own standards, the talents and reliability and loyalty of their comrades.

I have said also that there must be witnesses. But in a sense, there always are witnesses, because these delinquents specialize in forays, in group adventures in which more than two boys participate. It is important, apparently, that accredited observers attest the prowess, hardness, strength, courage, cruelty, imagination of any single participant. It would be an absolutely idle waste of energy to commit any of the crimes that are committed and to go unnoticed.

I should like to approach this observation in another way. In my opinion, in the large urban centers in which delinquency is most flagrant (and somewhat less noticeably in smaller cities), juvenile gangs constitute the most coherent, publicly self-conscious, and vigorous communities that can be found. I discount businesses, churches, schools, the police and other similar groups as not, properly, forming neighborhoods. The gangs actually live together as social ensembles, the perfection of their communities marred here and there by the impinging adult world. The city is the locale of disintegrating neighborhoods (in the traditional sense) and, conversely, the locale of a rising, novel and peculiarly mobile neighborhood. In short, increasingly in our cities (as well as in certain of the cities of Europe and Asia) the most effective and powerful neighborhoods that exist are juvenile neighborhoods. They are the ones, ironically, that preserve some measure of face-to-face community living. And they are themselves aware of it, at least in that revealing lapse by which their members boldly attack innocent people without fear of reprisal. The law-abiding adult world is distinctly inert, from their point of view, providing only an endless variety of occasions and targets for the exhibition of the skills that are prized within the gang. Even the unfriendly press provides gratuitous and welcome confirmation of the gang's own chronicles. And, periodically, the forays themselves lead to large-scale rumbles, which, as is well known, are advertised to all except the police and others interested in law enforcement.

So the adult world is abdicating in large part its neighborhood responsibility and authority and, by its increasing inertia, has allowed control to pass into the hands of vigorous and ardent youngsters, whose code, however, does not promise to preserve the law-abiding values of the old neighborhood. It also happens that cities spring up without ever having had the experience of the old neighborhood solidarity; but this hardly is designed to prevent the rise of the new gangs.

I have put forward what I take to be two important clues for any suitable interpretive model of the sort required. I should like to say something now about such a model. The adult world thinks of these delinquents as deviants, outlaws, irresponsibles; and it is baffled by its inability to contain them. But the juveniles themselves actually form a string of genuine and relatively stable neighborhoods, with a day-to-day code of conduct, a system of sanctions and rewards, a calendar of community life, an educational program, and facilities for communications and the provision and distribution of goods and services. It is a simple society in which everyone is known by name and face and accomplishment; it is an aristocratic society—frequently monarchical—but in any case ruled by the most talented persons (discounting the perversity of the talents preferred). It is in fact *the* society to which these juveniles belong. The adult world, from their point of view, is vaguely defined and alien, usually threatening in its intermittent contact with their own; although, of course, the juvenile cannot ever be entirely free of a subordinate participation in that adult world.

The juvenile neighborhood has, I should say, two principal rituals to perform. It is, as a matter of fact, overwhelmingly concerned with ritual forms. But the two I have in mind bear most directly on the terror and violence that have so shocked the adult world. One is the initiation ritual, and the other is what I can only call the ritual sortie. They are essentially indistinguishable as far as overt behavior is concerned; they are different only in their purpose. The initiation ritual has to do with recruitment, the selection of suitable members of an elite society. The ritual sortie has to do with status and prestige within that society, both a requirement of members in good standing and an opportunity for the advancement of the ambitious and the talented. The society is usually, at its most audacious, a society of warriors and "free" souls who accept only those limitations upon conduct that, as a corporation, they themselves impose. But it is also a society of pranksters, gaming companions, exhibitionists, children, concerned as much with extremities of style in dress and speech as with murder and theft. It is always, however, a loyal brotherhood provided with a more or less clear schedule of honors. And it leads what is essentially a public life, protected as far as possible from the eyes of law-enforcement agencies.

If we are to understand this model, we shall find that we must look to some surprising parallels. I should suggest, because of its familiarity, that of the Knights of the Round Table, without at all ignoring the willingness of our own juvenile gangs to give themselves—in all candor and accuracy —sinister and evil and even repugnant names. It is important to notice that there are no ready models (even models that they might pervert) to be found in the law-abiding adult world. And it is important also to isolate that critical feature of their own way of life that is so entirely alien to the more or less official ideology of the adult world.

The feature in question may perhaps most succinctly be described as "climax-technique" (I borrow the term from the accounts of the code of life of the pagan Teutonic knights). I submit that our juvenile gangs implicitly subscribe to this significant principle, however corrupt their particular values may be said to be. Briefly, the routine of ordinary, unadventurous life is quite worthless, boring, idle to our juveniles; it is made supportable only by celebrating previous sorties and by preparation for others. In an odd sense, then, the juvenile does not wish to be idle—idleness is death to him. But, curiously, he considers the life of the adult world (and his submission to it) an idle life and, correspondingly, the adult world views his exploits also as a species of idling. The significance of his life lies exclusively in the climactic and perilous mountain peaks of the adventures he enters into so wholeheartedly (an important inversion of the purity of the soul we associate with, say, the devotion of the Round Table Knights). So he proves himself from episode to episode—whether by torture, theft, sexual liberties, murder, fighting, vandalism, drinking—always in accord with the strict code of his own society.

The values of the adult world have to do with docility and safety and, most important, with the merits of prolonged routine work. It is here, therefore, that we have the most dramatic evidence of the breakdown in the educational apparatus of the adult world, of the autonomy of the juvenile: we must acknowledge the existence of a subsociety that effectively recruits and instructs novices (willing or not) in a way of life that, in the most fundamental manner possible, is opposed to the values of an otherwise incredibly powerful society. The juvenile world is simply slipping through very strong nets; but, as it does, it is also managing to get control of the vital neighborhood. It repudiates the declared values of the adult world and, finding itself potentially in control of an unorganized neighborhood, simply reinforces the quite naturally intimate and sustained society of the young and moves to institutionalize its own values. It is necessarily parasitic, feeding on the wealth and skills and goods of the adult world, relieved therefore of any positive concern with the maintenance of the requisite routines; and thus relieved, it is almost entirely free to pursue those special ritual adventures by which it distinguishes itself.

The phenomenon of the delinquent gang is not an altogether new one. Gang and quasi-tribal patterns are quite familiar among adolescents, patterns at once compulsive and inclined toward outlawry. Still, we cannot fail to notice certain distinctive features of the current delinquency: the advanced decline in adult participation in the forming and maintaining of neighborhood policy, particularly with respect to the hour-to-hour activities of the adolescent, and the apparently easy accessibility of dangerous weapons. We may also remark the juvenile's interest in the publicized exploits of otherwise unfamiliar criminal "heroes." Delinquency appears to have taken on an epidemic quality, and the criminal achievements of newly discovered offenders invite appraisal and emulation. In fact, the ever-efficient press actually facilitates the standardization of juvenile conduct, hence that of juvenile crime. It has, for example, become altogether common for informal, small and inexperienced groups of juveniles spontaneously to attempt dangerous, violent sorties of the kind formerly reserved for the most desperate criminals: we hear every day of unbelievable crimes motivated by pure whim.

Although it would be madness to refuse to admit the threat posed by juvenile gangs and their responsibility for their own crimes, it would be a serious blunder to imagine that increasing the severity of penalties for juvenile criminals will in any way reduce their activity. Similar measures have not affected senior crime. Given the mentality of the juvenile types I have been trying to describe, such measures can only serve to make their lives more daring and more exciting, without at all disturbing the solidarity of their society. Punishment, then, is a force somewhat misapplied, since it aims at restraining the juvenile and not at recovering his allegiance. But it is precisely this allegiance that the adult world has lost.

CHAPTER FIFTEEN

Education

EDUCATION, like any other social institution, is sensitive to social change. Havighurst points out that this relationship has three aspects: (1) education helps to transmit traditional culture patterns; (2) it is an instrument for bringing about changes which society desires; and (3) in its search for truth it initiates change.

The current debate on education in America was brought to a focus by the question, "How did the Russians beat us into space?" We are told that American education must measure up to its responsibilities and meet the threat to our national security, and to our internal harmony and progress. Simmons' article shows that the Russians are also busy reassessing their educational goals. The Soviet educational system, which won the admiration of many Americans, has lately undergone complete revision as directed by Khrushchev and the Central Committee of the Communist Party.

[30] How Education Changes Society*

by ROBERT J. HAVIGHURST

When the future historian writes of the twentieth century, he will probably call it the century of world-wide social change. He will describe the hopes and frustrations, the visions and bewilderment of people who were caught up in the process, some desiring change and some resisting it.

While change is not a new thing in the world, there is a new modern element, which did not play an important role in the processes of social change in previous times. This new element is education. The notion of education as productive of change is a modern notion. This paper will explore some of the relations of education to change in the modern world, and touch on the basic question of the degree and manner of the *causal* action of education in the processes of change.

In discussing the influence of education on a society it would be well to begin by defining education broadly as that which the society teaches its young so as to enable them to be successful adults. Thus every society has a system of education, though it may not have specific educational institutions like our own schools and universities.

Education is carried on in all societies by the family and by religious, political and economic institutions; these will be called the "basic social institutions" in this discussion. Generally, as societies become more complex, they develop specific educational institutions to carry on some of the educational functions which in simpler societies were fulfilled by the basic social institutions. The education provided by schools, colleges and universities will be called *formal* education to distinguish it from the *informal* education carried on by these other institutions.

Education, when seen in relation to society, has two general aspects. First, it is a stabilizer or perpetuator of the society, and second, it is an agent for change. As a stabilizer, education mirrors what is already in the society and reflects it into the lives of the next generation. As an agent of change, education acts under the direction of technological or ideological forces to make each generation different from its parent.

The stabilizing, culture-perpetuating function of education is best seen in the simple societies which have not developed specialized educational institutions. Examples are to be found in the American Southwest, where the ancient and almost unchanging Pueblo Indian cultures exist side by

* Reprinted from *Confluence: An International Forum*, Spring, 1957 (Vol. VI, No. 1), pp. 85-96 *passim*. By permission of the publisher.

side with the dynamic American culture, and where many of the Pueblo Indians participate in both cultures. One of these Pueblo Indians, a member of the Hopi tribe who was born about 1890, has given us his autobiography.[1] This man received the traditional Hopi education as a young boy and then was sent to a government board school where he got a white man's education. He speaks of his early education, obtained through his family and the other basic social institutions, as follows:

Learning to work was like play. We children tagged around with our elders and copied what they did. We followed our fathers to the fields and helped plant and weed. The old men took us for walks and taught us the uses of plants and how to collect them. We joined the women in gathering rabbitweed for baskets, and went with them to dig clay for pots. We would taste this clay as the women did to test it. We watched the fields to drive out the birds and rodents, helped pick peaches to dry in the sun, and gathered melons to lug up the mesa. We rode the burros to harvest corn, gather fuel, or herd sheep. In house-buildings we helped a little by bringing dirt to cover the roofs. In this way we grew up doing things. All the old people said that it was a disgrace to be idle and that a lazy boy should be whipped.

The boy, who was later to fill the important position of Sun Chief, when he was six or seven years old went through the first initiation, in which all Hopi children learn the simplest of the religious mysteries. Before that he had received some of his early moral education through the visits of Katcinas (villagers disguised as supernatural beings). Of this he says:

I saw some giantlike Katcinas stalking into the village with long black bills and big sawlike teeth. One carried a rope to lasso disobedient children. He stopped at a certain house and called for a boy. 'You have been naughty' he scolded. 'You fight with other children. You kill chickens. You pay no attention to the old people. We have come to get you and eat you.' The boy cried and promised to behave better. The giant became angrier and threatened to tie him up and take him away. But the boy's parents begged for his life and offered fresh meat in his place. The giant reached out his hand as if to grab the boy but took the meat instead. Placing it in his basket, he warned the boy that he would get just one more chance to change his conduct. I was frightened and got out of sight. I heard that sometimes these giants captured boys and really ate them.

We can see how deeply the traditional, non-changing Hopi culture was implanted in the boy by the family and the other basic social institutions, thereby enabling him to do his share in carrying on the culture unchanged.

The same culture-perpetuating function is present in the highly-developed educational systems of modern societies, and especially in the

[1] L. W. Simmons, Editor, *Sun Chief* (New Haven, Conn., Yale University Press, 1942), pp. 45, 51-2.

elementary schools, which teach the traditional reading, writing and arithmetic, and the basic loyalties to family, community and nation.

Education is seen most clearly in its other aspect—as an agent of change—after a successful revolution, when the revolutionary government seeks to use it to re-form the society in its own revolutionary image. For instance, the Russian Revolution of 1917 was followed by a widespread use of adult education and by a reformation of the schools. Since the Communist regime did not trust the Church and to some extent mistrusted the Russian family, it removed the teaching function entirely from the Church and as far as possible from the family. The State, collaborating with the Labor Unions, reorganized the formal education of the country and supplied a corps of teachers who were in sympathy with the revolutionary purposes.

A society that is changing in a slower, evolutionary way also uses education to promote change; in fact, it relies on education more fully than does a revolutionary society, which has other more drastic means of bringing about the desired changes. To see how formal education is related to these various aspects of change in the basic social institutions, we will have to modify the simple distinction already made between education as a perpetuator of society and education as an agent for change. Formal education in a contemporary society is not one or the other of these— it is both of them at the same time. In some areas of culture education works for change, while in other areas it may resist or ignore change.

The kinds of social change most effectively promoted by education are those (1) which can be taught readily, and (2) which the society generally approves. Therefore new kinds of technical skills and knowledge and new occupational techniques are readily introduced through education into a society, as also are new material modes of living. For instance, the training of engineers and medical practitioners has changed greatly, with general social approval. And the use of automobiles, of electrical gadgets in the home and of vitamin pills are examples of social changes for which education is effectively used.

The areas of social change least open to educational influence are those in which there is (1) a taboo, or (2) a controversy. As an example of taboo, let us take sex relations. It seems clear that social and physical relations between the sexes have changed a great deal in the past century in the Western civilization, and are changing rapidly now. But formal education has generally either neglected this area or has taught conservatively so as to preserve the older forms of sex relations.

An example of the difficulty of using education to promote social change in areas of controversy is seen in the conflict over foreign policy in the

United States. This is an area in which education could and should play
a large part; certainly there have been major efforts to use education as
an agent of change, especially through adult education projects such as
those of the American Foreign Policy Association and through courses
given in universities and colleges. But the secondary schools in many communities have been prevented from being entirely candid in their treatment of international relations because the subject is controversial. As a
result, the teacher either ignores this area or treats it "safely"—which generally means conservatively and in such a way as to avoid change. . . .

The modern national State uses education to change itself—and this,
too, is a comparatively recent phenomenon. The nation-states which began to arise in the sixteenth century in Europe achieved unity through
political and military rather than educational means. Then, with the coming of the industrial revolution, the national states were caught up in vast
social changes profoundly affecting their rapidly growing populations.
This was the signal for the development of national systems of education,
aimed to make the people literate and more efficient both as workers and
citizens, and to inculcate national loyalties. At first the national governments ventured gingerly into the field of formal education, limiting themselves to assisting the Church and various philanthropic educational
organizations to provide a free education for the children of the poor. This
was the practice of the British Government in the first half of the nineteenth century, and was elequently supported by John Stuart Mill in his
Essay on Liberty, where he argued that the State should limit itself so
far as possible to enforcing universal education, while the family and the
Church provided this education in a wide variety of ways which would
guarantee individual liberty. He cited objections against State education,
saying, "that the whole or any large part of the education of the people
should be in State hands, I go as far as any one in deprecating. All that
has been said of the importance of individuality of character and diversity
of opinions and modes of conduct, involves, as of the same unspeakable
importance, diversity of education. A general State education is a mere
contrivance for making people to be exactly like one another: and as the
mould in which it casts them is that which pleases the predominant power
in the government, whether this be a monarch, a priesthood, an aristocracy, or the majority of the existing generation, in proportion as it is
efficient and successful, it establishes a despotism over the mind leading
by natural tendency to one over the body." [2]

Despite the logic of this reasoning, it seems quaint today, when every

[2] John Stuart Mill, edited by R. B. McCallum, *On Liberty* (Oxford, Basil Blackwell,
1946), p. 95.

national state provides a general State education which is regarded as an essential part of the task of maintaining a successful government, whether it be a democracy or some other type. The national state operates within a changing society, and uses education to adapt its people to change and to control change in favor of the values of the society. . . .

The economic institutions of a society also use education to effect change. Industry looks to the educational system for the training of workers who will be adaptable to change and for the education of its professional workers—engineers, scientists and business administrators who are the key personnel in modern industrial development. Furthermore, industry uses educational means to train its own personnel for the specific jobs they will perform. Thus a giant corporation like the International Harvester Company, doing business throughout the world, maintains a kind of private university for training its employees for important executive and sales positions.

It is clear that formal education, in school or university, is an essential instrument for the promotion of change in a changing society, and is so used by the basic institutions of family, church, government and economy. On the other hand, a society which is not changing rapidly, such as that of Medieval Europe, employs education primarily as a stabilizer to perpetuate the status quo. Such a society has less use for formal education than does the society which is "on the march."

Formal education is most fully used to promote social change in the modern urban industrial societies. To see the reason for this it is useful to look at Brazil, a great nation passing through changes which Europe and North America have already known. From its colonization in the early sixteenth century until it became a republic at the close of the nineteenth century, Brazil made its living by extracting things from the earth and exporting them—brazil wood, sugar, gold, diamonds, coffee, rubber, cotton. This was done by a small aristocracy and a large working class consisting mainly of slaves. During all that time, education tended to preserve this type of social structure. About 1900, Brazil began to industrialize rapidly, a process which was hastened by the two World Wars. With this came the growth of large cities, the movement of population from the country to the industrial centers, and most important of all, the development of a middle class of professional and managerial people who were *educated* for their leading roles. Thus a modern system of education became essential to Brazil's development into a modern industrial nation. In Russia there is a variation on the same theme in the rise of a class of educated managers and technical experts who spearhead the social changes. The political structure in which the changes operate is different from that of most other countries, but the goal is the same. . . .

The argument so far has tended to indicate that the forces making for change in a society operate *through* education but not as a planned result of it. For instance, when technology develops to the point where it needs more engineers, the educational system produces more engineers. But the educators do not of their own accord get together with the industrialists and decide whether in the interest of society there should be more engineers at some future date.

Generally speaking, the formal education of a society mirrors and reflects what is already in the society, including those forces and movements making for change. Thus one might think of education as simply an instrumentality, a set of processes that go on in schools and universities and the minds of men in response to the decisions of powerful people who themselves are moved by changes which demand action.

This seems to be very true of the Technical Assistance programs by which a number of nations are now changing themselves. Through the Technical Assistance Program of the United Nations, and the analogous programs of various nations including England, Russia and the United States, the leaders of the less developed countries are deliberately creating change in their own societies. Much "technical assistance" is essentially education: either training people to carry on certain new methods of working or educating the general public to follow new modes of living. The government of Puerto Rico, for example, in planning major improvements in the lives of its people, uses education to help achieve them. . . .

Yet it is not the whole truth to say that education operates as an instrumentality for change after the decision has already been taken that change is desirable. There is also a drive for change implicit in education as we know it today. Schools and universities present facts and ideas to their students; ideas are active. Research workers discover new knowledge; knowledge gives power. Who can say that the idea of an electromagnetic field which occurred to physicists in the early nineteenth century and gave rise to the electric generator was not more influential in promoting social change than any act of government or the formation of any great industrial enterprise? Einstein's equation which asserts the equivalence of energy and matter was only an idea for a good many years, but it was a necessary idea on the road to the discovery of the secret of releasing atomic energy. These great and fruitful ideas were at one and the same time the products of changing times and the products of men's minds. They were not produced through any planned process.

Education certainly is capable of originating change as well as of promoting changes already planned. But perhaps it must always originate change blindly, as seems to have been the case in the past. The human intellect, when working in an educational milieu and focussing either on the physical world, the social world or the world of ideas, has always come out with some new truth, and the new truth has very often worked to change the society. It seems a reasonable conclusion that under present conditions education will always work for change, whether in the industrial processes of a society, its religious beliefs, its esthetic standards or other areas of life.

In working for material improvement, education will be performing a well-accepted and relatively well-understood function in society. But in discovering new truth which makes for change in the non-material aspects of life, education will operate somewhat blindly, the results of its influence will not be easily foreseen, and it will enter into controversial areas.

Can education be so organized and directed as to prevent social change and to perpetuate or stabilize a particular social order or social structure?

Education certainly is used successfully to conserve traditional values. But in modern society this very act of conserving values seems to require changes in society which are fostered by education. For example, to conserve certain values of the family in a changing society it may be necessary to change certain things in the family. To conserve and to achieve the values of democracy it may be necessary to change modern societies in far-reaching ways.

Two general statements can be made about education in relation to social change. First, education is a powerful instrument for social change in a society which knows what kinds of changes it wants. Generally, such changes are in technology and in material modes of living. The contemporary Technical Assistance programs work for such changes in the less-developed countries.

Second, education as the search for truth also results in social change, but generally such changes are not planned in advance, and sometimes they are not welcomed by the people and groups of people who are in power.

There seems to be no place in the world today where education is simply a perpetuator of traditional ways of behaving and believing. The world is caught up in a vast and varied process of change, in which education may be either instrument or originator.

[31]   *The Change in Soviet Schooling**

by ERNEST J. SIMMONS

"Chekhov was loved and is loved not only by Russians, but also by Western readers," recited Galya, a ninth-grade student in a Leningrad school. "The famous foreign writer, Dresden . . ."

The class pricked up its ears. The teacher looked inquiringly at Galya. "No, I mean Dryden."

Her classmates began to smile.

"Perhaps you mean Dreiser?" the teacher asked.

"No, it's someone else, but I've forgotten who," Galya replied in some embarrassment.

The teacher, reporting this incident in a recent article in *Izvestia*, explained that Galya really had in mind Bernard Shaw.

"You should be ashamed of yourself," the teacher admonished. "Not knowing Shaw!"

"What do I need to know that for?" Galya defiantly asked. "I'll be going to work in a factory all the same. I have no use for literature."

Galya's plaint may well be echoed by countless Soviet school children who are now destined to work in factories or on collective farms in order to justify their claims to a higher education in this land where the intellectual is more revered than the movie actress or sports champion. In fact, the sweeping changes in education which have recently been announced may turn out to be more significant for the Soviet future than the orbiting of the first Sputnik.

The Soviets have always regarded education as a matter of supreme importance for the future of the state and have lavishly supported its development. After the progressive experimentation of the early years of revolutionary upsurge, education settled down to a national pattern in the 1930's. A profound utilitarian emphasis dominated the pattern: boys and girls were encouraged to think of education as a means of acquiring skills desperately needed by the state in its drive to achieve industrial reconstruction and agricultural collectivization. Hundreds of technical schools and institutes to educate specialists sprang up.

The efficacy of Soviet scientific education is really the fruit of some thirty

---

* From *The Atlantic Monthly*, October, 1959, pp. 74-76. Reprinted by permission of the author.

years of intense emphasis on such studies. Honors and attractive material rewards were held out to those who made a career of science. The 250,000 scientists now at work in the Soviet Union and the 94,000 engineers who graduated in 1958, more than twice as many as did in the United States, offer some measure of Soviet success over the years in popularizing science education.

A strong note of dissatisfaction with the prevailing system of education was first heard at the 20th Party Congress in 1956. Instruction was divorced from life, speakers declared, and graduates had little notion of the importance of socially useful labor. Decisions were taken to introduce polytechnical education in the ten-year schools. Students in the fifth to seventh grades were assigned two hours a week in school workshops and those in the eighth to tenth grades two hours a week of practical training in agriculture and industry. Further, applicants to institutions of higher learning were informed that preference would be given to those who had already achieved a record of employment in manual labor.

In addition, an experiment in fifty ten-year schools in 1957 called for three days a week of regular studies and three days of application to a job specialty of the student's selection. With the cooperation of industrial plants and, in rural areas, of collective farms, students learned to read blueprints and were trained to be universal-lathe operators, patternmakers, electricians, winders, draftsmen, and designers. They then continued their formal education over an eleventh year, but spent half of their time in regular employment at the plant in their acquired trades.

Results of the experiment were praised on every hand. Teachers claimed that student participation in the work and in all the activities of the plant had a beneficial effect on their studies, especially on their science courses, in which they did much better than the average in examinations. The directors of plants asserted that the students acquired occupational skills faster than workers without a secondary-school education, students were gratified by this dual participation in learning and practical work, and parents were convinced that their children displayed a new interest in the process of being educated.

Encouraged by the success of these preliminary experiments, inner circles of the Party decided upon a comprehensive reorganization of the whole national system of education. Khrushchev himself sounded the keynote in a ringing speech at the 13th Congress of the Young Communist League on April 18, 1959. He pointed out that, because institutions of higher learning can admit approximately 450,000 a year, and only half of these to full-time study, some 2,200,000 secondary-school graduates between 1953 and 1956 could not qualify for advanced education. Yet they knew nothing about work in industry and agriculture.

Khrushchev called for the introduction of vocational training, with direct work experience, in all the ten-year schools and evening courses. Institutions of higher learning should be reorganized, he said, so that their programs would involve a combination of theoretical study and extensive work, manual or otherwise, though preferably in the student's own specialties. And these institutions should admit only students with labor records. It is wrong in principle and foreign to socialist society, he pointedly declared, to believe that only second-raters go into industry. Such reasoning is insulting to toilers. "All children entering school," he concluded, "must prepare themselves for useful labor, for participation in building a Communist society."

With customary unanimity, government educational authorities promptly supported the leader's position. In September, Khrushchev made a detailed report to the Presidium of the Central Committee of the Party on the need to reorganize the educational system, and two months later the Central Committee and the U.S.S.R. Council of Ministers published "The Party and Government Theses on School Reforms." The objectives as well as various details of the "Theses" were then discussed in numerous public meetings, in hundreds of articles and letters in the press, and in many speeches at the 21st Congress of the Communist Party. Finally, in December, the Supreme Soviet voted "The Law on Strengthening Ties Between School and Life." It called for initiating the reforms in 1959 and 1960 and for the completion of them within three to five years.

New study plans have already been formulated which require establishment of a compulsory eight-year school of general education instead of the old seven-year school. Substantial changes will be made in the usual general education courses: more time will be allotted to foreign language study, and its primary goal will be the acquisition of oral speech skills; the old geography course is being expanded, and new courses are being added in natural history and natural science; students will also be given a wider knowledge of mathematics, in which special attention will be paid to computing techniques and the solution of practical problems, and the physics course will be altered to include extensive material of an applied nature that will serve as a theoretical foundation for the study of such subjects as machine building and the fundamentals of electrical engineering.

The total program of the eight-year school will devote a third of the student's time to what is described as "training for socially useful labor." Among other things, the program will include the acquisition of elementary knowledge about major branches of production; skills in measuring, computing, reading of blueprints, and processing the most common materials; and manual work in study shops and on training-and-experimental sectors. From the third grade on there will be two hours a week of such work as cleaning classrooms and school grounds, repairing furniture, and working in school lunchrooms and libraries. In addition, home economics courses will provide instruction to girls from the fifth to the eighth grades in dressmaking, sewing, and cooking, and to boys in the fifth grade on how to take care of homes, clothing, and footwear.

The new study plans provide for continuity between the eight-year school and the new three-year labor-polytechnical high school. The content of the science courses on the secondary level, however, will be substantially changed to include the latest developments in science and technology. In general, more attention will be paid to the study of plastics, artificial and synthetic fibers, and rubber, and in the biology course emphasis will be placed on practical problems of agriculture and the latest achievements in agronomy.

As in the eight-year school, about one third of the total time from the ninth through the eleventh grades is assigned to the study of vocational training and production labor. Students will perfect their vocational training by working directly at industrial enterprises or on collective farms and in basic, not auxiliary jobs, and engineers, technicians, farm directors, agronomists, and skilled workers will be in charge of training them.

A network of evening schools and correspondence courses will provide ambitious graduates of the eight-year schools with essentially the same education as that of the three-year polytechnical schools. The organization of such evening schools will allow students to work full time as they learn. And similarly, evening programs in higher education will be offered to workers who have completed their secondary-school education. In fact, one of the main intentions of the whole reorganization plan is to make day and evening education on every level beyond the compulsory eight-year school virtually interchangeable in content, standards, and staff. The total picture projected by the reorganization is that of a whole nation continuously involved with improving itself by education, either day or night; but in this process study must always be combined with labor.

The law offers special privileges for those who elect to complete their higher education while working. Those in applied science fields which initially require a knowledge of complicated theoretical subjects and a heavy schedule of laboratory experience will be allowed to take time out from employment during the first two or three years. Thereafter, however, they will be expected to complete their education while engaged in practical work in staff jobs in production, laboratories, or design bureaus. In training agricultural specialists, the educational programs will be conducted in institutes organized on the basis of large state farms which possess model instructional facilities and where the farm work will be done by the students themselves.

The future scientists, economists, philosophers, lawyers, and literary scholars will also be compelled by law to acquire "a certain amount of experience in socially useful labor," which may not necessarily have any relation to their special fields of study. Even for medical students, instruction must be "combined with continuous practical work in medical and prophylactic institutions or institutions of hygiene."

The prolongation of the whole period of formal education, an inevitable consequence of combining employment with learning, is in no sense regarded as a disadvantage by the Soviets, who argue that the completion of formal education at a more mature age will prove beneficial to the majority of young people.

The only exceptions recognized are gifted students whose unusual abilities in the arts and sciences are manifested early in life. The reorganization plan will encourage them to finish their formal education as soon as possible and then qualify for special schools in mathematics, the natural sciences, and the arts. But even these students will be expected, while learning, to engage in a certain amount of "socially useful labor."

The reasoning supporting the educational reorganization is studded with statements concerning the need of training a people capable of developing and keeping abreast of future advances in automation, electronics, synthetic chemistry, and atomic energy. Vast labor reserves will be required if the goals of the new economic Seven Year Plan are to be achieved. But millions of students who finished their education at the end of the old seven-year schools or even ten-year schools and entered the labor force are now regarded as inadequately trained to cope with the future demands for technically skilled workers. The educational reorganization is designed to eliminate this deficiency on all levels. Soviet leaders are also aware of the economic gain to the country that would result from having all students employed while they are learning.

As the standard of living has risen, the Party leaders have become increasingly worried about the growing cleavage between the privileged managerial and intellectual class and the working classes. For the children of this privileged class, education has meant a way of avoiding manual labor and of developing ideas and tastes incompatible with Communist ideology and morality. The student disturbances at the time of the Polish and Hungarian uprisings signified to Party leaders that education was failing to inculcate in youth a proper respect for the grand design of Communism and an unwillingness to abide by the Party blueprint of Soviet life. The main cause of this failure, it was argued, was a contempt for toil. The antidote, Party leaders reasoned, was to make toil a prescribed function of all forms of education in the conviction that extensive contact with workers on the part of students would temper them and assure their loyalty to Communist ideals. "This way," declared Khrushchev in his speech to the Young Communist League, "it will no longer be possible to say that Vanya, for instance, does not have to go in for industry, while Kolya here has no other choice."

failing to inculcate in youth a proper respect for the grand design of Communism and an unwillingness to abide by the Party blueprint of Soviet life. The main cause of this failure, it was argued, was a contempt for toil. The antidote Party leaders demanded was to make toil a prescribed function of all forms of education in the conviction that extensive contact with workers on the part of students would temper them and assure their loyalty to Communist ideals. Thus, say, declared Khrushchev in his speech to the Young Communist League, "it will no longer be possible to say that Vanya, for instance, does not have to go to the factory, while Kolya here has no other choice."

PART THREE

Economic Organization and Social Problems

CHAPTER SIXTEEN

Economic Behavior and Its organization

M AN *must meet his basic economic needs for food, clothing, and shelter in order to survive. Over the centuries his economic activities and his methods of organizing them have changed, but in all societies people are still faced with the necessity of earning a living.*

In "Economics and Economic Wants" Weiler and Martin answer such questions as, What does economics *mean? Who makes economic decisions? and What determines our economic wants? Nordin and Salera explain the importance of planning in every society. They also suggest that individuals with a tradition of liberty will prefer to avoid both the "jungle" of little or no planning and the "jail" of complete central planning. Rostow, in the third selection, analyzes the developments necessary for a country to enter a period of sustained economic growth.*

[32] Economics and Economic Wants*

by E. T. WEILER and W. H. MARTIN

"The poetry of earth is never dead," sang the poet of long ago. And a significant part of the ceaseless poetry of earth is the never-ending activity of mankind associated merely with "making a living." The world over, from the beginning of time, men have had to combine the resources at their disposal to provide for themselves the means of livelihood and the additional comforts that they desire. In some times and places, the result has meant little more than the mere material requirements of subsistence; at others, it has meant a different scale of living far above the "subsistence" level for the bulk of the population. The effectiveness of economic activity is reflected in the living standards of the people.

Why is it that some societies have been able to achieve higher living standards than others? This is one of the important questions which we plan to investigate later. But first let us see, in a broader fashion, what is involved in the study of economics.

Economics has been defined as the study of that part of human behavior associated with the activities of "making a living." But such a definition does not limit our subject matter by very much because so many activities are associated with making a living. The housewife, for example, when she purchases her week's supply of groceries, is engaged in economic activity; not only is she acquiring a portion of the economy's output, but her purchases also directly affect employment opportunities in the food-producing industries. The father who selects Christmas toys for his children makes an economic decision; he indicates that a part of the nation's economic resources shall be used to produce toys rather than the topcoat which he has decided not to buy.

The comprehensive character of the study of economics has been indicated by Alfred Marshall, one of the great economists of the past:

Political Economy or Economics is a study of mankind in the ordinary business of life; it examines that part of individual and social action which is most closely connected with the attainment and with the use of the material requisites of well-being.

Broad as Marshall's definition is, it does serve to indicate the point of view from which economic behavior is approached. After all, such activi-

* From Weiler and Martin, *The American Economic System*, pp. 3-8, *passim*. © 1957 by E. T. Weiler, W. H. Martin, and used with the permission of The Macmillan Company.

ties as buying and selling could be studied from the point of view of the social psychologist, who may be interested in the development of group habits. Or they could be studied by the sociologist, who would be interested in the development of economic institutions and their effect on group living. In the study of economics we are interested in human behavior as it affects "the material requisites of well-being" (as Marshall put it) of society.

The outstanding feature of economic well-being, in the eyes of economists, is that there has never been enough food, clothing and housing so that everybody might have all that he wanted. Even with our own highly productive economy operating at the level of full-employment, having more clothing means having less food, and having more cars and highways means having fewer schools and hospitals. To be sure, there are times when shortages of goods are due in part to the malfunctioning of the economy, as when we are plagued by depression and unemployment. But speaking more generally, such shortages are due to the scarcities of economic resources such as human labor, capital and natural resources. As a society, we must *economize* in the amount of labor and other resources used to produce clothing in order to have more of other products such as food. Our limited resources will not permit us to have as much of both as we would prefer. So, economics may be thought of as the study of human behavior from the point of view of the material well-being of mankind, where such well-being is limited by the availability of economic resources.

Economists, as Economists, Are Not Concerned with Questions of "Ought." Now economics, and for that matter, all the social and natural sciences, are essentially descriptive. Their purpose is to describe so completely that it will be possible to say, "If A should occur, then B will follow." There is nothing in the study of economics which tells us what *ought* to be, what kinds of goods people ought to want, what kind of world is best to live in, or what ends in life should be valued most highly. These are problems of a philosophical nature, problems which can be answered only by reference to philosophical and religious propositions regarding the nature of man and his needs.

An example may be in order. Suppose that a comprehensive "cradle-to-the-grave" social security system were proposed and that economists were called upon to make an appaisal of it. As *economists* they might state that the proposed scheme would have a certain effect on the way the economy would operate. They might be willing to hazard a guess about its effect on the total output of the economy. But as *economists* it would not be their place to say whether or not it should be adopted. For the sake of argument let us assume that the economists could demonstrate rather conclusively that the enactment into law of such a comprehensive social security system would reduce the output of the economy by, let us say, $100 per capita. The basic question would still remain: Which is better, more personal security and less output, or less personal security and more output? This question is essentially a philosophical one, involving as it does an opinion as to which is better for man, security or wealth. Society, and not the economists, must make the choice.

Another way of putting the same thing is to say that economics is primarily concerned with means and not with ends. Once the ends are given (the result of social decisions), the economist is in a position to give advice as to how they can best be achieved—how, for example, the resources of a nation can be best used to fight a war, to build pyramids, or to alleviate poverty.

The Family Is the Basic Social Unit in Our Society. Although the economist does not pass judgment on the ultimate aims or values of society, he must nevertheless take account of them. In many cases, such values become basic data for the study of economic phenomena. For instance, as our society is presently constituted, the family is the fundamental social unit. We are first and foremost likely to consider ourselves members of families before we consider ourselves to belong to any other kind of social unit. Although this is a characteristic of our own society, it need not, of course, be true of all societies. It is easy to imagine, for example, a society (in fact such societies do exist) where the care and training of the young are entrusted to groups composed especially for the purpose, rather than to let such tasks devolve upon the biological parents of the children. Our society has made a choice, proceeding from the values of a more or less "basic" philosophical scheme, which is different in fundamental respects from the basic philosophies which govern social organization in other societies. And, of course, even in our own society the role assigned to the family changes continuously as the introduction of new cultural elements alters the structure of "basic" values. It is true, nevertheless, that the family is the fundamental social unit of our present society.

Individual Choice Is Given a High Priority in Our Society. Our society, too, places a rather high value on individual choice in human behavior. To be sure, freedom of choice is circumscribed by the requirements of the laws, customs, and traditions of the society, but within the limits thus imposed there remains a wide area of choice regarding the social behavior of individual persons and individual families. But again, the degree of individual choice permitted by society is not something fixed and given for all times and places. In some societies a great variety of social decisions are made by political leaders; in other societies these same decisions are made by citizens acting for themselves, or at least independently of a central political authority. In our own society, of course, the degree of freedom permitted to individual choice is subject to change, which is sometimes rather rapid, with the alteration of underlying social values. Even so, we accept as a characteristic of our present-day society that its values are such as to permit a relatively wide latitude of choice to the individual. . . .

An Economy Provides the Goods and Services Wanted by the Community. We accept as a starting point that, in a society whose major values correspond to our own, the eventual purpose of economic activity is to meet the needs, or "wants," of the society. Now, we do not picture the specific wants of persons as something inherent in all mankind. The particular wants of the members of a community are themselves socially determined. A family wants what it does because it is living within a society which includes other families. Even the so-called necessities turn out to be no such thing at all on close examination. As members of a society, families do not want simply food, clothing, and shelter; they want particular *kinds* of food, of clothing, and of housing. And the kinds of each that they want depend to quite a large extent on such things as custom and fashion. To a degree that would be difficult to exaggerate, we want the things we do because of the values imposed on us by our associations with other persons.

The values which guide our wants depend also on what the economy is presently capable of producing. People did not "want" radios and refrigerators before such articles were produced by the economy (although they did want entertainment and ways of preserving foods). Economic wants and economic production are interrelated, that is to say, people "want" what the economy produces, as well as the other way around.

Thus, personal wants are not things sprung once and for all on the economy. Instead, wants change continuously in accord with continuously changing tastes and preferences, reflecting the changing values of society. Furthermore, our wants grow larger along with their more adequate satisfaction: it seems to be literally true that "the more we have, the more we want." And again this seems, partially at least, to reflect the values of our society. Where status and accomplishment are measured largely by a person's success in acquiring material things, it seems destined that wants shall ever outrun the means of satisfying them.

The question as to how peoples' values and wants are influenced by the society in which they live is a significant area of study in itself, but one which we as economists shall say little about. In any event, it is clear why economic organization is of crucial importance to our modern society: An economy must supply the goods and services needed to meet as fully as possible the ever-changing wants which can never be completely satisfied. . . .

[33]   *Economic Planning**

by J. A. NORDIN and VIRGIL SALERA

You will have noted the extensive use of economic planning in the contemporary world. Individuals, firms, groups of firms, and nations actually must plan economic activity. This does *not* mean that there must be full-blown and nation-wide economic planning by an all-powerful bureaucracy in Washington. Far from it.

By economic planning we mean individual or social action taken to determine economic goals, and the selection and use of means to attain these goals. In this sense, even the most rugged individualist is an economic planner. He decides what it is that he wishes to achieve economically—be it the exploitation of oil-bearing sands in a barren part of the state of Wyoming or the development of a chain of self-service gasoline stations in Los Angeles. After deciding what to do, he must find effective means of accomplishing his objective. His planning may or may not be successful in the economic sense. His undertaking involves more or less risk of loss. For instance, his attempts to find oil in Wyoming may result in only one more dry hole, well lined with the finest steel pipe that money can buy. But he has had the advice of geophysicists and old-timers in the petroleum business. In risking some or all of his capital in this drilling operation, he is one cog in a giant machine that allocates our resources without centralized control.

* From J. A. Nordin and Virgil Salera, *Elementary Economics,* pp. 826-831. © 1950, Prentice-Hall, Inc., Englewood Cliffs, N.J. Reprinted by permission.

The economic planning that most people hear about, and that is so derisively lampooned in some newspapers is, of course, that of Soviet communism and some forms of socialism. We have said, however, that economic planning includes even the actions of individuals in a so-called free enterprise economy. Economic planning is involved, then, all the way from economies that are capitalistic to those that are fascistic or communistic. This does not mean that there are no differences among the economic planning operations involved in these cases. The differences are, in fact, very great. In general, we may say that the differences lie in the (*a*) purposes, (*b*) degree, and (*c*) implementation of planning.

The Purposes of Economic Planning.   There are a number of purposes for which individuals, groups, and nations plan their activities. Let us describe them briefly. First, they may plan in order to control their private economic operations or to achieve a technically more efficient plant. These are the planning activities of individuals and firms. The operations are planned in order to avoid aimless drift or a hit-or-miss approach to production. Hence plans are drawn, with the aid of engineers and other technicians, and attempts are made to conform to the plan while carrying out the project that is involved. Planning with respect to plant size is mainly an engineering problem. This includes the selection of different kinds of equipment, power facilities, plant layout, and so forth.

Second, planning may be undertaken to release the constructive powers of individuals and to suppress their predatory tendencies. Illustrative of such planning is political action in the form of constitutional guarantees against seizure of property acquired legally by the individual, laws against theft, fraudulent business behavior, and the antitrust laws. The purpose of such planning is to give rein to the full and free expression of individual talent.

Third, planning may be undertaken for the purpose of increasing community well-being and thus, indirectly, the nation's economic productivity. Such planning takes many forms in the United States. For example, consider city planning to avoid blighted areas and slums. We have zoning ordinances that help to accomplish this objective. Other ordinances sometimes exist to insure that there will be enough safe streets for children, plenty of ventilation in residences, properly located community shopping centers, ample park space in each residential area, well constructed homes, and the amenities of life in each neighborhood. Cities planned this way have lower juvenile delinquency rates, lower accident rates, a more healthy population, a more contented people, and a record of high productivity. To date, we have only scratched the surface in this field of planning.

Fourth, there may be planning to shape the course of a national economy by essentially impersonal means. In this type of planning, the individual as such is not subject to direct restrictions by government. Monetary, fiscal and public works policies are perhaps the best examples of planning undertaken for this purpose. The aim of such policies, as we have seen, is to limit the swings of business activity, employment, and production over the years. This is conspicuous planning, but it is a relatively small part of total planning activity in the economy. The great bulk of the nation's planning is carried out by individuals and firms on a truly decentralized basis. Individual responsibility is great, centralized planning modest.

Fifth, we may have centralized planning of basic industries. When this is carried out under public ownership, the system is essentially that of socialism. Most of the planning is centralized. Only the relatively unimportant units of economic activity are left to operate on the basis of decentralized plans. Strictly private enterprise is confined to the field of small-scale business. But in the aggregate, private business may make up more than half of the economy.

Finally, the purpose of planning may be to lodge in the hands of a small dictatorial group full control over every aspect of a nation's economic life. Planning is fully centralized and private activity nonexistent in the economic field.

The Degree of Economic Planning. Our discussion of the purposes of planning has indicated somewhat the degree of planning that can exist under different economic systems. It is obvious that the six purposes for which planning may be used differ greatly in the degree of centralized planning involved. When the planning is by the individual or the firm, there are numerous planning units but each has little, if any, control over the activities of other individuals and firms. Resource allocation occurs under the influence of impersonal market forces, and the variety and quantity of production and the income of producers are governed in the last analysis by dollar votes cast in the stores and shops of the nation by consumers of all kinds.

At the other extreme, there are only a few subordinate planning units and one master unit at the top. Strict centralization of planning is characteristic. The nation's resources are allocated by the planning bureaucracy, and the distribution of the social product is also the result of central planning decisions. Consumer sovereignty, as we know it, is absent. Rather, consumers are given only limited money voting power in the stores. They are compelled to buy the type and quantity of goods that are made available as a result of bureaucratically planned production.

Implementation of Planning. We turn now to a discussion of the manner in which economic planning is carried out. It is obvious that the various degrees of economic planning involve different implementations. Individual and firm planning are based on personal self-interest, under a system which releases the constructive powers of individuals. It relies on the drives of individuals, each seeking his own ends. History and critical analysis both suggest that, under the system of private enterprise, the nation produces goods and services with great effectiveness. We all benefit from the immense store of widely scattered special experience and information in the economy. It is this fund of special knowledge, coupled with mobility of resources and the rapidity of adjustment to dynamic conditions, that makes for a very effective use of our resources. Such a system has one major weakness, however. General economic activity tends to proceed by jerks—with booms and depressions. As we have seen, appropriate measures of economic stabilization probably can eliminate or offset most of the disturbances of this kind.

In contrast, the system of centralized planning of the entire economy relies on a combination of planning skill and a tight discipline of the citizenry. It relies on the obedience of the citizen and not on the drives of the individual. Resources are committed to specific uses in advance so that there is a low mobility of resources over short periods. For the same reason, adjustment to dynamic conditions is slow. To the extent, however, that people are disciplined to carry out orders from the top, there tends to be only a small element of change that is not subject to control.

Even with the tightly disciplined citizenry of the police state, the centrally planned system does not necessarily grow in a well balanced manner. It is difficult to have the various industries grow at a synchronized pace. This is because each industry is forced to operate under a system of controlled prices, controlled investment, and controlled wages. If, as often happens, these prices, investment schedules, and wages get out of line with each other, there tends to be too much of some goods and too little of others. Such distortions are not quickly corrected. Corrective action, when taken, may easily err by producing a new set of distortions.

Under controlled capitalism, however, freedom of prices to move in response to market forces tends to insure balanced growth. Prices are continually changing in relation to one another. Such changes stimulate the output of one product and contract the production of another. The result is that the right amount of each product is available at the right time and place.

The Jungle and the Jail. As we have seen, the choice of modern man is not between planning and no-planning. There must be planning in the individual and social arenas. There is, however, one real and very important choice in the field of planning. It is how much centralized planning we want and how much individual responsibility we are to have.

There is, of course, individual responsibility in even the most centrally planned system, say, that of the Soviet Union. But the responsibility is limited in numerous ways. In particular, it is limited to minor details on the production front—to what may be referred to as the interest of the individual in having his cog in the production machine function well. The individual cannot undertake economic activity on his own, even if he should have a wonderful idea. He is not free to acquire the means of production. All he can do is contribute whatever skill he may have to a pool of labor and skill, after which his responsibility is limited by the requirement that a plan be fulfilled.

On the consumption side, individual responsibility is largely a matter of self-preservation—making the most of limited income to buy a restricted list of products. In effect, the individual's responsibility is restricted to a budgeting program. His consumption pattern cannot be shaped with an eye to undertaking, for example, an investment program. The situation is less extreme in a system of partial central planning, like some forms of socialism. Then the individual can consider both consumption and investment programs in the spending of his income. The broadened scope of his activities, compared with the system of completely centralized planning, tends to make for a greater individual responsibility.

The essential question of this age seems to be how much centralized planning is to be combined with the individual responsibility. It has been suggested that societies are moving in the direction of either the jungle or the jail. Citizens steeped in a tradition of individual liberty will prefer to avoid either of these extremes. In the jungle, of course, there is no central planning: There can be only individual planning, and then only under precarious and hazardous conditions. In a well run jail, on the other hand, individual planning is futile—escape routes are all blocked off. Should individual planning be successful, it will reflect only the weakness of the central (jail) plan. There are "wide open spaces" between the jungle and the jail. Probably the average American wants to put himself and his resources to fruitful and satisfying use in such spaces, steering clear of both extremes.

[34]   "Take-off" into Economic Growth*

interview with W. W. ROSTOW

Q *Prof. Rostow, what distinguishes a growing society from a nongrowing one?*

A What essentially distinguishes a growing society from a nongrowing one is its ability to produce and apply a regular flow of modern technology. Before this can happen, a great many prior changes must occur. There must be a prior revolution in agricultural productivity in order to supply food to the growing cities. There must be a big build-up of social overhead capital—schools, roads, health facilities, etc. And, usually, there must be some changes in production which will bring in more foreign exchange.

Q *In your recent book, "Stages of Economic Growth," you have described certain societies, where no sustained growth takes place, as "traditional" societies. What do such traditional societies have in common?*

A Traditional societies vary greatly from African tribes to the grand ebb and flow of the dynasties of China or the Roman Empire. These societies have not usually been static. Often they developed all the preconditions for growth "take-off"—except one. They improved their agriculture with irrigation. They built roads and other forms of social overhead capital. They engaged in trade and even did a certain amount of manufacturing. But what ultimately triggered their decline was the invariable absence of a scientific attitude toward the physical world, and a social and technical inability to *regularly* allocate first-rate talent to breaking the bottlenecks. In other words, they did not have a *flow* of modern technology.

Q *And this was the fatal flaw?*

A The fatal flaw, yes. Of course, many patterns have marked the crises of these traditional societies, but behind them lay the fact that they could not break through into a stage of economic development where technology could substitute for adequate supplies of land and meet the requirements of a growing population.

* From *Challenge* (May, 1960), pp. 30-37, a publication of the Institute of Economic Affairs, New York University. Reprinted by permission.

Q *Does this mean that there was no possibility of a take-off before you had industrial technology?*

A That is right. While growth is not a function of modern technology, *sustained* growth is.

Q *What changes have to take place before a traditional society is ready for the take-off?*

A From the time that a traditional society is intruded upon from the outside and the time it is ready for its take-off, enormously complex and revolutionary changes—social, political, economic and psychological—have to take place. While there are certain uniformities in the problems —technical, social and psychological—that have to be faced, the lesson of history is that every case is unique. Some societies, such as Japan, have found it possible, for largely accidental reasons of social structure and culture, to make the changes necessary for take-off rather quickly. Others had to go through a most terrible torment, like China from the time of the Opium Wars down to 1949.

Powerful Spreading Effects of the New Technology

Q *Let us assume that a society has reached a stage where it is ready for the take-off. What is involved in getting it off the launching pad, as it were?*

A What is required is not only that modern technology be applied to some leading set of economic factors but, even more important, that the society react positively to the powerful spreading effects of this new technology. Let me give you an example. The take-offs of the United States, France and Germany during the mid-19th century, and those of Canada and Russia shortly before World War I, all stemmed from railroads. Now, the railway potentially leads to growth take-off because it has a number of very important "spread" effects. Railways set up a demand for coal, iron and heavy engineering industries. Railways spread out into the countryside and, if the countryside responds, they can accelerate agricultural specialization.

Q *But railways have not always resulted in an economic take-off?*

A No, they have not. In China, India and Argentina, the development of railways did not lead to a take-off. If the society, in the widest sense, does not actively respond, the building of railways will not have these self-generating effects. Society must be equipped with a set of institutions and values capable of responding to modern technology.

Q *What does this involve?*

A It involves several things. First, there must be a group of private or public entrepreneurs able and willing to exploit the new possibilities of productive activity or profit set in motion by the new technology. There must also be an adequate core of trained people who can perform the technical jobs necessary to exploit these opportunities. Finally, there must be a government which, either actively (as is true in most cases) or passively (as was the case in Britain in the late 18th-century cotton textile take-off), will do all that is necessary to encourage the technological breakthrough.

Q *If all this is done, the chances are that such technological developments will spread into other sectors of the economy.*

A Correct. Modern techniques can spread backward—that is, they can stimulate old industries in the way that the railways encouraged the coal and iron industries. They can spread laterally—by setting up requirements for new cities and new social overhead capital. But most important, they can spread forward by creating new industries. In this way, the steel industry came into its own as a result of the need for steel rails when it was discovered that iron rails wore out too fast. Now, the leading sector in the take-off has varied widely—from textiles in England to railroads in the United States and Germany, to timber in Sweden, to import substitution industries in Argentina and India. Each society will have its own set of leading sectors depending on its resources and on the stage in technological history when it comes into the game.

Q *Most of the take-offs we have discussed so far took place in the 19th century. But the technology required for a similar take-off in mid-20th-century Southeast Asia may be quite different. If the leading sectors are no longer, say, railroads, but mass irrigation and power projects, does this call for a larger government initiative during the take-off period?*

A Let us get one thing clear. No country—not even Britain during the 18th century—has ever been able to get itself ready for take-off without the government playing a very large role. That role has varied, of course. In the case of the U.S., government played an extremely important role. Prior to the Civil War, most of the social overhead capital was built by the state and local governments rather than by the federal government. While we had less of an agricultural problem than most countries, since we had ample supplies of good land, we did devise a public land policy especially to exploit this resource. Moreover, our land-grant colleges were a conscious act of federal policy designed to improve our agricultural technology. And, of course, we had a deliberate foreign exchange policy in the form of protective tariffs. Similarly, government played an extremely important role in the preconditioning of 19th-century Canada, Czarist Russia and Meiji Japan.

Q *So the underdeveloped countries today follow this same process?*

A Yes, but in a more extended form. Only very unhistorical economists can argue that government played no role in Western take-offs, or that what we are now witnessing in underdeveloped countries is something new and ideologically peculiar.

The Responsibility of Industrialization

Q *Well, what other factors may determine the extent of government intervention during the take-off period?*

A A lot depends on whether you have a solid commercial middle class ready to move in and assume the responsibility of industrialization. Where such a middle class did not exist, as in Japan, Turkey and Czarist Russia, governments often initially took a direct hand in stimulating industry. But, contrary to the expectations of ideologists, it is not true (outside of Communist countries) that governments never relinquish their hold on a particular industry. Governments which are not compulsively committed to economic control for power reasons often find that the public interest does not require them to maintain total ownership and operational control of the private fabricating sector. In fact, what we are rediscovering is that the public interest can be safeguarded by means other than having the government run industry, which, as many underdeveloped countries are beginning to find out, can be a great headache.

Q *Then the necessary degree of government intervention will vary with each society?*

A Of course. If, as was true with the Japanese and British, there is no very severe problem with social overhead transport capital because these islands have coastal shipping, the government's role in this area will be light. In countries like Russia and Canada, on the other hand, you had a very great transportation problem, and the government had to play a preponderant role. And the same variations exist in the fields of agriculture and foreign exchange. The extent of technically appropriate state intervention will vary with each situation.

Q *But, in the context of competitive coexistence, the growth rates themselves have become an important ideological issue. Will this not mean* *that even in societies where there is no ideological compulsion for state intervention, such as India, the initial performance of totalitarian societies may seem so impressive that the temptation to emulate totalitarian institutions may prove irresistible?*

A This is possible, but not very probable. I do not believe that people are quite as silly as professors sometimes are. What will matter in the competition between India and China, for example, is not whether the Indian growth rate matches the Chinese. If India, in the next decade, can move into a genuine take-off sufficient to give its people a real sense of improvement, if it can begin to make a dent on the unemployment problem, if it can improve agricultural productivity and provide her urban masses with a more stable food supply, I don't think Indians will care if they read in the newspapers that the Chinese GNP is increasing faster than theirs. A great deal—including, in my opinion, the fate of Communist China—hinges upon the Indian government's ability to give her people concrete evidence of material improvement.

Self-Sustained Growth Is Not a Smooth Process

Q *Let us assume that a country has successfully accomplished an economic take-off. Does this success assure it of permanent growth?*

A The answer to that is both yes and no. Certainly, no country that has once achieved a successful take-off has ever relapsed into stagnation or decline for more than a limited period. On the other hand, self-sustained growth is not a smooth process. Growth consists of a constant repetition of the take-off in the sense that leading economic sectors are constantly decelerating. Only by creatively introducing *new* leading sectors into the economy can we sustain over-all economic growth.

Q *Is the transition from one leading sector to another always smooth?*

A History is full of cases where certain leading sectors declined *before* a new set of leading sectors took hold. There was such a gap during the 1880s, for example, when railways could no longer lead growth in many countries. There was another such gap, at least in Western European history, during the interwar years when the potentialities for growth from the prevailing leading sectors—steel, steel ships, coal, iron and heavy chemicals—could no longer carry growth forward. At the same time, Western Europe was not quite able to adapt itself to the age of high mass consumption—that is, the age of automobiles, ball bearings, electricity, strip steel and gadgets. In fact, it was not until the 1950s that Europe finally moved into the same stage that we had already been in since the 1920s.

Q *But you believe that once a take-off has been achieved, new leading sectors will always emerge?*

A Well, that seems thus far to be the lesson of history.

Q *In your book you describe the U.S. as having reached the most highly developed stage of economic growth—the stage of high mass consumption. Can we expect other societies, like the Soviet Union, for example, to enter this stage irrespective of what their leaderships may desire?*

A In theory, I can see no reason why all cultures should choose to make the same use of a mature industrial machine and of modern technology that we do in the U.S. In the U.S., we have been able to see what happens in a society where 80 per cent of the people have cars and 70 per cent have their own houses. In the U.S., at least, people have opted for larger families and, perhaps, for a certain "retreat into leisure"—do-it-yourself projects, trips to national parks, long-playing records, and the like. But, there is nothing about the American choices which has been decreed by nature.

Symbols of Privacy and Mobility

Q *Still, wouldn't you say that increasing awareness that such a style of living is possible must have a political effect on the middle classes of more advanced Communist countries?*

A Well, my hunch is this. Once people enjoy a certain level of food, shelter and clothing, and have some measure of security, the two things they want next are privacy and mobility. Consider what the Russian middle class is now doing with its income. It, too, wants a *dacha* in the country and a *Moskvich* to get there—the perfect symbols for privacy and mobility. And the same thing is happening in Japan, except that there they ride Japanese motor scooters instead of automobiles. In fact, the trend may well turn out to be universal. Certainly, recent studies comparing consumption patterns here and in Western Europe show only trivial variations in demand once adjustments have been made for price and income differences.

Q *But countries like the Soviet Union are not free to follow consumer preferences in this matter.*

A That is true. While I believe that Communist countries would, if left free to follow consumer preferences, go the same way as the rest of the industrialized world, the major purpose of the Soviet government at present is to control the consumption process so as to prevent this from happening. This is not only a question of saving resources for capital equipment and armament. The mass automobile, for example, diverts resources for roads, gas stations and hamburger stands; it also provides a means whereby the Soviet citizen can obtain mobility and privacy. Khrushchev has formally announced that he does not intend to imitate the West in this matter. Instead of the private automobile, the Soviet government will go in for fleets of government-controlled taxicabs equipped, as was significantly explained to me, with transistor radios. In this way, the privacy involved in owning your own automobile will have been eliminated.

Q *Do you think that the Soviet government will get away with this?*

A My guess will be that it will—for perhaps a generation. But sooner or later the Russians will want to hit the road on their own with their families, just like the rest of the human race.

Q *If, as you say, the Soviet Union will move increasingly in the direction of more consumption—and more private property—won't this diversion of resources for private ends tend to limit the aggressiveness of Soviet policy?*

A To a very limited extent the official sanctioning of these consumption values may diminish the aggressiveness of the Soviet government. But, given the current Soviet growth rate, there is no reason why consumption cannot expand substantially without placing any limits on the resources available for military and political purposes. I believe that higher consumption in Soviet society can, in itself, make only a very minor contribution to world peace. Much more important, in this context, is the diffusion of power (both nuclear power and, beyond that, industrial power) into parts of the world which neither the U.S. nor Russia can control. If the free world maintains a strong stance, I believe it will gradually be driven home on the Russians that any dream they may have of world domination —and even ideological domination—is based on a rather hopeless illusion. For, in this matter, time is against her. In the end, Russia will have to accept her destiny as one substantial major power among a group of such powers in a world where domination is increasingly difficult.

Q *Thank you, Prof. Rostow.*

[CHAPTER SEVENTEEN]

The American Economy

*T*HE high productivity of the American economy has made our standards of living the envy of the world. How did this come about? Various
attempts have been made to explain it. Many believe that vigorous competition has accounted for much of the growth of our economy; but some
also think that in recent years competition has been declining.

Sumner Slichter argues that this latter idea is a fallacy and that, on
the contrary, competition has been increasing. John Jewkes, a noted English economist, finds the reasons for the high productivity of our economy
not only in the pervasiveness of competition but also in the diversity and
flexibility which result from our free economic institutions. Hans Morgen-
thau sees our most important economic problems as political rather than
strictly economic, because he believes that government is playing an ever-
increasing role in economic affairs.

[35] The Growth of Competition*

by SUMNER H. SLICHTER

One of the most widely held misconceptions about the American economy is the belief, fostered by the conspicuous growth of large companies, that competition is gradually being supplanted in many industries by monopoly. Probably no single belief has done more to undermine confidence in the future and to convince many people that socialism is inevitable.

If competition in fact were dying out, the matter would be most serious. But, as inquiry will show, competition is steadily spreading and growing in vigor, despite the fact that the business world is full of groups that wish strong competition for the other fellow but desire restraints on rivalry among their own members.

The evidence that competition has been spreading and growing in vigor falls into five parts:

The disappearance of conditions that have limited competition. Those who believe competition is declining look back to an imaginary age when the country was made up of thousands of small concerns all vigorously competing with one another. These conditions never existed. When population was sparse and transportation poor and expensive, most communities could afford few businesses and were pretty completely cut off from other places.

What a transformation has occurred! The growth of population has made possible several competing stores or dealers where formerly there was room for only one. The automobile and good roads have enabled buyers to switch from one seller to another, indeed from one town to another, to take advantage of buying opportunities within 50 miles or more. Never have consumers been so independent of the merchants of any particular town.

Improved transportation has also exposed producers to competition from new and distant sources of supply. Refrigeration in vessels and railroad cars has put the winter fruits and vegetables of the South in competition with the canned fruits and vegetables of the North; coal from West Virginia and Pennsylvania must compete in the East with gas piped halfway across the continent from Oklahoma and Texas.

The rise of new business methods and new types of business organiza-

* From *The Reader's Digest,* January, 1954, and *The Atlantic Monthly,* November, 1953. Reprinted by permission.

tions that increase competition. The rise of mail-order selling has brought vigorous competition into thousands of communities, no matter how isolated. Back in the days of Adam Smith there was no selling by mail. Today one may buy by mail not only apparel, food and furniture but also trailers, boats, insurance and prefabricated houses.

Then came the chain store and the supermarket. Each is based on the discovery that cutting traditional retail markups produces rapid turnover of stocks and good profits. The supermarkets are selling cigarettes, toys, phonograph records, hardware, underwear, nylon hosiery. They are even invading the fields of the drugstore, previously the great disregarder of business boundary lines, and in some communities the drugstores have retaliated by selling groceries.

The motel has arisen to compete with the hotel, the book club with the retail bookstore, the vending machine with the retail store. Savings banks, within the last 50 years, have had to meet stiff competition for the savings of individuals from life-insurance salesmen, credit unions, mutual funds and even Government savings bonds. Of particular importance in increasing competitiveness are the recently developed venture-capital companies. These concerns help promising companies get started by putting capital and in some cases managerial assistance into them.

The increase in the number of products, services and processes. In the period 1940-1951, when the output of our economy increased by about five percent a year and population was growing less than one percent a year, output and sales of television sets grew 113 percent a year, freezers 71 percent, dishwashers 21 percent, frozen foods 19 percent. New industries which grow faster than the average are a constant threat to the established industries, forcing them to keep prices down and values up.

Too, the number of commodities and services battling for the same market is constantly increasing. Today oil competes with coal, and gas with oil. Cotton and wool face the ever-growing competition of artificial fibers, paper competes with glass and cloth, the bus and the privately owned automobile with the railroad, the radio with the newspaper, television with the movies, the trailer with the apartment or dwelling house.

Changes in conditions that intensify old forms of competition. Today people have more personal possessions than formerly, and this intensifies competition between the new and the old. In the early days of the automobile industry, for example, there was little competition between new cars and old ones—nearly all the cars purchased were new ones. Today the prospective buyer has the choice of buying either a good secondhand car or a new one, or indeed, unless the newer cars are sufficiently more attractive than his old one, of using his old car a year or two longer.

What is true of automobiles is true of other durable goods—refrigerators, vacuum cleaners, radios, television sets. Most of the possible buyers already possess earlier models which serve the essential purpose and are not discarded until the new models are sufficiently superior—one reason why producers place so much emphasis upon improving the quality of their goods rather than simply reducing the price.

The expansion of technological research. Half a century ago industry depended for inventions and discoveries largely upon enterprising and daring individuals (a Morse, McCormick, Bell, Goodyear, Edison, Marconi or Ford) who operated on their own with such resources as they had or could beg or borrow. But during the last 20 years the search for new and better products and methods has become a normal part of company operations. In 1950 private industry spent about $1,100,000,000 on technological research—nine times as much as in 1930—and employed more than four times as many scientists.

This spectacular growth of research and the huge sums now spent every year on improving products and cutting costs refute the assertion that the economy is becoming less competitive. Never in history have existing products and methods encountered a greater challenge. The very fact that one enterprise is using research to cut its costs or to improve its products means its rivals must do the same thing or be left behind. It is competition at its best.

There are number of ways to encourage competition still further:

Avoid reimposing the excess-profits tax except in time of war. This tax hits hardest the very person who needs to be encouraged—the successful innovator. He will become a more formidable competitor if he is permitted to plow back a large part of the profits of his successful innovation.

Forbid agreements by which manufacturers control retail prices. Such agreements prevent efficient retailers from underselling their less efficient rivals and thereby limit competition.

Withdraw undue protection to American industries against foreign competition. Although American industries are exposed to all kinds of competition in the domestic economy, some direct competition from abroad would be stimulating.

Encourage able young executives to go into business for themselves. The persons best qualified to start new enterprises—namely, successful young executives in established concerns—usually have such good prospects with their present employers that they are little inclined to take the enormous risks inherent in striking out on their own. The new venture-capital companies are an important step toward encouraging able executives to go into business for themselves by helping them obtain much needed funds.

Changes could also be made in the corporate-income-tax laws that would make working for a new and struggling concern a more attractive gamble than it is today. An executive who gives up a secure job with an established enterprise is now compelled to sacrifice the pension rights he has earned during his service. This is unfair, and it is bad for the economy —pension rights become a form of industrial serfdom. Company contributions to pension plans should not be permitted to be counted as an expense in computing tax liability unless the plan vests with any employee of, say, ten years' service or more the right to claim all payments made on his behalf.

Expand the Government's support of research. There are limits on the kind of research that private industry can support, because the results of much research soon become available to everyone. Therefore, much of the support for research should come from the Government, not only to aid defense but to help make the economy more productive and competitive.

The growing competitiveness of the economy causes one to be confident that industry will continue to be progressive. The development that gives most reason for confidence is that the support of invention and discovery has become a normal part of business operations. True, each innovator is attempting to discover something unique, to become a sort of monopolist. But the public need not fear this sort of monopoly. Each would-be monopolist is limited in his power by the fact that he has many rivals. And this rivalry assures us that our fund of technical knowledge will grow rapidly and that the economy will be tough, adaptable and well prepared for any emergency.

[36]   Strengthening Free Institutions in the United States*

by JOHN JEWKES

A problem can be defined as an unsettled question and, for me, the most intriguing unsettled question about the future of the United States is whether the causes of the great economic achievements of the past can be unravelled and the knowledge applied to preserve and strengthen the habits and institutions which have made for economic growth. Will American success prove to have an end, be destined to pass away as mysteriously as it has made its appearance? Or can the upward trend, subject always to the inevitable short period oscillations, be maintained by conscious contrivance based upon a thorough understanding of the sources of the wealth of a nation?

The power of the American economic system to provide standards of living unequalled anywhere else in the world has become so familiar that its extraordinary features are often overlooked. The accomplishments of this vast concourse of people, admittedly now possessed of a substantial proportion of the capital equipment of the world but equipment which, after all, they have created for themselves, should not be taken too much for granted, especially when it is further remembered that all has been brought to pass without resort to the seductive short cuts of totalitarian methods. In recent years, indeed, niggling statisticians have sought to belittle American economic performance and sour-grape sociologists have suggested that what has been done may not have been worthwhile. But here two facts seem decisive: the first is that it is to the United States that investigators flock to plumb the secret of industrial efficiency; the second is that it is from the United States that international aid has flowed so strongly since the end of the war.

How much real progress has been made in detecting the reasons why the United States has so far outstripped other countries? I doubt whether the explanations commonly advanced have as yet reached the heart of the matter. It is sometimes said that America has the advantage of being a

* Reprinted from *Problems of United States Economic Development*, Vol. I, January 1958. Published by The Committee for Economic Development, 711 Fifth Ave., New York 22, N.Y.

large country. But is not India a large country? Is it not true that some quite small countries—Sweden, Switzerland, Belgium, Holland, New Zealand—stand high in any list of countries graded by their income per head? Is it not the case that the United States has not always been a large country, measured by population or output or income; if its size is a result of its growth, how then can it also be argued that its growth is a consequence of its size? Again it is claimed that the United States has derived benefit from its extensive free trade area. But the relatively high transport costs in a large land area have often put limits to such benefits—in the Russian economy, for example, the crucial bottleneck is transport. May it not be argued that the American conquest of distance through the expansion and cheapening of carriage by rail, road and air is an outstanding instance of the overriding of a natural adversity? It is frequently asserted that America has been fortunate to have ample supplies of many natural resources within her borders. It would be idle to deny this; but it must not be forgotten that the natural richness of a country depends upon two things: the original presence of the resources and the skill and energy shown in finding what is there and in making the best use of it. Again, the scale of expenditure on research and development has been put forward as a primary cause of American power. This, to my mind, overlooks the very high proportion of such expenditure devoted to purely military ends. In any case, large scale commercially-supported research is far too new a thing to explain the longish trends that have to be accounted for.

Finally, it is maintained that the United States is, par excellence, the home of large scale production and that therein lies the secret of success. This in itself is a vast subject upon which it is difficult to make useful comment within the compass of a few sentences. It is not to be doubted that the American genius for mass production and the presence in the United States of industrial organisations of a size not found elsewhere have made a great contribution towards efficiency. Nevertheless, I suggest that this is not the unique feature of the industrial system, it is simply one aspect of a more general truth. The characteristic of American industry to which there is not, and never has been, a counterpart seems to me to be the *diversity* of the industrial units. If America is the home of large scale production it is also the home of small scale production. It has a greater range in size, type and composition of industrial units than any other country in the world. It may, indeed, have the largest factories but, nevertheless, the average size of factory is small, is certainly not tending to increase quickly and may be no bigger than that found in some other countries. It may possess firms which in size and multiplicity of product cannot be matched elsewhere but, despite this, the average size of manufacturing firm does not appear, in terms of employment, to be increasing significantly and the total number of firms is not declining. International comparisons in this field are always tricky and often impossible but to me what puts the American industrial system into a class by itself is the fact that there are to be found there 300,000 manufacturing firms, spread over an enormous range of size and pattern, with a high rate of entry and exit.

The reasons normally given for American economic strength, therefore, even when taken together, seem to be too slight to account for the results we are trying to understand. They do not go deep enough. I will not presume to try and fill this gap in knowledge but I suggest that the *direction* in which the fuller answers are most likely to be found will be in the study of what has made the American economy so *flexible*. It begs the question to say that the American people are more enterprising, more disposed to take risks and to make mistakes and quicker to learn and recover from them than other peoples (although all this is true). But why are they so? Not, I am convinced, because they are born so. I can offer no better suggestion than that, whether by good chance or by design, the United States has created within itself a set of institutions which implants in its citizens the habits and arts of adjusting themselves to the ever-changing facts of life and of recovering in resilient fashion from the blows of fortune.

Economic experience, and especially recent experience, suggests that the world is a very unsure place and that survival depends upon the disposition and power to face the insecurities. There is no rational way of predicting future economic situations, the range of possibilities is too vast and complicated, too constantly subject to chance incident and unexpected conjunctures ever to be mapped. But this need not provide grounds for despair. Even if the future must always be dim, it will still be true that some ways of preparing to meet the unknown, some attitudes towards reality, will be more effective than others. "Life is like a game of cards; you cannot control the cards, but of such as turn up you must make the most."

In the past quarter of a century the American economic system has operated in closer accord with that truism than the system of any other country. Of all other countries it may be said that, in proportion as they have sought to shut their eyes to the truism, they have failed to make the most of their economic potentialities. (Indeed it is one of the tragic comedies of modern times that so many poorer countries, seeking to emulate the economic achievements of the United States, have been prepared to imitate everything and anything except the things that matter.) The crucial peculiarities of the American economic system are not difficult to pick out though much remains to be learnt of just how and why they produce the effects they seem to produce. In the United States a wider range of economic decisions and adjustments are made under the direction of price movements than elsewhere—although Germany is rapidly becoming an exception to this generalisation. Competition within and between industries is more pervasive and more persistently forces every industrial unit to justify itself and its deeds than elsewhere. The diversity of the industrial structure, mentioned above, makes it the more likely, in every unexpected contingency, that somewhere there will be found a type of institution best fitted to master the new conditions. Industrial diversity offers a better chance that somewhere and somehow the ideas of innovators will at least be given a trial and provided with the facilities for development. In brief, a flexible economic system is one which at one and the same time engenders the need for changes and provides the means for carrying out these changes swiftly.

The same point may be put in another way. What strikes an outside observer of the American scene is the *speed* with which new routes are followed and awkward obstacles circumvented. This is tacitly implied in the opinion, widely held in Europe, that even new scientific and technical ideas of European origin are frequently first developed and exploited commercially in the United States. It is well illustrated by the rapid large scale marketing of new products and processes: nylon, Dacron, penicillin, air conditioning units, frequency modulation radio, television, continuous hot strip steel rolling, diesel electric traction, fluorescent lighting, the helicopter, the long-playing record, automatic transmissions, power steering, synthetic detergents, shell moulding, the new insecticides—cases where the original scientific discoveries were not invariably made in the United States. It is equally well exemplified by the frequency with which one organisation or another will be found grimly pushing on with a new idea, the future of which is by no means established, as, for instance, color television, pay-as-you-go broadcasting or the continuous casting of steel.

It would, therefore, be a really worthwhile task for economists in the next two decades to return to a study of economic competition in order to try to clarify the indisputable association which exists between it and high standards of living, to determine whether this association is indeed cause and effect and, if so, what precisely are the causal links. It is all the more reasonable to make this suggestion because in the past twenty years so much of the energy of economists, too much some would say, has been devoted to a most painstaking examination of the defects, however minor or peripheral, of competition and of private enterprise as a system for production and distribution.

With that might properly go studies from the opposite angle: how economies, formerly flexible, gradually lose their virtues with time so that the growing points become fewer and are more frequently nipped, resistances to change slowly accumulate, the switching of resources becomes sluggish. It is easy to recognise the forms in which "bureaucracy" makes itself evident. When the contributions of individuals tend to be belittled or ignored and exaggerated claims are made for the virtues of team work; when change is frowned upon unless it can be introduced in a neat and tidy way; when the short period pains of readjustment are unduly magnified and longer period benefits discounted; when institutions are allowed to be both advocate and judge of their own cause; when the responsibility for making decisions, or failing to make them, can be so deeply buried within a hierarchical organisation that no one can ever be held to be individually responsible for anything—in all such cases we know we are in the presence of something which is destructive of growth. But, considering its importance, this subject has been woefully neglected by those whose studies are concerned with the wealth of nations and, indeed, it has been left to a Russian novelist, Dudintsev in "Not by Bread Alone," to provide for the world the clearest modern analysis and fullest description of what is meant by bureaucracy.

Bureaucracy, naturally, flourishes most freely and becomes most deeply rooted where the government makes itself responsible, largely or wholly, for the economic life of the nation. It would, however, be a mistake to assume that only under such circumstances can it take a hold. It seems essentially to be associated with the size of institutions and the status which age itself may confer upon them. In the twentieth century as much harm as good has probably been done to economic efficiency in the name of large scale operation. The damage which it may cause is most likely to be found where attempts are made, by organisation, to force the pace of those human activities which are not organisable or are organisable only to a relatively minor degree. One good though minor illustration of that is provided by the lamentable results of the efforts to nationalize such services as road transport in Britain. Another more general case is the present tendency to organise research to too high a degree, to try to multiply fundamental innovation by large scale operations and by what amounts almost to administrative coercion. I fancy that, among the Western countries, such ideas have been most readily accepted in the United States and that some of the adverse consequences are already observable in the shape of decreasing returns in which masses of smaller improvements and refinements may appear but the bigger breaks-through in knowledge get fewer and fewer. Inventions, the really path-breaking ideas, cannot be sought for under a systematic and cut-and-dried plan. It seems unlikely that their flow will be increased by grouping the major part of the highly trained scientists and technologists in a few large organisations where the opportunities of following odd hunches and dimly perceived conceptions must necessarily be limited. In the long run it is equally frustrating when university workers are expected to devote themselves to tasks set for them from above by those who must, in the nature of things, constantly be pressing for results. It seems to me highly paradoxical that in the United States, where so much attention is devoted to the maintenance of small scale manufacture (and in this, as I have made clear, I believe there is a deeper wisdom) much less seems to be heard of the crucial need to provide room for the individual inventor, the free lance technologist, the uncommitted scientist. And yet, on the good antibureaucratic principle of organising no human activity beyond the point of increasing returns, this might well seem to be one of the requisite foundations for economic growth.

[37]   *The State and the Economic System**

by HANS MORGENTHAU

The most important economic problem which the United States is likely to face in the next twenty years is political rather than economic in the strict technical sense. This seeming paradox results from the decisive influence which political factors exert, and are likely to exert in the foreseeable future, upon the economic life of the nation. We are in the presence of the revival of a truly political economy, whose major economic problems are political in nature.

This interconnectedness of the political and economic spheres is not peculiar to our age. Even in the hey-day of nineteenth-century liberalism,

* Reprinted from *Problems of United States Economic Development*, Vol. I, January 1958, published by The Committee for Economic Development, 711 Fifth Ave., New York 22, N.Y.

the strict separation of the two spheres was in the nature of a political ideal rather than the reflection of observable reality. The monetary, tax, and tariff policies of the government had then, as they have now, a direct bearing upon the economic life; and so had the outlawry of the association of working men as criminal conspiracy. Yet the ideal of strict separation served the political purpose of protecting the economic forces from political control without impeding the former's influence in the political sphere.

What is peculiar to our age is not the interconnectedness of politics and economics but its positive philosophic justification and its all-persuasiveness. The State is no longer looked upon solely as the umpire who sees to it that the rules of the game are observed and who intervenes actively only if, as in the case of the railroads, the rules of the game favor one player to excess and thereby threaten to disrupt the game itself. In our age, the State, aside from still being the umpire, has also become the most powerful player, who, in order to make sure of the outcome, in good measure rewrites the rules of the game as he goes along. Neither the government nor society at large rely any more exclusively upon the mechanisms of the market to keep the game going. Both deem it the continuing duty of the government to see to it that it does.

The State pursues three main purposes in the economic sphere: observance of the rules of the game, maintenance of economic stability, and national defense.

The rules of the game are oriented toward the pluralistic objectives of American society. Thus they seek to prevent any sector of the economy from gaining absolute power vis-à-vis other sectors of the economy, competitors, or the individuals as such, by controlling and limiting its power. Regulatory commissions, legislation controlling and limiting the strong and supporting the weak, tariff and monetary policies serve this purpose.

While the State started to assume responsibility for the rules of the game in the last decades of the nineteenth century, it made itself responsible for economic stability in the nineteen thirties. Economic stability, in this context, signifies the mitigation, if not the elimination in certain sectors, of the business cycle. Its main positive characteristics, as conceived by the government of the United States, are stability of employment, of the value of the dollar, and of agricultural prices. A plethora of legislative and administrative devices serve this purpose.

Since the end of the Second World War, technological research and industrial production have become to an ever increasing extent the backbone of military defense. The regular annual expenditure by the government of close to forty billion dollars on national defense, its decrease or increase from year to year, its shift from one sector of the economy to another, all exert a sometimes drastic influence upon the economic life of the nation. They have made the government the most important single customer for the products of the national economy. In addition, many tax and monetary, price and wage policies are determined by considerations of national defense.

With the government thus exerting an enormous controlling, limiting, and stimulating influence upon the economic life, the ability to influence the economic decisions of the government becomes an indispensable element in the competition for economic advantage. Economic competition manifests itself inevitably in competition for political influence. This political influence is exerted through two channels: control of, and pressure upon, government personnel.

The most effective political influence is exerted by the direct control of government personnel. The economic organization which has its representatives elected to the legislature or appointed to the relevant administrative and executive positions exerts its political influence as far as the political influence of its representatives reaches. Insofar as the latter cannot decide the issue by themselves, the competition for political influence and, through it, economic advantage will be fought out within the collective bodies of the government by the representatives of different economic interests. While this relationship of direct control is typical in Europe, it is by no means unknown in the United States. State legislatures have been controlled by mining companies, public utilities, and railroads, and many individual members of Congress represent specific economic interests. Independent administrative agencies have come under the sway of the economic forces which they were intended to control. The large-scale interchange of top personnel between business and the executive branch of the government cannot help but influence, however subtly and intangibly, decisions of the government relevant to the economic sphere.

However, in the United States the most important political influence is exerted through the influence of pressure groups. The decision of the government agent—legislator, independent administrator, member of the executive branch—is here not a foregone conclusion by virtue of the economic control to which he is subject. His decision is in doubt, for he is still open to divergent economic pressures. The competition for determining the decisions of the government takes place not among the government agents themselves, but between the government agent, on the one hand, and several economic pressure groups, on the other. Only after this latter competition has been settled one way or another, the former will take place, provided the issue is still in doubt.

The political struggle, ostensibly fought for victory in periodical elections by political parties, reveals itself in good measure as a contest of economic forces for the control of government action. In consequence, the decision of the government and, more particularly, of legislatures ostensibly rendered "on the merits of the case," tends to reflect the weight of economic influence and, at worst, to give political sanction to decisions taken elsewhere. Legislators and administrators tend to transform themselves into ambassadors of economic forces, defending and promoting the interests of their mandatories in dealing with each other on behalf of them. The result is a new feudalism which, like that of the Middle Ages, diminishes the authority of the civil government and threatens it with extinction by parcelling its several functions out among economic organizations to be appropriated and used as private property. And just like the feudalism of the Middle Ages, these new concentrations of private power tend to command the primary loyalties of the individual citizens who owe them their livelihood and security. In the end, the constitutionally established government tends to become, in the words of Chief Justice Marshall, a "solemn mockery," glossing over the loss of political vitality with the performance of political rituals.

If giant concentrations of economic power, in the form of corporations and labor unions, were thus to become laws unto themselves, deciding with finality the matters vital to them and using the government only for the purpose of ratifying these decisions, they would not only have drained the life blood from the body politic but also destroyed the vital energies of the economic system. For the vitality of the American economic system has resided in its ability to renew itself on new technological opportunities, unfettered by the interests identified with an obsolescent technology. Seen from the vantage point of the individual enterprise, this is what we call freedom of competition. This freedom of competition has been a function of the rules of the economic game, as formulated and enforced by the State.

Yet the new feudalism, if it is not controlled and restrained, must inevitably tend to abrogate these rules of the game in order to assure the survival of the economic giants which, in turn, tend to take over the functions of the State. The consummation of this development, possible but not inevitable, would be a state of affairs in which for those giants the rule of life would not be freedom of competition, which might jeopardize their survival, but freedom from competition in order to secure their survival. The dynamics of the American economic system, continually destroying and creating as life itself, would then give way to a gigantic system of vested interests in which the established giants would use the State to make themselves secure from competitive displacement, only to die the slow death of attrition.

It is the measure of the quandary which American society faces in this problem, insoluble by any simple formula, that the only visible cure raises issues as brave as the disease. That cure is a State strong enough to hold its own against the concentrations of private power. In good measure, such a State already exists. It is the State whose importance for the economic life of the nation we have referred to above. Insofar as this State is able to act as an independent political force, controlling, restraining, and re-directing economic activities, it is indeed the strong State, capable of keeping the concentrations of private power in check. Yet such a State, by being strong enough for this task, cannot fail being also strong enough to control, restrain, and re-direct the economic activities of everybody. In other words, as the American political tradition correctly assumes, a strong government, whatever else it may be able to accomplish, threatens the liberties of the individual, especially in the economic sphere.

Thus America is faced with a real dilemma: a government which is too weak to threaten the freedom of the individual is also too weak to hold its own against the new feudalism, and a government which is strong enough to keep the new feudalism in check is also strong enough to destroy the liberties of all. What, then, must it be: the new feudalism of private power or the new despotism of the public power? Or is there a third way in the form of an intricate system of checks and balances within the economic sphere, within the political sphere, and between both— combining, in the spirit of *The Federalist,* the ability to perform the functions of government, private and public, with those restraints upon government action upon which the liberties of all depend?

The next twenty years are likely to pose these questions in different guises, but with ever increasing urgency. The answers we are able to give to these questions will determine both the political and economic system under which we shall live.

[CHAPTER EIGHTEEN]

Economic Stability and Full Employment

*J*OHN *Maynard Keynes was the outstanding economist of the first half of the twentieth century. As Slichter notes, he "contributed invaluable tools of analysis" to economics; but he was unduly influenced by the period of the great depression. His belief that highly developed industrial countries must suffer from a chronic shortage of demand and hence from chronic unemployment has not been borne out by experience, and in the first article below Slichter explains why.*

Our second selection is a debate. In it Braverman, a socialist, argues that major depressions cannot be avoided in a capitalist economy. Lerner, an able economist who employs Keynesian techniques of analysis, maintains that we not only can but will prevent them, and he explains the reasons for this belief.

[38] The Passing of Keynesian Economics*

by SUMNER H. SLICHTER

John Maynard Keynes ranks with Adam Smith and Karl Marx among economists in the influence that his views have exerted on the general public. He had the vision to see that economics lacked a general theory of demand, and he proceeded with boldness and brilliance to construct one.

His theory produced the startling conclusion that highly developed industrial countries suffer from a chronic deficiency of demand, and that this deficiency is bound to grow worse as countries become richer. Hence, Keynes called upon government to assume a new responsibility and a new function—that of closing the growing gap between the power of progressive economies to produce and the size of effective private demand. Keynes suggested two general lines of action—that of controlling the size of the gap through changes in the distribution of income and that of offsetting the gap through greater government spending.

Keynes's theory contributed invaluable tools of analysis to economics and started hundreds of able economists in many lands studying the important problems that the theory opened up. No one in the history of economics has done as much as Keynes to stimulate good work. But Keynes's theory has turned out to have been wrong in all its essentials. Although intended to be a "general" theory, applicable to all conditions, it was unduly molded by the depressed thirties, the period when Keynes composed it. Advanced economies do not suffer from a chronic deficiency of demand—they suffer from a chronic *excess* of demand. It would be hard today to find an advanced economy that is not struggling to control demand, and most of them are having only partial success.

It is among the undeveloped economies, precisely where Keynes did not expect to find a chronic shortage of demand, that unemployment is endemic and most severe. Keynes's theory that unemployment is caused by an excessive disposition to save obviously does not explain the high unemployment in countries which are too poor to have any savings at all. The high unemployment in undeveloped countries is best explained by Marx's theory of unemployment—that men lack work because savings are

* From *The Atlantic Monthly*, November, 1959. Reprinted by permission.

268

insufficient to provide the growing labor force with the tools of production.

The Consumer's Role. Why has Keynes turned out to have been so completely wrong? He made two basic mistakes. In the first place, he assigned to consumers a relatively passive role in determining the demand for goods. In the second place, he overlooked the fact that the development of investment opportunities is itself an expanding industry carried on for profit and able to supply the community with a rapidly growing number of investment outlets.

Keynes thought that consumers play a rather passive role in determining the demand for goods because he believed that the amount spent on consumption depends pretty completely upon the size of the national income. Hence, the dynamic influences in the economy, the influences that make the national income and the total demand for goods change, must be found, according to Keynes, outside the spending habits of consumers. Keynes found a single dominant dynamic influence in the rate of investment, which by rising and falling determines whether the economy expands or contracts. As business increases or cuts its buying of investment goods, incomes will rise or fall, and as they rise or fall consumption too will rise or fall.

Had Keynes lived in the United States, he would perhaps have seen that consumers do not let their consumption be determined so completely by the size of their incomes. American consumers, with their strong desire to live better and with their freedom from customs and traditions that decree what ways of living are suitable for people in certain stations, have always been ready to cut their rate of saving, to draw on their capital, or to go into debt in order to buy new things.

Particularly in recent years, consumers have developed a growing willingness to incur short-term debts in order to buy goods. Since the boom year of 1929 there has been an almost sevenfold increase in consumer credit, from a mere $6.4 billion at the end of 1929 to a whopping $41.9 billion at the end of 1956. During this period consumers were obviously not limiting their spending by their incomes. Their spending was being determined, as one would expect it to be, by their total resources, which include their credit, not merely by their incomes. Instead of playing the passive role ascribed to them by Keynes, consumers have been a powerful dynamic influence accelerating the expansion of the economy.

The Ethics of Borrowing. Consumers have been encouraged to play a dynamic role in the economy by the rapidly growing consumer credit industry. This industry is based upon the discovery, only recently made, that consumers are far better credit risks than anyone had dreamed them to be. As a result, there has been a rush by finance companies, banks, mail order houses, automobile dealers, department stores, airplane and steamship lines, and many others to persuade consumers to buy goods on credit. At first consumer credit was limited to tangible goods with a rather definite resale value, such as automobiles or household appliances, but now one may finance trips and vacations on the installment plan. And the proportion of sales made on credit steadily rises. Sears Roebuck reports that in 1954, 39 per cent of its sales were made on credit. Last year the proportion was 44 per cent. With consumers behaving as American consumers are accustomed to behave, Keynes's fear that people will insist on saving too much seems farfetched.

Incidentally, with the discovery that consumers are better risks than had been previously suspected, there has developed a marked change in attitudes toward personal loans—a real change in the ethics of borrowing. Time was when personal indebtedness, except for a few emergencies and to provide the necessary furnishings for a home, was regarded as imprudent or reckless. Today it is seen that debt is a stabilizing and stimulating influence, and that it is a good thing for most young men, particularly married men, to have at least a moderate volume of debts that they are paying off.

The Demand for Capital.   Although Keynes thought that the dominant dynamic influence in the economy is investment, he conceived of businessmen as a surprisingly unenterprising and helpless lot—unable to do much about the scale of investment. Keynes was obsessed with the fear that, as the country's stock of capital became larger and larger, outlets for savings would be harder to find, and he expressed his fears quite eloquently. He said that he felt sure that the demand for capital is strictly limited in the sense that it would not be difficult to increase the stock of capital to the point where its ability to produce a return would fall to a very low figure.

Keynes's belief that the return on capital would drop very drastically as the stock of capital increased must be ascribed to his failure to appreciate the significance of modern technology. Though a man of affairs, and a highly successful one at that, he failed to see what others saw, the large and growing capacity of industry to discover investment opportunities— a capacity that is far greater in highly developed countries than in undeveloped ones and that grows as the economy becomes richer and more industrial. Technological discoveries are the most important single influence on investment in advanced industrial economies, and yet Keynes's brilliant work contains no discussion of technological research.

The Industry of Discovery.   It is ironic that at the very time that Keynes was proclaiming his pessimistic views on the shortage of investment opportunities, the rise of technological research was producing a revolutionary change in the economy. Technological research was becoming an industry. It is convenient to call it the industry of discovery. It consists of many captive laboratories which work only for the company which owns them and a rapidly growing number of firms which do research under contract. The industry of discovery is one of the most rapidly growing industries in the country. Industry spent $116 million of its own money on research and development in 1930, $234 million in 1940, and about $1.5 billion in 1953, and it has been making even larger outlays under government research contracts. Outlays on research and development would grow even faster were they not limited by the shortage of engineers and scientists.

The revolutionary nature of the rise of the industry of discovery is not appreciated even by economists. Until recently, discoveries have been made mainly in two ways: by the efforts of operating men (incidental to their regular work), who have seen opportunities to improve methods of production or products, and by the efforts of "inventors" who, using their own resources and often driven by much stronger motives than hope of gain, have made industrial applications of scientific knowledge. The revolutionary change is that it has become possible to find a large number of problems or areas of investigation on which money may be spent with a reasonable expectation that the outlay will produce enough useful information and understanding to justify the expense. This means that it has become possible to apply the economic calculus—the balancing of expected expenses against expected gains—to an important new area of human activity, and to have the organized pursuit of gain take over a field of activity where formerly there had only been haphazard individual activities. . . .

Many thousands of able men now make their living by disturbing our lives and by forcing us to discard old equipment, old methods, and old ways of doing things. The more they disturb us, the better living they make. And the vested interests of the people who live by making discoveries cause them to strive to improve the methods and instruments of investigation, thus steadily raising the capacity of the economy to develop investment opportunities. The danger that Keynes feared—namely, that we shall run out of investment opportunities—grows more remote every day, and it becomes most remote in the highly developed economies, precisely where Keynes erroneously believed that it would be greatest.

The Outlook for Production. How does the world look when Keynes's theory of demand, constructed in the midst of the great depression, is replaced with one based on the developments of the last twenty years?

On the whole, it appears to be a far better world than the one described by Keynes's theory—though not a world from which tough economic problems are absent. The specter of chronic unemployment, slowly growing as wealth increases and as the rate of saving rises, has pretty completely disappeared, at least as far as the industrially developed countries are concerned. Only a series of major blunders in policy could produce the chronic unemployment that Keynes dreaded. Consumers are a far more dynamic influence than Keynes ever suspected, and industry has far greater power to create demand for goods, mainly through technological discoveries, than anyone a generation or so ago dreamed it might have —and this power is growing. . . .

New Confidence in Free Enterprise.   The discovery that our economy has far greater capacity to increase the demand for goods than Keynes suspected has naturally produced a great resurgence of confidence in capitalism and private enterprise. Rising confidence in the effectiveness of capitalistic institutions has had the interesting result of causing radicals and conservatives alike to abandon extreme positions. As attacks on capitalism have moderated, the defense of capitalism has become less doctrinaire. In the United States there has been a marked growth of "middle-of-the-road" opinion. The same thing has happened in Western Europe where the Labor and Socialist parties have shifted from advocating nationalization of industry to championing the welfare state—the operation of private enterprise within a comprehensive framework of public policies—and where the principal conservative parties have also accepted the welfare state.

We should be grateful that the world is what it is rather than what Keynes pictured it as being. It is a world in which the energies and aspirations of men are stimulated by expanding opportunities rather than depressed by the constant threat of chronic unemployment. Most important of all, it is a world in which the rapidly growing industry of discovery is creating the possibility of a great cultural revoluton. For the first time in history, the high productivity of some countries is enabling their people to have sufficient income, sufficient education, and sufficient leisure so that the good life is ceasing to be the privilege of a favored few and is being brought within the reach of all members of the community.

[39]   Can We Cure Depressions?*

a debate between ABBA P. LERNER
and HARRY BRAVERMAN

HARRY BRAVERMAN:

It's pretty widely agreed that there is an instability in a capitalist economy. That wasn't something that was agreed upon twenty-five years ago. At that time, most economists went on the theory that there couldn't be a serious and prolonged depression, as the economy was guided by some kind of "invisible hand," a set of laws which saw to it that things turned out right. With the Great Crash of 1929, that point of view was pretty decisively repudiated. So I don't believe Dr. Lerner and I will have a lot of argument about that point.

Now, I'll state why I think the economy tends to get out of whack. The very dynamics of the capitalist system when it's in a period of boom, the drive to produce an ever larger amount with less and less labor per unit of production, alters the proportions of the parts of the economy to each other. There is a tendency to expand production and capacity as though the sky were the limit, while on the other side expanding consumption and purchasing power in a relatively limited way. That disproportion leads to a bust in the boom. That's been the history of every big upswing in the business cycle up to now, and I believe that that's the tendency in the economy at the present time.

The government spent during the war some $180 billion more than it took in in taxes, giving a terrific stimulus to the economy by throwing in purchasing power that wouldn't otherwise have been there. Then consumer credit in the eight years following the war added another $200 billion, this time in private indebtedness. In the decade and a half after 1940, some $400 billion of additional debt was piled up in this country that hasn't been repaid. I know we've all gotten badly jaded by many of the astronomical figures, but if you stop to think what $400 billion of credit buying means, you can quickly see that, measured against our average national income during that same period, it represents roughly an additional year's purchasing power for every ten; within ten years, there was about eleven years of buying, by borrowing ahead on future income.

* Reprinted from *The American Socialist*, April 1958, Vol. 5, No. 4, pp. 6-8.

If you see this picture clearly, you must realize how lame our formerly self-reliant capitalism is getting, and the kind of props it needs. The question also arises whether this kind of a credit splurge can be repeated every 15 years. Even if the government could repeat, the consumer cannot add much more to his credit load.

That is what I think is a chief defect in Dr. Lerner's theory of functional finance. Perhaps I should leave this to Dr. Lerner to explain, as he is the originator of the theory, but it's necessary for my presentation to say a few words about it. The thought is that a national debt is a useful proposition. In times of depression, the government should spend what it hasn't got, or in other words borrow. Business gets an impetus to pick up. Then when you have a major boom going on, the government can repay some of its indebtedness, and in that way it will prevent the boom from getting too exuberant. In theory, the valleys and peaks of the business cycle get leveled off somewhat. That, at any rate, was the hope.

Well, if symmetry is a virtue in a theory, this is one that has great beauty. But the symmetry has not been displayed in real life. Instead of being able to pay off a good part of our indebtedness during the boom, even in this time of prosperity after the war, the government had to pile up another $30 billion of debt. Now what that means to me, is that the mechanism which Dr. Lerner or other followers of John Maynard Keynes speak of does tend to work if it is applied in massive enough doses, *but these economists have underestimated the downward trend of the capitalist economy.* The way their theory actually worked out in practice has required continual spending—for armaments, as we all know—to keep the boom going.

This big flow of government and consumer spending set off an investment boom—which has been historically the last stage in all our major upswings. There was a great stimulus to investment in new plant and equipment. Because the whole effort is, quite naturally, to turn out more with less labor, there was no comparable stimulus to consuming power. Consumption has been growing at a slow and leveling-off rate, and has begun to decline recently. Over the last year or two, Leon Keyserling calculated, expansion of plant and equipment was about eight times as fast as the increase of consuming power.

This jibes with the theory I presented at the start. The McGraw-Hill Department of Economics has done some surveys of this and come up with startling results. Where, in the first six, seven years after the war, the economy was running at well over 90 percent of capacity—with the exception only of the slump year of 1949—the economy was operating at

82 percent of capacity in 1953, 81 percent in 1954, 84 percent in 1955 (our top boom year), 80 percent in 1956 and at the end of 1957. They revised these figures somewhat upwards later, but the revisions were just a point or two.

As distinguished from the twenties, there are certain stabilizers in the economy, cushions to consumer income. Economists, government officials, businessmen have some confidence in these shock absorbers to *slow* a decline, but they don't expect them to *prevent* a decline. These stabilizers have one important feature in common, that they have less effect the deeper a recession gets and the longer it goes on.

A major argument of the "new economists" is that they today know a great deal more than we used to. They know how income and investment ought to be shifted, how the different forces in the economy ought to be balanced to prevent or cure a depression. Admittedly, if you have the power to shift anything in the economy any way you wanted, you can readjust the proportions to get it working again. That all goes on the assumption that the only thing we were lacking in the past was knowledge. But can anyone tell me of a capitalist country where disinterested political scientists are running the government, and economists are running the economy? The major decisions in our economy are still being made in the same old way: *by the self-interest calculations of private firms*. Politics and economics encompass fierce struggles between contending interests. That is why it is foolish to predict an end to depressions because of the growth in economic knowledge.

The subtitle for this debate is: "Can America Avoid Depression and Maintain Free Enterprise?" and I'll answer that question this way: First I would alter the question to read "capitalism," or "private enterprise," as we don't have any such thing as the free enterprise this country used to know a century or more ago. It's a highly trustified, cartelized, monopolized economy. With that correction, I would answer to the question that, in the long run, we cannot maintain capitalism and enjoy prosperity.

That is the conclusion that emerges no matter from what angle you choose to view the technical-economic debate. Look at the experience of the last twenty-five years: We went into the deepest depression in our history, we finally climbed out of it, not by any ordinary government intervention, not by welfare spending, but when the big military spending started. We wound up then with a government sector of the economy amounting to some 20 percent of the total—mostly tied to the military. Now, how many more depressions or recessions can we climb out of that way and still maintain a capitalist system? Mind you, I'm not saying that's the way this country will get socialism—I doubt it very much, but that's

another discussion. But I am saying that even this method of curing depression is one that bodes ill for the future of capitalism. So even the
Keynesian theory, when tested against the experience of the past quarter
century, tends to show that capitalism is not a viable or desirable proposition for the people of this country.

ABBA P. LERNER:

I want to thank Mr. Braverman for a very pleasant, polite, patient, and
clear discussion, with about nine-tenths of which I find myself in agreement. But unfortunately the one-tenth with which I find myself in disagreement rather spoils what comes out at the end.

The essential part of Mr. Braverman's argument is that there is "an
inherent instability." That's a very nice-sounding word, but I think we
ought to try to look at it a little more closely and deal with it in more
ordinary language. Economists used to believe that it isn't necessary to
have any policy to prevent depressions; that they will cure themselves.
But it is no longer believed, as Mr. Braverman clearly pointed out, that
depressions can't happen—that an "invisible hand" looks after these
things. The "invisible hand" doesn't prevent depressions and we need to
have a policy.

The essentials of this policy are very simple. If depressions are caused
by people not spending enough money—and this is the only kind of depression which we have discussed so far—the cure is to see to it that
enough money is spent. The government can always do that by spending
money itself. It's no use telling me, or Mr. Braverman, to spend more
money because we haven't got the money to spend. And we are not in
the position of printing more money to spend because if we do they'll put
us in jail. But the government can print as much money as it likes—nobody can put the government in jail—and so the government can provide
all the money that is necessary to keep people spending, and if the government wants to do that, nobody can stop it. Such a policy is "functional
finance."

Mr. Braverman correctly described functional finance as a policy by
which the government undertakes action to maintain spending at the
required level, but he imposed a limitation which I never recognized. It
is therefore, I'm afraid, necessary for me to give Mr. Braverman a further
lesson on functional finance. The essential point about functional finance
is that the *only* judgment as to whether the government should or shouldn't
provide more money is: how it works—how it functions. If more money
is needed to maintain full employment, why then it should provide more,

and if not, then it shouldn't, and if a reduction in money spending is required to prevent inflation then there should be a reduction.

Actually a lot of people have made exactly the same mistake as Mr. Braverman though they didn't call it functional finance and did not attribute it to me. The Swedish economists in particular made the same mistake when they went part of the way towards functional finance. They very properly said: The idea of balancing the budget every year is not a very sensible one. Why should the necessity of the government to encourage and discourage spending just balance out in the 365¼ days that it takes the earth to go round the sun? Spending is a matter of economics, not of astronomy. And indeed 365¼ days is no more relevant than the ninety minutes it takes the sputnik to go around the earth. Nobody thus far has been suggesting that we balance our budget every ninety minutes, nor should we balance it every year. But the Swedes slipped when they said: "Maybe it should be balanced every ten years." And they had long-term budgets. This is just like Mr. Braverman's "limitations." However they soon realized that ten years made no more sense than one year, and so they wiggled themselves out of the error in a very complicated way. They spoke about having a "cyclical budget," and a "capital budget," and other kinds of budgets; then they had a lot of footnotes saying that if necessary, something else can be done—which means they didn't really believe in any of these budget balancings but just left them in for window-dressing so that people like Mr. Braverman who felt strongly the budget should be some way, somehow, or sometime brought into balance, shouldn't feel too bad about it.

Functional finance says clearly that there are no such limits, and that is why all of the argument Mr. Braverman made here just disappears. There is no reason why the government should stop spending short of achieving and maintaining full employment. I once wrote an article, called "Functional Finance and the Federal Debt," on what happens if the government keeps on increasing federal debt. Will the debt grow so big that it would destroy the economy? It wouldn't because in the first place we owe the debt to ourselves, not to any other nation. If we owed the debt to the Germans or to the Japanese the payments on its interest and principal could ruin us. But since we owe it to ourselves we also get the payments, and so we are not impoverished. We can still consume all that we produce and that's what really matters; as long as we can produce a great deal, we're all right.

In the second place the debt will not grow indefinitely. Supposing the government found there wasn't enough spending—people didn't invest enough or consume enough—and so the government had to provide some more spending. Then either the national debt would increase, or the volume of money would increase, or more probably both would increase. As the amount of money in the economy grew larger and larger, the public would have more and more money in their pockets. As the amount of debt grew larger and larger, the public would own more U.S. bonds and government debt certificates. These people look at their bankbooks and debt certificates and they feel rich. As the growth goes on, they feel richer and richer, and they can afford to spend more. And since they spend more, *they* fill the gap in spending and it isn't necessary for the *government* to come in. So *the debt automatically stops growing* when people have become sufficiently rich in cash and in government debt certificates. If this is overdone and causes *too much* spending, then you apply functional finance in reverse, create a budget surplus and pay off some of the debt. But there is no need to get to that point, because the government doesn't need to keep on increasing spending if people are spending enough. So there is no need to worry about the difficulty or danger of debt growth.

There's only one more point which I think is important here, and that is the last point that was made by Mr. Braverman; namely: Even if the economists know what ought to be done, will the government do it? If the government doesn't, then all this knowledge, I agree, is of no use. However, I think the government is extremely interested in doing it, because—one peculiar thing about governments—they like to be re-elected. And no government is going to be re-elected if it has a depression. You can find much better reasons why we shouldn't have depressions: People shouldn't be out of work and hungry; a depression would make more people believe that the Russian system is better than the American system. But even if our politicians didn't care about the people, and didn't care about America and Russia, they still care about being re-elected, and so they will do whatever they can to stop a depression. Even politicians who are worried about an unbalanced budget and who think functional finance is wicked, find themselves pressured in deficits, because, if there is unemployment, not only the politicians and the economists, but everybody, almost, in America knows, that the government can provide jobs by spending money—they've seen it happen.

When the war broke out, as Mr. Braverman pointed out, in spite of the New Deal, in spite of Keynes, we still had many millions of people unemployed, because, when Keynes said you should spend $30 billion, the government said, $30 billion is too much, let's try $3 billion, and so we got some reduction in unemployment, but we didn't effect a cure. And then the war came, and the government spent $30 billion and $50 billion and $100 billion, and everybody saw what happened. Everybody was working; we were able to produce all the goods we wanted, we were able to maintain our standards of living and still produce all the airplanes and armaments and guns for ourselves, for our allies, for Russia, because we were spending enough money. Having seen this happen the public knows that government spending can prevent depression and governments cannot avoid their responsibility for providing enough spending and still be re-elected. I am confident we are not going to have a bust; mainly because I have great confidence in the eagerness of politicians to be re-elected.

CHAPTER NINETEEN

Economic Inequality and Social Security

IN recent years we have made only moderate progress toward reducing inequalities of income in the United States, but we have made substantial progress in raising the average of all incomes and in providing greater security for individuals and families.

Soffer describes the progress of private industry in providing security for workers; the article from United States News & World Report describes the Canadian plan for hospital care. The latter is of special interest because there are strong demands in this country for adding hospital and medical care to our own Social Security system.

[40] *Fringes Are Not Frills**

by BENSON SOFFER

To most people "fringe benefits" connote a miscellaneous collection of frills and benefits adding minor costs to industry's wage bill. In fact, the so-called "fringes" usually account for 25 per cent of payroll costs and support such important items as: (1) a major part of group health and life insurance costs for nearly all employees and their families; (2) the entire cost of unemployment benefits; (3) half of the contributions to the Social Security Program (covering 90 per cent of our population); (4) almost all the funds from which supplementary pension benefits are paid; and (5) paid vacations and holidays.

None of these are included in hourly wage statistics. Half the "fringe package" represents wage increases taken as time off the job, or extra wages for work under special conditions. A three-week paid vacation, for example, adds five and three-quarters per cent to payroll costs and reduces the average workweek by three and one-third hours.

It is currently fashionable to criticize "organization men" and their concern for economic security. And the fact remains that, in relation to direct wages, income security has grown steadily in economic importance. Some critics of this trend foresee adverse effects on incentive, individual free choice, prudence and eventually on economic growth. Others fear that the growth of private benefit plans discourages improvements in government Social Security and that private insurance ties the worker to one employer.

Both sides, however, see many problems in private responsibility for "security" in a dynamic, unstable economy.

Union members have worked through their leaders to expand the scope of collectively bargained benefits because of the eroding effects of inflation on similar government sponsored programs. Union demands for supplementary benefits seek to maintain the "benefit-to-income" relationships established in the depression. Even before income-security programs were developed, workers looked for a lifetime job with a single employer. Now, seniority has been broadened to give plant-wide, area-wide and even company-wide employments rights in large, multi-plant corporations.

The plans themselves are not revolutionary, but are based on the true

* From *Challenge* (March 1960), pp. 61-65, a publication of the Institute of Economic Affairs, New York University. Reprinted by permission.

281

economic advantages of group insurance of good-risk employees. And employers have come to realize that such plans are an essential part of the personnel policies needed to achieve a permanent labor force.

Practicality and Need.   Both the practicality of and the need for such "social insurance," and the desire of both labor and management to meet this need, have accounted for the rapid growth of private income security plans. What were once the prerogatives of only some salaried (and far fewer manual) employees have, in a decade, come to be standard conditions of employment in most major industries.

Have these new benefits worked as well in practice as they do in theory? When one considers the constant experimentation conducted in the field of benefit plans and the rapid extension of these plans to companies unacquainted with them, the record is remarkable. In spite of the inevitable difficulties, no area of labor-management relations has been so free of controversy and abuse as the negotiation and administration of these programs. Costs have been estimated conservatively, benefits have been kept well within income, and responsibility has been shown in seeking meaningful benefits and efficient administration of them. There has also been a considerable amount of innovation in devising methods of spreading benefit coverage to those whose employment is irregular. And, all in all, abuse and malingering by workers have been surprisingly low.

In this responsible and constructive spirit, many "principles" which once loomed as sources of conflict have disappeared, and practical solutions to problems have been found. The employer's ability to gain tax advantages by financing noncontributory plans has encouraged the spread of this type of benefit plan. New pension benefit formulae (based on flat amounts or percentages of recent earnings) have eliminated the possibility of retirement income lagging behind current wage levels. Almost all pension plans are funded, and past service liabilities are generally being reduced at the maximum rate allowed. Although benefits (such as pension vesting) are steadily being liberalized, payments are still below the income level of pension and supplementary unemployment benefit funds.

Rapid Cost-Inflation.   The serious problems remaining are related to specific types of benefits—the gravest of these being the rapid inflation of medical and hospital costs. The doubling of both health insurance costs and out-of-pocket expenses in a decade casts a shadow over the actual value of all hospitalization benefit programs.

It is easy to look for a villain, but the cause of this problem is neither unnecessary treatment of the insured nor exorbitant medical fees; although instances of these abuses are not rare. The problem stems from a shortage of hospital facilities, a shortage underscored by the fact that 22 million Americans were short-term hospital patients in 1959. Medical progress raises quality, but it also raises costs. At the same time, the organization of medical care is poorly coordinated since it places the cost of research and training on the sick. While the AMA now admits there is a shortage of doctors and encourages the expansion of medical schools, union health centers attempting the economies of group practice and preventative medical care still meet sharp resistance.

Nevertheless, little can be accomplished without the cooperation of doctors and the community organizations controlling hospitals. The newest answer is major medical insurance covering very costly illness; but under this plan the patient bears a substantial share of the cost. In 1959, 123 million Americans having health insurance received a total of $4.7 billion from the insuring companies for medical expenses. But another $12 billion was not covered by this insurance. It will be possible, but difficult, to solve a problem of this magnitude.

Limited in Coverage. Supplementary unemployment benefits remain very limited in coverage, primarily to members of the automobile and steel unions, and such plans would not exist at all had not unions been willing to forego wage increases for them. Employers have insisted that there be no employment guarantees and that under these plans benefits for lower seniority workers (who need them most) be restricted. The result was that in the 1958 recession, only 30 to 40 per cent of the laid-off workers were eligible for the SUB benefits.

Even fewer workers have employment guarantees. Although many employers have stabilized employment, most industries have made only limited progress. Expansion of SUB coverage will, therefore, require sizable cost increases and unions will continue to meet resistance to these plans.

Some industries, companies and plants are burdened with income security costs for the "old" work forces who find re-employment in other industries difficult for many reasons. Chief among these is that the relatively short work life remaining to older workers makes their pension and training costs disproportionately large. Multi-plant companies in such situations are often tempted to close obsolete plants when they face financial difficulty. Workers "hang around" (as in the coal fields), hoping to work enough to preserve their pension benefits. Under very adverse conditions, income security plans do not work well, but the same might be said for almost any kind of similar program.

Reasonable Protection. These difficulties do not justify the fears of critics. Supplementary pension and unemployment benefits do not create a privileged class. Since there is little possibility that legislatures will ever agree to setting government benefits at 50 to 60 per cent of wages, private benefit plans do give reasonable income protection to high wage earners. Indeed, the improvements in government benefit programs urged by the unions occurred *after* the collectively bargained programs had been started. Nor do these benefits sharply reduce labor mobility—they accentuate the already serious immobility of older, less-educated workers in declining industries which use skills that are becoming obsolete. They do not affect the mobility of the more versatile, better educated, younger workers. (The sensible approach to this immobility of labor is a positive one—for example, retrain labor through government-industry cooperation.)

Those who have feared decreasing work incentives and the growth of "legal malingering" should now realize that they were misled by class bias. Older workers have not requested unemployment pay instead of jobs. Like most other Americans, when unemployed they feel the loss of status, self-respect and income that cannot be replaced by fairly comfortable lay-off pay. In fact, older workers have fought through their unions to relax compulsory retirement rules in many companies.

Security does reduce economic growth in some respects, but it probably increases growth over-all. Protection against the adverse effects of change contributes substantially to widespread worker cooperation or ready acceptance of technological change in a dynamic economy. Both private and government insurance funds help stabilize the economy and thus encourage longer-run, more rational business and consumer decisions. Fund balances are not a net loss to the economy as they are invested in securities.

Sensible Course.   Present systems of income security are "paternalistic," but voluntary saving has never been adequate. Without these programs, we would still have paternalistic care for the improvident and unfortunate. Then either all taxpayers would be forced to pay for relief, or some individuals would be forced to carry the burden of private relief. It is much easier and more sensible to prevent poverty than to cure its many evil effects.

We are much better off in our struggle to improve our systems of income security than we were a decade ago without adequate protection against the unavoidable economic hazards of modern life. There is a price to pay, but in return for planning and effort we can obtain higher quality working forces, improved management, sounder industrial relationships, and better hospital and medical care. The cost is not a serious burden if we maintain a healthy and growing economy.

Our ability to protect the employee against the vicissitudes of the modern business and industrial world may well determine the success of our free enterprise system.

[41]   *The Canadian Plan*
*for Hospital Care**

by U.S. NEWS & WORLD REPORT

People of Canada now are taking a long step along the road of socialized medical care. How well they make out is expected to have a big part in determining whether the United States takes a similar course.

Just a few days ago, on April 13, the U. S. Congress got a report on the cost of free hospital insurance for only one group of Americans—those on Social Security pensions.

The Department of Health, Education and Welfare reported that such insurance would cost a billion dollars a year at the start, and lead to demands for broader aid to other groups. Legislation for the insurance is strongly backed by U.S. labor unions.

In Canada, free, or nearly free, hospitalization has begun in seven of 10 provinces. Two more provinces are expected to join this summer, leaving Quebec the only holdout. The high and rising cost of hospital care had led four provinces into earlier experiments with Government subsidies. A system that is nearly nation-wide has followed.

Most Canadians who are ill today are assured of bed and board in a hospital ward with no limit on the length of stay. In two provinces— Alberta and British Columbia—a "deterrent charge" of $1 to $2 a day is made. In other provinces, the service is free.

Other free services include: all necessary nursing, X rays, laboratory

* Reprinted from *U.S. News & World Report* (April 27, 1959), an independent weekly news magazine published at Washington. Copyright 1959 United States News Publishing Corporation.

and diagnostic services, use of operating rooms, anesthetics, routine surgical supplies, drugs, when administered in hospitals; blood transfusions; use of radio-therapy and physical therapy, when equipment is available.

If "medical necessity" requires it, a patient is entitled to a private room and special nursing care. The attending physician decides upon "medical necessity." Otherwise, such extras as a special nurse or a private room must be paid for by the patient.

"State Medicine"? Not Yet. Canada is undertaking to provide for everyone broader hospital care than that offered by privately financed hospital insurance in the United States. Canadians point out, though, that they are stopping short of "state medicine."

The following services, provided free in Great Britain, are not available without charge to the people of Canada: payment of doctors' bills or surgeons' fees; private nurses, except for "medical necessity"; ambulance service; dental care; false teeth; eye examinations; eyeglasses; hearing aids; crutches, canes and wheel chairs.

The Canadian plan also excludes, in most provinces, the type of special care and treatment that patients get in tuberculosis sanitoriums, cancer clinics, mental hospitals, old-age homes and rehabilitation centers. In most provinces, there are other arrangements for these services. . . .

The federal share comes out of the Federal Treasury. The provinces have adopted a variety of taxes to meet their share. . . .

Total cost of hospital insurance is estimated by Canadians to come high. The Federal Government is expected to provide 160 million dollars as its share for the fiscal year that ends March 31, 1960. The provinces are expected to provide at least that much or more.

Ontario, for example, estimates that the first year of the plan will cost the province 233 million dollars, with 75 million coming from federal funds, 71 million from the provincial treasury, and 87 million raised from the premiums deducted from payrolls.

The plan is designed to provide hospital insurance for each one of the 17.3 million persons in the Canadian population. Basic hospital care is to be offered regardless of income, or financial resources. Most of the voluntary hospital-insurance programs, such as Blue Cross, have been taken over by the provincial governments. These private organizations, however, are continuing to operate on a reduced scale by offering "superior accommodations" not included in the Government program.

More Hospitals Coming? Hospitals also are expected to be freed from annual deficits and financial worries. Each hospital accepted by provincial authorities submits a budget and, after the budget is approved, its costs are reimbursed.

The program is expected to lead to more hospital construction on a nationwide basis. Agreements signed between the provinces and the Government in Ottawa call for minimum standards which all hospitals are supposed to meet. And the Federal Government agrees to help the provinces with special grants to meet hospital needs.

The "Financial Post" of Toronto estimates that the total cost of hospital insurance and new construction will be more than 3 billion dollars in the next five years. This program is being adopted in a country where the annual budget has never exceeded 5.4 billion dollars.

Private doctors are being relied on to keep hospital costs within bounds. The relations of doctors and patients are not disturbed by hospital insurance, but Government authorities expect that doctors will not be too lenient in recommending hospital treatment. If they are, officials say, costs will get out of bounds.

[CHAPTER TWENTY]

Labor Relations and the Public Welfare

NO area in our economy is the source of more problems than that which involves the relations between employers and organized labor. To give the reader some concept of the significance of the modern labor movement, we have chosen for our first selection a chapter from a recent book by Daniel Bell. In this chapter he deals with what he considers to be the unique characteristics, the problems, and the underlying philosophy of American trade-unionism. For our second selection we have included a paper by George Terborgh in which he explains the widely-held theory that union pressures for higher wages are an important cause of inflation.

[42] The Capitalism of the Proletariat: A Theory of American Trade-Unionism*

by DANIEL BELL

Trade-unionism, said George Bernard Shaw, is the capitalism of the proletariat. Like all such epigrams, it is a half-truth, calculated to irritate the people who believe in the other half. American trade-unionism would seem to embody Shaw's description, but in fact it only half-embodies it— at most. True, the American labor leader will mock socialism and uphold capitalism; yet he has built the most aggressive trade-union movement in the world—and one, moreover, that has larger interests than mere economic gain. Abroad, the European Marxist hears the labor leader praise the free enterprise system as the most successful method yet devised for a worker to obtain a fair, and rising share, of the country's wealth; within the United States, the American businessman listens to the labor leader denouncing him in wild and often reckless rhetoric as a greedy profiteer, monopolist, and exploiter. How reconcile these contradictions? One U.S. labor leader sought to do so in these terms: *to* your wife, he said, you talk one way; *about* your wife, you talk another. Very clever; but, one might add, another half-truth—at most.

William James once said that whenever you meet a contradiction you must make a distinction, for people use the same words but mean two different things. One way out of this seeming contradiction, therefore, is to see American trade-unionism as existing in two contexts, as a *social movement* and as an economic force (*market-unionism*), and accordingly playing a different role in each. The social movement is an *ideological* conception, shaped by intellectuals, which sees labor as part of a historical trend that challenges the established order. Market-unionism, on the other hand, is an *economic* conception, a delimiting of role and function, imposed by the realities of the specific industrial environment in which the union operates.

Any labor movement finds itself subject to all the ideological pressures of the "left," whether social, communist, or syndicalist. After all, it is in the name of the workers that these social movements proclaim their slogans; and the labor movement itself is one of the chief vehicles of social change. But in the United States, the image of trade-unionism as

* From *The End of Ideology* by Daniel Bell, pp. 208-221, Glencoe, Ill., *The Free Press.* Copyright © 1960 by *The Free Press,* a corporation. Reprinted by permission.

a social movement took a unique course, as plotted in the theory—inspired largely by the "Wisconsin school" of John R. Commons and Selig Perlman —of "Laborism." The theory argues that the trade-union movement, although fashioned ideologically, has a different source of cohesion than the radical movement, i.e., the limited, day-to-day, expectation of social improvement. By its concentration on the specific issues at hand, it must necessarily reject the far-flung socialist and radical ideologies; unlike them, it is both in the world and *of* the world. In its operation, it can indeed become a force for social change, but only by "sharing" power rather than seeking the radical transformation of society. This sharing of power takes place both in the factory—through bargaining on wages and working conditions, and sometimes on production standards—and in the larger society, through seeking legislation for the increased welfare of the worker.

"Laborism" is the dominant ideology, to the extent that there is one, of the American labor movement. In the past it has been the conservative defense of the unions against the recriminations of the radicals; it was a rationalization of the purely economic role of the unions. Yet, despite its theorists, even it has come to have a political force of its own. Pale ideology though it is, it still conceives of unionism as a social movement, and it still conceives of itself as being opposed to the employer class as a whole. Contemporary American unionism could only have flourished with the aid of a favorable political—and social—climate, which was provided by the New Deal. More importantly, the Roosevelt Administration provided, through law, two extraordinary protections: first, the legal obligation of employer to bargain collectively with unions; and second, the granting of *exclusive* representation rights to a *single* union within a defined bargaining unit. This, plus the growth of various union security devices (e.g., maintenance-of-membership clauses, union shop, etc.) gave the unions a legal protection that few union movements enjoyed anywhere. "Laborism" is associated usually with the New Deal and Fair Deal, and with the left wing of the Democratic party. It calls for improved social-welfare benefits, for a tax program which falls mostly on the wealthy, and it cries out incessantly against "monopolies."

But here lies an anomaly and the source of a contradiction; for *market-unionism*, collective-bargaining unionism, can only exist in monopoly situations, a monopoly created either by the employers or by the unions. In fact, the only industries in the United States where unionism is strong today are those where a monopoly situation, industry- or union-created, exists.

The reason is fairly simple. *The chief purpose of market-unionism is to eliminate wages as a factor in competition.* Where an industry is only partially unionized and wages therefore can be utilized as a competitive lever, a union must either impose a monopoly or go under; the erosion of the American textile unions is a case in point.

The pattern of monopoly follows that of the different markets. In oligopolistic markets, i.e., in industries dominated by a few giant firms, the unions eliminate wages as a competitive factor by "pattern bargaining," that is, by imposing wage agreement on all firms in the industry. While, theoretically, bargaining is still done with individual firms, in practice (as is seen in the case of steel) the agreement is industry-wide. In the highly competitive or small-unit-size fields, the unions have stepped in and provided a monopoly structure to the market, limiting the entry of firms into the industry, establishing price lines, etc. This has been true most notably in the coal industry, in the garment industry, and in the construction trades.

In coal, where the industry could not do it itself, the miners' union has enforced a basic price floor for the entire industry. This has been done in various ways: through legislative price-fixing, as in the Guffey Coal Act of the first years of the New Deal; outright production-restriction schemes, as in Pennsylvania, which limit the tonnage of anthracite that can be mined in the state; by keeping the mines open only three days a week; by staggered strikes in order to reduce coal surpluses, etc.

The garment unions have established a fixed series of price lines, or grades, for men's clothing and women's dresses, thus bringing order out of chaotic competition. By limiting the number of contractors who can sew and finish dresses for a single manufacturer, and by stopping firms from moving out of a fixed geographical area, the International Ladies' Garment Workers' Union has been able to restrict the number of firms in the industry and to police the market.

The most elaborate form of market stabilization exists in the construction trades. The power of the unions resides in the fact that they serve as a work contractor, i.e., as the labor-force recruiting agent, for the employer. Few of the firms that bid on the heavy construction work (dams, power stations, roads, factories, atomic installations, etc.) maintain a permanent labor force; nor do they know the local labor market; they rely on the union to supply experienced and skilled men. Even the small home-builder needs the union to provide stability. The major factor in the cost of each competing home contractor is the wages he must pay. In northern California alone, there are 12,000 construction firms bidding on various home constructions. The union is in no position to bargain with each single contractor. Therefore the union organizes an *employers'* association and enforces stability in the market by holding wage rates constant over a period of time.

Long ago, the construction unions and the contractors were quick to realize the monopoly advantages to be gained by mutual co-operation. Thus, on many local projects, outside contractors are kept out because the unions refuse to supply them with labor; or if they win a bid, they find themselves afflicted by strikes or slowdowns.

Often the union, as in the case of coal, can decide the fate of firms and the future of an industry. Because of competing fuels, like natural gas and oil, the demand for coal has shrunk almost a third in the last ten years. John L. Lewis and the union faced a choice. Either they could seek to restrict output and force all the firms in the industry to share the dwindling market, thus saving the marginal firms, or they could allow the marginal firms to go to the wall. In the decisive coal negotiations of 1952 the Southern coal producers, owners mostly of smaller mines, offered to meet all the union demands if Lewis would order three-day production in the industry. The large mechanized mines opposed this move since it meant higher overhead costs for unutilized equipment. Lewis, reversing a previous course, chose to line up with the large mechanized mines and their desire for continuous output. The decision meant higher wages for the men but a permanent loss of jobs in the industry. The union could accept that because of the natural attrition of an aging mine work force. Other unions could not solve the dilemma so easily.

Thus it is that a trade-union, operating in a given market environment, necessarily becomes an ally of "its" industry. Less realized is the fact that, in the evolution of the labor contract, the union becomes part of the "control system of management." He becomes, as C. Wright Mills has put it, a "manager of discontent."

It is difficult for a manager, faced with an aggressive group of union leaders across a bargaining table, to realize that the trade-union performs a vital function *for him.* All he can think of is that, because of the union, he has lost some of his power. And to a great extent this is true: he cannot fire a man at whim, promotions are on the basis of seniority, a foreman cannot make job transfers—these are performed by the union.

But in taking over these powers the union also takes over the difficult function of specifying priorities of demands, and in so doing, it not only relieves management of many political headaches but becomes a buffer between management and rank-and-file resentments. The union, particularly on the local plant level, is not a monolith but a web of interest groups which reaches far down to the lowest unit of plant organization, the work group. These interests often conflict: skilled vs. unskilled, piece-work vs. hourly-paid, night-shift vs. day-shift, old vs. young. In formulating its demands, the union has to decide: should a wage increase go "across the board" (i.e., be equal for everybody) or should it be on a percentage basis in order to maintain the differentials in skill?

The second fact is that the union often takes over the task of disciplining the men, when management cannot. This is particularly true during "wildcat strikes," when the men refuse to acknowledge the authority of management but are forced back to work by the union leaders who, by the logic of a bargain, have to enforce a contract.

Managing these discontents becomes difficult not only at bargaining periods but throughout the year as well. During a time of layoffs, the question of which type of seniority is to be followed (whether by particular type of work or by a plant-wide list) becomes a bread-and-butter struggle. But the major headache arises when workers, in order to keep a company competitive, and thus safeguard jobs, cut their wage rates, tighten their time assignments, and accept increased production loads. In effect, they disrupt the uniform patterns which the union has been seeking to impose throughout the industry. The problem of "my company first" is one that has plagued the United Auto Workers: should the national office seek to maintain uniform standards, and if so, to push the marginal company to the wall? Or should it protect the employment of the men by allowing them to cut wages and reduce standards? In recent years, the UAW has chosen to safeguard employment.

The question of "my company first" has its counterpart in this "my industry first" attitude of different unions. Thus the interest conflicts become raised to national levels. The teamsters oppose government favors for the railroad. The coal union seeks higher tariffs against foreign oil production and unites with the railroads—since the railroads gain a large share of their income from hauling coal—in joint lobbying ventures. The machinists, whose strength is in the aircraft industry, will lobby for more planes, while the boilermakers, who construct ships, urge a larger navy. More generally, unions will often engage in joint promotional campaigns with an industry in order to stimulate demand and save jobs. This is as true for the "socialist" Ladies' Garment Workers as for the narrow, craft-minded plasterers' union. In these, as in many other instances (e.g., trucking, glass, etc.), the initiative has come from the unions, since they are more powerful and more market-conscious than any single firm.

In effect, then, the logic of market-unionism leads to a limited, uneasy partnership of union and company, or union and industry; uneasy because in many cases employers would still prefer to exercise sole power, although the more sophisticated employers know the value of such powerful allies as the union in safeguarding their interests; uneasy, too, because there is still the historic tendency of labor, acting as a social movement, to oppose the employers as a class. This tendency derives from the ideological conception of labor as the "underdog." More specifically, it has been reinforced by the political alliances, forged in the early days of the New Deal, which enabled labor to obtain legislative protection for its organizing activities. These political alliances lead necessarily to wider areas of group or class conflict: tax policy, subsidized housing, medical insurance, and the whole range of welfare measures which add up to a more or less coherent philosophy of liberal politics.

The distinction between the *social movement* and *market-unionism* is not, as might seem at first glance, a distinction between political and collective-bargaining unionism. In present-day society, the latter division no longer exists. All unions are, willy-nilly, forced into politics. The problem is what sort of politics will be played. Will the AFL-CIO simply be a political arm for market-unionism, protecting the various interest groups that are its members, or will it become part of a genuine social movement?

Some clue to the answer may be found from American labor's past. In the nineteenth century there were four main strands: fraternalism, cooperation, political action, and collective bargaining. While one easily assumes that collective bargaining is the unique form of American unionism, it took nearly a half a century of debate and experiment to come to this form. United States labor was always reluctant to accept the wages system. Its early organizers sought escape in free land, money reform, and failing that, in the creation of producer co-operatives. The vast power of industry, and the openness of the political system, caused many individuals to feel that political action, rather than economic bargaining, was the easier road to better conditions. The large movement for shorter hours, for example, in the 1880's, was almost entirely a political movement. But the unwillingness of the Socialists to modify their goals, and the insistence by Gompers on separate trade organization which could achieve an integral role in the market, turned American labor to its bargaining role. But, always, concurrently, there was the image of the social movement. If we apply the distinction between social movement and market-unionism to the past, we derive the following periodization:

(1) From 1860 to 1880, U.S. labor was primarily a social movement. The socialist and anarchist influences were paramount. There was a high degree of political activity, and many efforts to create labor parties. Unions built producers' co-operatives and supported many reform schemes. The extent of organization, however, was small.

(2) From 1880 to 1920, the two tendencies were in conflict: the AFL

represented the narrow conception of market-unionism, while such groups as the Socialists, the IWW, and other anarcho-syndicalist elements sought to build radical labor movements. The AFL won out.

(3) From 1933 to 1940 (the period of the 1920's was one of stagnation), labor once again assumed the role of a social movement. The emerging CIO, faced by the attacks of the industrial combines, tended to take on an ideological coloration. The influx of the intellectuals, particularly the Socialists and the Communists, heightened this radical political quality. Support by the federal government gave labor an awareness of the necessity for political action. And John L. Lewis, a shrewd and dynamic labor leader, realized the possibility of welding together a new political bloc.

(4) From 1940 to 1955, labor lost this ideological flavor and concentrated, instead, on market-unionism. There were several reasons. First, the sense of national unity created by the war. Second, the acceptance by large industry of trade-unionism, at first because of the need for uninterrupted production, later because of the realization that the unions could not be broken directly. Third, the need of the newly built unions to consolidate their collective-bargaining position in the plant. Fourth, the attack on the Communists in the unions, beginning in 1947, and the eventual elimination of their influence.

And the future? Where U.S. labor goes from here is a difficult question, for the trade-union movement is now at an impasse. The source of its difficulty lies deep in the facts of present-day American life.

1. *Union membership has reached its upper limit.* In the last seven years U.S. unions have ceased to grow. In fact, the proportion of the unionized in the work force has actually declined.

Today there are roughly 16 million workers (plus another 850,000 members of Canadian affiliates) belonging to American trade-unions as against 2 million a quarter of a century ago. Measured against a labor force of 65 million persons, this is slightly under 25 per cent; seen more realistically as a porportion of the wage and salaried persons (i.e., excluding farmers, self-employed professionals, and small businessmen), the unions have organized about 30 per cent of the employee group of the society. But in organizing this 30 per cent, they have reached a saturation mark; they have organized as much of their potential as they can.

If one distinguishes between blue-collar and white-collar workers, then it is likely that about 75 per cent of the blue-collar force—factory workers, miners, railway men, building craftsmen, and laborers—belong to unions. In coal and metal mining, in railroad and construction, in public utilities, unions have organized between 80 and 90 per cent of the blue-collar force. In basic manufacturing—auto, aircraft, steel, rubber, ship, glass, paper, electrical equipment, transportation equipment—about 80 per cent of plant production workers are organized. The remaining obstacle in the unorganized units is their small size. A UAW survey, for example, showed that 97 per cent of the unorganized plants within the union's "jurisdiction" have less than fifty workers. These plants are extremely difficult to organize. The social relations within a small firm are very different from those in a large one: the identification with an employer is greater; employer counter-pressure is easier; the cost to the union of reaching and servicing these places is very high and often "uneconomic," since unions, as business organizations, have their cost and efficiency problems as well. The only unorganized *industries* are oil, chemicals, and textiles. In oil and chemicals, wages are extraordinarily high because labor costs are only a slight element in total costs, and workers are organized in independent unions. In textiles, the old paternalistic and Southern mill-village pattern has been strong enough to resist unionization.

What then of the other fields? In the trade and service fields, employing about fifteen million workers, unions have only a slight foothold—in restaurants, hotels, laundries—but usually only in the metropolitan centers where other unions have been able to help organization. Most of these units are small, and thus difficult to organize. With the expansion of the *distributive field,* general unions, such as the Teamsters, are bound to grow, particularly since the Teamster method of organization is often to organize employer associations and "blanket" the workers into the unions. But this growth will be offset by the shrinkage in the *industrial* work force.[1]

In the white-collar and office field (banks, real estate, insurance, as well as the office forces of the large industrial companies), unions have failed signally. In plants where the blue-collar force is organized, the firm usually follows the practice of granting tandem wage increases to the office workers, so that the latter have no need or incentive to join a union. In the insurance companies and in white-collar employment generally, there is a high turnover. Jobs are held by young girls, recruited directly from school, who leave for marriage after five or six years and who are reluctant to join a union. In general, white-collar workers in the U.S., for status reasons, fear to identify themselves with the dirty-handed blue-collar workers. In European and Asian countries, teachers and civil service employees may consider themselves the leaders of the working class.

---

[1] It is likely that many craft and industrial unions, in order to resist shrinkage, will become "general" unions taking in whatever workers are at hand. This is what John L. Lewis tried with his District 50 of the Mine Workers, and this is what Hoffa is doing in 1959.

In the U.S. these groups seek to emphasize the differences between them.

2. *Unions have reached the limits of collective bargaining.* This may be a startling statement, but yet it is one of the most important facts tending to reshape the American labor movement. By the "limits of collective bargaining" I mean simply the growing awareness by unions that they can obtain wage and welfare increases equal only to the increases in the productivity of the country. Such a story may be an old one to unions in Europe, who are sensitive to the trade positions of their countries, but it is new in the United States.

Even the *idea* of productivity is a relatively recent one. (It is, perhaps, one of the reasons why Marx's analysis of capitalism has been proven wrong. For Marx, wealth was gained through "exploitation." Now we can see that wealth, private corporate wealth and national wealth, increases only through increases in productivity.) The turning point in American labor history, I think, came with the idea of the annual productivity wage increases. This is the conception that the workers are entitled *each year* to a wage increase, above and beyond the change in the cost of living. One may argue about how much productivity has advanced —whether it is 2 per cent, 3 per cent, or 4 per cent; these are statistical questions. What is settled is the fact that each year the living standard of the worker will advance—in the case of the auto workers, about 3 per cent. (If one compounds the 3 per cent increase, then the living standards will have doubled in a little over twenty-five years.) Curiously, the idea of the productivity wage increase was not a union but a corporation innovation, by General Motors. The company offered such a wage increase in return for a five-year contract, guaranteeing labor peace.

Today the idea of the productivity wage increase has spread throughout most of basic American manufacturing. In this way a strong demand factor is built into the economy, thus holding off a downturn of the business cycle. But wage rises are geared to the most productive sector of the economy, while inefficient firms, or industries which by their nature cannot increase productivity (barbers, waiters, etc.), have to match these increases. This leads to a strong inflationary impact on the economy.

Such questions aside, the importance of the productivity wage increase is that, despite the lingering rhetoric of militancy, unions have accepted the idea of limits to what can be obtained through economic bargaining. I do not mean to suggest that there will be no more bargaining. But we have here the *bureaucratization* of bargaining in the establishment of limits.[2]

[2] Arthur Ross has noted "the withering away of the strike," the fact that in the U.S. and almost every country there is a secular decline in the number of strikes. This is, I suggest, a consequence of such bureaucratization and the knowledge of limits.

3. *The rise of the salariat.* A third crucial change in the nature of the American labor movement arises from the shifting composition of the work force. Briefly put, the *proletariat* is being replaced by a *salariat,* with a consequent change in the psychology of the workers. The trend arises in part from the fact, as Colin Clark long ago noted, that with increasing productivity, greater output is being achieved with a smaller industrial work force, while the demand for new services, entertainment, recreation, and research means the spread of more and new middle-class occupations.

But we have appreciated less the changes in the work force *within* the giant manufacturing firms themselves. For with the increases in production have come increases in research, merchandising, sales and office force, etc. In the chemical industry, for example, from 1947 to 1952, production increased 50 per cent; the blue-collar force increased 3 per cent; the white-collar force by 50 per cent. In the fifteen largest corporations in the country, the salaried work force is already one-third to one-half of the hourly-paid production force. . . .

The change to a "salariat" has been intensified in the 1950's by two principal developments: the enormous rise in research and development within American industry, creating a new technical class, and the expansion of automation processes which result in the upgrading of skilled workers. From 1947 to 1957, the number of professional and technical workers increased by 60 per cent, the highest growth rate of any occupational group in the post-World War II period. In the next decade, this group increased an additional 43 per cent, or two-and-a-half times as fast as the labor force as a whole. While the semi-skilled group remained almost constant over ten years (from 12.2 to 12.9 million workers), the technical and professional, the non-production worker, has increased over 50 per cent in the same period. If one excludes the service fields, the number of white-collar workers in the United States by 1956, for the first time in U.S. history, exceeded the number of blue-collar workers.

These salaried groups do not speak the old language of labor. Nor can they be appealed to in the old class-conscious terms. Their rise poses a difficult problem for the leadership of the American labor movement.

4. *The loss of* élan *and the disfavor of the public.* The labor movement, in its present form, is less than twenty-five years old, and the men on top are the men who built it. But they are no longer young—the average age of the AFL-CIO executive council is in the middle sixties—and they have lost their *élan*. The organizing staffs, too, are old, and there is no longer the reservoir of young radicals to rely on for passing out leaflets at the plant gates.

But more than this, there is a crisis in union morality and public confidence. It is not simply a problem of racketeering.[3] Racketeering is shaped by the market. It has always had a hold in the small-unit construction trades, the longshoremen, and the teamsters, where the chief cost to an employer is "waiting time" and where one can therefore easily exact a toll from employers. And one finds no racketeering in the mass-production industries. Even in the fields where "shakedowns" are common, racketeering is on a considerably smaller scale today than twenty-five years ago, when the industrial gangster flourished in the U.S. The real sickness lies in the decline of unionism as a moral vocation, the fact that so many union leaders have become money-hungry, taking on the grossest features of business society, despoiling the union treasuries for private gain. And where there has not been outright spoliation—typical of the teamster, bakery, textile, and laundry unions—one finds among union leaders an appalling arrogance and high-handedness in their relation to the rank and file, which derives from the corruption of power. Such gross manifestations of power have alienated a middle-class public which, for twenty years, was tolerant of, if not sympathetic to, unionism.

The future of any movement depends upon the character of its leaders, the strength of its traditions (the impelling force) and the sharpness of its goals (the compelling forces), and the challenges of the society of which it is a part.

Certainly the radical tradition of the labor movement has almost vanished, and of those individuals who came out of the Socialist or left-wing movement, such as Dubinsky, Potofsky, Rieve, Curran, Quill, and Reuther, only Reuther still has the drive and desire to widen labor's definition of its goals. The men at the top of labor unions today have little energy for intensive political action or a desire to take a leading political role. At the middle levels, which reflect themselves largely in the state and city rather than national scenes, many of the younger labor leaders are eager for means to enhance their status and power, and it is quite likely that these men will step into the political arena in order to gain recognition and will do so by becoming more active in the Democratic party.

On the national level, the men who hold the stage are George Meany, Jimmy Hoffa, and Walter Reuther. Meany, by taking command of a reunited labor movement, has already written his page in history. Hoffa is ambitious, but other than consolidating his power over a strong union

[3] Given my distinction between *market-unionism* and the *social movement,* one can say that racketeering is a pathology of market-unionism, while communism is the pathology of the social movement.

and thus thumbing his nose at his detractors, there is little he can do politically. He is anti-intellectual, uneasy with ideas and those who articulate them because of his own inferiority in these realms, and lacking in any political or moral perspective. He can, on occasion, preach a primitive class war, more raw than anything Walter Reuther could or even would say, but this is a reflex of his temperament, which is to resolve all issues by action rather than ideas. He has extraordinary drive and ambition, but no direction. And the effort of various aides to provide him with one fell under Hoffa's own impatience. What ultimately will curb Hoffa is a craving for respectability, which is masked under the veneer of toughness. But it is there nonetheless; and this will tame him. Walter Reuther cares little for the respectability—the flattery of the press and the business community—which other labor leaders have sought; he has, still, a sense of mission (though the dogmatic edges have been dulled) and the respect of the liberal community which he gained twenty years ago. At age fifty (in 1958) Reuther still has a long future ahead of him. He is not popular with his labor peers. He makes them uncomfortable. He will not relax. His vices are few and his energies are great. Like the Jansenist confronting the "whiskey priests," his example calls them to account for their own moral failures. Yet, there is no one else in sight who can lead them. And Reuther temperamentally is an ideologist, though his skills are eminently practical; he can temper vision to reality, and his conception of the labor movement is a social one.

It is quite possible that the labor movement may sink, slowly, slothfully into the market role of being a junior partner to industry, as is now the case with the building trades. But it is more likely, in my opinion, that in the years ahead we will find U.S. labor seeking to redefine itself as a social movement.

Apart from the possible role of Reuther, one reason is that, with politics becoming so intertwined with bargaining, the need to extend labor's political power means that the unions will have to play a more direct role in the Democratic party and will have to build a liberal coalition in order to strengthen their own position in that party. If collective bargaining has reached a limit, then politics becomes an important arena.

A subtle change in the political process itself, molded by the spread of mass media and mass communication, reinforces this tendency. This is the emergence of what may be called "symbol" groups (or those bearing ideological tags), as against the "interest" groups (with their single focus on protecting the specific tangible interest of a specific, tangible group). For in a mass society, where public opinion is king, various groups are more than ever forced to assume some coherent identity and to clothe their aims in national or general-interest terms. This is particularly true where the poll concept of democracy takes hold, for polls can only formulate problems in symbolic terms, such as: what should *The Farmer* do? (without worrying about the complication that "The Farmer" is a whole spectrum of persons); or what should *Labor* do? (without enquiring further about the meaning of such a generic term as "Labor"). However, not only the nature of polls but also the new process of informal group representation in government becomes a shaping element in this fusion of coherent identities. Thus "Business" is asked to name its representatives to a government advisory board; and "Labor" is asked likewise. Political issues become national in scope, and "Labor," as a symbolic group, is asked to define "its" attitude toward such issues; and it has to learn to compose its internal differences in doing so. One of the pressures for unity between the AFL and CIO, for example, was the need to have a single set of spokesmen to speak for "labor" on various national issues.

A third element is the rise of "status anxieties" in the business community, a rising concern about the threat of "Big Labor" and its political influences at a time when the trade-union movement is ideologically exhausted and beset with hardening of its organizational arteries. The agitation over the "right-to-work" laws bore all the marks of an emotional crusade rather than a national *interest* attempt to deal with labor power. A study in 1958 by Frederic Meyers for the Fund for the Republic of the effects of the right-to-work law after five years in Texas showed that it had no effect at all. Unions were not hurt, industrial relations were no different than before, but employers had gained emotional satisfaction from the fact that a law which labor had fought was on the books. The right-to-work campaigns in California, Ohio, and other states in 1958 were sponsored predominantly by middle-sized concerns, while big business, with the exception of General Electric, stood aloof. For these employers, many of whom run multi-million-dollar industries, were clearly motivated by resentment of union power, even though that power had become stabilized and the pattern of industrial relations had become settled. It may well be that the business community thought that with the election and re-election of Dwight Eisenhower and the Republican party, the unions would roll over and surrender. But the unions didn't. The choleric reaction of many employers to the name of Walter Reuther—especially those who have never dealt with him and the UAW but to whom he is the symbol of perhaps new labor power—indicates that, on the national and political level, the labor-management tensions are no longer fired by interest-group conflict, though this exists, but in symbolic and emotional terms.

If American labor does develop more as a social movement in the next decade, what will be the political and ideological content of this new unionism? This is difficult to say. The "left" ideology has in recent years become utterly exhausted; and the idea of nationalization holds no appeal. Most likely we shall see the re-emergence of a rather more emphatic version of "Laborism," insisting more vigorously than ever before on such benefits as better housing, more schools, adequate medical care, the creation of a more "humanistic" work atmosphere in the factory, and the like. These are generally prosaic in nature, and it takes great skill on the part of an individual to dramatize them. The question is, who among the labor leaders could fire the imagination of the union leadership and rank-and-file? Walter Reuther thinks he can, but it is problematic whether he will be given the opportunity. The opposition to him, among his labor peers, is so great that if he assumed the leadership of the labor movement, following the retirement of George Meany, a split might ensue. To avoid one, it seems likely that the AFL-CIO would choose a middle-of-the-road individual such as Albert J. Hayes, of the Machinists. And it is possible that Walter Reuther, like John L. Lewis, might become one more "lost leader" of labor. To the extent that personality and imagination count in social action—and I think their weight is great—this would be a loss indeed.

[43]   *Wage Induced Inflation**

by GEORGE TERBORGH

The next couple of decades promise plenty of economic problems for the United States and a choice of the most important is not easy. No one problem can be expected to remain continuously pre-eminent over so long a period, for relative urgencies will shift with changing conditions. The choice, I take it, should turn on relative importance over the period as a

* Reprinted from *Problems of United States Economic Development*, Vol. I, January 1958, published by Committee for Economic Development, 711 Fifth Ave., New York 22, N.Y.

whole. On this assumption I have selected a long-range problem that promises to be with us most of the time over the next 20 years, and that from all present appearances may well be with us at the end. I refer to the problem of maintaining a satisfactory level of production and employment without creeping price inflation.

While this problem has other aspects, the heart of it is a lop-sided balance of power between management and labor in modern collective bargaining. With the privileges and immunities that labor unions now enjoy, it has become impossible, under conditions of reasonably full employment and expanding production, to hold the average rise in labor costs to the average rise in productivity. The inevitable result is a creeping advance in the general indexes of prices and living costs.

We hasten to say that this proposition implies no criticism either of union leaders or of the rank and file. The labor movement represents a cross section of the American public, no better and no worse than the rest. Nor does it concern the so-called "abuses" of unionism, recently dramatized in the activities of Dave Beck, Jimmy Hoffa, and Johnny Dio. Deplorable as they may be, these abuses have comparatively little to do with the problem. They could be totally eradicated and it would still be with us. For it arises, not from the *unlawful*, but from the *lawful,* operations of unionism.

This is not an essay on demonology, therefore; it is on social institutions. The fault lies in the lop-sided balance of power created by these institutions, not in human wickedness. Nothing is sillier than to blame unions for taking advantage of the power that is lawfully theirs, and certainly nothing is more futile than to hope that they will voluntarily forego its exercise. The remedy lies rather in institutional reforms that will create a non-inflationary balance of power in collective bargaining, that is to say, a balance that will hold the general advance in labor costs to the general rise in the productivity of the economy.

I have nominated the problem of wage-induced inflation as the most important for the next 20 years, in part because the remedy seems so far away. For a condition precedent to remedial action is an agreed diagnosis. At present there is none. Union leadership still denies that the problem exists. The upcreep of prices is attributed to the excessive profits of greedy employers, who could absorb wage increases if they only would. It is still possible to find university professors who insist on theoretical grounds that collective bargaining cannot raise costs and prices above the level that would obtain in its absence. But even among those less obviously self-interested or doctrinaire, there is as yet no clear agreement on the problem. Public opinion remains either confused or non-existent. As for the politicians, a subject so politically delicate as excessive wage demands is avoided if possible, and is mentioned if necessary only in terms of studied equivocation.

The standard posture of the politician in addressing this issue is a straddle. He implies he really doesn't know whether price inflation is due to excessive wage settlements or to excessive profits. So far as he can tell, both are equally to blame. He proceeds therefore to pious admonition to both labor and management, urging the one to be moderate in its wage demands, the other to be moderate in its pricing policy. It goes without saying that the public gains no enlightenment whatever from this political balancing act.

This is said, not to blame the politicians—I do not ask them to be heroes—but simply to confirm the absence of any strong sentiment against excessive wage settlements. There does not yet exist the necessary basis in public opinion for an attack on the problem.

We are the victims of a cultural lag. In this day of huge, monolithic labor monopolies, endowed with special privileges and immunities by the state, we still retain the attitudes and sentiments of an earlier day when a weak union movement was struggling against heavy odds. Labor is still regarded by most people as the underdog, and the public reaction to union wage demands is still, in the main, indiscriminately favorable. Thus when a powerful union leader in an already high-wage industry announces that he is going to exact 45 cents an hour in the next contract, the announcement is greeted, not with anguished protest, but with acquiescence or even positive approval.

This reaction is due not only to long emotional conditioning, but also to widespread acceptance of the myth, sedulously propagated by union leadership, that wage increases can come out of profits. They may come out of profits for brief periods of time in particular situations, but they cannot do so generally and for long without killing off production and precipitating a recession. We have had enough wage increases in the last 10 years to wipe out profits many times over, but they are still with us. Industry has passed on to the market in higher prices substantially all of the increase in labor (and other) costs not offset by rising productivity, and it will have to continue to do so if we are to maintain a prosperous economy. The notion that wage increases in excess of productivity can be "absorbed" is a popular delusion.

Another reason for the indulgent attitude of the public toward excessive wage demands is the common belief that wage increases initiated in one industry or sector of the economy will spread to others, with benefit to workers not directly involved. This belief can be summed up in the slogan "We'll get ours later." To what extent and under what conditions this expectation is valid, is a matter of debate into which I need not enter. For the point is simply this. Even if the expectation were completely valid—even if everyone were to keep pace with the wage leaders—the result would still be inflation. And inflation is the problem I am talking about.

Since the necessary climate of public opinion for an attack on wage-induced inflation does not yet exist, I can only conclude that we will have to live with the problem for a good many years. This does not mean that the upcreep of living costs will be continuous and uninterrupted. There may be times when falling raw-material prices (for example, the falling farm prices of 1951-55) will mask the effect of rising labor costs in fabrication and distribution. There may be periods of economic recession when the march of hourly wage rates slows up and profit margins are squeezed. But in conditions of prosperity and full employment—which it is the policy and obligation of the federal government to maintain so far as possible—we may expect that in general the cost of living will creep irregularly but persistently upward.

The basic problem, as I have said, is a lop-sided balance of power in modern collective bargaining. We will live with this problem until we have the wit to diagnose it and the courage to do something about it. In the meantime, we must be careful that in our desire to suppress the consequences of this disbalance of power we do not overwork anti-inflationary policies designed to cope with other problems.

I refer primarily to credit and fiscal policies. These are appropriate for dealing with the kind of price inflation that results from excessive demand for goods and services—from a generally taut and overstrained economy —but it has still to be demonstrated that they can effectively prevent the price consequences of modern collective bargaining without generating worse evils in the process.

Credit and fiscal policies can undoubtedly reduce the bargaining power of unions, but they do so only by slackening the economy itself. In a slack economy, cost increases are harder to pass on. Management resists wage demands more strenuously, and strikes are harder to win. But how much slack is required to hold wage increases, on the average, to increases in productivity? How large a figure for unemployment does this imply? And what is the price in lost production? More important still, is the maintenance of this degree of slack politically and socially tolerable?

There is another angle to this problem. The last question implies that it is within the power of credit and fiscal management to let the economy down to a certain level—the level at which wage increases average no more than productivity increases—and then to hold it there. No one with the slightest knowledge of economic affairs will believe this. It is simply not in the cards. The danger is ever-present that the momentum of the retreat will carry the economy beyond the target level and call for counter measures, the aftereffects of which will defeat the purpose of the policy.

So long as we have not solved the basic problem of the excessive bargaining power of unions, we will have to "roll with the punches." We will have to accept some degree of inflation as the price of prosperity and growth. A fanatical determination to stabilize the cost of living by credit and fiscal policies, come what may, risks worse evils than it attempts to cure. Until the axe is laid at the root of the tree, we will continue to harvest its bitter fruit.

[14] "Farm Policy
The Problem and the Choice
by JOHN KENNETH GALBRAITH

[CHAPTER TWENTY-ONE]

Agriculture and the Public Welfare

ONE *of our most difficult economic problems in the United States is to develop satisfactory public policies for dealing with the "farm problem." Should we or should we not attempt to protect the incomes of farmers? And if we decide to protect them, what methods should we employ?*

Galbraith believes that we have used the wrong methods of supporting farm prices and income, but that some kind of government support is needed. Hughes, on the other hand, believes we should abandon all attempts to "legislate farm income." He argues, however, that the government should do certain other things which in the long run would be of real benefit to the farmer.

[44] Farm Policy:
The Problem and the Choices*

by JOHN KENNETH GALBRAITH

I

In the last 20 years we have achieved something. We have come close
to agreement on at least two of the underlying causes of the farm problem. We agree, first of all, that a remarkable technological and capital
advance has remarkably increased output from given land and labor. A
great many changes—improved machinery and tillage, more and better
power, hybrids, plant foods, improved nutrition, and disease control—
have all contributed to this result.

Secondly, there is agreement that this great increase in the efficiency
of farm production and the resulting increase in output has occurred in
a country which has a relatively low absorptive capacity. In the economist's language both the price elasticity and the income elasticity of
farm products is small. Because of limited price elasticity an unusually
large crop does not move readily and easily into use when there is a modest reduction in prices. For the generality of farm products only a large
reduction in price will much expand consumption. Some are unresponsive
to almost any likely movement. Needless to say, this makes price cutting
a painful way of getting expanded consumption.

Such is the meaning of low price elasticity. Low income elasticity
means that as the incomes of people rise—urban incomes in particular—
they spend more on clothing, on transportation, on recreation, and on
other things but not a great deal more on food. The meaning of this will
be evident to everyone. While expanding prosperity and increasing purchasing power would be a cure for overproduction in other industries,
they are not similarly the salvation for agriculture.

I now come to another and, in some respects, more vital cause of our
farm difficulties. This is also one which is much less clearly perceived.
And much of what I have to say later on depends on a clear perception of
this point.

Unlike most industry and unlike most parts of the labor market, agri-

* From address by John Kenneth Galbraith before the National Farm Institute, Des
Moines, Iowa, February 14, 1958. Reprinted in *Congressional Record*, March 6, 1958,
pp. 3109-3111. By permission.

culture is peculiarly incapable of dealing with the problems of expanding output and comparatively inelastic demand. This incapability is inherent in the organization of the industry. Agriculture is an industry of many small units. No individual producer can exercise an appreciable influence on price or on the amount that is sold. As a result, it is not within the power of any individual producer—and since there is no effective organization to this end, it is not within the power of the agricultural industry as a whole—to keep expanding farm output from bringing down prices and incomes. And given the inelasticity of these markets, a large increase in supply can obviously be the cause of great hardship and even demoralization.

All this, you will say (or some will say), is inevitable. It is the way things should be. This is the free market. This is competition. Perhaps so. But it is a behavior that is more or less peculiar to agriculture. In the last 30 or 40 years there have been important technological improvements in the manufacture of automobiles, trucks, and tractors. The moving assembly line, special-purpose machine tools of high speed and efficiency, and automation have all worked a revolution in these industries. Did it lead to a glut on the market and a demoralization of prices? Of course it did not. It did not because the individual companies, very fortunately for them and perhaps also for the economy, were able to control their prices and regulate their output. This is a built-in power; it goes automatically with the fact that there are comparatively few firms in these industries. The steel industry is currently running at some sixty percent of capacity because it cannot sell a larger output at a price which it considers satisfactory. This it accomplishes easily without the slightest fuss or feathers. If farmers had the same market power they could, if necessary, cut hog production back by 40 percent in order to defend, say, a $20 price.

The power to protect its market that is enjoyed by the corporation is also enjoyed in considerable measure by the modern union. Early in this century American workers worried, and not without reason, lest the large influx of European migrants would break down their wage scales. They were in somewhat the same position as the farmer watching the effect of a large increase in supply on his prices. But now the unionized worker is reasonably well protected against such competition. Even though the supply of labor may exceed the demand, he doesn't have to worry about his wages being slashed. He, too, has won a considerable measure of security in the market.

Thus it has come about that the farmer belongs to about the only group—certainly his is by far the most important—which is still exposed to the full rigors of the competitive market. Or this would be so in the absence of Government programs. Government price protection, viewed in this light, is, or at least could be, only the equivalent of the price security that the modern corporation and the modern trade union have as a matter of course. There is this important peculiarity of the farmer's position. Because of the comparatively small scale of his operations, his large numbers, and the fact that agricultural production is by its nature scattered widely over the face of the country, he can achieve a measure of control over supply and price only with the aid of the Government. If one wishes to press the point, the market power of the modern corporation—deriving as it does from the State-issued charter—and the market power of the modern union both owe much to the State. But their debt is rather more subtle and better disguised than that of the farmer to the Agricultural Marketing Service and the CCC. So it is overlooked or perhaps conveniently ignored.

The meaning of this argument is also clear. It means that those who talk about returning the farmer to a free market are prescribing a very different fate for him than when they talk about free enterprise for General Motors or free collective bargaining for labor. In the free market the corporation and the union retain their power over prices and output. The farmer does not. What is sauce for the corporation is sourdough for the farmer. In its recent report, *Toward a Realistic Farm Program,* the Committee for Economic Development says that farm programs must have the basic objective of bettering the condition of the commercial farmer by means consistent with free markets and the national well-being. This means inevitably the particular kind of free market which farmers have. To prescribe the same kind of market for GM, one would have to recommend splitting the company up into a hundred or a thousand automobile-producing units. None of these would then have more influence than the average corn farmer on price; an improvement in technology would mean expanded output and lowered prices, and a glut of autos for all. And this recommendation applied to the labor market would mean the dissolution of unions. The CED is a highly responsible body. It would never think of making such silly recommendations for industry or labor. Yet this is what, in effect, it prescribes for the farmer when it asks that he be enabled to free himself from Government subsidy and control.

The special rigor with which the free market treats the farmer has always seemed to me self-evident. I have been struck by the general unwillingness to acknowledge it. While it is not usually fruitful or even wise to reflect on the reasons for the unwisdom of others, I do think some economists have resisted the idea for reasons essentially of nostalgia. Economic theory anciently assumed a market structure similar to that of agriculture. There were many producers selling in a market which none could influence or control. This was the classical case of free competition. There has been a natural hesitation to accept the conclusion that what was once (supposedly at least) the rule for all is now the rule only or chiefly for the farmer.

Also once we agree that the market operates with particular severity for the farmer we are likely to ask what should be done about it. The door is immediately opened to talk of Government programs. And that talk is not of temporary expedients but of permanent measures. Those who find such ideas abhorrent realize, perhaps instinctively, that to talk of free markets is the best defense.

I should also add that no one ever gets into trouble praising the virtues of the free market.

Finally, in recent times, the beneficence of unregulated markets has acquired some of the overtones of a religious faith. It is hinted, even though it is not quite said, that divinity is on the side of the free market. Support prices, although they may not be precisely the work of the devil, are utterly lacking in heavenly sanction. I must say I regard this whole trend of discussion not only as unfortunate but even as objectionable. I am not an expert in theology, but I doubt that providence is much concerned with the American farm program. Certainly it seems to me a trifle presumptuous for any mortal, however great or pious, to claim or imply that God is on his side. I would suggest that, following an old American tradition, we keep religion out of what had best be purely secular discussion.

II

It will be plain from the foregoing that expanding output, in the presence of inelastic demand, and in the absence of any internal capacity to temper the effect, can bring exceedingly painful and perhaps even disastrous movements in farm prices and incomes. And not only can it do so but on any reading of recent experience is almost certain to do so. And there is the further possibility that these effects may be sharpened by shrinking demand induced by depression. What should we do?

Within recent times, so it seems to me at least, we have come to understand more clearly the choice that confronts us. This choice rests on an increasingly evident fact of our agriculture. It is the very great difference in the ability of different classes of farmers to survive satisfactorily under the market conditions I have described. As I say, this is something of which we are only gradually becoming aware. Let me explain it in some detail.

For purposes of this explanation we may think of three classes of farmers in the United States. The first group are the subcommercial or subsistence farmers. These are the people who sell very little. Their situation is characteristic in the southern Appalachians, the Piedmont Plateau, northern New England hill towns, the cutover regions of the Lake States, and the Ozarks. Their income is inadequate less because prices are low than because they have so little to bring to market. It is plain that if these families are to have a decent income 1 of 2 things must happen. They must be assisted in reorganizing their farm enterprises so that their output is appreciably increased or they must find a better livelihood outside of agriculture. For the family grossing less than $1,000 or $1,500 from agriculture, of which there are still a great many in the United States, one or another of these remedies is inevitable. I doubt the wisdom of those who seek to make political capital out of statements of public officials which recognize this choice.

But it seems clear that we must now recognize two separate groups within the category that we are accustomed to call commercial farmers. We must distinguish the case of the very large commercial farm which, there is increasing evidence to show, has been able to return its operators a satisfactory income in recent years from that of the more conventional family enterprise which is in serious trouble. In the nature of things the dividing line here is not very sharp and it undoubtedly varies from one type of farming to another. But the growing income advantage of the large farm—the very large farm—is strongly indicated. It is shown by the trend toward farm consolidation. It is strongly suggested by farm management budgeting and programming studies. And it is borne out by the statistics. Speaking of commercial farms, Koffsky and Grove, of the United States Department of Agriculture, conclude in their recent testimony on agricultural policy for the Joint Economic Committee that between 1949 and 1954-55, although the evidence is not entirely conclusive, "net income on farms with an annual value of sales of $25,000 or more was fairly well maintained, while incomes of smaller operations, although still in the high-production category, showed substantial declines." That the large farms would even come close to maintaining their income in this period was highly significant.

We can conclude, I believe, that in many areas at least, modern technology has come to favor the large farm enterprise. Agriculture has become an industry where there are substantial economies of scale. The most successful units may, indeed, be very large by any past standards—

in some areas the investment will be from half or three-quarters of a million dollars upward. This is an important point, for there is still more than a slight reluctance to admit of the size of these units and to explore the full extent of the change that is involved. We hear scholars, Professor Schultz among them, speak of the need for a further large-scale withdrawal of the human factor from commercial agriculture. But we hear less of the massive reorganization of the farm units which this withdrawal implies. The huge scale of the resulting units is not recognized—or this part of the conclusion is soft pedalled. Yet, if many fewer people run our farm plant it can only mean that each person is operating a far larger firm.

For let there be no mistake, an agriculture where the average unit has a capitalization of a half million dollars or upward will be very different, both in its social and economic structure, from the agriculture to which we are accustomed. Not many can expect to start with a small or modest stake and control a half million or million dollars of capital during their lifetime. If these are the capital requirements of the successful farm, we shall have to accept as commonplace the separation of management from ownership. Owner-operation will be confined, with rare exceptions, to those who were shrewd enough to select well-to-do parents. We shall develop in our agriculture what amounts to an aristocratic tradition. There will no doubt also be closer integration with industrial operations with capital borrowed from industry and with closer control by industry. Modern broiler feeding is a sign.

Perhaps this development will not be so bad. But we should face up to its full implications. Those who now talk about adjustments and reorganization of commercial agriculture are talking about means without facing up to results. Those who praise the free market and the family farm in one breath are fooling either themselves or their audience. As I have noted, it is the very large farm, not the traditional family enterprise, which from the evidence has much the greater capacity to survive.

We should also recognize that the adjustment to high capitalization agriculture will not be painless. It will continue to be very painful. And we should spare a thought for the trail of uprooted families and spoiled and unhappy lives which such adjustment involves. I would especially warn colleges, now interesting themselves in these problems, against using the word "adjustment" as though it described a neutral and painless process.

III

Suppose we do not wish an agriculture of large, highly capitalized units. What is the alternative? The alternative is to have a farm policy in which the smaller commercial farm—what we have long thought of as the ordinary family enterprise—can survive. Given the technological dynamic of agriculture, the nature of its demand and the nature of the market structure, we cannot expect this from the market. It will come only as the result of Government programs that are designed to enable the family enterprise to survive. It has to be a Government program. Self-organization by farmers, of which some people are now talking, to regulate supply and protect their incomes is a pipe dream. Those who advocate it only advertise their innocence of history, economics, and human nature and their refusal to learn from past failure. I also confess my skepticism of individual commodity programs now so much in fashion. I very much fear that they will prove to be only a way of magnifying the tendency of farmers to disagree with each other—a tendency that is exceedingly well-developed—and thus to insure no action of any kind. I also deplore the belief that is currently so popular that if everyone just thinks hard enough someone, someday, will come up with a brilliant new idea for solving the farm problem and insuring everyone an adequate income. That is not going to happen either. Farmers are reputed to be hardheaded people. But a surprising number still have a sneaking faith in magic. The soil bank should stand as a warning. The good ideas have already occurred to people. So, of course, have the bad ones.

Or, to be more precise, the choices in farm policy are not very great. Any policy must provide a floor under prices or under income. As I have said on other occasions, a farm policy that doesn't deal with these matters is like a trade union which doesn't bother about wages. There must be production or marketing controls and these must be strong enough to keep the program from being unreasonably expensive. They will also inevitably interfere somewhat with the freedom of the farmer to do as he pleases. Nothing is controlled if a man can market all that he pleases. But we should also bear in mind that life involves a choice between different kinds of restraints. Inadequate income also imposes some very comprehensive restraints on the farm family.

I have long felt that there is a right way and a wrong way to support farm prices and income and that since World War II we have shown an unerring instinct for the wrong course. Production payments, either generally or specially financed, would be far more satisfactory. And since payments can be denied to overquote production, they fit in far better with a system of production control. But this is another story.

IV

The choice today is not the survival of American agriculture, or even its efficiency. The great and growing productivity shows that these are not in jeopardy. What is at stake is the traditional organization of this industry. We are in process of deciding between the traditional family enterprise of modest capitalization and widely dispersed ownership and an agriculture composed of much larger scale, much more impersonal, and much more highly capitalized firms. This is not an absolute choice. We shall have both types of farm enterprises for a long time to come. But a strong farm program will protect the traditional structure. The present trend to the free market will put a substantial premium on the greater survival power of the large enterprise.

My own preference would be to temper efficiency with compassion and to have a farm program that protects the smaller farm. But my purpose tonight is not to persuade you but to suggest the choice.

[45]   *Let's Set the Farmer Free**

by EARL M. HUGHES

For a quarter of a century Congress has been trying to legislate farm prosperity by bribing the farmer *not* to produce. Via one futile farm program after another, it has attempted to hold prices up and production down. But the spending of more than 11 billion taxpayers' dollars has only put the farmer deeper in the hole than he would have been without such help, and resulted in inevitable demands for still more billions to bail him out.

Many Congressmen admit privately: "We have a bear by the tail. We can't let go for fear it will bite us at the polls. Where do we go from here?"

I believe the cure which Congress so desperately seeks is plainly emerging. The solution, I think, is this:

Abandon the impossible job of trying to legislate farm income through direct price supports.
Stop the senseless flow of crops into the government's bulging bins.

*From *The Reader's Digest,* March, 1958, pp. 90-95. Copyright 1958 by The Reader's Digest Association, Inc. Reprinted by permission.

Make it government's main job to help find new uses and markets for our farm products.

Then turn farmers loose to produce in response to free market prices.

But can we really use what farmers produce? Listen to what Dr. Herrell DeGraff, noted Cornell University food economist, says: "Over the past 35 years, during which so-called surpluses have been almost chronic, a modest two-percent increase in livestock could have eaten up all of the surpluses. This *would* have happened had agriculture been free."

Let's take a hard look at where we are today after 25 years of controls on price and production:

Surpluses, caused by attempts to raise farm prices, are in fact *depressing* farm income (because they knock down the price of farm products) by two billion dollars a year, according to Department of Agriculture economists. And because the handling of surpluses is costly, the taxpayer has been hit hard. When I was in Washington I helped sell, trade, barter and give away seven billion dollars' worth of farm surpluses; but at the same time we moved this out the front door, we had to take in 10½ billion dollars' worth of new surpluses at the back door.

Today, as we try to whittle down Surplus Pile No. 1, a federal law is all set to build up Surplus Pile No. 2. To illustrate: if we can get rid of about 800 million bushels of government corn, the Secretary of Agriculture must immediately raise the support price to 90 percent of parity and boost acreage allotments from 37 million to at least 58 million acres. Higher guaranteed prices and more acres, plus the often overlooked fact that higher prices automatically reduce the size of the market, would soon have corncribs spilling over again.

Federal farm expenditures are getting bigger; they totaled more than five billion dollars last year. Borrowings by Commodity Credit, the government corporation set up to finance price supports and related programs, cost taxpayers close to a million dollars *daily* just in interest!

To run this bigger farm program, "big government" has got bigger: 11,412 full-time employees, plus thousands of part-time workers, have been added to the Department of Agriculture payroll since 1953.

The soil bank, our most recent effort to bail out previous bad programs, has many of the same old flaws. It has failed to reduce over-all farm production: we had 28 million acres idle in the soil bank last year, yet equaled our biggest harvest in history. It is a nightmare to administer: can you imagine the difficulty of setting "normal yields" for each farm? It is expensive: it cost about 600 million dollars last year. It masquerades as something it isn't: letting land lie idle doesn't save soil.

Despite the obvious bankruptcy of past policies, dozens of new "cures" which ignore these failures will be introduced during this session of Congress. There will be arguments for higher price supports—some from organizations which make millions off government storage—and pleas for the two-price plan, which proposes to sell at a high price at home and dump what we can't sell abroad. The Brannan Plan will be dusted off: it would make direct payments to farmers totaling at least seven to ten billion dollars a year!

Have we learned anything from the past? I fervently hope so. Here are a few basic facts which I feel should be borne clearly in mind in mapping future legislation.

Free commodities are in a healthier position today than those under controls. Commodities for which government has tried to do the most (corn, wheat, cotton, tobacco, rice, peanuts) are in the worst trouble today. Yet livestock farmers, unhampered by controls (although hurt by government meddling in feed grains), are still relatively prosperous.

U.S. cotton growers have lost markets both at home and abroad. Today they can plant only 40 percent of the cotton acreage they had in 1930. While the United States moved backward, the world cotton demand jumped 32 percent in the past seven years. Our farmers got none of these new markets abroad and lost further to synthetics at home.

Meanwhile, soybean producers, with no acreage restrictions, beat the drums for markets at home and abroad. They're now growing 3400 percent more beans than 25 years ago.

Food consumption can be increased and diet upgraded. Example: At the sharp break in the price of beef in 1953 there were howls that Congress should fix prices on beef cattle. But most cattlemen figured that the real answer was to sell more beef to the housewife, not to the government larder. They joined with packers, retailers, farm groups and government in an intensive promotion effort. The housewife got a bargain, and we ate our way out of the beef glut. In the past five years beef consumption has jumped from 62 to 85 pounds per person per year. If the government had stepped in to fix prices and control production, we would have had a beef scandal to dwarf the 500-million-dollar potato fiasco of 1947-51, when millions of bushels were given away or destroyed with kerosene. And we'd have a sick beef industry today.

Animal agriculture is the true "ever-normal granary." Livestock gives farmers 54 percent of their income; it's the traditional balance wheel of our national food economy. Half of our total harvested crops are fed to livestock, which convert five to seven pounds of feed into one pound of highly nutritious meat, milk, poultry or dairy products. Our food supply is enormously elastic: we can stretch it by eating more grain and feeding less livestock, or we can shrink it by merely feeding more livestock. So we can use all of our food surpluses if we upgrade our diets to use more meat, poultry and dairy products.

There is real farm opportunity today in a free market. We can learn something from Clarence Chappell, Jr., the hustling Star Farmer of America for 1958, a young man of 21 who used this animal-agriculture approach to success. And what success! At 21, he paid income tax on $7500; his net worth is $71,000.

Living near Belvidere, N. C., Chappell farms 225 acres of the home place with his dad, rents another 350 acres. He has no land in the soil bank—"I can't afford it." He raises hogs, dairy cows and beef cattle, plus the crops to feed them. He farms mainly outside the farm program because, he says, "This leaves me free to make my own management decisions and build a volume of business where we can operate efficiently."

There is no *political* solution to what is essentially an *economic* problem. Individual farmers can get more income by improving efficiency and their biggest single means of doing this is to increase their volume. Government can't increase individual farmers' income except by handouts.

When the government encourages inefficient farmers, by handouts of a few dollars, to continue in poverty on a subsistence farm rather than to seek better opportunity off the farm, it hurts everyone concerned. There are more than a million farmers who gross less than $2500 a year, and eke out a subsistence living of $15 to $20 a week net. No farm program has helped them, and none will, unless it is a direct cash handout. And then it becomes not a *farm* program but a welfare program. The voluntary movement of such families off the land, or to jobs off the farm, will do more than any law Congress could possibly pass.

For the day of the small horse-and-mule farm is no more. Today's farm *must* make use of specialized machinery, which is best used on large acreage; the small farm is inevitably inefficient. Yet more than one third of all cotton farmers, for example, have been squeezed down to five acres or less. How can such a farmer afford a $5000 (the lowest priced) cotton picker?

What, then, should our farm program be? What should Congress do in the present session?

We must quit trying to fix farm prices. It is politically impossible to set price supports low enough to stop the flow of commodities to government. And government is not a market. It merely holds the stuff for a while, then disposes of it in competition with farmers and private trade.

Let's face it: The only sure way of getting government out of our business is to get rid of price supports entirely.

We must free the farmer from the shackles of acreage controls and marketing quotas. Turn him loose to build a volume of business which will enable him to operate efficiently. Let him manage his own resources and make adjustments on his farm as the free market dictates.

We must get rid of our surplus hoard gradually, protecting the farmer against the price-depressing effects of this liquidation.

At the same time, the government can help the farmer to enlarge his markets by action on three fronts:

1. Promotion at home. We claim to be well-fed, yet the United States is ranked 15th among nations in milk consumption, 5th in meat eating (per capita). Even in Iowa, heart of the food belt, Iowa State College nutritionists found that two thirds of the women over 30 need an extra glass of milk daily to get sufficient calcium. It would take 25,000 gallons of milk per day just to give Iowa schoolgirls the calcium they need.

Can we get people to eat more of the right sort of foods? There are many proofs that we can:

Poultry producers have jumped sales by packaging all white meat, all thighs, no necks. The citrous people have done an equally effective job with high-vitamin frozen juices. An automatic milk-dispensing machine sells 6000 half-pints of milk monthly in a 450-student high school near my home. Thousands of schools, factories, office buildings are potential milk markets.

Says Dr. Herrel DeGraff: "If we ate half a pound more meat per person per week, it would bring full balance between our production and consumption, and nutritionists agree it would mean better health and more vigor for our people."

2. Promotion abroad. "There is a big opportunity to sell vast amounts of feed grains to many countries that have a rapidly growing livestock population," says Francis C. Daniels, vice-president of the Commodity Credit Corp., who has just completed a round-the-world survey.

Here are two examples of how the government is already using our surpluses to build markets:

It subsidized the export of surplus poultry products to Germany. The Germans like the taste of chicken and have now allocated dollars to buy more.

Japan has a rapidly growing population with little acreage to produce the rice she needs. We're now shipping surplus wheat to convert the Japanese into wheat-eaters. It looks as though they may acquire a taste for it.

3. Finance research on new crops and new uses for old crops. Promising research now under way uses corn, for example, to make alcohol which in turn is used to make rubber. If successful, this may consume 200 million bushels of corn per year. Another project now in the development stage aims at taking the starch from millions of bushels of wheat and corn and using it to improve concrete for our highways. New crops— sesame, safflower, bamboo—may replace old ones on thousands of acres.

Industry now takes five to seven percent of our farm production. Research is the key to increasing this volume. Both parties have already introduced bills in Congress to budget 100 million dollars for such research.

No Secretary of Agriculture, no farm leader, can lead us out of the mess we're in. Only courageous leadership from within Congress can do this job. And if we voters don't back up Congress in repudiating price supports and acreage restrictions, we must share the blame for more wasted billions, more useless surpluses and, in the long run, higher food prices and a leveling of family farms to peasant-like mediocrity.

CHAPTER TWENTY-TWO

The Consumer

*T*HE *welfare of consumers is affected by many factors, including advertising, merchandising methods, taxes, and government expenditures. In the selections which follow, first Fuchs discusses the alleged social gains and losses that result from modern advertising. Next Jarrell describes in humorous and sometimes sardonic vein the disproportionate importance which "things" seem to have assumed in our society. To be happy and to keep the wheels of the economy turning, we must always be buying something; and to make sure that we do this our advertising media keep training us to want more and more.*

Whatever may be the reason, it is true that most American consumers, despite the highest average income in the world, have a strong desire for many more things than they can afford. Galbraith, however, thinks that much of our private spending is on things that are relatively unimportant. He believes that our greatest economic problem is to shift a substantial portion of it to government spending for essential public services.

[46] *Advertising on Trial**

by VICTOR R. FUCHS

A growing number of advertisers are questioning the amount of money they are investing in advertising.

Media, with a few distinguished exceptions, have abdicated their responsibilities to refuse advertising not in the public interest.

Had these charges appeared in a consumers' association house organ, a muckraking popular journal or an esoteric economics textbook, they might be dismissed as the work of ignorance, prejudice or faulty analysis. But when they appeared in *Printers' Ink,* the widely read "weekly magazine of advertising and marketing," it became obvious that all is not well on Madison Avenue. This $11-billion industry is under an attack sharper and more penetrating than ever before. The answers it gives, or fails to give, may well determine its future role in our society. The most basic point at issue is the question of the *value* of advertising to the individual businesssman, the economy and society.

From the businessman's point of view, advertising has value only insofar as it contributes to profits, present or future. The question, "How much advertising should a firm do?" can be answered theoretically in terms of economic concepts of marginal cost and marginal revenue. A profit-maximizing firm should increase expenditures for advertising until the last (marginal) dollar spent brings in only one extra dollar of profit. The economist agrees completely with that successful pioneer in advertising, Gerard B. Lambert, who wrote, ". . . when sales of a product and the advertising are both running along on a level, a company can wisely spend an *additional* dollar on advertising, even if that dollar brings in net only an additional dollar and one cent." Implementing this marginal principle, however, is difficult, because it is frequently impossible to determine the portion of sales and/or profits attributable to advertising expenditure.

This is not always the case. The effectiveness of direct mail advertising, keyed coupon ads and department store newspaper ads can frequently be measured with great accuracy. But for the billions of dollars poured into TV and magazine ads, the best that can be hoped for is to measure the number of people "exposed" to the message. This leads to the tremen-

*From *Challenge* (March, 1960), pp. 17-21, a publication of The Institute of Economic Affairs, New York University. Reprinted by permission.

dous emphasis on circulation and TV audience rating scores. More sophisticated practitioners in the field are, of course, aware that many things other than "exposure" affect the sales-producing effect of advertising, but a clear-cut, measurable connection between advertising expenditures and profits has yet to be established.

In desperation, advertisers cling to such questionable measuring rods as "How much are my competitors spending for advertising?" Or they make ad appropriations after allowing for all other costs. Relying on industry-wide averages as guides to advertising appropriations bothers the scientific-minded businessman and reinforces the nagging notion that if less were spent, all would benefit. Advertising agencies can, like Salvation Army lassies utilizing fallen men, point to backsliders who have attempted to abandon or decrease advertising appropriations with disastrous results. But negative proofs are never the most convincing, and inevitably the question arises: Would sales have fallen off so precipitously if all competitors had cut back, rather than just one? . . .

Informative and Educational. The strongest arguments for advertising are that it is informative, and that it lowers distribution costs and makes possible inexpensive mass media of entertainment and education free from government or political control. Often exaggerated by defendants of advertising, the first point is frequently underestimated by its critics. Most department store newspaper ads, for example, are primarily informative and clearly help to enhance consumer satisfaction. Similarly, consumer knowledge about new products, ranging from cameras to cookie mixes, depends to a considerable extent upon advertising. On the other hand, it is highly unlikely that the expenditure of over $900,000 on 19 different pages of a single issue of *Life* (December 14, 1959) was necessary to inform the public of the pleasant feelings which follow the imbibing of alcoholic beverages.

Analyzing the role of branded advertised products in lowering distribution costs is both theoretically and empirically difficult, but it can be generally agreed that, under certain conditions, these costs *are* lowered by advertising and that these conditions are probably present in some American industries. Anyone who has ever shopped in an Oriental bazaar can appreciate some of the commonly accepted conveniences of branded products.

Perhaps advertising's most secure claim to a permanent role in our society is its part in subsidizing mass media. Advertising provides more than two-thirds of the total revenue of the publishing media and absorbs all the costs of broadcasting. While this relationship may lead to other abuses, it has enabled the public to enjoy some high quality news coverage, discussion and entertainment at modest or zero prices. The early history of newspaper publishing in this country, when most papers served as voices for political parties, is not a pretty one. The prospect of state control of publishing, Russian style, is not appealing; although the British Broadcasting Company provides some evidence that it is possible to have a tax-supported public information medium function free of political pressures and prejudice.

The principal arguments against advertising are, not surprisingly, the opposite of those in its favor. It has been argued, first, that advertising decreases consumer satisfaction by misleading claims and charges; secondly, that advertising increases the cost of goods; and, finally, that advertising exercises undue control over mass media, and that this control results in the distortion of truth and the debasement of taste.

The extent to which advertising misleads the consumer cannot be accurately measured, but the number of claims and counterclaims made by many of the largest advertisers suggest that attempts to deceive or at least mislead are widespread. Questions such as "Does aspirin upset the stomach?," "Which gasoline gives the most miles per gallon?" and "Do cigarettes cause cancer?" are not likely to be answered impartially by advertisements. And when four competing brands of cigarettes boast that each is "lowest in nicotine," three are surely conveying *mis*information.

Impact Exaggerated. The public generally tends to exaggerate the impact of advertising costs on the final price of goods and services. Nevertheless, it is true that ad outlays are currently running at close to four per cent of personal consumption expenditures. It is also true that this percentage has increased every year since 1947. Should this trend continue, the allocation of resources to advertising could become serious. At present, advertising does not impose a major burden on the prices of most commodities; but it is extremely important in selected fields such as proprietary medicines, cosmetics and some specialty food items.

Chicanery and Ethics. Probably the most serious charge facing advertisers—the one largely responsible for their current predicament—is that they control the advertising media and hence are responsible, for example, for the low quality of most TV programs and for the chicanery and unethical practices revealed in the operation of that medium. That advertising agencies and sponsors do control TV programs at present can scarcely be denied. Whether they should be permitted to control them is subject to debate, and to most outside observers the arguments for eliminating this control are persuasive. . . .

Two-Edged Sword. What effect does advertising have on the general propensity to consume? This question has scarcely been touched by serious research. Simon Kuznets' data suggest that consumption has tended to be a fairly stable percentage of income over a very long period of time, including decades of negligible advertising expenditures. To the extent that advertising increases total spending out of any given amount of income—rather than divert it from one form to another, as many economists believe—the argument can be a two-edged sword for the industry. For surely the most persistent problem of the postwar period has been inflation, not unemployment, and the argument suggests that one way to restrain excessive spending and avoid inflation would be to curb advertising. Similarly, insofar as advertising increases our preoccupation with consumption and the material pleasures of life, it is destructive of those higher values which the philosophers and teachers of all ages have assured us are at the core of social progress and individual fulfillment.

Actually, it is in the sphere of moral and social values that advertising will ultimately be judged. And the criticisms made of advertising in this respect are often misplaced. The addiction to alcohol or tobacco, for example, did not begin with advertising nor would it disappear if advertising were abolished. The wearing of cosmetics is as old as civilization. Madison Avenue did not invent lust, greed, envy or fear any more than did our religious leaders invent love, faith or charity. If we hold one calling in higher repute than the other, it is because it appeals to that which we regard as the "better side" of man.

A verdict at this point would be premature. We really know little about advertising—its impact on consumers, its effect on prices, its role in the business cycle and economic growth, its social and political implications. The most compelling conclusion which emerges is the need for objective research on these questions.

[47]   *A Sad Heart at the Supermarket**

by RANDALL JARRELL

The Emperor Augustus would sometimes say to his Senate: "Words fail me, my Lords; nothing I can say could possibly indicate the depth of my feelings in this matter." But I am speaking about this matter of mass culture, the mass media, not as an Emperor but as a fool, as a suffering, complaining, helplessly nonconforming poet-or-artist-of-a-sort, far off at the obsolescent rear of things: what I say will indicate the depth of my feelings and the shallowness and one-sidedness of my thoughts. If those English lyric poets who went mad during the eighteenth century had told you why the Age of Enlightenment was driving them crazy, it would have had a kind of documentary interest: what I say may have a kind of documentary interest.

> The toad beneath the harrow knows
> Exactly where each tooth-point goes;

if you tell me that the field is being harrowed to grow grain for bread, and to create a world in which there will be no more famines, or toads either, I will say, "I know"—but let me tell you where the tooth-points go, and what the harrow looks like from below.

Advertising men, businessmen, speak continually of "media" or "the media" or "the mass media"—one of their trade journals is named, simply, *Media.* It is an impressive word: one imagines Mephistopheles offering Faust media that no man has ever known; one feels, while the word is in one's ear, that abstract, overmastering powers, of a scale and intensity unimagined yesterday, are being offered one by the technicians who discovered and control them—offered, and at a price. The word, like others, has the clear fatal ring of that new world whose space we occupy so luxuriously and precariously; the world that produces mink stoles, rockabilly records, and tactical nuclear weapons by the million; the world that Attila, Galileo, Hansel and Gretel never knew.

And yet, it's only the plural of "medium." "Medium," says the dictionary, "that which lies in the middle; hence, middle condition or degree. . . . A substance through which a force acts or an effect is transmitted.

*From *Daedalus* (The Journal of the American Academy of Arts and Sciences) Spring, 1960, pp. 359-364, 371-372, *passim*. Abridged and reprinted by permission of the author and publisher.

. . . That through or by which anything is accomplished; as, an advertising *medium*. . . . *Biol.* A nutritive mixture or substance, as broth, gelatin, agar, for cultivating bacteria, fungi, etc." Let us name *our* trade journal *The Medium*. For all these media (television, radio, movies, popular magazines, and the rest) are a single medium, in whose depths we are all being cultivated. This medium is of middle condition or degree, mediocre; it lies in the middle of everything, between a man and his neighbor, his wife, his child, his self; it, more than anything else, is the substance through which the forces of our society act upon us, make us into what our society needs.

And what does it need? For us to need . . . Oh, it needs for us to do or be many things—to be workers, technicians, executives, soldiers, housewives. But first of all, last of all, it needs for us to be buyers; consumers; beings who want much and will want more—who want consistently and insatiably. Find some spell to make us no longer want the stoles, the records, and the weapons, and our world will change into something to us unimaginable. Find some spell to make us realize that the product or service which seemed yesterday an unthinkable luxury is today an inexorable necessity, and our world will go on. It is the Medium which casts this spell—which is this spell. As we look at the television set, listen to the radio, read the magazines, the frontier of necessity is always being pushed forward. The Medium shows us what our new needs are—how often, without it, we should not have known!—and it shows us how they can be satisfied: they can be satisfied by buying something. The act of buying something is at the root of our world: if anyone wishes to paint the beginning of things in our society, he will paint a picture of God holding out to Adam a checkbook or credit card or Charge-A-Plate.

But how quickly our poor naked Adam is turned into a consumer, is linked to others by the great chain of buying!

> No outcast he, bewildered and depressed:
> Along his infant veins are interfused
> The gravitation and the filial bond
> Of nature that connect him with the world.

Children of three or four can ask for a brand of cereal, sing some soap's commercial; by the time that they are twelve they are not children but teen-age consumers, interviewed, graphed, analyzed. They are on their way to becoming that ideal figure of our culture, the knowledgeable consumer. I'll define him: the knowledgeable consumer is someone who, when he goes to Weimar, knows how to buy a Weimaraner. He has learned to understand life as a series of choices among the things and services of this world; because of being an executive, or executive's wife, or performer, or celebrity, or someone who has inherited money, he is able to afford the choices that he makes, with knowing familiarity, among restaurants, resorts, clothes, cars, liners, hits or best-sellers of every kind. We may still go to Methodist or Baptist or Presbyterian churches on Sunday, but the Protestant ethic of frugal industry, of production for its own sake, is gone. Production has come to seem to our society not much more than a condition prior to consumption: "The challenge of today," writes a great advertising agency, "is to make the consumer raise his level of demand."

This challenge has been met: the Medium has found it easy to make its people feel the continually increasing lacks, the many specialized dissatisfactions (merging into one great dissatisfaction, temporarily assuaged by new purchases) that it needs for them to feel. When, in some magazine, we see the Medium at its most nearly perfect, we hardly know which half is entertaining and distracting us, which half making us buy: some advertisement may be more ingeniously entertaining than the text beside it, but it is the text which has made us long for a product more passionately. When one finshes *Holiday* or *Harper's Bazaar* or *House and Garden* or *The New Yorker* or *High Fidelity* or *Road and Track* or—but make your own list—buying something, going somewhere seems a necessary completion to the act of reading the magazine. Reader, isn't buying or fantasy-buying an important part of your and my emotional life? (If you reply, *No*, I'll think of you with bitter envy as more than merely human; as deeply un-American.) It is a standard joke of our culture that when a woman is bored or sad she buys something to make herself feel better; but in this respect we are all women together, and can hear complacently the reminder of how feminine this consumer-world of ours is. One imagines as a characteristic dialogue of our time an interview in which someone is asking of a vague gracious figure, a kind of Mrs. America: "But while you waited for the Intercontinental Ballistic Missiles what did you *do?*" She answers: "I bought things."

She reminds one of the sentinel at Pompeii—a space among ashes, now, but at his post: she too did what she was supposed to do. . . . Our society has delivered us—most of us—from the bonds of necessity, so that we no longer need worry about having food enough to keep from starving, clothing and shelter enough to keep from freezing; yet if the ends for which we work, of which we dream, are restaurants and clothes and houses, consumption, possessions, how have we escaped? We have merely exchanged man's old bondage for a new voluntary one. But *voluntary* is wrong: the consumer is trained for his job of consuming as the factory worker is trained for his job of producing; and the first is a longer, more complicated training, since it is easier to teach a man to handle a tool, to read a dial, than it is to teach him to ask, always, for a name-brand aspirin—to want, someday, a stand-by generator. What is that? You don't know? I used not to know, but the readers of *House Beautiful* all know, and now I know: it is the electrical generator that stands in the basement of the suburban houseowner, shining, silent, until at last one night the lights go out, the freezer's food begins to—

Ah, but it's frozen for good, the lights are on forever; the owner has switched on the stand-by generator.

But you don't see that he really needs the generator, you'd rather have seen him buy a second car? He has two. A second bathroom? He has four. He long ago doubled everything, when the People of the Medium doubled everything; and now that he's gone twice round he will have to wait three years, or four, till both are obsolescent—but while he waits there are so many new needs that he can satisfy, so many things a man can buy.

> Man wants but little here below
> Nor wants that little long,

said the poet; what a lie! Man wants almost unlimited quantities of almost everything, and he wants it till the day he dies.

We sometimes see in *Life* or *Look* a double-page photograph of some family standing on the lawn among its possessions: station wagon, swimming pool, power cruiser, sports car, tape recorder, television sets, radios, cameras, power lawn mower, garden tractor, lathe, barbecue set, sporting equipment, domestic appliances—all the gleaming, grotesquely imaginative paraphernalia of its existence. It was hard to get them on two pages, soon they will need four. It is like a dream, a child's dream before Christmas; yet if the members of the family doubt that they are awake, they have only to reach out and pinch something. The family seems pale and small, a negligible appendage, beside its possessions; only a human being would need to ask, "Which owns which?" We are fond of saying that something-or-other is not just something-or-other but "a way of life"; this too is a way of life—our way, the way.

Emerson, in his spare stony New England, a few miles from Walden, could write:

> Things are in the saddle
> And ride mankind.

He could say more now: that they are in the theater and studio, and entertain mankind; are in the pulpit and preach to mankind. The values of business, in an overwhelmingly successful business society like our own, are reflected in every sphere: values which agree with them are reinforced, values which disagree are cancelled out or have lip-service paid to them. In business what sells is good, and that's the end of it—that is what *good* means; if the world doesn't beat a path to your door, your mousetrap wasn't better. The values of the Medium (which is both a popular business itself and the cause of popularity in other businesses) are business values: money, success, celebrity. If we are representative members of our society, the Medium's values are ours; even when we are unrepresentative, nonconforming, our hands are (too often) subdued to the element they work in, and our unconscious expectations are all that we consciously reject. (Darwin said that he always immediately wrote down evidence against a theory because otherwise, he'd noticed, he would forget it; in the same way we keep forgetting the existence of those poor and unknown failures whom we might rebelliously love and admire.) *If you're so smart why aren't you rich?* is the ground-bass of our society, a grumbling and quite unanswerable criticism, since the society's nonmonetary values *are* directly convertible into money. (Celebrity turns into testimonials, lectures, directorships, presidencies, the capital gains of an autobiography *Told To* some professionel ghost who photographs the man's life as Bachrach photographs his body.) When Liberace said that his critics' unfavorable reviews hurt him so much that he cried all the way to the bank, one had to admire the correctness and penetration of his press-agent's wit: in another age, what mightn't such a man have become!

Our culture is essentially periodical: we believe that all that is deserves to perish and to have something else put in its place. We speak of "planned obsolescence," but it is more than planned, it is felt—is an assumption about the nature of the world. The present is better and more interesting, more real, than the past; the future will be better and more interesting, more real, than the present. (But, consciously, we do not hold against the present its prospective obsolescence.) Our standards have become, to an astonishing degree, those of what is called "the world of fashion," where mere timeliness—being orange in orange's year, violet in violet's—is the value to which all other values are reducible. In our society "old-fashioned" is so final a condemnation that a man like Norman Vincent Peale can say about atheism or agnosticism simply that it is old-fashioned; the homely recommendation of "Give me that good old-time religion" has become after a few decades the conclusive rejection of "old-fashioned" atheism. . . .

But why go on? I once heard a composer, lecturing, say to a poet, lecturing: "They'll pay us to do *anything*, so long as it isn't writing music or writing poems." I knew the reply that, as a member of my society, I should have made: "So long as they pay you, what do you care?" But I didn't make it—it was plain that they cared. . . . But how many more

learn not to care, love what they once endured! It is a whole so comprehensive that any alternative seems impossible, any opposition irrelevant;
in the end a man says in a small voice, "I accept the Medium." The Enemy
of the People winds up as the People—but where there is no Enemy, the
People perish.

The climate of our culture is changing. Under these new rains, new
suns, small things grow great, and what was great grows small; whole
species disappear and are replaced. The American present is very different
from the American past: so different that our awarness of the extent of
the changes has been repressed, and we regard as ordinary what is extraordinary (ominous perhaps) both for us and the rest of the world. For
the American present is many other peoples' future: our cultural and
economic example is, to much of the world, mesmeric, and it is only its
weakness and poverty that prevent it from hurrying with us into the
Roman future. Yet at this moment of our greatest power and success, our
thought and art are full of troubled gloom, of the conviction of our own
decline. When the President of Yale University writes that "the ideal of
the good life has faded from the educational process, leaving only miscellaneous prospects of jobs and joyless hedonism," are we likely to find it
unfaded among our entertainers and executives? Is the influence of what
I have called the Medium likely to make us lead any good life? to make
us love and try to attain any real excellence, beauty, magnanimity? or
to make us understand these as obligatory but transparent rationalizations, behind which the realities of money and power are waiting?

Matthew Arnold once spoke about our green culture in terms that have
an altered relevance (but are not yet irrelevant) to our ripe one. He said:
"What really dissatisfies in American civilization is the want of the *interesting*, a want due chiefly to the want of those two great elements of the
interesting, which are elevation and beauty." This use of *interesting* (and,
perhaps, this tone of a curator pointing out what is plain and culpable)
shows how far along in the decline of the West Arnold came; it is only
in the latter days that we ask to be interested. He had found the word
in Carlyle. Carlyle is writing to a friend to persuade him not to emigrate
to the United States; he asks, "Could you banish yourself from all that is
interesting to your mind, forget the history, the glorious institutions, the
noble principles of old Scotland—that you might eat a better dinner, perhaps?" We smile, and feel like reminding Carlyle of the history, the
glorious institutions, the noble principles of new America, that New
World which is, after all, the heir of the Old. And yet . . . Can we smile
as comfortably, today, as we could have smiled yesterday? listen as un-
concernedly, if on taking leave of us some tourist should say, with the
penetration and obtuseness of his kind:

I remember reading somewhere: that which you inherit from your fathers you must earn in order to possess. I have been so much impressed with your power and possessions that I have neglected, perhaps, your principles. The elevation or beauty of your spirit did not equal, always, that of your mountains and skyscrapers: it seems to me that your society provides you with "all that is interesting to your mind" only exceptionally, at odd hours, in little reservations like those of your Indians. But as for your dinners, I've never seen anything like them: your daily bread comes *flambé*. And yet—wouldn't you say?—the more dinners a man eats, the more comfort he possesses, the hungrier and more uncomfortable some part of him becomes: inside every fat man there is a man who is starving. Part of you is being starved to death, and the rest of you is being stuffed to death. . . . But this will change: no one goes on being stuffed to death or starved to death forever.

This is a gloomy, an equivocal conclusion? Oh yes, I come from an older culture, where things are accustomed to coming to such conclusions; where there is no last-paragraph fairy to bring one, always, a happy ending—or that happiest of all endings, no ending at all. And have I no advice to give you, as I go? None. You are too successful to need advice, or to be able to take it if it were offered; but if ever you should fail, it is there waiting for you, the advice or consolation of all the other failures.

[48] *The Use of Income Resulting from Economic Growth**

by JOHN KENNETH GALBRAITH

To defend one's selection of the central economic problem in the years ahead one must, first of all, show cause for excluding some of the obvious alternatives. Thus I exclude, as a problem, the grinding poverty of Asia, Africa, and South America and the means to its amelioration. This poverty

*Reprinted from *Problems of United States Economic Development*, Vol. I, January 1958, published by Committee for Economic Development, 711 Fifth Ave., New York 22, N.Y.

is, indeed, a question for the United States, and in some ultimate sense it is conceivably the central one. But the terms of the question seem to exclude such an answer. These are not precisely the problems of the internal American economy.

I also exclude the economic problems that would accompany a major war. This is not because anyone can entirely eliminate this hideous possibility from his thoughts. Rather such a war would reduce the economic problem to the stark and pristine simplicity of the caveman's struggle for survival if, indeed, it did not simplify it even more by eliminating the survivors. If such war is our destiny, we will not need economists to identify the resulting problems.

Two more possibilities, both less calamitous, can also, it seems to me, be set aside. These are unemployment and inflation. Neither is improbable or benign, but both are of a lower order or urgency than other questions we seem likely to face.

Specifically, in measures to control aggregate spending in the economy —the management of public spending and taxation—we have a remedy for unemployment. We have also, I believe, the requisite agreement on these measures. And they are in the broad current of political acceptability. To increase spending or to reduce taxes is not politically unpalatable. Were unemployment to rise substantially in the years ahead, we may assume that, by enlarged public outlays, more generous social security, and by tax cuts we should seek to compensate for the falling income and thus to counter the increase in unemployment.

Inflation is, without question, a more stubborn problem. Nor should we underestimate the damaging effects of long-continued price increases, of persistent and never-ending deterioration in the value of the currency. Savings, public services, law abidance, public morality all suffer. However, inflation can be prevented. It is well within the range of strong public policy on taxes, restraints on profligate borrowing, and limited direct control. We should recognize that, at the moment, we are in a peculiarly unfortunate position on this question. On the employment side the economy must conform to a very high standard—any unemployment much in excess of two or two and a half million is politically unacceptable. We take it for granted that corporations and unions will have considerable power over their prices, and it is plain that this power can be used to increase prices whenever the economy approaches full employment. In this situation price stability requires a strong policy on numerous fronts. This we have not yet recognized. On the contrary, we have chosen this particular moment to turn our back on strong policy and to return to the ancient hope that, by manipulation of the interest rate and the hopeful but unrevealed magic of monetary policy, price stability can somehow be achieved without effort or pain. But we shall learn again, as we have before, that much as we could do with some magic in economic management, none is available.

Finally, I do not take seriously the ponderous cliché that economic growth is our major problem. Such growth, it is held, is essential if we are to keep pace with the Russians. Basic industrial capacity was no doubt relevant to an old-fashioned war. In economics as in strategy we always find it most agreeable to fight the last war or the one before that. But the general relevance of industrial capacity to power in the nuclear age is less than clear. It becomes wholly unclear when we see that in our case growth consists, overwhelmingly, in capacity to produce our remarkable array of consumer's goods. Growth means that we will have more television sets than the Russians; that we will have longer, lower, and more elaborately painted automobiles; that nothing in Russia will match the hotels on Miami Beach; that we are far better equipped than they with washing machines, clothes driers, garbage grinders, and flannel suits, and that we are rapidly catching up on vodka. These things are not to be deplored. But they seem hardly an imperative of national policy. Yet those who talk so solemnly about the need to outproduce the Russians are talking about such goods, for it is of such goods, in the main, that our increased production consists.

So much then for the negative side of the case. If these are not to be the economic problems, what are?

One, of course, could argue that there will be none. A rich man has no economic problem in the sense that the poor man has. Wealth is the opposite of privation. So it is with a nation. And if war and depression be excluded we shall, of course, be rich. However, the analogy is not without flaw. Although as a nation we can be rich, a certain number of people can and most likely will be appallingly poor. I would be disposed to give this problem of residual poverty a position of priority in any list of problems. We have congratulated ourselves too long on the rising average. We have thought too little of those who remain at the lower extremity. Nor can these people be dimissed as the inevitable examples of individual inadequacy or shiftlessness, for in very large measure this poverty afflicts whole communities. In numerous areas the Southern Appalachians, the old South, the Ozark plateau, as well as in mountain towns in New England, and the cutover counties of the Lake States such poverty is endemic. In some ways it is more serious and blighting than its more visible counterpart in the urban slum. One cannot readily argue that whole communities or areas suffer from the deficiency or unemployment of their people.

However, there is a more important—although not unrelated—problem. The rich man, however rich, must still decide what to do with his wealth. And, if he uses it unwisely or corruptly or to excess in one direction, there will be question as to whether it serves his pursuit of happiness. This, I suspect, is also our problem as a nation. We have our wealth. We have yet to learn how to use it.

One measure of our failure is the surviving poverty just mentioned. Did we know how to use our wealth well, we would know how to eliminate such poverty. But there are simpler and more obvious aspects of this shortcoming. The newspapers day-by-day as this is written chronicle our increased output of goods—of automobiles, electronic entertainment, human plumage, bedeviling surpluses of food, and the myriads of other blessings and preoccupations. But the same papers tell just as urgently of our poverty in other things. They tell of the shortages of schools, the shortage of teachers, the inability of police and welfare workers to deal with juvenile crime, the failure of the sanitation services to keep abreast of the litter from the increasingly elaborate packages in which our products come, the losing battle for breathable air and potable water. The modern novelist or sociologist, in search of the human frustration which is his stock-in-trade, now goes unerringly to the new suburbs—to the world of tiny houses and peeling paint, crowded schools, septic tanks, and bad drainage. Obviously, we are not so distributing our wealth as to equalize need.

A millionaire who has six Cadillacs, a superb cigarette lighter, and an admirably caparisoned wife as not really well off if his children have no school and he must live with them in a chicken coop.

Much of the trouble obviously lies along the line between private goods and public services. We are well supplied with the first; our poverty in the second, even in the elementary ones like schools, roads, and public services, is patent. But it is also clear that some industries are badly related to their task. Housing and community design, in particular, have serious shortcomings.

Nor does it appear that we are close to an understanding of the problem. There is no reason why a community should not seek to satisfy its public needs with the same vigor and enthusiasm and the same sense of achievement and gratification that it views its satisfaction of private wants. The building of schools is not inherently inferior to the production of television sets. The building of roads is not inherently inferior to the building of the cars that use them. There is even a likelihood that a rapidly increasing population gives a special urgency to the provision of social capital.

Yet the satisfaction of public needs continues to be regarded as a burden. To build cars is an opportunity. To supply the roads is an unfortunate necessity. Whatever the deficiencies in our public services, they still cost too much, and the cost should be reduced. Business incentives are damaged although the years of high taxes since World War II have, it is conceded, been years of unparalleled growth. The democratic decision to spend for public goods and services is even held to be undemocratic.

And it is a measure of the road that we have yet to travel that even most enlightened of organizations have voiced these stereotyped alarms in face of the obvious imbalance of our wealth. The CED, remarkably redeemed, one must hasten to say, by its willingness to give voice to the other side, has recently observed: "It is the CED's view that the nation would benefit more from tax reduction than from a number of government programs. . . . We should remember that reliance on the free decisions of individuals, including their decisions about how they will spend their incomes, is fundamental to our democratic process."

PART FOUR

Political Organization and Social Problems

[CHAPTER TWENTY-THREE]

The Role of Government

THERE have been a number of theories of the origin of government, some of them purely fictional. MacIver believes that government began in the primitive family, and that it developed gradually to meet the universal need of societies for regulation. He attempts to trace the development of government and law from their simple forms in primitive societies to their complex forms in modern multi-group societies.

[49] *Man and Government**

by ROBERT M. MacIVER

. . . Government is a phenomenon that emerges within the social life, inherent in the nature of social order. Man's social nature is a complex system of responses and of needs. In the relation of man to man everywhere there is the seed of government. It takes different institutional shapes according to the interplay of these relations. Sometimes, in the simplest communities, it has no ministers or agents, but is sufficiently maintained by the spontaneous reaction to the prevailing folk-myths. Always it is guarded by these myths, however elaborate the machinery through which it operates. Wherever man lives on the earth, at whatever level of existence, there is social order, and always permeating it is government of some sort. Government is an aspect of society.

Since we know of no more universal or more elemental form of society than the family, we can learn some primary lessons about the roots of government if we begin by observing how within that minimum society the rudiments of government are already present.

THE FAMILY AS REALM

When we speak of government without a qualifying adjective we mean political government, the centralized organization that maintains a system of order over a community large or small. Political government is one form of social regulation, but by no means the only form. This point must be remembered when we raise questions about the origins of government. Regulation is a universal aspect of society. Society means a system of ordered relations. The system may be informal, folk-sustained, uncentralized, and without specific agencies, or it may be highly organized. But social regulation is always present, for no society can exist without some control over the native impulses of human beings. Political government appears when social regulation is taken over or begins to be presided over by a central social agency. At first the business of regulation is mainly a family concern, broadly protected by the custom of the inclusive group. To ascribe the beginnings of government to force or to contract or to some particular conjuncture is to ignore the fact that al-

*From Robert M. MacIver, *The Web of Government,* pp. 20-35, 61-71, 421-430 *passim.* Copyright 1947 by Robert M. MacIver and used with permission of The Macmillan Company.

ready in the family, the primary social unit, there are always present the curbs and controls that constitute the essence of government. Government is not something that is invented by the cunning or the strong and imposed on the rest. Government, however much exploitation of the weak by the strong it may historically exhibit, is much more fundamental than these explanations imply. It is the continuation by the more inclusive society of a process of regulation that is already highly developed within the family. . . .

The same necessities that create the family create also regulation. The imperative of sex has for human beings no pre-established harmony with longer-range imperatives, with the upbringing of the young and the maintenance and enhancement through the generations of the mode of life that the group, on whatever level, has acquired. The long dependence of the human young necessitates the establishment of some kind of control over sexual relations. There must be rules, and against so powerful an appetite, against the recklessness and the caprice of desire, these rules must be guarded by powerful sanctions. They must have back of them the authority of the community, bulwarked by such myths as the prevailing culture can devise against so formidable a danger.

Here is government in miniature and already government of a quite elaborate character. For sex is so closely inwrought with other concerns, and particularly with those of possession and inheritance, that its control carries with it a whole social code. The existence of the family requires the regulation of sex, the regulation of property, and the regulation of youth. . . .

In showing how the nature of the family necessitated the regulation of sex and the regulation of property and how the family itself was the primary agent in the maintenance of the customary law that determined its particular being we have not yet fathomed the significance of the family in the generation of the habits and patterns of government. Nor would that significance be adequately revealed if we went on to explain how the family was the locus of the altar as well as of the workshop, of the school as well as of the tribunal. Beyond all such associations there lies the elemental fact that man is born the most helpless and unwitting of animals, the least armed with ready instincts to fit him for survival, the slowest to develop his potentialities of autonomy; and at the same time the most receptive, the most imitative, the most educable, the most richly endowed. The family receives this amorphous being and through the long years of childhood shapes the mentality and orients it into social attitudes, imprinting on the impressionable organism the habits that become the foundation for all its later activities. . . .

So far as the child is concerned the imperium of the home is always absolute at the first, and only the length of time through which it holds undisputed sway differentiates in this respect one form of culture from another. For the child the magic of the law begins as soon as it becomes aware of others and of its relation to others. What is right and what is wrong, the things it must not do and the things it must do, are delivered to it from on high, as the law was delivered to Moses. It is so ordained, it is the eternal way of things. It is incorporated in the rites and religious observances of the community. Beyond it there is no other law.

It is easy then to see how "the habits pertaining to government" are bred in childhood, and how the family itself is always, for the child at least, a miniature political realm. . . .

In the light of these facts we see also how superficial and inadequate are those doctrines that find the origin of government in some particular occurrence or conjuncture, such as war, conquest, or exploitation. The danger of these doctrines is that by presenting government as something that supervenes in human society, something merely accessory to it, or something that actually perverts it they misinterpret the service and minimize the necessity of government. They give plausibility to the absurd notion of anarchism, to the deluding fancy of a "stateless society." So men can cherish the dogma that in some happier future the state will "wither away" and government as an organizing principle cease to control. But no one who cares to examine the role of government in the primal and universal society of the family can be so grossly deceived.

FROM FAMILY TO STATE

Before we proceed to show how government grew up from its cradle in the family we shall pause over a matter of definition. We have been speaking about "government," but the word "state" has crept into the argument. What is the difference? When we speak of the state we mean the organization of which government is the administrative organ. Every social organization must have a focus of administration, an agency by which its policies are given specific character and translated into action. But the organization is greater than the organ. In this sense the state is greater and more inclusive than government. A state has a constitution, a code of laws, a way of setting up its government, a body of citizens. When we think of this whole structure we think of the state. Later on we shall see that the *political* structure is not coextensive with the *social* structure but is a particular system relative to and dependent upon a more inclusive system. But for the present we are content to point out that the political structure itself, with its usages and traditions, with its framework of institutional relationships between the rulers and the ruled, should not be identified with its organ of government.

Under certain social conditions, particularly in the simpler societies, it is not appropriate to speak of a state. The political structure may be embryonic or rudimentary. Similarly there may be no structure properly called a church, even though a religion prevails and there are special officers of religion, priests or prophets. The terms "state" and "church" apply to specific associational forms that emerge at a later stage, and characterize more complex societies. . . .

In the simplest societies we know the main locus of government is the family circle. This circle is more inclusive than the unitary family of modern civilization. It is a primary kin-group fulfilling the functions essential to the family and many others besides. It has a definite head, whether the paterfamilias, the patriarch, the maternal uncle, or some other member. Within this circle the specific business of government is carried on. It makes and enforces the rules that are needed to meet the various contingencies that arise. Its ability to do so depends, of course, on the customs that are common to a community composed of a number of such families. The community is held together by the understanding that each family exercises this role, and since the community is itself a more inclusive group of the kin there is an accepted mode in conformity to which the role is exercised. This mode is authoritative, as the result of the sociopsychological processes of adaptation that have worked continuously on the kin-group. But the authority is guarded by the rule of custom as it is applied by each family unit. The operations of government are not yet centralized. If there is a headman, or chief, he is not yet a ruler but only *primus inter pares,* a man of somewhat higher prestige or distinction. But his functions tend to increase as changes bring new problems, as the size of the community grows, as relationships with neighboring tribes become more difficult or more important, and so forth.

We cannot cope with the ramifications and vicissitudes of the process in which government became institutionalized, in which the state-form emerged. It is a process that begins before there is any light of history and it is one that is still far from being fulfilled. Under endlessly varied circumstances the "habits pertaining to government," which at first were centered in the family and the kin-circle, found a locus in the inclusive community. We must be content to take a few glimpses, perhaps sufficient to show the more obvious steps that led to the extension and centralization of authority.

Frequently we find that the government of a tribe or of a locality is in the hands of the "old men," or, in patriarchal society, of "the fathers." In many languages, as in our own, such expressions as "the elders," "the city fathers," "the seigniory," "the senate," and so forth, connote authority. It is easy to understand how the heads of families would come together to discuss and administer inter-family concerns, or perhaps first to settle some trouble or compose some quarrel arising between members of their respective households. In such meetings some patriarch, some forceful personality, would assume the role of leader. The meeting becomes a council, and the leader becomes its head, the chief. As chief, he superintends the organization of the community for particular purposes, to carry on a trading expedition, to stage a festival or a ritual, to arrange a hunt, to reallocate lands, to seize some booty from a neighboring tribe, to defend the community against enemies. For these purposes the chief at length gathers about him a group of assistants or henchmen, a bodyguard. So he becomes elevated above the other "fathers." His prerogatives become gradually defined, his particular honors, his lion's share of the booty, the ceremonies proper to his office. Custom is always at work turning example into precedent and precedent into institution.

An important step in this process is the turning of chieftainship into hereditary office. An aggressive or ambitious leader is likely to use his prestige so as to favor the appointment of his son or near-of-kin as his successor. Thus one family is singled out from all the rest, the ruling family. With this elevation the distinction between chief and subjects is developed, the distance between the chief and the other "fathers" is widened, with consequent new accretions of ceremony and ritual to corroborate the change.

Along such lines the institutions of government must have developed, though with many variations. . . .

GOVERNMENT AND LAW

Without law there is no order, and without order men are lost, not knowing where they go, not knowing what they do. A system of ordered relationships is a primary condition of human life at every level. More than anything else it is what society means. Even an outlaw group, a pirate ship, a robber gang, a band of brigands, has its own code of law, without which it could not exist. The picture of the "lawless savage," running wild in the woods, is wholly fictitious. The "savage" is never lawless, he clings to his own laws more tenaciously, more blindly, than does the civilized man. Only the completely *déraciné*, the man torn from his social environment, or the extreme sophisticate, or the tyrant who emerges in a time of confusion, can be described approximately as lawless. The law of the "savage" is not our law, and there is no law between him and the outsider—a situation that still exists, in times of war, for civilized peoples. The world has been, and up to the present has remained, a collocation of areas of lawfulness, communities with no law binding the one to the other.

To the primitive his law is sacred. It is unchallengeable. For him the law is not something made by chief or legislator or judge. It is timelessly ordained. He can no more disown it than he can disown his tribe. No chief can interfere with it, or he becomes lawless himself. It does not indeed follow that the primitive never disobeys his law, only that he rarely doubts and practically never disbelieves its rightfulness. A man may firmly believe in God, and still break under temptation what he believes to be God's commandments. The primitive finds ways of evading the law and under strong impulsion will directly violate it. But it is still the law of his life. It is not like our civilized law, a specialized body of *legal* rules. It is one with custom, it is the way of the folk, hallowed by tradition, breathing the very spirit of the folk. It is unwritten law, and that sometimes raises troubles, for on particular points the interpreters may differ. It has little or no legal form, and that sometimes causes difficulties, for, as has been said of the law of the Cheyenne Indians, its conclusions do not fall "into easily accessible patterns to draw minor trouble-festers to a head, and so to get them settled. This shows again and again in smoldering irritations over points of fact." But it is the firmament of order in society.

To the primitive his folk-law is not something men can make and remake. It is as much given to him as the earth he lives on. He scarcely recognizes it for what it is, a cultural product that changes imperceptibly with the changing culture. But of course Thomas Hobbes was right when he explained that law in human society is not like the law that rules the communities of ants or of bees. It is not in that sense "natural," not biologically determined but socially constructed, a folk-creation. Hence there is still the need for social sanctions. The errant member of the flocks must be disciplined, or his example will weaken respect for the law. Sometimes the folk itself is the sufficient guardian of its ways. The disrepute it attaches to the offender, the ostracism with which it penalizes more serious transgressions, or the direct punishment it inflicts when strongly aroused —as when the people turned against the offender Achan and "all Israel stoned him with stones"—these reactions serve in place of the machinery of law. But, as we have seen, there is always leadership, even for the seemingly spontaneous responses of the folk. The habit of personal government that developed in every family circle would be enough, apart from other considerations, to stimulate the establishment of personal government over the larger community. At first the chief might merely settle disputes, but in doing so he was unconsciously changing and making law. The government thus set up, the chief or the council of elders, came easily to be regarded as the guardian of the folkways. It was in effect an executive and judicial authority, rather than a legislative one. Its direct law-making activity was at most minor, incidental, and sporadic. Occasionally, at a more advanced stage, the heroic figure of a "law-maker" appears, like Lycurgus or Solon or Hammurabi or Moses. But the Great Legislator is usually represented as being either a codifier of the laws or a prophet who receives them from God. . . .

In a modern society we distinguish between custom and law, and recognize that custom and other non-legal principles control a great sector of human behavior. In simple societies there is no clear-cut distinction between custom and law. The specific legal code, with its specific machinery of enforcement, has not yet developed. Consequently such government as existed was not regarded as making rules for the community, but only as administering its affairs, settling disputes, and guarding the folkways against the dangerous violator. Where, however, communities expanded in population and resources, where they extended their boundaries, through war or otherwise, and took under their dominion other groups or communities, where by reason of such conditions the tempo of social change was accelerated, and especially where serious conflicts and maladjustments arose between the more demarcated economic categories or social classes of the larger society, there the old-established folkways no longer gave the needed guidance. Government took on the job of *legislation.*

Often the strife between privileged classes and oppressed or exploited classes caused intolerable unrest and dissension. To allay it a whole new system of laws was necessary. This was the task to which the famous lawgivers of the ancient world devoted themselves. In Athens, for example, when strife became acute between the oligarchic families or Eupatridae and the discontented population, Draco came forward with a system of ruthless penal laws that failed to achieve their purpose. Solon followed and abolished many of the privileges of the Eupatridae, setting up at the same time an entirely new apparatus of government. Later Cleisthenes appeared and sought to unify a still divided people by establishing a remarkably democratic constitution, giving to the citizen body as a whole the most complete right to control the entire policy of the state.

But neither the most famous law-giver nor the most powerful despot abrogated the general pattern of law-ways already existent among their peoples. The great law-giver was mostly concerned with reforming the constitution, the broad framework of government, the respective shares of different groups in the making of policy, the powers and privileges possessed by different classes of the community. The main body of laws and law-usages remained and, where necessary, was readjusted to the new order. The despot scarcely tampered with the laws at all. The typical dynast of China or of Egypt or of Babylonia disposed freely of men and of things, but he did little to change the code. Even if he personally violated the laws he still did not alter them. There was an established order, in part set out in the terms of law but in much larger part expressed in folkways. The folkways derived their authority not from the monarch but from the folk—or from God. They were invested with sanctity. The ruler, no matter how despotic he might be, had no power over them. He might "protect" them but he could not overthrow them. Emperor or rajah or sultan lived, like their peoples, under the aegis of the sacred law. . . .

Not only in primitive society but also in the ancient civilizations and in the mediaeval world it was accepted doctrine that the ruler was subject to the laws, not above them, and that the body of laws was something scarcely touched by the fiat of authority. The law is the law of the community, not the law of the ruler. Sometimes the law was regarded as expressive of the will of God, as among the Hebrews; sometimes it was regarded as emanating from the whole people. . . .

The same doctrine held throughout the Middle Ages. It was differently oriented to correspond with the different social structure. The mediaeval king or emperor did not make laws or decrees of his mere pleasure, but with the consent of his council. His council was supposed to stand for the community. His authority was always presumed to be derived from the community, and, as Bracton put it, the law was the bridle of authority. Furthermore, the notion of natural law as the abiding model of human law prevailed in the thought of the times. And of course there was the constant admonition to the ruler that he was subject to the law of God. In the Middle Ages there was no lack of accepted ethical and religious standards to which political authority was "in principle" subject. It is true that the approach of practice to principle was often remote. Perhaps there has been no great period of history wherein ethical prescriptions were so clearly formulated and so universally espoused while yet the behavior of those in power seemed in effect regardless of them. "The king stands below the law of nature," "the prince cannot change the law of nature," "any act that violates the law of nature is null and void"—such expressions recur in the writings of mediaeval thinkers but they neither deterred princes from their ambitions nor protected the people from arbitrary power. Abstract rights could give small comfort against concrete wrongs. . . .

With the Renaissance we find the rise of another doctrine concerning the relation of government and law, a doctrine that in its fulfillment denied the older conception of the basis of order in society and at times shook and even cracked the whole firmament of law. This was the doctrine that set the ruler above the law and made his single will the very source of law. . . . Political thinkers of the sixteenth century in Western Europe, and particularly in France, were engaged in buttressing the authority of the king, since their age was weary of the old wars of feudal barons within the disunited realm and of the new and more embittered wars of religious sects that threatened to destroy whatever unity the realm still possessed. The solution was to elevate the monarch to a commanding height above all other men and leaders of men and to invest him with complete supremacy over them all. So the doctrine of sovereignty was re-devised and greatly amplified and elaborated. The king, formerly the defender of the community-made law, now became the supreme lord who gave its law to the community. Hitherto the king had owed, in the thought of learned and ignorant alike, his authority to the law; now the law owed its authority to him. . . .

But there was a serious flaw in the new doctrine, and it was manifest from the first. The sovereign was one, indivisible, omni-competent. What then of the claims of religion? There were many who on this ground resisted the new exaltation of the king. Among them was the great Jesuit leader, Suarez, who vindicated the autonomy of the spiritual realm against the state, asserting again the higher authority of the former and the right of men to wage war against tyrannical rulers. Where there were no religious divisions within the greater state the problem could be somehow met. The king could still be by God appointed, invested with the divine right of kings, entering into a concordat with the church and acting as defender of the faith. But how could the adherents of one faith accept as sovereign over their religious brotherhood a ruler of another faith? How could they accept the principle of the treaty of Augsburg, that the religion of the prince held for the territory over which he ruled? The religion of every group proclaimed that it was better to obey God than man. Only three years after Bodin's work on *The Republic* there appeared also in France the famous Huguenot treatise, *Vindiciae contra tyrannos,* the author of which asserted that the sovereign becomes a tyrant, whom it is the duty of the magistrates to resist, if his commands run counter to true religion and the law of God.

From the time of the Reformation the number of religious sects was on the increase. In some countries the ruler was Roman Catholic, in others he was Protestant. Everywhere there were religious groups that suffered persecution for their faith. The age had not yet discovered that the ruler need not meddle with the religion of his subjects or that it was unnecessary to make a particular religion a condition of civic rights or that, when citizens were divided by religious differences, the firmament of order was not weakened but on the contrary much strengthened if each group was free to worship in its own way or to worship its own God. The new myth of sovereignty blocked, instead of promoting, the solution of this sharpening issue.

Meanwhile, although the states of Western Europe—France, England, and Spain—consolidated the monarchy, making the throne strong against the crumbling claims of the feudal hierarchy, their internal order was threatened again and again by religious strife. Bodin's trust in the law of nature gave no comfort to oppressed minorities, subject to the omni-competent sovereignty of ruthless kings. He himself believed in toler-ance and detested religious fanatacism. But his doctrine of sovereignty merely gave to a fanatical age a new doctrinal sword. The religious group that had the monarchy on its side was only too ready to attribute to the secular arm the defence of the faith. In this there was no difference between the reformist Luther or Melanchthon, the Presbyterian Calvin or Beza or Knox, the Anglican bishops who in their *Convocation Book* de-clared that any rebellion against king or magistrate, for any cause what-soever, is "a sin very detestable against God," and the Catholic Bossuet. When, as happened often enough, the situation was reversed and their own faith was persecuted, the same groups were apt to invoke the law of God against the tyrant, and to declare, with many scriptural supports, that "to obey man in any thing against God is unlawful and in plain dis-obedience." So wrote, for example, Christopher Goodman in his work *How Superior Powers Ought to be Obeyed*. So said Calvin and Knox re-garding monarchs who professed other faiths than their own.

The Massacre of St. Bartholomew, the "English Terror" organized by Thomas Cromwell under Henry the Eighth, the persecution of Protestants under "Bloody Mary," and the numerous "wars of religion" high-lighted the omni-competence of sovereignty. Revolts of the middle economic classes, especially in England, began to increase the confusion that hith-erto had centered in the religious issue. The old bases of authority were menaced, the firmament of order was threatened. A new kind of society was developing within the greater state, a society no longer, like feudal society, uni-centered in its faith nor uniform in its economic pattern. It was the dawn of modern multi-group society. The authoritarian order, whether the feudal type or the new type of royal absolutism, was no longer appropriate, could not much longer be maintained. But the doctrine of the new order was not yet developed. The idea of "toleration," as a concession to non-conformist faiths, was wholly inadequate. Men felt the need for a new basis of order but old traditions yielded slowly. . . .

THE MULTI-GROUP SOCIETY

Our main argument to this point is that the relation of man to the many groups and forms of organization to which he is more nearly or more distantly, more deeply or more superficially, attached is not solved by making one of these, whether the state or any other, the sole or inclusive object of his devotion, the one social focus of his being. There are other forms of order than the simple uni-centered order. There is the order of the balance and inter-adjustment of many elements. The conception of the all-inclusive all-regulating state is as it were a pre-Copernican conception of the social system. It appeals to the primitive sense of symmetry. As we explore more deeply the social universe we must discard it and frame a conception more adequate to social reality. In this exploration we learn, among other things, to understand better the nature of the multi-group society of modern man.

With this theme we shall deal here very briefly. We start from the fact that men have many different kinds of interest, that some of these are universal, in the sense that they are pursued by all men everywhere—all seek alike the satisfaction of certain elementary needs—while some are particular, making appeal to some men and not to others. Now since organization conveys power men learn to join with others so as to pursue their interest more effectively, each for each as well as each for all. Some of these interests are purely distributive, as are most economic interests. These we may speak of as like interests. The benefits of organization then accrue to each separately, so that the proceeds become private dividends, privately enjoyed by each. Other interests are *common,* in such wise that what each receives does not divide the product of the collectivity or lessen the benefits available to all the rest. To this class belong our cultural interests, the advance of knowledge, the exploration of art, of thought, of literature, of religion, and so forth. While the individual explorer or creator may receive particular awards, honors, or emoluments, the things that he explores or creates are potentially for all men. The wells of knowledge and of inspiration are not less full for the number who drink of them. When a man makes shoes it is for private use. When he makes a work of art or literature it is generally available, in one way or another, for the enjoyment of those who care for it.

Thus we can distinguish two types of organization, according to the nature of their product, leaving aside those that are intermediate or that in some manner combine both functions. Let us consider particularly the character of the second type. The cultural interests of men are exceedingly diverse and they exist on every level from the highest to the lowest. Many men have many minds. Children subjected to the same conditions and to the same influences react in very different ways. The attitudes of every group differ from the attitudes of every other. There is much incompatibility of outlook, of opinion and belief, of interpretation, of enjoyment, of the whole realization of life. Different men find very different sustenance within the fields of culture. In the seeking of this sustenance they are most themselves, most alive, most creative. Whether the sustenance be refined or vulgar, ample or meager, it is always that through which man seeks fulfillment. Everything else on earth is for the spirit that is in man nothing but apparatus or mechanism.

To satisfy this need men weave manifold relationships with their fellows. These extend from the give-and-take of love or comradeship through informal neighborly groupings for recreation, gossip, and so forth, up to the world-wide religious brotherhoods. There are two conclusive reasons why the numerous organizations thus engendered cannot be coordinated, over any range of territory great or small, under the aegis of the state.

One is that the various organizations of the same cultural species are not only dissimilar in viewpoint, in method, in system of values, but actually antipathetic, alien, or hostile to one another in these respects. The differences are not reconcilable, nor are they so unimportant that they could be omitted from some universal charter or creed that would seek to embrace the different faiths within a single organizational fold. There are schools and styles in every form of art, in every field of cultural expression. The followers of any one abjure the other schools and styles. They take delight in their own, in the difference itself. Religions may alike proclaim the brotherhood of man or the fatherhood of God, but each has its own conception of the fatherhood. To co-ordinate them all into one would be to destroy their characteristic qualities, to drain them of their vitality. Co-ordination could be imposed only by sheer compulsion, and there is essential truth, even if the statement be too strongly worded, in the comment of the absolutist Hobbes, "Belief and unbelief never follow men's commands."

Here we reach the second reason why neither the state nor any other form of organization can be all-embracing. Every way of life and every way of thought is nourished from within. It is the conviction that counts, the habit of mind, the devotion to a cause, the impulse to artistic expression, the congeniality of the group. It cannot be controlled from without, it cannot be directed by an indifferent or alien power. The creative force of all culture lies in its own spontaneity. It is killed by compulsion, reduced to a lifeless mechanism. Only the arrogance of the tyrant or of the dogmatist denies this truth. The dogmatist, secure in his own faith, would refuse other men the right to theirs, blindly seeking to destroy in them the same spirit of devotion from which he nourishes his own being.

This truth was appreciated by T. H. Green, Hegelian though he was. In his *Lectures on the Principles of Political Obligation* he put forward the thesis that the state should not command the doing of things the value of which depends on the spirit in which they are performed and not on the mere externals of performance. This thesis is relevant to the whole area of cultural pursuits, though of course there arise marginal issues. We may put forward as a corollary of this thesis the further point that wherever actions are of such a kind that the performance of them by one group in one manner or style does not impede the performance of them by other groups in a diverse or contradictory manner or style such actions should not be on intrinsic grounds subject to co-ordination by the state or any other collectivity. When we say "on intrinsic grounds" we mean that, for example, no one should be forbidden to worship in his own way because the ruling powers entertain a religious objection to that form of worship. If however the worship involved, say, head-hunting or any other interference with the liberties of other men or any infringement of a criminal law that itself was not motivated by religious considerations but only by regard for public safety, then the performance would be subject to ban or control on extrinsic grounds. Our formula applies to the whole business of the expression of opinion, to the great realms of art and of thought in every form. One man is not precluded from advancing his opinion because another man has a contrary opinion. One man is not prevented from worshipping his own God because another man worships a different kind of God. Thus the objective conditions of public order do not demand uniformity in the cultural realm.

There is some contrast here between the cultural realm and the realm presided over by the organizations that fall predominantly within our second type. Economic activities, for example, cannot be left to the free arbitrament of individuals and groups without serious interference with public order. Thus an employer cannot lower the wages of his employees below the prevailing rate without seriously affecting the business of other employers who may have more concern for the welfare of their workers. He cannot extend the hours of labor without doing harm to his fellow employers as well as to his employees. He cannot "run his own business in his own way" as though it were a private imperium islanded from the rest of the world. No more can a man rightly claim to use his property in any way that seems good to him. His property not only is the fruit of co-operative labor of many men but also it is the potential if not the actual source of the livelihood of others. If he neglects it, lets it run to waste or ruin, or actually destroys it he is injuring his fellows. He does the same thing if, say, he buys a patent from an inventor so as to prevent its exploitation, for the sake of his own greater profit. But there is no end of such examples. The economic order is a vast network of interdependence.

It might be claimed that a like statement could be made concerning the cultural order. A man cannot ventilate his opinions, cannot write a popular novel, cannot even worship his God without having some influence somehow on others. But there is a crucial difference. One man influences another in this manner because the other is freely responsive to that influence. We may adjudge the influence good or bad. We may condemn and oppose it. That also is our right. Opinions and creeds are forever in conflict. Every man must find and respond to his own. There is no other way save compulsion, and we have already shown how alien and perilous that is. Moreover, with respect to economic relations the effect of one man's action on that of another is external and even automatic. The effect is measurable. We have a common standard, an objective index. Economic advantage, economic prosperity, has the same meaning for all men, even though some are more devoted to it than others. Thus the main objections that apply to the control of opinion are not relevant here. There is in fact only one relevant limit to specific economic controls, and that is precisely the consideration how far such controls conduce to the general economic welfare, how far they are efficient, how far they may go without restraining the spirit of initiative and enterprise, the spring of energy, vision, and responsibility, without which organization degenerates into the wasteful routine of bureaucracy.

Let us return, however, to our first conclusion, that the many cultural organizations of society have not and cannot have any one focus, cannot without losing their identity and their function be amalgamated and absorbed as mere departments of the state. Now we face the question of the inter-adjustment of all these organizations, and of the groups who maintain them, within the ordered yet free life of the community. Here is the essential problem of our multi-group society.

In every range and at every stage of social life this problem exists. In the simplest societies it is embryonic, and it reaches its full proportions only in the ambit of the modern nation. In the world of Western civilization it first became acute when various religious groups broke away from the universalism of the mediaeval church. The assumption that every community, every state, must have a single religion had a tremendous hold over the minds of most men. Only the sheer impossibility of maintaining this assumption at length persuaded them that they could live decently together, as members of one community, with those who professed a different faith. Centuries of persecution, war, and civil strife were needed to achieve this result. Manifestations of the old intolerance persist in the more liberal states while new forms of it, not associated with a religious principle, have appeared in some other states and shown a virulence not surpassed by the most extreme instances of earlier times.

The full requirement of cultural liberty has rarely, if ever, been realized. In democratic countries it is now *politically* established. These countries have advanced far since the days when the king of one of them announced that he would "make the extirpation of the heretics his principle business." Gradually they passed from persecution to toleration and from toleration to the position that a man's religion is no concern of the state. The Edict of Nantes in 1598 was the first acknowledgment of a Roman Catholic government that "heretics" should be accorded civil rights, but even as late as 1776 the greatest of French radicals could assert that it was "impossible for men to live at peace with those they believe to be damned." In Protestant countries Roman Catholics were at length "tolerated," but it was only in 1819 that even England admitted them to citizenship. As for Jews, they have suffered longer and more grievously from persecution and the denial of civil rights than those who professed any other religion.

The principles set out in the First Amendment of the United States Constitution, that no law shall be enacted respecting an establishment of religion, has in effect been accepted by most democratic countries as well as by some others that cannot be placed in that category. But the problem of the multi-group society is not solved merely by the formal recognition of equality before the law. Such equality can exist while nevertheless minority groups or groups in an inferior economic or social position may be subject to such discrimination that they are practically excluded from participation in the life of the community. An outstanding example is the situation of the Negroes in the United States, particularly in the South. Other groups suffer discrimination to different degrees. The Jewish people are exposed to it but so in a measure are various ethnic groups, especially those of Eastern European countries, while yet stronger disabilities are applied against the Chinese, the Japanese, and the people of India. If we add to these groups the American Indians, the Filipinos, the Mexicans and other Latin-Americans we get the picture of a country constitutionally dedicated to the equality of men that nevertheless exhibits a complex pattern of rifts and fissures ramifying across the life of the community.

In different countries the problem takes different shapes. While in the United States minority groups are dispersed throughout the population, in some other countries they have a territorial locus, as in the Balkan area. Sometimes ethnic differences are associated with differences of religion. Often the disadvantaged groups occupy an inferior economic status. Not infrequently there is political as well as social and economic discrimination. This situation is found in its extreme form in colonial possessions, where the usual relation of majority and minority is reversed in favor of a dominant alien group.

Under all conditions the discrimination of group against group is detrimental to the wellbeing of the community. Those who are discriminated against are balked in their social impulses, are prevented from developing their capacities, become warped or frustrated, secretly or openly nurse a spirit of animosity against the dominant group. Energies that otherwise might have been devoted to constructive service are diverted and consumed in the friction of fruitless conflict. The dominant group, fearing the loss of its privileges, takes its stand on a traditional conservatism and loses the power of adapting itself to the changing times. The dominated, unless they are sunk in the worse apathy of sullen impotence, respond to subversive doctrines that do not look beyond the overthrow of the authority they resent. Each side conceives a false image of the other, denying their common humanity, and the community is torn asunder.

There is no way out of this impasse, apart from revolution, except the gradual readjustment of group relations in the direction of equality of opportunity—not merely legal equality. Since this readjustment requires the abandonment of habits and traditions, the breaking of taboos, the reconstruction of the distorted images cherished by each group of the other, and the recognition that the narrower interests and fears and prides that stimulate discrimination and prejudice are adverse to the common good and often empty or vain, its achievement can be affected only through the arduous and generally slow processes of social education.

The sense of community, dissipated by the pervading specialization of interests, needs to be reinforced. The common values of the embracing culture need to be reasserted and again made vital. The provision of equality of opportunity will not of itself bring about any such result. It will serve chiefly by removing a source of division that stands obdurately in the way of social cohesion. Only when this obstacle is removed can the positive values of the multi-group society be cultivated— if we have the wisdom to seek and to find them.

The sense of the need of community, if not the sense of community, is still alive and seeks embodiment. It is witnessed to by men's devotion to the nation and by their attachment to some local community they feel— or once felt—to be their home. But these bonds do not satisfy the need, do not sufficiently provide the experience of effective solidarity. The nation is too wide and too diverse. The local community is too heterogeneous, if it is large, or too limited, if it is small. Often the attachment to it is nostalgic or merely sentimental. So the unit gropes for a more satisfying unity, seeking to recover the spirit of co-operative living that animated the uni-group society. Sometimes men seek to recover it by methods that would re-impose the old order on the new. They would restore the myth of the uni-group society; they would make the all-inclusive state the sufficient focus of our moral and spiritual being; they would even, as totalitarians, ruthlessly co-ordinate out of existence our cultural heterogeneity. But there is no road back. The course of civilization is as irreversible as time itself. We have left behind the one-room social habitation of our ancestors. We have built ourselves a house of many mansions. Somehow we must learn to make it ours.

CHAPTER TWENTY-FOUR

Democracies and Dictatorships

CHANGE *is universal in human societies, and this applies to social ideologies and forms of government as much as to other aspects of culture. In the first selection below, Carr, an Englishman, traces the change from earlier forms of democracy to the "mass democracy" found in our present-day society. Because this is a new phenomenon—"a creation of the last half-century"—many new problems have entered the picture. He believes that making mass democracy work will require not only creative effort by responsible leaders, but a society educated to such a point as to close the gap between the electorate and the leaders.*

In opposition to democracy stands the totalitarian theory of government. Brewster explains why all totalitarian states are dictatorships, even though not all dictatorships are totalitarian.

[50] From Individualism to Mass Democracy*

by EDWARD HALLETT CARR

The problem of political organization in the new society is to adapt to the mass civilization of the twentieth century conceptions of democracy formed in earlier and highly individualistic periods of history. The proclamation by the French revolution of popular sovereignty was a serious challenge to institutions which had grown up under quite different auspices and influences. It is no accident that Athenian democracy, which has been commonly regarded as the source and exemplar of democratic institutions, was the creation and prerogative of a limited and privileged group of the population. It is no accident that Locke, the founder of the modern democratic tradition, was the chosen philosopher and prophet of the eighteenth-century English Whig oligarchy. It is no accident that the magnificent structure of British nineteenth-century liberal democracy was built up on a highly restrictive property franchise. History points unmistakably to the fact that political democracy, in the forms in which it has hitherto been known, flourishes best where some of the people, but not all the people, are free and equal; and, since this conclusion is incompatible with the conditions of the new society and repugnant to the contemporary conscience, the task of saving democracy in our time is the task of reconciling it with the postulate of popular sovereignty and mass civilization.

Modern democracy, as it grew up and spread from its focus in western Europe over the past three centuries, rested on three main propositions: first, that the individual conscience is the ultimate source of decisions about what is right and wrong; second, that there exists between different individuals a fundamental harmony of interests strong enough to enable them to live peacefully together in society; third, that where action has to be taken in the name of society, rational discussion between individuals is the best method of reaching a decision on that action. Modern democracy is, in virtue of its origins, individualist, optimistic and rational. The three main propositions on which it is based have all been seriously challenged in the contemporary world.

In the first place, the individualist conception of democracy rests on a

*From *The New Society* by Edward Hallett Carr, pp. 61-79. Published by St. Martin's Press, Inc., New York, and Macmillan & Co. Ltd., London, 1957. Reprinted by permission.

belief in the inherent rights of individuals based on natural law. According to this conception, the function of democratic government is not to create or innovate, but to interpret and apply rights which already exist. This accounts for the importance attached in the democratic tradition to the rights of minorities within the citizen body. Decision by majority vote might be a necessary and convenient device. But individuals belonging to the minority had the same inherent rights as those belonging to the majority. Insistence on the rule of law, preferably inscribed in a written and permanent constitution, was an important part of the individualist tradition of democracy. The individual enjoyed certain indefeasible rights against the society of which he was a member; these rights were often regarded as deriving from a real or hypothetical "social contract" which formed the title-deeds of society. Just as the individualist tradition in *laissez-faire* economics was hostile to all forms of combination, so the individualist tradition in politics was inimical to the idea of political parties. Both in Athenian democracy and in eighteenth-century Britain, parties were regarded with mistrust and denounced as "factions."

The French revolution with its announcement of the sovereignty of the people made the first serious assault on this view of democracy. The individualism of Locke's "natural law" was replaced by the collectivism of Rousseau's "general will." Both Pericles and Locke had thought in terms of a small and select society of privileged citizens. Rousseau for the first time thought in terms of the sovereignty of the whole people, and faced the issue of mass democracy. He did so reluctantly; for he himself preferred the tiny community where direct democracy, without representation or delegation of powers, was still possible. But he recognized that the large nation had come to stay, and held that in such conditions the people could be sovereign only if it imposed on itself the discipline of a "general will."

The practical conclusion drawn from this doctrine, not by Rousseau himself, but by the Jacobins, was the foundation of a single political party to embody the general will. Its logical conclusions were still more far-reaching. The individual, far from enjoying rights against society assured to him by natural law, had no appeal against the deliverances of the general will. The general will was the repository of virtue and justice, the state its instrument for putting them into effect. The individual who dissented from the general will cut himself off from the community and was a self-proclaimed traitor to it. Rousseau's doctrine led directly to the Jacobin practice of revolutionary terror.

It would be idle to embark on a theoretical discussion of the rival merits of the two conceptions of democracy. Individualism is an oligarchic doctrine—the doctrine of the select and enterprising few who refuse to be merged in the mass. The function of natural law in modern history, though it is susceptible of other interpretations, has been to sanctify existing rights and to brand as immoral attempts to overthrow them. A conception based on individual rights rooted in natural law was a natural product of the oligarchic and conservative eighteenth century. It was equally natural that this conception should be challenged and overthrown in the ferment of a revolution that proclaimed the supremacy of popular sovereignty.

While, however, the beginnings of mass democracy can be discerned in the doctrines of Rousseau and in the practice of the French revolution, the problem in its modern form was a product of the nineteenth century. The Industrial revolution started its career under the banner of individual enterprise. Adam Smith was as straightforward an example as could be desired of eighteenth-century individualism. But presently the machine overtook the man, and the competitive advantages of mass production ushered in the age of standardization and larger and larger economic units. And with the mammoth trust and the mammoth trade union came the mammoth organ of opinion, the mammoth political party and, floating above them all, the mammoth state, narrowing still further the field of responsibility and action left to the individual and setting the stage for the new mass society. It was the English Utilitarians who, by rejecting natural law, turned their backs on the individualist tradition and, by postulating the greatest good and the greatest number as the supreme goal, laid the theoretical foundation of mass democracy in Britain; in practice, they were also the first radical reformers.

Before long, thinkers began to explore some of the awkward potentialities of mass democracy. The danger of the oppression of minorities by the majority was the most obvious. This was discerned by Tocqueville in the United States in the 1830's and by J. S. Mill in England twenty-five years later. In our own time the danger has reappeared in a more insidious form. Soviet Russia has a form of government which describes itself as a democracy. It claims, not without some historical justification, to stem from the Jacobins who stemmed from Rousseau and the doctrine of the general will. The general will is an orthodoxy which purports to express the common opinion; the minority which dissents can legitimately be suppressed. But we are not concerned here with the abuses and excesses of the Soviet form of government. What troubles us is the question how far, in moving from the individualism of restrictive liberal democracy to the mass civilization of today, we have ourselves become involved in a conception of democracy which postulates a general will. The question is all around us today not only in the form of loyalty tests, avowed or secret, or committees on un-American activities, but also in the form of the closed shop and of increasingly rigid standards of party discipline.

In a speech made to a regional Labour party conference at the time of Mr. Aneurin Bevan's resignation in April, the Minister of Defence denounced "absence of loyalty" in the party: "The loyalty of our party," exclaimed Mr. Shinwell, "is superior to any exhibition of political private enterprise. . . . No person, I don't care who he is, can be allowed to interfere with the democratic structure of this party." Lenin used strikingly similar phrases at the Bolshevik party congress in March 1921. We have moved far from the conception of truth emerging from the interplay of divergent individual opinions. Loyalty has come to mean the submission of the individual to the general will of the party or group.

The second postulate of Locke's conception of society, the belief in a fundamental harmony of interests between individuals, equally failed to stand the test of time, and for much the same reason. Even more than natural law, the harmony of interests was essentially a conservative doctrine. If the interest of the individual rightly understood coincided with the interest of the whole society, it followed that any individual who assailed the existing order was acting against his own true interests and could be condemned not only as wicked, but as short-sighted and foolish. Some such argument was, for instance, often invoked against strikers who failed to recognize the common interest uniting them with their employers. The French revolution, an act of self-assertion by the third estate against the two senior estates of nobility and clergy, demonstrated—like any other violent upheaval—the hollowness of the harmony of interest; and the doctrine was soon also to be powerfully challenged on the theoretical plane.

The challenge came from two quarters. The Utilitarians, while not making a frontal attack on the doctrine, implicitly denied it when they asserted that the harmony of interests had to be created by remedial action before it would work. They saw that some of the worst existing inequalities would have to be reformed out of existence before it was possible to speak without irony of a society based on a harmony of interests; and they believed in increased education, and the true liberty of thought which would result from it, as a necessary preparation for establishing harmony. Then Marx and Engels in the *Communist Manifesto* took the class struggle and made out of it a theory of history which, partial though it was, stood nearer to current reality than the theory of the harmony of interests had ever done. Social and economic pressures resulting from the breakdown of *laissez-faire* illustrated in practice what Marx had demonstrated in theory.

But in Great Britain it was reformist Utilitarianism rather than revolutionary Marxism that set the pace. The flagrant absence of a harmony of interests between competing and conflicting classes more and more urgently called for state intervention. The state could no longer be content to hold the ring; it must descend actively into the arena to create a harmony which did not exist in nature. Legislation, hitherto regarded as an exceptional function required from time to time to clear up some misunderstanding or to rectify some abuse, now became normal and continuous. It no longer sufficed to interpret and apply rights conferred on the individual by the laws of nature. What was expected of the state was positive and continuous activity—a form of social and economic engineering. The substitution of a planned economy for *laissez-faire* capitalism brought about a radical transformation in the attitude towards the state. The functions of the state were no longer merely supervisory, but creative and remedial. It was no longer an organ whose weakness was its virtue and whose activities should be restricted to a minimum in the interests of freedom. It was an organ which one sought to capture and control for the carrying out of necessary reforms; and, having captured it, one sought to make it as powerful and effective as possible in order to carry them out. The twentieth century has not only replaced individualist democracy by mass democracy, but has substituted the cult of the strong remedial state for the doctrine of the natural harmony of interests.

The third main characteristic of Locke's conception of society—a characteristic which helped to give the eighteenth century its nicknames of the Age of Reason or the Age of Enlightenment—was its faith in rational discussion as a guide to political action. This faith provided the most popular nineteenth-century justification of the rule of the majority as the basis of democracy. Since men were on the whole rational, and since the right answer to any given issue could be discovered by reason, one was more likely, in the case of dispute, to find right judgment on the side of the majority than on the side of the minority. Like other eighteenth-century conceptions, the doctrine of reason in politics was the doctrine of a ruling oligarchy. The rational approach to politics, which encouraged leisurely argument and eschewed passion, was eminently the approach of a well-to-do, leisured and cultured class. Its efficacy could be most clearly and certainly guaranteed when the citizen body consisted of a relatively small number of educated persons who could be trusted to reason intelligently and dispassionately on controversial issues submitted to them.

The prominent rôle assigned to reason in the original democratic scheme provides perhaps the most convincing explanation why democracy has hitherto always seemed to flourish best with a restrictive franchise.

Much has been written in recent years of the decline of reason, and of respect for reason, in human affairs, when sometimes what has really happened has been the abandonment of the highly simplified eighteenth-century view of reason in favour of a subtler and more sophisticated analysis. But it is none the less true that the epoch-making changes in our attitude towards reason provide a key to some of the profoundest problems of contemporary democracy.

First of all, the notion that men of intelligence and good will were likely by process of rational discussion to reach a correct opinion on controversial political questions could be valid only in an age when such questions were comparatively few and simple enough to be accessible to be educated layman. It implicitly denied that any specialized knowledge was required to solve political problems. This hypothesis was perhaps tenable so long as the state was not required to intervene in economic issues, and the questions on which decisions had to be taken turned on matters of practical detail or general political principles. In the first half of the twentieth century these conditions had everywhere ceased to exist. In Great Britain major issues of a highly controversial character like the return to the gold standard in 1925 or the acceptance of the American loan in 1946 were of a kind in which no opinion seriously counted except that of the trained expert in possession of a vast array of facts and figures, some of them probably not available to the public. In such matters the ordinary citizen could not even have an intelligent opinion on the question who were the best experts to consult. The only rôle he could hope to play was to exercise his hunch at the election by choosing the right leader to consult the right experts about vital, though probably still unformulated, issues of policy which would ultimately affect his daily life.

At this initial stage of the argument reason itself is not dethroned from its supreme rôle in the decision of political issues. The citizen is merely asked to surrender his right of decision to the superior reason of the expert. At the second stage of the argument reason itself is used to dethrone reason. The social psychologist, employing rational methods of investigation, discovers that men in the mass are often most effectively moved by non-rational emotions such as admiration, envy, hatred, and can be most effectively reached not by rational argument, but by emotional appeals to eye and ear, or by sheer repetition. Propaganda is as essential a function of mass democracy as advertising of mass production. The political organizer takes a leaf out of the book of the commercial advertiser and sells the leader or the candidate to the voter by the same methods used to sell patent medicines or refrigerators. The appeal is no longer to the reason of the citizen, but to his gullibility.

A more recent phenomenon has been the emergence of what Max Weber called the "charismatic leader" as the expression of the general will. The retreat from individualism seemed to issue at last—and not alone in the so-called totalitarian countries—in the exaltation of a single individual leader who personified and resumed within himself the qualities and aspirations of the "little man," of the ordinary individual lost and bewildered in the new mass society. But the principal qualification of the leader is no longer his capacity to reason correctly on political or economic issues, or even his capacity to choose the best experts to reason for him, but a good public face, a convincing voice, a sympathetic fireside manner on the radio; and these qualities are deliberately built up for him by his publicity agents.

In this picture of the techniques of contemporary democracy, the party headquarters, the directing brain at the centre, still operates rationally, but uses irrational rather than rational means to achieve its ends—means which are, moreover, not merely irrational but largely irrelevant to the purposes to be pursued or to the decisions to be taken.

The third stage of the argument reaches deeper levels. Hegel, drawing out the philosophical implications of Rousseau's doctrine, had identified the course of history with universal reason, to which the individual reason stood in the same relation as the individual will to Rousseau's general will. Individual reason had been the corner-stone of individualist democracy. Marx took Hegel's collective reason to make it the corner-stone of the new mass democracy. Marx purported to reject the metaphysical character of Hegel's thought. But, equally with Hegel, he conceived of history pursuing a rational course, which could be analysed and even predicted in terms of reason. Hegel had spoken of the cunning of reason in history, using individuals to achieve purposes of which they themselves were unconscious. Marx would have rejected the turn of phrase as metaphysical. But his conception of history as a continuous process of class struggle contained elements of determinism which revealed its Hegelian ancestry, at any rate on one side. Marx remained a thorough-going rationalist. But the reason whose validity he accepted was collective rather than individual.

Marx played, however, a far more important part in what has been called "the flight from reason" than by the mere exaltation of the collective over the individual. By his vigorous assertion that "being determines consciousness, not consciousness being," that thinking is conditioned by the social environment of the thinker, and that ideas are the superstructure of a totality whose foundation is formed by the material conditions of life, Marx presented a clear challenge to what had hitherto been regarded as the sovereign or autonomous reason. The actors who played significant parts in the historical drama were playing parts already written for them: this indeed was what made them significant. The function of individual reason was to identify itself with the universal reason which determined the course of history and to make itself the agent and executor of this universal reason. Some such view is indeed involved in any attempt to trace back historical events to underlying social causes; and Marx—and still more Engels—hedged a little in later years about the rôle of the individual in history. But the extraordinary vigour and conviction with which he drove home his main argument, and the political theory which he founded on it, give him a leading place among those nineteenth-century thinkers who shattered the comfortable belief of the Age of Enlightenment in the decisive power of individual reason in shaping the course of history.

Marx's keenest polemics were those directed to prove the "conditioned" character of the thinking of his opponents and particularly of the capitalist ruling class of the most advanced countries of his day. If they thought as they did it was because, as members of a class, "being" determined their "consciousness," and their ideas necessarily lacked any independent objectivity and validity. Hegel, as a good conservative, had exempted the current reality of the Prussian from the operation of the dialectic which had destroyed successively so many earlier historical forms. Marx, as a revolutionary, admitted no such absolute in the present, but only in the future. The proletariat, whose victory would automatically abolish classes, was alone the basis of absolute value; and collective proletarian thinking had thus an objectivity which was denied to the thinking of other classes. Marx's willingness, like that of Hegel, to admit an absolute as the culminating point of his dialectical process was, however, an element of inconsistency in his system; and, just as Marx was far more concerned to dissect capitalism than to provide a blue-print for socialism, so his use of the dialectic to lay bare the conditioned thinking of his opponents lay far nearer to his heart, and was far more effective, than his enunciation of the objective and absolute values of the proletariat. Marx's writings gave a powerful impetus to all forms of relativism. It seemed less important, at a time when the proletarian revolution was as yet nowhere in sight, to note his admission of absolute truth as a prerogative of the proletariat. The proletariat was for Marx the collective repository of Rousseau's infallible general will.

Another thinker of the later nineteenth century also helped to mould the climate of political opinion. Like Darwin, Freud was a scientist without pretensions to be a philosopher or, still less, a political thinker. But in the flight from reason at the end of the nineteenth century, he played the same popular rôle as Darwin had played a generation earlier in the philosophy of *laissez-faire*. Freud demonstrated that the fundamental attitudes of human beings in action and thought are largely determined at levels beneath that of consciousness, and that the supposedly rational explanations of those attitudes which we offer to ourselves and others are artificial and erroneous "rationalizations" of processes which we have failed to understand. Reason is given to us, Freud seems to say, not to direct our thought and action, but to camouflage the hidden forces which do direct it. This is a still more devastating version of the Marxist thesis of substructure and superstructure. The substructure of reality resides in the unconscious: what appears above the surface is no more than the reflexion, seen in a distorting ideological mirror, of what goes on underneath.

The political conclusion from all this—Freud himself drew none—is that any attempt to appeal to the reason of the ordinary man is waste of time, or is useful merely as camouflage to conceal the real nature of the process of persuasion; the appeal must be made to those subconscious strata which are decisive for thought and action. The debunking of ideology undertaken by the political science of Marx is repeated in a far more drastic and far-reaching way by the psychological science of Freud and his successors.

By the middle of the nineteenth century, therefore, the propositions of Locke on which the theory of liberal democracy were founded had all been subjected to fundamental attack, and the attack broadened and deepened as the century went on. Individualism began to give way to collectivism both in economic organization and in the forms and practice of mass democracy: the age of mass civilization had begun. The alleged harmony of interests between individuals was replaced by the naked struggle between powerful classes and organized interest groups. The belief in the settlement of issues by rational discussion was undermined, first, by recognition of the complex and technical character of the issues involved, later and more seriously, by recognition that rational arguments were merely the conditioned reflexion of the class interests of those who put them forward, and, last and most seriously of all, by the discovery that the democratic voter, like other human beings, is most effectively reached not by arguments directed to his reason, but by appeals directed to his irrational, subconscious prejudices. The picture of democracy which emerged from these criticisms was the picture of an arena where powerful interest-groups struggled for the mastery. The leaders themselves were often the spokesmen and instruments of historical processes which they did not fully understand; their followers consisted of voters recruited and marshalled for purposes of which they were wholly unconscious by all the subtle techniques of modern psychological science and modern commercial advertising.

The picture is overdrawn. But we shall not begin to understand the problems of mass democracy unless we recognize the serious elements of truth in it, unless we recognize how far we have moved away from the conceptions and from the conditions out of which the democratic tradition was born. From the conception of democracy as a select society of free individuals enjoying equal rights, and periodically electing to manage the affairs of the society, a small number of their peers, who deliberate together and decide by rational argument on the course to pursue (the assumption being that the course which appeals to the majority is likely to be the most rational), we have passed to the current reality of mass democracy. The typical mass democracy of today is a vast society of individuals, stratified by widely different social and economic backgrounds into a series of groups or classes, enjoying equal political rights the exercise of which is organized through two or more closely integrated political machines called parties. Between the parties and individual citizens stand an indeterminate number of entities variously known as unions, associations, lobbies or pressure-groups devoted to the promotion of some economic interest, or of some social or humanitarian cause in which keen critics usually detect a latent and perhaps unconscious interest.

At the first stage of the democratic process, these associations and groups form a sort of exchange and mart where votes are traded for support of particular policies; the more votes such a group controls the better its chance of having its views incorporated in the party platform. At the second stage, when these bargains have been made, the party as a united entity "goes to the country" and endeavours by every form of political propaganda to win the support of the unattached voter. At the third stage, when the election has been decided, the parties once more dispute or bargain together, in the light of the votes cast, on the policies to be put into effect; the details of procedure at this third stage differ considerably in different democratic countries in accordance with varying constitutional requirements and party structures. What is important to note is that the first and third stages are fierce matters of bargaining. At the second stage, where the mass persuasion of the electorate is at issue, the methods employed now commonly approximate more and more closely to those of commercial advertisers, who, on the advice of modern psychologists, find the appeal to fear, envy or self-aggrandizement more effective than the appeal to reason.

Certainly in the United States, where contemporary large-scale democracy has worked most successfully and where the strongest confidence is felt in its survival, experienced practitioners of politics would give little encouragement to the idea that rational argument exercises a major influence on the democratic process. We have returned to a barely disguised struggle of interest-groups in which the arguments used are for the most part no more than a rationalization of the interests concerned, and the rôle of persuasion is played by carefully calculated appeals to the irrational subconscious.

This discussion is intended to show not that mass democracy is more corrupt or less efficient than other forms of government (this I do not believe), but that mass democracy is a new phenomenon—a creation of the last half-century—which it is inappropriate and misleading to consider in terms of the philosophy of Locke or of the liberal democracy of the nineteenth century. It is new, because the new democratic society consists no longer of a homogeneous closed society of equal and economically secure individuals mutually recognizing one another's rights, but of ill co-ordinated, highly stratified masses of people of whom a large majority are primarily occupied with the daily struggle for existence. It is new, because the new democratic state can no longer be content to hold the ring in the strife of private economic interests, but must enter the arena at every moment and take the initiative in urgent issues of economic policy which affect the daily life of all the citizens, and especially of the least secure. It is new, because the old rationalist assumptions of Locke and of liberal democracy have broken down under the weight both of changed material conditions and of new scientific insights and inventions, and the leaders of the new democracy are concerned no longer primarily with the reflexion of opinion, but with the moulding and manipulation of opinion. To speak today of the defence of democracy as if we were defending something which we knew and had posssessed for many decades or many centuries is self-deception and sham.

It is no answer to point to institutions that have survived from earlier forms of democracy. The survival of kingship in Great Britain does not prove that the British system of government is a monarchy; and democratic institutions survive in many countries today—some survived even in Hitler's Germany—which have little or no claim to be called democracies. The criterion must be sought not in the survival of traditional institutions, but in the question where power resides and how it is exercised.

In this respect democracy is a matter of degree. Some countries today are more democratic than others. But none is perhaps very democratic, if any high standard of democracy is applied. Mass democracy is a difficult and hitherto largely uncharted territory; and we should be nearer the mark, and should have a far more convincing slogan, if we spoke of the need, not to defend democracy, but to create it.

In my second and third lectures I discussed two of the basic problems which confront the new society—the problem of a planned economy and the problem of the right deployment and use of our human resources. These problems are basic in the sense that their solution is a condition of survival. The old methods of organizing production have collapsed, and society cannot exist without bringing new ones into operation. But those problems might conceivably be solved—are even, perhaps, in danger of being solved—by other than democratic means: here the task of mass democracy is to meet known and recognized needs by methods that are compatible with democracy, and to do it in time. The central problem which I have been discussing today touches the essence of democracy itself. Large-scale political organizations show many of the characteristics of large-scale economic organization, and have followed the same path of development. Mass democracy has, through its very nature, thrown up on all sides specialized groups of leaders—what are sometimes called élites. Everywhere, in government, in political parties, in trade unions, in co-operatives, these indispensable élites have taken shape with startling rapidity over the last thirty years. Everywhere the rift has widened between leaders and rank and file.

The rift takes two forms. In the first place, the interests of the leaders are no longer fully identical with those of the rank and file, since they include the special interest of the leaders in maintaining their own leadership—an interest which is no doubt rationalized, but not always justly, as constituting an interest of the whole group. The leaders, instead of remaining mere delegates of their equals, tend in virtue of their functions to become a separate professional, and then a separate social, group, forming the nucleus of a new ruling class or, more insidiously still, being absorbed into the old ruling class. Secondly, and most important of all, there is an ever-increasing gap between the terms in which an issue is debated and solved among leaders and the terms in which the same issue is presented to the rank and file. Nobody supposes that the arguments which the leaders and managers of a political party or a trade union use among themselves in private conclave are the same as those which they present to a meeting of their members; and the methods of persuasion used from the public platform or over the radio will diverge more widely still. When the decision of substance has been taken by the leaders, whether of government, of party or of union, a further decision is often required on the best method of selling the decision. Broadly speaking, the rôle of reason varies inversely with the number of those to whom the argument is addressed. The decision of the leaders may be taken on rational grounds. But the motivation of the decision to the rank and file of the party or union, and still more to the general public, will contain a larger element of the irrational the larger the audience becomes. The spectacle of an efficient élite maintaining its authority and asserting its will over the mass by the rationally calculated use of irrational methods of persuasion is the most disturbing nightmare of mass democracy.

The problem defies any rough-and-ready answer. It was implicit in Lincoln's formula of government "of the people" (meaning, I take it, belonging to the people in the sense of popular sovereignty), "by the people" (implying, I think, direct participation in the business of government) and "for the people" (requiring an identity of interests between governors and governed only obtainable when such participation occurs). It was implicit in Lenin's much-derided demand that every cook should learn to govern and that every worker should take his turn at the work of administration. The building of nineteenth-century democracy was long and arduous. The building of the new mass democracy will be no easier. The historian can here only look back over the way we have come, and analyse the fundamental questions which are being presented to the coming generation. He may be able to throw some light on the nature of the answers that are required; but he cannot define or prescribe them.

For myself, it seems inconceivable that we can return to the individualist democracy of a privileged class; and, by the same token, we cannot return to the exclusively political democracy of the weak state exercising only police functions. We are committed to mass democracy, to egalitarian democracy, to the public control and planning of the economic process, and therefore to the strong state exercising remedial and constructive functions. On the fundamental rôle of reason I shall say something in my last lecture. Here I will say only that I have no faith in a flight into the irrational or in an exaltation of irrational values. Reason may be an imperfect instrument; and we can no longer take the simple view of its character and functions which satisfied the eighteenth and nineteenth centuries. But it is none the less in a widening and deepening of the power of reason that we must place our hope. Mass democracy calls just as much as individualist democracy for an educated society as well as for responsible and courageous leaders; for it is only thus that the gap between leaders and masses, which is the major threat to mass democracy, can be bridged. The task is difficult but not hopeless; and just as Great Britain has done more than any other country during the last five years to mark out new lines of social and economic advance, so I believe that she has better opportunities than any other country to lay the foundations of an educated mass democracy.

[51]   The Totalitarian Theory of the State*

by R. WALLACE BREWSTER

Recency of the Application of Totalitarian Theory.   Not until the present century was an attempt made to apply the totalitarian theory of the state. Although its *philosophy* is rooted in the past, never before was it worked out so completely and tried in actual operation. The totalitarian idea found its fullest expression in Italy and Germany under the direction of the Fascist and Nazi Parties, respectively, following World War I. The Japanese government easily adapted many established fascist ideas and practices and cooperated fully with the totalitarian countries of the Western world until defeated at the close of World War II. Japan retained, however, some elements of a non-totalitarian nature which made it a rather poor example of totalitarian theory. Russia and her satellites, too, can be classed as supporters of totalitarian theories and practices as well as Spain.

Because totalitarian theory was best exemplified in Italy and Germany, we shall use them as illustrations of totalitarian doctrines. There were some differences between the Italian and German versions, but they were relatively incidental matters of emphasis. Technically, we speak of Italian Fascism and German Nazism, but in general practice the single term "fascism" is applied to both, a usage that will be followed here.

*From *Government in Modern Society* by R. Wallace Brewster, pp. 98-99, 102-103, *passim*. Reprinted by permission of Houghton Mifflin Company. Copyright 1958.

Russia will not be used here as an example of totalitarian theory because of the confusion between basic Marxian communism and the interpretations of it made in Russia by Lenin and his successors. The task of adjusting theory and practice needed to explain the nature of Soviet totalitarianism is too long for the space available. Then, too, Marx never glorified the state as did the exponents of fascism. In fact, he asserted that the state is an evil and predicted that it would eventually "wither away" after a communist society had been established following the liquidation of the old order. Not only the failure of the Russian state to "wither away" but the use as well of totalitarian practices on a scale perhaps even greater than in fascist Germany and Italy, complicates the problem of description. One leading analyst of Soviet institutions indicates how impossible it is for Soviet leaders to follow the Marxian theory of the state. "The 'withering away' thesis in Soviet ideology is conspicuous by its irrelevance . . . and the thesis that the state will wither away once capitalist encirclement is liquidated cannot be taken seriously."

In this connection, a study of various totalitarian systems, both fascist and communist, by two Harvard scholars, Carl J. Friedrich and Z. K. Brzezinski, led them to conclude that a common pattern exists throughout all of them. They are: an official ideology, a one-party governing system, a terroristic secret police, a monopoly on communication, exclusive access to weapons, and a nationally planned economy. It represents what William Ebenstein calls a "way of life" which characterizes totalitarian society. . . .

Why Dictatorship Is Essential. The totalitarian state leaves no room for democratic liberalism with its insistence on rule by the "people." The masses are held to be incapable of deciding what is best for themselves, to say nothing of the national welfare. Furthermore, the people do not know what the state's will is. Parties merely represent hostile groups which tear the nation asunder and reduce the efficiency of group activity. There must be only one party representing the united nation.

In the place of bungling government by talk, they say, a government of action must be established which is clothed with the unlimited authority to make decisions *for* the people. Mussolini once summed it up by saying that "Fascism denies that the majority, by the simple fact that it is a majority, can direct human society; it denies that numbers alone can govern by means of a periodical consultation, and it affirms the immutable, beneficial, and fruitful inequality of mankind, which can never be permanently leveled through the mere operation of a mechanical process such as universal suffrage." [1]

[1] Benito Mussolini, *The Political and Social Doctrine of Fascism*, p. 9.

Effective governmental action, it is asserted, can be assured only through a leader clothed with unlimited powers and responsible legally to no one. He is the sole source of authority in the state; neither the legislature nor the courts can limit anything he does. His successor is designated by him and not elected. His will is the law under the fiction that it embodies the will of all members of the nation. This omnipotent power of the chief executive of the state is absolutely necessary for the good of the nation; anything less would mean the best interests of the people could not be served. Since anything benefiting the nation is good and anything injuring it is bad, dictatorship is morally necessary. A . . . quotation from a Nazi is illustrative:

The Führer is the bearer of the people's will; he is independent of all groups, associations, and interests, but he is bound by laws which are inherent in the nature of his people. . . . The Führer is no "representative" of a particular group whose wishes he must carry out. He is no "organ" of the state in the sense of a mere executive agent. He is rather himself the bearer of the collective will of the people. In his will the will of the people is realized. He transforms the mere feelings of the people into a conscious will. . . . Thus it is possible for him, in the name of the true will of the people which he serves, to go against the subjective opinions and convictions of single individuals within the people if these are not in accord with the objective destiny of the people. . . . He shapes the collective will of the people within himself and he embodies the political unity and entirety of the people in opposition to individual interests. . . .[2]

The fact that Fascist and Nazi doctrines call for a dictatorial (autocratic) form of government as an absolute essential does not mean that all countries which have dictatorships are necessarily totalitarian in their philosophy. By the same token, dictatorship does not necessarily mean the existence of a totalitarian state. There have been many dictatorships which did not represent totalitarian states, ranging from those of Alexander the Great, through Caesar, on to Napoleon. The same can be said for many Latin-American dictatorships. In other words, all totalitarian states have a dictatorial form of government but not all dictatorships operate within a totalitarian state.

[2] Ernest Rudolf Huber, *Constitutional Law of the Greater German Reich*, quoted in *National Socialism*, pp. 34-36.

[CHAPTER TWENTY-FIVE]

Democratic Government in America

*T*HE Federalist papers are a classic series of essays on the nature of the government of the United States as outlined in the Constitution. They were written in 1787 and 1788 when ratification of the Constitution was under consideration by the States. The authors were Alexander Hamilton, James Madison, and John Jay. In Number 14 Madison argues that, in spite of the wide territory covered, union of the thirteen states as proposed in the Constitution is both practical and desirable. In Number 37 Madison presents the major difficulties faced by those who drew up the Constitution, and explains the necessity for making many compromises.

In "America's Big Tug-of-War" Sidney Hyman gives a lively and graphic picture of how our governmental system of "checks and balances" works in practice. His emphasis is on the role of the Supreme Court.

[52] Excerpts from "The Federalist"

An objection drawn from the extent of country answered.

[NO.] 14 by JAMES MADISON

WE have seen the necessity of the Union, as our bulwark against foreign danger; as the conservator of peace among ourselves; as the guardian of our commerce, and other common interests; as the only substitute for those military establishments which have subverted the liberties of the old world; and as the proper antidote for the diseases of faction, which have proved fatal to other popular Governments, and of which alarming symptoms have been betrayed by our own.

All that remains, within this branch of our inquiries, is to take notice of an objection that may be drawn from the great extent of country which the Union embraces. A few observations on this subject, will be the more proper, as it is perceived, that the adversaries of the new Constitution are availing themselves of a prevailing prejudice, with regard to the practicable sphere of republican administration, in order to supply, by imaginary difficulties, the want of those solid objections, which they endeavour in vain to find. . . .

As the natural limit of a democracy, is that distance from the central point, which will just permit the most remote citizens to assemble as often as their public functions demand, and will include no greater number than can join in those functions: so the natural limit of a republic, is that distance from the centre, which will barely allow the representatives of the people to meet as often as may be necessary for the administration of public affairs. Can it be said, that the limits of the United States exceed this distance? It will be said by those who recollect, that the Atlantic coast is the longest side of the Union; that, during the term of thirteen years, the representatives of the States have been almost continually assembled; and that the members, from the most distant States, are not chargeable with greater intermissions of attendance, than those from the States in the neighborhood of Congress. . . .

Favourable as this view of the subject may be, some observations remain, which will place it in a light still more satisfactory.

In the first place, it is to be remembered, that the general Government is not to be charged with the whole power of making and administering laws: its jurisdiction is limited to certain enumerated objects, which concern all the members of the republic, but which are not to be attained by the separate provisions of any. The subordinate Governments, which can extend their care to all those other objects, which can be separately provided for, will retain their due authority and activity. Were it proposed by the plan of the Convention, to abolish the Governments of the particular States, its adversaries would have some ground for their objection; though it would not be difficult to show, that if they were abolished, the general Government would be compelled, by the principle of self preservation, to reinstate them in their proper jurisdiction.

A second observation to be made is, that the immediate object of the Federal constitution, is to secure the Union of the thirteen primitive States, which we know to be practicable; and to add to them such other States, as may arise in their own bosoms, or in their neighbourhoods, which we cannot doubt to be equally practicable. The arrangement that may be necessary for those angles and fractions of our territory, which lie on our northwestern frontier, must be left to those whom further discoveries and experience will render more equal to the task.

Let it be remarked, in the third place, that the intercourse throughout the Union will be daily facilitated by new improvements. Roads will everywhere be shortened, and kept in better order; accommodations for travellers will be multiplied and meliorated; an interior navigation on our eastern side, will be opened throughout, or nearly throughout, the whole extent of the Thirteen States. The communication between the western and Atlantic districts, and between different parts of each, will be rendered more and more easy, by those numerous canals, with which the beneficence of nature has intersected our country, and which art finds so little difficult to connect and complete.

A fourth, and still more important consideration, is, that as almost every State will, on one side or other, be a frontier, and will thus find, in a regard to its safety, an inducement to make some sacrifices for the sake of the general protection: so the States which lie at the greatest distance from the heart of the Union, and which of course may partake least of the ordinary circulation of its benefits, will be at the same time immediately contiguous to foreign nations, and will consequently stand, on particular occasions, in greatest need of strength and resources. It may be inconvenient for Georgia, or the States forming our western or northeastern borders, to send their representatives to the Seat of Government; but they would find it more so to struggle alone against an invading enemy, or even to support alone the whole expense of those precautions, which may be dictated by the neighbourhood of continual danger. If they should derive less benefit therefore from the Union in some respects, than the less distant States, they will derive greater benefit from it in other respects, and thus the proper equilibrium will be maintained throughout.

I submit to you, my fellow citizens, these considerations, in full confidence that the good sense which has so often marked your decisions, will allow them their due weight and effect; and that you will never suffer difficulties, however formidable in appearance, or however fashionable the error on which they may be founded, to drive you into the gloomy and perilous scenes into which the advocates for disunion would conduct you.

Concerning the difficulties which the Convention must have experienced in the formation of a proper plan.

[NO. 37] by JAMES MADISON

AMONG the difficulties encountered by the Convention, a very important one must have lain, in combining the requisite stability and energy in government, with the inviolable attention due to liberty, and to the republican form. Without substantially accomplishing this part of their undertaking, they would have very imperfectly fulfilled the object of their appointment, or the expectation of the public: yet, it could not be easily accomplished, will be denied by no one who is unwilling to betray his ignorance of the subject. Energy in government, is essential to that security against external and internal danger, and to that prompt and salutary execution of the laws, which enter into the very definition of good government.

Stability in government is essential to national character, and to the advantages annexed to it, as well as to that repose and confidence in the minds of the people, which are among the chief blessings of civil society. An irregular and mutable legislation is not more an evil in itself, than it is odious to the people; and it may be pronounced with assurance, that the people of this country, enlightened as they are, with regard to the nature, and interested, as the great body of them are, in the effects of good government, will never be satisfied, till some remedy be applied to the vicissitudes and uncertainties, which characterize the State administrations. On comparing, however, these valuable ingredients with the vital principles of liberty, we must perceive at once, the difficulty of mingling them together in their due proportions. . . .

How far the Convention may have succeeded in this part of their work, will better appear on a more accurate view of it. From the cursory view here taken, it must clearly appear to have been an arduous part.

Not less arduous must have been the task of making the proper line of partition, between the authority of the General, and that of the State governments. Every man will be sensible of this difficulty, in proportion as he has been accustomed to contemplate and discriminate objects, extensive and complicated in their nature. The faculties of the mind itself have never yet been distinguished and defined, with satisfactory precision, by all the efforts of the most acute and metaphysical philosophers. Sense, perception, judgment, desire, volition, memory, imagination, are found to be separated, by such delicate shades and minute gradations, that their boundaries have eluded the most subtle investigations, and remain a pregnant source of ingenious disquisition and controversy. The boundaries between the great kingdoms of nature, and still more, between the various provinces, and lesser portions, into which they are subdivided, afford another illustration of the same important truth. The most sagacious and laborious naturalists have never yet succeeded, in tracing with certainty the line which separates the district of vegetable life, from the neighboring region of unorganized matter, or which marks the termination of the former, and the commencement of the animal empire. A still greater obscurity lies in the distinctive characters, by which the objects in each of these great departments of nature have been arranged and assorted.

When we pass from the works of nature, in which all the delineations are perfectly accurate, and appear to be otherwise only from the imperfection of the eye which surveys them, to the institutions of man, in which the obscurity arises as well from the object itself, as from the organ by which it is contemplated; we must perceive the necessity of moderating still further our expectations and hopes from the efforts of human sagacity. Experience has instructed us, that no skill in the science of government has yet been able to discriminate and define, with sufficient certainty, its three great provinces, the legislative, executive, and judiciary; or even the privileges and powers of the different legislative branches. Questions daily occur in the course of practice, which prove the obscurity which reigns in these subjects, and which puzzle the greatest adepts in political science. . . .

To the difficulties already mentioned, may be added the interfering pretensions of the larger and smaller States. We cannot err, in supposing that the former would contend for a participation in the Government, fully proportioned to their superior wealth and importance; and that the latter would not be less tenacious of the equality at present enjoyed by them. We may well suppose, that neither side would entirely yield to the other, and consequently that the struggle could be terminated only by compromise. It is extremely probable, also that after the ratio of representation had been adjusted, this very compromise must have produced a fresh struggle between the same parties, to give such a turn to the organization of the Government, and to the distribution of its powers, as would increase the importance of the branches, in forming which they had respectively obtained the greatest share of influence. There are features in the Constitution which warrant each of these suppositions; and as far as either of them is well founded, it shows that the Convention must have been compelled to sacrifice theoretical propriety to the force of extraneous considerations.

Nor could it have been the large and small States only, which would marshal themselves in opposition to each other on various points. Other combinations, resulting from a difference of local position and policy, must have created additional difficulties. As every State may be divided into different districts, and its citizens into different classes, which give birth to contending interests and local jealousies: so the different parts of the United States are distinguished from each other, by a variety of circumstances, which produce a like effect on a larger scale. And although this variety of interests, for reasons sufficiently explained in a former paper, may have a salutary influence on the administration of the Government when formed; yet everyone must be sensible of the contrary influence, which must have been experienced in the task of forming it.

Would it be wonderful if, under the pressure of all these difficulties, the Convention should have been forced into some deviations from that artificial structure and regular symmetry, which an abstract view of the subject might lead an ingenious theorist to bestow on a constitution planned in his closet, or in his imagination? The real wonder is, that so many difficulties should have been surmounted; and surmounted with an unanimity almost as unprecedented, as it must have been unexpected.

[53] *America's Big Tug-of-War**

by SIDNEY HYMAN

It should be easy these days for civics teachers to make their subject throb with life by connecting the textbook accounts of our government of checks and balances to the front-page storm that has been beating against the Supreme Court. For in this storm—aroused not alone because of the Court's school desegregation decisions, but for other reasons as well—almost every power rivalry present in our system of checks and balances has come into play.

State governors have clashed with the federal Chief Executive. State chief justices have rebuked the federal Supreme Court. Regions have clashed with regions.

Amid the strife between the Republican and Democratic parties on a national scale, each has been torn internally by clashes between rival wings. Within the federal government recently, the executive clashed with the Congress during its 85th sitting. There too, the committees of the Congress clashed with the full membership of each chamber. The House as a whole clashed with the Senate as a whole. And so on.

To be sure, this is not the first time that the Supreme Court has been the center of a great storm. Still, what makes the current event so significant is that it differs from the general pattern of such controversies. In the past, it was generally a President who led the attack on the Supreme Court, as was the case in the 1937 furor over Franklin D. Roosevelt's "court packing" plan.

A strong President, then bent on domestic reform, had met successive Supreme Court vetoes. His first reaction was to lecture the "Nine Old Men" from afar, calling their outlook a relic of horse and buggy days. When the lectures failed to impress the Supreme Court, Mr. Roosevelt had a bill introduced in Congress whose practical effect would have allowed him to appoint new members to the high tribunal. Presumably, the new ones would lift all judicial bars to his reform measures.

But the conservative members of the Congress, as a tactic in their own war against the President, sprang to the defense of the imperiled judges. They then argued that the Supreme Court was the only Con-

---

* From *The Chicago Sun-Times*, September 7, 1958, Sec. II, pp. 1-2. Reprinted by permission of the author and publisher.

stitutional arm we have that can protect the rights of individuals from arbitrary uses of executive or legislative power. The Congress then killed the "court-packing" plan.

In the current controversy, however, it is not a reforming President who has brought the court under siege. This attack has been mounted by "conservatives" occupying various centers of power in our divided system of government.

In the recent 85th Congress, for example, three conservative legislative task forces sponsored a number of bills aimed at curbing the Supreme Court. One of these three was formed of Southern Democrats, including those who had been most vocal in the 1937 defense of the Supreme Court's independence. Only now they enlisted themselves in the anticourt army, either from personal hostility to the school desegregation decisions, or under the pressure of inflamed local sentiments stemming from the same cause.

The second task force was formed of Northern Republicans, the guiding spirits being congressional investigators in the heyday of McCarthyism. Their activities then had resulted in contempt citations which the Congress voted against various persons, followed by convictions in the lower federal courts.

These "civil liberties" or "security" cases had travelled the full distance of appeals until they came before the Supreme Court.

With few exceptions, that court moved to protect the constitutional rights of persons violated in some form. The original convictions were set aside.

To congressional investigators this meant the court was "soft on communism." So Congress had to "curb the judiciary" if the republic was not to be "undermined" by the Supreme Court which, one would believe, had its decisions written in the Kremlin.

The third conservative legislative task force attacking the Supreme Court was formed of men who felt it had been an all too potent instrument through which federal regulatory powers were encroaching on, and displacing, state and local powers. Their attack was mounted on behalf of local interests who wanted to throw off the yoke of federal authority, and deal only with the regulatory powers of pliant state governments.

Many anticourt bills emerged from these punitive expeditions. One forbade the Supreme Court to pass on the pertinency of questions asked witnesses by congressional committees. Such a committee then could conduct a legislative trial of an individual on any pretext. If the committee influenced the Congress to vote a contempt citation, the courts would be under a virtual legislative directive to find the individual guilty of contempt, and punish him according to the criminal code.

Another anticourt bill, provided that no federal statute, past or present, should be construed by the Supreme Court to be supreme over state law, unless the Congress specified such an intention, or unless there was a "direct and positive conflict" between federal and state law. The so-called "states rights" bill, would have overturned 169 years of constitutional practice under which federal law is paramount over state law, generally as a matter of course. Southern states then would have a freer hand in a broad range of local matters involving civil rights. And again, local economic interests across the land would feel themselves liberated in some degree from federal power.

None of the anticourt bills were enacted by the 85th Congress. They were defeated after a dramatic interplay of various "checks and balances" in our system of government. The executive as a whole opposed the Congress as a whole, when Atty. Gen. William Rogers plainly implied that the President would veto the "states-rights" bill if it was enacted. The House as a whole opposed the Senate as a whole, when the House passed all the punitive bills, only to have them die in the Senate.

In the Senate, a majority of the judiciary Committee favored the immediate enactment of the punitive bills, though a majority of the full membership of the Senate eventually wanted them tabled or killed outright. Northern and border state Democrats broke away from their Southern colleagues to join in killing the bills along with New England and urban state Republicans—who had broken away from their Midwestern and Rocky Mountain state brethren.

Also, Senate Majority Leader Lyndon Johnson (D-Tex.) had resisted two strong demands. One was from Northern Democrats who wanted him to pigeonhole the anticourt bills without allowing them ever to come to a vote. The other was from Southern Democrats who wanted him to bring the bills to a vote early in the session. That the national Democratic party should be spared a long and blood-letting North-South fight, Johnson waited until the Congress was rushing pell-mell for adjournment before he brought the court bills forward for a sharp but short three-day contest on the floor of the Senate.

Still, if the Supreme Court survived the attack mounted in the 85th Congress by three strong legislative task forces, within hours after the Congress adjourned another power center in our system of checks and balances mounted a new and perhaps more impressive attack.

The striking arm this time was a Los Angeles conference of state chief justices representing the state judiciary (as distinct from the federal judiciary), these jurists by a vote of 36 to 8 approved a 10-man committee report containing neither apology nor deference in sharply taking the U.S. Supreme Court to task.

By this means the state chief justices accused the U.S. Supreme Court of making "hasty, impatient" decisions, frequently reversing its own decisions, and of adopting "the role of a policymaker without proper judicial restraint." They observed that in constitutional cases, unanimous decisions of the U.S. Supreme Court are "comparative rarities," and that divisions on a 5-4 basis are quite frequent. Nor was this all.

The state chief justices asserted that "at times, the U.S. Supreme Court manifests, or seems to manifest, an impatience with the slow working of our federal system." It therefore needed to be reminded that in the field of federal-state relations, the divisions of power should be "more diligently preserved." And finally, the U.S. Supreme Court should exercise "the power of judicial self-restraint" in interpreting the Constitution, and not to give effect to what the court might deem "desirable or undesirable."

The judges from the South voted solidly in favor of this stern rebuke. But many others who voted with them came from states with a long tradition of racial equality, and where secure tenure shielded the judges from popular outrage. Many of these last had been nettled because their own decisions had been reversed in no uncertain terms, by the U.S. Supreme Court. And in this they were joined by still other judges who mirrored the discontent of law journals, where writers criticized recent Supreme Court decisions upsetting what had long stood as the next best thing to Divine Revelation.

The eight state chief justices who disagreed with the other thirty-six were from the urban North. In essence, what they said to their colleagues ran to this effect: It would be well if the state chief justices practiced the judicial restraint they were preaching to the U.S. Supreme Court. Moreover, if the quality of justice was to be improved, the last way to improve was by a vote of a judges' association critical of the decisions of other justices. The best way to improve it was still the customary way. It was to have a judge, legally responsible for a decision, make the decision. Then, afterward, the matter could be reviewed by a higher court with responsibilities of its own.

But this was not the end of the storm raging around the Supreme Court. U.S. District Court Judge Harry J. Lemley had given the school board of Little Rock, Ark., a 30-month breathing spell before trying again to integrate Central High School. Then the Eighth Circuit Court of Appeals overturned his ruling, but granted a stay of its own decision. The purpose here was to permit Little Rock to appeal to the U.S. Supreme Court.

In the immediate sequel, Gov. Orval Faubus of Arkansas called his State Legislature into special session, to secure from it special powers to prevent integration from taking effect—regardless. And an extraordinary special session of the U.S. Supreme Court granted the Little Rock School Board a delay until Sept. 11 to show cause why the decision of the court of appeals, overturning Judge Lemley's decision and ordering the integration of the high school, should not be sustained.

Nor did this exhaust the complications arising from our divided government, based on a system of checks and balances. At a White House news conference, President Eisenhower stated in clear terms that he had a presidential duty to enforce the court's desegregation decision. But he refused to commit himself on the question of whether he personally agreed or disagreed with the principle of desegregation. Seven days later he again refused to express himself on the principle of desegregation. But he hinted that perhaps the actual process of school desegregation should go forward a bit more slowly.

However, it developed that neither his solicitor general nor his attorney general were so shy in speaking about the merits of the case. At the special session of the Supreme Court, the solicitor general argued the case for immediate integration with great eloquence. With equal eloquence, the attorney general told the American Bar Assn. that desegregation of the public schools was morally, legally and politically right and proper.

All this raised the question of whether the executive branch of the government was split on the question of school desegregation. It raised the further question whether a special kind of political "checks and balances" was operative: whether Vice President Richard Nixon was speaking through his close friend the attorney general, in opposition to the President.

Leaving out of account the burning question of school desegregation (where the Supreme Court's original decision was unanimous), what about the present position of the Supreme Court in other matters? Has it given the appearance of monolithic solidarity? Far from it. In many of its decisions it has given new form and focus to a fundamental split between the "activists" and the "passivists" which goes far back.

The take-out point for this split is the fact that the Constitution itself is most vague in locating and specifying the role of the court in relation to other branches.

Within the framework of this uncertainty, now as in time past, the judicial "activists" want the Supreme Court to be a positive force, with a social point of view of its own. That is, it should stand ready to use judicial power to fill political vacuums neglected by legislative or executive power. Or if these vacuums have been filled in wrong-headed ways, then the court should set matters right.

In 1933-37 the "activists" on the court were "conservatives," using their social point of view to veto New Deal legislation. Today, ironically, the leading "activists" are called "liberals."

The judicial "passivists," on the other hand, have felt in times past, and feel now, that the Supreme Court should place itself under a self-denying ordinance. It should not undertake to make up for political deficiencies of the Congress or the President; within the four corners of the Constitution, it should allow them a right to exercise their own judgments—good or bad. If circumstances arise where an interposition of judicial judgment is unavoidable, then the Supreme Court should rest its case on the narrowest of possible grounds.

In times past, the judicial "passivists" were the great "liberal" judges like Justice Holmes, Brandeis and Cardozo. Their leading heir on the present court is Justice Felix Frankfurter.

One final comment seems in order. If the teachers of American civics and their young students get discouraged as they follow all the intricacies of what "checks and balances" mean in actual practice, let them take heart from this fact. One hundred and sixty-nine classes before them, starting in 1789, had to study and master the same difficult subject matter. Still, despite the difficulties, the proof that they could and did master it, finds its evidence in the truth that the American system of government is now the oldest in the world from the standpoint of unbroken continuity in its basic form.

[CHAPTER TWENTY-SIX]

Political Parties and Elections

O NE of the most common criticisms of the American political system is that the two major parties do not stand for anything. Their platforms, it is said, are similar and consist of vague generalities; their only real purpose is to win elections.

While this concept of our political parties is an exaggeration, it contains an important element of truth. Fischer, however, instead of regarding this lack of clear-cut division on major issues as a weakness, considers it one of the great elements of stability in our political system. He explains why, in his judgment, it protects the vital interests of divergent groups and minimizes conflict. As a result of it, he believes, when major government decisions are actually made, they are usually supported by a "concurrent majority."

[54] Government by Concurrent Majority*

by JOHN FISCHER

Every now and then somebody comes up with the idea that the party system in American politics is absurd because our two great parties don't stand for clearly contrasting principles, and that we would be better off if we had a conservative party and a radical or liberal party. It is a persuasive argument, especially for well-meaning people who have not had much first-hand experience in politics. You have probably heard it; it runs something like this:

"Both of the traditional American parties are outrageous frauds. Neither the Republicans nor the Democrats have any fundamental principles or ideology. They do not even have a program. In every campaign the platforms of both parties are simply collections of noble generalities, muffled in the vaguest possible language; and in each case the two platforms are very nearly identical.

"Obviously, then, both parties are merely machines for grabbing power and distributing favors. In their lust for office they are quite willing to make a deal with anybody who can deliver a sizable block of votes. As a result, each party has become an outlandish cluster of local machines and special interest groups which have nothing in common except a craving for the public trough.

"This kind of political system"—so the argument runs—"is clearly meaningless. A man of high principles can never hope to accomplish anything through the old parties, because they are not interested in principle. Moreover, the whole arrangement is so illogical that it affronts every intelligent citizen.

"We ought to separate the sheep from the goats—to heard all the progressives on one side of the fence and all the conservatives on the other. Then politics really will have some meaning; every campaign can be fought over clearly defined issues. The Europeans, who are more sophisticated politically than we simple Americans, discovered this long ago, and in each of their countries they have arranged a neat political spectrum running from Left to Right."

This argument pops up with special urgency whenever a third party

*From *Unwritten Rules of American Politics* by John Fischer, *Harper's Magazine*, November, 1948, pp. 27-36 *passim*. Reprinted by permission.

appears—Theodore Roosevelt's in 1912, Robert LaFollette's in 1924, or Henry Wallace's in 1948. And it sounds so plausible—at least on the surface—that many people have wondered why these splinter parties have always dwindled away after the election was over. Indeed, many veteran third-party enthusiasts have been able to account for their failure only by assuming a perverse and rock-headed stupidity among the American electorate.

There is, however, another possible explanation for the stubborn durability of our seemingly illogical two-party system; that it is more vigorous, more deeply rooted, and far better suited to our own peculiar needs than any European system would be; that it involves a more complex and subtle conception than the crude blacks and whites of the European ideological parties. There is considerable evidence, it seems to me, that our system—in spite of certain dangerous weaknesses—has on the whole worked out more successfully than the European. Perhaps it is the very subtlety of the American political tradition which is responsible for the almost universal misunderstanding of it abroad. . . . The most useful discussion of this tradition which I have come across is the work of John C. Calhoun, published nearly a century ago. Today of course he is an almost forgotten figure, and many people take it for granted that his views were discredited for good by the Civil War. . . .

Calhoun summed up his political thought in what he called the Doctrine of the Concurrent Majority. He saw the United States as a nation of tremendous and frightening diversity—a collection of many different climates, races, cultures, religions, and economic patterns. He saw the constant tension among all these special interests, and he realized that the central problem of American politics was to find some way of holding these conflicting groups together.

It could not be done by force; no one group was strong enough to impose its will on all the others. The goal could be achieved only by compromise—and no real compromise could be possible if any threat of coercion lurked behind the door. Therefore, Calhoun reasoned, every vital decision in American life would have to be adopted by a "concurrent majority"—by which he meant, in effect, a unanimous agreement of all interested parties. No decision which affected the interests of the slaveholders, he argued, should be taken without their consent; and by implication he would have given a similar veto to every other special interest, whether it be labor, management, the Catholic church, old-age pensioners, the silver miners, or the corngrowers of the Middle West.

Under the goad of the slavery issue, Calhoun was driven to state his doctrine in an extreme and unworkable form. If every sectional interest had been given the explicit, legal veto power which he called for, the government obviously would have been paralyzed. (That, in fact, is precisely what seems to be happening today in the United Nations.) It is the very essence of the idea of "concurrent majority" that it cannot be made legal and official. It can operate effectively only as an informal, highly elastic, and generally accepted understanding.

Moreover, government by concurrent majority can exist only when no one power is strong enough to dominate completely, *and then only when all of the contending interest groups recognize and abide by certain rules of the game.*

These rules are the fundamental bond of unity in American political life. . . . Under these rules every group tacitly binds itself to tolerate the interests and opinions of every other group. It must not try to impose its views on others, nor can it press its own special interests to the point where they seriously endanger the interests of other groups or of the nation as a whole.

Furthermore, each group must exercise its implied veto with responsibility and discretion; and in times of great emergency it must forsake its veto right altogether. It dare not be intransigent or doctrinaire. It must make every conceivable effort to compromise, relying on its veto only as a last resort. For if any player wields this weapon recklessly, the game will break up—or all the other players will turn on him in anger, suspend the rules for the time being, and maul those very interests he is trying so desperately to protect. That was what happened in 1860, when the followers of Calhoun carried his doctrine to an unbearable extreme. Much the same thing, on a less violent scale, happened to American business interests in 1933 and to the labor unions in 1947.

This is the somewhat elusive sense, it seems to me, in which Calhoun's theory has been adopted by the American people. But elusive and subtle as it may be, it remains the basic rule of the game of politics in this country—and in this country alone. Nothing comparable exists in any other nation, although the British, in a different way, have applied their own rules of responsibility and self-restraint.

It is a rule which operates unofficially and entirely outside the Constitution—but it has given us a method by which all the official and Constitutional organs of government can be made to work. It also provides a means of selecting leaders on all levels of our political life, for hammering out policies, and for organizing and managing the conquest of political power.

The way in which this tradition works in practice can be observed most easily in Congress. Anyone who has ever tried to push through a piece of legislation quickly discovers that the basic units of organization on Capitol Hill are not the parties, but the so-called blocs, which are familiar to everyone who reads a newspaper. There are dozens of them —the farm bloc, the silver bloc, the friends of labor, the business group, the isolationists, the public power bloc—and they all cut across party lines. . . .

Now it is an unwritten but firm rule of Congress that no important bloc shall ever be voted down—under normal circumstances—on any matter which touches its own vital interests. Each of them, in other words, has a tacit right of veto on legislation in which it is primarily concerned. The ultimate expression of this right is the institution—uniquely American— of the filibuster in the Senate. Recently it has acquired a bad name among liberals because the Southern conservatives have used it ruthlessly to fight off civil rights legislation and protect white supremacy. Not so long ago, however, the filibuster was the stoutest weapon of such men as Norris and the LaFollettes in defending many a progressive cause.

Naturally no bloc wants to exercise its veto power except when it is absolutely forced to—for this is a negative power, and one which is always subject to retaliation. Positive power to influence legislation, on the other hand, can be gained only by conciliation, compromise, and endless horse-trading.

The farm bloc, for instance, normally needs no outside aid to halt the passage of a hostile bill. As a last resort, three or four strong-lunged states-men from the corn belt can always filibuster it to death in the Senate. If the bloc wants to put through a measure to support agricultural prices, however, it can succeed only by enlisting the help of other powerful spe-cial interest groups. Consequently, it must always be careful not to an-tagonize any potential ally by a reckless use of the veto; and it must be willing to pay for such help by throwing its support from time to time behind legislation sought by the labor bloc, the National Association of Manufacturers, or the school-teachers' lobby. . . .

This process of trading blocs of votes is generally known as log-rolling, and frequently it is deplored by the more innocent type of reformer. Such pious disapproval has no effect whatever on any practicing politician. He knows that log-rolling is a sensible and reasonably fair device, and that without it Congress could scarcely operate at all.

In fact, Congress gradually has developed a formal apparatus—the committee system—which is designed to make the log-rolling process as smooth and efficient as possible. There is no parallel system anywhere; the committees of Parliament and of the Continental legislative bodies work in an entirely different way.

Obviously the main business of Congress—the hammering out of a series of compromises between many special interest groups—cannot be conducted satisfactorily on the floor of the House or Senate. The meetings there are too large and far too public for such delicate negotiations. Moreover, every speech delivered on the floor must be aimed primarily at the voters back home, and not at the other members of the chamber. Therefore, Congress—especially the House—does nearly all its work in the closed sessions of its various committees, simply because the committee room is the only place where it is possible to arrange a compromise acceptable to all major interests affected.

For this reason, it is a matter of considerable importance to get a bill before the proper committee. Each committee serves as a forum for a particular cluster of special interests, and the assignment of a bill to a specific committee often decides which interest groups shall be recognized officially as affected by the measure and therefore entitled to a hand in its drafting. "Who is to have standing before the committee" is the technical term, and it is this decision that frequently decides the fate of the legislation.

Calhoun's principles of the concurrent majority and of sectional compromise operate just as powerfully, though sometimes less obviously, in every other American political institution. Our cabinet, for example, is the only one in the world where the members are charged by law with the representation of special interests—labor, agriculture, commerce, and so on. In other countries, each agency of government is at least presumed to act for the nation as a whole; here most agencies are expected to behave as servants for one interest or another. The Veterans' Administration, to cite the most familiar case, is frankly intended to look out for Our Boys; the Maritime Board is to look out for the shipping industry; the National Labor Relations Board, as originally established under the Wagner Act, was explicitly intended to build up the bargaining power of the unions.

Even within a single department, separate agencies are sometimes set up to represent conflicting interests. Thus in the Department of Agriculture under the New Deal the old Triple-A became primarily an instrument of the large-scale commercial farmers, as represented by their lobby, the Farm Bureau Federation; while the Farm Security Administration went to bat for the tenants, the farm laborers, and the little subsistence farmers, as represented by the Farmers Union. . . .

Calhoun's laws also govern the selection of virtually every candidate for public office. The mystery of "eligibility" which has eluded most foreign observers simply means that a candidate must not be unacceptable to any important special interest group—a negative rather than a positive qualification. A notorious case of this process at work was the selection of Mr. Truman as the Democrats' Vice Presidential candidate in 1944. As Edward J. Flynn, the Boss of the Bronx, has pointed out in his memoirs, Truman was the one man "who would hurt . . . least" as Roosevelt's running mate. Many stronger men were disqualified, Flynn explained, by the tacit veto of one sectional interest or another. Wallace was unacceptable to the business men and to many local party machines. Byrnes was distasteful to the Catholics, the Negroes, and organized labor. Rayburn came from the wrong part of the country. Truman, however, came from a border state, his labor record was good, he had not antagonized the conservatives, and—as Flynn put it—"he had never made any 'racial' remarks. He just dropped into the slot. . . ."

The stronghold of Calhoun's doctrine, however, is the American party —the wonder and despair of foreigners who cannot fit it into any of their concepts of political life.

The purpose of European parties is, of course, to divide men of different ideologies into coherent and disciplined organizations. The historic role of the American party, on the other hand, is not to divide but to unite. That task was imposed by simple necessity. If a division into ideological parties had been attempted, in addition to all the other centrifugal forces in this country, it very probably would have proved impossible to hold the nation together. The Founding Fathers understood this thoroughly; hence Washington's warning against "factions."

Indeed, on the one occasion when we did develop two ideological parties, squarely opposing each other on an issue of principle, the result was civil war. Fortunately, that was our last large-scale experiment with a third party formed on an ideological basis—for in its early days that is just what the Republican party was.

Its radical wing, led by such men as Thaddeus Stevens, Seward, and Chase, made a determined and skillful effort to substitute principles for interests as the foundations of American political life. Even within their own party, however, they were opposed by such practical politicians as Lincoln and Johnson—men who distrusted fanaticism in any form—and by the end of the Reconstruction period the experiment had been abandoned. American politics then swung back into its normal path and has never veered far away from it since. Although Calhoun's cause was defeated, his political theory came through the Civil War stronger than ever.

The result is that the American party has no permanent program and no fixed aim, except to win elections. Its one purpose is to unite the largest possible number of divergent interest groups in the pursuit of power. Its unity is one of compromise, not of dogma. It must—if it hopes to succeed —appeal to considerable numbers on both the left and the right, to rich and poor, Protestant and Catholic, farmer and industrial worker, native and foreign born.

It must be ready to bid for the support of any group that can deliver a sizable chunk of votes, accepting that group's program with whatever modifications may be necessary to reconcile the other members of the party. If sun worship, or Existentialism, or the nationalization of industry should ever attract any significant following in this country, you can be sure that both parties would soon whip up a plank designed to win it over.

This ability to absorb new ideas (along with the enthusiasts behind them) and to mold them into a shape acceptable to the party's standpat-ters is, perhaps, the chief measure of vitality in the party's leadership. Such ideas almost never germinate within the party itself. They are stolen— very often from third parties.

Indeed, the historic function of third parties has been to sprout new issues, nurse them along until they have gathered a body of supporters worth stealing, and then to turn them over (often reluctantly) to the major parties. A glance at the old platforms of the Populists, the Bull Moosers, and the Socialists will show what an astonishingly high percentage of their once-radical notions have been purloined by both Republicans and Demo-crats—and enacted into law. Thus the income tax, child-labor laws, mini-mum wages, regulation of railroads and utilities, and old-age pensions have all become part of the American Way of Life.

While each major party must always stand alert to grab a promising new issue, it also must be careful never to scare off any of the big, estab-lished interest groups. For as soon as it alienates any one of them, it finds itself in a state of crisis.

During the nineteen-thirties and -forties the Republicans lost much of their standing as a truly national party because they had made themselves unacceptable to labor. Similarly, the Democrats, during the middle stage of the New Deal, incurred the wrath of the business interests. Ever since Mr. Truman was plumped into the White House, the Democratic leader-ship has struggled desperately—though rather ineptly—to regain the con-fidence of business men without at the same time driving organized labor out of the ranks. It probably would be safe to predict that if the Republi-can party is to regain a long period of health, it must make an equally vigorous effort to win back the confidence of labor. For the permanent veto of any major element in American society means political death— as the ghosts of the Federalists and Whigs can testify.

The weaknesses of the American political system are obvious—much more obvious, in fact, than its virtues. These weaknesses have been so sharply criticized for the past hundred years, by a procession of able analysts ranging from Walter Bagehot to Thomas K. Finletter, that it is hardly necessary to mention them here. It is enough to note that most of the criticism has been aimed at two major flaws.

First, it is apparent that the doctrine of the concurrent majority is a negative one—a principle of inaction. A strong government, capable of rapid and decisive action, is difficult to achieve under a system which forbids it to do anything until virtually everybody acquiesces. In times of crisis, a dangerously long period of debate and compromise usually is necessary before any administration can carry out the drastic measures needed. The depression of the early thirties, the crisis in foreign policy which ended only with Pearl Harbor, the crisis of the Marshall program all illustrate this recurring problem.

This same characteristic of our system gives undue weight to the small but well-organized pressure group—especially when it is fighting *against* something. Hence a few power companies were able to block for twenty years the sensible use of the Muscle Shoals dam which eventually became the nucleus of TVA. An even more flagrant example is the silver bloc, representing only a tiny fraction of the American people. It has been looting the Treasury for a generation by a series of outrageous silver subsidy and purchase laws.

The negative character of our political rules also makes it uncommonly difficult for us to choose a President. Many of our outstanding political operatives—notably those who serve in the Senate—are virtually barred from a Presidential nomination because they are forced to get on record on too many issues. Inevitably they offend some important interest group, and therefore become "unavailable." Governors, who can keep their mouths shut on most national issues, have a much better chance to reach the White House. Moreover, the very qualities of caution and inoffensiveness which make a good candidate—Harding and Coolidge come most readily to mind—are likely to make a bad President.

An even more serious flaw in our scheme of politics is the difficulty in finding anybody to speak for the country as a whole. Calhoun would have argued that the national interest is merely the sum of all the various special interests, and therefore needs no spokesmen of its own—but in this case he clearly was wrong.

In practice, we tend to settle sectional and class conflicts at the expense of the nation as a whole—with results painful to all of us. The labor troubles in the spring of 1946, for instance, could be settled only on a basis acceptable to *both* labor and management: that is, on the basis of higher wages *plus* higher prices. The upshot was an inflationary spiral which damaged everybody. Countless other instances, from soil erosion to the rash of billboards along our highways, bear witness to the American tendency to neglect matters which are "only" of national interest, and therefore are left without a recognized sponsor.

Over the generations we have developed a series of practices and institutions which partly remedy these weaknesses, although we are still far from a complete cure. One such development has been the gradual strengthening of the Presidency as against Congress. As the only man elected by all the people, the President inevitably has had to take over many of the policy-making and leadership functions which the Founding Fathers originally assigned to the legislators. This meant, of course, that he could no longer behave merely as an obedient executor of the will of Congress, but was forced into increasingly frequent conflicts with Capitol Hill.

Today we have come to recognize that this conflict is one of the most important obligations of the Presidency. No really strong executive tries to avoid it—he accepts it as an essential part of his job. If he simply tries to placate the pressure groups which speak through Congress, history writes him down as a failure. For it is his duty to enlist the support of many minorities for measures rooted in the national interest, reaching beyond their own immediate concern—and, if necessary, to stand up against the ravening minorities for the interest of the whole.

In recent times this particular part of the President's job has been made easier by the growth of the Theory of Temporary Emergencies. All of us —or nearly all—have come around to admitting that in time of emergency special interest groups must forego their right of veto. As a result, the President often is tempted to scare up an emergency to secure legislation which could not be passed under any other pretext. Thus, most of the New Deal bills were introduced as "temporary emergency measures," although they were clearly intended to be permanent from the very first; for in no other way could Mr. Roosevelt avoid the veto of the business interests.

Again, in 1939 the threat of war enabled the President to push through much legislation which would have been impossible under normal circumstances.

Because we have been so preoccupied with trying to patch up the flaws in our system, we have often overlooked its unique elements of strength. The chief of these is its ability to minimize conflict—not by suppressing the conflicting forces, but by absorbing and utilizing them. The result is a society which is both free and reasonably stable—a government which is as strong and effective as most dictatorships, but which can still adapt itself to social change.

The way in which the American political organism tames down the extremists of both the left and right is always fascinating to watch. Either party normally is willing to embrace any group or movement which can deliver votes—but in return it requires these groups to adjust their programs to fit the traditions, beliefs, and prejudices of the majority of the people. The fanatics, the implacable radicals cannot hope to get to first base in American politics until they abandon their fanaticism and learn the habits of conciliation. As a consequence, it is almost impossible for political movements here to become entirely irresponsible and to draw strength from the kind of demagogic obstruction which has nurtured both Communist and Fascist movements abroad.

The same process which gentles down the extremists also prods along the political laggards. As long as it is in a state of health, each American party has a conservative and a liberal wing. Sometimes one is dominant, sometimes the other—but even when the conservative element is most powerful, it must reckon with the left-wingers in its own family. At the moment the Republican party certainly is in one of its more conservative phases; yet it contains men who are at least as progressive as most of the old New Dealers. They, and their counterparts in the Democratic party, exert a steady tug to the left which prevents either party from lapsing into complete reaction.

The strength of this tug is indicated by the fact that the major New Deal reforms have now been almost universally accepted. In the mid-thirties, many leading Republicans, plus many conservative Democrats, were hell-bent on wiping out social security, TVA, SEC, minimum-wage laws, rural electrification, and all the other dread innovations of the New Deal. Today no Presidential aspirant would dare suggest the repeal of a single one of them. In this country there simply is no place for a hard core of irreconcilable reactionaries, comparable to those political groups in France which have never yet accepted the reforms of the French Revolution.

This American tendency to push extremists of both the left and right toward a middle position has enabled us, so far, to escape class warfare. This is no small achievement for any political system; for class warfare cannot be tolerated by a modern industrial society. If it seriously threatens, it is bound to be suppressed by some form of totalitarianism, as it has been in Germany, Spain, Italy, Russia, and most of Eastern Europe.

In fact, suppression might be termed the normal method of settling conflicts in continental Europe, where parties traditionally have been drawn up along ideological battle lines. Every political campaign becomes a religious crusade; each party is fanatically convinced that it and it alone has truth by the tail; each party is certain that its opponents not only are wrong, but wicked. If the sacred ideology is to be established beyond challenge, no heresy can be tolerated. Therefore it becomes a duty not only to defeat the enemy at the polls, but to wipe him out. Any suggestion of compromise must be rejected as treason and betrayal of the true faith. The party must be disciplined like an army, and if it cannot win by other means it must be ready to take up arms in deadly fact.

Under this kind of political system the best that can be hoped for is a prolonged deadlock between parties which are too numerous and weak to exterminate one another. The classic example is prewar France, where six revolutions or near-revolutions broke out within a century, where cabinets fell every weekend, and no government could ever become strong enough to govern effectively. The more usual outcome is a complete victory for one ideology or another, after a brief period of electioneering, turmoil, and fighting in the streets; then comes the liquidation of the defeated.

Because this sort of ideological politics is so foreign to our native tradition, neither Socialists, Communists, nor Fascists have ever been accepted as normal parties. So long as that tradition retains its very considerable vitality, it seems to me unlikely that any third party founded on an ideological basis can take root. The notion of a ruthless and unlimited class struggle, the concept of a master race, a fascist élite, or a proletariat which is entitled to impose its will on all others—these are ideas which are incompatible with the main current of American political life. The uncompromising ideologist, of whatever faith, appears in our eyes peculiarly "un-American," simply because he cannot recognize the rule of the concurrent majority, nor can he accept the rules of mutual toleration which are necessary to make it work. Unless he forsakes his ideology, he cannot even understand that basic principle of American politics which was perhaps best expressed by Judge Learned Hand: "The spirit of liberty is the spirit which is not too sure that it is right."

[CHAPTER TWENTY-SEVEN]

Government Finance and the Social Welfare

BARBARA Ward believes that in the United States far too much is
spent by individuals on non-essentials, and far too little is spent by government on public services. She implies that, if defense expenditures
cannot be reduced, ways must be found to raise taxes. Chamberlin, on the
other hand, suggests that we have done rather well in providing more
funds for public services. He notes the very rapid increase in taxes and
government spending in recent years, and especially the great increase
in spending on education; and he includes a quotation from the First
National City Bank Letter in which the fear is expressed that higher taxes
would discourage individual initiative and check economic growth. By
implication this might, in the long run, mean relatively less rather than
more funds for public services. Finally C. Northcote Parkinson, writing
humorously but with underlying seriousness, propounds "Parkinson's
Second Law." He suspects that increased government revenue is apt to
mean more inefficiency and waste rather than more or better services;
and he maintains that the total tax burden cannot be allowed to exceed
certain limits without endangering the social structure.

[55]   The Gap Between Social Needs and Public Expenditures*

by BARBARA WARD

Every assessment of America's future economic problems will presumably begin with the most dynamic factor in the American community—the bounding birth rate. It is now a conservative estimate to expect a population of some 220 millions by 1975. If the three and four child family becomes the pattern of the future, the estimate should be considerably higher.

In any normal, responsible family the arrival of more children leads to a change in habits of spending. More money will be set aside for education, for health, for insurance, for housing. Parents cut down some less essential expenditure—smoking, perhaps, or drinking—or postpone desirable purchases—new drapes, a new automobile.

When, in the great family which is the nation, a cataract of new babies pours into the community, it would not be unreasonable to expect something of the same kind of shift in spending. Housing, health, education—these would claim more of the national income, a wide range of consumer goods rather less.

This reasonable assumption is, however, a little complicated by the fact that some of the higher expenditures made necessary by America's growing population come out of the public purse. The millions and millions of new houses which must be built when the babies born in the great upsurge of population in the early 1940's begin to marry and form their own homes will be financed in the main by the families themselves. But the streets, the water supplies, the sanitation, the urban and suburban amenities, the policy and fire protection which help to turn four walls and a roof into a functioning unit in a civilized community must all come from tax money. Health payments and insurances will be mainly private, but much more public money will be needed for hospital-building and for various forms of preventive medical services. Education, by the fundamental decision to provide all Americans with a free birthright of learning, must come to an overwhelming degree from public funds.

All this is obvious enough—although the scale of social expenditure

*Reprinted from *Problems of United States Economic Development*, Vol. I, January 1958, published by The Committee for Economic Development, 711 Fifth Avenue, New York 22, New York.

the new families will make necessary almost certainly is not. But there are one or two other factors which affect the scale of necessary social capital. It is not only the rising population that swells the need. There is a heavy backlog of unsatisfied demand. Smaller expenditures during the depression, the enforced economy of the war years, have left the community with a legacy of obsolete schools, houses, hospitals, and indeed whole urban areas, which, with the passage of each year, calls more urgently for replacement and lengthens the list of necessary new construction.

To give only the most fateful instance—that of education—the position today is that in spite of building 50,000 new classrooms each year, the authorities are not keeping pace with the new entries to school. The deficit is growing by thousands every year, and today it stands at 75,000 classrooms. At the same time, perhaps 20 per cent of existing school buildings are strictly obsolete—a euphemism used to cover, in some cases, insanitary firetraps.

The steady increase in *density* of population also underlines the need for higher social expenditure. It may be that the cheapest method of housing the new millions is to leave private demand and the real estate and construction interests to surround existing urban centers with ring after ring of outward-growing suburbs. The nineteen-seventies may be not only the decade when America passes the 250 millions mark but when Boston is finally linked to Washington in one continuous "conurbation." To decentralize industry to smaller communities, to consider the creation of entirely new cities in growing areas such as the Pacific Northwest—such policies might well be more costly in terms of a whole range of urban and environmental services, but conceivably they might have some relevance to a basic American right, "the pursuit of happiness" and hence a basic economic necessity, a healthy and intelligent working force.

Implications such as these of a growing density of population may be hard to assess. But not all are so. It is clear that in the next decades, the most precious of all America's resources—pure water—must become steadily more costly as it becomes more scarce.

Can one make any estimate of the scale of need for social capital in the coming decades? The survey published by the Twentieh Century Fund in 1955 attempted a comprehensive assessment and carried its forecasts to 1960. Its conclusion was that in virtually every field of publicly-financed community need, there would be deficits in the 1960's. In terms of the 1950 dollar, these would run at the level of over $5 billions a year in education, over a billion for health and hospitals, nearly a billion for the preservation of natural resources, over a half a billion for sanitation and water supply, and another half billion for police, fire protection, and postal services. But these figures leave out another urgent social need—to bring American housing, with nearly two million sub-standard units, up to a reasonable level.

According to the estimates made in the Fund's Survey, a full housing program would entail a total capital outlay of between $80 and $90 billions. This figure does not include any estimate for urban redevelopment and new urban centers; nor does the Survey distinguish between public and private expenditure. But the cost of parts of the program, such as the acquisition of sites in slums and blighted areas and some low-cost housing, would certainly fall on the public authorities. The Survey makes no estimate of the public share but it would perhaps be not unreasonable to add between a quarter and a half billion extra dollars to the annual "general welfare" budget to cover publicly-financed housing and urban needs. The figure implies a spread of the program over two decades and allots to public funds one-eighth of the extra cost.

The Survey's figures thus suggest that America will enter the sixties with a gap between social need and actual public expenditure of the annual order of $9 billions—or even $11 billions if one includes social insurance. But this estimate is, in fact, too low. It is stated in 1950 dollars while the purchasing power of the dollar has shrunk 14% since 1950. The Survey's estimates of the growth of population have, like all other population estimates, proved too conservative. And the figures assumed no downward trend in public spending. Since 1953, however, federal expenditure on the general welfare—as a percentage of gross national product—has fallen from 10 to 6 per cent and this decline could offset the rise in tax yields from an expanding national income. Yet $9 billions is in all conscience high enough, much higher than any sum that is likely to be financed in present conditions.

The problem of meeting this social outlay must differ radically according to the trend—towards continued hostility or potential appeasement—in the world at large. The weight of personal income tax which seems in 1957 the burden the American voter resents most strongly is largely determined by defence and its related expenditures. If military and international outlays could return to the $17 billions spent in 1950, an extra $9 or $10 billions for the general welfare budget would still leave room for a vast abatement in taxation.

But there is no such prospect in sight. Must the conclusion therefore be that, with income and property taxes standing at what the voter feels to be the outside limit, and more rapid inflation threatened by any budgetary deficit, the fate of the American community in the next decades is, with its jet-propelled birthrate, to combine expansion in some types of consumption and well-being with a marked deterioration in others—better refrigerators in badly serviced houses, two car garages and two shift schools, good clothes and poor sanitation, enough alcohol but not enough water— the line being decided by the financial origin of the goods and services, the "tax dollar" resented and resisted, the private and personal dollar accepted and prized?

The answer cannot be given in economic terms. Unquestionably a community which spends more on cosmetics than on sanitation, eight or nine times as much on liquor as on water supplies, at least 25% more on automobiles, gasoline and auto-servicing than upon education, and which has almost doubled its cigarette smoking (per capita) in the last twenty years has some small margin of postponable personal consumption with which, even under cold war budgeting, it can ensure that the children of tomorrow are not, in a technological society demanding even higher standards of competence, worse schooled and taught than their grandparents. And, in spite of the growing place occupied by the sales tax in the structure of state taxation, the limit of this mode of transfer from the private to the public sector has probably not been reached.

The question whether some cuts in consumption could in fact secure more money for community needs is not, however, an economic problem. It depends upon the political decision of the voters.

Nor, if against all expectation, the cold war ceased and defence expenditure were more than halved, would the availability of social capital be an *economic* question. In terms of the maintenance of employment, the economic argument is strong in favour of maintaining a high level of public expenditure. Private spending by way of tax reduction could not expand on a scale sufficient to absorb an annual fall in public expenditure of $20 billions. A domestic program ready prepared for schools, hospitals, transportation and urban redevelopment is therefore the logical accompaniment of all serious attempts at disarmament.

But the program itself involves political, not economic decisions. If tomorrow's citizens believed education to be as essential to national survival as are today's weapons of defence, there would be no fear of a shortfall either in social capital or in high levels of employment. But democracy, in America or elsewhere, has not yet reached such a decision.

[56]   *Truth vs. Myths**

by WILLIAM HENRY CHAMBERLIN

Hard it is for a fact to run down a myth, especially when that myth is entwined in a cliché.

The favorite current myth of U.S. "liberals" is that Federal and state governments in this country are shamefully poor, while American citizens are shamefully rich, that public spending is outrageously stinted while private spending soars on luxurious consumer goods. And this myth is just one of several weightless propositions that the American Left has long been firing at the nation. . . .

The leading myth of the moment is that Federal and state governments in America are somehow getting short-changed while individuals prosper.

The First National City Bank of New York, in its monthly Letter, subjects this picture to the test of facts and figures.

The results reveal what a good many Americans would have suspected without necessarily having all the relevant data at their finger tips. The share of public spending in the national income has been steadily and rapidly increasing, not only absolutely, but relatively. This share, representing the amount of Federal, state and local taxation, grew from 10.8% in the mid-1920's to 20.8% in 1940 and to 31% in the late Fifties.

A specific comparison with 1927 shows that Federal cash income is up more than 20 times, while personal disposable income (after taxes) has grown about four times and state and local revenue more than five times. Federal cash expenditures were $9.6 billion in 1940, $94.8 billion in the late Fifties; state and local expenditures in this period went up from $10.3 billion to $48.8 billion, and gross national product from $95.6 billion to $463.8 billion.

A favorite contention of those who would vastly increase public spending is that education is starved; some very loose, misleading and downright false comparisons have been drawn with Soviet education. Yet expenditures on education rose from $2.8 billion in 1940 to almost $17 billion in the late Fifties. Total public and private expenditures on education in the United States in 1959 was $22 billion, a figure unmatched, absolutely or on a per capita basis, anywhere in the world. . . .

The National City Bank Letter points to a vicious circle which develops

* From *The Wall Street Journal,* July 1, 1960, p. 4. Reprinted by permission.

when impoverishment through excessive taxation leads to a demand for more Government subsidies, which leads to more taxation which leads. . . . And it draws this sound conclusion from its array of facts and figures:

"There are beyond doubt some government programs suffering from lack of sufficient funds. If this is so, it is hardly because the people are too rich, or inadequately taxed, but because government is trying to do more things than it can handle with real competence. The real point at issue is how much farther—if at all—we can safely go toward discouraging individual initiative, self-reliance and industrious habits. The barrage of complaints over inadequate economic growth would seem to suggest that we need to concern ourselves more, rather than less, with the human aspirations that make the economy go."

It is good to have in convenient form the facts of vastly expanded taxation and steadily increasing proportions of Federal and state expenditure to refute the myth of America as a country where the individual citizen rolls in wealth while public authorities are denied essential funds.

[57]   *Parkinson's Second Law**

by C. NORTHCOTE PARKINSON

An extremely wealthy man underwent an extremely serious operation at the hands of an extremely distinguished surgeon. Ten days afterwards the surgeon asked how his patient was progressing. "Doing fine," said the nurse. "He has already been trying to date Nurse Audrey, a sure sign of convalescence."

"Nurse Audrey?" asked the surgeon quickly. "Is that the blond girl from Illinois?"

"No," the nurse assured him, "Nurse Audrey is the redhead from Missouri."

*From *The Law and the Profits* by C. Northcote Parkinson, pp. 2-8, 14-16, 242-246, *passim*. Boston, Houghton Mifflin Company, and London, John Murray (Publishers) Ltd. © Copyright 1960 by C. Northcote Parkinson. Reprinted by permission.

"In that case," said the surgeon, "the patient needs something to steady his pulse. I shall tell him what the operation cost."

The patient sobered down under this treatment and did some rapid calculations on the back of his temperature chart.

"Your fee of $4000," he finally concluded, "represents the proportion I retain from the last $44,500 of my income. To pay you without being worse off would mean earning another $44,500 more than last year; no easy task."

"Well," replied the surgeon, "you know how it is. It is only by charging you that much that I can afford to charge others little or nothing."

"No doubt," said the patient. "But the fee still absorbs $44,500 of my theoretical income—no inconsiderable sum. Might I ask what proportion of the $4000 you will manage to retain?"

It was the surgeon's turn to scribble calculations, as a result of which he concluded that his actual gain, after tax had been paid, would amount to $800.

"Allow me to observe," said the patient, "that I must therefore earn $44,500 in order to give you $800 of spendable income; the entire balance going to government. Does that strike you as a transaction profitable to either of us?"

"Well, frankly, no," admitted the surgeon. "Put like that, the whole thing is absurd. But what else can we do?"

"First, we can make certain that no one is listening. No one at the keyhole? No federal agent under the bed? No tape recorder in the—? Are you quite sure that we can keep this strictly to ourselves?"

"Quite sure," the surgeon replied after quickly opening the door and glancing up and down the corridor. "What do you suggest?"

"Come closer so that I can whisper. *Why don't I give you a case of Scotch and so call it quits?*"

"Not enough," hissed the surgeon, "but if you made it *two* cases . . . ?"

"Yes?" whispered the patient.

"And lent me your cabin cruiser for three weeks in September . . ."

"Yes?"

"We might call it a deal!"

"That's fine. And do you know what gave me the idea? I studied Parkinson's Law and realized that excessive taxation has made nonsense of everything!"

"Rubbish, my dear fellow. Parkinson's Law has nothing to do with taxation. It has to do with overstaffing—of which, by the way, this hospital provides some interesting examples. In parasitology, for—"

"Like all medical men, you are out of date. You are referring to Parkinson's *First* Law. I am referring to his *Second* Law."

"I must admit that I never heard of it. It concerns taxation, you say?"

"It concerns taxation. It also concerns you. Now, listen . . . listen carefully. *Expenditure rises to meet income!*"

Expenditure rises to meet income. Parkinson's Second Law, like the first, is a matter of everyday experience, manifest as soon as it is stated, as obvious as it is simple. When the individual has a raise in salary, he and his wife are prone to decide how the additional income is to be spent; so much on an insurance policy, so much to the savings bank, so much in a trust fund for the children. They might just as well save themselves the trouble, for no surplus ever comes into view. The extra salary is silently absorbed, leaving the family barely in credit and often, in fact, with a deficit which has actually increased. Individual expenditure not only rises to meet income but tends to surpass it, and probably always will.

It is less widely recognized that what is true of individuals is also true of governments. Whatever the revenue may be, there will always be the pressing need to spend it. But between governments and individuals there is this vital difference, that the government rarely pauses even to consider what its income is. Were any of us to adopt the methods of public finance in our private affairs, we should ignore the total of our income and consider only what we should like to spend. We might decide on a second car, an extension of the home, a motor launch as well as a yacht, a country place and a long holiday in Bermuda. All these, we should tell each other, are essential. It would remain only to adjust our income to cover these bare necessities; and if we economize at all, it will be in matters of taxation. A government by contrast, which applied the methods of individual finance to public expenditure would begin by attempting to estimate what its actual revenue should be. Given so much to spend, how much should be allocated to what? A federal government which decided upon this novel approach to the subject would be responsible for a revolution in public finance. It is the chief object of this book to suggest that such a revolution, of which we have seen some hint in California, is now generally overdue.

Governmental as opposed to individual income is historically linked with the incidence of war. In all systems of revenue there has always been provision for the temporary expenses of conflict. During a time of emergency, with our interests, our beliefs, our pride or even our existence at stake, we agree to pay almost anything as the price of victory. The war ends and with it the temporary expenses which everyone has seen to be more or less inevitable. In theory the revenue should fall to something like its previous level. In practice it seldom does. While the governmental income remains almost at its wartime level, peacetime expenditure rises to meet it. In times past the action of this law was slightly restrained, to be sure, by two considerations which no longer apply. In the first place, it was usually felt that taxes had to be reduced somewhat in time of peace in order to allow of their being raised again in time of war. During a century, however, when each successive war is judged to be the last, this theory finds no further support. In the second place, there are types of extravagance which yield only a diminishing return. To the provision of banquets and the enjoyment of dancing girls there is (eventually) a physical limit. The same is not true, unfortunately, of departmental and technical luxuriance. Economic and cultural advisers can multiply beyond the point at which concubines might be thought a bore; beyond the point even at which they might be thought unbearable. Financially as well as aesthetically, the situation has become infinitely worse.

In countries like Britain and the United States the initiative in public finance comes from subdepartments of government which decide each year on their needs for the year that is to come. After allowing for present costs and future developments the experienced civil servant adds 10 per cent to the total, assuming (not always correctly) that his bid will be challenged at some stage by the financial branch. Assuming, however, that the expected wrangle takes place, the added 10 per cent is deleted at departmental level when the combined estimate comes to be drawn up. To this estimate the head of the department adds 10 per cent again, assuming (not always correctly) that his bid will be challenged by the Treasury. After the expected dispute, the revised estimate is laid before the responsible Minister, in England the Chancellor of the Exchequer, who consolidates all the departmental demands in a grand total and decides how the revenue can be made to equal the expenditure. With the agreement of his colleagues, he presents the nation with the bill. Here is the sum total of what the government needs, and these are the taxes which the people will have to pay. . . .

To summarize the position, the public revenue is regarded as limitless and expenditure rises eternally to meet it, and the various devices which are supposed to check expenditure fail to do so, being wrongly conceived and imperfectly motivated. The problem is a serious one and would seem to merit our attention. What is to be done? The modern instinct is to frame new regulations and laws, of which there are already more than enough. The better plan, less fashionable today, is to remotivate the people actually concerned, penalizing the extravagance we now reward and rewarding the economy we now penalize. As a first step toward redirecting the flood, we need to reverse the whole process of government finance. Ministers should not begin by ascertaining what the departments need. They should begin by asking what the country can afford to spend. We do not base our personal budget on what our past extravagances have taught us to like but on the income we can fairly expect to receive. We do not, in short, plan to spend what we have not got. The same principle should apply to public as it does to individual finance. The first question to decide is the ratio between the revenue and the gross national product. What proportion of the national income should the government demand? What proportion of the individual's income can the government safely take? And what happens when that proportion is exceeded? Economists (with one notable exception) have fought shy of this problem, allowing it to be assumed that, where government expenditure is concerned, the sky is the limit. It is one aim of this book to suggest that there are other and lower limits; a limit beyond which taxation is undesirable, a limit beyond which it is dangerous and a limit (finally) beyond which it is fatal. And these limits are clearly indicated by both economic theory and historical fact. . . .

CONCLUSION

The first task of a government should be to decide upon the proportion which they can safely take of the national income. In time of emergency, with the national existence at stake, the proportion can be high. At other times it should be low, allowing scope for increase when a crisis should arise. What, in normal circumstances, should that proportion be?

History tells us that governments of the more remote past have tended to exact about 10 per cent of the people's income. We learn, further, that tax demands above that level have often driven people to emigrate, at least in circumstances where migration was possible. Where flight has been for some reason impracticable, taxes of 20 per cent or more have been collected without much difficulty. As against that, taxes rising from 33 to 50 per cent have been the occasion for revolt or the cause of ruin. Taxes fixed at these high levels have characterized regimes of dwindling importance, their decay in strength being accompanied by decline of their literature and arts. During the present century, levels of taxation have risen toward the point at which previous disaster has been known to occur. Populations which have become largely literate are exposed to modern methods of tax collection which are based upon their literacy and upon their inability to escape. Democracy has given political power to those who, taxed themselves at the lower rate, will gladly support the penal taxation of the wealthy. The result has been the disproportionate or progressive system of direct taxation by which fortunes are largely confiscated. Taxation of this kind can be pushed to any extreme and there is at present no accepted level at which its upper limit can be fixed. It is currently assumed, rather, that the amount of revenue to be raised will be related in some way to the estimated total of public expenditure.

The drawback in thus attempting to adjust revenue to expenditure is that all expenditure rises to meet income. Parkinson's Second Law, a matter of common knowledge so far as the individual's finances are concerned, is also applicable to the government. But whereas the individual's expenses rise to meet and perhaps exceed an income level which is at least known, government expenditure rises in the same way toward a maximum that has never been defined; toward a ceiling that is not there. It rises, therefore, unchecked, toward levels which past experience has shown to be disastrous. In several modern countries the symptoms of approaching catastrophe are already obvious; and in none more so than in Britain. But this is not a matter in which Americans can afford to feel complacent. They are moving in the same direction even if they have not gone as far. They too have failed to fix a limit beyond which taxation must not go.

Where should the peacetime limit be drawn? It should be fixed at 20 per cent of the national income, well short of the point (25 per cent) at which the tax will cause inflation and further from the point (30 per cent) at which a country's international influence must begin to decline. From such a peacetime level the taxes can be safely raised in time of war, provided only that they are reduced again when the conflict ends. The perpetual danger, however, is that the wartime tax level will be afterwards maintained—peacetime expenditure having risen to meet it—with long-term disaster as the inevitable sequel.

To any such proposal as this, limiting national expenditure to the amount which the country can afford, there will be opposition from those who fear a reduction in the social services which they would rather see developed. How are low taxes compatible with the Welfare State? Will not cheaper government be worse? The answer is that cheaper government is better. The effect of providing government with unlimited funds is merely to clog the wheels of administration with useless officials and superfluous paper. All that we buy with higher taxes is additional administrative delay.

There are directions in which greater public expense would be fully justified—as, for instance, in the rebuilding of our obsolete cities—but this is no argument for heavier taxation. Funds for this and for every other enlightened purpose could be made available through the elimination of waste. Like taxation, waste has its origin in war. It continues after peace is made, and especially in the channels of expenditure which war has opened up. It continues as a torrent of needless expense, as a toil erosion of the deadliest kind. Waste is the enemy. It is the spectacle of public waste that seems to justify, if it does not cause, the widespread avoidance (or even evasion) of tax. It is the spectacle of public extravagance which seems to justify, if it does not cause, the nation-wide fashion in individual indebtedness. Toward serving the nobler purposes of the state, while at the same time easing the burden of taxes, an essential step is to eliminate waste; and the waste not merely of material but of talent and of time. But nothing of this sort is possible unless the whole process of public finance is reversed. There can be no economy while the public revenue is made roughly equal to the sum of the departmental demands. Economy must begin with fixing the revenue as a proportion of the national income and informing each department of the total expenditure it must not exceed. With every incentive to internal economy and with automatic dismissal following every deficit, we should soon find that much can be done with little and more, very often, can be done with less. Put an absolute limit to the revenue and then let expenditure rise to meet it. These are the profits of experience and from these profits we should derive our law.

International Relations

[CHAPTER TWENTY-EIGHT]

The World Community of Nation-States

*W*HAT *makes a group of people into a nation? How are nationalism and patriotism fostered? In the first selection Schuman traces the origins of the modern nation-state, at the same time describing vividly the emotion-laden cult of patriotism which gives nations so much of their individuality, vitality, and power.*

The second selection, by Sydney Bailey, deals with some of the activities of the United Nations. It might have been placed in the chapter on "The Search for Peace," since the primary purpose of the United Nations is to avoid war. The reason we include it here is that it throws light on the present status of the community of nations, and on the changes which are taking place in this community as new nations continue to be formed.

[58] The Making of Nations*

by FREDERICK L. SCHUMAN

NATIONAL patriotism is the firm conviction that the best country in the world is the one you happened to be born in.—G. B. Shaw

Universal conscript miltiary service, with its twin brother universal suffrage, has mastered all Continental Europe—with what promises of massacre and bankruptcy for the 20th Century!—Hippolyte Adolphe Taine, Les Origines de la France contemporaine, *1891.*

The major political trait of the peoples of the Western State System is their devotion to the "nations" into which they have got themselves divided. The Western peoples and their Oriental and African imitators are keenly aware of themselves as "nationals" of particular nation-states, already in existence or striving to be born. Millions are influenced more in their emotions and behavior by a sense of national solidarity and fellow feeling with their fellow nationals than by their racial, religious, economic, esthetic, or recreational interests. This becomes most apparent in wartime, when governments demand and usually receive unswerving and undivided allegiance. But war merely brings to the surface and makes plain through pathological exaggeration what already exists in peace: an almost universal disposition to place the nation before all other human groupings.

Education for Citizenship. The cult and creed of patriotism are instilled into people in every nation by an elaborate process of inculcation. Nationalism is close to the heart of the cultural heritage handed down from generation to generation in every modern society. Upon the eager minds of little children, as upon a blank slate, are written at an early age the large characters of "mother," "home," "heaven," "flag," "fatherland," and "patriotism." The first impressions of the Great Society outside the family, the neighborhood, and the kindergarten are associated with national emblems, heroes, and myths. Every child in the Western world, before he has learned how to read and write his national language, has learned how to respond to the gaily colored banner which is the flag of his fatherland, to the stirring rhythm of the song which is his national anthem, to the names and legends of the great nation-builders who are revered as men like gods. Awe, reverence, and enthusiasm toward the nation-state and its symbols are inculcated from infancy.

*By permission from *International Politics* by Frederick L. Schuman, pp. 336-341, 370-371 *passim*. Copyright, 1958. McGraw-Hill Book Company, Inc.

Next comes the primer, with its quaint little tales of national glory and achievement, and then the elements of national history and geography. In later childhood there is nationalistic history with a vengeance, patriotic exercises, Flag Day celebrations, festivals and fun for Independence Day, or Constitution Day, or Bastille Day, or Guy Fawkes Day. Puberty brings membership in the Boy Scouts or the Girl Scouts, outings and parties and training in citizenship. In adolescence the young citizen becomes acquainted with the alien tongues and customs of enemies and strangers. He studies the national literature, the national history, the national *Kultur*. He becomes politically conscious and emotionally inspired by a fuller appreciation of his identity with his fatherland. *La Patrie* becomes father, mother, mistress, or lover in the heart of the youthful patriot; he (or she) is taught to swear undying allegiance to that which is more sacred even than truth, honor, or life itself. And at length, in early adulthood, comes, in most lands, military service for the young man, romantic attachments to soldier-lovers for the young woman, the right to vote and pay taxes, and a deep sense of loyalty and devotion to that half-real, half-mystical entity which is the nation-state.

The techniques of civic education through which this result is attained have been analyzed in many States by scores of assiduous scholars. The initiation rites of the tribe or clan through which the rising generation is made a participant in the social group are repeated with elaborate variation in the educational processes of every modern nation. Youth is conditioned to allegiance—no longer to the tribe, the clan, the class, the caste, the province, or the city, but to the nation, which demands an allegiance above all other allegiances and a loyalty requiring, if need be, the supreme sacrifice on the altar of patriotism. What youth has been taught, age seldom forgets—and all modern States are nations of patriots whose rulers may ordinarily rely upon the unswerving devotion of the great masses of the citizens to the mighty traditions of the national past. Each State thus develops and enriches its own personality by perpetually recreating itself in its own image. Each State perpetually models its figures of earth and gets them more and more to its liking. Each State becomes symbolized as an anthropomorphic deity to which are attributed the national virtues and vices, the national achievements and frustrations. Each patriot, like a new Narcissus, is enthralled by the beauty of his own image, which he sees reflected in the national mirror; and he feels himself to be one with the nation.

The Genesis of Modern Patriotism. An understanding of the process of manufacturing patriots, however, does not in itself serve to explain why national patriotism has come to occupy such an all-pervading place in Western culture. Hans Kohn, ablest contemporary student of modern nationalism, points out that the new creed "as we understand it, is not older than the second half of the 18th Century." Early tribalism in Israel and Athens gave way to a universalism which has persisted almost (but not quite) to our own times. The great "national" leaders and writers of the Enlightenment, degraded to the stature of tribal patriots by later generations, were nothing of the kind. Frederick the Great made a Frenchman President of the Prussian Royal Academy and declared himself content to have lived in the age of Voltaire. Johann Gottfried Herder denounced Prussia, praised Czechs and Russians, and proclaimed: "The human race is one whole; we work and suffer, sow and harvest, each for all." Hans Kohn concludes:

Nationalism, taking the place of religion, is as diversified in its manifestations and aspirations, in its form and even its substance as religion itself. . . . Yet in all its diversities it fulfills one great task—giving meaning to man's life and justifying his noble and ignoble passions before himself and history, lifting him above the loneliness and futilities of his days, and endowing the order and power of government, without which no society can exist, with the majesty of true authority. . . . [But] nationalism is only a passing form of integration, beneficial and vitalizing, yet by its own exaggeration and dynamism easily destructive of human liberty. . . . From Jerusalem and Athens shine also the eternal guiding stars which lift the age of nationalism above itself, pointing forward on the road to deeper liberty and to higher forms of integration.

It seems probable that conflicts among culturally divergent populations played a significant role in producing within each community that sense of its own identity, that feeling of solidarity and common interest, that conception of the personality or ego of the group which is of the essence of national patriotism. Contacts of war would seem to be most effective in producing the type of group cohesion which lies behind nationalism. No emotion unifies a group so readily as hatred for a common enemy. International relations in the formative period of nationalism were for the most part those of war. Anglo-Saxon England attained unity for the first time when Alfred the Great rallied his subjects to resist the Danish invasion. Norman England was already an embryonic national State, with a Government of considerable authority and a population increasingly impressed with its "Englishness" by virtue of chronic conflicts with Scots, Irish, and French. In France, provincialism gave way to a common consciousness of "Frenchness" in the course of the Hundred Years' War, when its inhabitants at last organized themselves for effective resistance against English invaders and found a fitting symbol of the cause in the person of Jeanne d'Arc. In Spain, constant warfare against the Moors gave birth to Spanish nationalism and produced that blending of patriotic sentiment and crusading Catholicism which became its distinctive characteristic. In every case nationalism was born of war against alien groups.

All the later nationalisms between the 15th Century and the 20th were similarly born of conflicts between societies already differing from one another in language, religion, and institutions and made more aware of these differences by increased contacts with aliens. Dutch nationalism attained full flower in the long war against Spanish rule of the Netherlands. Swiss nationalism emerged out of conflicts with Austria. Sweden became a nation through struggles with Russians and Poles and Germans. American nationalism was generated by the War of the Revolution. In the 19th Century, Italian nationalism won unity for Italy as a result of common resistance to foreign invasion and common conflicts with Austria. The German nation became a unified State through battles with Danes, Austrians, and Frenchmen, after the "War of Liberation" earlier in the century converted Prussians, Bavarians, Swabians, and Wurtembergers into "Germans." The peculiarly intense nationalism of the Balkan peoples was the product of armed revolt against the Turks and of the presence within the Peninsula of many divergent groups, each of which became aware of itself through contact and conflict with neighbors. Irish, Turkish, Japanese, Indian, and Chinese nationalisms were likewise products of conflict against alien rulers, alien invaders, or alien foes across the frontier.

This suggests that the process whereby a community acquires a sense of its own identity and national personality bears a certain resemblance to the process whereby an individual growing up in society acquires a self, or ego, of his own. Social psychologists are generally agreed that an individual growing up to biological maturity in complete isolation from his fellows would not have a human "personality." The individual becomes humanized by social interaction with his fellows. His innate impulses are inhibited, directed, and conditioned through social pressure—until his personality becomes, in the language of the psychoanalyst, a fusion of instinctive biological drives (the "Id"), the conscious thinking and acting self (the "Ego"), and the unconscious controls and repressions of Id and Ego drives (the "Super-Ego"). The individual becomes aware of himself and develops distinctive personality traits by "taking the role of the other," by socialized experience with other persons.

Similarly, a nation acquires its ego by contacts with other nations. It becomes acutely aware of its own identity to the degree to which such contacts are intimate, rich, and varied. Contacts of war would seem to promote national solidarity more effectively than contacts of peace, for war requires cooperation in the interest of self-preservation. It dramatizes the flags, songs, slogans, traditions, and leaders which give unity to the group and distinguish it from other groups. National patriotism is the most complete expression of ethnocentrism. Its devotees are imbued with an intense consciousness of the collective personality of the national community, and this collective personality emerges out of social interaction between divergent groups not dissimilar to those between single human beings which produce and enrich the individual personality. The history of this process remains to be written by social psychologists with historical training or by historians who are also social psychologists.

The Cult of the Tribal Gods. Nationalists everywhere exalt the nation-state as the highest form of social organization. The national community must achieve political independence. It must incorporate within its frontiers all peoples speaking the language and having the culture of the national society. It must compel conformity to the dominant language and culture on the part of alien groups within its frontiers. It must attain unity, uniformity, solidarity. It must assert its rights vigorously and protect its interests energetically in contacts with other national groups. It is the all in all, the *ne plus ultra*, the final and perfect embodiment of social living for all loyal patriots. It is beyond good and evil, right or wrong; for its interests are supreme and paramount, and all means toward its greater glory and power are justified by the end. "A true nationalist places his country above everything; he therefore conceives, treats, and resolves all pending questions in their relation to the national interest." His object is "the exclusive pursuit of national policies, the absolute maintenance of national integrity, and a steady increase of national power —for a nation declines when it loses military might." To the patriot the nation-state is a great goddess to be worshipped, to be loved, to be served —and all sacrifices in her service are noble and heroic. She calls out to her worshippers:

Lord! Let the beautiful ships which are on their way to our Africa arrive safely at their port. Grant that our soldiers on the sunny roads on the other side of the sea have fortune as their guiding star and glory as their goal. Grant that they may crown with fresh laurels the old, glorious flags of Vittorio Veneto, which now wave under the tropic sky. Let the culture of the new Rome of Mussolini fuse with that of Caesar's Rome to a poem of greatness. Let the Italian Empire dreamed of by our great men and our martyrs become reality in the near future. Lord! Let our lives, if Mother Italy demand it, become a joyful sacrifice on the altar of Thy holy and just Will. [Prayer for the Ballila Boys, *L'Azione coloniale*, Rome, 1935.]

[Again,] as a spokesman of one of the newest (and oldest) national-isms of our time, Ilya Ehrenburg to the Red Army, 1943:

Together with you marches the frail little girl, Zoya, and the stern marines of Sevastopol. Together with you march your ancestors who welded together this land of Russia—the knights of Prince Igor, the legions of Dmitri. Together with you march the soldiers of 1812 who routed the invincible Napoleon. To-gether with you march Budenny's troops, Chapayev's volunteers, barefooted, hungry and all conquering. Together with you march your children, your mother, your wife. They bless you! . . . Soldier, together with you marches Russia! She is beside you. Listen to her winged step. In the moment of battle, she will cheer you with a glad word. If you waver, she will uphold you. If you conquer, she will embrace you. . . .

The New Nationalisms. Imitation, someone observed once upon a time, is the sincerest form of flattery. The national patriots of the North Atlantic communities painfully discovered in the middle years of the 20th Century that their prolonged and highly successful efforts to im-pose their power upon the "lesser breeds" were no longer successful in the face of the revolt of the victims. These, in turn, found no better way to resist their erstwhile masters than the way of copying Western nationalism and adapting it to their own purposes. In this wise, the Western cult of the nation-state has become in our time the universal faith of all man-kind, with all of its glories, frustrations, and aberrations, plus some unique features of achievement and failure in the making of nations attributable to the legacy of colonialism and to the special circum-stances of the human condition among those long disinherited and still impoverished.

Take a world map or, better, a globe, and trace a long line eastward and southeastward from the coast of Africa south of Gibraltar to the equatorial islands northwest of Australia. Along this line, if we exclude China, dwell almost 800,000,000 people, or nearly one-third of the human race—thinly scattered in the deserts and coastal plains of North Africa and the Levant, and densely crowded in the lush plains of southern and southeastern Asia and in what Westerners once called the "Spice Is-lands." Among these peoples African and Asian nationalisms, faithfully imitating earlier European prototypes, have come to full flower in our era. The peoples of the region thus delineated have nothing in common, linguistically, culturally, and religiously—and nothing in common politi-cally save a common rebellion against Western rule. The followers of the faith of Islam, to be sure, are to be found along the line all the way from Morocco to Indonesia. But Islam was never a unity nor is it now. Its disciples are interspersed along our perimeter of demarcation with millions of Christians and Jews and with many millions of Hindus and Buddhists.

Yet all the inhabitants of this vast expanse, intercepted by 20° north latitude, have more in common than they know. They know, indeed, very little beyond their local problems, fears, and hopes, for almost all of them are illiterate, ignorant, poor, and miserable as were all their ancestors for ages past. Many among them are peasants, still exploited by landlords in the ancient "feudal" pattern of human relations. In our time all are animated, dimly or brightly, with new dreams of a better life begotten by Western example. Whether their dreams are capable of fulfillment is a problem best deferred. Here it is in order to note that all these peoples have been moved by misery and resentment to adopt Western nationalism as a weapon against the West.[1]

[59]   *The Changing Character of the United Nations**

by SYDNEY BAILEY

Last December, during the strike of newspaper deliverers in New York City, I had a curious dream. By some means which I did not fully understand (but which did not, at the time, strike me as odd) the dispute between the newspaper publishers and the deliverers had been submitted to the General Assembly of the United Nations. There had been the usual spate of partisan speeches, and the usual draft resolutions. One of the resolutions called peremptorily on the strikers to return to work without delay. Another, equally peremptorily, insisted that the publishers concede what the strikers had been demanding. A third would have set up a fact-finding commission. A fourth requested Secretary Gen-

[1] Professor Schuman wrote this about 1957, just before the emergence of many new nations among the Negro peoples south of the Sahara Desert.

*From *The Progressive*, June, 1959, pp. 37-39. Reprinted by permission.

eral Dag Hammarskjold to use his good offices to promote an agreement. Finally, a compromise resolution had been put forward by countries whose names all began with the letter I (India, Ireland, Iceland, Iran, Iraq, Israel, and Indonesia); this resolution called upon the parties to negotiate a settlement in accordance with the Constitution of the United States and to report, jointly or separately, to the next session of the General Assembly. I am glad to report that this compromise was accepted by 53 votes to 9, with 19 abstentions, and I was therefore able to wake up feeling that justice had been done.

My dreams are invariably absurd, and any similarity between them and real life is purely coincidental. But at least this particular dream reminded me forcibly of two troublesome features of contemporary diplomacy.

In the first place, a large part of international diplomacy is now conducted publicly. I have in mind not only the debates in organs of the United Nations and other inter-governmental bodies. I am thinking of the notes, the letters, the speeches, the press conferences, the trial balloons, the calculated indiscretions, the "leaks," the journalistic speculations, the official denials or confirmations, the legislative hearings in Washington, the parliamentary questions at Westminster, the election speeches in the Kremlin—indeed, the whole paraphernalia of public activity which nowadays precedes or accompanies negotiation of the Berlin or any other question. One cannot help wondering whether these public activities may not so reduce the area of maneuverability by the time serious negotiations begin that, in many cases, the possibility of an agreed settlement is virtually eliminated. It is not that it is impossible to discover a concrete solution in the mutual interests of the parties, but that the parties have committed their prestige to goals that are largely unrealizable.

A second practice of contemporary diplomacy, and one which would doubtless puzzle a diplomat of the Eighteenth or Nineteenth Centuries, is that of trying to settle an international issue by voting. I am not suggesting that voting in inter-governmental bodies should or could be dispensed with; my point is that a majority vote by sovereign nations does not, of itself, "solve" anything. A vote may facilitate a solution; it may also obstruct one.

In a cohesive and homogeneous society, it is generally accepted that a minority should have its say and a majority should have its way; but because minorities have a habit of becoming majorities, a prudent majority will moderate its goals and ambitions. That is an essential element of the party system in a constitutional democracy. Moreover, the two-party system usually impels both parties to seek the favor of the uncommitted voters in the center. The system fosters the search by both parties for a policy with a wide appeal, thus discouraging extremism.

But perhaps the most important reason why voting can be used successfully in democratic countries is that the instruments of physical coercion are in neutral hands. Hitler demonstrated how democracy can be destroyed when political parties have private armies.

The nation-states have not renounced the instruments of coercion. Indeed, they have added new weapons to their arsenals: a voice and a vote in an organ of the United Nations or some other international body. This may not be as immediately decisive as a physical weapon, but there is no denying that it has a compulsive character. No nation can afford to be consistently contemptuous of the opinions of mankind. I recall how, a couple of years ago, Krishna Menon of India pleaded in the Security Council for the rejection of a particular resolution on Kashmir. To adopt it, he said, would merely "reagitate this question. This merely sows the apple of discord once more . . . To record another resolution which reaffirms something that one party has rejected . . . is, in our submission, not calculated to promote the purposes of the United Nations." This sort of thing is constantly said at the United Nations—by France in connection with Algeria, by the Soviet Union in connection with Korea and Hungary, by South Africa in connection with apartheid. Yet the very fact that these pleas are made with such earnestness reveals how seriously U.N. resolutions are taken.

One difficulty with a U.N. vote is that there is no necessary correspondence between votes and power, using the word "power" in its widest sense, to encompass the military, economic, political, and moral aspects of power. There have been proposals to modify the system of voting at the United Nations by "weighting" the votes in accordance with certain tangible manifestations of power. I must confess that I have not encountered any proposal for weighted voting that would seem to have the slightest chance of general acceptance, though it may be noted that the Yalta formula for giving the Soviet Union three seats in the U.N. Assembly is, in effect, a form of weighted voting. With this exception, the principle of "one state, one vote" prevails.

Until 1956, the political complexion of the U.N. Assembly favored the West. There were 50 founder-members of the organization, and Poland was permitted to acquire founder-membership retroactively. During the first five years in the life of the organization, nine other states were ad-

mitted, bringing the total membership to 60. Of this total, there were
20 Latin American republics and 19 other countries which joined NATO,
SEATO, or the Bagdad Pact; with the addition of Nationalist China,
there was thus a group of 40 states which, on cold war issues, usually
supported the United States. The Soviet bloc originally had six members (including the Ukraine and Byelorussia), but this was diminished
to five after Yugoslavia broke with the Cominform in 1948. The floating voters numbered 14, of which several (Liberia, for example) usually
voted with the United States.

In December 1955, 16 new members were admitted to the U.N. in the
well known "package" arrangement, and seven further admissions took
place in 1956-58. (The union of Egypt and Syria to form the United
Arab Republic means that the Assembly now has 82 members.) The
effect of the increase in the number of members on the political complexion of the Assembly can be understood if one bears in mind that
the recent admissions comprised:

Communist countries	4
Countries of the Afro-Asian group	13
Members of NATO	2
Spain	1
European neutrals	3
Total	23

In an assembly of 82 nations, with a two-thirds majority required for
all important questions, a resolution can be adopted either because it
has the support of at least 55 countries or because there are sufficient abstentions or absences; for every vote short of 55, two abstentions or
absences are needed if the resolution is to get a two-thirds majority. Consider this situation in relation to some of the key votes during the 1958
regular session of the Assembly:

Sept. 23—U.S. proposal not to discuss Chinese representation—44 in
favor.

Nov. 4—17-power resolution on disarmament—49 in favor.

Nov. 14—13-power resolution on Korea—54 in favor.

Nov. 14—7-power resolution on the U.N. Emergency Force—51 in
favor.

Dec. 10—19-power resolution on increasing the size of the Economic
and Social Council—52 in favor.

Dec. 12—20-power resolution on the peaceful uses of outer space—53
in favor.

Dec. 12—37-power resolution on Hungary—54 in favor.

The United States resolution on Chinese representation was opposed by 28 countries (with nine abstainers) and thus was actually four votes short of a two-thirds majority, but it passed because it was technically a procedural rather than a substantive question ("The General Assembly . . . decides not to consider . . . any proposals to . . .").

Moreover, the membership situation is not static. New states are coming into existence every year and are being admitted to the United Nations, as dependent territories acquire sovereignty. Before the end of next year we may expect Cyprus, the Cameroons, Togoland, Nigeria, Somaliland, and possibly Western Samoa and some of the French overseas territories in Africa (such as Madagascar) to be accepted into U.N. membership. There seems no reason why the membership of the United Nations should not top the one hundred mark by 1970, if not sooner. This speculation takes no account of the possibility of some arrangements being worked out for U.N. membership for the presently divided countries of Germany, Korea, and Viet Nam. Outer Mongolia has also applied for membership. In fact, the only state which possesses the attributes of nationhood but which has not yet indicated any desire to join the United Nations is Switzerland.

The possibility that the United Nations will have one hundred or more members within the calculable future raises a number of physical problems at United Nations headquarters, but these are not insurmountable; it is not technically impossible to enlarge the physical plant. The political problems of a greatly increased membership are, however, considerable. Debates will tend to last longer because more states wish to participate. There will be more disagreement about the composition of subsidiary organs. There will be less deference to the great powers. There will almost certainly be a majority (and this may not be very far away) in favor of seating representatives of the Peiping government in the Assembly; the continued exclusion of Peiping is already causing substantial uneasiness in the Western camp.

But perhaps the greatest problem for Western countries will be to adjust to a situation in which half the votes in the Assembly will be cast by the new countries of Asia and Africa, most of which simply did not exist as sovereign states when the United Nations was founded. I suspect that on some major political questions it will become less and less easy as time goes by to rally a two-thirds vote in support of any clear position. The Assembly was unable to adopt resolutions on the Greek complaint about Cyprus or the Indonesian claim to West Irian in 1957, or on the Algerian question in 1958. What happens is that resolutions pass in committee by a simple majority and then fail in the plenary where a two-thirds vote is needed if they are to pass. This phenomenon is not new in itself; what is new is the cause.

Just as the Security Council has been unable to discharge the functions envisaged for it in the Charter because of the disunity of its permanent members, so the Assembly may find increasing difficulty in reaching firm conclusions on some of the major political questions. Moreover, the disparity between votes and power (again using the word in its widest sense) could become a source of irritation if votes are not cast responsibly. During the 1958 Assembly, a group of states, which between them contribute less than ten per cent of the budget of the United Nations, was able to get adopted in a committee of the Assembly a resolution incurring certain abnormal expenses. It may well have been in the interests of the organization that the expenses should be incurred, and certainly the amount was relatively trivial (about $16,000); my point is that a large number of non-responsible votes on major questions could lead to a substantial diminution of enthusiasm for the United Nations in the United States and other Western countries.

In my view, the mistakes have been to place too much emphasis on the United Nations Assembly as a debating forum, and to imagine that a problem is settled when a majority of states has voted for a resolution. To adopt a resolution may be an important event; it may lead some governments (especially those in the minority) to review their policies. But debates and votes do not "solve" anything.

If the United Nations is to be an instrument for achieving the lofty purposes of the Charter, there must be renewed emphasis on the opportunities which the U.N. provides for quiet diplomacy. A few months ago, a serious dispute arose between Cambodia and Thailand. A matter of this kind could have been submitted to an organ of the United Nations for public discussion. Instead, the parties agreed to ask Dag Hammarskjold to send a special representative to the area to work quietly with the governments. The operation was carried out without publicity and without the need for government to adopt public positions. It was brilliantly successful.

One reason why the administration of the U.N. Emergency Force in the Middle East has worked with so few hitches is that Dag Hammarskjold has had the opportunity of private consultation with a small and representative advisory committee established by the General Assembly. In more than two years of work, this committee has never had to vote.

The U.N. committee on the effects of atomic radiation, which includes scientists representing the United States, the Soviet Union, and India, has worked harmoniously and quietly for several years and has only once disposed of a difference of opinion by voting.

These three examples illustrate the fact that it is perfectly possible, within the general framework of the U.N., to devise techniques of negotiation which minimize unnecessary dissension. Basic differences of national interest remain, of course; the role of the U.N. in this regard is to enable governments to review their concept of the national interest in the light of what they take to be the national interests of others. This was an essential function of the U.N. in the Cyprus dispute, but it is significant that the final agreement was worked out by direct and private negotiations between the parties.

It is a paradox of politics that the solution of one problem so often carries conditions that lead to another problem. It has often been remarked that the creation of Israel helped to solve the Jewish refugee problem, but at the cost of bringing into being an Arab refugee problem. The liquidation of colonialism is causing a rapid increase in the number of sovereign states, but it may also be causing an increase in the number and complexity of international disputes. This development is taking place at a time when governments realize that the threat or use of force is unprecedentedly risky. A U.N. delegate whose judgment I value commented to me the other day that "the only alternative to co-extinction is a diplomacy of moderation."

The procedures of the United Nations can be adapted to the changing character of the membership of the organization and the changing nature of the questions submitted to it. This is possible without amending the Charter. It will happen as governments appraise more profoundly the potentialities and the limitations of the instrument they have created.

No single remedy is sufficient, and of course no change of practice will be adopted just because one U.N. member happens to favor it. Nevertheless, I suggest the following useful approaches:

1. A steady attempt, over a period of years, to reinvigorate the three Councils (Security, Economic and Social, and Trusteeship).

2. More restraint in public debate on contentious issues.

3. Less frequent resort to voting on matters on which the United Nations has no power to enforce its decisions.

4. Constant efforts to isolate the technical (e.g., legal, scientific) aspects of political issues for preliminary consideration by technical bodies.

5. Further development of the mediatory functions of the Secretary-General and his colleagues, particularly in matters where direct contact between the parties is difficult or impossible.

6. Willingness to experiment with a variety of forms of U.N. representation (non-combatant) in troubled areas.

[CHAPTER TWENTY-NINE]

International Economic Relations

A striking aspect of international economic relations since World War II has been the huge sums lent or given by the United States to aid friendly nations. Umbreit, Hunt, and Kinter argue that much of this aid would be unnecessary if we would remove tariffs and other restrictions on imports, and buy more goods abroad.

Jean Monnet, an outstanding European businessman and statesman, believes that the greatest economic problem of the United States in the next twenty years will be to make satisfactory adjustment to the international situation created by Soviet growth. As he sees it, this will involve patience, anticipating the needs of the underdeveloped countries, and cooperating with a new partner, the United States of Europe.

[60] Trade Not Aid*

by MYRON H. UMBREIT, ELGIN F. HUNT, and CHARLES V. KINTER

Even severe critics of American economic policy can hardly deny that the United States has been generous to the remainder of the world. The Marshall Plan and other foreign aid programs were a major contribution toward rehabilitating Europe from the ravages of the Second World War. They also helped check the spread of communism. Under the Marshall Plan, sixteen European nations, plus western Germany, Austria, and Trieste, received aid in the form of goods and services, purchased in the United States and elsewhere, with funds supplied by the United States Treasury. To administer the Marshall Plan the Economic Cooperation Administration was established in 1948. At the end of 1951 it was replaced by the Mutual Security Agency. This change reflected the fact that American aid was increasingly being directed toward strengthening the military establishments of friendly nations.

From V-J Day to the end of 1955 the United States gave or lent more than $53 billion to aid other nations, not only in Europe but also in other parts of the world. Most of this stupendous sum took the form of outright gifts; only about one-fifth of it represented loans repayable to our government. Though aid planned for the future is on a reduced scale, it is likely to be very substantial for some time to come. . . .

The question of granting financial aid to other nations has caused much controversy. It is often asserted that such aid is not a solution to the problem, for in essence it represents what might be termed a relief program. Many citizens both in this country and in others maintain that only in so far as such aid creates a basis for increased trade, once such grants are withdrawn, can these programs be considered economically successful. It is insisted, therefore, that what nations need is a "trade not aid" program, and that unless and until the United States is willing to increase its trade with other nations, and this means increasing its imports, the barriers to international trade cannot be removed.

Let us examine the "trade not aid" policy in the light of the economic and political conditions which prevail. We must, in the first instance, recognize the fact that it is easier to relax trade restrictions when the

*By permission from *Economics: An Introduction to Principles and Problems* by Umbreit, Hunt and Kinter, pp. 587-591 *passim.* Copyright, 1957. McGraw-Hill Book Co., Inc.

428

economies of the world are prosperous, that is, when they have achieved reasonably full employment or when employment is rising. In such a situation, if additional imports are allowed to enter a country, any workers who may be displaced will not have too much difficulty in finding other jobs. Today the United States and many other countries are so prosperous that adjustments should be possible.

How "Trade Not Aid" May Be Achieved. If the objective of "trade not aid" is to be achieved, world trade must be coordinated with internal trade relationships. In some countries such as England, exports and imports vitally affect internal trade, and hence internal trade policies must be geared to world trade. In the United States, imports and exports in total play such a small part in total trade that internal trade policies often more or less ignore them. In total, imports represent about 3 per cent of our total trade, and exports are about 7 per cent. Some industries of course are greatly dependent on world trade, but they are exceptions.

A number of nations, however, are so dependent on trade with the United States that a small decline in our imports may cause a depression in their industries. Because the United States represents more than a third of the purchasing power and the production of the world, any internal policy which may cause trade in our economy to fluctuate a few points tends to have serious repercussions in other countries.

How, then, can the United States, which possesses vastly more economic power than any other nation, aid in restoring world trade?

Several suggestions have been made for attaining this objective of "trade not aid." Most of these suggestions relate to the fundamental principles which were considered earlier. Let us observe how they apply.

1. The United States should open its markets more freely to the world, in the hope of greatly increasing imports. This would mean the removal, so far as possible, of tariffs and other trade barriers. A large increase in imports seems feasible for several reasons: (*a*) Our population is growing rapidly; hence more of everything is needed. (*b*) We are exhausting our supply of many minerals and other natural resources; hence we should conserve our own resources and draw upon the world supply. (*c*) There are many products which we do not and cannot produce. We should make full use of the world supply of these products, and stockpile some of the nonperishable minerals as a security measure in case of war.

2. In giving financial aid the United States should place emphasis on technical assistance, so that backward and underdeveloped countries could develop their resources and in turn make them available to the world. This would increase their purchasing power and their productivity and would therefore raise their standards of living. The United States

would benefit, for not only could it secure more and better raw materials, but it could also export more goods and services.

3. Ways and means must be found to foster and promote private foreign investment. Unless investors are free to develop new areas, trade will not expand as it otherwise might. Backward nations must be convinced that investment capital will not enter their countries if investors are in fear of expropriation, are prevented from transferring earnings, are required to become partners with the state, or are subjected to similar restrictive measures.

4. To the extent that synthetics are more costly than, or inferior to, the natural product, efforts should be made to return to the use of the latter. This would stimulate trade in rubber, silk, tin, and other products.

5. Because of the size of the internal trade of the United States, compared with its foreign trade, some adjustments in our internal trade should be accepted in order to stimulate imports. Special aid, for example, might be given to some industries so that they could shift from one kind of production to another in order to permit increased imports from certain countries. In fact, it is suggested that perhaps a dollar spent on rearranging our internal-trade pattern in order to foster world trade might be better spent than if devoted to our present program of direct aid to foreign countries. Actually, if changes were made gradually over a period of several years, our domestic industries might need little help in adjusting to them.

6. Since world trade has political as well as economic implications, the issue of containing communism must always be considered. One appeal that communism has had in Europe and Asia is that the communist nations always express their willingness to purchase goods from the free nations. Since so many free nations must export to live, they naturally are anxious to trade with Russia and its satellites. As long as the United States gives financial aid but restricts imports, it increases the capacity of other countries to produce but it does not help them as much as it might to expand their foreign markets. The communists take advantage of this situation and are able to gain at our expense. They may not actually buy much, but their expressed willingness to do so is a valuable propaganda weapon as long as we maintain important barriers.

Obstacles to "Trade Not Aid."   If we assume that a rational view of international trade leads to the conclusion that its expansion would be one of the best means for increasing standards of living in the world and for decreasing world tension, why cannot this objective be accomplished?

We have pointed to certain political reasons which prevent world trade from expanding as vigorously as it should. These include the rise of nationalism in underdeveloped countries; the Iron Curtain; differences in national objectives; the unwillingness of people in backward countries to build slowly the basic foundations needed for raising living standards; the fear of investors that their capital will not be safe in foreign countries; the fear of war; and the misconceptions which are held in many countries as to the nature and objectives of democracy as compared with those of communism.

Another basic obstacle to the expansion of international trade is that many people still do not understand its economic advantages. Though the basic gains from world trade are clear to the student of economics, there are great numbers of people who still believe that a nation benefits by keeping out foreign goods to protect home industries.

[61]   *U.S. Response to Soviet Growth**

by JEAN MONNET

To forecast now the United States of America's main problems in the next twenty years requires some adventurous guessing. Twenty years is an arbitrary period, and I have no pretensions as a crystal-gazer. All the same, given certain assumptions, I think we can outline the trend, whether or not it fits neatly into our chronological framework.

The assumptions, however, are essential; the failure of only one of them will invalidate any forecast: the first is that America will be growingly prosperous; the second is that it will retain its democratic way of life; the third is that there is no war between America and Russia.

The technical revolution of our century seems to be accelerating. The pressures of increasing change in political, economic and social relations which this is causing, call for increasingly intense adaptation of each nation to general world conditions. We are aware today mostly of the tensions created by the meeting of dissimilar traditions. But the last ten

*Reprinted from *Problems of United States Economic Development*, Vol. I, January 1958. Published by The Committee for Economic Development, 711 Fifth Ave., New York 22, N.Y.

years alone have shown how fast nations are growing interdependent. Only Russia and America are still free to make a wide range of choices of policy. Even they, however, are becoming increasingly unable to act alone in the world.

Twenty years ago, in 1937, the United States believed it could live in isolation from the world, cultivating its own vast garden. It was the biggest island in the world, believing in peace and prosperity so long as America kept free of foreign entanglements and of Europe's quarrels in particular. In fact, it could not avoid those entanglements. Americans were drawn into the Second World War because the United States themselves would have been threatened by an Allied defeat. They emerged from that war as the world's preponderant power, the only one that left the struggle immensely stronger and richer than it entered it. America has since been necessarily interested in all the tensions and conflicts of the world. It has intervened in Europe, helping our countries to get back on their feet, with Marshall Aid; in China; in Korea, when the Communists attacked; in Indochina; and now in the Middle East. No major event on the earth's surface—or in its atmosphere—can now leave America indifferent. The earth is becoming a unit.

For this very reason, I do not believe that American predominance can last. Sooner or later, the strongest nation must adapt itself to changing conditions around it. One of America's traits of greatness is, indeed, that it has never particularly aimed at such predominance. America's recent power has been due to the extraordinary, inherently temporary gap between her wealth and that of the rest of the world. At the end of the war, with 5% of the world's population, America has over 40% of its wealth, with power to act in consequence. As Europe recovered, as the mobilised Soviet states created new industries, and the ex-colonial areas of the world became conscious of themselves and of new ambitions, this disparity could not last. For America, as for smaller countries, adaptation to a changing world will, in the coming twenty years, be the greatest problem.

There will, I think, be three main forces demanding this adaptation: the growth of Russia and more generally, the Soviet world; the gradual unification of Europe; and the upsurge of the underdeveloped areas. The problems of adjustment raised by each will be quite distinct though in practice, of course, they will merge in a single policy.

The rapid, challenging evolution of the Communist third of the earth is clearly a source of change. The Sputniks mark Russia's coming of age as an industrial leader. The industrial machine which has made this feat possible will continue to grow rapidly, though not as rapidly as in the past. It is a power economy, not a consumer economy like these of our Western countries. It works for the State and not for the citizen voter. The Sputniks explain the amazing gap between the expansion of Russia's basic industries and her still low standards of living. The Russians have mobilised their resources to develop tomorrow's industries, not those of today, electronics not motorcars, nuclear power and advanced chemicals not refrigerators. Whatever their use or misuse of this ability to ignore today's Russian consumer, the Soviet's rate of investment, much higher than that of most Western countries, compels us to increase our own rates if we are not to be left behind, in quantity today, in quality tomorrow. The United States remains much the greatest industrial power on earth. But it has been developing more slowly during the fifties than either Russia which has a long way to catch up, or than Western Europe, which has been enjoying its first great boom since the early years of the century. It is idle to hope that America can grow as fast as new countries now scratching their resources for the first time. But I have the impression that in 1957 we see the so-called capitalist world once more in danger of resting on its laurels after its great recovery from the depression of the thirties. The free world cannot afford this. A greater investment effort, and the effort of political and social organisation it implies, are once more necessary.

Politically, in the next twenty years, I think the present, opposed conceptions of liberty and totalitarianism between ourselves and the Soviet States will tend to converge on a new view. Advanced industrial countries will face many common problems, whatever their starting-points, and may well discover mutual attractions they do not now suspect. The stirrings of public opinion in Eastern Europe and Russia itself have only just begun. Educated and materially satisfied men do not gladly accept authoritarian government: they will move nearer our notions of liberty. We can expect a certain liberalising of the Soviet regime. We, for our part, will be forced to organise our society more in order to ensure that all its scientific and engineering power is mobilised for new discovery. Yet, I think, we must also realise that accommodation with Russia and relaxation of tension will only be gradual. For many years still, the Russian's will be able to ignore the consumer, the voting citizen, to a far greater extent than any democratic regime. Totalitarian regimes being what they are, it will be hard to turn "competitive coexistence"— short of war—into real international understanding to live and let live. Having pursued power, Russia has now developed a vast state machine, uncontrolled by outside checks and balances, which is trained to work and think in terms of power. It will not easily be deflected.

Thus, for many years yet, American responses to Communist developments are likely to be reactions rather than harmonious adjustments. Such adjustments, in the sense of a growing unity of action will, I think, come in relations with our European countries, now on the way to forming a United States of Europe. The habits of life and politics are, despite differences, fundamentally the same in Europe and America, We are all industrial states owing accounts to citizen-consumer. There are all the inherited and acquired resemblances lacking between any of us and Russia, even though it too is becoming an industrial state.

It is a sign of the anachronism of the traditional notions of power, that the United States has, since the war, understood and encouraged the efforts to European unity. There is no precedent for a dominant nation's urging others to come together instead of trying to divide and rule them. Now the peoples of six European countries, and not the least, since they include France, Germany, Italy and the Benelux trio of nations, are actively uniting. In twenty years' time, Europe will be united. By Europe, I mean not only these six, but the other free democratic countries of Europe as well. Britain will necessarily be more and more closely associated with the union of the Six. So will the smaller countries of Europe. As that happens, the current will carry the United States also, closer to a Europe able at last to contribute its full share to the prosperity, the security and vigour of the whole Atlantic world.

America is already realising that it will need to cooperate with European brains. All the more so when our countries undertake over-all European programmes, such as the development of civil nuclear power, which will give them experience of a kind the United States can profit by. A united Europe will sell more to and buy more from the United States. In return, American firms are already showing signs of intense interest in increasing investment on the common market. Our two halves of the Atlantic world will become more and more interdependent. When America has a single dynamic Europe to deal with, it will be far easier than now to lower tariff barriers between us which will, in twenty years' time, be as anachronistic as tariff barriers in Europe today. In twenty years' time, we shall not only see problems, as we are beginning to see them now, in world terms, but we should approach them as an Atlantic community made possible because the United States of America and a United States of Europe can make more nearly equal contributions than America and our European nations separately. As an Atlantic community, we shall be far better armed to coordinate, increase and mobilise our joint resources than we are today, and to bear the necessary burden of helping backward countries to industrialise.

This will be the third great challenge to America's adaptability. The problem of the underdeveloped areas is, I think, probably the most explosive and important of the next twenty years. At present, the tensions between the advanced industrial countries and the underdeveloped ones are growing rather than diminishing. The wealth of the industrial regions of the world has been growing faster than that of the pre-industrial areas which are notable less for rising produce than for the ever-increasing number of their mouths to feed. Very slowly and gradually, the advanced countries are tending to free themselves of their dependence on raw materials and on the underdeveloped areas which supply them. This is a larger, slower trend than can be compassed in the next twenty years. But, even today, in a world where all prices are increasing, those of raw materials are falling. The advanced countries must avoid the temptation of a new kind of isolationism. This would only exacerbate the international "class war" which already exists between rich nations and the poor, ex-colonial ones that resent "not being accepted." The rich industrial countries should come together—all of them, including Russia, if possible—to solve this problem of speeding the development of backward areas which will ultimately affect them all equally. They should increase the credits offered so far. They should offer them in such a way that they are not free gifts—there is no more souring relationship than that of giver or receiver-nation—and in such a way that they are never a single country's offer to another.

I do not underrate the difficulties. Russia for many years will probably think it profitable to continue the competition between East and West for the political support of the underdeveloped areas. In our own countries, it will need a continuous, enlightened effort of leadership to persuade tax-payers to foot bills, the value of which is hard for them to assess (I think this will be easier, though not easy, if many nations contribute). But the effort is necessary and will not be lost. The world will benefit from the growing markets that the expansion of the underdeveloped areas creates. And it will be the only way of slowly (very slowly) delivering it from the nightmare of prolonged rivalries and tensions which could at any moment touch off untold destruction.

Behind all these changes, there lies, I believe, the common pressure which technical progress is putting on man to new forms of organisation. One sign of this is the change in the idea of force. Societies in the past tried to settle their problems by brute force because, relatively, they had so little of it. Now it becomes harder and harder as the means of destruction becomes too massive. The selfsame technical progress which is making war more and more unthinkable is pushing countries to cooperation on a regional, or even world-wide basis. The growing number of international agencies, on food or health, or atomics, and even to organise the coming Geophysical Year, however limited their real scope, are significant of new needs. In fifty years, when the changes in the world's organisation, such as technical revolutions which space-travel prefigures, have exerted their effects on society, they will probably seem ludicrously inadequate beginnings. But fifty years ago they would have been inconceivable.

If there is no war, the narrowing gap between our American and European standards of living and those, first of Russia, and then ultimately, of the other late-starters on the Industrial Revolution should help also to narrow the gap between our ideas of human relations and governments. As the technical world gives new possibilities and also requires a more and more complex organism, gradually, our ideas of nations, even ones as great as the United States, will become outmoded. I think it will ultimately be technically and psychologically impossible for men to penetrate space carrying with them anachronistic earthbound quarrels.

Though we may suspect this is the end of present trends, it is a considerable way off, and the problems of statesmen will, as always be those of proper timing. We cannot be sure that in the next twenty years, we shall come to terms with the New Russia, and we may be certain that we cannot settle the immense problems raised in the ex-colonial areas of the world in such a short period of time. During the next two decades, I think the unity of peoples will apply mainly among those having a similar form of life and with similar conceptions of the relationships between human beings.

In summary: America's main problem in the next twenty years, as I see it, is to develop and carry out firm, creative ideas which will enable the United States to adapt itself to Russia's growth; cooperate with a new partner, the United States of Europe; and anticipate the needs and problems of the underdeveloped parts of the world. Essentially, I believe it is a problem of constant and creative adjustment.

CHAPTER THIRTY

Nationalism, Imperialism, and Communist Expansion

IN "A New Look at Nationalism" Hans Kohn sees in the hyper-national-
ism of the twentieth century a force which deepens antagonisms and
which threatens individual liberty and the universality of human culture.
He notes that though extreme nationalism and imperialism are waning in
the West, they have taken a new lease on life in the communist worlds
and in some of the countries which have newly emerged from colonialism.

In "Some Reflections on Colonialism" Kohn emphasizes that imperialism
is no Western invention, and that in spite of its faults, Western imperial-
ism has brought lasting benefits to Asia and Africa. He urges Americans
to renounce anticolonial slogans. Though there is need for reform every-
where, he questions whether the breaking up of empires always advances
the cause of liberty and peace.

[62] A New Look at Nationalism*

by HANS KOHN

. . . The late great Dutch historian J. Huizinga wrote in his last work, *Geschonden Wereld*, that "nationalism, the exaggerated and unjustified tendency to emphasize national interests, has produced in our time the abominable fruit of hypernationalism, the curse of this century." It was in this very century that many new nationalisms and nation-states have come into being, filled with the spirit of the age. Thus nationalism has become a powerful political threat not only to international peace but also to human freedom, perhaps the most powerful threat because nationalism in our time by far excels other appeals to human emotions—social or religious appeals—by its impact on masses and individuals alike. Communist Marxism, originally an a-national and anti-national movement, had to take this into account and has lately developed into a new kind of national socialism. Nationalism today unleashes forces which deepen antagonisms and hallow them by appeals to an idealized and over-sentimentalized past. Thus nationalism has tended to become what it originally had not been, a threat to individual liberty and to the universality of human culture.

After the First World War many peoples were "liberated" and created independent nations. Often these peoples had rightful complaints about the inequality of their status and the curtailment of their individual freedom. But before the First World War, following the example set by Britain in Ireland, South Africa, and India, the trend all over the earth went in the direction of greater equality of status and of growing recognition of individual rights. The creation of the new nation-states in 1918 in many cases reversed this trend. Nationalities which had demanded release from oppression became oppressors themselves, and sometimes worse oppressors, as soon as they were independent. Innumerable disputes about historical and natural frontiers sprang up. National traditions and national interests were idolized and absolutized at the expense of concern for neighbor and consideration for mankind. In the new nation-states racially closely related peoples felt oppressed, Ukrainians in Poland, Slovaks in Czechoslovakia, Croats in Serb-controlled Yugoslavia. Poland had bitter frontier disputes with Lithuania, Germany, Czechoslovakia, Russia—the frontiers of Yugoslavia and Italy, of Hungary and

*From *The Virginia Quarterly Review*, vol. 32 (Summer, 1956), pp. 321-332. Reprinted by permission.

Rumania, of Bulgaria and Yugoslavia were "bleeding" wounds and "unredeemed" populations continued to clamor for independence. This continued nationalist temper in central and eastern Europe helped in almost all the countries to undermine the respect for individual liberty: the deep hostility among the new nation-states facilitated German expansion first, Russian expansion later. The new Europe after 1918 offered the spectacle neither of peace nor of the progress of liberty and human civilization. The great hopes of Mazzini and Woodrow Wilson in national self-determination as a vehicle for democracy and harmony among peoples were not realized.

Twenty-five years later, nationalism became the dominant emotional force all over the globe. Nationalism is in itself neither good nor bad, as little as capitalism, socialism, or imperialism are. It would be disastrous to rational thought and individual liberty to regard a rethinking of nationalism or capitalism as a prelude to a sophisticated justification of exploitation or domination. But neither is it to be supposed—a position toward which modern British and North American humanitarian sensitivity inclines—that the underdog in a given situation is right and morally superior. There is no easy general rule. Phenomena of utmost complexity and variety, capitalism and socialism, nationalism and imperialism, differ in content and consequences with historical circumstances. But two paradoxical situations emerge from the study of nationalism. Thanks to its rapid spread all over the globe, the peoples of the earth are beginning to build, at least outwardly, their life on similar foundations of nationalism, of popular education, of industrialization. Modern schools and machines, the forms of popular elections, the emancipation of women, and the idea of national loyalty and service to the nation have penetrated everywhere. Modern inventiveness has afforded the technical means to a degree unimaginable a few decades ago for making cultural interdependence and intercourse even easier than economic interdependence. But at the same time peoples newly awakened to nationalism have begun to stress and to overstress their self-hood and independence, their cultural particularities and self-sufficiency. In the age of the awakening or the revolt of the masses, collective passions and utopian expectations have centered around the newly awakened nationalism to such a degree that ever new barriers disrupt the international community.

The other paradoxical situation is presented by the fact that nationalism is more or less on the wane in the lands of its origin, in the West, where the peoples are seeking ways for supra-national political organization and ever closer cultural integration, and this at the very time when nationalism has grown to a fever pitch in Eastern Europe and in

Asia. The same is true of Marxian socialism. Marx lived in England and he found his first great mass following in Germany. But today socialism in these countries as throughout the West has more or less openly abandoned Marxism as its theoretical foundation and its practical guide. The discrepancy between Marxian theory of the middle of the nineteenth century and the surrounding Western reality of the middle of the twentieth century has become too glaring. Only in the lands outside the Western historical community has Marxism tremendously gained in influence and prestige, a process which no Marxist at the end of the last century would have thought possible. And these two paradoxical developments are seen in one when we realize that nowhere is the emphasis on national sovereignty and its sanctity today as strong as in Communist society. In this atmosphere of paradoxical and unexpected developments strange myths are produced and uncritically accepted by the West. There were in history many predatory empires whose road was destructive of civilization and freedom. But there were other empires which with all their glaring human —all too human—shortcomings formed a protective shield under which peace and culture, freedom and law could grow. The Roman Empire of the second century and the British Empire of the later nineteenth century belonged to this category. It was the strength of these empires which made these two centuries the relatively happiest which mankind has known in its long story of devastating wars and lamentable misfortunes.

Communism uses today anti-imperialism and nationalism as two of its strongest ideological weapons in the war against freedom. Communist propaganda profits from the fact that many Western intellectuals have accepted Lenin's strange theory that imperialism is the product of late capitalism, that capitalist nations are by necessity imperialist, and that imperialism means above all economic exploitation. The Soviet Union or Communist China being by definition anti-capitalist must therefore be by definition anti-imperialist and free from exploitation. All these wondrous definitions cover up a reality in which Ukrainians and Georgians, Latvians and Uzbeks are oppressed to a degree hardly reached anywhere else in modern times, whole peoples are uprooted and transplanted as they were in the Assyrian Empire, and Tibet and the Mohammedan peoples of Sinkiang are refused their independence and even not allowed to voice their desire for it. Communist and Asian nationalist mythology have fused in propagating the fairy tale that imperialism is a special vice of the white man. Even Professor Toynbee's Reith Lectures on "The World and the West" seem to accept the legend of Russia and Asia as the victims of Western aggressiveness. In reality the West has been attacked by Asian forces throughout the longer part of recorded history, from the

Persian wars against Greece to the Second Siege of Vienna by the Turks in 1683. But it has not been in history a question of European against non-European peoples. There has been always oppression within Europe. And Asian and African peoples are as human as the European peoples are: they fought and exterminated each other, and enslaved and exploited each other, before and after the coming of the white man to those continents. The imperialist and nationalist conflicts among Asians and Africans will go on after the last vestiges of the relatively short Western imperial rule have disappeared. Yet the brief contact with modern Western civilization has vitalized the stagnant civilizations of Asia and Africa, has reinvigorated them and aroused in them a desire for liberty and human dignity, as contact with the same Western civilization had done a century before in Russia.

The myths about capitalist imperialism and the virtues of nationalism have brought many Asians to deny the existence of Soviet imperialism and of national independence movements in Communist or Asian empires. Little sympathy is expressed for the struggle of the Soviet nationalities or of the South Moluccans who demand their independence from Indonesia, or for the Karen national defense movement in Burma. The Indonesian government has repressed native insurgent forces in North Sumatra and in parts of Java and Celebes with a ruthlessness which would have been severely condemned in Western countries if it had been done by Western imperial administrations. Nor is this a tale of recent woes. Burmese conquerors have from the twelfth to the eighteenth centuries repeatedly invaded Thailand, destroyed the Thai capitals and led part of the population as slaves into captivity. Burma's threat to Thailand ended only when Britain imposed her rule upon Burma. Nor did the Thai kings refrain from military conquests in Laos. Similarly, racial superiority complexes are nothing peculiar to the white race. They are ethically reprehensible and politically unwise wherever they appear. But group superiority feelings are in different forms a general human failure. The Manchu conquerors of China enforced strict racial segregation and prohibited all intermarriage. Japanese colonial administrators imitated and outdid the exterior trappings of the quickly vanishing caste of British colonials. The Mohammedans in Chinese northwestern territories fought valiantly in many uprisings for independence until the ghastly repressions in the nineteenth century drowned all their efforts in an ocean of blood. A moral superiority complex based on an inverse racialism and on bitter resentments can produce intellectually and ethically unsound attitudes. Imperialism is today on the wane in the West, but it may be reviving outside the West, shunning the name, preserving the substance. To many observers India's attitude to Kashmir reveals no respect for national self-determination nor an absolute horror for imperial considerations. The Indians have taken over Britain's "advisory role" in Nepal and like all "advisors" they are not too welcome. Chinese throughout southeast Asia and Indians in East Africa and Surinam show little inclination to integrate with the natives of the countries of their residence: potentially some of them present the danger which the Auslandsdeutshe presented not so long ago.

Cultural freedom can only exist if intellectual life is guided by an effort at critical and objective thinking. The greatest threat to such thinking, and therefore to cultural freedom, was represented centuries ago by authoritarian and absolutized religion. Today it is represented by nationalism, above all in its over-resentful or semi-totalitarian forms. But everywhere in the free world, outside the confines of Communist rule and perhaps even there under cover, the critical forces which were born in the seventeenth century in northwestern Europe are at work to combat the exclusivism and egocentrism of modern nationalism. None has spoken more strongly against the cult of one's own nation or nationalism than Vladimir Solovyev in Russia or Rabindranath Tagore in India, both men deeply rooted in the spiritual tradition of their community and yet wide open to the critical insights of the West. Everywhere most of us have allowed our thinking to be channeled into widely accepted stereotypes about nationalism and its relation to liberty. In this time of mental and verbal confusion when general political terms have become so emotionally fraught that they cover disparate realities, we have to start rethinking many concepts in their historical context and in their concrete application. One of the chief concepts about which this rethinking has to be done in the interest of human freedom and of the possibility of cultural intercourse and universal rationality is the concept of nationalism.

[63]   *Some Reflections on Colonialism**

by HANS KOHN

. . . The issue of anti-colonialism has been used for some time in the international power struggle, and not only by the U.S.S.R. Anti-imperialism and anti-colonialism are widespread among independent nations of Latin America, which have seen for a long time in the United States the leading imperialist and colonial nation, American imperialism being chiefly though not exclusively "dollar imperialism." Argentina, an independent nation for over a century, very proud of its independence and hardly in danger of imperialist aggression, has used the issue of anti-colonialism as a weapon in her struggle against the United States for leadership at least in the southern and middle parts of the western hemisphere. The United States has used the issue of anti-colonialism in its rivalry with, or dislike of, Britain for very many decades. Now the Soviet Union is using the same issue in her rivalry with, and hatred of, the United States. But there is hardly anything fundamentally new in it except that the Western nations, especially Britain, have by now set many nations in Asia and Africa free, and that it is above all among these nations which are now independent that the issue of anti-colonialism is raised.

It is a widespread propaganda slogan that imperialism introduced wars, poverty, racial and economic exploitation to Asia and Africa. That is not the case. Poverty has existed in Asia and Africa since time immemorial, as it has existed in Europe until the rise of liberalism and capitalism. Poverty in Asia and Africa was for reasons of climate and temperament greater than in Europe. As far as historical memory goes, there has been perpetual warfare in Asia and Africa; one Asian nation or king enslaved other Asian peoples; African tribes enslaved and exterminated other African tribes. Imperialism is no Western invention. For many centuries Asian tribes and empires have endangered Europe. An accident saved Europe, but not Russia, from Mongol domination in the thirteenth century. As recently as 1683 the Turks were at the gates of Vienna, and Turks and Berbers enslaved Christian Europeans.

Western imperialism has had only a brief day in history. Its sun is now setting, and though this sun has been shining over many injustices and cruelties, in no way worse than the normal cruelties in Asia and Africa, it

*From *Review of Politics*, XVIII, 259 (July 1956). Reprinted by permission.

has brought lasting benefits to Asia and Africa, as the imperialism of Alexander the Great and of the Romans did for their empires, and has awakened and vitalized lethargic civilizations.

Now the tide of Western imperialism is definitely receding, due not so much to external pressure as to Western ideas themselves—but it has been on the whole a period of which the West and especially Britain has not to be ashamed. It would be wrong to apply twentieth century standards and principles of international law to preceding centuries. By doing that—and it should not be forgotten that these new twentieth century standards were developed by the Western world and only by the Western world— the West suffers from a bad conscience; the anti-Western propaganda is exploiting these guilt feelings. The extension of European control into American, Asian and African lands came not as the result of any peculiar iniquity but as the result of a sudden great disparity in cultural energy and economic productivity. Today, largely due to Western influence, this disparity is vanishing. A difficult readjustment is due—it will not be helped by any feeling of guilt or need for indemnity.

After 1918 Germany successfully exploited Western guilt feelings about Versailles; this false historical perspective, imposed upon a wrongly contrite West, was one of the main reasons why Hitler could rise and why the Germans started to threaten the West in their second hegemonial war of the twentieth century. The communists similarly have exploited the West's guilt feelings about many things, not only about colonies, for the last thirty-five years.

Reduced to its barest outline colonialism is foreign rule imposed upon a nation. Apart from the fact that no nations existed in most cases where colonialism was established often with the connivance of the colonial peoples themselves, it must be emphasized that this phenomenon of "foreign" rule has nothing to do with *European* control of Asia. Within Europe there has been rule of one people over another, or rather of one government over several peoples, and this has been resented as strongly and often, using the very same words as the anti-colonialists in Asia do today, who have learned their slogans and their tactics from European nationalist movements. This has nothing to do with race or race superiority, one of the most bewildering myths of the present time. Closely related peoples opposed each other, Norwegians against Danes or Swedes, Crotians against Serbs, Slovaks against Czechs, Ukranians against Russians, Catalans against Castilians, etc., and most bitterly resented what they regarded as political dominion, economic exploitation and relegation to a status of inferiority.

Nor will Asian aspirations for independence and conflicts resulting from it be solved by the dissolution of the existing Western empires and their replacement either by nation states or by Asian empires. The recent riots in Bombay in which the Indian police had to intervene in the very same way as under the British Raj and in which the number of victims was apparently greater than in any single riot or uprising against the British Raj since 1957, were caused by the fact that the Maharashtri population found itself or believed itself politically and economically exploited by, and subordinated to, the Gujerati population. It should not be forgotten that it was a Maharashtra who assassinated the Gujerati Gandhi.

The people of southern India, who speak Dravidian languages, of which Tamil is the most important, have formed the Dravida Kazhagam and the Dravida Munnetra Kazhagam (Dravidian Federation and Dravidian Progressive Federation) to prepare their separation from Aryan India. They feel themselves exploited and wish to establish Dravida Nadu (the Dravidian nation). "The social exploitation," one of their leaders writes, "we have endured for so many decades from Brahminism and the decay of our cultural literature due to this force is responsible for our attitude. Not only does Brahminism result in casteism; it has kept us for many a century on the lower rungs of the social ladder. That is why we say that the poisonous teeth of the Brahmin snake must be taken out."

These words only repeat what the Brahmins said—with less justification—against the British. The Indian government will probably suppress any attempt for independence on the part of some of the peoples of India with much greater ferocity than the British ever tried. Nor would it be fair to compare the position of the Negro in the United States to that of the outcasts in India. Though the position of the Negro is by far not yet what it should be, it is infinitely better than that of the Indian Untouchables. In the new Asian nations movements for independence continue: the territorial conflicts between India and Pakistan, between Pakistan and Afghanistan, the independence movements of the Karens in Burma and of the South Moluccans in Indonesia, the division between south and north in the Sudan and in Nigeria—these are some examples of continuing unrest after "imperialism" has gone. The Indian element in East Africa and the Chinese in Southeast Asia may create great hardship for the natives, once imperial protection is removed.

If the anti-colonial issue is brought up, the Western speakers should not put themselves on the defensive, but state the facts as they are. There have been Mongol, Chinese, Indian, Ottoman empires with their subject peoples as there has been a British empire. Which was "better" history will tell. Much is bad in many colonies, but much is bad in independent countries too. The British colony of Basutoland is much more progressive and salutary for the natives than the independent Union of South Africa which nevertheless claims Basutoland. British Hongkong is an oasis of order and liberty in the Far East, entirely due to British efforts and ideas. In the case of Cyprus the strategic interests of the Turks and their well-founded fears should be taken as much into consideration as French interests and fears in the Saar. There is no reason to assume that the New Guinean Papuas would fare better under the administration of Indonesian rulers, with whom they have no affinity in race, language, or religion, than under Dutch administration. All that does not mean that all colonial countries or all dependencies, whether in Europe or in other continents, should remain in this status. *Change and reforms are due everywhere.* Some colonial administrations like the French in North Africa and in Madagascar have been bad for the last decade, partly on account of over-centralization and of staffing even the lower echelons of the administration with Frenchmen. The question about the desirability of national independence, of the formation of new nation-states is in no way confined to Asia or Africa. It may be well asked whether the application of the principle of national independence—instead of transformation and reform of supranational empires and political entities—has helped the cause of liberty and peace in Europe. The most important maxim guiding our actions in all parts of the world should be the recognition that gradual reforms are necessary everywhere, that there is no panacea, and that each case must be judged on its own merits, according to its historical setting.

The people of the United States should not only renounce the use of the anti-colonial slogans, they should also give up the vain endeavor of competing in promises and panaceas with the Soviets. The Soviet short cuts for achieving economic well being and social happiness are naturally attractive, and they provide spiritual satisfaction to an intellectual elite which has abandoned its own traditional values and has turned against those of the West. But the Soviet heaven can come only *after* the total revolution which is not reversible. We cannot promise a Utopia like that either for ourselves or for others, and should in all decency stress the fact. Sound progress can come only slowly and by great efforts and self-control. In Asia the moral and social conditions do not exist to make the Asians in any foreseeable future as rich as we are. This fact may be deeply regrettable, but it cannot be attributed to our or to anybody's fault. Yet the only thing which would apparently satisfy the emotional dissatisfaction of some Asian intellectuals seems to be the lowering of our and the British standards to theirs. That we cannot do. We are not free because we are rich; it has been our long and hard developing tradition of individual liberty and responsibility which has made it possible for us to become rich. . . .

CHAPTER THIRTY-ONE

The Search for Peace

*I*N the past various explanations have been given for the prevalence of
war, including conflict of economic interests and the competitive building
up of armaments. Today the primary danger of war seems to come from
the existence of two great power blocs and from the fact that one of them
—Soviet Russia and its allies—has as its objective world domination.

Niemeyer believes that when nations act with persistent hostility toward
one another, chances are that the guns will go off sooner or later. We may
hope for, and attempt to bring about better relations with Russia; but
meanwhile we should assume that we are in a struggle for global supremacy, one likely to end in a violent showdown. Middleton, on the other
hand, thinks that a major war is unlikely for a long time to come. Russians
and their allies believe that the triumph of communism is inevitable, and
that it can be brought about by political, ideological, and economic penetration. Why, then, he asks, should they fight when in the long run everything seems to be coming their way?

[64]   The Probability of War in our Time*

by GERHART NIEMEYER

. . . As we focus our attention on the probability of war in the kind of relation that exists between the United States and the Soviet Union, let us remember, as a matter of general experience, that when nations (or other political groups) act with persistent hostility toward each other, regard each other's power as a real menace to themselves, are unwilling to let each other be within given areas, and point loaded guns at each other, chances are that the guns will go off sooner or later. Thus, an observer of American-Japanese relations could with confidence have predicted war as the likely outcome of the policies both countries pursued prior to Pearl Harbor. The understanding of the situation would not have been invalidated had circumstances combined to avoid the outbreak of war. What the observer would have understood is the potentiality of violence in a situation of sustained hostile intent of nations toward each other.

Groups and nations, no less than private individuals, often immerse their whole beings in conflict to a point where a solution by violence is inherent in their reciprocal wills and deeds a long time before it actually occurs. Perceptive reading of such a pattern of conflict enables the observer to anticipate probable war without in the least committing himself to any political theory positing the "inevitability of war."

Relations between the U.S. and the U.S.S.R. combine the characteristics of pre-Pearl Harbor relations between the U.S. and Japan with those of pre-Fort Sumter relations between North and South. Each side sees the other's aspirations as a threat to itself and begrudges the other the power it now enjoys. Each side is arming, and arming with an eye exclusively to the other. Each states its objectives in terms obviously unacceptable to the other. Each regards the other's power as a denial of its most basic values, a threat to its social order, and a death warrant for its leaders. Anyone who supposes that such a relationship can be changed merely by an effort of will has only to reflect upon our own conduct and the depth of conviction that determines it. Even our best-intentioned *demarches* vis-à-vis the Soviet Union have been characteristic assertions of our values, which no Soviet government can accept without admitting

*From *Orbis*, I, 161 (July 1957). Reprinted by permission of publisher and author.

political defeat. Having in fact conceded a Soviet sphere of influence in Eastern Europe, we have insisted on Western-style elections there, thus showing a disposition to inject Western political values into what the Soviets have some reason to regard as their own domain. We have confirmed this decision in favor of intervention by assisting Tito at the time of his quarrel with Moscow, by launching Radio Free Europe, by sympathizing with the rioting workers of East Germany and of Poland, by delivering food to East Germany, and by proposing a UN investigation of forced labor camps. We have taken the UN—based as it is on essentially Western, free-world concepts of right and wrong, law and order, majority rule and civil rights—and brandished it as a standard that the communists must accept. The UN concept of aggression, for example, itself introduced an "unlimited" Western objective into the Korean war, in the sense that we found ourselves pursuing not merely territorial or military objectives but the further objective of forcing the enemy to amend his character and accept our entire concept of international order. Similarly, our disarmament proposals, based as they have been on international inspection and open information, have amounted to a denial of the Soviet type of society. To put this a little differently: even in our most conciliatory moods, we cannot bring ourselves to show or feel respect for Soviet interests by giving up active objection, for example, to Soviet oppression of the satellite peoples, the police management of Soviet internal affairs and the clear Soviet policy of eliminating politically hostile groups in neighboring countries. At the same time, however, we insist that such policies as the Marshall Plan, NATO, SEATO, MSA, European integration, etc., are justified, though we know them to have aroused violent Soviet objections. Moreover, we have taken great pains to have some of these policies endorsed by majority resolutions of the UN.

This description is not intended to imply any criticism of our policies. We cannot act otherwise, since international law, majority rule, civil rights, free elections, open information, contractual labor, etc., are values that we cannot renounce without ceasing to be ourselves. But that is precisely the point. We mean no harm, but every time we seek to realize a goal that we believe to be good, just, and humane, we issue a declaration of war to Soviet society. And the same thing is true in reverse.

Beyond these value commitments in our foreign policy, moreover, we have in our domestic affairs launched on a path of relentless campaign against the communists that cannot fail to affect our feelings and actions toward Soviet Russia: witness the Smith Act, the McCarran Act, the periodic renewal of the House Committee on UnAmerican Activities, the successive measures calculated to tighten the Executive Loyalty Program, the Medina trial and its sequels, etc. All of these actions reflect a determination on the part of the American people to eliminate from its society persons of a certain persuasion. The measures mentioned amount to an announcement—by most Americans to the communist few among them—not that they must be silent but that they must either undergo a change of heart or be regarded—and treated—as enemies. Regardless of how we look upon this by now deep-rooted and persistent attitude, we cannot deny that it represents a basic decision on the part of the American people, and we cannot afford to ignore or even belittle its predictable effect on Soviet-American relations. We have here a manifestation of the deep-seated and almost instinctive abhorrence which Americans feel regarding communism and communists, an abhorrence that cannot help but arouse the abolitionist instincts that have played so great a part in American history.

There is no evidence that we are deliberately setting out to start a war with Russia; but we are behaving—and are by our deepest convictions constrained to behave—in such a way that a "we or they" of war is implied in the entire character of our intercourse with Soviet Russia. Similarly, one can dispense with the question whether the evidence points conclusively to a Soviet plan to start war at such and such a time, since they, even more than we, are committed by their entire view of history and society to the "we or they" choice. Given such a relationship, neither side can feel at peace so long as the other has the capacity to do it harm. Must not each side then assume that sooner or later the other will resort to war? And would not concern for our safety counsel that, instead of asking *whether* the struggle will culminate in a violent showdown, we begin by asking when and under what circumstances this could happen and by what means and methods we could be victorious?

Against this conclusion, the following argument is often advanced:

In our age of "mega-deaths" one cannot assume that the conflict of two hostile national wills locked in bitter, active and continuous antagonism will lead to violence as that kind of conflict has usually done in the past. General historical experience cannot any longer serve as a guide under present circumstances. The nature of war has so changed that, even in their bitterest struggles, modern nations will shrink from it because it is so certain to bring utter destruction to both sides.

Let it be noted that this argument does not deny the lessons of past experience as here mentioned. It admits that up to the present it has been correct to infer eventual violence from a pattern of evident, active and determined mutual hostility between nations. But, it asserts, in the face of modern military technology, one should not assume war to result from the clash of hostile national wills. The argument thus is based not on experience but on speculation—one could even say on optimistic speculation. War has so outgrown any proportion to any of its conceivable ends that deliberate resort to it is inconceivable. Many feel that assuming the possibility of war is but the first step toward willing war. Hence they reject even the assumption that it could happen, and much more the assumption that it is likely to happen.

Now, one cannot exclude the possibility that the nature of modern war has indeed imposed restraining fears on all governments to the extent that this fear overshadows all other motives of conflict. But, before discarding historical experience, one would do well to demand evidence that such a change has in fact taken place. Some such evidence seems to be available. The Western press abounds with declarations to the effect that "co-existence is the only alternative to no existence." War, we are frequently told, would mean the end of all civilization or even the end of all life on this planet. The President of the United States himself uttered the phase "There is no alternative to peace." Before rushing to the conclusion that such words are reliable proof of a fundamentally changed attitude toward war, let us consider other evidence.

Both the Soviet Union and the United States are engaged in an arms race. The fact that neither has been attacked by the other at the existing level of armaments does not cause them to maintain that level as adequate for their security. As the race continues, the hazards of the competitive relationship increase. Nevertheless, both sides are willing to risk these hazards and to bank on their capacity to win decisive military superiority. Both sides, despite protestations of defensive intentions, seek superiority in offensive weapons. On both sides, moreover, statements at the highest level have contradicted the declarations mentioned above. The Soviets never cease to accuse the United States of war mongering; at the same time, they assure their own people that an atomic war would destroy capitalism but not socialism. On our side high-ranking persons have similarly expressed their confidence that we rather than the Soviet Union would survive an atomic bombardment. There has been no dearth of warnings against a Soviet policy of atomic blackmail. In the negotiations on arms reductions since 1946, both sides have been well aware of each other's positions, yet both sides have insisted on conditions which they knew to be unacceptable to the other side. If attitudes toward war have changed, actions on both sides give little evidence.

One could, to be sure, point to the repeated "brink of war" risks which both sides took without actually going over the brink. Before attributing the restraint shown in Azerbaijan, Berlin, Korea, Indochina, Quemoy and Matsu, etc., to a changed attitude toward war, one would do well to consider another explanation for such restraints: We are in the presence not only of weapons of unprecedented power but also of a bipolar concentration of political forces. In other words, the clash, if and when it comes, will be more than a passing test of force. The clash will decide the fate of the world in the sense that either mankind will pass entirely under communist rule, or the will of the free peoples will prevail and destroy communist power. It may well be the finality of the showdown which causes the antagonists to hesitate in situations in which the military prospects do not favor them beyond any doubt. Inasmuch as the true cause of such restraint as we have witnessed is not certain, we cannot conclude confidently that attitudes toward war have fundamentally changed.

A violent showdown as the *ultima ratio* of the Soviet-American conflict could be ruled out if one could be confident that both the enemy and we are determined to suffer any marginal loss in prestige, power, security, self-respect, and freedom rather than fight. In other words, we could be virtually certain that "war is now impossible" if we were confident that, given the nature of modern war, both sides will know that they will end up losers. Even if one assumes that war in the atom age will necessarily result in wholesale destruction, it is hard to argue this thesis with conviction. Let him who would attempt to argue it aver that he would not prefer defeating the Soviet Union in an atomic war to being defeated by it! As long as it makes a decisive difference at which end of the one remaining gun one finds oneself after an infinitely devastating war, one cannot be sure that war will by tacit agreement be ruled out of the relations between two basically antagonistic nations. Must we not therefore assume that a time may come when one side or the other will so fear the consequences of further delay that it may prefer to take the chance of a violent showdown?

Suppose—so one might contend at this point—that neither of the two opponents will ever find himself pressed to a point where he must make the ultimate choice? Suppose, in other words, that the moment will never come when "further delay" appears to entail, for either side, such fearful penalties as a decisive loss of security and, ultimately, of freedom? Will not "further delay" then continue to be preferable to a "violent showdown," and can we not confidently assume that both sides will opt for what is and remains the less disastrous alternative? Recent events, both in the satellite countries and in the Middle East, have shown that the equation of East-West power is not likely to remain stable. The relations are such that each side must continuously fear that the other will seek to increase its strength to a level sufficient to accomplish not only certain international ends but a revolutionary change within its own frontiers; at the same time, neither side can safely enjoy the *status quo* so long as defections from its own ranks can swell those of the other side. The *status quo* is inherently unstable and total revolution lies (for the loser) at the end of the race for power advantage: is this not sufficient reason for each side to assume that in this developing power equation there is a point of no return? And when that point, in its estimation, seems to be approaching, will not loss of all that is valuable seem the inescapable price for letting it pass? And if this is so, dare we count on an indefinite postponement of the fateful decision by both sides? It is an extremely hazardous assumption to make, one that amounts to every bit as fateful a decision as that of going to the opposite extreme. . . .

Ponder as we may the issues of our time, the agonizing questions still are with us. The nature of war has utterly changed. Its power of destruction has so diminished the advantages traditionally attributed to victory that rational persons find it impossible to contemplate war as a policy assumption. Why should not war be ruled out as a conceivable alternative? And, even if others do not abhor war enough to abjure it, why should not we, on our part, renounce violence unilaterally?

Such arguments overlook the fact that, not only is war different now, but also the nature of our opponent and the consequences of defeat. The Soviet state differs from other great powers in history. It has declared its military hostility against all societies not dominated by it and its determination to destroy any opposition by dictatorial force. It now controls a formidable military establishment equipped with atomic weapons. Since World War II it has rapidly expanded its dominion and is devoting all its energies to develop capabilities superior to those of all other nations.

Wherever triumphant, Soviet power has proceeded to change not only governments, economies and social institutions, but also human nature itself. It has aimed at transforming the mind of man into an unquestioning servant of party leadership. It has proclaimed the identity of truth with party pronouncements. It has systematically destroyed all personal values, loyalties and allegiances, and supplanted them with new loyalties maintained by ceaseless indoctrination. It has subordinated not only the common good but also the human personality to the strategic aims of the Communist Party's struggle for total power.

Losing the struggle to such an opponent entails a penalty which is out of proportion with the traditional consequences of conflicts in the past. Before, a nation bested by another either diplomatically or in war suffered loss of territory, wealth, prestige, power and rank. At the very worst, it had to endure the yoke of a foreign victor—of a victor, however, who did not disrupt, or attempt to transform radically, the normal processes of life and government in the vanquished nation. Being bested by the Soviet Union, however, means the perversion of the very purposes of government, distortion of all moral standards and dissolution of all organic bonds.

Thus the struggle between the United States and the Soviet Union combines a clash of ideologies with a great power conflict. The outcome of the struggle depends on the capabilities of these two nations, because the might of each remains the real obstacle to the undisputed sway of the other. If the Soviets are to have peace on their terms, they must necessarily weaken the United States to the point where it could never again oppose their will. No nation could then, on penalty of extinction, deny the writ of the Kremlin. On its part, the United States can attain peace on terms other than the Soviets' only if it strengthens itself to the point where it can force the masters of the Kremlin to change their ways and their system.

The contest for power between the United States and the Soviet Union is strongly affected by the ideological climate throughout the world. Since ideological allegiances are subject to profound and sudden shifts, the boundaries of conflict are in constant flux, and the insecurity on both sides is deep and chronic. There is no escape from the conflict. The alternatives are a violent showdown or a bloodless and abject defeat.

This article, it must be emphasized, has attempted to state assumptions on which our foreign policy should be based. It should not be mistaken for a prescription for a certain course of action or for a prediction.

Understanding a relationship and deciding what to do about it are two different things. If we assume that the Soviet-American conflict implies eventual war, there is still a range of choices available for mapping the wisest American policy under the circumstances. For instance, on this premise we may decide that, in self-defense, we must precipitate the showdown. But the logic of the assumption does not by any means confine us to this one policy but admits of certain other alternatives. One of these might be called a "decision by stages," an attempt to exert pressure and violence through successive limited action in the hope that their cumulative effect will achieve victory. Or one might derive from the same assumption the concept of a "double track" policy which, while always prepared for and not shrinking from open violence, would pursue the ultimate objective of U.S. policy by all means short of a violent clash. The fact that these and a number of other conceivable policies can be based on the same assumption does not mean that they are equally wise or feasible. It does mean, however, that the decision as to which of these alternatives we should follow ceases to be a question of weighing basic ends and expectations, and becomes one of making estimates of concrete political, military, and economic factors as they fit into the framework of these basic ends and expectations.

Nor, on the other hand, should the assumptions formulated in this article be confused with predictions. True, an attempt to analyze a relationship involves a number of expectations which serve as a guide for policy, and several such expectations have been stated on these pages. Moreover, it is submitted that they are "correct," in the sense that behavior based on them is what the situation calls for. In other words, the expectations are, according to our best knowledge of Soviet-American relations, based on solid ground. These expectations, however, should not be taken as a commitment to historical "inevitability." Future events may change the grounds for our assumptions in ways that cannot now be foreseen. But while the unexpected must not be ruled out categorically, it is most important to keep in mind that we *cannot*, from our present vantage point, foresee these changes. If they come, they may be for the better: but they may also be for the worse. All that we can say at the present is that, should we find ourselves in a new situation, we would then have to revise our policy assumptions accordingly. In the meantime, the known situation and the expectations it implies should govern the assumptions from which our policy proceeds. No other course could be justified in terms of sober and realistic thought.

It is possible to go even a step farther. If the stated policy assumptions do not rule out future changes in the entire pattern of Soviet-American relations, as well as of the Russian regime—even though such changes cannot be foreseen or indeed be regarded as probable—neither do they rule out active efforts to bring about such changes deliberately. Policies having this aim would, of course, if adopted, be only a shot in the dark, and we would not be able to assume rationally that the hoped-for results were within the realm of possibility, much less of probability. In other words: Even though we might hope to change for the better our relations with a powerful socialist Russia, we should in sober reason continue to *assume* that we are in a struggle for the stake of global supremacy, one likely to end in a violent showdown. In this sense, the relationship should best be characterized as "war," although a war that is still in a "cold" phase.

What then is the rational basis for policies aiming at some fundamental changes in this relation? In any war, a purpose in the waging of it (one could even say the central purpose) is so to alter the opponent's will that the pattern of relationship is transformed from one of mutual, active hostility into something else. If this is true in a context of open violence, there is no reason why it should not be true of a "cold" war. We should remember, though, that while we may *aim* for a change of the opponent's will, we must not, on penalty of disastrous defeat, stop assuming that it has not changed until the actual moment when his fighting determination is assuredly broken. We should also bear in mind that the time and occasion of such a change cannot be predicted. While we can *try* to force the relationship into a different pattern we cannot base current policy on any assumptions about the success of these efforts, the more so since two can play at this game. Furthermore, in considering the prospect of a fundamental change in Soviet-American relations, we should guard against treating that prospect as a ray of hope until we have counted the cost of bringing it about. From our point of view, the pattern of Soviet-American relations would not appear to have changed until the Russian regime had stopped being actively hostile to the non-communist world or, in other words, until Russia's rulers have ceased being Leninist-Marxists. If we asked what kind of action on our part could possibly bring this to pass, we would surmise that it would take, at the margin, nothing less than potential strength adequate for victory, maximum preparedness, determination to face the worst the enemy could do to us, strong moral and political convictions, and possibly a violent test of strength—in other words, policies and actions based on precisely the assumptions stated in this article. In short: the assumptions about Soviet-American relations arrived at above would have to be considered the correct basis for our policy even while we might be trying to change the entire pattern of that relationship by our efforts.

[65]   *War or Peace: What Are the Chances?**

by DREW MIDDLETON

The rattle of machine-gun fire down a rainy Budapest street. The swoop of Canberras out of the African sun onto an Egyptian airfield. The journeyings of Ministers and Secretaries of State, reflected in big, black headlines. The stricken face of a young mother who hears, above the cocktail party's buzz, the monosyllable: war.

All these are expressions of the final breaking up of the post-war world. We may not, as some suggest, now be living in a pre-war world. But we certainly are living in one presenting new problems and unexplored ideological attitudes; a misty valley in which the accepted signposts of the past decade are meaningless and the superhighways leading to "peace" or "security" dwindle into rough cart tracks.

The break-up has been going on for three and a half years, or ever since the death of Joseph Stalin freed the Western world from the immediate danger of military aggression by the Union of Soviet Socialist Republics. The centrifugal forces then set in motion began to tear at the alliances, international concepts and political formulae evolved in the "cold war." The process was accelerated by the wide acceptance in the free world of the pleasing but inherently dangerous idea that possession of nuclear weapons by the United States, the Soviet Union and the United Kingdom ruled out, by a kind of balance of fear, the possibility of a major war.

There was another important factor in the dissolution of the post-war pattern. During the climactic years of the "cold war" with Russia, new nations emerged, particularly in Asia and Africa. The most important of these nations had been part of the British, French or Dutch empires, and a natural consequence of their independence was that these three powers, among the strongest and most reliable allies of the United States, faced increased difficulties in what remained of their imperial domains.

All of these factors have contributed to the new world situation in which a host of individual problems—often national rather than purely ideo-

*From *New York Times Magazine* (November 18, 1956). Reprinted by permission of the publisher and author.

logical—face individual nations instead of one major problem facing a group of nations, as Soviet expansion confronted the NATO countries. In such a situation, the probability of minor wars and armed conflicts is greater. The Israeli invasion of Egypt, British and French intervention in the Suez Canal Zone, the Soviet Union's murder of Hungary's liberty, all these are symptoms of the new world situation.

The question is: What is the danger of a small war becoming a major one, that is, a conflict involving the United States, Britain, and the U.S.S.R. as combatants?

Minor wars do not automatically develop into big ones. The Spanish Civil War did not. Germany's wars of the nineteenth century were localized. But the danger that other nations will become involved is always real.

The interdependence of the modern world makes small wars, no matter how remote, dangerous to the peace of the rest of the world community. This interdependence is not merely a matter of modern communications. It reflects economic relations as well. The basic reason for the willingness of Britain and France to risk world odium and invade Egypt was an economic one. It can be summed up by one word: oil. Faced with the prospect of a major conflict between Israel and the Arab states, a conflict that would disrupt the Middle East for years and shut off their oil supplies at the source, the British and French Governments were ready to act now rather than to pay later.

However, it does not follow that the situation either there or in Hungary must develop into general war. The reality of the situation in Hungary, a situation that may be repeated in other satellites, is that this small war could not become a large war without the active intervention of the United States.

Only military action by the United States, the most powerful and independent of Russia's opponents, could give any substance to the parallel so often drawn between what has been happening in Hungary and the resistance movements of occupied Europe in World War II. These resistance movements started early in the German occupation. But heroic and gallant as the latter were from the outset, they did not really trouble the high command of the German armed forces until two conditions were fulfilled.

The first of these was the supply of arms, information and wireless sets from Britain and the United States. The second was the arrival in Europe, roughly from the summer of 1943 onward, of Allied forces whose presence encouraged hope of final victory. These conditions presented a portion of the peoples of the occupied nations with the material and psychological elements necessary to accelerate their long, brave fight against Nazi tyranny.

These conditions do not apply to Hungary today. However, there is a very good chance that, if the United States did intervene in the satellites, either through large-scale delivery of arms to patriot groups or through active military intervention in their support, a general war would result.

As for the Middle East, there is little reason to think that the Soviet Union would allow a war involving Egypt and other Arab states to lead Russia into a general war. But if active military operations by the Western powers spread into Turkey and Iran, two nations whose frontiers are contiguous with the Soviet Union's, then a situation similar to that in Eastern Europe would be created. Russia would feel bound to intervene militarily to protect its own frontier.

The prospects of a small war becoming a major war are greatest, then, when military operations involve nations on the periphery of the Soviet Union.

There are, of course, many reasons for this Russian policy. But the fundamental one is military. No Russian Government, given the strong, almost pathological, fear of the Russian people of invasion from the West, can allow the satellites to fall into unfriendly or even neutral hands. If we accept this premise, we must contemplate a series of small wars or punitive actions by the Soviet Union against any satellite states that show any independence. Similarly, I think we can expect that the reunification of Germany under political conditions hostile to the Soviet Union would lead immediately to the strengthening of ties between Russia and her fearful satellites and ultimately to military action against the united Germany.

In more general terms, there are other powerful arguments against the possibility of major war. Before we examine them, it is discomforting to recall that there always have been. In peace men have invariably consoled themselves with the thought that new weapons or fear of economic ruin made war impossible. None the less, governments have gone blithely to war and, in most instances, the crowds have been available to shout "*Nach Paris*" or "*A Berlin.*"

The argument now most often advanced against the possible outbreak of such a conflict is that nuclear weapons make it impossible, that each prospective combatant knows it could not win. This seems a fallacious argument when it is considered in the context of totalitarian behavior.

The Soviet Union has the same weapons as the West. And there is no reason to believe that the leaders of the Soviet Union accept the idea that Russia could not win a nuclear war with the United States.

If Russia decides to go to war with the United States the first punch may well be the last. It will be unannounced, catastrophic and directed not solely at major centers of the United States but at our principle bases abroad as well.

Thus, there are good reasons for believing that the pleasant equation, Western nuclear strength plus Soviet nuclear strength equals peace, is incorrect. Rather, the principle argument against the start of a major war under present world circumstances is political and economic.

What does the Soviet Union seek? Certainly, world domination by communism is the main objective. Nuclear war is one means of obtaining it, but a very costly one. There are other means.

The Soviet Union has studied Germany's two attempts to seize the mastery of Europe. One often overlooked lesson of World War I and World War II is that Germany was on its way to winning through political and economic means as much as or more than she could gain by war.

Even Hitler's dream of German hegemony in a Nazi Europe might have been realized, as the political influence of the Third Reich followed the expansion of the nations economic influence. But twice Germany tried the military short cut to the goal and twice she was defeated and turned back.

On the basis of Russian actions in the last three years it can be assumed that the Soviet Union has benefited from Germany's example. The opportunity for grasping world domination by economic and political means is even more promising for Russia now than it was for Germany in 1939.

Since then, India, Pakistan, Burma and Indonesia have emerged as nations in Asia. Egypt, Morocco and Tunisia are independent states in Africa and to the south one can hear, beneath the brash talk of the Boer burghers, a continent in ferment.

All these new nations, having thrown off alien rule, are receptive to influences from Moscow. They need technical and economic assistance and they are just as willing—often more willing—to take it from Communists as they are from capitalists.

Here, then, is a marvelous opportunity for the Soviet Union. Why should its rulers contemplate war with the United States, even though they may think that war could be won? If communism can be extended step by step into southern and southeastern Asia, up the Nile into black Africa and across the poverty-stricken North African littoral, soon there will be no need to fight. For Russia will have gained almost all that Communist doctrine proclaims as its goal.

The United States will then peer out into a greatly changed world. Raw materials and markets may become scarcer. American diplomatic influence in large areas of the world may dwindle. Old and trusted allies may turn eastward toward the Soviet Union and increase their economic dependence on the Eurasian colossus, believing that they can maintain their political independence just the same. Our isolation will increase. But it will be unwelcome. We must ask ourselves if in the last ten years we have demonstrated the moral resources to halt this process.

Basically, the argument against a major war now is simple: Why should the Soviet Union fight when, over the long run, which is how Russians consider their prospects, everything seems to be moving their way? It is an uncomfortable argument, but on the basis of the international situation it is a valid one.

Do the Russians accept the validity of the argument? Their whole policy over the last three years has indicated that they do.

Communist activity in Western Europe has been toned down. Why? Because if the Soviet Union gains control of the Middle East and all Asia by political and Economic means, Western Europe will have to dance to its tune anyway. The Soviet Union is seeking to expand its trade with the free nations of Western Europe. Why? Because its leaders know that economic ties between those nations and the Soviet Union may eventually prove stronger than their political ties with the United States. NATO already is falling apart, largely as a result of the withdrawal of the immediate military threat to the West.

The conclusion which must be drawn from this situation is that, although the Soviet Union is not heading toward military conflict and hence a major war seems remote, the West is in for a war just the same. To halt the Soviet Union's political, diplomatic, ideological and economic penetration of the uncommitted nations will demand as much ability, courage and, in the long run, sacrifice as a major war. It will also demand infinitely more patience.

From the military standpoint it can be safely said that world sentiment opposes war. But one-sixth of the globe and 200,000,000 people in the Soviet Union are being directed toward another kind of war. Certainly, the Soviet Union has its troubles at home and abroad. But to the leaders of Russia and their active lieutenants in the Communist party, the troubles in Hungary and the ills of their nation's agriculture and industry are only relatively minor impediments to fulfillment of a vast ideological blueprint. The chances are that they will go on fighting *their* kind of war.

The Shape of the Future

[66] The Human Condition: Prologue*

by HANNAH ARENDT

In 1957, an earth-born object made by man was launched into the universe, where for some weeks it circled the earth according to the same laws of gravitation that swing and keep in motion the celestial bodies— the sun, the moon, and the stars. To be sure, the man-made satellite was no moon or star, no heavenly body which could follow its circling path for a time span that to us mortals, bound by earthly time, lasts from eternity to eternity. Yet, for a time it managed to stay in the skies; it dwelt and moved in the proximity of the heavenly bodies as though it had been admitted tentatively to their sublime company.

This event, second in importance to no other, not even to the splitting of the atom, would have been greeted with unmitigated joy if it had not been for the uncomfortable military and political circumstances attending it. But, curiously enough, this joy was not triumphal; it was not pride or awe at the tremendousness of human power and mastery which filled the hearts of men, who now, when they looked up from the earth toward the skies, could behold there a thing of their own making. The immediate reaction, expressed on the spur of the moment, was relief about the first "step toward escape from men's imprisonment to the earth." And this strange statement, far from being the accidental slip of some American reporter, unwittingly echoed the extraordinary line which, more than twenty years ago, had been carved on the funeral obelisk for one of Russia's great scientists: "Mankind will not remain bound to the earth forever."

*Reprinted from *The Human Condition* by Hannah Arendt by permission of The University of Chicago Press. © 1958 by The University of Chicago.

Such feelings have been commonplace for some time. They show that men everywhere are by no means slow to catch up and adjust to scientific discoveries and technical developments, but that, on the contrary, they have outsped them by decades. Here, as in other respects, science has realized and affirmed what men anticipated in dreams that were neither wild nor idle. What is new is only that one of this country's most respectable newspapers finally brought to its front page what up to then had been buried in the highly non-respectable literature of science fiction (to which, unfortunately, nobody yet has paid the attention it deserves as a vehicle of mass sentiments and mass desires). The banality of the statement should not make us overlook how extraordinary in fact it was; for although Christians have spoken of the earth as a vale of tears and philosophers have looked upon their body as a prison of mind or soul, nobody in the history of mankind has ever conceived of the earth as a prison for men's bodies or shown such eagerness to go literally from here to the moon. Should the emancipation and secularization of the modern age, which began with a turning-away, not necessarily from God, but from a god who was the Father of men in heaven, end with an even more fateful repudiation of an Earth who was the Mother of all living creatures under the sky?

The earth is the very quintessence of the human condition, and earthly nature, for all we know, may be unique in the universe in providing human beings with a habitat in which they can move and breathe without effort and without artifice. The human artifice of the world separates human existence from all mere animal environment, but life itself is outside this artificial world, and through life man remains related to all other living organisms. For some time now, a great many scientific endeavors have been directed toward making life also "artificial," toward cutting the last tie through which even man belongs among the children of nature. It is the same desire to escape from imprisonment to the earth that is manifest in the attempt to create life in the test tube, in the desire to mix "frozen germ plasm from people of demonstrated ability under the microscope to produce superior human beings" and "to alter [their] size, shape and function"; and the wish to escape the human condition, I suspect, also underlies the hope to extend man's life-span far beyond the hundred-year limit.

This future man, whom the scientists tell us they will produce in no more than a hundred years, seems to be possessed by a rebellion against human existence as it has been given, a free gift from nowhere (secularly speaking), which he wishes to exchange, as it were, for something he has made himself. There is no reason to doubt our abilities to accomplish such an exchange, just as there is no reason to doubt our present ability to destroy all organic life on earth. The question is only whether we wish to use our new scientific and technical knowledge in this direction, and this question cannot be decided by scientific means; it is a political question of the first order and therefore can hardly be left to the decision of professional scientists or professional politicians.

While such possibilities still may lie in a distant future, the first boomerang effects of science's great triumphs have made themselves felt in a crisis within the natural sciences themselves. The trouble concerns the fect that the "truths" of the modern scientific world view, though they can be demonstrated in mathematical formulas and proved technologically, will no longer lend themselves to normal expression in speech and thought. The moment these "truths" are spoken of conceptually and coherently, the resulting statements will be "not perhaps as meaningless as a 'triangular circle,' but much more so than a 'winged lion'" (Erwin Schrödinger). We do not yet know whether this situation is final. But it could be that we, who are earth-bound creatures and have begun to act as though we were dwellers of the universe, will forever be unable to understand, that is, to think and speak about the things which nevertheless we are able to do. In this case, it would be as though our brain, which constitutes the physical, material condition of our thoughts, were unable to follow what we do, so that from now on we would indeed need artificial machines to do our thinking and speaking. If it should turn out to be true that knowledge (in the modern sense of know-how) and thought have parted company for good, then we would indeed become the helpless slaves, not so much of our machines as of our know-how, thoughtless creatures at the mercy of every gadget which is technically possible, no matter how murderous it is.

However, even apart from these last and yet uncertain consequences, the situation created by the sciences is of great political significance. Wherever the relevance of speech is at stake, matters become political by definition, for speech is what makes man a political being. If we would follow the advice, so frequently urged upon us, to adjust our cultural attitudes to the present status of scientific achievement, we would in all earnest adopt a way of life in which speech is no longer meaningful. For the sciences today have been forced to adopt a "language" of mathematical symbols which, though it was originally meant only as an abbreviation for spoken statements, now contains statements that in no way can be translated back into speech. The reason why it may be wise to distrust the political judgment of scientists *qua* scientists is not primarily their lack of "character"—that they did not refuse to develop atomic weapons—or their naïveté—that they did not understand that once these weapons were developed they would be the last to be consulted about their use—but precisely the fact that they move in a world where speech has lost its power. And whatever men do or know or experience can make sense only to the extent that it can be spoken about. There may be truths beyond speech, and they may be of great relevance to man in the singular, that is, to man in so far as he is not a political being, whatever else he may be. Men in the plural, that is, men in so far as they live and move and act in this world, can experience meaningfulness only because they can talk with and make sense to each other and to themselves.

Closer at hand and perhaps equally decisive is another no less threatening event. This is the advent of automation, which in a few decades probably will empty the factories and liberate mankind from its oldest and most natural burden, the burden of laboring and the bondage to necessity. Here, too, a fundamental aspect of the human condition is at stake, but the rebellion against it, the wish to be liberated from labor's "toil and trouble," is not modern but as old as recorded history. Freedom from labor itself is not new; it once belonged among the most firmly established privileges of the few. In this instance, it seems as though scientific progress and technical developments had been only taken advantage of to achieve something about which all former ages dreamed but which none had been able to realize.

However, this is so only in appearance. The modern age has carried with it a theoretical glorification of labor and has resulted in a factual transformation of the whole of society into a laboring society. The fulfilment of the wish, therefore, like the fulfilment of wishes in fairy tales, comes at a moment when it can only be self-defeating. It is a society of laborers which is about to be liberated from the fetters of labor, and this society does no longer know of those other higher and more meaningful activities for the sake of which this freedom would deserve to be won. Within this society, which is egalitarian because this is labor's way of making men live together, there is no class left, no aristocracy of either a political or spiritual nature from which a restoration of the other capacities of man could start anew. Even presidents, kings, and prime ministers think of their offices in terms of a job necessary for the life of society, and among the intellectuals, only solitary individuals are left who consider what they are doing in terms of work and not in terms of making a living. What we are confronted with is the prospect of a society of laborers without labor, that is, without the only activity left to them. Surely, nothing could be worse.

To these preoccupations and perplexities, this book does not offer an answer. Such answers are given every day, and they are matters of practical politics, subject to the agreement of many; they can never lie in theoretical considerations or the opinion of one person, as though we dealt here with problems for which only one solution is possible. What I propose in the following is a reconsideration of the human condition from the vantage point of our newest experiences and our most recent fears. This, obviously, is a matter of thought, and thoughtlessness—the heedless recklessness or hopeless confusion or complacent repetition of "truths" which have become trivial and empty—seems to me among the outstanding characteristics of our time. What I propose, therefore, is very simple: it is nothing more than to think what we are doing.

"What we are doing" is indeed the central theme of this book. It deals only with the most elementary articulations of the human condition, with those activities that traditionally, as well as according to current opinion, are within the range of every human being. For this and other reasons, the highest and perhaps purest activity of which men are capable, the activity of thinking, is left out of these present considerations. Systematically, therefore, the book is limited to a discussion of labor, work, and action, which forms its three central chapters. Historically, I deal in a last chapter with the modern age, and throughout the book with the various constellations within the hierarchy of activities as we know them from Western history.

However, the modern age is not the same as the modern world. Scientifically, the modern age which began in the seventeenth century came to an end at the beginning of the twentieth century; politically, the modern world, in which we live today, was born with the first atomic explosions. I do not discuss this modern world, against whose background this book was written. I confine myself, on the one hand, to an analysis of those general human capacities which grow out of the human condition and are permanent, that is, which cannot be irretrievably lost so long as the human condition itself is not changed. The purpose of the historical analysis, on the other hand, is to trace back modern world alienation, its twofold flight from the earth into the universe and from the world into the self, to its origins, in order to arrive at an understanding of the nature of society as it had developed and presented itself at the very moment when it was overcome by the advent of a new and yet unknown age.

[67]   *Planning for the Year 2000**

by J. BRONOWSKI

London

A specter is haunting the Western world—yes, today as in 1848. But it is no longer the one that was paraded in the Communist Manifesto. Today the name of the specter is automation.

In every industrial country, men are looking with alarm at the installation of new automatic machines. They see the machines taking over work which, until a few years ago, seemed to need the most delicate human judgment. For the new machines do not merely replace the brute power of the muscle—machines have been doing that for nearly 200 years, ever since first the water wheel and then the steam engine were brought into the factory. The new machines are beginning to replace a gift which is neater and more specifically human: the ability of the eye to measure, of the hand to adjust, of the brain to compare and to choose. When the Luddites smashed factory engines in 1811, they were fighting, hopelessly, against their mere physical power, which dwarfs the strength and with it the output of a man. But the specter of automation points its long shadow at his intellect.

In the United States as in England, and in most industrial countries, the automatic control of machine operations has gone farthest in the making of motor cars. This may be because, whenever anybody wants a car, everybody wants one; and alas, it is equally true that whenever anybody does not want a car, then all at once nobody wants one. That is, the motor industry is peculiarly sensitive to good times and to bad times; and in England, it was putting in automatic machines just when the times turned abruptly from good to bad. The result was panic among employers, a bitter but divided strike by the workmen, and bewilderment (heavily lathered with platitudes) in the Government. No one is clear whether the dispute reached back to automation, or was merely a by-product of the credit squeeze; and was the strike a protest against *any* dismissal of workers, or only against their sudden dismissal?

Questions like these are never answered in the day-to-day of politics. A compromise is reached, a crisis is settled for the moment; and when the next crisis comes, we suddenly find that what had been a midnight

*From *The Nation*, March 22, 1958, pp. 248-250. Reprinted by permission.

compromise has become a permanent principle. For example, the strike of Britain's auto workers was settled by paying some of them compensation for the loss of their jobs. This is a new principle in English industry. Is it really good government, is it good sense, to invent such a principle on the spur of the moment in order to get on with the export of motor cars?

There are political thinkers who believe that it *is* good sense, or at least that it is inevitable, that issues are decided in this way. They say that all acts of state are particular acts, and that they do not conform to a principle but rather, one by one, combine to form the principle which wise historians read into them after the event. It is useless, these thinkers say, to ask statesmen in advance whether men who are displaced by machines should or should not be paid compensation: that will be decided at the historical moment when the change comes, almost by accident, by the strength of the two sides, and by the social backing they can muster.

But surely it is possible for men, even if they are historians, to be wise before the event. I think that there are some changes in the structure of our society which can be foreseen now. It can be foreseen that in the year 2,000 more people will do one kind of job and fewer will do another; that one kind of thing will be valued and another will not. That is, we can draw now the bony skeleton of any industrial society in the year 2,000. It may be a world society or a city state; it may live in a settled peace or still under the threat of war; it may be democratic or totalitarian. Whatever it is, I believe that life in it will have certain large features.

First, it is of course plain that everyone will have at his elbow several times more mechanical energy than he has today. The population of the world must be expected nearly to double itself by the year 2,000. But the rate at which energy is being added, particularly in the industrial countries, is much faster than this. The four billion people who will be alive in the year 2,000 will not all have the energy standard of Western Europe today, where every inhabitant commands the mechanical equivalent of about five tons of coal a year. But they can be expected to average about half this standard—say, the equivalent each of two tons of coal a year.

The use of energy per head is closely linked with the standard of living, and the rise that I have forecast is therefore in itself the mark of a massive advance in living standards. But more than the crude figures, it is the whereabouts, the distribution of this energy that is significant. Most energy of this kind is generated in electric-power stations, and today these stations run, nearly all of them, on coal. The real difficulty in getting energy to Central India or Northern Australia or the Copper Belt in Africa is the difficulty of carrying coal there. In the year 2,000, the greater part of the world's electrical energy will be generated from nuclear fuels. A nuclear fuel such as uranium or heavy hydrogen is over a million times more concentrated than coal; one ton of it does the work of more than a million tons of coal. Therefore it will be possible to carry the fuel, and to generate the energy, wherever it is wanted. There will no longer be a reason for the great industrial concentrations in the Ruhr, in Northern England, and in the Eastern United States. And what is as important, it will at last be as simple to have energy for agriculture as for industry.

Second, there will be advances in biological knowledge as far-reaching as those that have been made in physics. For fifty years now, we have been dazzled by a golden rain of exciting and beautiful discoveries about matter and energy—the electron, the quantum, relativity, the splitting of the atom, the proton, the neutron, the mesons—the bright list seems to have no end. But do not let us be blinded by them to the work which has been done in the last twenty years in the control of disease and of heredity. We are only beginning to learn what happens when we use a selective killer of weeds or breed a new strain of corn, when we feed anti-biotics to pigs or attack a cattle pest. That is, we are only beginning to learn that we can control our biological environment as well as our physical one. For the year 2,000, this will be critical. Starvation has been prophesied twice to a growing world population: by Malthus about 1800, by Crookes about 1900. It was headed off the first time by taking agriculture to America, and the second time by using the new fertilizers. In the year 2,000, starvation will be headed off by the control of the diseases and the heredity of plants and animals—by shaping our own biological environment.

And third, I come back to the haunting theme of automation. The most common species in the factory today is the man who works or minds a simple machine—the operator. By the year 2,000, he will be as extinct as the hand-loom weaver and the dodo. The repetitive tasks of industry will be taken over by the machines, as the heavy tasks have been taken over long ago; and mental tedium will go the way of physical exhaustion. Today we still distinguish, even among repetitive jobs, between the skilled and the unskilled; but in the year 2,000, all repetition will be unskilled. We simply waste our time if we oppose this change; it is as inevitable as the year 2,000 itself—and just as neutral.

But its implications go very deep. For it will displace the clerk as well as the fitter; and the ability to balance a ledger will have no more value, or social status, than driving a rivet. This is the crux in the coming of automation, that it will shift the social standing of those who do different kinds of work. And this is why these speculations about the year 2,000 are in place: because the shift is already going on, and it is our business to foresee now where it is certain to take us.

In themselves, the changes I have described will not determine whether by the year 2,000 Africa will become industrialized, whether the nations will still be testing bombs, or whether we shall live under totalitarianism or under democracy. They will not even determine whether we shall live in large communities or small ones.

This last point is odd and easily overlooked, but I think that it is important. For 200 years now, it has been the rule that, as a nation has grown in industrial strength (and with it in industrial complexity), so more and more of its workers have had to move together into large cities. In the sixteenth century, Queen Elizabeth I of England passed laws to prevent the growth of London, yet today Greater London houses nearly one-fifth of the population of Britain, and carries on about a quarter of all her industries. The same process of industrial concentration has been at work in France, in Germany and in America.

There are several forces which prompt this process. One is the hunger of industry for power; and in the past, power has been cheap only where it has been made on a massive scale. A second force has been the growing specialization of agriculture. And a third has been the sheer physical need to have large numbers of people to handle manually semi-finished goods through the many stages of manufacture.

Not one of these reasons need have force fifty year from now. The atomic-power plant need not be large; if it can reasonably drive a submarine now, it can reasonably power a community then. In the same way, biological control of the heredity and the disease of plants and animals will make it possible in the year 2,000 to grow our food in smaller units. But potentially the most powerful influence on the size of future communities, of course, is the coming of automatic machines. They make it possible for a few men to take a complex product such as a drug or an engine through all the stages of its manufacture. By using automatic machines, quite small communities can live in the elaborate world of industry; and they can do so either as the makers of some one product for a nation or, what is more difficult, as units which are self-contained and self-sufficient.

I have stressed the change which is possible in the size of the community, because this happens to be an historical subject as well as a critical one. Back in the 1820s, the pioneer of an idealistic socialism in Britain, Robert Owen, insisted that the industrial revolution of his day ought in the end to lead to smaller, not larger, communities. He hoped that societies of between 1,000 and 1,500 people, working co-operatively, could survive, and he actually founded some in America. In the setting of his time, Robert Owen was premature; but he was not wrong. There are now industrial developments which open the way to smaller communities, if we choose to take that way. Atomic energy and automation are among them; and so are the radio-telephone and the helicopter and the microfilm, because they all help to make it possible for the man in the village to be physically and intellectually as well equipped as the man in the metropolis. The size of the future community really depends only on the rarest skill which it needs to support on the spot—the surgeon, the brilliant teacher, or the matinee idol. Fifty years from now, a community of 10,000 may well be large enough to afford that.

But what such a community cannot afford is the unskilled worker. The atomic-power plant, the agricultural station, the automatic factory—none of them has a place for him. In the small community, each unskilled man is a heavy burden.

In a profound sense, therefore, the choice ahead of us is this: If between now and the year 2,000, we can, step by step, turn the men who now do our repetitive work into men with individual skills, then we have a prospect of living in small and homogeneous communities. But if we remain with a large reservoir of unskilled men, then society will continue to move towards larger and larger concentrations.

To my mind this is a profound political choice; it is the choice which we must make now, every day, in a hundred tiny actions. We are about to have introduced, day by day, here and there, another and another automatic machine. One will do the work of ten typesetters, another will displace a hundred auto workers; and soon, a third will take the place of a thousand clerks. I have said repeatedly that automation today is coming to do the work of the brain, and therefore is taking the place of the white collar worker. If these men are permanently reduced to unskilled work, they will become the material for a new army of Brownshirts. Hitler's squads were recruited in just this way, from unemployed men whose collars had once been white.

That is already the danger in the short term. And it remains a danger in the long term, too, threatening the generations ahead of us. If we allow the survival of a permanent reservoir of unskilled workers, then we do two things: we insure that our cities will get larger and larger; and we connive at a permanent war in society between the skilled and the unskilled. It seems to me most likely that a society of this kind, concentrated in large units and divided between top dogs and under dogs, will fall into a totalitarian form of government. I do not need to look to the year 2,000 for that; George Orwell looked only so far as 1984, and saw it.

Technical foresight is a necessity; our political actions depend on it. And they do not depend on taking the short view; they depend on the long view, on looking far beyond the years of which we can speak positively— they depend on seeing the large features of a future whose detail is still unformed. We cannot escape the large bony features: atomic energy, biological control, automation. But the body of society is not all bone; a good many different bodies clothe that skeleton. It is possible on that skeleton to have either a totalitarian or a democratic society. I think that it can be foreseen that the future society will be totalitarian if it contains many unskilled men working in large cities, and will be democratic if it consists of skilled men working in small communities.

Changes toward one or another of these future schemes are not brought about by some instant illumination, a thunderclap of universal conversion. They are brought about by our small daily acts, if we know in what direction we are trying to act. And I have given two general directions to which we should bend whatever we do, whenever we have the choice.

[68] *The Economic Revolution**

by BARBARA WARD

Three quarters of the human race today is involved in a vast movement of revolutionary economic upheaval. They are attempting to modernize their economies—to move from the old patterns of static agriculture and limited commerce which made up the general pattern of the human economy for millennia on to the new productive, dynamic economy of modern industry, technology and science. The change is not so much a matter of choice as of stark necessity. Everywhere among the emergent peoples,

*From *The Saturday Evening Post*, May 14, 1960, pp. 43, 52, 57-58, *passim*. Reprinted by permission of the author.

populations are doubling every generation or so. Resources must at least keep pace if even present standards are to be maintained—and these, incidentally, allow each person an average income of no more than $120 a year. If life is to be a little more secure and healthy, a little better nourished, housed and clothed, a trebling of resources would hardly be sufficient. But there is no possibility of such expansion under the old economic methods. Static agriculture has only one means of growth—to take in more land. But in most of Asia there is no more land. Unless economic methods are radically recast, the outcome in the next forty years must be deepening misery, anarchy and despair.

This world-wide revolution of economic modernization is one in which the wealthy West is fundamentally involved. It was in the Atlantic area that the revolution began. It was under western influence that the first impact of the new methods reached the other continents and determined decisively the conditions under which they in their turn would seek to modernize their economies. Thus to ignore or to be indifferent to the present world-wide movement of economic change would be the equivalent of canceling at least 300 years of western experience. Worse, it would entail withdrawal from the greatest contemporary human effort to remold society and remake the face of the earth. And it is a fact of history that those who seek to withdraw from its great experiments usually end by being overwhelmed in them.

We cannot fix a date for the origins of the modern economic revolution. A hundred different conditions, influences and decisions set it in motion, and the changes came cumulatively over several centuries. In part, it was rooted in medieval Europe's constitutional development which gave the merchant what he never had in the Orient—status, security and inducements to save. Calvinism played its part, teaching that hard work in pursuit of profit was blessed by God and that money so earned should be saved, not spent in luxury. The scientific temper of the eighteenth century encouraged progressive landowners and aspiring artisans to experiment with new methods of production. In Britain toward the end of the eighteenth century all these separate streams—of acquisitiveness, of work, of invention—had begun to flow together into that flood of economic and technological change which we loosely call the Industrial Revolution.

The men who made this revolution did not know what they were doing in any general sense. Each pursued his own interest and profit, and the sum of interests made up the working of the system. But with our hindsight we can disentangle the essential principles, the changes without which dynamic growth is impossible—the preconditions, therefore, of modernization anywhere else.

The two most important principles underlying the revolution of economic growth are productivity and saving. Productivity results from any method which helps men to produce more goods for the same output of effort and resources. The decisive changes in productivity in Britain's early industrial revolution were better agricultural methods and the application of a new form of power—steam from coal—to machines made by new processes of iron founding. The new machines began to flood the market with cheaper consumer goods—which incidentally wiped out handicrafts imported from Asia. Expanding trade created the need for better transport, bigger towns and harbors. New industrial techniques called for steadily increasing education.

These were the first steps. Since then invention has multiplied a thousandfold the effect of every instrument of growth. Above all, vast new sources of energy have been discovered—electricity, the atom. But the basic requirements of modernization have not changed. Now, as then, they are better farming, more education, "infrastructure"—roads, power, ports—and industrialization.

All these techniques of greater production depend upon saving—that is, upon the postponement of consumption. In the eighteenth century, Coke of Holkham postponed direct returns on his farms when he experimented with crop rotation. The fourfold increase in output paid him back handsomely and provided capital for further ventures. Similarly, when the duke of Bridgewater built the first canal to Lancashire, he took laborers and materials away from the immediate tasks of farming. When, as a result of the saving on transport, the price of coal in Manchester was halved, resources were available to recompense the duke and to provide for further experiment. John Wilkinson used his savings—and other people's—all his life to pioneer new methods of iron founding and new uses for cast iron. One result was the steam engine and the first fundamental revolution in energy, that greatest of all sources of productivity.

Even the most primitive economies save a little—putting aside seed corn for the next harvest. Perhaps 5 per cent of national income is saved in this way. Economists reckon that, as a general rule, when the level of productive saving has reached about 15 per cent of national income, the economy has reached the point of "break-through" and can generate each year enough savings to insure the expansion of both savings and consumption in the future. This process—the process of self-sustaining growth—is the ultimate objective of all developing economies today.

One can see that it works in a cumulative way. The more techniques of progress there are—better methods, more powerful machines, more skilled labor—the easier it is to save. Yet there is always a period during which the original investments have to be made. Consumption is postponed for the first investment in better farming, for the first machines, for the first expansion in power. As a general rule, increases in capital at this stage have come from agriculture because in all pre-industrial societies farming is the occupation of nearly 90 per cent of the people. And the chances are that the process will entail great hardships for them. Saving is, after all, not-consuming. Farming people in a static economy are not, in general, very rich. Their surpluses are small. If they are to consume less and send off their surplus to the towns, they are likely to be poorer, unless—as in America and later in Japan—farming is actually expanding at the time of the transfer.

Nor is this the end of the difficulties inherent in beginning to save. If in Britain after 1810 all the output of the new machines had been consumed at once by the thousands of workers herding into the new industrial cities, there would have been no margin for further expansion. The organizers of the new wealth—the rising industrialists, the bankers, the landowners—kept the surplus created by the machines and devoted it to increased investment. In Britain between 1820 and 1860, little of the new production directly benefited the bulk of the workers. It was not until the system was fully established and goods began to pour out from the new processes—and workers themselves were beginning to organize and bargain for better wages—that a general rise in living standards began.

Since then Britain's national income has increased on the average by more than 3 per cent a year; and this is the general figure for the industrial West. In recent decades the pace has even quickened a little owing to higher levels of investment, both public and private, and new methods in technology. Today, therefore, the harsh times of original saving are quite forgotten. America's 176,000,000 people enjoy a national income of nearly $500,000,000,000. For years now 15 per cent and more of this income has been set aside for further investment while the citizens' own consumption has steadily increased. But in free Asia, in Africa and Latin America more than 1,000,000,000 people have a total income of only $120,000,000,000. Take 15 per cent of this for investment, and every form of consumption has to be cut. Saving is as harsh a discipline as it was in Britain in the 1850's. In fact, it is harsher, for the pressure of population is greater and the task of cutting consumption correspondingly more drastic.

It is in the context of these early grinding days of forced saving that we can best grasp both the origins and the continued appeal of Communism.

All Marx's thinking was conditioned by the grim conditions of early industry in Britain. His contemporaries, as we have seen, had no very clear picture of the forces molding the new economy—nor apparently had Marx. He saw that a vast release of productive forces was taking place and gave the industrialists credit for it. But his attention and energy were fixed on the appalling conditions of the workers, and he denounced, like an ancient Hebrew prophet, the ugly fact of exploitation.

In part, he was right. The organizers of the new wealth were undoubtedly rewarding themselves handsomely—as commissars were to do a century later. But he missed the other facet of their policy—that the saving sweated from the workers provided the necessary capital for extending the whole base of the economy. In fact, Marx did not grasp *how* in practical terms a modern industrial society had to be built. He assumed that the *bourgeoisie* would first look after that; then the workers would take over a functioning machine once their deepening misery had driven them to revolt. There are thus no blueprints in *Das Kapital* for a modern economy, and when in 1917 the Communists found themselves with the whole of Russia on their hands, it was to their own pragmatism, not to Communist theory, that they had to look for guidance.

Russia had some beginnings of modernization. But the country was flattened by war and revolution. The first efforts of Communism—turning the factories over to the workers—made the confusion worse. In 1921 Lenin in fact decreed a modified acceptance of the market economy, hoping that peasants and traders would get the economy somehow back into motion. But by this time a fully integrated industrial society existed in the West which could be copied. The tremendous armaments built up by governments in the First World War showed what central direction could do to accelerate heavy industry and to mobilize the people's savings and work. It was Stalin's fateful achievement to use total state power to transpose to Russia the techniques of production evolved in the industrial West. The first Five Year Plan and its successors established the "infrastructure" and the heavy industry of a modern advanced economy by government fiat. At the same time it set in motion the vast schemes for education which would keep trained manpower in step with the machines. At first technicians and engineers were borrowed from abroad. But within a decade Russian development was self-sufficient. The break-through had been achieved—and at horrifying cost.

Communist Russia could not, any more than could capitalist Britain, avoid the iron necessity of beginning to save. There had to be capital—for the new sources of energy, the new factories, the new machines—and only the people at large could do the saving. But driven by his totalitarian daemon, Stalin pushed the percentage of national income devoted to saving far above the western figure. He compelled the Russians to save not 15 but 25 to 30 per cent of the fruits of their labors. Nor was this the end of the matter. Fearing an independent peasantry, he forced the farms to deliver their entire surplus to the government. They revolted, killed their animals and starved during the terrible imposition of collective farming. Far from agricultural techniques improving, output actually fell. But relentlessly the saving went on. Conditions in Russian farms and Russian cities were more appalling than in Victorian slums. Consumption was less, the "trickle down" even slower. For a decade at least, the great foes of exploitation exploited their own people as no capitalist had ever done, and squeezed out of them the last kopeck of saving.

But this is only one side of the story. Russian modernization was accomplished at breakneck speed. It had advanced far enough by 1941 to withstand Hitler's invasion. It achieved prodigies of postwar reconstruction. It has driven expansion onward at a rate of some 7 per cent a year. In four decades it has come within sight of America's military and industrial power. Today, even consumption is at last improving. To the peoples in emergent lands the speed and vigor of the transformation, accomplished in so few decades, is a matter of hope as well as fear. The times of iron discipline and ruthless saving in Russia are receding. What is more in evidence today is the growth and power. Inevitably the Soviet achievement seems to present an alternative to the slower traditional western method of reaching the point of "economic break-through." Among the preindustrial societies of today, China has already chosen the Russian route. And few other governments can hope to escape indefinitely from the dilemma of this choice.

The western nations are more or less aware of how much they, too, have at stake in the decision. If a third of the human race despaired of the open society with its flexible experimental methods and mild disciplines, and chose instead the iron path of total Communist control, the balance of freedom in the world would be perilously upset. Not only would the emergent peoples lose their liberty. The West itself might suffer from that loss of nerve and breakdown in confidence which occurs when societies have the impression that their ways are not the ways of the future—that history is leaving them behind.

What is perhaps less clearly realized is the extent to which the West has influenced and, if it will, can still influence the outcome. The conditions today under which the emergent peoples are trying to modernize their economies have been brought about almost entirely by western policies and western influence. As late as 1939 most of the world was still controlled either by settlers of European stock—as in all of America —or by the colonial rulers of the same origin. In Asia, it is true, the westerners came out to trade, and it was only where local authority collapsed—as in Java and India—that they took over political control. But their economic influence undermined Manchu power in China, and Japan could not have resisted them after 1850 if it had not forcefully westernized itself. In short, western control or western influence determined virtually the entire pattern of development in Asia from the seventeenth century to the end of the last war. Africa in the last hundred years has similarly been under total western domination.

The western contribution to the four levers of modernization proved uneven. Peasant agriculture remained static, and the new plantations mainly benefited western interests. Modern education began—especially in India—but in 1936 there were still only 516 university students among Java's 40,000,000 people. A start was made on infrastructure, roads, railways, ports and power—again, India led the rest—but industrialization lagged far behind.

At this point we reach one of the consequences of the western impact which, though unintended, may have given a decisive setback to Asian development. Until the nineteenth century China and India were exporters to Europe of manufactures—hand-loom textiles, silks, pottery. In addition, peasant income all through the vast countryside was supplemented by local handicrafts. In Britain such centers of artisan enterprise were often the starting points of mechanized industry. In Japan after 1870, they were to prove so again as thousands of small workshops were moving to production with power and machines. But in India and China as the nineteenth century developed, this widespread preindustrial system of manufacture was wiped out by the flooding in of machine-made textiles and gadgets from the West. Local centers were extinguished. Peasant income fell. Indigenous growth ceased. Later in the century, modern factory industry began; but often, as in China, it was overwhelmingly foreign. In India, given Britain's doctrines of free trade and *laissez-faire,* Indian enterprise did not secure full tariff protection until after the First World War. Industrialization was thus slow in spreading and would have been even slower if two world wars had not hastened it a little.

The small extent to which modernization was encouraged by western colonial control can best be illustrated by the opposite experience of Japan, the one Asian country to exclude the westerners. After 1870, a policy of thoroughgoing modernization was carried through by the Japanese themselves. A land reform gave the peasant a stake in production, extension services helped him to increase output by 50 per cent between 1870 and 1910. Most of this surplus was transferred to the towns, where the state expanded roads and ports, railways and power, began a drive for universal literacy, sent young men overseas to train, established industries, sold back the big concerns to the clans—the Zaibatsu—and encouraged cottage industry to supplement them. Every lever of modernization was thus brought into service, and in a few decades the Japanese economy was within sight of self-sustaining growth, saving enough each year to increase the volume of savings thereafter—and this in spite of a population which was increasing as rapidly as any in Asia.

We cannot fairly assess the western impact without this background of population pressure. China already had a vast population and gross rural poverty when western economic influence became predominant after 1850. But in India and Java it was western control that helped the spurt. A hundred years of peace probably doubled India's population between 1800 and 1900. In Java the numbers grew from just over 3,000,-000 in 1795 to nearly 30,000,000 by 1914. In the twentieth century, sanitation and medical services began to speed the rate of growth. Keeping pace with this increase would have required measures as vigorous as those of Japan to insure that economy and population grew together, each kind of growth stimulating the other as it did in the West. But under the impact of partial modernization—which best sums up Asia's western inheritance—population growth in most of the Asian countries began to accelerate before the economy had reached a position of self-sustaining growth. And this is perhaps the most fateful of all the legacies from the West.

Saving, it must be repeated, means not-consuming. The more mouths there are to feed in a static economy, the harder it is to postpone consumption. The only answer is to save more drastically and thus achieve growth. But how can this drastic saving be done when—after a century of rapid growth in population, combined with economic stagnancy— per-capita income has sunk to the margin? How can a government increase savings to 15 per cent of national income if—as in India—the citizen's average income is only sixty dollars? This is the dilemma which most of Asia has inherited from the West. And this is the dilemma which could lead—as it has done in China—to the choice of the Communist alternative. In Communist discipline, in Communist techniques of forced accumulation, in Communist readiness to wring the last ounce of saving from the countryside, there seems to be a possible escape from the Asian impasse.

Equally the dilemma of saving could give the key to an effective western policy. The broad aim over the next two or three decades should be to bring the flow of investment in the emergent lands up to the level needed for self-sustaining growth. Thereafter there would continue to be foreign investment on a normal business basis; but the period of emergency help, designed to overcome the obstacles created by partial modernization, would have to come to an end.

If the present position is taken as a starting point, one can broadly estimate that the emergent peoples in the free world—1,000,000,000 of them—with their annual income of about $120,000,000,000, manage to save the 5 per cent traditional in static economies. To this $6,000,000,000 is added each year about $3,000,000,000 of outside capital, public and private. These figures are roughly half of what is needed. But they cannot be doubled immediately because the local people lack the margins for tougher saving and because the ground is not yet prepared—in public utilities, in transportation, in technical training—to absorb a sudden startling increase from outside.

The process is essentially long term. But a reasonable aim might be to double the flow of capital from outside over the next two decades. If this extra injection of saving—of the order of $6,000,000,000 a year, both public and private—were used to increase local skills and infrastructure, domestic capacity to save would certainly increase, although a doubling of the level is perhaps too optimistic. But even if domestic savings increased by 50 per cent over the ten years, the next decade would open with total savings at least within sight of the goal of 15 per cent of national income. The second decade could complete the transformation of the local economies, and thereafter special assistance would taper off.

Such a scheme is, of course, no more than a statement of intent. The actual content of the program would vary from country to country and region to region, and would reflect the varying degrees of modernization achieved during the period of direct western control or influence.

Since the old colonial governments were not very active in the field of basic agriculture, most underdeveloped areas require at least a quintupling of expenditure on the land so that men and resources can be transferred from it to other sectors without imposing Stalinlike controls. Education, particularly in Africa, also needs really ambitious expansion. On the other hand, the colonial record of infrastructure is normally more lavish. Roads, railways, public utilities exist. It is usually a question not of starting from scratch, but of extending an existing system sufficiently to permit a frontal attack upon industrialization. Infrastructure is, incidentally, pre-eminently an aria for public investment, since private enterprise is not attracted by the low returns over long periods which public services provide.

The sphere of private enterprise now as in the past is likely to be the development of raw materials for export and all the myriad forms of industry—processing plants, consumer goods—which expanding wealth can support.

Not all the emergent peoples are ready for all these policies at once, but where—as in India—much of the infrastructure in both men and services already exists, investment plans can be more immediate and ambitious, and outside assistance can be mobilized on a larger scale. In fact, India might well be made the model of a speedy, efficient, coordinated effort of internal investment and outside help. In spite of their desperate poverty, the Indians have increased their domestic savings by 50 per cent in the last decade and hope to have doubled the annual rate by 1966. Even so, it still falls below the 15 per cent needed for self-sustaining growth. If, however, outside capital from all sources—public, private, international, national—could reach $1,000,000,000 a year during the third Five Year Plan, the point of break-through would be in sight at the end of the period; and the largest free community in Asia, in which live 40 per cent of the free world's emergent peoples, would have demonstrated that without totalitarian discipline, without the suppression of freedom or the imposition of forced saving on a murderous scale, an underdeveloped land can achieve full modernization and the possibility of sustained growth.

There is one proviso to this hope. At some point in the next decades there must be a check to the rate at which India's population is increasing—a need of which the Indian Government is well aware. But, in fact, the connection between rapid economic development and a more stable birth rate is exceedingly close. In a desperately poor society the birth of many children is an insurance against tragic rates of infantile mortality and, in some measure, an economic investment as well. It is only when parents, convinced of the chance of better health and rising standards, can hope to give their children surer prospects of survival and nurture, that they will feel inclined to raise a smaller family. It need hardly be stressed that in a free society, whatever measures are pursued by government, the decisive choice rests with the parents. Thus—as in the West—a measure of economic advance and expectation is virtually a precondition of a slackening in the population's rate of growth.

A target therefore may be set for the western nations of $5,000,000,000 to $6,000,000,000 a year in investment of all forms—public and private, from national and international agencies—with an immediate plan to allot $1,000,000,000 of this sum each year to India's crucial experiment in growth. That such an aim is easily within the West's resources requires little demonstration. It is no more than 1 per cent of the combined national incomes of the western nations; and since the recent rate of growth of these incomes is of the order of 4 per cent a year, to allot 1 per cent to a world investment project requires no diversion of resources. It merely entails a slight postponement in the rate at which consumption is actually increasing. To call this a strain or a sacrifice is an abuse of language.

But the mere availability of resources will not determine the result. The fundamental political question has to be decided—whether or not the western powers accept the need for a sustained, long-term policy of world investment and world growth. The arguments from self-interest seem overwhelming. We are beginning—after a decade of uncertainty—to see that the direct political appeal of Communism is on the wane. Hungary and Tibet are reminders that Communism can be the stalking horse of a new form of imperial control. Communism's chief appeal is therefore social and economic—that it can throw out the landlords, revolutionize agriculture, build industries at breakneck speed and achieve modernization in a decade. To people caught in the impasse between saving and rising population, its techniques of forced accumulation can still appeal—unless there is an alternative, the alternative of western aid. Sustained world investment is thus a fundamental weapon in the struggle against Communist expansion. . . .

But more than national security is at stake. In this century, owing to the work of historians and archivists, of archaeologists and explorers, we know more than men have ever known about the fate of civilizations. Our western forefathers could take their society for granted as the end product of a unique historical progress in which, little by little, the inventiveness and faith of free men had come to set up a world society under western influence and control. Today we know that progress is at best a fluctuating line; and that along the march of humanity many proud experiments in political organization, many essays in empire, many great and affluent societies have foundered by the way. We know, too, that again and again they failed not from an inherent lack of means and resources, but from something more subtle—a failure of the spirit, a loss of nerve or faith or inner control. . . .

There is no greater defeat for a man or a society than to set a great experiment in motion and then to abandon it before it is half done. The modernization of the world is such an experiment. Casually, unconsciously, but with deadly effectiveness, western man all round the globe destroyed the traditional gods and the ancient societies with his commerce and his science. Now that the old world is dead, is he to make no special effort to bring the new world to life? He has plowed up the continents and scattered the seeds of new methods and hopes and ambitions. Is he indifferent to the harvest? Does it mean nothing to him if great areas of the world, where western influence has been predominant, emerge from this tutelage unable to return to the old life, yet unfitted for the new? It is hard to believe that the future could ever belong to men demonstrating irresponsibility on so vast a scale.

But the greatest challenge is also the simplest. The element above all others which western man has brought into history is the belief in its moral dimensions. When one considers the rise and fall of empires, the predatory imperialism, the violence, the irrational destructiveness which has marked so much of mankind's story, one is tempted to see in it only "sound and fury, signifying nothing." But in the Christian, rational and humane tradition of the West, the attempt has been made to rescue wider and wider areas of human existence from the tyranny of man's grasping, irrational and violent instincts—and a fundamental element in this search for moral order, of which Communism itself is a perverted by-product, is the belief that men should not prey on other men but that they are, in very truth, their brother's keeper.

In the past this principle has been limited by the few resources available in any society for active help. Private charity could lessen misery, but the levers of economic growth were not available for a frontal attack on poverty itself. The Industrial Revolution has removed this inhibition. Within western society the principle that the wealthier, luckier and healthier should assist the less privileged to acquire the education and well-being needed to advance themselves—the principle of general welfare —has brought about a wider and wider sharing of the new wealth.

Today resources exist in such abundance that a world-wide extension of the principle of welfare is physically possible. All that is lacking is the political decision to do so. Is it possible that a society which boasts of its humanity and its Christian inspiration should ignore the challenge? Is it conceivable that such a society, having done so, should deserve to survive?

[69] *The Future As History**

by ROBERT L. HEILBRONER

I. A RECAPITULATION

We have been concerned with the great currents by which the future environment is being shaped and formed. Now it is time to step back, and in the light of the historic outlook, to consider again a question with which we began our investigations. This is our *state of mind* about the future—the philosophy of expectations with which we orient ourselves to its challenges, and beyond them, to the sweep of history itself.

In the past, as we know, we have approached the future with the sustaining beliefs of a philosophy of optimism. That is, we have always conceived of the future in terms of its benignity, its malleability, its compatibility with our hopes and desires. But if our preceding pages have had any purpose, it has been to demonstrate the inadequacy of this belief today. It is no longer possible for America to commit itself trustingly into the hands of a deity of history whose agent forces are comfortably circumscribed and comfortingly familiar. If one thing is certain it is that history's forces have reached a power utterly unlike that of our sheltered past, and that the changes those forces portend are very different from the propitious historic transformations they brought about in our past.

Let us briefly recapitulate what some of those changes are likely to be:

1. As a consequence of the new weapons technology we have not only lost our accustomed military security, but also any possibility of enforcing a military "solution" to the problem of communism. The weapons stalemate has thus magnified the influence of the non-military determinants of the central struggle of our times. The "historic forces" of politics and economics, of technologies and ideologies, are therefore of crucial importance in the resolution of this contest.

2. The trend of these forces is not an encouraging one. In the huge continents to the East and South we have witnessed an explosive awakening of hitherto ignored or abused peoples, who now seek a rapid redress of their age-old grievances. This has led the underdeveloped nations into

a desperate effort for economic development—an effort which, in the environment of underdevelopment, turns naturally in the direction of economic collectivism. There are strong possibilities that this collectivism will veer far to the left, whether or not it falls directly under communist hegemony. It is likely as well to discard the frail structures of democracy, and to maintain its morale by an exaggerated nationalism. Finally, we must not ignore the possibility that American economic growth, by widening the gap between the underdeveloped peoples and ourselves, may place America at the focus of the frustration and resentments which economic development is likely at first to generate.

3. At the same time, the drift of Western society is itself away from the traditional forms of capitalism. In all nations, including our own, a framework of "socialist" planning is replacing the unregulated market mechanism. In Europe this drift into planning is made more significant by the fact that European capitalism, unlike American, is not a self-assured and unchallenged social order.

4. However, within our own nation there are strong tendencies which move us away from the traditional, and now perhaps nostalgic idea of American society. One of these is the rampant technological and scientific development which marks our time. This development manifests itself in a proliferation of institutions needed to "support" the increasingly dependent individual, and in the rise of bureaucratic apparatuses needed to control the technological machinery itself. The rise of the welfare state, on the one hand, and of the military bureaucracy, on the other, are instances of the manner in which technology is enforcing a socialization of life.

5. There are also visible other tendencies which are transforming our society, particularly in its economic aspect. There is a strong likelihood that a radical redefinition of the limits of public economic activity will be enforced by the pressure of events. Over the near future this is likely to be provided in disguised form by the enlarging military sector, but in the longer run we shall probably be forced to find civilian outlets to replace the military. Somewhat further ahead lies the still more difficult problem of providing internal economic discipline in a society in which the usual market control mechanisms are increasingly weakened by widespread social abundance.

6. All these collectivist trends are accelerated by our main historic movement—our growth. The problem then is the degree to which our blind economic momentum makes it impossible to respond effectively

to the technological, political, and economic forces which are bringing about a closing-in of our historic future. This is a question to which dogmatic answers cannot be given. But it must be pointed out that an effective control over the historic forces of our times would require changes not only in the structure of power but in the common denominator of values, which do not seem likely to occur, at least for a considerable period.

The probabilities, in other words, are that "history" will go against us for a long time, and that the trend of events, both at home and abroad, will persist in directions which we find inimical and uncongenial. It would be foolish to pretend to a degree of prescience about the future which no amount of analysis can provide, or to be doctrinaire about the evolution of events. Yet surely, to hope for the best in a situation where every indication leads us to expect a worsening, is hardly the way to fortify ourselves against the future. Optimism as a philosophy of historic expectations can no longer be considered a national virtue. It has become a dangerous national delusion.

But if our optimism fails and misleads us, what shall we put in its place? How shall we prepare ourselves for the oncoming challenges of the future? What might be the character of a philosophy suited to our times? These are the deeply meaningful questions to which we now turn.

2. THE FAILURES OF OPTIMISM

It may help us to formulate answers to these questions if we ask ourselves what it has been about the recent past for which optimism as a philosophy of historic expectations has failed to prepare us. The answer is explicit in the theme of this book. It is an outlook on the future *as history.*

This is not to say that optimism does not contain—albeit tacitly—an estimate of the future "as history." We have already endeavored to show its roots in the technological, political, and economic forces that have generated modern history, and its unconscious assumptions about the automatic progress which those forces effect. But what is missing from the philosophy of optimism is a conscious recognition of the special circumstances of history from which it arose and about which it generalizes. It is a failure to see itself as the product of a unique and sheltered historic experience which could not be enlarged into a model for all historic experience irrespective of its setting.

As a result, optimism has misled us in two particulars. First, it has caused us to overestimate the degree of our freedom in history. Because it mirrors an historic experience in which our conscious efforts to "make" history coincided with and were aided by the movement *of* history, optimism has given us the notion that history is only, or largely, the product of our volitions. Thus it has deluded us as to our power when the forces of history run not with, but counter to, our designs. It has filled us with a belief that everything is possible, and has made it not a sign of wisdom but a suspicion of weakness to think in terms of what is impossible.

Secondly, optimism has given us a simplistic idea of the forces of history. Assessing those forces in terms of their eighteenth- and nineteenth-century manifestations, it has failed to alert us to the possibility that the identical basic forces, in another environment, might lead to very different results from those which we assume to be their natural outcome. Thus the philosophy of optimism has presented the idea of technical progress solely in terms of the enhancement of man's productive powers—which was indeed its outstanding attribute in the past—rather than in terms of the social repercussions of technology which may well be its principal impact upon us in the present and future. Similarly, the optimistic outlook has taught us that the impetus of popular political aspiration leads naturally to the development of democratic governments, as it did in the cradle of history in which it was nurtured, but has failed to alert us as to the turning which those self-same aspirations can take—and have already taken—in an environment in which the preconditions for Western parliamentary democracy are totally absent. Finally, in the terms of the optimistic philosophy, the consequences of economic progress have been perhaps the most artlessly conceived of all. Quite aside from whether it correctly judged the outcome of the internal mechanics of capitalism, the optimistic outlook made economic advancement itself an unambiguous and self-evident social goal—a point of view which, however justified by the conditions of insufficiency of the nineteenth century, entirely obscures the new problems, both of organization and of values, which the achievement of abundance itself brings into being.

Thus if we are to suggest the attributes of a philosophy of expectations better adapted to our times than that of optimism, we shall have to explore more fully the two main areas in which optimism is deficient. First we shall have to ask: What is possible at this moment in our history? What are the limits of intervention into, what are the "necessities" of the historic process? Secondly, we shall have to inquire: What attributes of the forces of history are neglected by the philosophy of optimism? How can we prepare for their unexpected and often unwelcomed repercussions? In a word, how can we think about the future as history?

3. THE LIMITS OF THE POSSIBLE

Everyone who considers the first of these questions—what is "possible" and "impossible" in history—soon comes up against a classic dilemma. This is the dilemma of "free will"—or in terms of the historic process, of determinism versus historic freedom. It is the dilemma of choosing between a world where everything is "possible" and therefore where nothing can be counted on, including the most basic necessities for the continuance of the human community; and a world where nothing is possible, and therefore where nothing can be hoped for except that which is inevitably and immutably fixed and beyond alteration. It is a choice between history as chaos and history as a prison.

This is a dilemma which still exercises philosophers and historians. But the dilemma has more to do with the limitations of abstract thought than with the experience of history itself. For when we turn to the living reality of history, we do not encounter a dilemma, but a *problem*—which is a very different thing. And this problem is not to formulate the meaning of historic freedom in general and forever, but to determine in the light of the actualities of the moment how much of history lies within our grasp and how much lies beyond.

Once we approach the matter in this direct and pragmatic fashion, the idea of what is "possible" in history presents itself intelligibly enough before us. We then find ourselves confronted, as a condition of life, with a situation which may be logically awkward but which is not at all awkward as a fact. This is the coexistence of freedom and necessity in history— the simultaneous existence of its glacial imperturbability, its "laws," its "necessities" on the one hand, and its "freedom," its openness, its amenability to our wills on the other.

The point at which we can divide freedom from necessity also comes to us with reasonable clarity. We all know that there are some historic events—such as, for instance, the internal politics of Soviet rule—which it is virtually impossible for us to affect. We recognize another class of events that lie directly—or at least to an important degree—within the scope of our control and responsibility. The "possibility" of war, for instance, is a matter in which we are quite sure that our free decisions play an immense and probably determinative role—all the more so, since so many aspects of the "historic" situation clearly set the stage for war.

This is, however, only one way of assessing what is historically possible for us. For what we deem to be "historic events" by no means exhausts the aspects of change and development in history. As Karl Popper reminds us, "There is no history of mankind, there is only an indefinite number of histories of all kinds of aspects of human life";[1] and when we turn to those aspects of history with which this book has been primarily concerned—the aspects of social change rather than of immediate political conflict—we find our possibilities of history-making sharply curtailed. In our society, the "history" of technological progress and penetration, or the "history" of political belief and economic development are not facets of human life which we normally subject to "history-making" decisions. In general we allow these aspects of history to follow their autonomous courses, and to evolve by their unguided interactions. Thus we limit our idea of what is possible in history by excluding from our control the forces of history themselves.

This is a very different situation from that which obtains in a more collectivistic society. The enormous national effort of Russian growth or the wholesale alterations in the social structure of China are instances of historic change whose possibility was initially discounted by observers who had in mind the limitations of historic intervention in our own kind of society. The point, then, is that there are no fixed and immutable limits to what is historically possible. Rather, different organizations of society define for themselves the limits of what is and what is not within reach of conscious history-making choice. Authoritarian societies, as a generality, have a much more comprehensive direction of the "forces" of history than open societies. On the other hand, open societies, through their democratic apparatus, retain a wider degree of control over the course of their "heroic" history, i.e., over the policies of their leaders.

4. THE POSSIBILITIES BEFORE AMERICA

What does this imply for the "possibility" of altering the historic outlook that lies before us?

To the extent that we are concerned with those aspects of the future which will be molded by the anonymous forces of technology, political ideology, and economic evolution, we must accept the conclusion that the possibilities of major intervention are not great. For the portents of the future spring, in the main, from underlying pressures of ideologies and from the fixed structures of institutions whose conscious manipulation does not now lie within the reach of our accepted "history-making" pow-

[1] *The Open Society* (London, 1952), vol. II, p. 270.

ers. Of course we can make small changes in the superstructure of our institutions. But if, for example, we really want to undo the "creeping socialism" of our time, we should have to do more than legislate away our institutions of social welfare and economic control. To remove these institutions without removing the massive technology and the economic instability which have produced them would only be to open the way for a social explosion which would probably swing even further leftward. Essentially, the only way to halt the creep of "socialism" is to return to an atomistic economy with small-scale technical and economic units, and with a wholly different climate of political and social beliefs. This it is obviously impossible for us to attempt, without a degree of historic intervention which is entirely alien to our social philosophy.

It may even be that with the most violent assault upon "history," with the most revolutionary intervention into institutions and ideologies, it would still not be possible to reverse the basic direction of our historic momentum. In our time, we have seen extraordinary attempts to reshape the social forces of history, and extraordinary results in imposing a heroic, revolutionary will upon social history.[2] Yet the changes which were inaugurated were in nearly every instance in accord with the drift and temper of world history as a whole. There has been no successful revolution against the forces of technology, of popular political aspiration, and of socialism, although it is obvious that the slogans of "democracy" and "socialism" have been put to cruel use. No revolutionary has been able to preach anti-industrialism, or the inequality of classes, or the ideals of capitalism. Gandhi, who came closest to being an exception insofar as his dislike of technology was concerned, was nonetheless unable to keep India closed off from modern technology. The few nations which have sought to stand against the political trend—like Spain—have been in a state of exhaustion and have had no subsequent important historic development. There have been few major revolutions since 1945 which have not flown the banners of socialism.

Thus there seems indeed to be a basic character to world civilization in our times from which no vital historic effort can depart very far in its essentials, and the fact that even revolutions have had to conform to this pattern makes it unlikely in the extreme that a non-revolutionary society, such as our own, will succeed in resisting it. To what ultimate ends this "inevitable" direction of historic forces may carry society we do not know, for such questions take us far beyond the horizon of the "given" historic situation. What may be the final impact of science and technology on

[2] For an excellent discussion of this problem in general, cf. Sidney Hook, *The Hero in History* (Boston, 1943), esp. Chap. XII.

civilization, the end effect of our egalitarian political ideals, or the ultimate organization of collectivism, we do not know. All that we do know is that, for the moment, these general historic tendencies are firmly in the saddle, and that short of the profoundest change in the character of our civilization, or an incalculable redirection of events, they bid fair to dominate the social environment of the future.

But the fact that the *main direction* of historic movement is too deeply rooted to be turned aside does not mean that our future is therefore caught in a deterministic vise. It is not just necessity, but a mixture of necessity and freedom which, as always, confronts us as a condition of historic existence. If the idea of the future as history tells us what it is not "possible" for our kind of society to do, it also makes clear what *is* possible.

For example, the spreading hegemony of scientific technology may be an inescapable general tendency of our times, but the social consequences which we have previously discussed do not follow as an inescapable corollary. They are largely the result of *non-intervention* before the historic closing-in of science and technology. But non-intervention is not the only possible response to this historic force. It is rather a kind of abdication before the problem itself. It leads us to ignore the very thought that there may exist other controls over the technological revolution than the economic calculus which is at present our main device for regulating its admission into our lives. One need hardly say that a society which consistently ignored considerations of economics would seriously jeopardize its own well-being. But this does not mean that a society cannot, however imperfectly, attempt to weigh the non-economic advantages and disadvantages, the non-economic costs and benefits that seem likely to accrue from major alterations in its technological apparatus, and allow these considerations to balance, offset—and on occasion, even to veto—the guide of profitability. Thus the actual impact of science and technology on our social existence will depend not merely on the presence of these overriding forces in our age, but on the influence which we *unavoidably* exert on their social application—including the passive influence of permitting economic criteria to exert their sway largely unchallenged.

The same general conclusion is true with respect to the possibilities of influencing the other main forces which affect our future. There is little doubt, for instance, of the overwhelming power of popular aspirations in the underdeveloped nations, or of the likelihood that those aspirations, in the frustrating conditions of underdevelopment, will lead toward economic collectivism and political dictatorship. But the fact that there is very little we can do about this is very different from saying that we therefore have no control over this aspect of the future. On the contrary, it is only by understanding the "inevitable" outlook that we can hope to devise policies which have some chance of exerting a lasting and positive effect on the course of economic development. Similar alternatives confront us in dealing with the trend of all industrialized nations, ourselves included, toward some form of economic collectivism. To continue to set ourselves adamantly against this trend is to minimize rather than maximize our possible historic influence. The possibility poised by history is not that of denying the advent of planning, but of seizing control of it to assure the kind of collective economic responsibility we want.

Thus the outlook on the future as history does not pave the way for an attitude of passivity and still less for defeatism. Those who would reject the idea of the "inevitable" future for these reasons are in fact more likely to object to the bold measures to which it points as the only means of rescuing our future from the category of "inevitable fate." It is unquestionably true that the exercise of such historic control is fraught with risk. *But so is the exercise of non-control.* The issue is not the simple and clear-cut one of a greater or lesser freedom. It is the difficult and clouded choice of a subservience to the necessities imposed by the forces visibly at work in our midst, or the perilous freedom of an exercise of historic control over ourselves.

How we shall behave in the face of this difficult choice of historic paths, it is not easy to say. Whether in the end we shall remain passive before the enveloping changes of history, or attempt to adapt our institutions so as to minimize their impact, is a question whose answer inevitably involves subjective biases. The degree to which the "common sense," the "basic instincts" of the people can be relied upon, the flexibility and farsightedness of the powers that be—these are matters about which purely objective judgments are impossible. All that one can say is that the challenges are very subtle; that the requisite changes in institutions, while not revolutionary, are nonetheless very great; and that the required degree of farsightedness is correspondingly high. Thus it is not difficult to conclude that the possibilities of historic intervention will not, in fact, be put to use. A critic who assesses the American scene in terms of its alertness to the underlying challenges of our times can scarcely fail to be struck by the general poverty of the prevailing outlook: the men of wealth and power, mentally locked within their corporate privileges; the middle classes, more Bourbon than the Bourbons; the working classes, unable to formulate any social program of purpose beyond "getting theirs"; the academicians, blind to the irrationalities of the society they seek to rationalize.

Yet it is one of the disconcerting facts of an open society that it offers so many opportunities for facile generalizations and so little sure ground for generally valid ones. As long as there is still visible in American society a continuing evidence of new thought and dissent, a self-control with respect to the use of political power, and above all, a nagging awareness that all is not right, it would be arrogant and unjust to shrug away our future as a hopeless cause. There are, after all, great traditions of responsibility and social flexibility in America. In them there may yet reside the impetus to seize the historic possibilities before us, and to make those changes which may be necessary if the forces of history are not to sweep over us in an uncontrolled and destructive fashion. But it is useless to hope that this will happen so long as we persist in believing that in the future toward which we are blindiy careering everything is "possible," or that we can escape the ultimate responsibility of defining our limits of possibility for ourselves.

5. THE IDEA OF PROGRESS

In our last section we have been concerned with the problems of historic possibility and impossibility, of freedom and necessity, which a philosophy of optimism tends to obscure. Now we must turn to a second shortcoming of our traditional outlook on history. This is the tendency of our philosophy to present the workings of the forces of history in an overly simplified manner—a manner which has entirely failed to prepare us for the actual turnings which history has taken. If we are to sum up the shortcoming in a phrase it would be this: *The optimistic philosophy equates the movement of history's forces with the idea of progress.*

Whether there is such a thing as "progress" in history depends, of course, on what we mean by the word. It is clear enough that there has been, particularly in the last three centuries, a steady and cumulative accretion of technical virtuosity and scientific knowledge which permits us to speak of "progress" in these fields in a fairly specific sense. One particularly important aspect of this progress has been the measurable lengthening of the longevity of man and the improvement of his capacity to alleviate his bodily ills. A second instance of definable progress has been in the rise of the level of well-being of the masses in the West—although this can be said to be more than offset by an actual decline, over the last century, of the "well-being" of the teeming masses of the East. A third instance, less easily indexed, but no less demonstrable in the large, is the historic progress from a society in which man is born into his status toward a society in which he is able to define his status for himself.

It is with these aspects of the forces of history that optimism identifies progress, and so long as the meaning of "progress" is restricted to such reasonably definable movements, there can be no objection to the word. But it is also apparent that we cannot generalize from these specific concepts of progress to the larger idea of an all-embracing progress of "society." There is no reason to believe that today's private morality, level of social ethics, and general nobility of public ideals are in any sense superior to much of the recorded past, if indeed they are equal to the best of American Revolutionary times or to the heights reached in the golden ages of Greece and Rome. Our cultural and aesthetic public existence is hardly at an historic high point. And if, with all his gains in health, well-being, or status, the average person is "happier," more serenely or creatively engaged in life than in the past, this is not apparent in the happiness, serenity, or creativity of our age. We often imagine that "life" is much better today than, say, in the Dark Ages, but this depends very much on whose lives we conjure up in these two periods. After all, we live at a time when German brutality reached what may be, statistically, a record for the systematic extermination of life, and when Russian despotism at its worst took us back to the level of morality of the crueler Biblical kings.

Yet these somber considerations do not dispose of the idea of progress. Rather they raise the question: Why is it that the forces of history, which are indisputably the carriers of potentially beneficial political and economic and technological change, have not resulted in a corresponding improvement in the human condition? What are the attributes of these forces, as agents of change, which the optimistic philosophy glosses over? Let us try to identify some of these attributes which are omitted in the optimistic notion of progress.

6. THE INERTIA OF HISTORY

Because we live in a time of great change, and because our philosophy of optimism makes us expectant of and receptive to change, we may easily overlook a deeply important aspect of historic development. This is its quality of inertia. It is a quality which is manifest not only in resistance to change—although that is one of its more important aspects—but in the viscosity which is imparted to history because people tend to repeat and continue their ways of life as long as it is possible for them to do so.

We do not usually call inertia to mind when we seek the great molding forces of history. And yet this humble characteristic is responsible for more of "history" than all the campaigns, the movements, the revolutions we readily call to mind. The simple, but quintessential fact that human beings persist in living their lives in familiar ways, which are the only ways they know how, is the very lifeline of social continuity itself.

This inertia which exerts so powerful a drag on history undoubtedly has its biological and psychological roots. But it is more than just an "innate" human characteristic. It is also the outcome of the historic social condition of man. For the persistence of habit acts as a protective reflex for the overwhelming majority of men who know very little except that life is a fragile possession, and that tried and true ways, however onerous, have at least proved capable of sustaining it. A mulish perseverance in old ways is not without reason when life is lived at the brink of existence where a small error may spell disaster. An instance in point was provided some years ago when a team of United Nations agricultural experts sought in vain to persuade Turkish farmers to improve their crops by removing the stones from their fields. Finally a few of the younger ones consented—whereupon, to the chagrin of the experts, their yields promptly *declined*. In the arid climate of Turkey, the stones had served the function of helping to retain the scanty moisture in the soil.[3]

Inertia shows itself as well in a general reluctance to embrace new social ideas. Reformers throughout history have deplored the tenacity with which the privileged classes have clung to their prerogatives—even when it was no longer in their "best interests" to do so. This is not so surprising when we view the enormous gulf which has normally separated the privileged and the unprivileged. What is far more striking is the difficulty which reformers have had in making even the most miserable and oppressed classes "see" the inequity of their lot, and in persuading them to rise in protest. The fact that our historic glance is easily caught by a few *jacqueries* obscures the fact that revolutions are remarkable in history not for their frequency but for their rarity, even though the "normal" condition of man has always been harsh enough to warrant revolutionary sentiments. We must conclude that whenever it has been possible the human being has *wished* to believe in the rightness and fixity of the situation in which he has found himself.

The inertia of ideologies as well as of institutions is often taken as a lamentable fact. It is the despair of the social engineer, the *bête noir* of the utopian planner. Nonetheless we must remember that there is a constructive role which this inertia also plays. A society without ideological inertia would live from instant to instant in peril of a fatal turning. The fixity of our voting habits, our customary beliefs, our stubbornly held ideas, even when these are wrong, serves a purpose in protecting and

[3] *Cultural Patterns and Technical Change,* ed. Margaret Mead (New York, 1955), p. 186.

stabilizing the community. The reformer who despairs because people will not listen to reason forgets that it is this same suspicion of change which helps to prevent people from heeding the Pied Pipers for whom society never lacks. We may make progress only by freeing ourselves from the rut of the past, but without this rut an orderly society would hardly be possible in the first place.

This historic undertow of inertia warns us against facile conceptions of "progress" in two respects. In the first place it disabuses us of the notion of the "ease" of social change. For most of the world's peoples, who have known only the changelessness of history, such a stress on the difficulty of change would not be necessary. But for ourselves, whose outlook is conditioned by the extraordinary dynamism of our unique historic experience, it is a needed caution. Contrary to our generally accepted belief, change is not the rule but the exception in life. Whether it is imposed from above or imposes itself from below, change must reckon with the reluctance of humankind to relinquish habits not only of a lifetime, but of life itself. This is the reason why even such enormous transformations as those we have dealt with in this book are slow, stretched out over generations, invisible from one day to the next.

Second, the drag of inertia warns us against the overestimation of the effects of change. The optimistic conception of progress calls our attention to the sweeping improvements which can be brought about by technology or democracy or economic advance. All that is certainly true as far as it goes. No one can doubt the capacity of history's forces to legislate beneficial changes in society. But there is a level of social existence to which these forces penetrate last and least. This is the level at which "society" is visible only as the personal and private encounters of each of us with his fellow man. It is the level at which life is *lived,* rather than the level at which it is abstractly conceived.

Here, at this final level of personal experience, the inertia of history is most apparently manifest. It is here that the revolutionary, having brought about tremendous changes in "society," comes to grips with the petty irritations of inefficient colleagues and apathetic clerks, of the "human factor" which like sand in a machine, has wrecked so many well-planned enterprises. It is not that revolutions, or the more gradual changes of historic evolution, make these daily frictions of life any worse. It is rather that so much of life remains the same, regardless of the new boundaries in which it is contained.

In this grinding persistence of the "human factor" lies the reason for much of the disillusion which so frequently follows a passionate attempt to bring about social progress. As Ignazio Silone has written: "Political regimes come and go; bad habits remain." [4] The underlying sameness of life, the reassertion of old established ways, of "bad habits," is an aspect of history which must not be lost to sight amid the more dramatic changes of the superstructure of society. An appreciation of the fact of human inertia must not lead us to understate the extent to which change is possible in society, but it should caution us against identifying this change with the equivalent "progress" of human life at a fundamental level.

7. THE HERITAGE OF THE HUMAN CONDITION

We have seen that optimism misleads us with respect to the possibilities of "progress" because it tends to underestimate the difficulty and to overestimate the consequences of historic change. But it compounds that shortcoming with a second and perhaps even more important failure. This is its lack of realism as to our starting point in the making of history. It is its failure to confront truthfully and unflinchingly the condition of the human being as it now exists.

Optimism tacitly views that condition in a favorable light. The very assumption that the growth of technical skill, political equality, or economic well-being will automatically lead to "progress"—rather than to increased destructiveness, heightened social disorder, or vulgar opulence—already takes for granted an environment in which rationality, self-control, and dignity are paramount social attributes.

But this is hardly the impression one gets from an examination of the panorama of human existence. If there is such a thing as an average human being, he is to be found among the majority of mankind which lives in the continents of the East and South. The chasm which divides the average life on these continents from our own is so wide that we can barely imagine existence on the other side. To be an Indian villager, a Chinese peasant, an African mine-worker is to be in a human condition whose dark and narrow confines cannot be penetrated by a Western mind.

But life on our side of the chasm is also very far from presenting a heartening vista. In the United States, for example, preventable disease and even deformity are still widespread. Mental aberration identifiably touches a tenth of the population. Criminality, in various social forms from murder to tax evasion, is prevalent among all classes. The urban environment in which life is mainly lived is crowded, often unspeakably ugly, and in its spreading slums, vicious. The average education is barely adequate to allow the population to cope with the technological complexities of the age, and insufficient to allow all but a few to understand them.

[4] "The Choice of Comrades," *Voices of Dissent* (New York, 1958), p. 325.

Large numbers of families do not know or care how to raise their children, as witness the epidemic incidence of juvenile disorders.

The list could be extended without difficulty. But what characterizes many, if not all of these degradations of life, is that they are unnecessary. Most of them could be vastly alleviated by a sustained and wholehearted effort. Yet such an effort—as to whose immense "value" all would agree— seems impossible to undertake. Indeed, the very suggestion that these areas of need should carry an absolutely overriding priority, taking precedence over any and all more "profitable" activities, smacks of a suspicious radicalism. We are simply not concerned, beyond a mild lip-service, with mounting an all-out effort to raise the level of national health or civic virtue, or mass living conditions or average education or upbringing. Looking at some of the institutions we nourish and defend, it would not be difficult to maintain that our society is an immense stamping press for the careless production of underdeveloped and malformed human beings, and that, whatever it may claim to be, it is not a society fundamentally concerned with moral issues, with serious purposes, or with human dignity.

The point, however, is not to berate ourselves for our obvious failure to produce anything like a "good society." The point is rather that, with all its glaring and inexcusable failures, the United States is still probably the most favored and favorable place on earth for a child to be born and to grow up.

These melancholy facts must assume their rightful place in any evaluation of the prospects for "social progress." For in such a social atmosphere the forces of history do not lead automatically in the direction which optimism assumes. In an atmosphere of neglect of and indifference to human capabilities, it is not at all surprising that technology should result in the trivialization of life and the stultification of work. It is certainly not remarkable that, in the harsh and primitive setting of underdevelopment, popular political aspirations press toward extreme and violent "solutions" to the problems of underdevelopment; nor that, in the more advanced societies, they mold society in the image of the mediocrity of mind and sentiment they represent. Nor, given the prevalence of physical poverty in the backward nations and of psychological poverty in all nations, is the pre-eminence of materialistic drives and goals to be wondered at. In sum, today as in the past, the half-educated, half-emancipated state of human society assures that there will be a long continuation of the violence, the instability, the blatant injustice, which are the most grievous aspects of the human tragedy. This is the true heritage of the human condition, and its bitter legacy.

What is perhaps the most sorrowful aspect of this tragedy is that its victims are chosen arbitrarily and at random. There is no guilt or innocence, no measure of culpability or responsibility in the fate meted out by a world which is still more brute than man. Those who fall in wars do not "start" the wars. The victims of Hitler or Stalin were not those who raised these dictators to power. Nor will there be a fine balancing of accounts when the crimes of South Africa eventually exact their terrible retribution, or when the indignities of the American South work their full damage to the American social fabric. In a world in which conscious morality can be regarded with derision, and reason with suspicion, this random toll of social tragedy cannot be avoided. It is the consequence of a situation in which, as Albert Camus writes in *The Fall:* "We cannot assert the innocence of anyone, whereas we can state with certainty the guilt of all."

To raise these dark thoughts is not to sermonize that man is "wicked" or to avoid the conclusion that some men are much more guilty than others. Neither is it to maintain that there is no hope for a betterment of the human condition. On the contrary, there is today a greater long-term prospect for such betterment than humanity has ever known before. But the heritage of the past is too deep to be overcome in a matter of a few generations. It will be a long while until the human condition has been substantially improved. Not to face up to this fact with compassion and concern is only to cringe before reality. And while this should urge us on with all the strength at our command to support every effort to improve the condition of man, it cannot but chasten us as to the reasonable expectations of the "progress" which that condition will permit.

8. THE AMBIGUITY OF EVENTS

In the very idea of progress, as we commonly accept it, is contained the notion of goals. We strive for specific objectives, located in the future, and imagine that each objective gained is a recognizable step toward "progress." As a result we find ourselves confounded when, having reached an objective, what we encounter is not the "progress" we anticipated but a new set of problems stemming from the very advance itself.

This disconcerting aspect of experience can be described as the ambiguity of events. By this we mean that every event in history has a Janus-like quality—one face which regards the past, and one which looks ahead; one aspect which is the culmination of what has gone before, and another which is the point of departure for what is to follow.

Simplistic ideas of progress see only the near face of events when they look to the future. Hence such views of the future typically underrate its complexities. They do not consider that the solution of one problem is only the formulation of the next. What an awareness of the ambiguity of events thus subtracts from the optimistic view of progress is the luxury of believing that progress is a simple pyramiding of success. The two-sided nature of future events does not deny that our problems may be our opportunities but it asserts with equal conviction that our opportunities may become our problems.

There is no more dramatic example of this than the impact on world history of that most "unambiguous" of all evidences of progress: the development of modern medicine. It is not necessary to spell out the enormous benefits which medical science has brought to mankind. Yet no assessment of the over-all impact of modern medicine on our age can ignore the fact that it has also been the "cause" of an immense amount of additional suffering in the world. By its success in reducing the scourges of mass disease and infant mortality, the "progress" of medical science has crowded the already overpopulated villages and cities of Asia and South America with still more mouths, and has thus aggravated the very human suffering it set out to relieve.

Needless to say, not every instance of progress cancels itself out in so direct and distressing a fashion as this. The point, rather, is that progress does not merely consist in the surmounting of a previous problem, but inherently consists in the emergence of a new problem which, although different, may be quite as grave as the old. In the course of this book, for example, we have seen such new problems emerging from the advance of technology or from the achievement of abundance in our own society. These new problems do not gainsay the advances which technology or economic growth bring us. But it may well be that the consequences of our technological captivity, or the control problems of economic abundance will be just as humanly crushing as the problems of insufficiency or technical inadequacy from whose solution they emerged. There is no reason to believe that the successive problems of "progress" pose easier challenges; indeed it is probable that the overcoming of the "simpler" problems of poverty and disease opens the doors on progressively more profound, elusive, and insoluble human dilemmas.

Marx and Hegel called this ambiguous aspect of progress the dialectic of history. Marx, however, brought his dialectical analysis to a halt with the achievement of communism as the "terminus" of the history of class struggle. Ironically enough, it is probable that there is no aspect of future history which today more desperately needs dialectical clarification than the achievement of the communist—or for the West, the socialist—goal.

It is clear that as the "near side" of socialism approaches, it is the "far side" which becomes of ever greater interest and importance. To consider socialism as a "goal" of social history is to fall prey to the optimistic delusion that goals are milestones in history from which the next stage of development promises to be "easier" or unambiguously "better" than the past. To rid oneself of this comforting notion is not to lessen one's ardor to resolve the difficulties of the present, but to arm oneself realistically for the continuance of the human struggle in the future.

9. THE GRAND DYNAMIC OF HISTORY

Is there then no possibility for progress?

As it must by now be clear, much depends on what one means by the question. If by "progress" we mean a fundamental elevation in the human estate, a noticeable movement of society in the direction of the ideals of Western humanism, a qualitative as well as a quantitative betterment of the condition of man, it is plain that we must put away our ideas of progress over the foreseeable vista of the historic future. For whereas there is no question but that the forces of our time are bringing about momentous and profound changes, it is only optimistic self-deception to anticipate, or even to wish for, the near advent of a perceptibly "better" world as a result. Taking into account the human condition as it now exists, the laggard slowness with which improvements in institutions are followed by improvements in "life," the blurred and ambiguous fashion in which history passes from problem to problem, it is certain enough that the tenor of world history will remain much as it is for a long while to come.

Indeed, from the point of view of the West and especially of America, it may seem to be deteriorating. As we have seen through the pages of this book, many of the tendencies of world history are likely to manifest themselves to us as a worsening of the outlook. We may well be tempted to interpret this growing intractability of the environment as the metamorphosis of progress into retrogression.

Against this dark horizon it is hardly possible to cling to the sanguine hopes and complacent expectations of the past. And yet if we can lift our gaze beyond the confines of our own situation, it is possible to see that every one of these changes is essential and inescapable if the present condition of humankind is to be surpassed. Until the avoidable evils of society have been redressed, or at least made the target of the wholehearted effort of the organized human community, it is not only premature but presumptuous to talk of "the dignity of the individual." The ugly, obvious, and terrible wounds of mankind must be dressed and allowed to heal before we can begin to know the capacities, much less enlarge the vision, of the human race as a whole.

In the present state of world history the transformations which are everywhere at work are performing this massive and crude surgery. We have dwelt sufficiently in the preceding pages on the violence and cruelty, the humanly deforming aspects of the changes about us. Now we must see that in their ultimate impact on history it is the positive side of these great transformations which must be stressed. However unruly the revolution of the underdeveloped nations, it is nonetheless the commencement of a movement away from the squalor and apathy which three-quarters of the human race still consider to be life. With all its disregard for Western standards of justice and liberty, the forced march of communism is nevertheless retreading the essential, but now forgotten path of early industrial development of the West. Whatever its capacity for the destruction or the diminution of man, the perfection and application of industrial technology is withal the only possible escape from the historic indenture of man. And no matter what its difficulties, the painful evolution beyond present-day capitalism is indispensable if those nations which have gained the benefits of material wealth are now to cope rationally with its administration.

Thus the blind and often brutal impact of the historic forces of our day can still be said to point in the direction of optimism and of progress. Only in our present situation, the West is no longer the spearhead of those forces, but their target. What is at bottom a movement of hope and well-being for the inarticulate and inadequate masses of mankind is a fearful threat to the delicate and now gravely exposed civilization of the articulate and advanced few.

No member of the Western community who loves its great achievements and who has enjoyed the inestimable value of its liberties and values can confront this outlook of history without anguish. Of all those who will feel the blows of the future, none will suffer more than the heirs of the long tradition of Western humanism, and none will more acutely feel the delays and the recession of "progress" as the world endures its protracted ordeal.

More aware than the rising masses of the world of the destination to which their inchoate revolution may hopefully carry them, it is the humanist spirits of the West who will feel most betrayed by the violence and excess which will likely accompany its course. Ever hopeful of the re-entry of the communist nations into the Western community of thought, it is the Western intellectuals and idealists who will bear the full agony of watching for and waiting for signs of change which may be very long in coming. Alive to the immense potential benefits of the technical virtuosity of their age, it is again the guardians of the humanist tradition who will most despair at its continued misapplication; just as it will be they rather than the masses who will wish for a more responsible form of economic society and who will chafe at the continuance of the old order.

This prospect of disappointment and delay may give rise to a tragedy greater than the tragic events of history itself. This would be the disillusion of Western thought and the abandonment of its hopes for and its distant vision of progress. It would be the surrender of the very ideals of the West before the crushing advent of history, and the adoption of an indifference, or worse, a cynicism before the march of events.

If this tragedy is to be avoided, the West will have need of two qualities: fortitude and understanding. It must come to see that because this is not a time of fulfillment does not mean that it is a time of waste. It is rather a time when the West must take upon itself a new and more difficult role in history than in the past: not that of leading in the van of history's forces under the banner of progress, but that of preserving from the ruthless onslaught of history's forces the integrity of the very idea of progress itself.

Particularly for Americans will this long period of abeyance provide a test of the spirit. Accustomed by our historic training to expect a mastery over events which is no longer possible, we are apt to interpret the intransigence of history as a kind of personal betrayal rather than as a vast and impersonal process of worldwide evolution. Thus there is the danger that we may abandon our optimism for a black and bitter pessimism, or for a kind of "heroic" defiance.

But neither pessimism nor defiance, any more than optimism, will give us the fortitude and understanding we require. For this we need an attitude which accepts the outlook of the historic future without succumbing to false hopes or to an equally false despair; a point of view which sees in the juggernaut of history's forces both the means by which progress painfully made in the past may be trampled underfoot, and the means by which a broader and stronger base for progress in the future may be brought into being.

Such an attitude may retain its kernel of optimism. But more is needed for the display of stoic fortitude than a residual faith in the idea of progress. Above all there is required an understanding of the grand dynamic of history's forces in preparing the way for eventual progress. There is needed a broad and compassionate comprehension of the history-shaking transformations now in mid-career, of their combined work of demolition and construction, of the hope they embody and the price they will exact.

Only from such a sense of historic understanding can come the strength to pass through the gauntlet with an integrity of mind and spirit.

What is tragically characteristic of our lives today is an absence of just such an understanding. It is very difficult while America and the West are at bay to feel a sense of positive identification with the forces that are preparing the environment of the future. Less and less are we able to locate our lives meaningfully in the pageant of history. More and more do we find ourselves retreating to the sanctuary of an insulated individualism, sealed off in our private concerns from the larger events which surround us.

Such an historic disorientation and disengagement is a terrible private as well as public deprivation. In an age which no longer waits patiently through this life for the rewards of the next, it is a crushing spiritual blow to lose one's sense of participation in mankind's journey, and to see only a huge milling-around, a collective living-out of lives with no larger purpose than the days which each accumulates. When we estrange ourselves from history we do not enlarge, we diminish ourselves, even as individuals. We subtract from our lives one meaning which they do in fact possess, whether we recognize it or not. We cannot help living in history. We can only fail to be aware of it. If we are to meet, endure, and transcend the trials and defeats of the future—for trials and defeats there are certain to be—it can only be from a point of view which, seeing the future as part of the sweep of history, enables us to establish our place in that immense procession in which is incorporated whatever hope humankind may have.